LOGICAL

PROGRAMMING

WITH SYSTEM/360

DON H. STABLEY

JOHN WILEY & SONS, INC.

NEW YORK | LONDON | SYDNEY | TORONTO

PREFACE

Few professional fields directly serve as many other diverse professions as does computer programming.

This book was developed to fill the existing need for a comprehensive treatment of System/360 and Third Generation programming concepts. Assembler Language is the best choice of the System/360 programming languages for the following reasons:

1. Assembler Language relates directly to all of the concepts of System/360.

2. Nearly every System/360 installation will require Assembler Language programmers, regardless of other languages which that installation might be using.

3. Certain other high-level languages, such as PL/I, are capable of producing an Assembler Language listing of program instructions. That listing represents the generated coding of the program statements and may be effectively used for program analysis and interpretation.

In order to establish the characteristics of the book it was first necessary to define the audience for which it was intended. After reviewing the advice of recognized professionals in data processing education, the decision was made to use a straight-forward approach in the basic terminology of the programming profession. Therefore, this text has been prepared to accommodate technical schools, universities, colleges, and industrial and commercial training programs, rather than as a specialized presentation for a particular type of educational program. Prepublication testing of the effectiveness of the manuscript has already proved its potential application within a wide range of educational environments. It is assumed that the reader has completed a general high school education and has a working knowledge of program logic flowcharting.

The opening chapters present a generalized coverage of System/360 computer hardware and terminology. This basic knowledge makes it possible to develop an understanding of the subsequent presentations of System/360 concepts, Assembler Language instructions, and programming techniques. These items are approached in the logical sequence of the System/360 number systems (Base-2, Base-10, Base-16), data representation concepts, the individual Assembler Language instructions, and the programming techniques in which each of these are applied. The final chapters present an overview of the concepts of file organization and data retrieval. These structures are discussed in their relationship to the System/360 data management routines, including sequential, indexed sequential, and random file organizations and access methods. A glossary of terms, designed to aid the reader with an expendient reference source, appends the main portion of the text.

In my opinion, it is as important for the student to be able to measure his progress as it is for the instructor who teaches him. Practice exercises must be an integral part of a good textbook. Unlike a written examination or a formal quiz, these should be designed to point out any weakness, even at the lowest level of the student's knowledge and understanding of the subject material. Absolute detail, rather than conceptual responses, are required. The development of the unique review exercises and examples contained within this text have almost automatically evolved as a part of my involvement in the sophisticated environment of large-scale computer systems and programming; an environment in which every professional is a perennial student, part-time instructor, and lecturer. You will find these exercises to be based almost entirely upon the necessity of extracting the student's understanding of the detailed and explicit performance of each of the individual Assembler Language instructions. This effort to emphasize minute details of language performance should result in greater efficiency when applied by the student to actual programs.

The logical arrangement of language instructions into a program structure must also be practiced. Just as review exercises are important to a good textbook, the coding of practice programs is essential to the success of a programming course. Unfortunately, this presents unique problems. What is the "correct" answer to a practice program problem? Speaking in broader terms, what are the "most acceptable" instruction statements that should comprise a particular program? There is a standing statement, "If 500 programmers were given an exact set of requirements for a program, the finished product would be 500 unique programs." A large number of those programs would be quite similar in content, but that would depend greatly upon the similarity in education of the programmers. Based on this assumption, it is appropriate for the practice coding programs to originate with the individual instructors who utilize this book. This will allow each instructor to establish his own evaluation of the correctness or inefficiencies of the student's application of the language. Therefore, the coding of complete practice programs has not been included.

Because of the inherent flexibility of System/360 and the vast range of its possible hardware and system configurations, it has been necessary to exclude certain areas of technology which might otherwise be desirable. Such material would include input/output control statements, macro-instructions, job control language, and other types of instruction or parameter definitions that might depend wholly upon a specific operating system or hardware configuration. Regardless of the apparent need for such information, it is not unreasonable to exclude it from this text. Just as the content of a single program would vary when written by different programmers, computer centers vary in the configuration of the computer systems they maintain. It must therefore be assumed that the required control statements for input/output operations, data management, and file descriptions will be supplied to the student by the instructional staff of the computer center with which he is affiliated.

Any attempt to list completely the names of persons and organizations to whom acknowledgments and statements of appreciation are due would most certainly result in numerous, although inadvertent, omissions. Many persons have contributed directly and indirectly to this book. Within this particular profession, knowledge is not singularly extrapolated from any one source or individual—it is derived from the day-to-day contact with associates, whether they are students, trainees, or seasoned professionals. My statement of appreciation, therefore, must be directed to all of those with whom I have shared the challenge of the constantly evolving technology of electronic data processing.

Photographs of System/360 computer hardware units have been furnished through the courtesy of the IBM Corporation.

Don H. Stabley

Rochester, N. Y.
December 17, 1969

CONTENTS

ix

Part III

LOGICAL APPLICATIONS OF ASSEMBLER
LANGUAGE

Part IV

ACCESS METHODS AND DATA SET FORMATS

Part V

TABLES AND GLOSSARY   527

LOGICAL PROGRAMMING WITH SYSTEM/360

PART I

INTRODUCTION TO SYSTEM/360

THE PROGRAMMER
AND THE COMPUTER

A. AN INTRODUCTION TO THE COMPUTER PROGRAMMER

The present-day computer is probably the most misunderstood aid to man that has ever been developed. Revered by many, disliked by others, it has been the target of both humor and serious attack, based conversely on its tremendous capabilities and its supposed shortcomings.

When Mr. Average Citizen receives his monthly account statement from the local credit emporium and finds that it is in error, the computer is spotlighted as the culprit; a computerized payroll system deducts too much money from the paychecks of all of the employees and the computer becomes infamous for its sins. This goes on and on—the rocket that goes astray, the purchase order that is automatically written for 1 million gizmos instead of 100, the lines of conglomerate gibberish that suddenly appear in

the middle of the latest news story in the evening newspaper—these are all accredited as the antics of a wayward computer.

Unfortunately, it will probably be many years before the general public recognizes and understands the overall concept of computers and their capabilities. Until that time, however, this fascinating maze of electronic equipment will have to continue to bear the brunt of the puns and disdain of those who have supposedly suffered from the whims of its flashing lights and massive memory banks. Someday, perhaps, the responsibility for all of the intangible evils of the computer will be finally accepted by that element which indeed spawns those same misdeeds —the human element.

The programmer has nearly as much to learn about human nature as he does about the nature of the computer that is to do his bidding. The programmer can slyly attempt to bypass the responsibility for a program abortion by blaming it on a "computer malfunction"—by the inability to generate a truly unique thought, the computer, therefore, becomes the "fall guy" for many a programmer's errors, and it cannot defend itself to the data processing manager. It would be extremely interesting to know the infinitesimally small percentage of processing errors for which the computer itself is truly responsible, in comparison to the overwhelming number of errors for which it is blamed.

Gradually, the computer programmer is gaining justifiable recognition as an artist in his own right. Programs can literally be a true work of art, an efficient masterpiece of the use of man's logic processes—or they may be a collection of *garbage* (a term frequently used in data processing), a monument of misguided concepts and misapplied techniques. Once computer programming has been accepted as a constructive challenge, it offers a wealth of potential originality to the programmer. What he makes of this challenge is the difference between the professional programmer and the ordinary "coder."

Throughout this book, the references to a programmer or programming student are stated in the masculine gender. This is merely a means of expression and is not intended as a "slight" to the feminine world of programmers which, incidentally, has proved to be a vast membership of computer enthusiasts who are equally as skilled, and sometimes even more knowledgeable, than their male counterparts.

B. SYSTEM/360—
A THIRD GENERATION
COMPUTER SYSTEM

Modern data processing concepts possibly originated with the advent of the punched card applications in which the cards were stored, sorted, and arranged according to the desired sequence by the existence of holes in the cards. This type of equipment really preceded the birth of what was to become the First Generation of computer hardware.

The term *generation,* as used in reference to computers, is frequently identified as the period of time during which the internal electronics of the computer utilized certain electronic principles and equipment. In this context, the First Generation computers were those that contained vacuum tubes for electronic circuitry power and processing. These forerunners of the present-day computers were literal "ovens," giving off heat in such quantities that it was difficult to maintain a reasonable temperature within the computer rooms.

With the initial application of the transistor came the Second Generation of computers, capable of greater storage and faster logic processes, yet requiring less room than its older brother. As the electronics industry progressed in the design of yet smaller and smaller components, microcircuitry became a reality. Solid-state devices were miniaturized to a point where an entire electronic logic circuit was smaller than the flat surface of a lump of sugar; "chip" transistors were created so small that 50,000 of them would fit into an ordinary sewing thimble. These components are the type of electronic equipment that were used in the design and production of todays computers—the Third Generation.

There are several definitions of computer generations, depending on who is making the analysis of the term. Some say that the Third Generation of computers really represents the satisfactory merge of a scientific computer and a commercial application computer into one modular system. This may be explained by stating that prior to the Third Generation equipment, it was not unusual for data processing installations to procure a particular type of computer based on the scientific versus commercial applications for which it was to be used. In this respect, System/360 appears to satisfy the needs of both the scientific and research programmer and the commercial data processing installations.

As the circuitry within the new computers became more compact, the internal processing speeds increased. Electric pulses and electronic data flow had less distance to travel between logic sections of the computer, allowing a performance that became more and more difficult to comprehend. Terms such as *nanoseconds* and *picoseconds,* representing billionths of a second and trillionths of a second respectively, were now associated with certain internal functions of the computer. Accordingly, it became necessary to design peripheral support equipment, such as the input/output devices for a computer system, which could perform data transmission at speeds that would not adversely degrade the performance of the computer processing functions. To expect that peripheral equipment to physically match the speed of the computer itself would be unrealistic; such equipment utilizes physical movement of some type as a part of its operational functions and, therefore, could not be expected to keep pace with a processing unit that depends solely on electronic circuitry. However, disk storage devices were developed that provided data transmission speeds at the rating of 312,000 characters per second, and drum-type storage devices were implemented that were capable of 1,200,000 characters per second data transmission.

One of the primary advantages of System/360 is the "modular" concept by which it is designed, allowing *upgrading* of the computer itself and the addition of peripheral equipment as the users' needs increase for such equipment. For example, assume that a particular data processing department has installed a System/360 computer system configurated as follows:

System/360 Model 50 Central Processing
   Unit, with 256K (262,144) bytes core
   storage capability
Console Typewriter
Card Reader/Punch
4 Tape Drive Units (7-Track 800-BPI
   models)
2   2311 Direct Access Storage Devices
Appropriate Control Units Where Required

As the computer center work load increases, it is subsequently decided that additional direct access devices are needed, so management now requests that a 2314 Direct Access Storage Facility be ordered. A multipro-

gramming system is to be implemented in the near future and it is now desirable to have an additional 256K bytes of core storage as well as another printer unit. Even later, the company management decides to increase magnetic tape processing output, so two of the 7-track tape drive units are released and six of the 9-track 1600-BPI tape drive units are ordered.

After all of these modifications have been completed, the computer system is now configurated as:

System/360 Model 50 CPU, with 512K
   (524,288) byte core storage capability
Console Typewriter
Card Reader/Punch
2 Printer Units
2 Tape Drive Units (7-Track 800-BPI)
6 Tape Drive Units (9-Track 1600-BPI)
1   2314 Direct Access Storage Facility
   (233,000,000 byte storage capacity)
2   2311 Direct Access Storage Devices
Appropriate Control Units Where Required

The original system has now been modularly incremented to a rather powerful computer system that would be capable of performance satisfactory to many data processing installations. The ability to upgrade a computer system in this manner is highly desirable so that the ever-expanding requirements of computerized business systems and research projects may be accommodated.

The so-called prophets of the workingman have been warning for years that the computer spells doom to the security of many jobs, yet the spiral of the net manpower required as computers are installed continues on an upward trend, not downward as forecast. In all fairness it must be noted that the increase in net manpower results in a much greater output of the data that is necessary for rapid management decisions and customer service. An order may be placed with a sales representative in Los Angeles in the morning and by evening the distribution center in New York City could have the shipping orders prepared and the ordered material waiting for shipment to the customer—all of the related functions have been expedited by means of a computerized telecommunications system for order processing.

As implied, the Central Processing Unit (CPU) of a computer system (see Figs. 1-1 and 1-2) is merely a well-planned maze of electronic circuits, incapable of any self-initialized action. In order for these circuits to be activated and perform in a predictable pattern, the computer must be provided with a master control program, often referred to as the *Supervisor* or *Monitor*. The Supervisor, as well as the computer system, may also be considered to be modular in that it consists of fixed and optional sets of smaller modules and control programs. The completed package of any given Supervisor control program is generally dependent on the following.

1. The operating system to which it is related.

2. The control modules required by that operating system.

3. The hardware configuration of the computer system.

4. The selection of optional data management routines.

The overall Supervisor package is created by a process of merging and extracting programs that is referred to as a *System Generation* or *SYSGEN*. A "system generation" by the using installation is necessary in order for the completed system to meet the needs of the requirements of their unique hardware configuration. Each of the operating systems may be generated in many different ways. These variations are created through the inclusion or exclusion of data parameters at the time the system generation is accomplished. By utilization of the packaged routines provided by the computer manufacturer, the selected optional routines and modules for the desired system are specified, processed through the computer, and compiled onto some type of storage media as the completed Supervisor. This becomes the

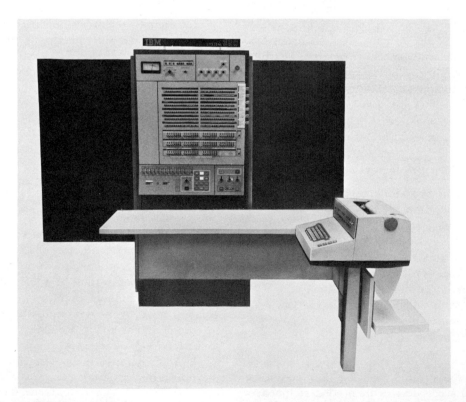

Figure 1-1. IBM System/360 Model 65 showing Central Processing Unit Control Panel and Console Typewriter.

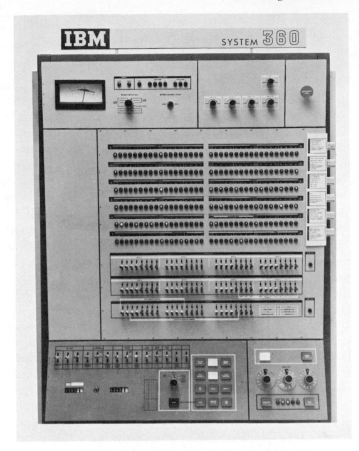

Figure 1-2. Central Processing Unit Control Panel for IBM System/360 Model 65.

master control program that is "loaded" into the computer CPU and supervises the day-to-day performance of the users' programs.

The Supervisor will differ considerably between the various operating systems—the Basic Operating System (BOS), the Tape Operating System (TOS), the Disk Operating System (DOS), and the full Operating System (OS). Each of these systems may be considered to be designed for computer equipment of different physical capabilities and scope, although in many instances a particular computer system configuration could possibly utilize a choice of several operating systems.

The Basic Operating System is assumed to be intended for relatively small System/360 computer systems, but contains all of the necessary functions that are required to derive the maximum performance that can be provided by a computer system of that size.

The Disk Operating System is applicable to computer systems in a range of sizes, but appears to be most applicable to those that principally employ direct access storage devices. Magnetic Tape Drive Units may be included in a computer configuration that is operated under the control of a Disk Operating System.

Tape Operating Systems are maintained by a tape-oriented Supervisor and are applicable to a range of medium-sized computer systems. A Tape Operating System cannot be utilized on a computer whose configuration includes direct access storage devices.

The largest and most flexible of all of the operating is the "full" Operating System. It is compatible on a practical basis with

System/360 computers that range from medium-small to the largest available. It offers the data processing installation a wealth of variation in support programs, access methods, file organization systems, and potential for assorted hardware configurations. Depending on the choice of elective options selected to comprise the Supervisor package for the Operating System, the OS Supervisor could logically range in size from 30,000 bytes to greater than 120,000 bytes of required core storage area. It is a very powerful operating system and will simultaneously support all variations of peripheral hardware—magnetic tape drives, drums, printers, display units, telecommunication equipment, and related terminals.

Each of the operating systems utilize control programs that differ somewhat from the other operating systems. Even a particular access method, although it may be supported by more than one operating system, is activated by somewhat different macroinstruction statements between the supporting systems. It is for this reason that the contents of this book cannot possibly attempt to become involved in explaining input/output macroinstructions, job control language, or functional system and language macroinstructions. Not only would it be impossible to anticipate the unique hardware configurations and corresponding variation of operating systems of the computer installations where this text might be used, but the attempt to explain and evaluate all of these variations would be prohibitive in terms of written volume alone. The educational center, university, college, or industrial complex that finds this text to be valuable for the education of their programmers must, therefore, bear the respective responsibility for providing the necessary technical information. As indicated, this data would consist of applicable job control language, device references and addresses, and the macroinstructions that are available for their operating system, language levels, and access methods.

C. NOMENCLATURE AND TERMINOLOGY

The study of System/360 programming will bring with it a host of new words and terms that may be totally unfamiliar to the student programmer. Certain words may be entirely within the scope of everyday language, yet when they are used in association with computer programming they take on an entirely different interpretation and context. For example, drum, word, channel, core, terminal, register, bit, switches are all standard nouns and verbs within the grasp of anyone not familiar with computer systems. When these same terms are used to relate to System/360, they assume the identity of a noun that has a peculiar and distinct interpretation. Mention a drum and the initial mental picture response by a noncomputer-oriented person would be that of either a percussion muscial instrument or a metal barrel type of container; yet to the programmer it is a direct access storage device! In order to aid in the understanding of computer-related terms, a glossary has been provided at the end of this text. It contains the majority of terms and descriptive nomenclature that may be of assistance to the student.

Some of the nomenclature for System/360, as with other computers, requires additional explanation and discussion. Such is the case of the terms "hardware" and "software," as related to computer systems. Computer *hardware* is considered to be any physical device or piece of equipment that is a part of the overall configuration of the computer system itself. The CPU, direct access devices, display units, cables, tape drives, control units, printer units, console typewriters, and such related equipment are all considered to be hardware. The term *software* is associated with peripheral utility programs or with any or all sets of control programs that are required by the computer in order for it to act on the users' programs in a desired manner. Although software is often related directly

The Programmer and the Computer

to the specialized control programs furnished by the computer manufacturer, it is equally applicable to specialized programs written by the using installation, which provide a particular service to the operating system or to the everyday user. A program of the latter type might be an accounting routine of computer usage that accumulates the run time for each particular job during the day, records that job time to a particular charge number on an accounting log, and prints a message on the run scroll for each job as to the extent of time that was required for completion of that task. A software program could also be one that is available to all users in order to aid them in performing a certain function within their operational programs. This might take the form of a set of routines, activated by a "call" from the users' program, which would perform special arithmetic calculations based on parameter values passed to it by the "calling" program, including the subsequent return of resulting values as determined by that calculation.

Throughout this text, certain terms and phrases will be used that might not be sufficiently described at that point, or that might not have been previously clarified to the reader's satisfaction. In such instances, it is recommended that the reader refer to the Glossary of Terms.

COMPUTER SYSTEMS IN GENERAL

A. PROGRAMMING LANGUAGES

In order for the programmer to communicate the logic of his program to the computer, he must state the information in such a way that it might be understood by the computer control programs. The common ground for this understanding between man and machine is the programming language that is used to state the program logic.

A programming language, in reality, does not constitute a direct link with the computer. It is only the programmer-related portion of a two-step communication process that will define the action to be accomplished. Using the parameters and limitations related to the language that is being used, the programmer specifies the task to be performed by coding language source statements. Upon completion of this coding, he has established a series of steps that must be translated into the type of instruction

representation that is understood by the internal functions of the computer on which that task is to be performed. This translation is accomplished by a *language compiler,* or language assembler.

The *compiler,* or language compiler, is a portion of the control program packages contained within the operating system. Each language, or level of a language, requires a separate compiler program in order to translate the source language coding that is submitted for compilation. The operating system used by any given computer installation needs only to contain a compiler for each of the specific languages or level thereof that will be compiled and used at that installation.

The language source statements, together with the necessary control cards to identify the language compiler that is to be used, are input into the computer system, where the processing of those source statements then takes place. Once all of the source coding has been introduced into the compiler work area, the compiler itself begins to identify each statement and relate it to a function that is to be performed by the computer at program execution time. When a statement has been related to a specific function, the compiler translates that action into one or more machine-language instructions. After all the source statements have been translated, the resulting data is considered to be an *object module,* the program that will be linked to the system control programs and executed.

The object module may be punched into cards as an *object deck* or it may be written onto a data set as part of a *program library.* After completion of the execution of the language compiler, a print-out is created that lists the source statements from which the object module was compiled. This listing will usually "flag" any coding errors and, in some language compilers, it will issue warnings related to possible error conditions that might occur during the execution of the object program.

Programming languages generally fall within two categories—*low-level* or *high-level* languages. A low-level language is one that is very closely related to the actual machine-language, almost on a one-for-one basis of programming language to machine-language. Within System/360, Assembler Language is considered to be the low-level language.

A high-level language is usually referred to as a *statement* language or as an *expression* language, wherein each coded instruction statement might generate many machine-language instructions. A high-level language instruction statement might appear as, "If A Equals B then do C until Y equals Z."

There are many valid arguments for both low-level and high-level languages, but too often one is chosen without consideration for the benefits of the other. There is a definite place and a definite need for both types of languages in almost every computer installation. It is the personal opinion of the author that it is of a definite advantage to the programmer to first learn a low-level language because of the direct relationship

of such a language to the working concepts of the computer itself. Indications are that this conclusion has also been arrived at by others, as evidenced by an apparent trend among data processing and programming educational centers toward low-level languages. Once the student programmer has grasped the use of the low-level language, simultaneously absorbing the concepts of the computer with which he is working, any subsequent training required in high-level languages should be more easily comprehended.

As mentioned, Assembler Language is a widely used low-level language for System/360. What then are the high-level or statement-level languages applicable to this computer? Rather than list all of these, it will suffice to state that PL/I, COBOL, FORTRAN, and ALGOL are perhaps the most commonly used. The name COBOL is derived from COmmon Business Oriented Language; FORTRAN from FORmula TRANslation; ALGOL from ALGOrithm Language; and PL/I, an IBM-developed language, from Programming Language I (One). COBOL, as its name suggests, is generally used for business and commercial applications, FORTRAN and ALGOL are very strong for scientific and engineering applications, and PL/I contains many features of the previous three.

Present high-level languages, such as the four mentioned here, are continually in the process of being improved and updated in their techniques. Undoubtedly, new languages of this type will be introduced from time to time, as well as new versions of the existing languages.

There are no fixed standards to determine the type of programming language that should be used by any computer installation. About the only type of predictable forecast that can be assumed is a possible separation of high-level languages between a scientific or engineering environment and the commercial or business programming environment. Certain high-level programming languages are directed more specifically to a particular type of application, but this does not preclude their use for other purposes.

Assembler Language, as a low-level language, enjoys the privilege of being applicable in any type of programming environment, whether it be in commercial, scientific, computer research, or software development applications.

B. PERIPHERAL HARDWARE EQUIPMENT

As a part of every computer system, there must be some type of hardware available that will provide input data to the operating programs and will be capable of receiving output data in return. The input and output functions need not both be handled by the same device; one type may facilitate the input data and another the output. This equipment may be quite varied in type and configuration, each computer system being structured to the needs of the user's installation. The peripheral I/O hardware, as it is referred to, may consist of several units of the same type or may be comprised of many units of numerous types. Each one of the devices has a channel (cable) connection with the Central Processing Unit, either directly to it or through a control unit that interfaces with the CPU.

Within the descriptions of the devices contained on the following pages you will find sufficient information to become familiar with the general physical characteristics and attributes of each and their common application in respect to a functional computer system. Because this text is intended for education in computer programming, rather than computer sciences, these descriptions will not delve deeply into the technical and electronic principles of this equipment.

1. Magnetic Tape Concepts

The use of magnetic tape for storing and retrieving data has been a generally accepted method of accomplishing these functions. Although it is now being challenged by the direct access devices of Third Generation computer systems, it remains the largest single media of data input/output operations.

Magnetic tape consists of a thin plastic film base that has been coated with an oxide surface. This oxide surface will accept electrical impulses that generate magnetic groupings of the oxide atoms, sometimes logically referred to as *bits*. The arrangement of these groupings represents the *bit arrangement* of the data that is contained on the tape, and will remain in that configuration until altered by a subsequent rearrangement. The bits contained on the tape surface are arranged in rows across the face of the oxide surface, from side to side. In some types of magnetic tape equipment, each row of bits represents a single byte of data; in some other equipment, it requires two rows of bits to represent a character. These rows of bits are also spaced differently in linear form among the various models of magnetic tape drives. This spacing between subsequent rows of bits is referred to as the *density* at which the tape was created. System/360, as a Third Generation computer, functions primarily with magnetic tapes created at a density of 800 BPI and 1600 BPI—BPI representing bits per inch, or rows of bits per inch of magnetic tape. A tape created at 1600 BPI density has 1600 rows of magnetized data bits for every inch of tape that contains data. The term BPI may be found to be described elsewhere as bytes per inch, nomenclature that is generally used when describing tape forms in which one row of data bits comprise a single byte of data.

Magnetic tape does not contain an unending string of contiguous data bit rows. After a logical block of data is *written* onto the surface of the tape, the system skips over a portion of the tape surface prior to writing the next logical block of data. This portion of the tape that has not been used is referred to as an *inter-record gap*, or *IRG*. Along with several other control functions, this gap is used by the system as a logical, and physical, means of distinguishing between blocks of data contained on the tape.

The magnetic tape drives, or tape units, are available in a wide variety of configurations and models within System/360 (see Fig. 2-1). Some units will process one particular density of magnetic tape, others will process two types of tape density. The speed at which

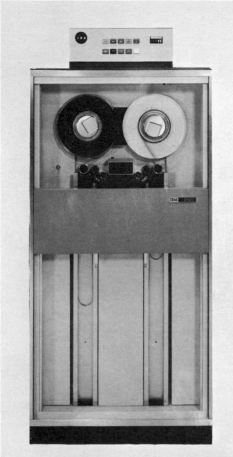

Figure 2-1. IBM Magnetic Tape Drive, Model 2401.

magnetic tape is processed by the tape drive units is measured as a *KBS* factor—or K bytes per second, wherein K is equal to a value of 1024. A tape drive unit that will process magnetic tape at a rating of 90 KBS is actually capable of 92,160 bytes per second. Some tape drive units process data at the rate of 15 KBS, others can process magnetic tape as fast as 180 KBS.

Magnetic tape represents a fairly inexpensive means of storing bulk data. The reels of tape may be readily filed or stored for safekeeping in vaults or tape file libraries, thereby protecting the data until it is needed. One of the very practical uses for magnetic tape is to use it as an output media in lieu of a printer unit; the data that is to be printed as the result of a program or system is instead written onto magnetic tape. The

print-out of that data may then be accomplished at a more convenient time or on another computer system or off-line printer system.

2. Card Reader/Punch Units

Data contained on punched cards is probably the oldest means of input/output media that is currently associated with computer equipment. Long before the days of magnetic tape, direct access devices, and display terminals, punched cards were being used to represent a system of storing data, as well as its present-day application of initial data input, source program coding input, problem program object modules, and task management control statements. Standard punched card concepts, as used in System/360, utilizes a flexible cardboard card that measures $3\frac{1}{4}$ by $7\frac{3}{8}$ inches, each card containing 80 columns. Each column consists of 12 vertical positions that may contain small rectangular holes punched into the card. The combination of holes, or single hole, punched into the vertical column is interpreted by the system as being representative of data content, either as hexadecimal, binary, or EBCDIC formatted.

The *reader* portion of a combination reader/punch unit transmits data to the CPU based on the "sensing" of the holes contained in each card as it passes by the sensing mechanism. The actual reading, or sensing, of the holes is usually accomplished by small wire brushes or by photoelectric-type cell units. In the brush-type mechanism, the card is passed under a set of 80 brushes, one brush for each vertical column on the card. If a hole is present on the card, the brush will make contact with a sensing plate beneath that hole and register an impulse. All of the impulses received for each vertical column are then interpreted by the control programs of the system and the next card is read. In reader units that use a light-sensing device, the light source replaces the function of the brushes and the photoelectric cells replace the function of the sensing plate. As the card holes pass over the sensor cells, the light passes through and the existence of the hole is recorded. (See Fig. 2-2.)

The *punch* portion of the reader/punch

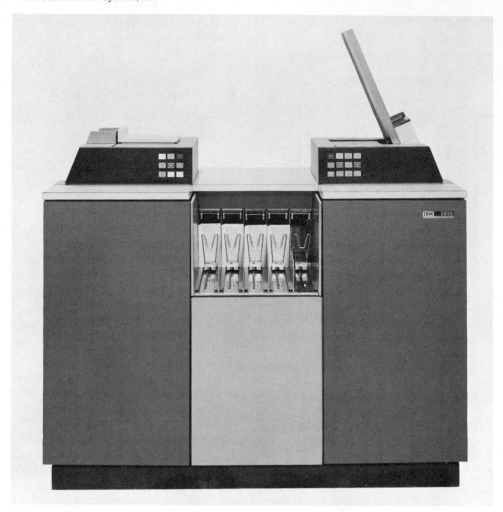

Figure 2-2. IBM Card Reader/Punch Unit, Model 2540.

combination unit generally has the reverse procedure of the reader logic, but is somewhat slower because of the necessity of physically punching the required holes into the cards. Data that is to be punched is converted into its card-code form and transmitted to the punch unit. As the card passes under the punch heads, the heads are electronically activated according to the positions of the holes that are to be punched into the vertical columns of the card. Cards that are punched as output data from one task are often subsequently used as input to another task or operation.

3. Printer Units

Printer units are a means of creating visual data output in *hard-copy* form, in single or multiple copies. The term *printer* most commonly refers to a unit that is used solely for the output of data. Under some circumstances, a typewriter-type of unit, capable of both input and output, may be loosely considered to be a printer, but because of the comparatively slow speed it is a very expensive means of printing output data. True printer units are generally a high-speed printing device utilizing either a type-bar or a type-chain/train mechanism to reproduce the data output.

The type-bar printer unit contains repetitive segments of printable characters mounted on a bar that moves back and forth horizontally in a straight-line motion. Each printable position on the printer unit has a print hammer that is used to drive a selected segment of the print bar forward against the printer ribbon, causing the impression of that character segment onto the paper. As the print bar shuttles back and forth, each print position hammer is activated when a print-bar segment, passing in front of it, corresponds to a similar character that is to be printed in that position as specified by core storage control programs. Many print positions may be "simultaneously" printed if the segments that are to be printed are properly aligned.

Printer units using either a *type-chain* or a *type-train* perform the printing function in basically the same manner, except that the physical characteristics of the type-transport are somewhat different. (See Fig. 2-3.)

A type-chain consists of a series of character-slugs, each slug containing two configurations, which are linked together to form a continuous chain. This chain, mounted on two gears and forming an oblong pattern, travels horizontally in one direction at a very high rate of speed. Similar to a type-bar unit, each print position is represented by a print hammer that is activated when the selected character to be printed is opposite the hammer. The actual print impression on the paper is created differently, however, in that the print hammer drives the paper against the interceding ribbon to the print character-slug.

A type-train differs from a type-chain in that the print-slugs, each containing three characters, are not interconnected. The print-slugs are consecutively mounted within a track in which they slide freely, driven in a horizontal oblong path by a drive gear at one end and an idler gear at the other. The print-slugs themselves contain the corre-

Figure 2-3. IBM Printer, Model 1403.

sponding teeth that are meshed with the drive gear to drive them along the track. The printing of each character is conceptually the same as with a type-chain, but the physical characteristics of the hammer mechanism are somewhat different.

The speed at which some printer units perform, such as 1100 lines per minute, is often more impressive to the spectator than the internal workings of the computer itself. The printer offers a mechanical operation that is more easily comprehended by the layman than the electronic workings of the processing unit; thereby he can relate the speed of the printer to real physical conditions.

Printer units normally utilize assorted widths of continuous-form paper that is perforated to create a fold-point for stacking and separation. The length of each assumed print-page is governed by the distance from one row of perforations to the next. Many paper suppliers are now producing specialized forms for computer printer applications, such as continuous-form envelopes, federal withholding tax statements, labels, invoices, checks, etc.

4. Direct Access Devices

Disks, drums, and data cells are the three classes of hardware units that are usually referred to as direct access devices. These units derive this name from the fact that they allow the operating system to directly access any single data record, block, or region without first processing all preceding data within the volume or data set. Most direct access devices are used in an application that requires the following.

1. The storage of large quantities of data.
2. The storage of data that is to be re-

Figure 2-4. IBM 2311 Disk Storage Drive.

trieved in some manner other than sequential processing only.

3. The storage of data that must remain actively accessible to a program or system.

It is not always one of these factors, but sometimes a combination of two or three, that dictates the requirements for a direct access device application.

In a manner somewhat similar to magnetic tape techniques, direct access devices magnetically record data on an oxide surface. For each of the three previously mentioned classes of device, however, the physical characteristics of the storage media is considerably different. Disk storage devices consist of one or more *platters,* resembling phonograph records, on which the data is stored on *tracks* or prealigned paths. Just as the platters resemble a phonograph record, the tracks may be thought of as being similar to the grooves on that record. The tracks do not spiral in toward the center of the disk, but rather each track is concentric—one complete circular path ending at an index marker point where it also started. A set of these removable platters is referred to as a *disk pack.* (See Fig. 2-4.)

Each disk platter has tracks on both the upper and lower surface, the number of tracks on either surface depending upon the type of device with which the disk pack is associated. For example, both the IBM 2311 DSD and the IBM 2314 DASF utilize disk packs that contain 200 addressable tracks per

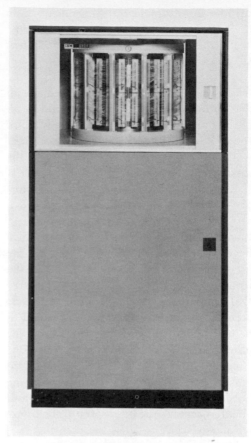

Figure 2-6. IBM 2303 Drum.

surface; the IBM 2302 DS disks contain 492 addressable tracks per surface, but it does not contain a removable disk pack. A *cylinder* is a term that is used to describe all of the addressable tracks residing in any one verti-

Figure 2-5. IBM 2314 Direct Access Storage Facility.

cal line. For example, if the outside track on the surface of the top disk was numbered 'zero', the next one in toward the center of the disk was '1', the next in toward the center was '2', etc., a cylinder would be all of the tracks in the same relative position on all disk surfaces. The first cylinder would be all of the outside tracks on all surfaces of all of the disks on that pack; the second cylinder would be all of the '1' tracks on all of the disks, etc. (See Fig. 2-5.)

Reading or writing of data on a disk storage device is accomplished by *read/write heads* attached to movable *access arm mechanisms.* Each recording surface has a read/write head, or heads, which are moved by the access arm mechanism to the track where the read/write operation is to occur. The 2311 DSD and the 2314 DASF each have one access arm mechanism—as a single track is being sought, all heads are aligned on the other tracks within that cylinder. The IBM 2302 DS units have two access arm mechanisms per module; one that accesses the outside 50% of the tracks on all surfaces and one that accesses the inside 50% of the tracks on all surfaces.

Drum storage units contain a single vertically mounted drum that is equal in diameter at all points. Unlike disk-type devices, there is only one recording surface, consisting of the outside circumference of the drum itself. The tracks, or recording paths, run horizontally around the drum, and each track has its own unmovable read/write head. As data is to be written onto, or read from, any particular track, the read/write head for that track is selected and the operation takes place. The fact that the heads are permanently positioned over each respective track saves any delay in accessing the data on that track, there is no need to wait for an access arm mechanism to move the head into the proper position for any track. (See Fig. 2-6.)

The IBM 2303 Drum records the data serially in the same manner as the disk storage devices. Data is written on only one physical, or logical, track at any one time, providing that device with a read/write

speed slightly faster than 300,000 bytes per second. In the application of the IBM 2301 Drum, however, one logical track is actually comprised of four physical tracks; data is written on the four physical tracks as logical groups of four bits, one bit per track. This characteristic of the 2301 Drum provides it with a capability of performing read/write operations at approximately four times the speed of the 2303 Drum unit, or approximately 1.2 million bytes per second.

The IBM 2321 Data Cell Drive utilizes functions of both magnetic tape and direct access devices. The data is stored on the oxide surface of strips of tape measuring approximately $2\frac{1}{4}$ inches wide by 13 inches long. This tape resembles standard magnetic tape, but the base material on which the oxide is coated is approximately three times thicker. The tape strips are stored in *subcells* within *cells,* each subcell containing ten strips and each cell containing 20 subcells or 200 strips per cell. As in the case of other direct access devices, the data is stored on tracks. There are one hundred 2000-byte tracks on each strip, or 20,000 tracks per cell. The entire Data Cell Drive consists of ten removable cell units, arranged in a circular mount, or array, which revolves in order to place any one of the cells in alignment with the access mechanism. (See Fig. 2-7.)

When an individual strip is to be accessed, the drive unit rotates the array of cells until the proper subcell is positioned beneath the access mechanism. That mechanism withdraws the proper strip from the subcell and wraps it around a drum, which in turn passes the strip beneath a series of read/write heads. The strip is then returned to the proper position within the subcell from which it was extracted. Although the 2321 Data Cell Drive does not access data quite as quickly as other direct access devices, it is an excellent means of mass data storage in that it is capable of containing up to 400 million bytes of data at any one time.

5. *Display Devices*

A relative newcomer to the commercial applications of computer I/O devices are the

Figure 2-7. IBM 2321 Data Cell.

cathode-ray tube display devices. These units contain a CRT that is quite similar to the "picture tube" in a home television receiver, but functions through a control unit that interfaces for it with the CPU of the computer. There are two basic types of CRT display devices associated with System/360—the IBM 2260 Display Station and the IBM 2250 Display Unit. Each of these two units are available in several different models and modified variations, but they generally contain the same basic concepts and techniques of operation for the CRT unit itself. The control units are considerably more variable and are the determining factor in the size, quantity, and performance of the actual CRT device. Data is transmitted to the control unit from the computer, or received from the display unit keyboard, and held in *buffers* employing a technique that is known as *delay-line buffering*. The data represented

within these buffers is effectively *painted*, or displayed, on the screen of the CRT and remains there until it is altered or deleted either by the problem program control or by a request from the display device keyboard.

The IBM 2260 Display Station has a character-formatted screen display and keyboard. It may be used as an input/outout data terminal for either *local* or *remote* mode applications. Local mode operations are transmitted via the control unit through a direct channel connection to the CPU; remote mode is when the display device and control unit transmit and receive data via transmission lines, such as telephone cables, and are interfaced with the CPU through a transmission control unit. This type of CRT display station has excellent potential and real application in data inquiry systems, on-line updating of data sets, and even real-time submission of data directly to the

Figure 2-8. IBM 2260 Display Station.

problem program in lieu of keypunching card input data. (See Fig. 2-8.)

The IBM 2250 Display Unit contains what might be referred to as a *grid-formatted* screen. The screen illumination of the grids can result in character data, illustrations, charts, drawings, and similar representations. In addition to the regular character keyboard, this unit offers a control-function keyboard and an optic-fiber light-pen. The control-function keyboard consists of a group of keys, each of which may be programmed to accomplish a particular function or a special subroutine related to the task being executed. The light-pen may be used to alter data on the screen—for example, a blueprint drawing of the circuitry of an electronic device may be displayed on the screen after being extracted from a direct storage device; by using the light-pen, components specified on that drawing may be altered or replaced and the corrected drawing returned to the storage device. (See Fig. 2-9.)

Although display units such as these do not perform at the same speeds that are normally thought of for computerized devices and functions, they are capable of very expedient processing. The inherent fact that

Figure 2-9. IBM 2250 Display Unit.

they are intended for on-line visual applications deters the need for extremely high-speed performance inasmuch as they need only be as fast as the ability of the display device operator to read, absorb, and produce the data that is to be transmitted.

PART II

INTRODUCTION TO ASSEMBLER LANGUAGE

NUMERIC REPRESENTATION AND NUMBER SYSTEMS

Within the scope of this text, there will be five types of numeric representation. Four of these represent number systems that probably are not familiar to the student programmer—hexadecimal, binary, fixed-point, and packed decimal. The fifth is the standard numeric character representation in its extended form, or EBCDIC.

The descriptions and explanations within this section are intended to be of an introductory nature. They should provide the reader with enough basic knowledge of the numeric structures of System/360 and Assembler Language to allow him to understand the logic and execution processes of the system. At certain points within the text these subjects will be reopened for review and additional information of a more technical nature will be presented.

A. BINARY VALUE REPRESENTATION

The "bi" of the word binary infers the entire basis of this scheme of numeric representation. The entire logic is based on two numeric values—0 (zero) and 1(one). Either of these digits, if written alone, expresses the value that it is intended to represent. However, when a series of these digits, such as '10010101', is being interpreted as a value, each successive digit position to the left is construed to represent a value of exactly twice that of the digit position to its right. This value is only counted as being an effective addition to the sum of all digit positions when it is a one-bit. This is known as the "Powers-Of-Two" binary representation and is in reality a "Base-2" number system. The contiguous bit positions of any half-byte, byte, or series of bytes may be evaluated as a "Powers-Of-Two" binary representation.

25

The potential Base-2 value of a series of such a set of bit positions is shown as:

This illustration represents the number of bit positions (16) contained within a two-

Respective bit position
from the right

Two Bytes

16	15	14	13	12	11	10	9	8	7	6	5	4	3	2	1
0	0	0	0	0	0	0	0	0	0	0	0	0	0	0	0

32768   8192   2048   512 256 128 64 32 16 8 4 2 1
    16384   4096   1024

Potential bit position
value in Base-2

byte field. As stated previously, the assumed value representation of any single bit position is not considered to be effective unless a one-bit occupies that position. Therefore, the preceding illustration can be considered

to be an absolute value of zero since there are no one-bits within the field. Using this same two-byte field, but containing various bit configurations, the following examples define the accumulation of the assumed

Example 1

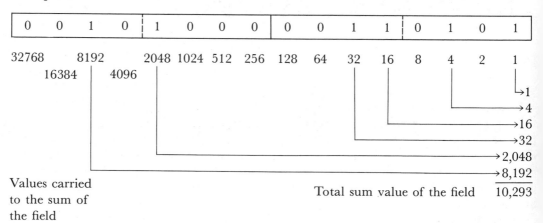

Values carried
to the sum of
the field

Total sum value of the field   10,293

Example 2

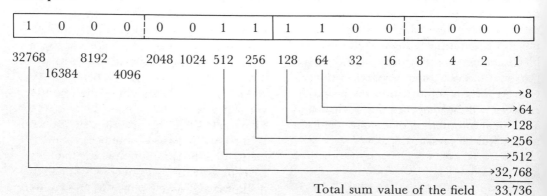

Total sum value of the field   33,736

Example 3

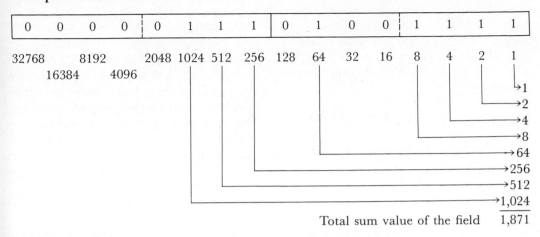

Total sum value of the field   1,871

one-bit values into the sum value of the entire field as a binary "Powers-Of-Two" notation.

The maximum potential Powers-Of-Two value of any field is limited to the number of bit positions within the field. This maximum value for various lengths of fields, in half-byte increments, is as follows:

Field Byte Length	Maximum Powers-of-Two Value
½	15
1	255
1½	4,095
2	65,535
2½	1,048,575
3	16,277,215
3½	268,435,455
4	4,294,967,295
4½	68,719,476,735
5	1,099,511,627,775

The assumed value of any single bit position within a 32-bit field may be determined by referring to the Powers-Of-Two table in Part V of this text. Each successive increment of that table represents the relative bit position of a binary field, from right to left.

A value expressed solely in true binary notation does not have a definitive sign; the sign of the value must, therefore, be considered to be positive. Because of the restriction of having only a positive assumption, true binary representation has limited use in itself as a means of expressing numerics. On the other hand, it is the entire basis for the fixed-point value system.

B. FIXED-POINT VALUE REPRESENTATION

The fixed-point value system is the principal arithmetic process employed by the operating system in maintaining addressing, displacements, and register assignments. It is available to the programmer as a means of compact and expedient arithmetic operations via AssemblerLanguage fixed-point instructions. The representation of a fixed-point value is based on binary value representation with the additional capability of expressing both negative and positive values. The sign of the fixed-point value is determined by the left-most high-order bit of the field. All other bits are combined in binary representation to create the integer value of the field. Using a 16-bit field as an example, the following illustration points out the single sign-bit and the 15 bits comprising the integer.

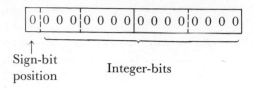

↑
Sign-bit
position   Integer-bits

Because a fixed-point value may commonly be expressed either as a halfword or as a fullword, depending on the size of the

value, the number of integer bits vary in accordance with the size of the field. A half-word fixed-point value contains 1 sign-bit and 15 integer-bits; a fullword fixed-point value contains 1 sign-bit and 31 integer-bits.

A positive fixed-point value is expressed as a 31-bit integer in true binary representation and a sign-bit consisting of a zero-bit. The significant digits of the integer are considered to represent the Powers-Of-Two value of their respective positions within the integer field and are summed together to arrive at the whole of the fixed-point value. Using halfword fixed-point values to illustrate this concept, the following examples are presented in the same manner as those for a binary value representation.

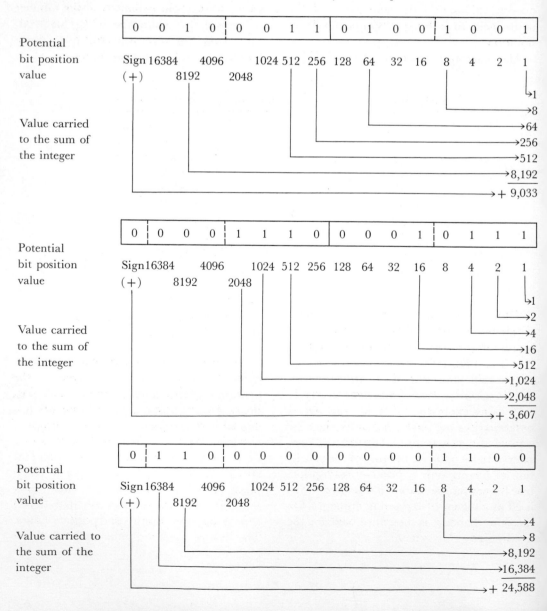

A negative fixed-point value is expressed as a 31-bit or 15-bit integer in *"Two's Complement Notation"* and a sign-bit consisting of a one-bit. In Two's Complement notation, a significant digit-bit is considered to be a zero-bit because it is the opposite of the sign-bit. The interpretation of a negative fixed-point value may be accomplished by:

1. Subtracting a one-bit from the low-order (right-most) bit position of the field.

2. Reversing the configuration of all bit positions.

3. Summing the representative value of all significant integer bits.

This process is indicated in the following illustrations.

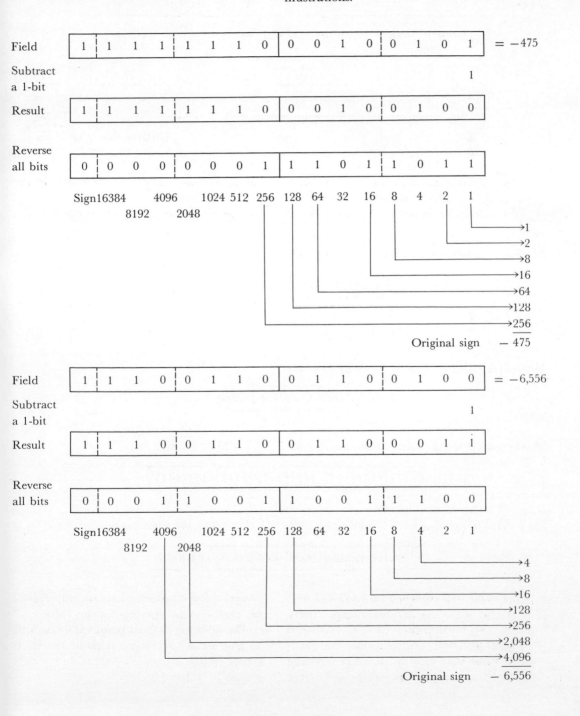

Field

| 1 | 0 | 0 | 1 | 1 | 1 | 1 | 1 | 1 | 1 | 1 | 1 | 1 | 0 | 1 | 1 |

= −24,581

Subtract
a 1-bit

| | | | | | | | | | | | | | | | 1 |

Result

| 1 | 0 | 0 | 1 | 1 | 1 | 1 | 1 | 1 | 1 | 1 | 1 | 1 | 0 | 1 | 0 |

Reverse
all bits

| 0 | 1 | 1 | 0 | 0 | 0 | 0 | 0 | 0 | 0 | 0 | 0 | 0 | 1 | 0 | 1 |

Sign 16384   4096   1024 512 256 128   64 32   16   8   4   2   1

8192   2048

→1
→4
→8,192
→16,384

Original sign   − 24,581

The maximum negative and positive values that can be contained within a half-word or fullword location, and the configuration of those values, are displayed in the examples below:

Note that the maximum positive fixed-

Maximum halfword positive fixed-point value = +32,767

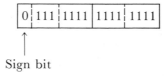

Sign bit

Maximum halfword negative fixed-point value   − 32,768

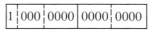

Maximum fullword positive fixed-point value   +2,147,483,647

Maximum fullword negative fixed-point value   − 2,147,483,648

| 1 | 000 | 0000 | 0000 | 0000 | 0000 | 0000 | 0000 | 0000 |

point value of a fullword (+2,147,483,647) is not so great as the maximum binary value representation of a fullword (+4,294,967,295). This is because the fixed-point value may only use 31 bit positions of the field as integer bits, whereas the true binary value representation can utilize all 32 bit positions as representing the value.

The addition of fixed-point values, as well as true binary representations of values, is based on the schedule of sums and results shown in Table 3-1.

TABLE 3-1. Bit Values

Field 'A'		Field 'B'		Sum	
0	plus	0	equals	0	
0	plus	1	equals	1	
1	plus	0	equals	1	
1	plus	1	equals	0	with a carry-over of 1 to the next higher bit position of either field.

The following illustration represents a series of additions of a value of +1 to a halfword fixed-point field.

Fixed-point subtraction is accomplished

Original field

| 0 | 0 | 0 | 0 | 0 | 0 | 0 | 0 | 0 | 0 | 0 | 0 | 0 | 0 | 0 | 0 |

Plus 1　　1

Equals 1

| 0 | 0 | 0 | 0 | 0 | 0 | 0 | 0 | 0 | 0 | 0 | 0 | 0 | 0 | 0 | 1 |

Plus 1　　1

Equals 2

| 0 | 0 | 0 | 0 | 0 | 0 | 0 | 0 | 0 | 0 | 0 | 0 | 0 | 0 | 1 | 0 |

Plus 1　　1

Equals 3

| 0 | 0 | 0 | 0 | 0 | 0 | 0 | 0 | 0 | 0 | 0 | 0 | 0 | 0 | 1 | 1 |

Plus 1　　1

Equals 4

| 0 | 0 | 0 | 0 | 0 | 0 | 0 | 0 | 0 | 0 | 0 | 0 | 0 | 1 | 0 | 0 |

Plus 1　　1

Equals 5

| 0 | 0 | 0 | 0 | 0 | 0 | 0 | 0 | 0 | 0 | 0 | 0 | 0 | 1 | 0 | 1 |

Plus 1　　1

Equals 6

| 0 | 0 | 0 | 0 | 0 | 0 | 0 | 0 | 0 | 0 | 0 | 0 | 0 | 1 | 1 | 0 |

Plus 1　　1

Equals 7

| 0 | 0 | 0 | 0 | 0 | 0 | 0 | 0 | 0 | 0 | 0 | 0 | 0 | 1 | 1 | 1 |

Plus 1　　1

Equals 8

| 0 | 0 | 0 | 0 | 0 | 0 | 0 | 0 | 0 | 0 | 0 | 0 | 1 | 0 | 0 | 0 |

Plus 1　　1

Equals 9

| 0 | 0 | 0 | 0 | 0 | 0 | 0 | 0 | 0 | 0 | 0 | 0 | 1 | 0 | 0 | 1 |

Plus 1　　1

Equals 10	0	0	0	0	0	0	0	0	0	0	0	0	1	0	1	0
Plus 1																1
Equals 11	0	0	0	0	0	0	0	0	0	0	0	0	1	0	1	1
Plus 1																1
Equals 12	0	0	0	0	0	0	0	0	0	0	0	0	1	1	0	0
Plus 1																1
Equals 13	0	0	0	0	0	0	0	0	0	0	0	0	1	1	0	1
Plus 1																1
Equals 14	0	0	0	0	0	0	0	0	0	0	0	0	1	1	1	0

by the system by first reversing the configuration of the subtrahend to its complement form of value and then adding the two fields together. (See Examples 1, 2, and 3.)

Notice that in Example 2 a negative value was to be subtracted from a positive value. The subtrahend (the negative value) was first reversed to its complement, resulting in the true binary notation form of a positive value.

It was then added to the first value (the minuend) and the correct difference was obtained.

C. HEXADECIMAL REPRESENTATION

The hexadecimal number system participates very actively in System/360 program-

Example 1

$$+245 \text{ less } + 83 = +162 \qquad OR \qquad +245 \text{ plus } -83 = +162$$

| 0 | 0 0 0 | 0 0 0 0 | 1 1 1 1 | 0 1 0 1 | +245

| 1 | 1 1 1 | 1 1 1 1 | 1 0 1 0 | 1 1 0 1 | plus   −83

| 0 | 0 0 0 | 0 0 0 0 | 1 0 1 0 | 0 0 1 0 | equals +162

Example 2

$$+175 \text{ less } -10 = +185 \qquad OR \qquad +175 \text{ plus } +10 = +185$$

| 0 | 0 0 0 | 0 0 0 0 | 1 0 1 0 | 1 1 1 1 | +175

| 0 | 0 0 0 | 0 0 0 0 | 0 0 0 0 | 1 0 1 0 | plus   +10

| 0 | 0 0 0 | 0 0 0 0 | 1 0 1 1 | 1 0 0 1 | equals +185

Example 3

$$+2938 \text{ less } +5961 = -3023 \qquad OR \qquad +2938 \text{ plus } -5,961 = -3023$$

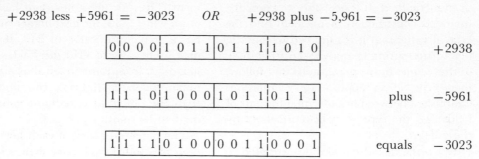

|0|0 0 0|1 0 1 1|0 1 1 1|1 0 1 0| +2938

|1|1 1 0|1 0 0 0|1 0 1 1|0 1 1 1| plus −5961

|1|1 1 1|0 1 0 0|0 0 1 1|0 0 0 1| equals −3023

ming. It is a *"Base-16"* numeric structure wherein every four bits of the binary configuration of the data or value is represented by a single hexadecimal digit. Core dumps, a printed listing of the contents of certain areas of core storage at a planned point in time or as the result of an abnormal termination of processing, are listed in hexadecimal format. Addresses and instructions on an Assembler Language compiler source listing are referenced in hexadecimals, as are many other functional values within the overall scope of System/360. Even fixed-point and true binary values are more easily interpreted when written in hexadecimal notation, as opposed to the format of individual bit configuration expressions. It is, therefore, of prime importance that the programmer obtain a very solid grasp on the fundamentals and concepts of the hexadecimal number system and hexadecimal arithmetic operations.

The range of hexadecimal digit representation is from 0 through 9 and from A through F. The configuration of each of these hex digits is shown in Table 3-2.

The decimal value of any hexadecimal digit is directly related to the Powers-Of-Two value of the significant bits within the four bit positions of the hexadecimal. This can be illustrated by using the true binary format

TABLE 3-2

Numeral	Hexadecimal	Bit Configuration
0	0	0 0 0 0
1	1	0 0 0 1
2	2	0 0 1 0
3	3	0 0 1 1
4	4	0 1 0 0
5	5	0 1 0 1
6	6	0 1 1 0
7	7	0 1 1 1
8	8	1 0 0 0
9	9	1 0 0 1
10	A	1 0 1 0
11	B	1 0 1 1
12	C	1 1 0 0
13	D	1 1 0 1
14	E	1 1 1 0
15	F	1 1 1 1

of the hexadecimal digit 'E' and interpreting its value by Powers-Of-Two summation.

A single hexadecimal digit may, therefore, represent any decimal value within the range of '0' through '15'. However, it is seldom that a single hexadecimal digit is used as a solitary value. More often multiple hex digits will be used to represent a value or set of data. A compound hexadecimal field, one which consists of more than one hexadecimal

Hexadecimal 'E' equals
Potential bit position value

Value carried to the sum
of the field

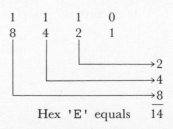

Hex 'E' equals   14

digit, may represent many kinds of character or numeric data. It is necessary to know the intended construction of the field and the type of value that it is supposed to contain, before attempting to analyze the magnitude of that value. In the paragraphs that follow, there will be an appropriate relationship established between hexadecimal formats of fields and the type of data represented by those fields.

When the hexadecimal digits are used to interpret the decimal value of a binary or a fixed-point value, each hexadecimal digit is considered to be a Base-16 unit of increment. The right-most hex digit has a maximum value of 15, the next higher-order digit has a maximum value of 240, the next a maximum value of 3840, etc. Each successive hex digit, from right to left, has a potential maximum value that is sixteen times greater than the potential maximum value of the digit to its right.

The potential range of each hexadecimal digit of a four-byte binary field is indicated in this illustration:

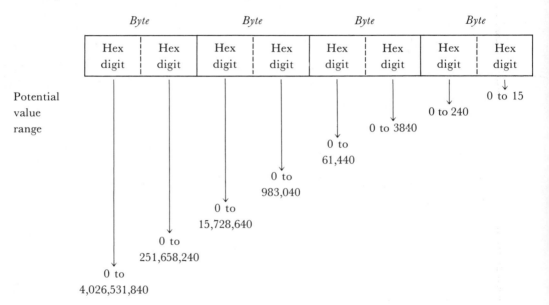

The Hexadecimal/Decimal Conversion Table (see Part V) should be used to aid in interpreting binary values that are comprised of more than one hexadecimal digit. It is an expedient method of converting the positional hex digits into their relative Base-16 value.

The following examples consist of binary values, illustrated in both their binary and hexadecimal format, which have been interpreted as the decimal value they represent by using the Hexadecimal/Decimal Conversion Table.

In using the table to interpret this ex-

Example 1

Binary	0000	1001	0010	0101
Hexadecimal	0	9	2	5

→5
→32
→2304
→0

2341

ample, the standard procedure of beginning at the right-most hex digit was used. The right-most hex digit of '5' assumes its own value. The next hex digit, '2', has its value determined by looking at the corresponding column of values within the table—0 = 0, 1 = 16, 2 = 32, etc. The next higher-order hex digit, '9', is evaluated by the corresponding table column—0 = 0, 1 = 256, 2 = 512, 3 = 768, etc.

Example 2

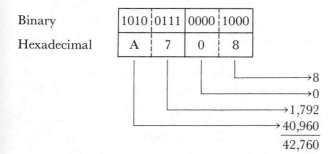

Binary

| 1010 | 0111 | 0000 | 1000 |

Hexadecimal

| A | 7 | 0 | 8 |

→8
→0
→1,792
→40,960
—————
42,760

Example 3

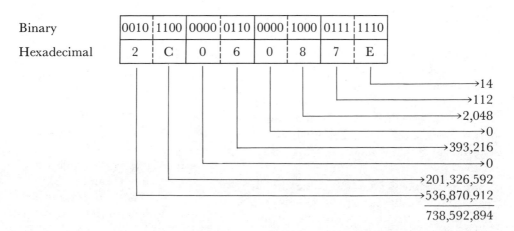

Binary

| 0010 | 1100 | 0000 | 0110 | 0000 | 1000 | 0111 | 1110 |

Hexadecimal

| 2 | C | 0 | 6 | 0 | 8 | 7 | E |

→14
→112
→2,048
→0
→393,216
→0
→201,326,592
→536,870,912
——————
738,592,894

It is quite likely that the programmer will want to accomplish a decimal-to-hexadecimal conversion process at some time or another. This too becomes a relatively easy task when utilizing the Hexadecimal/Decimal Conversion Table. The decimal value that is to be converted to hexadecimals is used to find a relative value range on the Conversion Table. The value sought on the table should be equal to the decimal value or else the next smaller value than the decimal value. The corresponding representative hex digit is recorded and the table value is subtracted from the decimal value. The remaining decimal value balance is now searched for and the process is repeated. A detailed example of this action is shown below.

The decimal value that is to be converted is 15,931.

Step a   15,931
Step b   12,288 = 3
          ————————
Step c   3,643
Step d   3,584 = E
          ————————
Step e   59
Step f   48 = 3
          ————————
Step g   11
            11 = B
          ————————
Step h   Hex value = '3E3B'

Step a. The decimal that is to be converted is written down.

Step b. The table is scanned to find a value that is equal to or nearest to, but less than, the value of 15,931. The closest value in the table is 12,288 (in column 4 from the right) so this number is set down to be subtracted from the decimal value. The hex digit '3' represents the value of 12,288 in that column of the table, so it is also recorded.

Step c. Subtract the table value from the original value, determining the balance of the original value that is yet to be converted.

Step d. The table is now scanned again, this time in order to find the value that is closest to, but not greater than, 3643. Secondary scans and all subsequent scans of the table should always be to the column of values that are one column to the right of the column in which the last value was found. In this example a value of 3584 is found in the column to the immediate right of the column in which the value of 12,288 was found. Being the nearest value to 3643, the table value of 3584 is noted along with its hexadecimal representation of 'E'.

Step e. Subtracting the value of 3584 from the previous remaining balance results in a new balance of 59. This amount will represent the value that will next be searched for on the table.

Step f. In looking for the value that is nearest to 59 in the next right column, the value of 48 is found. It is the single value within the table that is closest to, but not greater than, the balance value of 59. The value of 48 and its hexadecimal representation of '3' are recorded.

Step g. The newest value is subtracted from the latest balance, resulting in the newest balance. Because the search has now progressed to the right-most column of the table, the new balance cannot exceed a value of 15—otherwise a mistake has occurred during the conversion process. In this instance, the exact value of 11 is found on the table and its hexadecimal representation of 'B' is noted.

Step h. The hexadecimal digits recorded from the table are now taken from top to bottom and are set down from left to right

as a compound hexadecimal expression. This results in the hexadecimal '3E3B', which in Base-16 is exactly equal to a decimal value of 15,931.

In describing these steps it was mentioned that each time a value was found in a table column, the subsequent search should begin in the next column to the right. It must be carefully noted that if a satisfactory value is not found in that column during the subsequent search, a hex '0' digit should be recorded and the search should then progress to the next column to the right of that one. If a hexadecimal zero-digit is not recorded for each column in which a satisfactory value was not found, the resulting compound hexadecimal configuration will be grossly incorrect. The following examples illustrate the procedure of recording hex '0' digits during the conversion process.

Example 1. The decimal value that is to be converted is 47,621.

$$
\begin{array}{ll}
47,621 & \\
\underline{45,056} = B & \text{(Found in column 4} \\
2,565 & \text{from the right)} \\
\underline{2,560} = A & \text{(Found in column 3)} \\
5 & \\
 = 0 & \text{(No comparable value} \\
& \text{in column 2)} \\
\underline{5} = 5 & \text{(Found in column 1)} \\
\end{array}
$$

The hex value is expressed as 'BA05'.

Example 2. The decimal value that is to be converted is 36,908.

$$
\begin{array}{ll}
36,908 & \\
\underline{36,864} = 9 & \text{(Found in Column 4)} \\
44 & \\
 = 0 & \text{(No comparable value} \\
& \text{in column 3)} \\
\underline{32} = 2 & \text{(Found in column 2)} \\
12 & \\
\underline{12} = C & \text{(Found in column 1)} \\
\end{array}
$$

The hex value is expressed as '902C'.

Example 3. The decimal value that is to be converted is 11,863,712.

11,863,712

$\underline{11,534,336}$ = B (Found in column 6

329,376   from the right)

$\underline{327,680}$ = 5 (Found in column 5)

1,696

     = 0 (No comparable value

             in column 4)

$\underline{1,536}$ = 6 (Found in column 3)

160

$\underline{160}$ = A (Found in column 2)

0 = 0 (Found in column 1)

The hexadecimal value is expressed as 'B506A0'.

The importance of inserting a hexadecimal zero-digit when a value is not extracted from each successive column is reflected in these examples. If the zero-digit had not been placed into Example 1, the hex configuration would have resulted in 'BA5'—equal to a decimal value of 2981. If the zero digits had not been inserted in Example 3, the resulting hex configuration would have been 'B56A' —equal to a decimal value of 46,442. The general rule to follow is this: "Once the column containing the first value to be subtracted has been found, each successive column to the right must be represented by either a significant hex digit or a hex zero-digit." Even if the total decimal value has been reduced to a zero balance prior to exhausting all columns to the right, each of the remaining columns must be represented by zero-digits.

Decimal value to be converted is 720,896.

720,896

$\underline{720,896}$ = B (Found in column 5

             from the right)

0 = 0 (Found in column 4)

0 = 0 (Found in column 3)

0 = 0 (Found in column 2)

0 = 0 (Found in column 1)

The hexadecimal value is expressed as 'B0000'.

Fixed-point values expressed in hexadecimal format vary somewhat from true binary values similarly expressed, in that the value of the sign-bit is included in the high-order hexadecimal digit. By looking at that high-order hex digit, it can be immediately determined whether or not the fixed-point value is of a positive or a negative configuration. Because a positive value will contain a zero-bit in the high-order bit position of the high-order hex digit, a positive fixed-point value will always contain a high-order hex digit of '7' or less. Conversely, a negative fixed-point value will always contain a high-order hex digit of '8' or greater.

The positive-signed decimal equivalent of a positive fixed-point value is interpreted from hexadecimal digits as shown in the next examples.

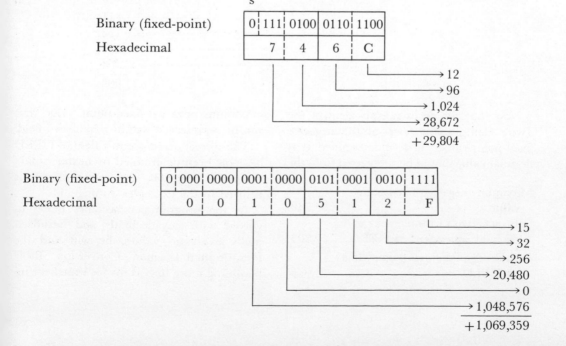

As shown in the above illustrations, there is no apparent difference between the process of interpreting binary values from hexadecimal fields or interpreting positive fixed-point values from hexadecimal fields. This can be attributed to the fact that a positive fixed-point value will always contain a zero-bit sign-bit. A negative fixed-point value will always contain a one-bit sign-bit, which is not considered to be a part of the overall value of the integer. Therefore, it is necessary to modify the representation of the high-order hexadecimal digit prior to manually converting the negative fixed-point values from hexadecimal to decimal. Because a negative value of this type is in Two's Complement form, the interpretation of the Base-16 values of the hex digits will not present the real negative value of the field. This problem may be circumvented by converting the hexadecimal digits of the negative value to the decimal equivalent of those digits and then subtracting that decimal value from the maximum negative fixed-point value containable in a field of equal length. For example, a negative value that is to be interpreted resides in a halfword storage location. The value is −14,965.

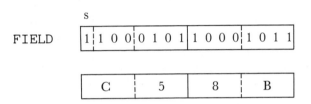

Because the high-order hex digit is greater than seven, it is known that the value must be of a negative power. In order to convert the integer value of this number, it is necessary to exclude the one-bit sign-bit from the value of the high-order hex digit; 'C' minus '8' (the hex value of the sign-bit) equals '4'. The hexadecimal digits could now be converted as:

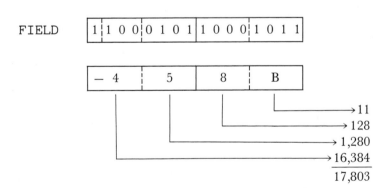

Now that the decimal equivalent of the Two's Complement form of the negative fixed-point value has been determined, that decimal value should be subtracted from the

Maximum negative fixed-point value	32,768
Subtract Two's Complement of decimal equivalent of FIELD	17,803
Actual negative fixed-point value of FIELD	14,965

maximum negative fixed-point value that can be represented within a halfword field.

The correct decimal equivalent of FIELD has now been determined by hexadecimal/decimal conversion. This same process is utilized in the examples on page 39.

As the programmer becomes more involved with hexadecimals and hexadecimally expressed values, he will find the Hexadecimal/Decimal Conversion Table becoming more important for expedient in-

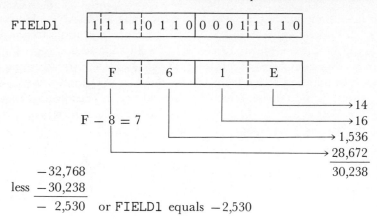

FIELD1

| F | 6 | 1 | E |

F − 8 = 7

→14
→16
→1,536
→28,672

30,238

− 32,768
less − 30,238
─────────
− 2,530   or FIELD1 equals −2,530

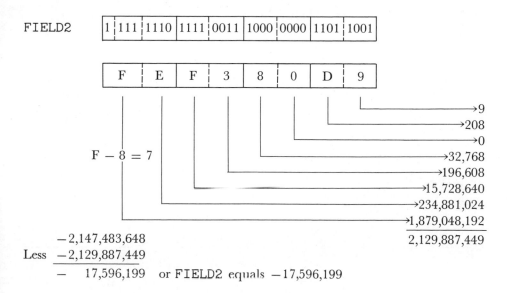

FIELD2

| F | E | F | 3 | 8 | 0 | D | 9 |

F − 8 = 7

→9
→208
→0
→32,768
→196,608
→15,728,640
→234,881,024
→1,879,048,192

2,129,887,449

− 2,147,483,648
Less − 2,129,887,449
─────────
−   17,596,199   or FIELD2 equals −17,596,199

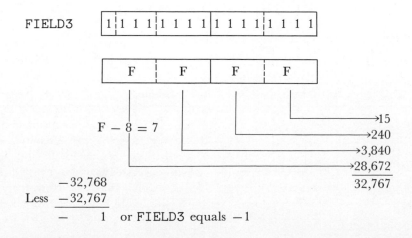

FIELD3

| F | F | F | F |

F − 8 = 7

→15
→240
→3,840
→28,672

32,767

− 32,768
Less − 32,767
─────────
−   1   or FIELD3 equals −1

terpretation. As he becomes more proficient with this type of arithmetic expression, the use of this table will become second nature and portions of it will probably be committed to memory. In addition to the table, there are procedures for adding and subtracting hexadecimals that will be of considerable assistance to the programmer in determining relocatable addresses, displacement factors, and table increments.

The rules for adding together any type of values follow the corresponding parameters for the "base" of those values. Accordingly, the addition of hexadecimal digits must follow the value parameters of a Base-16 concept. For example:

$$
\begin{array}{ccccc}
\text{F} & & \text{F} \ (15) & & \text{F} \ (15) \\
\underline{+\text{A}} & OR & \underline{+\text{A}} \ (10) & OR & \underline{+\text{A}} \ (10) \\
? & & ? \ (25) & & 19 \ (25)
\end{array}
$$

(25 less 16 equals 9 with a carryover of 1)

Carefully examine the following examples of multiple hexadecimal digit addition.

Subtracting hexadecimal digits follows the general rules of subtraction that apply to any

Example 1. Hex '0C3' plus Hex '175' equals?

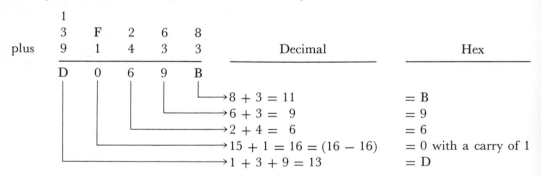

```
           1
           0   C   3
  plus     1   7   5                  Decimal                          Hex
          _____
           2   3   8
                    →5 + 3 = 8                                         = 8
                   →12 + 7 = 19 = 19 − 16                              = 3 with a carry of 1
                  →1 + 0 + 1 = 2                                       = 2
```

Example 2. Hex '3F268' plus Hex '91433' equals?

```
           1
           3   F   2   6   8
  plus     9   1   4   3   3              Decimal                          Hex
          _____
           D   0   6   9   B
                        →8 + 3 = 11                                       = B
                       →6 + 3 =  9                                        = 9
                      →2 + 4 =  6                                         = 6
                     →15 + 1 = 16 = (16 − 16)                             = 0 with a carry of 1
                    →1 + 3 + 9 = 13                                       = D
```

Example 3. Hex '29FD09' plus Hex 'F8030A' equals?

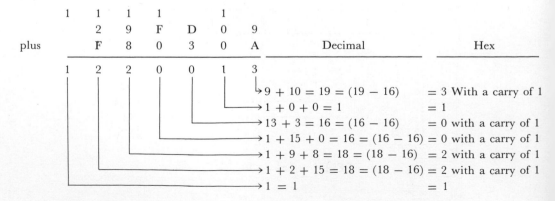

```
         1   1   1   1       1
         2   9   F   D   0   9
  plus   F   8   0   3   0   A              Decimal                          Hex
        _____
     1   2   2   0   0   1   3
                        →9 + 10 = 19 = (19 − 16)        = 3 With a carry of 1
                       →1 + 0 + 0 = 1                   = 1
                      →13 + 3 = 16 = (16 − 16)          = 0 with a carry of 1
                     →1 + 15 + 0 = 16 = (16 − 16) = 0 with a carry of 1
                    →1 + 9 + 8 = 18 = (18 − 16)         = 2 with a carry of 1
                   →1 + 2 + 15 = 18 = (18 − 16)         = 2 with a carry of 1
                  →1 = 1                                = 1
```

Example 4. Hex '49DE2' plus Hex '5F6' equals?

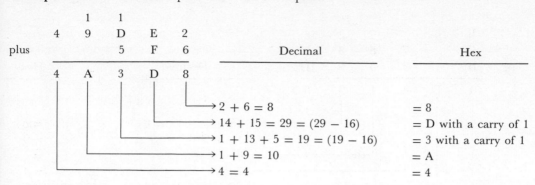

base number system. For example, when a unit is "borrowed" from the next higher hex digit it assumes a value of 16 to the column that is borrowing it.

The following examples illustrate the process of "borrowing" as it is applied during the subtraction of hexadecimal digits.

$$
\begin{array}{cc}
& \text{C} \quad 16 \\
\text{D} \quad 8 \qquad\qquad \not{\text{D}} \quad 8 \\
\quad OR \\
\text{less} \quad 1 \quad 9 \qquad\qquad \text{less} \quad 1 \quad 9 \\
\hline
? \qquad\qquad\quad \text{B} \quad \text{F}
\end{array}
\qquad
\begin{array}{cc}
\text{C} \\
\not{\text{D}} \quad 24 \\
OR \\
\text{less} \quad 1 \quad 9 \\
\hline
\text{B} \quad \text{F}
\end{array}
$$

$$(12 - 1 = 11 = B)\ (24 - 9 = 15 = F)$$

Example 1. Hex '39F48' less Hex '17058' equals?

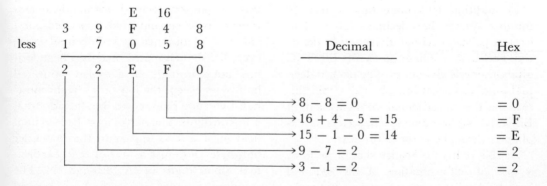

Example 2. Hex 'F20351' less Hex '30D21B' equals?

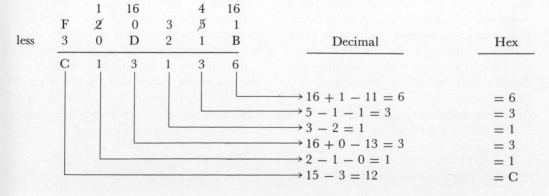

Example 3. Hex 'C27835' less Hex 'B4339D' equals?

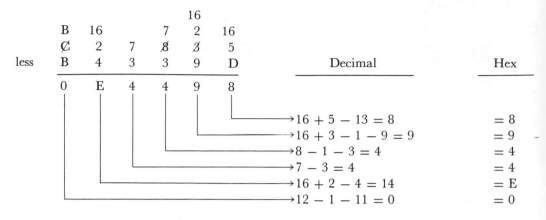

	16			16	2	16		Decimal	Hex
less	B	16		7	2	16			
	Ȼ	2	7	8	3	5			
	B	4	3	3	9	D			
	0	E	4	4	9	8			

$16 + 5 - 13 = 8$ = 8
$16 + 3 - 1 - 9 = 9$ = 9
$8 - 1 - 3 = 4$ = 4
$7 - 3 = 4$ = 4
$16 + 2 - 4 = 14$ = E
$12 - 1 - 11 = 0$ = 0

It is understandable that hexadecimals are often looked upon with apprehension by the student programmer. This is primarily because most number systems are comprised solely of numeric representation structures, rather than including alpha characters such as those utilized by hexadecimal logic. Once the programmer becomes accustomed to thinking of the hexadecimal alpha digits in their numeric sense, such as $A = 10$, $B = 11$, $C = 12$, etc., much of the apprehension of hexadecimal configurations should vanish.

In addition to representing a Base-16 number system, hexadecimals are used to express packed decimal digits and to define the half-byte configurations of EBCDIC alpha-numeric characters. The packed decimal number system is explained within this section; the hexadecimal configuration of EBCDIC alpha-numeric characters is explained throughout the entire text.

At this point the reader should perform a task of self-evaluation of his acquired knowledge of the concepts of hexadecimals. If the discussions presented within this section have not yet sufficiently provided a reasonable working knowledge of hexadecimal/decimal conversions and simple hexadecimal arithmetic operations such as subtraction and addition, it is strongly suggested that the entire section be reviewed.

D. THE PACKED DECIMAL NUMBER SYSTEM

The packed decimal number system utilizes the representation wherein the value field will usually consist of a single sign-digit and one or more numeric digits, all of which are represented by hexadecimal digits. In this type of application, the hexadecimal digit is not considered to be a Base-16 value, but instead it represents a self-expressing digit. Logically, since the packed decimal digits are represented by hex digits, each packed decimal number occupies only one-half byte. The configuration of a packed decimal value may be in signed or unsigned representation, but it must be a signed value if it is to be used in packed decimal arithmetic operations or is to be converted to a fixed-point value. In an unsigned packed decimal value, every half-byte is represented by a hexadecimal numeric digit; in a signed value, all half-bytes except the low-order (right-most) half-byte are represented by hexadecimal numeric digits. The sign of a packed decimal field must always appear in the low-order half-byte and must be one of the hexadecimal alpha digits of 'A' through 'F'. The standard positive $(+)$ sign for a packed decimal value is a hex 'C' or 'F'; the standard negative $(-)$ sign is a hex 'D'. Both signed and unsigned packed decimal values and their equivalent decimal values are contained in the illustration on page 43.

As indicated by these examples, the hexadecimal configuration of a packed decimal field is self-expressing as to the decimal equivalent of the packed decimal value. Fields 1, 3, and 5 are signed positive values; fields 6 and 8 are signed negative values; fields 2, 4, and 7 are unsigned values, assumed to be positive in lieu of a sign. The

Packed Decimal Fields

Assumed
Decimal equivalent

1.

| 0 | 3 | 5 | 5 | 6 | C |

+ 3,556

2.

| 9 | 9 | 7 | 5 |

9,975

3.

| 0 | 0 | 0 | 0 | 0 | C |

+ 0

4.

| 7 | 5 | 8 | 4 | 4 | 1 | 2 | 6 |

75,844,126

5.

| 9 | C |

+ 9

6.

| 0 | 0 | 0 | 0 | 1 | 8 | 8 | D |

− 188

7.

| 0 | 6 | 2 | 0 |

620

8.

| 1 | 9 | 5 | 3 | 3 | D |

− 19,533

latter three fields could not be used in conjunction with packed decimal arithmetic operations in their present format.

E. NUMERIC CHARACTER REPRESENTATION

The EBCDIC (Extended Binary Coded Decimal Interchange Code) numeral is the standard numeric character representation. A group of these numerals may be considered to be a numeric value or merely a set of characters that might be intended to create an identifier or identification. The composition of any EBCDIC character consists of eight binary bit positions; one full byte. The left-most four bits are considered to comprise the zone of the character; the right-most four bits comprise the numeric portion. Numeric characters may be signed or unsigned. An unsigned EBCDIC numeral is assumed to be a positive value (+) or a neutral numeric; a signed EBCDIC numeral represents a positive (+) or negative (−)

value, whichever configuration the sign is comprised of.

The unsigned EBCDIC numeral of zero through nine is represented by the hexadecimals digit sets of 'F0' through 'F9'. The entire range is shown in Table 3-3.

These unsigned numeric characters are considered to be positive values in lieu of having a signed configuration.

A signed EBCDIC numeral is referred to

TABLE 3-3

One Byte	Bit Configuration	Unsigned EBCDIC Numeral
F 0	1111 0000	0
F 1	1111 0001	1
F 2	1111 0010	2
F 3	1111 0011	3
F 4	1111 0100	4
F 5	1111 0101	5
F 6	1111 0110	6
F 7	1111 0111	7
F 8	1111 1000	8
F 9	1111 1001	9

as a *"zoned decimal"* configuration. The rightmost byte of a signed value expressed in EBCDIC numerics will be the only one containing a zoned decimal numeral. The positive and negative signed zoned decimals are represented in Table 3-4.

TABLE 3-4

	Signed Positive Zoned Decimals				Signed Negative Zoned Decimals		
Value	Hex	Bit Configuration	EBCDIC Character	Value	Hex	Bit Configuration	EBCDIC Character
+0	C 0	1100 0000	(Blank)	−0	D 0	1101 0000	(Blank)
+1	C 1	1100 0001	A	−1	D 1	1101 0001	J
+2	C 2	1100 0010	B	−2	D 2	1101 0010	K
+3	C 3	1100 0011	C	−3	D 3	1101 0011	L
+4	C 4	1100 0100	D	−4	D 4	1101 0100	M
+5	C 5	1100 0101	E	−5	D 5	1101 0101	N
+6	C 6	1100 0110	F	−6	D 6	1101 0110	O
+7	C 7	1100 0111	G	−7	D 7	1101 0111	P
+8	C 8	1100 1000	H	−8	D 8	1101 1000	Q
+9	C 9	1100 1001	I	−9	D 9	1101 1001	R

As indicated by these tables, a signed EBCDIC numeric (zoned decimal) creates a standard EBCDIC alpha character in all instances except for a zero. A signed zero, either negative or positive, creates a configuration for which there is no valid character representation.

Unsigned EBCDIC numeric fields:

Character Representation   *Assumed Numeric Value*

| 2 | 3 | 6 | 5 | 8 | 1 |

+236,581

| 3 | 9 | 4 | 7 | 8 |

+39,478

| 5 | 2 | 7 |

+527

| 2 |

+2

| 4 | 1 | 1 | 9 |

+4,119

Signed positive-value EBCDIC numeric fields:

Character Representation   *Assumed Numeric Value*

| 2 | 3 | 6 | 5 | 8 | A |

+236,581

| 3 | 9 | 4 | 7 | H |

+39,478

| 5 | 2 | G |

+527

| B |

+2

| 4 | 1 | 1 | I |

+4,119

Signed negative-value EBCDIC numeric fields:

| *Character Representation* | | | | | | *Assumed Numeric Value* |

| 2 | 3 | 6 | 5 | 8 | J |

−236,581

| 3 | 4 | 9 | 7 | Q |

−34,978

| 5 | 2 | P |

−527

| K |

−2

| 4 | 1 | 1 | R |

−4,119

Review Exercises

1. The binary number system is comprised of two numeric digits. These are the numbers __ZERO__ and __ONE__.

2. The high-order (left-most) bit position of an expressed fixed-point value is considered to contain the __Sign__-__BIT__. All other bit positions are considered to comprise the __INTEGER__. *4 bytes 32 bits*

3. The integer of a fullword value is construed as consisting of the right-most __Thirty-one__ bit positions.

4. The "base-16" number system utilized in System/360 is referred to as __HEXADECIMAL__ representation.

5. EBCDIC alphanumeric characters are represented as consisting of __8__ bit positions.

6. The hexadecimal digit 'C' represents a decimal value (base-10) of __12__.

7. Packed decimal digits are graphically represented as synonymous with __HEX__ digit representation.

8. An EBCDIC character that represents a signed (positive or negative) numeric value is referred to as a __Zoned__ __Decimal__.

9. Provide the bit configuration of the following *binary* values:

   a. 48,763

   b. 219,465

   c. 11,557

10. Determine the *fixed-point* value of each of the following fields and express them in decimal form:

   a. _____

S			
0	111	0000	0110	1101

   b. _____

S						
0	000	0000	0010	0001	1101	0011	0101	1101

   c. _____

S			
0	000	1010	0111	1110

   d. _____

S						
0	000	0000	1001	1111	0100	1000	0000	0011

   e. _____

S			
1	110	0010	0001	0101

   f. _____

S						
1	111	1111	1111	1011	1100	0011	1110	1110

11. Complete the bit configuration for the following *fixed-point* values:

   a. A halfword value of +26,715

   b. A halfword value of −8901

   c. A fullword value of +14,211,536

   d. A fullword value of −397,827

12. Determine the *binary* value of each of the binary-expressed fields and indicate that value in decimal form:

a. _____

| 1001 | 0001 | 1100 | 0000 | 1001 | 0111 |

b. _____

| 1111 | 1111 | 1111 | 1111 |

c. _____

| 0000 | 0000 | 0000 | 0000 | 0101 | 1000 | 1110 | 1100 |

d. _____

| 0110 | 0111 | 1000 | 0110 | 0101 | 1001 |

13. Add each of the following sets of hexadecimals, expressing the sum of each set in hexadecimal and in decimal (base-10) form.

	a.	2CA1	*b.*	59F	*c.*	600C	*d.*	A0FF
		3029		3082		514D		2B33
						2953		05C2
Hex		*5CCA*		*3621*		*D AAC*		*D1F4*
Decimal								

	e.	0C00	*f.*	6FF6	*g.*		*h.*	
		31D6		2A1D		A37		2001
		281C		2177		6C9F		300F
Hex		*65F4*		*BB8A*		*76D6*		*5010*
Decimal								

14. Complete the bit configuration for the following sets of hexadecimals:

a. 3FA6C1

| | | | | | |

b. D587

| | | | | | |

c. F347E

| | | | | | |

d. 189C4B

| | | | | | |

15. Subtract the following sets of hexadecimals, expressing the resulting difference for each problem in hexadecimal and as a positive decimal value:

	a.	2C356	*b.*	3A29	*c.*	A59F	*d.*	7B73D
		1D0F7		B36		34B5		42ACF
Hex								
Decimal								

16. Indicate the implied decimal value of these *packed decimal* fields:

a. _____

4	0	0	C

b. _____

0	0	3	0	9	7	0	D

c. _____

0	0	0	0	6	5	0	0	2	C

d. _____

0	8	7	0	0	D

e. _____

1	0	7	8	6	0	3	9

17. Define the implied numeric character value of the following *zoned decimal* character representations:

a. _____

3	0	2	2	5	7	0	6	4	R

b. _____

0	0	7	0	3	M

c. _____

5	5	8	A

d. _____

4	0	0	6	7	9	9	P

ASSEMBLER LANGUAGE INSTRUCTION FORMATS

The System/360 Assembler Language provides a means of program coding that enables the programmer to control the individual logic operations of a program to the smallest degree. It is technically referred to as a low-level language—that is, the structure and relationship of the actual coding instructions are quite close to the actual machine-language level. Although a single machine-language instruction may cause the computer to perform several internal functions, it is generally considered that a machine-language is the lowest level of instructions that can be coded for the computer.

The individual Assembler Language *instruction*, which may be considered to be a *command* or *statement* to the computer, generates a machine-language instruction, along with certain implied or specified parameters relating to that instruction. If the programmer attempted to code in pure machine-language, it would be necessary for him to maintain constant surveillance of boundary alignments, register applications and assignments, displacements, lengths, addresses, and many other features that he would soon find overwhelming. However, the Assembler Language compiler interprets the individual instruction statements in such a way as to supervise control of many of these functions. It is still the programmer's responsibility to assign and maintain register controls, but not nearly to the degree that would be required in machine-language coding.

Programming with Assembler Language will include the use of *macroinstructions* as provided by the operating system and access methods that are to be used. A macroinstruction is a unique instruction, or command, that may be stated with a variable number of operand parameters. A single macroinstruction will *generate* a series of Assembler Language instructions and macrocoding that will provide a service to the programmer without requiring him to become involved in complex coding. The term generate, as used here, may be somewhat misleading in that the macroinstruction does not really create any unique coding. All of the related instruction statements for each macroinstruction are contained in an operating system library if their inclusion was specified at system generation time. The use of a macroinstruction in the problem program results in a *call* to this library in order to provide the system with the instructions necessary to perform the task for which that macroinstruction was designed. The names, as well as the performance, of the macroinstructions may vary considerably between access methods and operating systems. This text will make no attempt to discuss macroinstructions other than an occasional use of one or two in examples of program coding routines. Even then the use of such macros will be referred to in the most general terms.

The individual Assembler Language instructions described in this text will be the Standard Instruction Set and the Decimal Feature Instruction Set. Floating-Point Logic and Floating-Point Feature Instructions of Assembler Language are not to be included in these discussions. In the author's opinion, floating-point arithmetic operations in Assembler Language are not required for the majority of programming students at this stage of their education; the complexity of floating-point applications lends itself to a high-level language of the nature of PL/I or FORTRAN. This could well be a controversial opinion, but with all due apologies, it is the basis on which this portion of the text is presented.

As the study of Assembler Language progresses, supplemented by the discussions and examples within this text, so will the individual's concept of the versatility and scope of System/360 progress. In learning the performance of these instructions, one cannot help but to derive a better understanding of the detailed processes used by the computer system control programs in executing those instructions.

The instruction format has two distinct variations. The first format may be interpreted as the way that the instruction statement is written by the programmer. The second format is the way that the system compiler interprets that coding and rearranges it into an executable machine-language sequence. Although these two format groupings are directly related, the programmer will at first need to be more thoroughly familiar with the coded instruction statement format. Once he has begun to write problem programs, he will find that the knowledge of the machine-language format of these instructions will assist in the analysis and interpretation of errors and coding problems.

A. THE INSTRUCTION STATEMENT CODING FORMAT

An instruction statement, as coded by the programmer, may consist of three sections of data. These are:

1. The *LABEL* or *SYMBOL*
2. The mnemonic *OP CODE*
3. The *OPERANDS,* consisting of from 1 to 3 per statement.

These three sections comprise an individual instruction statement in its maximum form. Of these, only the op code and the operands are required in order to create a valid statement, as will be brought out in the following paragraphs.

1. The Label or Symbol

The label is referred to as a symbol, a tag, a name, or an identifier, depending on the nomenclature to which the individual has been exposed. Overall, regardless of the reference to it, it is a name that is used to identify the address of an instruction statement, a defined area, a constant, or the beginning of a routine or subroutine. Whenever a label is used as a part of one of these, the compiler cross-references that label as the address point within the program for that data. Any separate references to that label would then be the same as to use the actual address to which the label relates. A label, therefore, is merely a convenient means of referring to a certain address for a section or a part of the problem program. If no reference is required, it is unnecessary to use a label for identification.

The actual configuration of the label has certain restrictions. The number of characters comprising the label varies between the different operating systems. For use within the full Operating System (OS), the label may consist of from 1 to 8 characters. Although these characters may be mixed alpha-numerics, the first character of the label must be alphabetic. The label may not contain special characters or embedded blanks. The following list consists of valid label references:

SKIP	PACKRT1
K23456	R
PTS32R	BRANCH
ADD	MOVE
M3M3M3	MVO

Note that the last label (MVO) is also the op code for the Move With Offset instruction. This is a valid label as long as it is coded in the proper position on the coding sheet. Any combination of alpha-numerics that the programmer can originate are valid if he follows the composition restrictions for a label. Because a unique label is used to reference any single address within the problem program, it is understandable that the same identical label may not be used to reference two different addresses within that program.

2. The Op Code

The op code is the mnemonic representation of the instruction that is to be performed by the instruction statement. It represents an activity that the system compiler is to translate into a machine-language instruction, telling the object program just what action is to be accomplished. The op code usually represents a single Assembler Language instruction, although it may also represent a macroinstruction identity. In most instances, it will be found that the alphabetic characters comprising the op code will have a noticeable relationship to the descriptive name for the instruction that it represents. This relationship is shown in the following op codes for Assembler Language instructions:

AR	Add Registers
CL	Compare Logical
EDMK	Edit & Mark
CVD	Convert to Decimal
LPR	Load Positive Register
STM	Store Multiple
DP	Divide Packed
EX	Execute

3. The Operands

Although a macroinstruction statement need not necessarily have any operands, for any single Assembler Language instruction the statement itself may consist of from 1 to 3 operand parameters. Each individual instruction has a specific number of operands required whenever that instruction is used to comprise an instruction statement. The operand(s) provide the problem program with the address of the field(s) or data that is to be affected by the execution of the op code. For example, the Move Characters (MVC) instruction requires two operands when it is coded into an instruction statement—an operand identifying the area from which the data is to be moved and an operand identifying the field into which the data is to be placed. The unique characteristics of the op code for each instruction determines the use and application of the address generated by the operands. In most instances, the contents, or value, specified by the second operand will be used to alter the contents, or value, of the first operand. There are exceptions to this performance, so it is necessary to be completely aware of the activity generated by each instruction.

Included with the individual summarized descriptions of the Assembler Language instructions within this text will be an item referred to as a *Format*. For that particular format description, the operands will be shown as consisting of elements, such as $R_1,D_2(X_2,B_2)$. In this instance the R_1 represents the first operand of a completed instruction statement and the $D_2(X_2,B_2)$ represents the second operand. The use of the parentheses indicates that the elements within them may be used to further modify the address generated by the D_2 portion of the operand.

The following is a complete listing of all of the elements comprising the operand formats.

B   Represents the *base register* to be used for the operand in which it is specified.

D   Indicates the *displacement;* an actual or symbolic address or value.

I   An *immediate* or self-defining character or value.

L   An explicit *length* attribute for the operand in which specified.

M   A *mask* value, defined as either a literal or a constant.

R   A *general register* used as an operand; or a label or symbol that has been equated to a general register.

X   An *indexing,* or incrementing, general register.

In order that these codes be related directly to the operand for which they apply, a numeric character is also used to identify the component of the instruction statement to which they belong.

1   The number *1*, paired with a format component of the instruction statement, identifies that component as being a part, or the whole, of the first operand.

2   The number *2*, paired with a format component, identifies that component as being a part, or the whole, of the second operand.

3   The number *3*, paired with a format component, identifies that component as being the whole of the third operand. This value is used only with multiple register operands and identifies the ending register in a sequential range of general registers. An instruction statement of this type will always contain the first operand, the third operand, and then the second operand, in that exact order.

Applying the information to actual coded instruction statements, the identity of the various operands and components would be considered to be as shown in Fig. 4-1.

The general forms taken by the instruction statement formats are grouped as follows.

1.   RR FORMAT:
   (a) R_1,R_2
       Both operands refer to general registers.
   (b) M_1,R_2
       The first operand is a *mask* value; the second operand is a general register.

2.   RS FORMAT:
   (a) $R_1,R_3,D_2(B_2)$
       R_1 and R_3 refer to general registers; $D_2(B_2)$ refers to a displacement or storage address, either as an actual value or as a symbolic reference to an address.
   (b) $R_1,D_2(B_2)$
       R_1 refers to a general register; $D_2(B_2)$ refers to a displacement or storage address, either as an actual value or as a symbolic reference to that address.

3.   RX FORMAT:
   (a) $R_1,D_2(X_2,B_2)$
       R_1 refers to a general register; $D_2(X_2,B_2)$ refers to a displacement or storage address, either as an actual value or as a symbolic reference to an address.
   (b) $M_1,D_2(X_2,B_2)$
       M_1 refers to a mask value; $D_2(X_2,B_2)$ refers to a displacement or storage address, either as an actual address value or as a symbolic reference to an address.

4.   SI FORMAT:
   (a) $D_1(B_1),I_2$
       $D_1(B_1)$ refers to a displacement or storage address, either as an actual value or as a symbolic reference to an address; I_2 refers to a self-defining or *immediate* character, value or reference.

5.   SS FORMAT:
   (a) $D_1(L,B_1),D_2(B_2)$
       Both operands refer to displace-

IBM System/360 Assembler Coding Form

X28-6509-2 U/M050
Printed in U.S.A.

| PROGRAM | | | PAGE | OF |
| PROGRAMMER | DATE | PUNCHING INSTRUCTIONS / GRAPHIC / PUNCH | CARD ELECTRO NUMBER | |

Name	Op Codes	Operand	Comments	Identification-Sequence
LABELS		OPERANDS		
GOTO	BC	8,THERE $\underset{M1}{}\underset{D2}{}$		
PASS12	MVC	FIELD1(10),FIELD2+6 $\underset{D1}{}\underset{L1}{}\underset{D2}{}$		
	STM	3,9,FULLWDS $\underset{R1}{}\underset{R3}{}\underset{D2}{}$		
	CLC	0(5,9),TABLE(7) $\underset{D1}{}\underset{L}{}\underset{B1}{}\underset{D2}{}\underset{B2}{}$		
MVI	MVI	SWITCH,X'00' $\underset{D1}{}\underset{I2}{}$		
	ZAP	FLD1+6(5),FLD2(3) $\underset{D1}{}\underset{L1}{}\underset{D2}{}\underset{L2}{}$		

Figure 4-1

53

ment or storage addresses, either as actual values or as symbolic references to addresses.

(b) $D_1(L_1,B_1),D_2(L_2,B_2)$
Both operands refer to displacement or storage addresses, either as actual values or as symbolic address references.

The operand components contained within the parentheses are optional—that is, they may be specified by their inclusion in the coding or they may be implied by their exclusion from the coding. For example, if the defined length of a field labeled AREA was six bytes, and the instruction statements were coded as:

```
MVC      AREA(4),DATA
MVC      AREA,DATA
```

the first statement would move four bytes of data from DATA into AREA because the length attribute of "4" was specified. The second statement would move six bytes of data because the implied length of AREA is six bytes.

B. CODING SHEET CONVENTIONS

While on the subject of the format of instruction statements, it is an appropriate point at which to describe an accepted practice of writing down the coded instructions. Although the Assembler Language compiler allows a certain amount of free-form instruction statement entry, it is far more desirable for the programmer to adhere to a clean, aligned form of coding. This would mean that the labels, op codes, and the first operand are nearly always aligned onto their own starting point, instruction statement after instruction statement.

Using the standard 80-column coding form provided by the IBM Corporation, this would be considered to be formatted as follows.

Column 1. The LABEL must always start in this column. It may be eight positions in length if written for the Operating System (OS).

Column 10. The OP CODE should begin in this column. Because a blank must always separate a label from the op code, this practice will assure that there is always at least one blank between the op code and a maximum-length label of eight bytes.

Column 16. The first character of the first operand should begin here. This allows at least one blank between the op code and the operands. In some instances wherein a macroinstruction op code is used, that op code may be longer than a regular Assembler Language instruction op code; therefore, in order to leave a blank prior to the first character of the first operand, that operand may have to begin in a higher-numbered column.

By following this suggested format, the source listing printed out by the compiler is quite easily read and interpreted. Using these standards, a set of coded instruction statements that are to be keypunched would appear as in Fig. 4-2.

As shown in this illustration, the labels, op codes, and operands are all consistently aligned in their respective starting positions. There have been several new items introduced in this example for the convenience of the programmer. Some of these are the two different ways of entering *comments* information on the coding sheets without affecting the compiler interpretation of the program instructions. In the middle of the example just presented there are four lines that contain an asterisk (*) in column 1. This symbol indicates to the compiler that these are "comments lines" that are to be included within the source compilation listing, but are not to be included as a part of the object module. As they are shown here, they are being used to create a visual separation between two subroutines, as well as to document the second routine by providing a "comment heading" for that routine. The programmer may write any type of information that he desires on such a line and he may insert these lines wherever he wishes—even between two lines of sequential instruction logic without any affect on the performance of his program.

The second type of "comment" entry is shown on the line labeled FINDIT, line

IBM System/360 Assembler Coding Form

X28-6509-2 U/M050
Printed in U.S.A.

Name	Operation	Operand	Comments	Identification-Sequence
START	MVC	FIELD1,DATA		0001
	STM	2,13,SAVEAREA		0002
	L	5,FWD1		0003
BRANCHED	BAL	6,FINDIT		0004
	ZAP	PACKFLD1,=PL1'0'		0005
	BCT	5,BRANCHED		0006
*				0007
**				0008
**		FINDIT LOOKUP ROUTINE		0009
*				0010
FINDIT	LA	9,10		0011
	CLI	0(9),C'S'		0012
	BCR	8,6	LOAD BASE REGISTER	0013
	MVI	0(10),C'X'		0014
	BCR	15,6		0015
*				0016

Figure 4-2

55

0011. The words "LOAD BASE REGIS-TER" are shown following the operands for this instruction, with several blanks between the comment and the end of the last operand. A comment that is to be written on the same line with an instruction statement may occupy up to, and including, column 71 of the coding sheet, but it must be separated from the operands by at least one blank position.

By using these two means of entering comments, the programmer can thoroughly document the logic of his coding; skipping spaces between subroutines, general headings and explanations of the routines, and a brief explanation of the intent of each instruction if that is desired. Good documentation of the source program is a highly desirable feature and, in many instances, it is a required standard set by data processing management.

Columns 73 to 80 of the coding sheet contain spaces for entering sequence numbers to the individual instruction statements or lines of coding. Any or all of these columns may be used for line identification. These identifications are punched into the source code cards at the same time that the coding statements are keypunched. The keypunched source statement cards now contain an identity that will allow the programmer to resequence them in the event that the card *deck* is dropped, or to change any single source statement by merely following the sequence numbers through the source deck until the proper card is located. The sequence numbers contained on the source deck cards are also listed on the compiled source listing so that the programmer may cross-reference any single source statement.

C. MACHINE-LANGUAGE INSTRUCTION FORMATS

Some knowledge of the format of the machine-language instruction, as created by the Assembler Language compiler, is helpful in analyzing program error conditions and interpreting *core dumps.* A core dump may be explained as a printed listing, in hexadecimal format, of the contents of the core storage areas occupied by the problem program and the related system Supervisor. A core dump is normally produced whenever the problem program encounters various types of programming infractions or data set inconsistencies that result in error interruptions. Such a core storage print-out may be requested by the programmer, requested by the computer operator, or automatically provided by certain error conditions. It is at that time that the programmer may find a need for understanding the machine-language instruction formats in order to follow the phase of programming accomplished immediately prior to the program termination.

These formats, by category of type of instruction, are as follows.

1. RR FORMAT

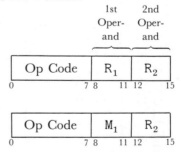

2. RX FORMAT

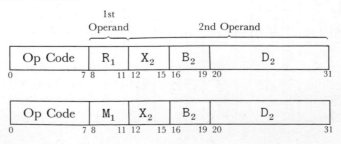

3. RS FORMAT

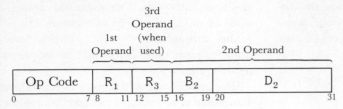

4. SI FORMAT

5. SS FORMAT

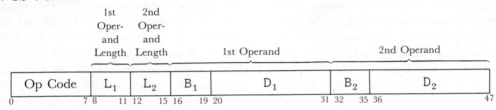

The small numeric figures under each example represents the relative bit positions occupied by that portion of the machine-language instruction format.

The component codes used for these formats are the same as those used for the instruction statement formats. An example of an RX formatted instruction (in machine-language format) can be followed through from the instruction statement format as shown in the following. The instruction statement is:

$$LA \quad 9,83$$

The machine-language format for this statement would be:

$$4\ 1\ 9\ 0\ 0\ 0\ 5\ 3$$

This would be interpreted in a diagram in the following manner:

OP CODE	R_1	X_2	B_2	D_2	
4 1	9	0	0	0 5 3	= Hexadecimal
0100 0001	1001	0000	0000	0000 0101 0011	= Binary
LA	9	0	0	+83	= Actual

D. CONDITION CODES

The *Condition Code* is represented by two bit positions (34 and 35) within the *Program Status Word* (PSW). It is, in effect, a type of indicator used to relate a condition that was created by, or resulted from, the execution of a previous instruction statement. By testing the configuration of the Condition Code the programmer is able to make program logic decisions based on the configuration. Not all Assembler Language instructions affect the bit configuration of the Condition Code bits, as will be noted during the discussion of the individual instructions. Some of the questions that can be answered by the Condition Code are:

1. Was the comparison high, low, or equal?
2. Was the resulting answer zero?
3. Was the resulting answer a positive value or a negative value?
4. Did an arithmetic overflow occur?

There are certain instructions that test the Condition Code and then react according to the parameters coded for that instruction statement. Although it is not necessary to become technically involved with the form and use of the Condition Code at this time, throughout this text there will be additional detailed information regarding the composition and utilization of the Condition Code. The chapter on "Program Branching Logic" will go into specific detail about the bit configuration of the Condition Code within the PSW and the means of coding those instructions in order to create a "branch" to another section of the problem program.

E. REGISTER CONCEPTS AND APPLICATIONS

System/360 has a set of internal storage areas that are referred to as registers. As a part of the system there are sixteen *"general registers,"* referenced by number as "0" through "15". In addition, if the hardware was so ordered, the user may have four additional registers that are referred to as *"floating-point"* registers, each of which have twice the physical number of bit positions of a general register. Because the floating-point registers are not a standard hardware feature on all models and because the floating-point operations are not to be included within this text, all further references to registers hereafter will imply a general register.

A general register is considered to be one fullword in length—4 bytes or 32 bit positions. They are located in a contiguous ar-

rangement, "0" through "15", similar to a chain of fullwords. The technical descriptions of the applications of registers will be found throughout this text, but a basic knowledge of their use should be acquired at this point.

The primary use of a register in Assembler Language is to establish a *"base"* range for referencing a set of instruction statements. When a register is used for this purpose it is referred to as a *"base register."* Simply expressed, the system requires that a base register be assigned for at least every 4096 bytes of object coding generated by the source coding. This includes the areas occupied by constants, literals, and program work fields. The base register creates a type of linkage between the various machine-language instructions contained within the 4096 bytes to which that register has been assigned. If a program is anticipated to generate more than 4096 bytes of object module coding, then enough base registers must be assigned to encompass the number of bytes generated. These assignments would normally be in increments of 4096 bytes.

There are a number of ways to establish base register assignments. If a programmer has the ability to estimate the object coding generated by the program statements, he may assign the base registers throughout the coding of the program as they are required. This can result in poor utilization of the registers because it is nearly impossible to determine the exact point within a program where a new base register assignment is necessary. A very convenient means of base register assignment is the "stringing" of base registers together at the beginning of the problem program coding. A rough estimate of the program size is all that is necessary to initialize several base registers at this point in the program. They are established in such a manner that each 4096 bytes covered by a single base register are consecutive in assignment to the next 4096 bytes. The manner of applying this technique is described within the section "Basic Program Initialization." Because all base register assignments are made at one point in the program, this method of creating the base register assignments allows the addition, or deletion, of extra base registers without difficulty.

A word of caution should be given on the use of certain general registers as base registers. The various operating systems use several of the general registers in order to perform special linkage tasks. When the system takes control of any one of these particular registers, it will destroy the previous value that was contained within that register. For example, when executing an Assembler Language program operating under OS (the full Operating System), it is almost a certainty that the system will use general registers 0, 1, 13, 14, 15 during the operation of that program. In addition, the Assembler Language Translate & Test instruction will destroy any prior contents of general register 2. Using this information as a guide, it is, therefore, safe to assume that general registers 3 through 12 are available to the OS programmer for his exclusive use, either as base registers, or as control registers that are to be used in conjunction with instruction statements.

The application of using registers as a part of the instruction statement is well defined within the description of each instruction to which it pertains. There are basic rules that pertain to this use of registers. Data being loaded into a register from a storage location must be from a storage area that is aligned on a *fullword boundary* address. A fullword boundary is any core location address, within the range of the problem program, that is divisible by four. Data being stored from a general register to a storage location must have the storage location residing on a fullword boundary address.

Registers are required for the performance of fixed-point arithmetic operations. Although the values to be used by fixed-point operations may reside in storage areas, *at least* one value must be loaded into a register in order to accomplish the arithmetic operation. Depending upon the type of fixed-point instruction to be performed, either 1, 2, or 3 general registers might be utilized by the instruction statement.

F. DATA FORMAT

Other than special coding or conversion of information created by the problem program, the *logical* concept of data is represented in three forms: EBCDIC character data, packed decimal numeric data, and fixed-point arithmetic data. As stated, these are the logical concepts of data format, although any one of these may be thought of as being comprised of binary bit configurations or hexadecimal digit configurations. As a rule, however, there will be a general relationship between the concept of the data format and the interpretation of which configuration it is comprised of.

Special codes or converted information created by the problem program must also be thought of in terms of one of the data formats or configurations. There is no standard for determining this information since it is the prerogative of the programmer as to how he believes it would be more easily decoded or reconverted to standard form.

1. Character Data

Character formatted data, as it is used within this text, is construed to be an alphanumeric or special character representation that is comprised of eight binary bit positions and constitutes a graphically defined number, letter, or symbol. This includes alphabetics "A" through "Z," numerics "0" through "9," and such symbol-characters as), (, #, ?, ', $, /, -, etc. A complete listing of the characters that comprise character formatted data can be found in the EBCDIC Character Table in Part V of this text. The letters EBCDIC (which may be pronounced E-BICK-DICK) stands for "Extended Binary-Coded Decimal Interchange Code. This represents a standard character-set code in which the graphic characters are comprised of unique bit configurations, the bit positions being numbered from 0 through 7, from left to right. Inasmuch as it requires eight bit positions to constitute a single EBCDIC character, it may be stated that a single graphic EBCDIC character requires one byte.

Using the letter "F" and the numeric "4" as examples of one-byte EBCDIC characters, the configuration comprising these characters can be thought of as existing in three ways.

		1 Byte		*1 Byte*	
Character format		F		4	
Hexadecimal digit configuration		C	6	F	4
Binary bit configuration		1100	0110	1111	0100

Although it is seldom necessary to know the binary bit configuration of character data, it is often useful to be able to remember the hexadecimal digit composition of alphanumeric characters. This is particularly true when interpreting problem program core dumps, which contain untranslated hexadecimal digits as the core storage representation.

As indicated, any character that is considered to be a standard EBCDIC graphic character consists of a unique eight-bit configuration. Even though a single byte can contain any one of 256 unique bit configurations, there are only 63 EBCDIC graphic characters. The remaining 193 unique bit configurations do not represent characters in the sense that character-formatted data implies.

2. Packed Decimal Data

Packed decimal data is in synonymous form with hexadecimal digit configuration; each packed decimal digit is comprised of four binary bit positions, equal to one-half byte or one *nibble*. The data itself consists of packed decimal numeric digits (0 through 9) and sign-digits (alphabetic hex digits A through F). Each validly signed packed decimal value may have a single sign-digit that must reside in the low-order (right-most) half-byte of the field occupied by that value. The remaining packed decimal digits comprising the whole of the value must be numeric digits only. It is possible to create a packed decimal value in which all digit positions are represented by numeric digits, but this type of packed decimal may not be used for packed decimal arithmetic operations.

Only validly signed packed decimal values may be used in conjunction with an Assembler Language packed decimal arithmetic instruction or operation.

Because of their hexadecimal digit configuration, packed decimal values are easily recognized whenever it is necessary to interpret hexadecimal-configurated core storage dumps. This will become evident in the analysis of the examples that follow within this section and others.

The packed decimal format may be considered to be a compressed means of expressing a conventional character-formatted decimal value. Each byte of packed decimal digits will contain two numeric digits except for the low-order byte, which will usually contain one numeric digit and one sign-digit. A series of decimal values along with the corresponding packed decimal format of these values as they would appear within a four-byte field, are shown in Table 4-1. Although the length of the fields shown for these values was four bytes in each instance, the length need only to be as many bytes as are required to contain the left-most significant (nonzero) packed decimal digit. Note that the sign-digit for the illustrated values varied for similar positive or negative configurations. A valid plus sign (+) may be represented by a hexadecimal 'A', 'C', 'E', or 'F'; a valid negative sign may be represented by 'D' or 'B'. The usual representation generated for a packed decimal value will be a 'C' for a signed positive value and a 'D' for a negative or minus value.

The purpose of creating packed decimal fields is for packed decimal arithmetic operations, compressing numeric data for file stor-

TABLE 4-1

Decimal Value	Equivalent Packed Decimal Value Format							
+254	0	0	0	0	2	5	4	C
+395,116	0	3	9	5	1	1	6	C
+0	0	0	0	0	0	0	0	C
+1	0	0	0	0	0	0	1	C
−45,926	0	0	4	5	9	2	6	D
−0	0	0	0	0	0	0	0	D
+0096	0	0	0	0	0	9	6	C
+7,134,298	7	1	3	4	2	9	8	C
−0	0	0	0	0	0	0	0	B
+3,655	0	0	0	3	6	5	5	A
+116,644	0	1	1	6	6	4	4	E
+00882	0	0	0	0	8	8	2	F

age, and for using editing instructions to put numeric digits to graphic output devices, such as a printer, display terminals, or typewriter terminals, in a formatted manner. Whenever eight-bit EBCDIC character data is packed, creating a packed decimal value, the left-most four bits of the EBCDIC characters are discarded. When that packed decimal value is unpacked into eight-bit EBCDIC character format, all character bytes, with the exception of the low-order byte, are supplied with the left-most four bits of a numeric character zone, a hexadecimal 'F'. It is useless, therefore, to attempt to compress EBCDIC alphabetics into packed decimal format; when that same data is later unpacked, it will have permanently lost its alphabetic identity and will appear as numeric character data.

The functions of packed decimal values

TABLE 4-2

Fullword	0	000	0000	0001	0000	0010	0000	0010	1001	+1,056,809

Fullword	1	111	1111	1111	0111	0011	1111	1001	0011	−573,549

Fullword	0	000	0000	0000	0000	1111	0010	1001	1110	+62,110

Halfword	0	000	0011	1111	0000	+1,008

Halfword	1	111	1111	1111	0111	−9

Halfword	0	000	0101	1001	1101	+1,437

and the means of converting them are thoroughly explained in the sections on "Packed Decimal Arithmetic Operations" and "Packed Decimal/Fixed-Point Conversion," as well as in a number of other places throughout this text.

3. Fixed-Point Data

Fixed-point data may be considered to be binary arithmetic values that are contained in increments of halfwords, fullwords, or registers. The data itself is not necessarily used for arithmetic operations, but may be used as an address, an increment, or an absolute value. Fixed-point values are thought of as a binary-configured integer in which

the *"Powers-Of-Two"* values of the bits within the contiguous bit positions are summed together to arrive at the overall value of the integer. In a fixed-point value, the sign of the value is represented by the left-most (high-order) bit position of the field or register. A one-bit in the high-order bit position indicates a negative integer value; a zero-bit indicates a positive integer value.

Utilizing the binary bit configuration of fixed-point values, Table 4-2 is representative of a logical concept of the signed integer expression. Using the last halfword illustrated in Table 4-2 (+1437), the summing of the "Powers-Of-Two" values of the one-bits would appear as:

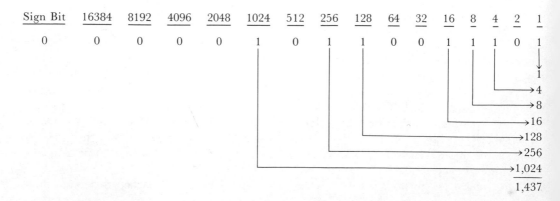

Sign Bit	16384	8192	4096	2048	1024	512	256	128	64	32	16	8	4	2	1
0	0	0	0	0	1	0	1	1	0	0	1	1	1	0	1

```
                                                                    1
                                                                →   4
                                                            →       8
                                                        →           16
                                              →                    128
                                        →                          256
                            →                                    1,024
                                                                 _____
                                                                 1,437
```

Specific detailed information about (1) interpreting fixed-point values, (2) translating negative fixed-point values, and (3) hexadecimal computation of fixed-point values may be found in the following sections of this text:

Fixed-Point Arithmetic Operations
Packed Decimal/Fixed-Point Conversions
Hexadecimal/Decimal Conversion Table
"Powers-Of-Two" Table
Comparing Data and Conditions

A direct and understandable relationship also exists between hexadecimal digit configuration (arithmetic base-16) and the binary bit configuration (arithmetic base-2) of fixed-point values. By using the Hexadecimal/Decimal Conversion Table (see Part V), the hexadecimal digit configuration of a fixed-point value can be calculated directly into the integer value of the number. This type of value conversion is extremely useful; fixed-point values and address generated by a problem program are accessible only as a hexadecimal configuration unless the programmer wishes to calculate the binary bit configuration and then sum the "Powers-Of-Two" values of those bits. It will be found that the hexadecimal conversion to fixed-

point value is considerably more expedient.

4. Special Data

Special data is not in itself a data format, but rather an interpretation of information that has been configured in any one of the three logical data format arrangements— character, packed decimal, or fixed-point. Quite often the desired information is expressed by the lowest possible configuration, binary bit format, and yet it could coincidentally comprise a valid packed decimal field or an EBCDIC character. This possibility can readily be illustrated: assume that the programmer has established a single byte of storage that is intended to contain eight condition switches, wherein each bit position of the byte is used as a "yes/no" indicator or switch. The bit positions, from left to right, are considered to be Switch 1 through Switch 8. If a switch position contains a one-bit, the implied condition is "yes"; if it contains a zero-bit, the condition is "no." It is quite probable that the circumstances would arrive at any time wherein a "yes" condition could be simultaneously reflected for Switches 2, 3, 4, 5, and 6. If this occurred, the bit configuration of the entire byte would appear as:

One Byte

0	1	1	1	1	1	0	0
Switch 1	Switch 2	Switch 3	Switch 4	Switch 5	Switch 6	Switch 7	Switch 8

This particular binary bit configuration also represents a hexadecimal configuration of '7C', as shown below.

Binary configuration

0 1 1 1	1 1 0 0

Hexadecimal configuration

7	C

It is coincidental that this representation may also be construed to be two other valid data formats.

7	C

= A one-byte packed decimal field for a value of +7.

7	C

= An EBCDIC character of '@'.

Insofar as the programmer's intent is concerned, however, the real configuration of this data is the "yes/no" condition reflected by the bit position digits. If the programmer were to use a data code consisting of hexadecimal digits, it is quite likely that this coded data would, at some time, assume the appearance of a packed decimal field or of EBCDIC character data.

Worthy of repeating is the fact that a strong recognition of hexadecimal configurations will be a valuable asset to any programmer. Any type of data format can be readily interpreted through its hexadecimal representation.

1. Two hexadecimal digits can represent an EBCDIC character.

2. Two or more hexadecimal digits can represent a packed decimal field.

3. The hexadecimal digits comprising a fixed-point value can be quickly converted into the sign-bit and integer combination.

4. Binary bit values are readily distinguishable from the hexadecimal digits they comprise.

Review Exercises

1. A general register has a byte capacity of ____4____ bytes, equal to one ____F____.

2. An Assembler Language Op Code, when used in conjunction with applicable operands, comprises an instruction __STMT__.

3. A name that has been used to designate an instruction statement, a defined area, a constant, or the beginning of a routine is referred to as a __Lbl__.

4. There are ____16____ general registers available to the Assembler Language programmer.

5. The first character of a label must be an __Alpha__ character.

6. What are the register numbers assigned to the general registers? _0,1,2 ... 15_

7. A byte consists of ____8____ bit positions.

8. The mnemonic representation of an Assembler Language instruction is referred to as an _OP_ _CODE_.

9. Packed decimal digits are the same configuration as __Hex__ digits.

10. Regular binary values are considered to be a __positive__ value even though they are not signed.

11. A fullword boundary is any core position address that is evenly divisible by ____4____.

12. An Assembler Language instruction statement may consist of a label, an op code, and from 1 to 3 __OPERANDS__.

13. Fixed-point values may be signed as either a __pos__ or a __neg__ configuration.

14. A halfword boundary is any core position address that is evenly divisible by ____2____.

15. When creating a label to define any portion of the program, the first character of the label must begin in column # ____1____ of the coding sheet.

16. A positive fixed-point halfword has a maximum value of __32767__; a negative fixed-point halfword has a maximum value of __-32768__.

17. An instruction statement that is expressed in RR format has a fixed-length attribute that will cause _____4_____ bytes of data to be affected.

18. A "comment" line may be indicated to the Assembler Language compiler by coding an _____*_____ in the first column of that line on the coding sheet.

19. An _Explicit_ length attribute may sometimes be utilized in order to alter or guarantee the number of bytes of data to be affected by an instruction statement.

20. The two op codes that are used to create data fields and work areas are the ___DC___ and the ___DS___.

21. An RR format instruction statement indicates that both operands of that statement should be ___Register___ operands.

22. A Define Storage statement   (does)   (does not)   clear the storage area that it defines.

23. The label of an area that has been defined by a DS or a DC statement addresses the first (high-order) byte of that area. (True) (False)

24. An area established by the following statement will create six 50-byte fields and each field will be singularly addressed by the label WORKFLD. (True) (False)

```
        WORKFLD    DS    6CL50
```

25. What would be the total number of bytes of storage reserved by the following statements? ___60___

```
        DATAFLDS    DS    0CL54
        DATA1       DS    CL20
        DATA2       DS    0CL34
        SUBDATA1    DS    CL15
        SUBDATA2    DS    CL12
        SUBDATA3    DS    CL7
        DATA3       DS    CL6
```

26. In the following set of instruction statements, will the field RECNO be aligned on a halfword, fullword, or doubleword boundary? (Use only the largest possible boundary) ___F___

```
                   DS    0D
        FIELDS     DS    CL6
        IDNO       DS    CL5
        CONSTIN    DS    CL1
        RECNO      DS    CL4
        SUBRES     DS    CL15
```

27. How many bytes of storage would be allocated by each of the following statements?
    a. ___6___   b. ___60___   c. ___ZERO___

```
        a. SAVEFLD     DS    9H
        b. WORDTABL    DS    15F
        c. PACKAREA    DS    0D
```

28. Place a check mark in front of each of the following names that could be used as valid labels.

____✓ SETDATA1   ____✓ DC   _____ ADDFIELDS
____✓ R6SET   _____ INTR'1'   ____✓ G
_____ 5TBARD   _____ BACK IN   _____ M3M265911

_____ ✓ FLDA1   _____ INITIATES   _____ ✓ 360SYS
_____ ✓ Z32MSG   _____ ✓ Y   _____ ✓ ORG

29. The maximum length of a C-type (character) constant is ___256___ bytes.

30. How many bytes of storage will be allocated to the constant shown below? ___3___

                    XFIELD   DC   XL3'5296874C'

31. A valid "blank" has a hexadecimal configuration of X'___40___'.

32. ___14___ bytes of storage would be allocated to this constant.

                    TITLE   DC   C'WAGES && TAXES'

33. Fill in the character contents (EBCDIC) resulting from this DC statement.

                         LINEHD   DC   CL8'START'

LINEHD | S | T | A | R | T | | | |

34. A total quantity of ___0___ storage bytes would be allocated to this DC statement.

invalid LBL   STATUSFLD   DC   15CL3'INTO'

35. Indicate the hexadecimal contents created by this constant.

                         VALUESET   DC   3XL2'5C'

VALUESET | 00 | 5C | 00 | 5C | 00 | 5C |

36. Define the bit configuration resulting from this constant.

                         BITSETS   DC   3BL1'100010001'

BITSETS | | | | | | |

37. Define the hexadecimal configuration resulting from this constant.

                         SETHALF   DC   H'15999'

SETHALF | | | |

38. The maximum length of a Z-type (Zoned Decimal) constant is _____ bytes.

39. What would be the hexadecimal contents generated by this constant?

                         PAKFLDS   DC   2PL3'15'

PAKFLDS | | | | | | |

SPECIFYING THE INSTRUCTION STATEMENT

The ability to properly interpret logic problems and apply the appropriate Assembler Language instructions are not the only prerequisites to becoming an efficient programmer. The logic path created by any programmer should be coded so that it may be easily interpreted and followed by another programmer of similar experience and training. Just as the Assembler Language instruction op codes are mnemonic to the interpretation of their performance, so should the labels and symbols used in the instruction statement relate to a program function or task. Compare the following instruction statements:

```
PT111      CLC     CMP1(3,8),R45
LOOKUP1    CLC     TABLE(3,8),KEY
```

For all intent and purpose both statements are performing an identical task. The first statement by itself gives no indication of what type of application is being performed.

The second statement clearly infers that it is a part of a look-up routine and is comparing a three-byte table segment to a key. This logical approach to creating labels and fields with names that are synonymous to their applications becomes more valuable with time. If a particular program has been operational for a year, and it is then determined that a change in the logic should be made in order to accept a new condition, even the author of the program would have to review the coding closely to refamiliarize himself with it. Quite possibly, the original programmer of this task is no longer responsible for its maintenance. It would now become evident that logical label and field name assignments are of considerable importance. This application, coupled with sufficient instruction line documentation (comments made on source coding lines), can reduce program maintenance and debugging time to the lowest possible level. Whenever coding a program, it is a good rule to consider that you may be asked to change it two years later; let the comments and logical naming techniques be a map to help you find your way through it at that time.

The unique naming of routines, subroutines, areas, and constants is the one option during the coding of instruction statements over which the programmer has the most control. There are other functions that also give the programmer a range of coding variations for any given instruction. These relate to the technical specification of the operands, which includes addressing elements, length specifications, and self-defining values. Although the results of compounded or complex operands must address or create a required value, the means of accomplishing that end can be properly applied in many ways.

A. ADDRESSING

Even though there are a number of ways to generate any given address within the problem program, the only concern at this time will be with the most obvious, and direct, means of doing so.

One of the methods of creating an address for any given point in a program is to *"tag"* that point with a label or symbol. Labels can be used to identify the address of a constant, a defined storage area, a routine or subroutine, a table, or any particular individual instruction statement. A label, by itself, will always generate an address that points to the left-most byte of a field or instruction; this represents the lowest point in storage of the area identified by the label. If the label points to a field of data, then this concept might be somewhat confusing—the address will be that of the left-most byte of that field, which in reality is the lowest point in core for that field, and yet that byte of the field may be referred to as the high-order byte. It is evident that there are two types of address values to keep clear and separate from each other—the core address value and the content value of the field itself. For any given field these might appear as:

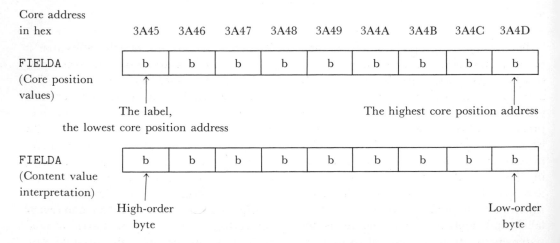

Any reference to an address generated by a nonmodified label reference will hereafter refer to the lowest-core position address of the overall field, or value, pointed to by that label. As the address of a label is *"modified"* or adjusted, such as FIELDA+5, it will be construed that the address to be generated is that of a point located that many bytes higher in core positions than the address of the label itself.

Address adjusting is usually applied to the task of locating a specific nonlabeled core position within a data field or to increment a search through a series of data segments. It can be used to modify the length attribute of an instruction, though this is recommended only after some experience in programming.

One example of address adjusting can be seen in the routine shown in Fig. 5-1. In this

IBM System/360 Assembler Coding Form

| PROGRAM | | | PUNCHING INSTRUCTIONS | GRAPHIC | | PAGE | OF | |
| PROGRAMMER | | DATE | | PUNCH | | CARD ELECTRO NUMBER | | X28-6509-2 U/M050 Printed in U.S.A. |

```
Name     Operation  Operand                       Identification-Sequence
8        10   14    16        20        25   30   73          80
*                                                             000001
CHEKFLD5 CLI       FIELD5,C'L'                                 000002
         BC        7,CHEK2                                     000003
         BAL       9,RTNEL                                     000004
CHEK2    CLI       FIELD5+1,C'A'                               000005
         BC        7,CHEK3                                     000006
         BAL       9,RTNEA                                     000007
CHEK3    CLI       FIELD5+2,C'M'                               000008
         BC        7,CHEK4                                     000009
         BAL       9,RTNEM                                     000010
CHEK4    CLI       FIELD5+3,C'P'                               000011
         BC        7,CHEK5                                     000012
         BAL       9,RTNEP                                     000013
CHEK5    CLI       FIELD5+4,C'S'                               000014
         BC        7,CHEKDUN                                   000015
         BAL       9,RTNES                                     000016
CHEKDUN  BC        15,ENDCHEK                                  000017
*                                                             000018
*                                                             000019
FIELD5   DC        CL5' '                                      000020
*                                                             000021
```

Figure 5-1

69

instance, a five-byte field contains five separate character positions. If certain configurations are found in each of those positions, the program logic intends to branch out to a respective subroutine, process some kind of information, and then return to the main routine again. At this point the logic will assume that the field, FIELD5, now contains data from an input stream.

The first instruction statement compares the first byte of FIELD5 to a character "L"; if the compare is unequal the logic branches to the next "compare" instruction, CHEK2. Each one of the compare statements is checking at an address that is one byte higher than that one addressed by the previous compare statement—FIELD5, FIELD5+1, FIELD-5+2, FIELD5+3, FIELD5+4—after which all five bytes of FIELD5 have been checked. If the byte addressed by the compare is not equal, a branch is taken to the next compare instruction statement. If the compare is equal, the program logic falls through to the Branch & Link instruction statement. The BAL instruction will cause the processing to go out to a unique subroutine, perform a task, and then return to the instruction immediately following the BAL statement. The address adjustments can be shown as:

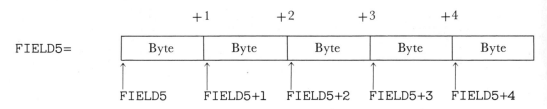

This type of address adjusting is not always practical to use, especially when incrementing through a series of data segments or a table of values. For that type of application, it is more efficient to load the address of the first segment into a general register and then add a value (equal to the length of a segment) to the register each time the logic wishes to check the next higher segment. The value of the register containing the address is then used as the base register with the operand specifying a zero displacement.

Assume that the problem program contains a very large table that is to be searched for certain values. The table is comprised of many segments, each segment being 10 bytes long. The table might be defined within the program as shown in Fig. 5-2.

The value that is to be searched for on the table is contained in the third and fourth bytes of each table segment. The basic way of coding the primary portion of the routine could be established in several ways. Two different sets of coding are shown in Fig. 5-3.

Statement 001, Example 1, loads the address of the *first* byte of TABLE into general register 9.

Statement 001, Example 2, loads the address of the *third* byte of TABLE into general register 9.

Statement 002, Example 1, compares the third byte of the current table segment to a literal. The third byte is addressed by a displacement of "0+2" plus the current address of TABLE as contained in general register 9. The "2", as contained in (2,9), signifies that the comparison is to be for a length of two bytes.

Statement 002, Example 2, performs the same comparison. Because the address loaded into general register 9 was that of TABLE+2, it is not necessary to specify any displacement factor other than zero.

Statement 003 for both examples will cause a branch to PASSBAL if the comparison in Statement 002 resulted in an unequal condition.

Statement 004 for both examples is a Branch & Link statement to an assumed subroutine.

Statement 005 for both examples is another compare of the same TABLE bytes used in Statement 002. The logic used in

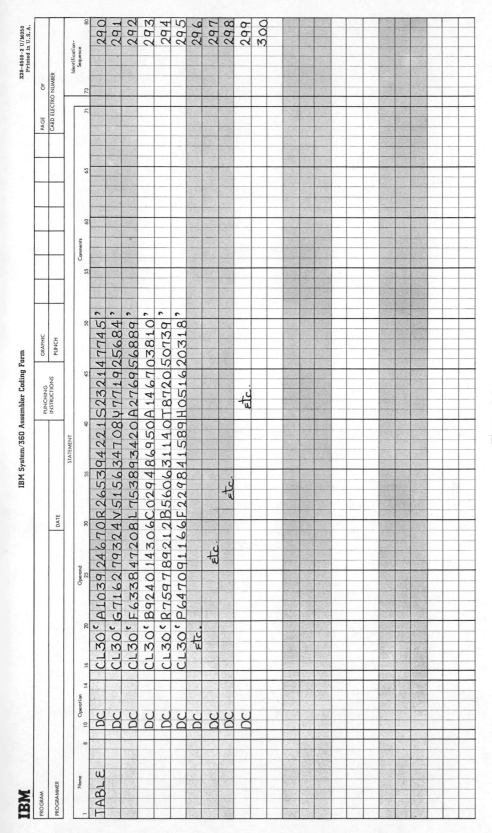

Figure 5-2

IBM IBM System/360 Assembler Coding Form

PROGRAM		PUNCHING INSTRUCTIONS	GRAPHIC			PAGE	OF
PROGRAMMER	DATE		PUNCH			CARD ELECTRO NUMBER	

X28-6509-2 U/M050
Printed in U.S.A.

STATEMENT

```
* EXAMPLE #1                                           001
*
ENTER   LA    9,TABLE                                  001
LOOP    CLC   0+2(2,9),=CL2'47'                        002
        BC    7,PASSBAL                                003
        BAL   3,FOUNDIT                                004
PASSBAL CLC   0+2(2,9),=CL2'99'                        005
        BC    8,END                                    006
        AH    9,=H'10'                                 007
        BC    15,LOOP                                  008

* EXAMPLE #2
*
*
ENTER   LA    9,TABLE+2                                001
LOOP    CLC   0(2,9),=CL2'47'                          002
        BC    7,PASSBAL                                003
        BAL   3,FOUNDIT                                004
PASSBAL CLC   0(2,9),=CL2'99'                          005
        BC    8,END                                    006
        AH    9,=H'10'                                 007
        BC    15,LOOP                                  008
```

Figure 5-3

Statement 002 is applicable for the respective examples.

Statement 006 for both examples is a "Branch On Equal Condition" instruction statement that tests the results of Statement 005 and decides whether or not to branch.

Statement 007 adds the value of the length of one table segment to general register 9. On the first pass through the LOOP routine, register 9 would contain an address equivalent to TABLE + 10 for Example 1 and TABLE + 12 for Example 2. On the second pass through LOOP, register 9 would contain an address equivalent to TABLE + 20 for Example 1 and TABLE + 22 for Example 2, etc.

Statement 008 for both examples is a *forced branch* back to the first instruction of the LOOP cycle routine.

Both of these coding examples would accomplish identical tasks. The only difference between them is the value of the address that was loaded into general register 9 by Statement 001 and the subsequent use of that address in Statements 002 and 005.

As shown in these examples, the address pointer register can be incremented by adding a halfword fixed-point value to the contents of that register. The value to be added in this case was the length of the table segments, or + 10. Any of the sets of instruction statements shown in Fig. 5-4 could have been used to replace Statements 001 and 007, and the end result would have been the same.

Statement Set *A loads the address of TABLE into general register 9. It then effectively states, "Load the actual address value of + 10, including the address presently contained in register 9, into register 9." If that general register first contained the address of TABLE as "30563," the instruction increment of general register 9 would create an operation as:

+ 10 plus register 9 (30563)

= register 9 (30573)

Statement Set *B also loads the address of TABLE into general register 9 as its first step. It then loads an absolute address value of + 10 into general register 4. The incrementing of register 9 is accomplished by an Add Register instruction statement that adds the increment value contained in register 4 (+ 10) to the address value in general register 9.

Statement Set *C has defined a fullword constant with a fixed-point value of + 10. After general register 9 has been loaded with the address of TABLE, the routine will increment that address by a fixed-point ADD instruction statement, adding the fullword constant of + 10 to the value contained in register 9.

B. LENGTH ATTRIBUTES

A length attribute is considered to be the controlling factor that determines the number of bytes to be affected by an instruction statement. Certain instruction op codes allow the programmer a choice of using either explicit length attributes or implied length attributes. Still other instruction op codes have a fixed length attribute. With the exception of packed decimal operation instructions, all of the Assembler Language Standard Instruction Set have a single length attribute control. Packed decimal instructions have two length attributes—one for each operand. It is quite important to be fully aware of the length attribute characteristics of each of the Assembler Language instructions. These are defined in the following paragraphs.

1. "Fixed" Length Attributes

Instruction op codes whose statement formats do not include an 'L' component, indicating that a length attribute may be specified, are considered to have a *"fixed"* length attribute. This means that these instruction statements inherently contain a length factor that cannot be altered during the coding of that statement. The actual number of bytes or fullwords controlled by the fixed length attribute varies between the different instruction op codes that fall within this category. This includes all of the RR, RX, RS, and SI formatted instructions. The majority

IBM

IBM System/360 Assembler Coding Form

X28-6509-2 U/M050
Printed in U.S.A.

PROGRAM				PAGE	OF
PROGRAMMER		DATE		CARD ELECTRO NUMBER	
	PUNCHING INSTRUCTIONS	GRAPHIC			
		PUNCH			

```
Name    Operation  Operand                          Comments          Identification-
                                                                       Sequence
*A
ENTER   LA   9,TABLE    (REPLACES STATEMENT 001)
        LA   9,10(9)    (REPLACES STATEMENT 007)

*B
ENTER   LA   9,TABLE    (REPLACES      STATEMENT 001)
        LA   4,10
        AR   9,4        (REPLACES STATEMENT 007)

*C
ENTER   LA   9,TABLE    (REPLACES STATEMENT 001)
        A    9,INCRMNT  (REPLACES STATEMENT 007)
*
INCRMNT DC   F'10'      (FULLWORD CONSTANT OF +10)
```

Figure 5-4

of the "register" instructions, such as CLR, AR, LTR, SR, etc., will affect only four bytes (a register or fullword) of data. The fixed-point arithmetic multiply and divide instructions will affect a pair of registers. Multiple Load and Multiple Store instructions will affect as many fullwords and registers as are covered by the range specified by, and implied between, the registers whose numeric representations comprise the R_1 and R_3 operands. The remaining instructions are those that will affect only one byte of data—such instructions as the CLI, STC, IC, and MVI.

Any attempt to specify a length attribute for an instruction that contains a fixed length attribute will result in either a program compile error or a misinterpretation of the intended use of the value; the compiler could interpret a length attribute to be a base register or a displacement register if the value specified was within the numeric range of between 1 and 15.

2. "Implied" Length Attributes

If a particular Assembler Language instruction format contains the option of specifying a length attribute, it is the programmer's decision as to whether or not the coded statement requires a length attribute specification. Should the programmer choose not to indicate the length attribute, it is considered to be *"implied."* In an instruction statement containing an implied length, the length is construed to be the length of the field addressed by the first operand in the statement.

Examine this set of instruction statements.

```
RECVR      DC      CL6'bbbbbb'
SEND1      DC      CL4'ABCD'
SEND2      DC      CL4'EFGH'
*
MOVEIT     MVC     RECVR,SEND1
```

The instruction statement labeled MOVEIT would result in the move of six bytes of data (ABCDEF) into the field labeled RECVR. The implied length for this statement's execution is the length of the first operand, which is six bytes. At the time this statement was executed, the system would commence sending data bytes from the point specified by the second operand and would continue until the implied length of the first operand had been fulfilled. This would result in the four bytes of data in SEND1 being moved, immediately followed by the first two bytes of SEND2. The opposite reaction to this is also true in an instance wherein the second operand field is longer than the first operand field.

```
RECVR      DC      CL3'bbb'
SENDR      DC      CL5'139B2'
*
MOVEDATA   MVC     RECVR,SENDR
```

As a result of the statement shown here, only the first three bytes of SENDR (139) would be moved into RECVR. Since the implied length of the first operand field determines the number of bytes of data to be moved, the move operation is terminated once the length of that operand has been exhausted. Note carefully that if address adjusting is used, such as . . . MVC RECVR + 2, SENDR . . . , the implied length of the receiving field is still effective. Three bytes of data, commencing at SENDR, would be moved into the three bytes of data commencing at RECVR + 2.

Packed decimal instructions are unique in that both operands of the completed statement may be considered to have implied length attributes. Because of this, executing packed decimal instruction statements containing fields of unlike length factors requires adequate knowledge of the peculiarities of those instructions. If the field length of the first packed decimal operand is greater than that of the second packed decimal operand, there is usually no difficulty in completing a satisfactory statement execution. However, if the field length of the second operand is greater than that of the first operand, packed decimal arithmetic routines can possibly result in a decimal overflow exception and a program interrupt. It might be suggested that the programmer acquire the habit of using explicit-length attribute coding for those instructions that allow a defined length characteristic.

3. "Explicit" Length Attributes

The use of explicit length attributes refers to the actual coding of a length value within an operand. This application may be used to confirm or ensure the stated length attribute of a field, or it may be used to change or alter the implied length. There are many instances in the average program in which this type of specification may be of considerable value. A large section of data may be held in storage under a single label, but through the use of address adjusting and explicit length attributes, small sections of that data field can be moved in or out of the area or manipulated as desired. Regardless of the length of any field of data, a length attribute as great as allowed by the particular instruction op code to be employed may be used to move data into that field, and subsequent fields if so desired. It must be remembered that an explicit length attribute can only be used within those Assembler Language instructions whose instruction statement format indicates the optional use of a length attribute.

The following set of examples illustrate some of the applications for which explicit length attributes may be applied.

Example 1. The data fields to be affected and the instruction statements to be performed are:

	+1	+2	+3	+4	+5	+6	+7	+8	+9
BIGFLD	1	2	3	1	2	3	1	2	3	0

SMALLFLD	4	5	6

```
BIGFLD      DC      CL10'1231231230'
SMALLFLD    DC      CL3'456'
*
            MVC     BIGFLD+3(3),SMALLFLD        001
            MVC     BIGFLD+9(1),SMALLFLD        002
```

Statement 001 is interpreted as stating, "Move three bytes of data (as indicated by the explicit length attribute of 3), from the field SMALLFLD into the fourth, fifth, and sixth bytes of BIGFLD (BIGFLD+3)." This performance would appear as:

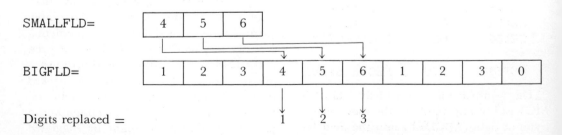

Statement 002 states, "Move one byte of data, as indicated by the length attribute parameter of '1', from the address generated by SMALLFLD into the tenth byte of BIGFLD (BIGFLD+9)." This action is illustrated on page 77.

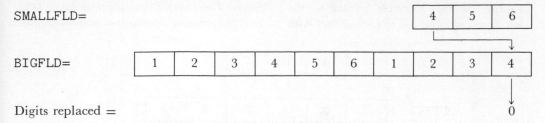

SMALLFLD=

BIGFLD=

Digits replaced =   0

This example has shown how a portion, or all, of a "sending" field may be moved into any portion of a receiving field for any explicit length, so long as the length attributes do not exceed the number of bytes allowed to be affected by that instruction.

Example 2. The definition of the data fields and the expression of the instruction statement is:

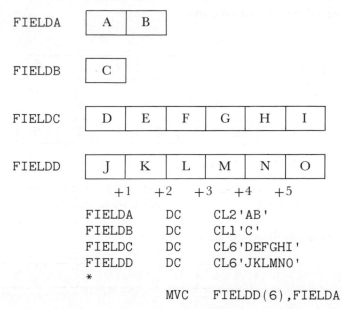

```
FIELDA    DC    CL2'AB'
FIELDB    DC    CL1'C'
FIELDC    DC    CL6'DEFGHI'
FIELDD    DC    CL6'JKLMNO'
*
          MVC   FIELDD(6),FIELDA
```

This instruction statement specifies that "Commencing at the address generated by FIELDA, move six bytes of data into FIELDD." Because this statement has specified a data length of six bytes is to be moved,

FIELDA (two bytes), FIELDB (one byte), and the first three bytes of FIELDC will be moved into the overall length of FIELDD. The performance of this statement can be illustrated as:

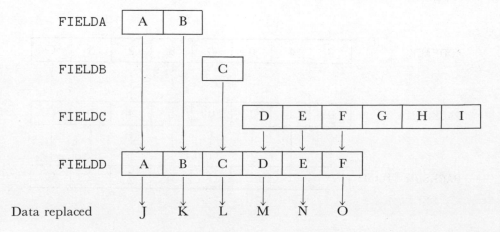

Data replaced   J   K   L   M   N   O

Example 3. This example relates to the comparison of a portion of each of two data fields. The overall definition of these fields and the ensuing instruction statement are:

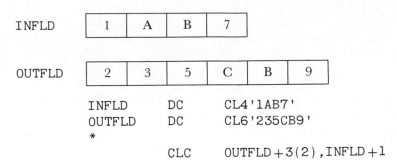

```
INFLD     DC      CL4'1AB7'
OUTFLD    DC      CL6'235CB9'
*
          CLC     OUTFLD+3(2),INFLD+1
```

The bytes of data that would be compared by the performance of this instruction statement would be:

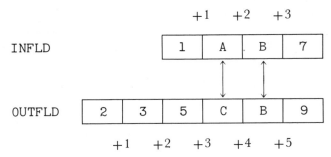

As shown, only the two bytes of alphabetic characters would be compared.

Example 4. This example illustrates how a part of a packed decimal field may be added to the whole of a larger packed decimal field. The data contained in the fields appears as:

ADDPACK

| 3 | 4 | 0 | 0 | 8 | 2 | 3 | C |

PACKSUM

| 0 | 1 | 1 | 0 | 5 | 4 | 9 | C |

The instruction statement that is to be performed is:

```
AP    PACKSUM(4),ADDPACK+2(2)
```

The operation of this statement may be shown by:

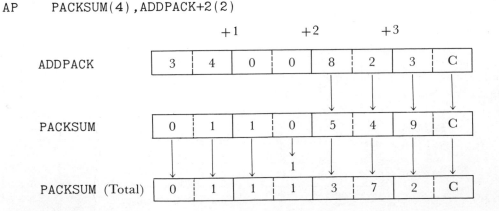

As illustrated, the last two bytes of ADD-PACK, containing a packed decimal value of +823, would be added to the whole of PACKSUM. The resulting sum would be considered to be contained in the entire four bytes of PACKSUM.

In addition to these examples of the use of explicit length attributes, many of the various other examples throughout this text will also demonstrate this application.

C. SELF-DEFINING CHARACTERS AND VALUES

A *self-defining* character or value is one that is written in its own representation as an operand. These are generally construed to be literals, immediate character representations, and absolute values. The attributes of each are defined in the following paragraphs.

1. Literals

Although another section of this text is devoted to the construction and composition of a literal, it is necessary to include a general overview of their functions at this point. As a rule, literals are a relatively small number of data bytes, or a self-defining value, that is to be used as an operand. This would be mostly applicable in instances where the intended value or data content of the literal are to remain unchanged. Because a literal does not have a label by which it may be referenced, it cannot be cross-referenced by the programmer at any other point within the problem program. If a literal of the same value is to be used at multiple points in the problem program, it must be rewritten in its entirety each place that it is to be used. A complete explanation of the various types of literals and their respective representations is contained within the section entitled "Defining Constants and Literals."

The instruction statements that follow each contain a literal. The use of the literal is defined following the statement in which it appears.

(A)

```
AP      PAKCNTR(3),=PL1'1'
```

This instruction statement specifies that a packed decimal value of +1, as represented by the literal, is to be added to a three-byte area referenced by the label PAKCNTR. The programmer could have established a labeled one-byte packed decimal constant and used the label as the second operand in this statement in lieu of the literal. This particular instruction might be part of the logic to keep count of, or control, the number of times that the logic processing passes through a given section of the program.

(B)

```
CLC     PACKFLD(3),=X'00000C'
```

This statement is comparing the three bytes of a field of packed decimals, addressed by the label PACKFLD, to a three-byte hexadecimal literal. The literal represents a three-byte packed decimal field of plus-zero (+0). In this particular instance, the programmer wants to know only if that field, PACKFLD, contains a bit-for-bit configuration of the +0 value. The programmer could have used the Compare Packed instruction except for the fact that the CP instruction considers a plus-zero and a minus-zero to be equal values.

(C)

```
CLC     RECORD+5(2),=CL2'ID'
```

In this instance, the statement is comparing the sixth and seventh bytes of a field defined as RECORD to a two-byte literal containing the alpha characters 'ID'. It is assumed that the data contents of RECORD will change every time a new data record is used by the program. The literal is used to check the contents of each new section of data for the characters 'ID', so it is just as practical to use that literal as to establish a two-byte constant containing 'ID'. It is often easier to follow the logic of a program containing this type of literal than it is to interpret a statement in which the second operand is a label that references a constant.

Compare the three sets of instruction statements in Fig. 5-5, each of which are expressed using a literal and similarly expressed using a label that addresses a constant of the same configuration as the literal.

IBM System/360 Assembler Coding Form

IBM

X28-6509-2 U/M050
Printed in U.S.A.

PROGRAM

PROGRAMMER

PUNCHING INSTRUCTIONS

GRAPHIC

PUNCH

DATE

PAGE   OF

CARD ELECTRO NUMBER

STATEMENT

Name	Operation	Operand	Comments	Identification-Sequence
*				
	ZAP	PKAREA,=PL1'0'		
	ZAP	PKAREA,PKZERO		
*				
	CLC	DATA+2(2),=CL2'MV'		
	CLC	DATA+2(2),DATACHEK		
*				
	MVC	CARDOUT(4),=CL4'0001'		
	MVC	CARDOUT(4),SEQNO		
*				

Figure 5-5

In each instance, the literal defines itself not only as to data content, but also as to format and length. The statements using the labeled data as the second operand are not self-explanatory as to the value or data content of that operand. Someone tracing these logical instructions in a problem program would have to find the location of the definition of the label of the second operand in order to acquaint himself with its characteristics and contents.

2. Immediate Characters or Values

As indicated in the descriptions of some of the Assembler Language instructions, certain instruction statement formats require the use of immediate data. The written configuration of immediate data is very similar to the manner in which a literal is written, with the following exceptions.

1. It is not preceded by an equal sign (=).
2. It may only consist of one byte of data.
3. It cannot be replaced by a constant or symbol.

The functional Assembler Language instructions that use an immediate character or representation are:

```
AND IMMEDIATE (NI)
EXCLUSIVE OR IMMEDIATE (XI)
OR IMMEDIATE (OI)
COMPARE LOGICAL IMMEDIATE (CLI)
MOVE IMMEDIATE (MVI)
TEST UNDER MASK (TM)
```

The configuration of the immediate data may be expressed in character, binary bit, or hexadecimal configuration. It may not be expressed as a "P," or packed decimal byte. The decision of which configuration to use would probably depend on the type of instruction statement being utilized. The CLI and MVI instruction statements would probably be written using character configuration. The remaining instructions would be more often written using a hexadecimal configuration or a binary bit configuration, inasmuch as the one byte of immediate data used for these instructions represents a mask that is comprised of binary bit conditions. Figure 5-6 presents instruction statements

using a single byte of immediate data. In each instance the statement is shown twice, utilizing two different configurations for the expression of the immediate data. Because all of these instructions are limited to acting on one byte of data, there are no length attributes reflected in these statements. Note that the data byte used to represent the immediate character must be self-representing. An immediate character of P'4' is not valid inasmuch as the compiler would have to convert it to a hex configuration of X'4C'. On the other hand, however, an immediate character expressed as X'4C' is valid.

Each statement within any of these sets will be interpreted by the compiler as identical to the other statement within the set. Therefore, the programmer has the option of configurating the byte of immediate data in whichever mode he prefers.

3. Absolute Values

An absolute value is construed to be a decimal self-defining term or expression. It is written in its basic numeric digit form and should contain no symbols that would indicate the "sign" of the value.

A typical example of the use of an absolute value may be found in its association with a Load Address instruction statement, such as when that statement is being used to load a loop control value into a register. This type of use is shown by:

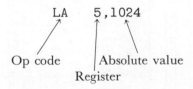

This instruction statement tells the system to load the absolute value of 1024 into general register 5. Upon completion of the execution of that instruction statement, general register 5 will contain a value of +1024.

An absolute value may also be used to indicate a displacement parameter in an operand of many Assembler Language instructions. Its most general application in this type of assignment is to reference an unlabeled point within a defined field, creating an explicit address.

IBM System/360 Assembler Coding Form

X28-6509-2 U/M050
Printed in U.S.A.

```
Name      Operation    Operand
*
          CLI          DATA,C'X'
          CLI          DATA,X'E7'
*
          XI           SWITCHES,X'04'
          XI           SWITCHES,B'00000100'
*
          MVI          TABLE+5,X'C1'
          MVI          TABLE+5,C'A'
*
          TM           ID,B'01011110'
          TM           ID,X'5E'
*
          CLI          AMNT,C'9'
          CLI          AMNT,X'F9'
*
          NI           TESTBIT,X'11'
          NI           TESTBIT,B'00010001'
*
          MVI          KEYBYTE,C'3'
          MVI          KEYBYTE,X'F3'
*
          OI           0+4(10),X'4B'
          OI           0+4(10),B'01001011'
```

Figure 5-6

82

```
TABLE      DC       50CL14'b'
*
MODULE     LA       6,TABLE
           MVC      4(2,6),=CL2'ID'
```

The constant TABLE is defined as consisting of 50 segments of 14 bytes each. The Load Address (LA) instruction statement has loaded the address of the first byte of TABLE into general register 6. The Move Characters (MVC) instruction states, "Into the address that represents the fifth byte of TABLE (a displacement of four plus the address of TABLE as contained in general register 6), move the two-byte literal supplied by the second operand." The MVC instruction statement is broken down as:

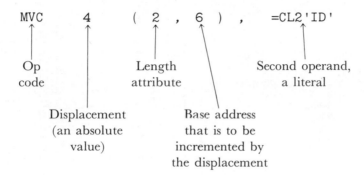

If, at program execution time, the decimal address of TABLE was 23410, then the first operand in the MVC instruction statement just shown would generate an address of 23414.

Logically the value used to represent a register (0 through 15) as a part of an operand, or as an operand in itself, is also an absolute value. This does not mean to imply that every time the compiler encounters a value in the range of from 0 through 15 that it will assume that value to represent a general register; this will only be effected when the value stated occupies a statement parameter that requires a register specification.

D. BASIC PROGRAM INITIALIZATION

As the programmer progresses through this text, he will probably desire to test out the knowledge of the concepts he has learned. Rather than requiring him to undertake the study of register assignments, *"save"* areas, control sections, etc., at the very beginning of this material, a set of basic coding is provided here that will establish the necessary housekeeping.

Using the instruction statements contained on the coding sheets shown in Fig. 5-7, the programmer may insert small coded routines within the control section and compile his program.

The first section, from the label INITL through to the label SAVEREG, is setting up the initialization of the program and the base register assignments. This model has been organized with three contiguous base register assignments of 4096 bytes each, so the programmer will have approximately 12,288 bytes of program logic area to work with.

Item 2, the label START, should contain the first instruction statement of the program that is to be tested.

Item 3 identifies the area where the programmer may place all of the instruction statements of his program. These should be stated between the statement labeled START and the one labeled FINIS.

Item 4 is a *"literal org"* statement that will assign the proper program alignments to any literals that the programmer may have included within his instruction statements.

Item 5 contains several "Equate" statements that are assigning symbolic references or labels to several general registers. Any other reference to these registers may be made by specifying the register only, or by

IBM System/360 Assembler Coding Form

IBM

Name	Operation	Operand	Comments	Identification-Sequence
INITL	CSECT			00001
BEGIN	SAVE	(14,12),,*		00002
	BALR	R3,0		00003
	USING	BR3,R3		00004
	L	R4,BR4		00005
	L	R5,BR5		00006
BR3	USING	BR3+4096,R4		00007
	USING	BR3+8192,R5		00008
	ST	R13,SAVEREG+4		00009
	LA	R13,SAVEREG		00010
	BC	15,START		00011
*				00012
*				00013
BR4	DC	A(BR3+4096)		00014
BR5	DC	A(BR3+8192)		00015
SAVEREG	DS	18F		00016
*				00017
*				00018
START	- -	- - - -		00019

(1) (2) (3)

Insert as many program logic statements here as necessary

Figure 5-7a

84

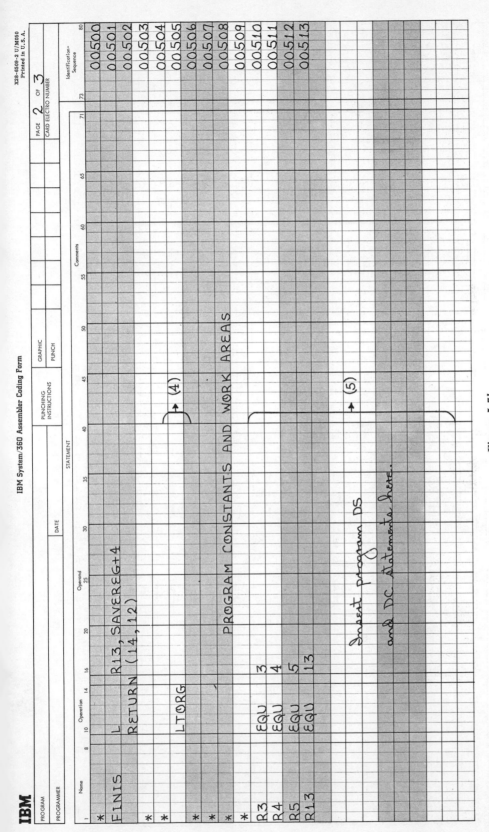

Figure 5-7b

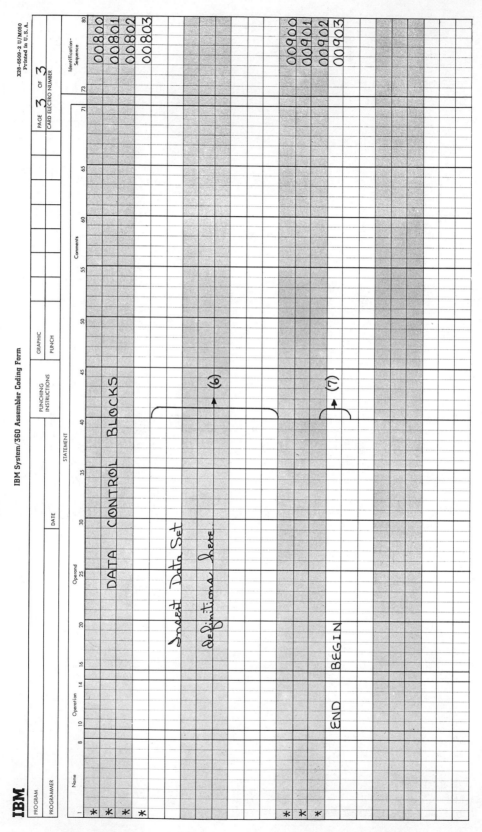

Figure 5-7c

specifying the symbolic label, such as shown in Item 1 of this set of coding. Also included here is the area into which the programmer should place all of the DS (Define Storage) and DC (Define Constant) statements to be used within his program.

Item 6 may contain the data control block statements for the input or output units that are to be used by the program. The exact form of these statements will depend on the type of operating system being used and the quantity and type of devices being used for input/output operations to the program. The requirements for the format of this data should, therefore, be supplied by the users' data processing installation.

Item 7, the END statement, is the final statement in the problem program. Any coding to be inserted by the programmer should have been included within the areas indicated, somewhere prior to this statement.

Both the compilation of the source module and the subsequent testing of the object program will require "Job Control Language" cards. These are necessary in order for the task to be identified by name, to advise the system what type of function is to be performed, which devices are to be used, and several other related types of information that the operating system will require for each task execution.

The statements within this set of coded logic have been formatted for use with a full Operating System. In the event that the programmer will be utilizing a different operating system, some of the instruction formats may have to be altered somewhat.

PART III

LOGICAL APPLICATIONS
OF ASSEMBLER LANGUAGE

CREATING WORK AREAS
WITHIN THE PROGRAM

A. ESTABLISHING STORAGE AREAS

The concept of storage areas, as discussed in this section, relates to the fields and work areas that will be used by the problem program to hold data, accumulate data, or to manipulate data within that area. This type of storage area might be used to hold input or output records, to build tables and indexes, as arithmetic work areas such as the Quotient-Remainder combination, register storage areas, or any other such fields in which the data will change during the execution of the program.

1. Defining the Areas

The op code that is used to reserve a contiguous number of bytes of storage area is the DS, representing the Define Storage instruction. The use of this instruction may reserve an allocation of core storage for use within the problem program. Unlike the Define Constant (DC) op code, it does not create a configuration of data within the area of storage that it is reserving. Until the problem program actually places some type of data into the area that was established by a DS instruction statement, the contents of that area would be totally unpredictable. Data stored in that particular area of core by a previous problem program would probably still be resident within that area.

A typical DS statement might appear as:

```
RECORD      DS      CL300
```

This particular statement would assign the label RECORD to 300 bytes of contiguous storage as a part of the problem program.

It is quite probable that the programmer may want to reference smaller units of storage within a large storage area without using address adjusting. Such an allocation might appear as:

```
DATAFLD     DS      OCL100
NAME        DS      CL20
ADDRESS     DS      CL40
PHONE       DS      CL9
DETAIL      DS      CL31
```

The statement for DATAFLD is assigning that label to 100 bytes of storage, but it is not actually reserving or allocating that storage. The zero (0) that precedes the 'CL' in the first statement is a parameter that may be used to indicate that no storage is to be allocated for this statement. It does indicate, however, that if 100 bytes of data are moved into the address that is referenced by DATAFLD, that data will be placed into the areas reserved by any subsequent DS or DC statement. The obvious logic for establishing this set of statements is that the program intends to place a 100-byte data record into the area that is addressed as DATAFLD. The detail contained within this record will consist of a name, address, telephone number, and some additional detail data. The data to be placed into this overall area can be moved there by referencing the label DATAFLD. Once that data is in storage, it can be referred to in whole by the label DATAFLD, or in part by referencing the

labels for the subfields. Take note that the aggregate storage area actually reserved by the subfield DS statements is exactly equal to the length of the DATAFLD label assignment—100 bytes. In this type of application, it is very important that the subfield space allocations are equal to the length of the area referenced by the primary label. If this rule is not followed, it is quite likely that storage data may be inadvertently destroyed or altered. For instance, the storage definition statements within a problem program might appear as:

```
DATE        DS      OCL6
MONTH       DS      CL2
DAY         DS      CL2
ENDCARD     DC      CL9'DELIMITER'
```

As shown here, the label DATE is used to reference six bytes of storage. The subfields defined within DATE have only declared four bytes of storage. Because of this, any reference to DATE would imply reference to MONTH, DAY, and the first two bytes of ENDCARD. At the time that the program was initialized, these fields, and the way that the labels would apply, would appear as:

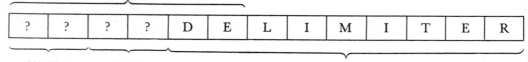

Now assume that the program intends to move some data from another area, which happens to contain "031569" (March 15, 1969), into the area that is referenced by the label DATE. It then intends to compare a card input area to the constant ENDCARD to see if the card input area contains the word "DELIMITER," indicating the end of the input card data stream. The instruction statements that are to be executed within the

problem program are coded as:

```
MVC     DATE,SOMEAREA       (001)
CLC     CARDIN,ENDCARD      (002)
BC      8,JOBDONE           (003)
```

Statement 001 is moving the data contained within SOMEAREA (031569) into the area that is addressed by DATE. The contents of DATE and ENDCARD would now appear as containing this data:

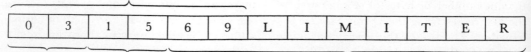

Because DATE was specified so as to reference six bytes of storage, all six bytes of data were moved from SOMEAREA to DATE. The last two bytes of SOMEAREA (69) have now overlayed and destroyed the first two bytes of the constant ENDCARD (DE).

Statements 002 and 003 are intended to compare a card input field to the contents of ENDCARD (which is supposed to be "DELIMITER") and then branch to the end-of-job routine on an equal condition. Even though the card input area (CARDIN) eventually would contain the word "DELIMITER," the comparison would not result in an equal condition due to the fact that the constant ENDCARD now would contain "69LIMITER." Accordingly, the appropriate branch to JOBDONE would not be taken and the program would probably terminate abnormally.

The nonreserving attribute of a DS statement may also be used within a previously defined or labeled area.

```
INRECORD   DS   OCL55
NAME       DS   CL15
ADDRESS    DS   OCL40
STREET     DS   CL15
CITY       DS   CL15
STATE      DS   CL5
ZIPCODE    DS   CL5
```

This set of statements is specifying a storage area that is to be used to hold input records of data. The overall length of the area is 55 bytes and it can be referred to in its entirety by the label INRECORD. The first subfield within INRECORD is the NAME field, consisting of the first fifteen bytes of INRECORD. Following the NAME field is a label reference, ADDRESS, which refers to the remaining 40 bytes of INRECORD. STREET, CITY, STATE, and ZIPCODE are the subfields of both INRECORD and ADDRESS, and they are actually reserving the storage positions that are referred to by ADDRESS and INRECORD. The cross-reference of all of these labels would now appear to be:

15 Bytes	15 Bytes	15 Bytes	5 Bytes	5 Bytes
	STREET	CITY	STATE	ZIPCODE
NAME	ADDRESS			
INRECORD				

The fields of STREET, CITY, STATE, and ZIPCODE can be moved or altered individually by referring to any one of those labels; or they can be moved or altered collectively by referring to the label ADDRESS. In the same manner, it is possible to move all of INRECORD at one time or any portion of it by the other labels.

DS statements and DC statements can be intermixed in the same manner as just shown for DS statements. The DS statement must be used if a label is to be tagged to an area that is to be subdefined in line without direct storage allocation for that label. An example of this type of application could be coded as:

```
DATAHOLD   DS   OCL9
PACKFLD1   DC   PL2'0'
SWITCH1    DC   X'40'
PACKFLD2   DC   PL2'0'
SWITCH2    DC   X'40'
CODE       DS   OCL3
PREFIX     DC   X'40'
SUFFIX     DC   X'4040'
```

The logical and hexadecimal configuration of the areas defined by these statements would appear as:

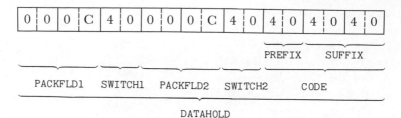

As these statements have indicated, the entire nine-byte area may be referred to by the label DATAHOLD. The fields labeled PACKFLD1 and PACKFLD2 will contain packed decimal values of +0, which would allow them to be used for packed decimal arithmetic operations by references to either label. SWITCH1 and SWITCH2 are each one-byte areas containing the hexadecimal configuration of a valid "blank." CODE, another subfield of DATAHOLD, is further subdefined by PREFIX and SUFFIX, and contains valid blanks.

2. Overlaying Field Descriptions

In some instances, the programmer may find it helpful to be able to define an area in several formats or in different subfields. This can be accomplished by the use of the DS statement and the ORG instruction. The ORG statement effectively causes the next assigned byte of storage to begin at the address specified by the single operand of the ORG instruction statement. A practical example of the combined use of the DS statements and ORG statements might be within a program that reads data cards into its logic. The normal definition of the card input field would usually suffice, but in this instance the program will be reading cards that are formatted in three different ways. The first character contained on the card identifies which of the three formats apply to that particular card. In order to efficiently work with the unique data fields on each type of card, the overall card input field is first defined in whole and then completely redefined for each of the three different content formats. Using labels that might be applicable to a purchasing system, the card layouts could be defined by the statements in Fig. 6-1.

As each card is brought into storage via the I/O (input/output) data management routines, it can be read into the area that is referenced by the label CARDIN. Once the card data resides in CARDIN, allowing it to be referred to by CARDIN, CODE, or DATA, it may also be referred to by any of the other labels indicated by the list of DS statements. If the card should happen to contain data pertaining to a purchase requisition, it will be a CODE1 data card. The information for that card will be aligned in the format of the labels shown for a CODE1 card and any field defined by those labels may be accessed by that definition. As indicated, a CODE2 card contains purchase order data and a CODE3 card contains receiving report information. Once the program logic has determined what type of data is contained on the card and has been passed to the program data input area, it would branch to one of three different routines. Each routine would be unique in such a way as to process the appropriate data representation contained on the respective cards.

Note that in each case the card format contains a different number of bytes of data and the unreferenced data bytes have been allowed for by the MT (empty) label for each code. This is the means that is used to account for all of the bytes that have been assigned to the next higher level of label reference. Even though these area definitions have effectively created unique representations for four different card format areas, including the basic input area, the net result has only allocated a total of 80 bytes of storage area.

It is not necessary that the ORG instruction statement refer to the first character byte in the data field that is to be subdefined. If a field is to be similarly defined in multiple

IBM System/360 Assembler Coding Form

X28-6509-2 U/M050
Printed in U.S.A.

PROGRAM

PROGRAMMER   DATE

PUNCHING INSTRUCTIONS   GRAPHIC   PUNCH

PAGE 1 OF 2   CARD ELECTRO NUMBER

Name	Operation	Operand / Comments	Identification-Sequence
*			0001
CARDIN	DS	0CL80	0002
CODE	DS	CL1	0003
DATA	DS	CL79	0004
*			0005
	ORG	CARDIN	0006
CODE1	DS	CL1	0007
REQSTNNO	DS	CL8	0008
PARTNO1	DS	CL12	0009
REQDATE	DS	CL6	0010
REQQTY	DS	CL8	0011
MT1	DS	CL45	0012
*			0013
	ORG	CARDIN	0014
CODE2	DS	CL1	0015
PURCHNO1	DS	CL7	0016
VENDOR	DS	CL6	0017
PARTNO2	DS	CL12	0018
PODATE	DS	CL6	0019
POQTY	DS	CL8	0020
BUYER	DS	CL8	0021
MT2	DS	CL32	0022
*			0023

Figure 6-1a

95

IBM

IBM System/360 Assembler Coding Form

PROGRAM

PROGRAMMER

DATE

PUNCHING INSTRUCTIONS — GRAPHIC / PUNCH

PAGE 2 OF 2

CARD ELECTRO NUMBER

X28-6509-2 U/M050
Printed in U.S.A.

Name	Operation	Operand / Comments	Identification-Sequence
	ORG	CARDIN	0024
CODE3	DS	CL1	0025
RECVGNO	DS	CL7	0026
PURCHNO2	DS	CL7	0027
PARTNO3	DS	CL12	0028
RECQTY	DS	CL8	0029
BACKORDR	DS	CL4	0030
MT3	DS	CL41	0031
*			0032

Figure 6-1b

subdefinitions, it can be referred to by the first label by which it was defined. This idea is shown in Fig. 6-2 using the same basic subdefinitions as in the previous set of DS statements.

In this instance, each subsequent subdefined area was able to use the same labels previously defined for other fields. In a side-by-side listing, these areas would overlap as:

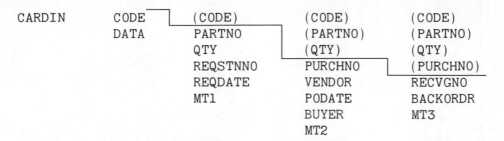

The labels within the parentheses do not appear in the statements because their interpretation and field length is identical to a previous definition. Notice that this type of definition is accomplished in a "step-down" mode, that is, each unique subdefinition must be accomplished at a lateral level or subsequent field level.

3. Boundary Alignments

Storage areas and data fields that are to be used directly in fixed-point arithmetic operations or in the performance of register instructions are required to be aligned on halfword, fullword, or doubleword boundary alignments, depending on the particular instruction statement to be executed. The valid boundary alignments are considered to be:

1. Halfword — A decimal core location that is divisible by 2.
2. Fullword — A decimal core location that is divisible by 4.
3. Doubleword — A decimal core location that is divisible by 8.

It is not anticipated that the average programmer would know exactly where each storage area or data area would be aligned when his program is compiled.

Therefore, the programmer is given the 'H', 'F', and 'D' type of operands for both the DS and DC op codes. These operands will automatically provide halfword, fullword, and doubleword boundary alignment respectively. The illustrations that follow provide examples of some of the ways that these operands may be expressed in a Define Storage (DS) statement.

```
FULLWD      DS      F
```

This statement is reserving four bytes of storage, aligned on a fullword boundary and referenced or addressed by the label FULLWD.

```
SAVEREG     DS      18F
```

This statement is assigning the label SAVEREG to 18 contiguous fullwords of storage—72 consecutive bytes. Every fourth byte of this overall area will be aligned on a core storage boundary location that is divisible by four. This is the type of storage area that is established in every problem program for the purpose of saving register contents at program initialization.

```
HAFWDS3     DS      3H
```

As suggested by the label, this statement is defining a storage area that will consist of six bytes—three consecutive halfword locations. Because it would not be known which halfword also happens to be aligned on a fullword boundary, it would be impractical to attempt to use any two of these halfwords as a fullword location.

```
ALIGN       DS      0F
DATABITS    DC      B'01001100'
CHEKBITS    DC      X'4C4C'
NULLBITS    DC      B'00000000'
```

The first statement in this group represents a means of establishing fullword boundary

IBM

IBM System/360 Assembler Coding Form

X28-6509-2 U/M050
Printed in U.S.A.

PROGRAM						PAGE	OF
PROGRAMMER		DATE		GRAPHIC		CARD ELECTRO NUMBER	
			PUNCHING INSTRUCTIONS	PUNCH			

Name	Operation	Operand / Comments	Identification-Sequence
*			0001
CARDIN	DS	0CL80	0002
CODE	DS	CL1	0003
DATA	DS	CL79	0004
*			0005
	ORG	DATA	0006
PARTNO	DS	CL12	0007
QTY	DS	CL6	0008
REQSTNNO	DS	CL8	0009
REQDATE	DS	CL6	0010
MT1	DS	CL47	0011
*			0012
	ORG	REQSTNNO	0013
PURCHNO	DS	CL7	0014
VENDOR	DS	CL6	0015
PODATE	DS	CL6	0016
BUYER	DS	CL8	0017
MT2	DS	CL34	0018
*			0019
	ORG	VENDOR	0020
RECVGNO	DS	CL7	0021
BACKORDR	DS	CL4	0022
MT3	DS	CL43	0023
*			0024

Figure 6-2

alignment for small segments of data that comprise less than a four-byte fullword. The statement labeled ALIGN will create a reference for that label to the nearest fullword boundary alignment from the point in the program at which the statement was encountered. It will not reserve those storage positions. The one-byte area, DATABITS, which immediately follows ALIGN, will commence at the fullword boundary specified by ALIGN. CHEKBITS (two bytes) and NULLBITS (one byte) will be allocated so as to complete the remainder of the fullword area. Although this entire set of statements could have been created with the same data by calculating the fixed-point value of the bit configuration and establishing a single fullword constant, this is considerably more expedient. In addition, each of the three defined subfields can be referenced directly by their own labels.

```
          DS    0D
DUBPAK    DC    PL8'0'
```

This set of statements is creating an eight-byte field, containing a packed decimal value of +0, aligned on a doubleword boundary. This is one way of establishing the typical packed decimal doubleword area that is required as an operand in all Convert To Binary (CVB) and Convert To Decimal (CVD) instruction statements. This area could also have been defined as:

```
DUBPAK    DS    D
```

This latter form of assignment would have required that the programmer use the ZAP instruction to move the packed decimal field into DUBPAK prior to a CVB instruction statement, or required that the field be formatted as packed decimal prior to an application requiring a packed decimal field.

B. DEFINING CONSTANTS AND LITERALS

1. What is a Constant?

Within programming terminology, the term *"constant"* would seem to imply, "An item of expression that maintains its con-figuration unless expressly altered." In Assembler Language this implication is justified. A constant consists of data such as a value, an expression, or characters, any of which have been defined within the problem program by a Define Constant statement. This data, once defined, may be referenced or used by any subroutine or routine within that program, retaining its defined configuration until directly altered by the program logic. Actual program storage locations are assigned to the constant so that it may be addressed by a symbolic label or by an actual address.

Because the existence of a constant is based on the assumption that some subroutine or statement plans to utilize its contents, it is logical that such reference be made via a symbolic label. It is much easier to address a constant by referring to its symbolic label than to state the address at which it would reside. Therefore, even though a Define Constant statement indicates that the symbolic reference of a label is optional, it is an accepted practice to "label" all constants.

The Define Constant is written as:

```
SYMBOLIC LABEL    DC    DATA
```

The purpose of the symbolic label has already been described. It may consist of any valid EBCDIC alpha-numeric character data, ranging from one to eight bytes in length for the full Operating System. The standard rules regarding the composition for labels applies equally to constants: (a) the first character must be an alphabetic letter; (b) remaining characters may be all alpha, all numeric, or any combination of these; (c) it may not contain any blanks within it; and (d) it may not contain any special characters.

Valid Symbolic Labels	Invalid Symbolic Labels
P124689	86523
RTE	GO THERE
ROUTINE2	3FINIS
GOTDATA	DATAFIELD
KX7RC6	NOW_GO
M345N346	244MASK

The mnemonic op code for the Define Constant instruction is written as DC. This advises the Assembler Language compiler that it is supposed to create the constant data specified in the data portion of the statement, and to assign the address where it is generated to the symbolic label.

The data portion of the DC statement may be comprised of four specification factors or subfields. These are:

(a) The duplication factor.
(b) The type of constant.
(c) The length modifier.
(d) The actual data or value expressed as the constant.

(a)   The Duplication Factor. The duplication factor defines the number of times that the constant is to be generated. If no duplication factor is specified the default is to one. Therefore, if only a single constant is required, the duplication factor may be omitted. To establish a constant that contained the characters "1234123412341234 1234" the DC statement would be written as:

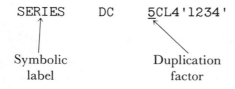

```
SERIES        DC        5CL4'1234'
```

Symbolic   Duplication
label   factor

In this instance the constant SERIES is to be generated as five groups of four bytes, each group containing the numeric characters '1234'.

(b)   The Type of Constant. The constant must be defined as to the type of data format that it is intended to represent. The identity

of the type of constant is a single character that provides the Assembler Language compiler with the proper information for creation of that constant in machine-language format. The types of constants, such as 'C' for character format, 'B' for binary, 'X' for hexadecimal, etc., will be fully discussed in this section. If a duplication factor is coded as part of the DC statement, the type of constant indicator immediately follows it; otherwise the type of constant is the first factor coded in the operand field of the statement.

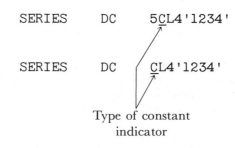

```
SERIES        DC        5CL4'1234'


SERIES        DC        CL4'1234'
```

Type of constant
indicator

(c)   The Length Modifier. The length modifier defines the actual length of the constant that is to be created. If no length modifier is specified in the DC statement, the created length of the constant will be equal to the length of the expressed constant itself or equal to the length implied by the type of constant specified. Certain types of constants do imply a given length, i.e., an 'F' constant implies a fullword, an 'H' constant implies a halfword, etc. The following list of DC statements provide some examples of lengths that are implied or specified as being assigned to constants.

```
CONST1   DC   C'NOW'
CONST2   DC   CL5'DATE'
CONST3   DC   F'23968'
CONST4   DC   H'1'
```

Implied length of three bytes
Specified length of five bytes
Implied length of four bytes
Implied length of two bytes

The manner in which the data is formatted and aligned within the various types of constants will be analyzed as each type of constant is discussed. There are four explicit types of length modifier factors.

1. Constant byte-length modifier.

2. Bit-length specification modifier.
3. Scale modifier for fixed-point values.
4. Exponent modifier for fixed-point values.

Because of their more general application in Assembler Language programming, types

1 and 2 will be discussed and illustrated throughout this section.

Type 1, the constant byte-length modifier, is used to state the number of actual bytes that are to be assigned to the constant regardless of its apparent or implied length. It is written as Ln, wherein "n" is a decimal value representing the number of bytes.

Type 2, the bit-length specification modifier, will state the actual number of bit positions that are to be assigned to the constant. It is written as L.n wherein "n" is a decimal value indicating the number of bit positions to be assigned to the constant. This type of length modifier would normally only be used with B, F, H, or D types of constants. If the value of the constant does not create a length equal to that indicated by the bit-length modifier, a sufficient number of additional high-order zero-bits will be added to the value of the constant in order to complete the bit-length specification.

It is important to know, and remember, that boundary alignments will not be provided when a length modifier is used within a fixed-point constant of a halfword, fullword, or a doubleword.

(d) The Actual Constant Data. The actual data that comprises the intended content of the constant is the last operand factor of the DC statement. If it is an A, S, V, or Y type constant, the actual data is enclosed within parentheses—all other types should have the actual data enclosed within apostrophes. Although many examples of all types of constants will appear throughout this section, a few are presented here in order to associate the components of the constant to the way that it is written.

1.	CHARCONS	DC	CL6'ABCDEF'	(Character)
2.	BINCON	DC	B'10110001'	(Binary)
3.	FIXDCON	DC	4F'398'	(Fixed-point)
4.	HEXCON	DC	XL3'DF236C'	(Hexadecimal)
5.	PACKCON	DC	PL4'253774'	(Packed decimal)
6.	ADCONST	DC	A(15975)	(Address constant)

*   *   *   *   *   *   *   *

1. CHARCONS is a character constant of six bytes containing the characters 'ABCDEF.' The modifiers determine the following:

    C A character-type constant.

    L6 An explicit length of six bytes.

  'ABCDEF' The actual data content of the six bytes.

When compiled, this constant would be generated so that it could be interpreted in any one of these formats:

Character	A	B	C	D	E	F
Hexadecimal	C | 1	C | 2	C | 3	C | 4	C | 5	C | 6
Binary	1100¦0001	1100¦0010	1100¦0011	1100¦0100	1100¦0101	1100¦0110

    *   *   *   *   *   *   *   *

2. BINCON is a one-byte binary constant. Because no length attribute was specified, the length of the constant defaults to the implied length of eight bit positions, one byte. The modifiers determine that this constant will be as follows:

    B A binary constant.

  '10110001' The binary configuration of the constant. Eight bits are specified with no conflicting specified length attribute; the constant is therefore compiled as one byte.

Binary	1 0 1 1	0 0 0 1		Hex	B	1

*   *   *   *   *   *   *   *

3. FIXDCON is a fullword fixed-point constant. The modifiers are interpreted by the compiler as:

    4 A duplication factor of four; whatever the single constant value is expressed as, it will be generated a total of four times in contiguous storage positions.

    F It is a fullword fixed-point constant. Because no explicit length modifiers are present the constant will consist of four bytes aligned on a fullword boundary.

    '398' A fixed-point value of +398.

Inasmuch as a duplication factor of four is applied to a constant consisting of four bytes, the overall storage allocation for FIXDCON will be 16 bytes; 4 times 4 bytes equals 16 bytes.

	4 bytes	4 bytes	4 bytes	4 bytes
FIXDCON	+398	+398	+398	+398

The first four bytes of FIXDCON, and each subsequent four-byte increment, would appear as:

Binary	0	000	0000	0000	0000	0000	0001	1000	1110

Hexadecimal	0	0	0	0	0	1	8	E

*   *   *   *   *   *   *   *

4. HEXCON is a three-byte hexadecimal constant. The compiler would interpret the modifiers as:

    X A hexadecimal constant.

    L3 A byte-length attribute of three bytes.

    'DF236C' The hexadecimal digits comprising the constant data.

Hexadecimal	D	F	2	3	6	C

Binary	1101	1111	0010	0011	0110	1100

*   *   *   *   *   *   *   *

5. PACKCON is a four-byte packed decimal constant containing a value of +253,774. The modifiers are interpreted as:

    P A packed decimal constant.

    L4 A byte-length attribute of four bytes.

    '253774' The packed decimal value of +253,774 that is to occupy the four-byte constant area.

Because the stated value is not sufficiently large enough to occupy the whole of the length specified for the constant, the high-order half-byte is padded with a hex zero-digit.

PACKCON
(Hexadecimal form)

0	2	5	3	7	7	4	C

*   *   *   *   *   *   *   *

6. ADCONST is an address constant. The lack of a specified length attribute will cause the length of the constant to default to a four-byte fullword. The modifiers are interpreted as:

A An address constant of four bytes.

(15975) An address contained within the fullword ADCONST as a fixed-point value.

ADCONST (Binary)

0	000	0000	0000	0000	0011	1110	0110	0111

(Hexadecimal)

0	0	0	0	3	E	6	7

A more thoroughly detailed examination of the various constants will be supplied during the discussions of each particular type of constant.

(e) The Literal Version of a Constant. The general interpretation of a constant is that a label, or a symbolic reference, is assigned to a particular configuration of data or value in order that it might be referenced via that label from any point within the problem program. A literal, however, is considered to be an "on-the-spot" constant—in other words, "A literal interpretation of the data or value that is expressed within an instruction statement." The same literal may be used any number of times within a program, but each time that it is used it must be expressed in its entirety and may not be cross-referenced from any other point within the program.

A literal is written in the same format as the operand portion of a constant except that it must be preceded by an *equal-sign* (=). Other rules regarding the use of a literal are stated below:

1. A literal may not specify multiple operands.

2. A duplication factor of zero may not be indicated.

3. Duplication factors and length modifiers must be expressed as self-defining, unsigned decimal values.

4. A literal may not specify an S-type address constant.

The two sets of instruction statements that appear in Figs. 6-3 and 6-4 reflect the difference between the use of a constant and the use of a literal.

In the first set of coding statements PACKS has been defined as a four-byte packed decimal constant with a value of +31,649. Any subsequent reference to that amount needs only to state the symbolic label that creates the address of that constant.

The second set of statements reiterates the entire value of the literal each time that it is used. It is somewhat obvious that defined constants can result in faster and more efficient program coding as well as lessening the chance for error in the repeated writing of the value. When a literal is compiled, the language compiler will not be able to tell if the value stated was correct or not, other than for general format. However, if the name of a constant is misspelled, the compiler will indicate an "undefined symbol error," as long as that misspelling does not create a symbolic reference that is validly designated elsewhere within the program.

If a value or character data is to be used only once or twice throughout the entire program, it is quite practical to use a literal in lieu of a constant.

(f) Expressing the Constants. The means by which a constant is expressed, and the interpretation of that expression by the compiler, depends largely on the type of

IBM

IBM System/360 Assembler Coding Form

| PROGRAM | | | | | PAGE | OF |
| PROGRAMMER | | | DATE | | CARD ELECTRO NUMBER | |

PUNCHING INSTRUCTIONS — GRAPHIC / PUNCH

X28-6509-2 U/M050
Printed in U.S.A.

Name	Operation	Operand	Comments
*		USING A CONSTANT	
*			
PACKS	DC	PL4'31649'	
*			
ROUTE1	AP	BIGFIELD,PACKS	
	SP	PACKTWO,PACKS	
	MP	PACKANSR,PACKS	

Figure 6-3

IBM | IBM System/360 Assembler Coding Form | X28-6509-2 U/M050 Printed in U.S.A.

PROGRAM | PUNCHING INSTRUCTIONS | GRAPHIC | PAGE OF
PROGRAMMER | DATE | PUNCH | CARD ELECTRO NUMBER

STATEMENT: Name 1–8 | Operation 10–14 | Operand 16– | Comments –71 | Identification-Sequence 73–80

```
*                         USING  A  LITERAL
*
ROUTE1    - -    - - - - - - -
         AP      BIGFIELD,=PL4'31649'
          - -    - - - - - - -
          - -    - - - - - - -
         SP      PACKTWO,=PL4'31649'
          - -    - - - - - - -
         MP      PACKANSR,=PL4'31649'
          - -    - - - - - - -
```

Figure 6-4

constant that is being created. This section will discuss the alternatives and requirements that are to be considered for the twelve most commonly used types of constants. These are shown in Table 6-1.

Each of the various types of constants has an intended application for which it was designed. However, they are by no means restricted to that particular application. It is often the programmer's personal choice that determines the type of constant that will be used for any given application, although it must be stated that this choice should be based on reasonable logic and clarity of definition. For example, if the program logic required a bit-by-bit binary configuration, the constant could readily be defined as a binary constant, a hexadecimal constant, or even as a halfword or fullword constant. Of

these four choices the hexadecimal format is most often preferential—it is not lengthy to write and yet the bit structure can be easily identified.

As the various types of constants are described on the following pages, attempt to visualize all of the practical applications for which they might be used.

2. The 'C' Constant (Character)

The character constant is the "workhorse" of most commercial programs. Data messages, output fields for printed data, data insertion, search arguments, and many other concepts equally utilize this type of constant. A character constant may have a length attribute range of from 1 to 256 bytes. The manner in which the constant is expressed, however, may limit the length to less than

TABLE 6-1

Code Character	Type Of Constant	General Application
C	Character	To define EBCDIC character representation, either as alpha, numeric, or symbols.
X	Hexadecimal	To express a binary format, a hexadecimal configuration, fixed-point values, or packed decimal values.
B	Binary	To indicate a bit-by-bit format of the constant.
F	Fullword	To define a four-byte fixed-point value aligned on a fullword boundary location. (It is aligned providing that no length modifier is specified.)
H	Halfword	To define a two-byte fixed-point value that will be aligned on a halfword boundary location if no length modifier is specified.
D	Doubleword	To define an eight-byte floating-point assignment. That value will be aligned on a doubleword boundary location if no length modifier is specified.
P	Packed decimal	To define a packed decimal value.
Z	Zoned decimal	To express a decimal value in extended zoned format wherein each digit occupies one byte, the right-most byte containing the sign of the field.
A	Address	To define an address constant, consisting of a four-byte fullword unless specified otherwise.
Y	Address	To define an address constant, consisting of a two-byte halfword unless specified otherwise.
S	Address	To define an address constant expressed in base-displacement form, consisting of a maximum of a two-byte halfword.
V	Address	To define a reserved storage area for the address constant of an external symbol. Although this would normally generate a four-byte fullword area, a smaller length may be specified.

256 bytes, a fact that is not readily pointed out in most texts. If the programmer attempted to create a Define Constant statement wherein the expressed constant itself physically occupied 256 positions on the Assembler Language coding form, the language compiler would flag the last two lines of the constant as an error. This is because the maximum number of continuation lines permissible for a regular instruction statement is two lines plus the original line, or a maximum of 165 bytes after allowing one byte to define the type of constant and one byte each for the opening and closing apostrophes that enclose the constant. (See Fig. 6-5.) If it is necessary to actually create a constant with a length greater than 165 bytes in which each and every byte must be relatively unique, it is possible to do so by creating two smaller contiguous constants. In order to use the overall combined data contained in both, it is only necessary to refer to the label of the first constant and state a specific length attribute of the combined length of both constants.

When a character constant is defined, each character indicated in the expressed constant will be compiled as a one-byte EBCDIC character. If a length modifier is not expressed, the assigned length of the constant will be determined by the number of characters that comprise the expressed constant.

If a length modifier is specified and it differs from the number of characters contained in the constant expression, one of the following will occur:

1. If the specified length attribute is less than the number of characters in the constant, any right-most bytes of the constant in excess of the specified length will be dropped.

2. If the specified length attribute is greater than the number of characters in the constant, the bytes to the right of the expressed constant will be supplied with blanks, X'40'.

An exception to the rule of "one character equals one byte" exists when an ampersand (&) or an apostrophe (') is to be included as a part of the constant itself. In order to include either of these characters within the constant, the character must be stated twice in succession—this would appear as && or ''. When considering the length of the constant, however, the two characters only count as one byte.

In the character-type constants that comprise the following examples, the DC statement is shown along with the resulting constant field that it would create. The individual units within all illustrated fields are considered to be in one-byte increments.

Example 1

```
DATA1      DC      C'RECORD'
```

DATA1	R	E	C	O	R	D

No length modifier was specified; consequently, the length attribute was determined by the number of characters in the constant expression.

Example 2

```
DATA2      DC      CL7'DEVICES'
```

DATA2	D	E	V	I	C	E	S

The length modifier and the number of bytes of constant data agree; therefore, the constant is established exactly as stated.

IBM IBM System/360 Assembler Coding Form

X28-6509-2 U/M050
Printed in U.S.A.

PROGRAM | PROGRAMMER | DATE | PUNCHING INSTRUCTIONS | GRAPHIC | PUNCH | PAGE OF | CARD ELECTRO NUMBER

STATEMENT: Name (1–8), Operation (10–14), Operand (16–), Comments (–71), Identification-Sequence (73–80)

```
BIGFIELD DC      C'ABCDEFGHIJKLMNOPQRSTUVWXYZ1234567890987654321ZYXWVUTSR*
               QPONMLKJIHGFEDCBABCDEFGHIJKLMNOPQRSTUVWXYZ1234567890987 6*
               54321ZYXWVUTSRQPONMLKJIHGFEDCBABCDEFGHIJKLMNOPQRSTUVWXY'
```

Figure 6-5

Example 3

```
DATA3      DC      CL6'123456789'
```

DATA3	1	2	3	4	5	6

Although the constant expression contained nine characters, the length modifier of L6 controlled the length of the compiled constant. The three excess bytes, '789', were ignored.

Example 4

```
DATA4      DC      CL10'SERIAL#'
```

DATA4	S	E	R	I	A	L	#	ƀ	ƀ	ƀ

A compiled constant of ten bytes was created from the specification of a length modifier of L10. Because the constant expression did not contain enough characters to fill the ten bytes, the right-most three bytes of the defined area were created as blanks. (The symbol 'ƀ' representing a blank.)

Example 5

```
DATA5      DC      C'TO&&FRO'
```

DATA5	T	O	&	F	R	O

The exception regarding ampersands (and apostrophes) is shown in this example. It was necessary to indicate a set of ampersands in order for the compiler to generate a single byte containing an ampersand. Even though seven characters appeared within the constant expression, the compiler recognized the single-byte implication of the double ampersand; therefore, only a six-byte constant was created.

Example 6

```
DATA6      DC      5CL2'A'
```

DATA6	A	ƀ	A	ƀ	A	ƀ	A	ƀ	A	ƀ

In this example a one-byte expression was used to create a two-byte single constant, resulting in a blank being placed in the right-most byte of the pair. In addition, a duplication factor of five was indicated, creating an overall field length of ten bytes.

Example 7

```
DATA7      DC      CL250'ƀ'
```

This constant would be compiled as a 250-byte area, each byte containing a valid blank, X'40'. The first byte of the area was created as a blank because of the 'blank' representation of the expression itself; the remaining 249 bytes were configured as blanks because the length modifier of L250 was greater than the specified characters in the constant expression.

The literal version of a character constant is written exactly the same as the constant operand fields except that it is preceded by an equal-sign. Literals used in instruction statements appear as:

```
MVC      DATARECD(4),=CL4'1222'
CLC      INPUT(5),=C'MERGE'
MVC      TABLE(20),=10CL2'DF'
```

3. The 'X' Constant (Hexadecimal)

The hexadecimal constant has many applications in creating data fields or values that are to be used throughout the program. It can be suitably used to originate mask configurations, fixed-point values of various lengths, or even to establish packed decimal values and fields.

The hexadecimal constant may have an overall byte length of from 1 to 256 bytes, equal to a range of from 2 to 512 hexadecimal digits. Any of the valid hexadecimal digits may be used to create the constant—0 through 9 and A through F.

The length of the generated 'X' constant is determined much like the 'C' constant, but with a slight variation. If a length modifier is stated, the constant will be generated in accordance with the specified length. If a length modifier is not stated, the hexadecimal expression will determine the constant length by one of the following rules.

1. If the number of hexadecimal digits expressed in the DC statement is an even number, the byte length of the constant will be generated at $\frac{1}{2}$ of that number. This is because there are two hex digits to every byte.

2. If the number of hexadecimal digits expressed in the DC statement is an odd number, the byte length of the constant will be generated as $\frac{1}{2}$ of that number plus one more byte. The left-most (high-order) half-byte will be supplied with a hexadecimal zero-digit. For example, 15 hexadecimal digits will compile into an 8-byte constant —$15 \div 2 = 7 + 1 = 8$.

In the event that the length modifier stated does not logically coincide with the number of hexadecimal digits expressed, one of the following will occur:

1. If the length modifier specifies a byte length in excess of the number of bytes required for the hexadecimal digits expressed within the constant, the high-order half-bytes will be supplied with enough hex zero-digits to complete the field.

2. If the length modifier specifies a byte-length less than that required to contain all of the expressed hexadecimal digits of the constant, any high-order half-bytes in excess of the length modifier will be ignored.

In the examples of hexadecimal constants that follow, the generated constant fields will be represented in half-byte increments. They could also be interpreted in character or binary format, depending on the use for which they were intended.

Example 1

HEXCON1	DC	X'39FD1E'

HEXCON1	3	9	F	D	1	E

In this example, the length of the generated constant was determined by the number of hexadecimal digits within the constant expression. No length modifier was stated, so there was no other confirmation, or confliction, of the length attribute implied.

Example 2

HEXCON2	DC	XL5'069F41'

HEXCON2	0	0	0	0	0	6	9	F	4	1

The length modifier specified a generated constant length of five bytes (L5). Because there were not enough hex digits to fill this length, the high-order unfilled half-bytes were supplied with hexadecimal zero-digits.

Example 3

```
HEXCON3     DC      X'FFFE1'
```

HEXCON3	0	F	F	F	E	1

The rule for creating a generated length for a constant containing an odd number of hex digits is demonstrated here—five digits divided by two equals a whole quotient of two bytes, plus one byte equals three bytes. The high-order additional half-byte that was required to complete the constant in full-byte format was supplied with a hex zero-digit.

Example 4

```
HEXCON4     DC      XL3'06914DE7C'
```

HEXCON4	1	4	D	E	7	C

The length modifier in this DC statement specified a total length of three bytes to be generated for the constant. Because nine hex digits were expressed as the constant, the high-order three hexadecimal digits ($1\frac{1}{2}$ bytes) were dropped by the compiler.

Example 5

```
HEXCON5     DC      3XL2'91C'
```

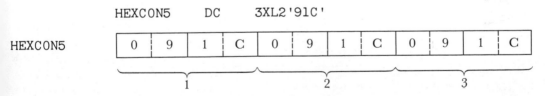

HEXCON5	0	9	1	C	0	9	1	C	0	9	1	C

Although the length modifier specified a length of two bytes for the configuration of the constant expression, only three hex digits were indicated. A high-order hex digit of zero was supplied to the constant in its singular form. The duplication factor of '3' caused the two-byte constant to be generated three times, requiring a total of six storage bytes.

Example 6

```
HEXCON6     DC      XL4'C'
```

HEXCON6	0	0	0	0	0	0	0	C

In this example, a valid four-byte packed decimal field containing a value of +0 has been created through the use of the X-type constant. The hex digit 'C' (a standard plus-sign for packed decimal values) was placed into the low-order half-byte and the remaining high-order half-bytes were supplied with hex zero-digits.

The hexadecimal literal may be written exactly the same as the operand portion of the hexadecimal constant except that it must follow the rule of literals by being preceded by an equal-sign. The following instruction statements include hexadecimal literals.

```
MVC    CHEXFLD(3),=X'050505'
MVC    PRTLINE(1),=X'40'
OC     SOURCE(4),=XL4'FEFEFEFE'
CLC    DATAFLD(2),=XL2'C1C2'
```

4. The 'B' Constant (Binary)

The binary constant is restricted to the use of bit-symbols in the expression of the actual constant data. This would mean that the constant must be expressed in 1's and 0's or all of either of these. The minimum length of a binary constant is one byte—the maximum length is 256 bytes. Experience has indicated that the binary constant may be cumbersome for coding purposes and that a hexadecimal constant would usually suffice as well. The unique ability to define small groups of bits, as provided by this constant, does justify its existence.

The implied length of a binary constant is in eight-bit bytes. If a fractional number of bits are expressed in the constant, the compiled constant will be padded on the high-order with sufficient zero-bits to complete a byte.

If the constant is given a specific byte length that does not agree with the logical number of bits expressing the constant data, one of two actions will occur.

1. If the specific byte count of the length modifier is greater than logically required to contain the number of bits expressed by the constant, the high-order undefined bit positions will be filled with zero-bits.

2. If the length modifier indicates a byte length less than that required to contain all of the expressed bits, a sufficient number of the bits of the high-order will be dropped to coincide with the specified byte length.

The following examples of binary constants relate these variations to their respective positioning within the byte fields. The generated fields are illustrated only in binary bit configuration format.

Example 1

```
BINCON1    DC    B'0110000010100101'
```

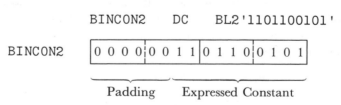

The implied length of this constant is exactly two bytes, or 16 bits.

Example 2

```
BINCON2    DC    BL2'1101100101'
```

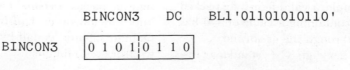

The length modifier of this constant specified a byte length of 'L2' (16 bits) even though only 10 bits were indicated as the expressed constant. The unspecified 6 bit positions were supplied in the form of 6 high-order zero-bits.

Example 3

```
BINCON3    DC    BL1'01101010110'
```

BINCON3 | 0 1 0 1 | 0 1 1 0 |

The explicit length attribute for this constant was stated as one byte (8 bits), although 11 bits were contained in the expressed constant data. Accordingly, the three high-order bits (0 1 1) of the expressed constant were ignored when the constant was compiled.

The literal version of the binary constant is expressed in the same manner as the operand portion of the DC statement. As in the case of all literals, it must be preceded by an equal sign. All of the rules conventional to the binary constant apply to the binary literal. Literals of this type would appear as:

```
CLC     HOLDBYTE(1),=BL1'1101'
MVC     INSERT(2),=B'1111000000001111'
IC      6,=BL1'10110011'
```

5. The 'F' Constant
(Fullword Fixed-Point)

The fullword constant is used to create a four-byte fixed-point value that is expressed in the constant statement as a decimal value. The fullword alignment is true under the condition that a length modifier is not specified within the constant. In the event that a length modifier is stated, the constant assumes that length and the boundary alignment is no longer effected.

Although there are many variations of the fullword constant (F), the halfword constant (H), and the doubleword constant (D), all of these variations will not be discussed. Constants involving scaling, scale modifiers, exponents, exponent modifiers, and implied or specified variable fractions are not considered by the author to be an integral requirement of the Assembler Language programming portion of this text. Any need for additional data on these factors may be easily referenced within the computer manufacturers' technical manuals.

The fullword constant may be expressed as a signed or unsigned decimal value. If the sign of the value is not specifically expressed, the value is considered to be positive.

As mentioned, a fullword constant may be given a length modifier, the maximum range of which is eight bytes. It would appear to be contradictory to create a fullword constant with a length specification of eight bytes, but this allows the programmer to originate a fixed-point value in a field larger than four bytes without first setting up a doubleword area and loading the fixed-point value into it.

The examples for the fullword constant consist of four-byte aligned fullwords including the variations of specifically-signed values. The decimal value in the expressed constant is converted to a fixed-point value expressed in both binary form and hexadecimal configuration.

Example 1

FULLWD1   DC   F'3295'
s

FULLWD1 (Binary)	0000	0000	0000	0000	0000	1100	1101	1111
(Hex)	0	0	0	0	0	C	D	F

Example 2

FULLWD2   DC   F'-661327'
s

FULLWD2 (Binary)	1111	1111	1111	0101	1110	1000	1011	0001
(Hex)	F	F	F	5	E	8	B	1

Example 3

	FULLWD3	DC	F'12593446'
	s		

FULLWD3 (Binary)

0000	0000	1100	0000	0010	1001	0010	0110

(Hex)

0	0	C	0	2	9	2	6

In each of the foregoing examples, the hexadecimal configuration of the resulting constant has been provided to enable a meaningful conversion of the fixed-point value to its decimal equivalent. This can be readily accomplished by the use of the Hexadecimal/Decimal Conversion Table.

The fullword literal follows the conventions of other literals, it is preceded by an equal sign and the context is that of the operand field of the constant.

```
A     10,=F'675021'
L     6,=F'32596'
LM    6,8,=3F'4096'
```

In the last statement, a Load Multiple instruction statement, the literal will generate three consecutive fullwords, each containing a fixed-point value of +4096. The first fullword will be loaded into general register 6, the second into general register 7, and the third into general register 8.

The maximum values that may be expressed in a four-byte fullword constant are +2,147,483,647 or −2,147,483,648.

6. The 'H' Constant (*Halfword Fixed-Point*)

Ignoring the same variations that were excluded from the description of the fullword constant, the halfword constant is generally used to establish a two-byte fixed-point value aligned on a halfword boundary location. A length modifier may be specified, in which instance the boundary alignment of the constant is no longer applicable. A halfword constant may contain a length specification of up to eight bytes.

The value of the constant may be expressed specifically as a signed value, or the sign may be implied, in which case the value is assumed to be positive. The maximum values than can be contained within a two-byte halfword are +32,767 or −32,768.

The following examples of halfword constants are considered to be two-byte aligned halfwords representing fixed-point values. The representation of the value is illustrated in both binary and hexadecimal form, the latter allowing a ready interpretation of the decimal conversion process.

Example 1

	HAFCON1	DC	H'15987'

HAFCON1 (Binary)

0011	1110	0111	0011

(Hex)

3	E	7	3

Example 2

	HAFCON2	DC	H'−896'

HAFCON2 (Binary)

1111	1100	1000	0000

(Hex)

F	C	8	0

Example 3

HAFCON3   DC   3H'10775'

HAFCON3 (Binary)	0010	1010	0001	0111	0010	1010	0001	0111	0010	1010	0001	0111
(Hex)	2	A	1	7	2	A	1	7	2	A	1	7

1   2   3

The halfword literal is preceded by an equal sign as shown in its application in the following instruction statements:

```
AH      5,=H'24'
LH      10,=H'-13006'
MH      6,=H'256'
```

7. The 'D' Constant (Doubleword)

Although a doubleword constant is generally assumed to be within the category of floating-point arithmetic operations, it has a very functional use in normal fixed-point applications. Because the need for a value in excess of the capability of a fullword is seldom found in the Assembler Language programming of commercial applications, the primary use of a doubleword constant might be considered to be the initialization of an eight-byte area containing zero-bits.

For example, the program logic might intend to create two individual fullword values within a defined doubleword constant and later place the overall doubleword, assumed to consist of two values, into two consecutive registers via the Load Multiple instruction. The creation of such a field, originally containing a zero value, would be coded as:

```
DUBCON    DC    D'0'
```

Each four bytes of this field would also be on fullword boundary alignment. Data or values could then be loaded out of, or stored into, and manipulated within any section or portion of this field by utilizing address adjusting or length specifications (wherever necessary) as a part of the instruction statement. This might appear as:

```
L       8,DUBCON+4
STM     5,6,DUBCON
```

```
CVB     9,DUBCON
MVI     DUBCON+7,X'00'
```

8. The 'P' Constant (Packed Decimal)

The packed decimal constant is probably the second most widely used type of constant in commercial programming with Assembler Language. Its form of expression is quite similar to that of hexadecimal constants in that each expressed digit occupies a half-byte of the compiled constant. The sign of the packed decimal constant may be expressed within the constant or omitted, which in the latter case it is assumed to be a positive value. When the compiler creates the packed decimal constant, the right-most digit of the expressed constant is paired with the sign of the constant to fill the right-most byte. The remaining bytes of the compiled constant are filled with the pairs of digits of the remaining expressed constant.

If the number of digits in the expressed value do not fit equally into the implied length of the constant, a single high-order hexadecimal zero-digit is provided to complete the high-order byte.

When an explicit length modifier is stated as part of the constant and the quantity of expressed decimal digits do not combine to a byte length equal to that of the length modifier, one of two events occur:

1. If the explicit length attribute is greater than the number of bytes required for the expressed value, excess high-order half-bytes are padded with hex zero-digits.
2. If the explicit length attribute is less than the number of bytes required for the expressed value, the surplus high-order digits of the expressed value are ignored.

The length of a packed decimal constant may be a minimum of 1 byte and a maximum of 16 bytes. For the purpose of data clarity and implied alignment, a decimal point may be expressed within the decimal value. This decimal point is entirely ignored by the compiler and the constant is compiled as though the decimal point had never existed in the DC statement. It is intended solely for the purpose of aiding the programmer in his interpretation of the value of the constant for alignment purposes. Other than the sign of the packed decimal value and the inclusion of a decimal point when so desired, the expressed constant must be written in decimal form.

The following examples of packed decimal constants contain the DC statement and a hexadecimal representation (half-bytes) of the data field that would be created by the compiler.

Example 1

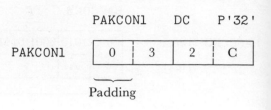

Even though the expressed constant contained only two digits, it was necessary to create the constant as a two-byte field. This was caused by the fact that the implied sign required the right-most half-byte of the compiled constant. When the length was forced to two bytes, there were not sufficient digits to fill the field. Accordingly, a hex zero-digit was placed into the vacant high-order half-byte.

Example 2

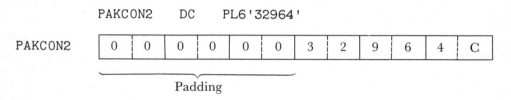

The length modifier of the DC statement forced the compiler to create a six-byte packed decimal constant field. The value of the expressed constant was not great enough to fill these bytes, so zero-digits were supplied to the additional high-order half-bytes.

Example 3

PAKCON3   DC   PL2'7968'

| PAKCON3 | 9 | 6 | 8 | C |

In this example, the programmer apparently did not give any consideration to the necessity of allowing a half-byte for the sign of the constant. An explicit length of two bytes was specified, which left only three half-bytes for packed decimal digits. Accordingly the high-order digit of the expressed constant was ignored.

Example 4

PAKCON4   DC   P'−25986'

| PAKCON4 | 2 | 5 | 9 | 8 | 6 | D |

The expressed constant was stated as a negative value. The constant, therefore, contains a standard negative sign applicable to packed decimals.

Example 5

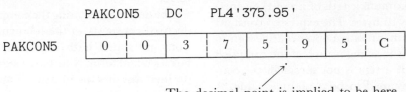

PAKCON5   DC   PL4'375.95'

The decimal point is implied to be here

The expressed constant in this example contains an embedded decimal point. The compiler has ignored the decimal point and has created the actual constant without it. The primary purpose of specifying the decimal point within the DC statement was to remind the programmer that any subsequent use of this constant should consider it to contain an implied decimal point at this position.

Example 6

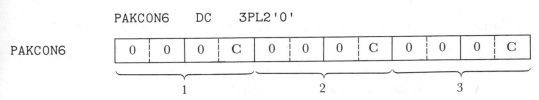

PAKCON6   DC   3PL2'0'

This DC statement has effectively created three two-byte packed decimal fields, each containing a value of +0. Each of the two-byte constants could be addressed separately, such as by PAKCON6, PAKCON6+2, and PAKCON6+4. If an operation was to be executed using any single field of the three, an explicit length attribute would have to be included in the instruction. This would appear as:

```
AP      PAKCON6+4(2),PAKDATA
```

The literal form of the packed decimal constant is written with an equal sign preceding it. All of the rules applicable to the generation of a packed decimal constant apply as well to its literal form. Examples of this type of literal would be:

```
AP      PACOUNTR,=PL1'1'
SP      BIGPACK,=P'32964'
CP      PAKCHECK(3),=PL3'-1597'
MP      PAKQUOT,=PL2'9.95'
DP      DIVPAK,=PL3'+17.82'
```

9. The 'Z' constant (Zoned Decimal)

The zoned decimal constant is used to create an EBCDIC numeric constant in which the right-most byte contains the sign of the decimal value expressed by the constant. Each digit of the constant expression of the DC statement will construct one byte of the compiled constant if the length attributes coincide.

If a length modifier is not stated, the compiled constant will have a length attribute equal to that implied by the number of digits within the expressed constant.

If a length modifier is specified that does not agree with the number of numeric digits contained within the expressed constant, one of the following will occur:

1. If the length modifier is greater than the number of expressed constant digits, the unfilled high-order bytes of the compiled constant will be supplied with EBCDIC zero numerics.

2. If the length modifier is less than the expressed constant digits, the excessive expressed digits will be ignored by the compiler.

The maximum length of a zoned decimal constant is 16 bytes. The expressed constant may contain a positive or a negative sign to determine the configuration of the compiled constant. If a sign is not specified, the constant is assumed to be a positive value. A decimal point may be written within the expressed constant, but only for the purpose of information and assumed alignment. The decimal point is ignored by the compiler and the constant is created without any reference to it.

The fields representing the compiled zoned decimal constants in the following illustrations are stated both in character and in hexadecimal form. Note that a signed, zoned decimal assumes the identity of an EBCDIC alpha character.

Example 1

```
ZONECON1    DC    Z'9236'
```

ZONECON1	9		2		3		F	
	F	9	F	2	F	3	C	6

The right-most character, 'F', represents a positive-signed zoned decimal of '6'.

Example 2

```
ZONECON2    DC    ZL6'2048'
```

ZONECON2	0		0		2		0		4		H	
	F	0	F	0	F	2	F	0	F	4	C	8

The right-most character, 'H', represents a positive-signed zoned decimal of '8'.

Example 3

```
ZONECON3    DC    ZL4'1651'
```

ZONECON3	1		6		5		A	
	F	1	F	6	F	5	C	1

The right-most character, 'A', represents a positive-signed zoned decimal of '1'.

Example 4

```
ZONECON4    DC    Z'-296883'
```

ZONECON4	2		9		6		8		8		L	
	F	2	F	9	F	6	F	8	F	8	D	3

The right-most character, 'L', represents a negative-signed zoned decimal of '3'.

Example 5

ZONECON5   DC   ZL5'763.13'

ZONECON5	7	6	3	1	C
	F 7	F 6	F 3	F 1	C 3

The right-most character, 'C', represents a positive-signed zoned decimal of '3'. The decimal point is not compiled as a part of the constant itself, but appears on the program source listing as a reminder to the programmer of its implied position.

The zoned decimal literal is written in the instruction statement in the same manner as that operand portion of a zoned decimal constant is written within a DC statement. As with all literals, it must be preceded by an equal sign.

```
MVC    DATAHOLD(5),=Z'23965'
CLC    ZONEDEC(2),=ZL2'99'
MVC    OUTPUT(4),=ZL4'+377.7'
```

10. The Address Constants—
A, S, V, and Y

The address constants are used to provide the program with storage address constants. The address that is used to generate the constant operand may be generally in absolute or relocatable form, such as a symbolic label. One of the principle applications of address constants is to aid in the initialization of the base register assignments for program storage. The symbolic label of the constant itself addresses the area containing the respective address of the symbol or value contained within the statement operand. Address constant expressions are contained within parentheses, rather than within apostrophes. Only the 'A' and 'Y' address constants may be expressed as literals.

(a)   The 'A' Address Constant. The 'A' address constant has an implied length of four bytes that will result in fullword boundary alignment. If an explicit length modifier is used, word boundary alignment is not applicable.

The 'A' type of address constant is written as:

```
START1    DC     A(BASE1)
START2    DC     A(BASE1+4096)
START3    DC     A(BASE1+8192)
SETADDR   DC     A(TABLE)
```

(b)   The 'Y' Address Constant. The implied, and maximum, length of a 'Y' address constant is two bytes. Unless a length modifier is specified, the constant will be aligned on a halfword boundary location. Any program that is to be processed and executed under the full Operating System (OS) of a System/360 computer *should not* contain any 'Y' address constants specified in relocatable form. This same restriction is applicable when the processing hardware CPU is of a core size of 32,767 bytes or more.

The 'Y' address constant might appear as:

```
SUBRTE    DC     Y(ENTRY1)
SUBRTEA   DC     Y(ENTRY1+16394)
```

(c)   The 'S' Address Constant. The 'S' type of address constant is compiled as a two-byte halfword if no length modifier is specified. It has a maximum length restriction of two bytes, and the presence of a length modifier will prevent forced halfword boundary alignment. When the constant has been compiled, the high-order four bit positions will indicate the base register assignment—the low-order 12 bit positions representing the displacement value.

The expressed constant itself may be specified either as:

1. A set of absolute expressions represent-

ing the displacement portion of the address and the base register assignment. This type of expression would appear as S(512(4)) wherein the '512' indicates the displacement value and the '4' indicates the base register.

2. It may also be expressed simply as an absolute or relocatable address factor, such as S(BASE1).

(d) **The 'V' Address Constant.** The 'V' constant differs somewhat from the other address constants in that it compiles with an absolute value content of zero. Its actual purpose within Assembler Language is to allocate storage space for the address of an external symbol. This address will not be provided until the program with the external symbol reference is loaded.

Unless a length modifier is specified, the 'V' address constant is compiled as a four-byte fullword, with proper boundary alignment of a fullword. The expressed constant itself is specified as a single relocatable symbol.

```
ADCONVA      DC      V(EXREF)
ADCONVB      DC      V(OUTMOD)
ADCONVC      DC      V(PROG2)
```

In each of these examples the constant expression contained within parentheses has no compiled identification within the program in which it was compiled.

Review Exercises

The following problems consist of constants that have been coded by the programmer via the use of DC instruction statements. Analyze the individual instruction statement and then complete the contents of the field for that constant as it would be generated by the Assembler Language compiler. Express the contents of each field as specified—in character, hexadecimal, or bit-by-bit configuration. Wherever there is insufficient room to place the length of an entire field on one line, subsequent lines represent the contiguous storage allocation for that field. Please note that the character form of a blank (X'40') is shown as ƀ.

1.   HEXCONA   DC   XL6'C1C2C3E7E8E9'

Character format

Hex format

2.   HEXCONB   DC   X'F7F8F9'

Character

Hex

3.   HEXCONC   DC   3XL3'F7F8C9'

Character

Hex

4.   HEXCOND   DC   XL5'5B4B4B6161'

Character

Hex

5.   HEXCONE   DC   XL2'4040'

Character

Hex

6.   HEXCONF   DC   2XL4'5BF6F1F0'

Character

Hex

7.   CHARA   DC   CL3'ABC'

Character

Hex

8.   CHARB   DC   5CL1'9'

Character

Hex

9.   CHARC   DC   2CL4'AØB'

Character

Hex

10.   CHARD   DC   CL2'$-'

Character

Hex

11.   CHARE   DC   CL6'ADHLPT'

Character

Hex

12.   CHARF   DC   4CL2'135'

Character

Hex

13.   CHARG   DC   3CL5'⌀'

Character

Hex

14.   PKONA   DC   4PL2'+225'

Hex

15.   PKONB   DC   PL6'−51983'

Hex

16.   PKONC   DC   PL3'610'

Hex

17.   PKOND   DC   2P'159.8762'

Hex

18.   PKONE   DC   5PL1'−.9'

Hex

19.   PKONF   DC   2PL3'+259877'

Hex

20.   ZCONA   DC   ZL6'−2158'

Character

Hex

21.   ZCONB   DC   2Z'+789'

Character

Hex

22.   ZCONC   DC   ZL5'+333'

Character

Hex

23.   ZCOND   DC   3ZL2'−5'

Character

Hex

24.   ZCONE   DC   ZL4'4172'

Character

Hex

25.   ZCONF   DC   ZL6'+85917'

Character

Hex

26.   BINCONA   DC   4BL1'01000000'

Hex

Binary

27.   BINCONB   DC   BL3'1101000111010010'

Hex

Binary

28.   BINCONC   DC   2BL.2'11111111'

Hex

Binary

29.   BINCOND   DC   3BL.1'11101110'

Hex

Binary

30.   BINCONE   DC   BL3'111111111111111111'

Hex

Binary

31.   FXCONA   DC   3H'32767'

Hex

Binary

Fixed-point
value   _____   _____   _____

32.   FXCONB   DC   2F'32768'

Hex

Binary

Fixed-point
value   _____   _____

33.   FXCONC   DC   D'0'

Hex

Binary

34.   FXCOND   DC   F'295315647'

Hex

Binary

35.   FXCONE   DC   H'-6153'

Hex

Binary

36.   FXCONF   DC   2F'-386995'

Hex

Binary

Fixed-point
value   _____   _____

COMPARING DATA
AND CONDITIONS

A. THE INSTRUCTIONS FOR COMPARING DATA

Before studying the general applications of the Assembler Language "compare" instructions, the technical composition and restrictions of each instruction must be presented. This same requirement is equally applicable to the subsequent chapters of this text in which the logical applications of other Assembler Language instructions are presented. Each of these chapters will, therefore, be preceded by an introductory section consisting of concise technical descriptions for all of the instructions that are to be introduced within that chapter.

It is advised that the reader thoroughly study the technical description for each of the instructions before proceeding to the application phase of the chapter. The introductory sections for these chapters may

thereafter be used as a quick technical reference guide to the Assembler Language instructions.

*　　*　　*

INSTRUCTION: COMPARE LOGICAL

Mnemonic	Hex Code	Operand Format
CL	55	$R_1,D_2(X_2,B_2)$

The Compare Logical instruction activates a binary comparison of the bit configuration of the first operand register to the second operand field. The comparison is from left-most bit to right-most bit. If an unequal condition is encountered prior to the end of the comparative fields, the compare is terminated and the Condition Code bits are set accordingly. The address generated by the second operand (D_2) must be a fullword boundary alignment.

CC	BC	Condition
0	8	The first and second operands are equal.
1	4	The first operand is less than the second operand.
2	2	The first operand is greater than the second operand.

* * *

INSTRUCTION:

COMPARE LOGICAL CHARACTERS

Mnemonic	*Hex Code*	*Operand Format*
CLC	D5	$D_1(L,B_1),D_2(B_2)$

The Compare Logical Characters instruction will cause the execution of a binary comparison of the storage data specified by the first operand to the storage data specified by the second operand. The comparison is bit-by-bit, from left-most bit (high-order) to right-most bit. If an unequal condition should happen to be encountered prior to the end of the comparative fields, the compare is terminated and the Condition Code is configurated accordingly. Up to 256 bytes of data may be compared with one instruction statement.

CC	BC	Condition
0	8	The first and second operands are equal.
1	4	The first operand is less than the second operand.
2	2	The first operand is greater than the second operand.

* * *

INSTRUCTION:

COMPARE LOGICAL IMMEDIATE

Mnemonic	*Hex Code*	*Operand Format*
CLI	95	$D_1(B_1),I_2$

The Compare Logical Immediate instruction creates a binary comparison of one byte of storage data (referred to by the first operand) to one byte of immediate data as defined by the second operand (I_2). The comparison is bit-by-bit, from left-most bit (high-order) to right-most bit. If an unequal

condition is encountered prior to the end of the comparative fields, the compare is terminated and the Condition Code bits are set to the representative configuration.

CC	BC	Condition
0	8	The first and second operands are equal.
1	4	The first operand is less than the second operand.
2	2	The first operand is greater than the second operand.

* * *

INSTRUCTION:

COMPARE LOGICAL REGISTERS

Mnemonic	*Hex Code*	*Operand Format*
CLR	15	R_1,R_2

The Compare Logical Registers instruction causes a binary comparison of contents of the first operand register to the contents of the second operand register. The comparison is from left-most bit to right-most bit. If an unequal condition is encountered prior to the end of the comparative registers, the compare is terminated and the Condition Code is set to the appropriate condition.

CC	BC	Condition
0	8	The first and second operands are equal.
1	4	The first operand is less than the second operand.
2	2	The first operand is greater than the second operand.

* * *

INSTRUCTION: COMPARE

Mnemonic	*Hex Code*	*Operand Format*
C	59	$R_1,D_2(X_2,B_2)$

This Compare instruction will compare the contents of the first operand register to the contents of the second operand (algebraically as 32-bit signed integers), and set the Condition Code bits as a result of that comparison. The operands are not altered by the execution of the instruction. The address generated by the second operand should be that of a fullword boundary alignment.

CC	BC	Condition
0	8	The first and second operands are equal.
1	4	The first operand is less than the second operand.
2	2	The first operand is greater than the second operand.

* * *

INSTRUCTION: COMPARE HALFWORD

Mnemonic	Hex Code	Operand Format
CH	49	$R_1,D_2(X_2,B_2)$

Prior to the actual compare operation, this instruction will expand the 16-bit value of the second operand contents to a 32-bit value by creating 16 additional high-order bits, each having the same value as the original sign-bit of the second operand. It will then algebraically compare the first operand register contents to the expanded second operand, as 32-bit signed integers, and set a Condition Code as a result of the comparison. The operands are not altered by the execution of this instruction. The address generated by the second operand should be located on a halfword boundary alignment.

CC	BC	Condition
0	8	The first and second operands are equal.
1	4	The first operand is less than the second operand.
2	2	The first operand is greater than the second operand.

* * *

INSTRUCTION: COMPARE REGISTERS

Mnemonic	Hex Code	Operand Format
CR	19	R_1,R_2

The Compare Registers instruction will compare the contents of the first operand register to the contents of the second operand register, algebraically as 32-bit signed integers. It will then set the Condition Code as a result of that comparison. The contents of the operands are not altered.

CC	BC	Condition
0	8	The first and second operands are equal.

CC	BC	Condition
1	4	The first operand is less than the second operand.
2	2	The first operand is greater than the second operand.

* * *

INSTRUCTION:

COMPARE PACKED DECIMALS

Mnemonic	Hex Code	Operand Format
CP	F9	$D_1(L_1,B_1),D_2(L_2,B_2)$

This instruction will compare the packed decimal contents of the first operand against the packed decimal contents of the second operand. The comparison is from right to left, through all digits of both operands. If the length attributes of the two operands are not equal, the shorter field is expanded to the length of the longer field by the insertion of high-order zero-digits. The actual bit configuration of the sign-zone nibbles (the right-most four bit positions of each field) is not checked other than to determine if the sign is a plus sign or a minus sign. Any valid plus sign compares equal to any other valid plus sign; any valid minus sign compares equal to any other valid minus sign. However, a plus-zero ($+0$) value of one field will compare equal to the minus-zero (-0) value of another field. The configuration of the operand contents are not altered by the execution of the compare. The maximum implied, or explicit, length for either field is 16 bytes.

CC	BC	Condition
0	8	The first and second operand contents are equal.
1	4	The first operand is less than the second operand.
2	2	The first operand is greater than the second operand.

B. THE APPLICATION OF THE "COMPARE" INSTRUCTIONS

It would be illogical to assume that a program could be written in which the execution of a comparison statement did not take place. Although not all comparison instructions or actions are under the programmers direct control (the operating system itself performs many decision functions based on comparisons), the average program will probably contain many decisions and decision points, the result of which are based on a comparison.

Since the majority of Assembler Language instructions set the Condition Code bits in the Program Status Word as a result of their performance, it could be loosely interpreted that each of these instructions, in their own way, are a "compare." If we were to disregard the setting of the Condition Code bits as the criteria for distinguishing a compare instruction, there are still a number of instructions that do not clearly define themselves as compare instructions by using that term in their names. Instructions such as Branch On Count, Branch On Index High, and Test Under Mask are quite logically a compare instruction. For the purpose of this section, however, the instructions and techniques to be explained will be only those that contain the term "compare" within their descriptive names. These will be set forth in three categories; logical compares, fixed-point compares, and packed decimal compare.

1. Logical Compares

The compare instructions that fall within the grouping of logical compares are the Compare Logical, Compare Logical Characters, Compare Logical Immediate, and Compare Logical Registers instructions. This type of compare instruction is not concerned with the character format of the operand fields on which the comparison is based. Each of these instructions starts at the leftmost bit position (high-order) of the operands fields and compares the binary bit position contents rightward. Each bit position in the first operand is compared to a corresponding bit position within the second operand. As soon as the instruction encounters a single unequal bit position, the compare will terminate and the Condition Code in the Program Status Word (PSW) will be set according to the status of the inequity. If an unequal condition is not found, the compare will continue through the length of the operand fields, bit position by bit position, until the implied, or explicit, length of the first operand is depleted. Since the logical compare is one in which the individual bit positions create the equal, or unequal, condition, a signed binary decimal integer of −365 would compare high to a signed binary decimal integer of +365. These two operand fields would appear as:

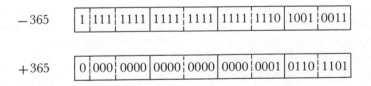

-365 | 1 111 1111 1111 1111 1111 1110 1001 0011

$+365$ | 0 000 0000 0000 0000 0000 0001 0110 1101

The first bit position to be compared would be the sign-bit, in which case the negative value of −365 would have a one-bit in the sign-bit position and the positive value of +365 would have a zero-bit in the sign-bit position. The logical compare would terminate at this point and the condition code would be set to indicate that the logical value of −365 (as a fixed-point value) was greater than the logical value of +365 in comparable format. This would be a true condition inasmuch as the comparison was made for the logical value of the operands, not the fixed-point arithmetic value.

(a) Compare Logical (CL). This instruction is used to logically compare the contents of a register to the contents of a fullword of data in storage. It could be used to logically compare the configuration of a general register to a preestablished bit configuration in a constant in order to determine if a particular condition or point within the program had been reached.

In order to understand the various representations that a data field might assume, the logical sequences of translation are shown in the following illustrations. Assume that a particular fullword in storage, referenced by the label CONA, contained the bit configu-

ration required to comprise the EBCDIC alphabetic characters "ABCD". The transition from EBCDIC format to an interpretation in bit configuration format for the contents of CONA would appear to be:

	A		B		C		D	
Character format	A		B		C		D	
Hexadecimal format	C	1	C	2	C	3	C	4
Binary bit configuration	1100	0001	1100	0010	1100	0011	1100	0100

Using this field as one of the operands, a compare statement was coded as:

```
CL      6,CONA
```

At the time of execution of this instruction statement, general register 6 contained a bit configuration of:

General register 6	1100	1010	1111	0101	1111	1100	1100	0100

The sequence of the comparison by bit positions would be:

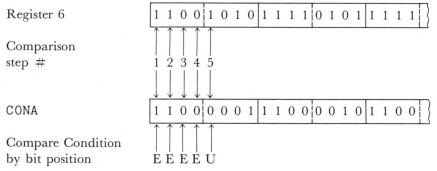

The compare action would terminate on the fifth comparison of the relative bit positions because an unequal condition was encountered. The Condition Code would then be set to reflect that general register 6 contained a bit configuration that was logically higher in value than the bit configuration of CONA.

Another illustration of the Compare Logical instruction, wherein CONA contains the same value but general register 6 contains a different value, might indicate the following steps of comparison:

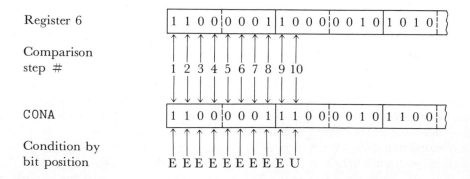

In this instance, the comparison would terminate on encountering the tenth relative bit positions. The Condition Code would then be set to indicate that general register 6 contained a bit configuration that was logically lower in value than the bit configuration of CONA.

(b) Compare Logical Characters (CLC). The CLC instruction would normally be used to logically compare the zoned alpha-numeric contents of two fields of storage data. The inference is that both fields of data contain EBCDIC data in character, numeric, or special character form, although it is not restricted to this. The instruction could be used to identify input data through the use of sets of control data, check fields for data stored prior to branching decisions, establishing criteria for the selection or exclusion of data to be processed, or any

unique use in which this instruction might lend itself to the programmer's intended logic path.

To illustrate the performance of this instruction in the following example, FIELDA and FIELDB both contain three bytes of EBCDIC character data. FIELDA contains the criteria control data on which the prefix fields in certain records are to be matched. If the prefix field for a record (FIELDB) creates an equal compare to FIELDA, the programmer might wish to use certain data from within the overall data record. The action of the Compare Logical Characters instruction can be interpreted as shown following this instruction statement.

CLC   FIELDA,FIELDB

The character-formatted contents are considered to be:

FIELDA (Control data)

P	O	S

FIELDB (Record prefix data)

P	R	S

The interpretation of the hexadecimal configuration of these fields would be:

FIELDA

D	7	D	6	E	2

FIELDB

D	7	D	9	E	2

The binary bit configuration of the fields and the resulting action of the CLC instruction statement might appear as:

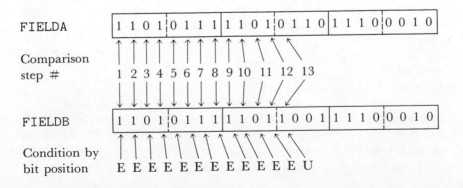

As indicated by this illustration, the compare action would terminate when the 13th bit position (from the left) was checked, because an unequal condition occurred at that point. The Condition Code would be set to indicate that FIELDA was of a lesser value than, or unequal to, FIELDB and, based on this result, the programmer's logic coding would determine what the program decision function would be.

Numerals in EBCDIC format can also be readily checked with this instruction. Assume that a programmer wished to check a three-byte field of data for its EBCDIC numeric contents to ascertain if these numerals were in excess of a value of 099. If the comparative value of 099 was a constant in a data storage area labeled NUMBRA and the data to be checked was in a field in data storage labeled NUMBRB, the instruction statement might appear as:

    CLC   NUMBRB,NUMBRA

If the comparative value of 099 was not already established as a constant, the programmer could use a literal in lieu of the second operand. At program compile time, the compiler would assign a storage address for the literal value. The instruction statement in this instance of the use of a literal would appear as:

    CLC   NUMBRB,=CL3'099'

In either case, the compare would be processed similarly if the contents of all fields in both instructions were comparable.

Character format:

NUMBRB	2	3	0

NUMBRA	0	9	9

Hexadecimal configuration:

NUMBRB	F	2	F	3	F	0

NUMBRA	F	0	F	9	F	9

The bit configuration and comparison action would be:

NUMBRB   1 1 1 1 0 0 1 0 1 1 1 1 0 0 1 1 1 1 1 1 0 0 0 0

Comparison
step #   1 2 3 4 5 6 7

NUMBRA   1 1 1 1 0 0 0 0 1 1 1 1 1 0 0 1 1 1 1 1 1 0 0 1

Condition by
bit position   E E E E E U

Upon encountering the seventh relative bit position of both fields, the instruction statement operation would find an unequal condition and terminate the compare. The Condition Code would be configured to indicate that field NUMBRB was unequal to, or higher than, field NUMBRA.

(c)   Compare Logical Immediate (CLI). Because this instruction will compare only fields of one-byte length, it can readily be used to test the "on-off" condition of a one-byte "switch" or to look for a one-byte control character in data fields. The first operand would contain the label or symbolic address of one byte of storage data; the second operand would be a one-byte self-defining (immediate) character or value.

For example, a program plans to check a one-byte control field on each record of input to determine if that byte contained an alphabetic "D" in EBCDIC format. This one-byte field, CHEXA, could be compared in any of the following ways, using the Compare Logical Immediate instruction.

```
CLI     CHEXA,C'D'
CLI     CHEXA,X'C4'
CLI     CHEXA,B'11000100'
```

In each of these three instruction statements, the comparison would be identical. Note that the configuration of the second operand, whether expressed as a character, as hex, or as binary, is interpreted as an alphabetic character "D" in all three instances. Assuming that CHEXA contained a character "X", the breakdown of the data could be construed to be:

Character format:

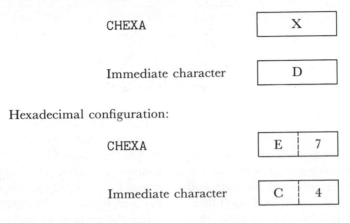

Hexadecimal configuration:

The action of the CLI instruction on the bit configuration of these two bytes would appear to be:

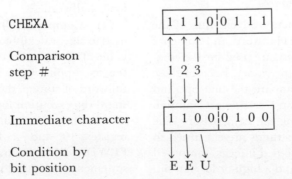

During the comparison of the third respective bit positions, the instruction statement would encounter the inequality of the bit values and terminate the compare. The resulting Condition Code setting would enable the programmer to determine that an unequal comparison was made, one in which the first operand contained the greater character value.

(d) Compare Logical Registers (CLR). The CLR instruction, as its title implies, will logically compare the bit configuration of the contents of two general registers. As with the other logical compare instructions, the respective bit positions are compared from left to right, bit by bit.

Assuming that general register 6 was to be compared to general register 8, the instruction statement would be coded as:

$$CLR \qquad 6,8$$

The following illustration defines the comparison action that might result from this instruction statement, depending on the contents of the registers.

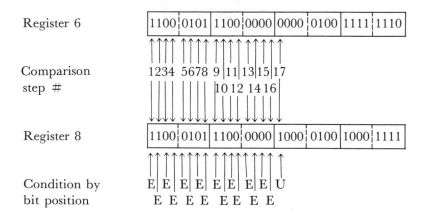

The bit configuration comparison would be equal until the 17th respective bit positions were encountered. At that time, the instruction statement would note the unequal condition, terminate the compare, and change the present Condition Code bits in the Program Status Word to indicate that general register 6 was of a lesser logical value than general register 8.

2. *Fixed-Point Compares*

A series of instructions, consisting of the Compare, Compare Halfword, and Compare Registers instructions, are used for the comparison of fixed-point values. Each of these instructions will compare the first operand to the second operand, setting a Condition Code as a result of the comparison. The contents of both operands are construed to consist of a 32-bit signed integer, comprised of a 31-bit integer and a high-order sign-bit. The actual comparison, therefore, is algebraic, based on the fixed-point value of each operand. In essence, the instruction determines the value of the 31-bit integers, evaluates the sign of each, and makes the com-

parison. The value of a positive-signed $(+)$ integer is determined by summing the Powers-Of-Two value for each bit position that contains a one-bit. The value of a negative-signed $(-)$ integer, expressed in two's complement form, can be determined by summing the integer as if it were a positive number and subtracting that value from the maximum negative value, which is $-2,147,483,648$ for a fullword and $-32,768$ for a halfword.

(a) Compare (C). This instruction is used to algebraically compare the fixed-point value of the contents of a general register to the fixed-point value of the contents of a fullword of storage data. In order to understand the execution logic of this instruction, assume that a comparison between general register 10 and a fullword in storage, FLWDA, is to be made. The instruction statement itself would be coded as:

$$C \qquad 10,FLWDA$$

The data that is to be compared by this instruction statement resides within the respective areas with this configuration:

Bit configuration:

Register 10

0	000	0000	0000	0000	0001	1100	1001	1101

FLWDA

0	000	0000	0000	0000	0011	1010	1000	1100

Hexadecimal configuration:

Register 10

+	0	0	0	0	1	C	9	D

FLWDA

+	0	0	0	0	3	A	8	C

The programmer can determine the value of these fields by converting the individual hexadecimal values, in their contiguous arrangement, to the fixed-point value that they represent. The Powers-Of-Two Table and the Hexadecimal/Decimal Conversion Table will aid in making this conversion. The method of making this conversion is as shown in the following illustration.

	Register 10		FLWDA	
Right to Left Order	Hex	Decimal	Hex	Decimal
First hex digit	D	13	C	12
Second hex digit	9	144	8	128
Third hex digit	C	3,072	A	2,560
Fourth hex digit	1	4,096	3	12,288
Integer value		7,325		14,988
Sign-bit		+		+
Signed fixed-point value		+7,325		+14,988

The algebraic comparison would indicate that the fixed-point value of FLWDA was greater than the value contained in general register 10. The Condition Code bits of the PSW would be set to indicate that the first operand of the instruction statement was of a lower value than that of the second operand.

Another example of this instruction, in which there are different values contained in the operands, is:

C   6,FLWDB

Bit configuration:

Register 6

0	000	0000	0001	0110	0000	0001	1101	0110

FLWDB

0	000	0000	0001	0001	1001	0010	1011	1010

Hexadecimal configuration:

Register 6

+	0	0	1	6	0	1	D	6

FLWDB

+	0	0	1	1	9	2	B	A

Hexadecimal to fixed-point conversion:

	Register 6		FLWDB	
Right to Left Order	Hex	Decimal	Hex	Decimal
First hex digit	6	6	A	10
Second hex digit	D	208	B	176
Third hex digit	1	256	2	512
Fourth hex digit	0	0	9	36,864
Fifth hex digit	6	393,216	1	65,536
Sixth hex digit	1	1,048,576	1	1,048,576
Integer value		1,442,262		1,151,674
Sign-bit		+		+
Signed fixed-point value		+1,442,262		+1,151,674

The execution of the Compare instruction statement would determine that the algebraic value of general register 6 was greater than the value contained in FLWDB. The Condition Code bits would be set to indicate that the first operand of the instruction statement was of a greater fixed-point value than that of the second operand.

It is necessary to understand the conversion of binary bit configuration to fixed-point values through the interpretation of the hexadecimal value arrangements in order to fully appreciate the mechanisms of fixed-point instructions. The previous two examples have illustrated the conversion of standard positive-signed (+) values. Of equal importance is the knowledge and understanding of the concept of two's complement values and their interpretation. Although the subject is adequately covered within other sections of this text, a repetition of some of the basic rules and fundamentals is in order. The negative-signed value of the contents of any fixed-point field may not be of direct and immediate importance to the programmer insofar as the coding of the Compare instruction statement is concerned; the coding is created in the same manner regardless of what the format of the contents of the operands might be. It is possible, however, that he might wish to verify the results of a Compare instruction statement in order to confirm the data that is being passed through his program logic. If one of the values that he is attempting to verify is a two's complement value, representing a negative fixed-point value, it may be interpreted in this manner.

Bit configuration:

Register 3 | 1 | 111 | 1111 | 1110 | 1100 | 0111 | 1001 | 1101 | 0010 |

Hexadecimal configuration:

Register 3 | — | 7 | F | E | C | 7 | 9 | D | 2 |

Fixed-point conversion:

Right to Left Order	Register 3 Hex	Register 3 Decimal	
First hex digit	2	2	
Second hex digit	D	208	
Third hex digit	9	2,304	
Fourth hex digit	7	28,672	
Fifth hex digit	C	786,432	
Sixth hex digit	E	14,680,064	
Seventh hex digit	F	251,658,240	
Eighth hex digit	7	1,879,048,192	(Excludes the sign-bit)
Integer value		2,146,204,114	
Maximum negative value of a fixed-point fullword			2,147,483,648
Integer value of general register 3			2,146,204,114
Difference			1,279,534
Sign-bit			−
Negative fixed-point value of register 3			− 1,279,534

The unsigned integer portion of register 3 can be verified by converting it back to a positive value by the reversal of the two's complement form. This can be accomplished as follows:

General register 3	1 111 1111 1110 1100 0111 1001 1101 0010
Subtract a one-bit	−1
Result	1 111 1111 1110 1100 0111 1001 1101 0001
Reverse the bit notation	0 000 0000 0001 0011 1000 0110 0010 1110
Convert to hexadecimal	+ 0 0 1 3 8 6 2 E

Right to Left Order	Register 3 Hex	Register 3 Decimal
First hex digit	E	14
Second hex digit	2	32
Third hex digit	6	1,536
Fourth hex digit	8	32,768
Fifth hex digit	3	196,608
Sixth hex digit	1	1,048,576
Integer value		1,279,534

In converting the negative configuration of general register 3 back to a positive value, the calculation has verified the accuracy of the original negative configuration interpretation.

(b) Compare Halfword (CH). The Compare Halfword instruction algebraically compares the contents of a general register to the contents of a halfword of storage data. The instruction statement first accesses the halfword location and picks up the data stored there. It will then expand that 16-bit halfword to a 32-bit fullword by creating 16 additional high-order bits of the same value as the halfword sign-bit. The instruction then proceeds with the algebraic comparison of the two operands.

The action of this instruction is demonstrated by the following illustrations.

$$CH \qquad 12,HAFWDA$$

Original bit configuration of the fields in this instance:

Register 12		0	000	0000	0000	0000	0010	0001	1110	1111

HAFWDA		0	100	1101	0110	0011

Bit configuration after expansion of the halfword HAFWDA:

Register 12	0	000	0000	0000	0000	0010	0001	1110	1111

HAFWDA	0	000	0000	0000	0000	0100	1101	0110	0011

Hexadecimal interpretation of these fields:

Register 12	+	0	0	0	0	2	1	E	F

HAFWDA	+	0	0	0	0	4	D	6	3

Hexadecimal to fixed-point conversion:

Right to Left Order	Register 12		Expanded HAFWDA	
	Hex	Decimal	Hex	Decimal
First hex digit	F	15	3	3
Second hex digit	E	224	6	96
Third hex digit	1	256	D	3,328
Fourth hex digit	2	8,192	4	16,384
Integer value		8,687		19,811
Sign-bit		+		+
Signed fixed-point value		+8,687		+19,811

The algebraic comparison would find that the value of HAFWDA was greater than that of register 12. The Condition Code bits in the PSW would be set to reflect this condition.

A halfword in storage that contains a negative value would be expanded by the addition of 16 additional high-order bits, each bit having the configuration of the negative sign-bit of the original halfword.

HAFWDB

Expanded HAFWDB

The value of HAFWDB has not changed, but it is now of a size to facilitate comparison with a register content. The original data, still stored at location HAFWDB, is not altered by the Compare Halfword instruction.

(c) Compare Registers (CR). The Compare Registers instruction is used to algebraically compare the fixed-point value of the contents of two general registers. The contents of the first operand register are compared to the contents of the second operand register. This instruction, as with the other fixed-point compare instructions, treats both operands as 32-bit signed integers, consisting of a sign-bit and a 31-bit integer.

The evaluation of the contents of two registers that are being used in a CR instruction statement could be accomplished by the programmer as follows:

$$\text{CR} \quad 6,9$$

Bit configuration of the registers:

Register 6

Register 9

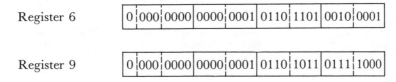

The Hexademical configuration of the registers:

Register 6 | + | 0 | 0 | 0 | 1 | 6 | D | 2 | 1 |

Register 9 | + | 0 | 0 | 0 | 1 | 6 | B | 7 | 8 |

The Hexadecimal to fixed-point conversion:

Right to Left Order	Register 6		Register 9	
	Hex	Decimal	Hex	Decimal
First hex digit	1	1	8	8
Second hex digit	2	32	7	112
Third hex digit	D	3,328	B	2,816
Fourth hex digit	6	24,576	6	24,576
Fifth hex digit	1	65,536	1	65,536
Integer value		93,473		93,048
Sign-bit		+		+
Signed fixed-point value		+93,473		+93,048

As a result of this comparison, the Condition Code bits in the PSW would be set to indicate that the first operand, general register 6, contained a value greater than the one contained in general register 9, the second operand.

Following are several other examples of the Compare Register instruction statement that indicate the interpretation of the values of the operands. In each instance, the interim illustration indicating the means of determining the value of the fields have been omitted.

CR   10,7

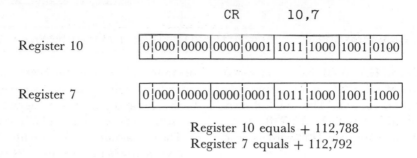

Register 10 equals + 112,788
Register 7 equals + 112,792

The condition reflected by the Condition Code bits would be that the value of the first operand, general register 10, was of a lesser fixed-point value than that of the second operand, general register 7.

CR   5,15

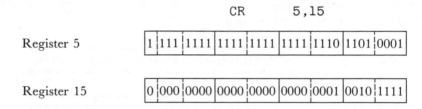

Register 5 equals − 303
Register 15 equals + 303

The Condition Code setting resulting from this instruction statement would indicate that the fixed-point value of the first operand, register 5, was less than the fixed-point value of the second operand, register 15.

3. The Packed Decimal Compare

The only instruction that falls within this category is the Compare Packed Decimals (CP) instruction. The comparison is between fields of storage data and follows the rules peculiar to packed decimal operations. The data is compared from right to left, one-half byte at a time. Inasmuch as a single hexadecimal digit is comprised of four binary bit positions (one-half byte, sometimes referred to as a nibble), the representations and discussions for this instruction will refer to packed decimal digits and hex characters synonomously.

(a)   **Compare Packed (CP).** The general action of this instruction has been basically covered by the preceding paragraph. It should be noted, however, that unlike other compare instructions, this one has length requirements for both operands. The maximum length for either operand is 16 bytes. If the operand fields are not of equal length, the instruction will expand the shorter field by adding additional bytes of hex zero-digits until the lengths of the two fields agree. The additional bytes are supplied to the high-order side of the shorter field.

As in the case of all packed decimal instructions, a plus sign (+) is construed to be a hex character 'A' (1010), 'C' (1100), 'E'

(1110), or 'F' (1111); a valid minus sign ($-$) is either a hex 'B' (1011) or 'D' (1101). The fields that are to be compared should be validly signed in their low-order nibble (half-byte) with one of these hex digits. Any hex digit with a value of less than ten (A) is construed to be a packed numeric digit and is not acceptable as a sign for a packed decimal field. Any one of the valid positive signs ($+$), hex 'A', 'C', 'E', or 'F', will compare as equal with one another. Accordingly, a negative sign ($-$) of hex 'B' will compare equal to a hex 'D'. Somewhat contrary to the general rules is the fact that a packed decimal value of $+0$ will compare as being equal to a packed decimal value of -0.

In the examples of this instruction, the binary bit configuration of the fields is not used as it was with the fixed-point compare interpretations. The hex digit representation for each nibble ($\frac{1}{2}$ byte) is used instead since this gives the clearest illustration of the values of the packed decimal fields. In some instances, the instruction operands will contain explicit length attributes. This is done to point out the length differences between operands and the manner in which the instruction adjusts the length of the shorter operand.

CP   PAXA , PAXB

PAXA		0	0	0	0	7	3	3	C

PAXB		0	0	9	8	2	4	2	D

As indicated, PAXA contains a packed decimal value of $+733$; the contents of PAXB is a packed decimal value of $-98,242$. As a result of the CP instruction statement, the Condition Code bit setting would indicate that the value of the first operand was greater than the value of the second operand.

CP   PACK1 , PACK2

PACK1		0	9	1	5	3	C

PACK2		0	9	1	5	3	F

The Condition Code bit setting resulting from this compare would indicate that both operands contained equal values—both the 'C' sign-digit and the 'F' sign-digit are valid plus signs for packed decimal fields.

CP   PACK3(2) , PACK4(3)

PACK3		3	9	7	C

PACK4		0	0	2	4	4	C

Prior to the actual comparison of the values, the instruction would extract the shorter field from its data storage location and expand it to match the length of the longer field.

PACK3	0	0	3	9	7	C

PACK4	0	0	2	4	4	C

The comparison shown here would have set the Condition Code bits to indicate that the packed decimal value of the first operand, PACK3, was greater than the packed decimal value of the second operand, even though the length attribute of the PACK3 field was the shorter one. The contents of the original storage field, PACK3, are not altered by the execution of the CP instruction statement even though the length of the field was expanded for purposes of comparison.

Review Exercises

1. The "logical" compare instructions begin their comparison with the ___High___-order bit position and compare toward the ___Low___-order bit position. The comparison will terminate as soon as a non-match is found between two corresponding ___bit___ positions.

2. The second operand of a CLI (Compare Logical Immediate) instruction statement must consist of an "___immediate___" character or value.

3. The Compare, Compare Halfword, and Compare Registers instructions are considered to be ___Fixed___-___point___ arithmetic comparisons.

4. What are the valid hexadecimal sign-digits for a negative packed decimal value? ___B___ ___D___

5. What is the maximum allowable length of a packed decimal field that is indicated as the second operand in a Compare Packed (CP) instruction statement? ___16 bytes___

6. A packed decimal sign-digit of X'C' will compare   (equal)   (unequal)   (high)   (low) to a packed decimal sign-digit of X'A'.

7. In executing a Compare Logical (CL) instruction statement, a fixed-point value of −39,510 would compare   (high)   (low)   (equal)   to a fixed-point value of +39,510.

8. The maximum lengths for any two fields that are to be compared by the Compare Logical Characters (CLC) instruction is ___256___ bytes per field.

9. The following two fields are being compared via a logical type of compare. Circle the single bit position in each field at the point at which the comparison would terminate.

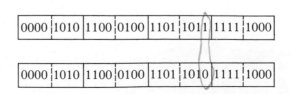

0000	1010	1100	0100	1101	1011	1111	1000

0000	1010	1100	0100	1101	1010	1111	1000

10. If a field labeled BYTE contained an EBCDIC alpha character "S," the following instruction statement would set the Condition Code bits to indicate that BYTE compared (high) (low) (equal) to the second operand literal.

> CLI   BYTE,B'11100010'

11. General register 6 contains a fixed-point value of +3,175,815. A fullword of storage, FWDTWO, contains a hexadecimal configuration of X'00307588'. After execution of the following instruction statement, the Condition Code bits would indicate that the value within general register 6 was (greater than) (less than) (equal to) the fixed-point value of the contents of FWDTWO.

> C   6,FWDTWO

12. A fixed-point value of zero can be represented in either positive or negative form. (True) (False)

Carefully analyze each of the following instruction statements. Place a check mark in front of the instruction statements that contain incorrect types of operands, incorrect length attributes, or that consist of incorrect operand formats. In most instances, register operands have been coded as R3, R4, R5, R6, R7, R8, R9, etc., indicating that the referenced register has been equated to such a symbolic label for the purpose of clarity and to assist the reader in determining which operands are registers.

13. _____	CP	DATAPAK,=X'03952C'
14. _____	CLR	R12,R15
15. _____	CLC	INDATA,0(5)
16. _____	CLI	VALUE,X'40'
17. __✔__	CL	DATAFLD,INPUT
18. _____	CR	R9,R8
19. __✔__	CH	HAFWD,R7
20. __✔__	C	DATA,0(8)
21. _____	CP	PACKSUM(6),DATAPAK(3)
22. _____	C	R8,=F'32957'
23. __✔__	CLC	0+5(3,9),R7
24. _____	CLI	7(5),B'10110001'
25. __✔__	CP	R13,DUBLPACK
26. __✔__	CL	R3,R2
27. _____	C	R12,FULLWD6
28. _____	CLR	R10,R11
29. __✔__	CLI	R6,F'6'
30. _____	CLC	DATA(95),BIGSET
31. __✔__	C	R3,R12
32. __✔__	CR	R6,DATA(9)

33. _____	CP	0+10(6,8),5+7(10,7)
34. _____	CLI	SWITCH,=C'X'
35. _____	CH	R9,HAFWD7
36. _____	CL	R6,FULLWD5RG
37. _____	CP	SETPACK+20(3),INSET+52(3)
38. _____	CLI	SETUP,C'1'
39. _____	CP	PACKIT(25),INPACK(25)
40. _____	CLR	SETVALUE,R6
41. _____	CLC	0(4,3),5(4,6)
42. _____	C	R10(7),FULLWD8
43. _____	CL	R6,4(8)
44. _____	CH	R3,FULLWD
45. _____	CLR	0(4,9),R3
46. _____	CLI	TWOBYTE(2,6),C'AB'
47. _____	CLC	INDATA+9(6),CONSTA
48. _____	CR	R3(6),R11
49. _____	C	R9,8(3)
50. _____	CP	PACKINITL+15(3),=PL3'519'
51. _____	CLI	0+95(11),X'C1'
52. _____	CLR	R9,R13
53. _____	CH	R12,HAFWD4

PROGRAM BRANCHING LOGIC

A. THE INSTRUCTIONS FOR PROGRAM BRANCHING LOGIC

INSTRUCTION:

BRANCH ON CONDITION

Mnemonic	Hex Code	Operand Format
BC	47	$M_1, D_2(X_2, B_2)$

The Branch On Condition instruction uses the bit configuration of the first operand mask as a comparator to the Condition Code setting that resides within the Program Status Word. If a matching condition is found, the instruction statement will cause a program logic branch to the address referenced by the second operand.

The condition Code setting is not changed by this instruction.

* * *

INSTRUCTION:

BRANCH ON CONDITION TO REGISTER

Mnemonic	Hex Code	Operand Format
BCR	07	M_1, R_2

The Branch On Condition To Register instruction will cause a program logic branch to be taken to the address contained within the second operand register if the bit configuration of the first operand mask compares equally to the Condition Code setting.

The Condition Code is not changed by this instruction.

* * *

INSTRUCTION: BRANCH ON COUNT

Mnemonic	Hex Code	Operand Format
BCT	46	$R_1, D_2(X_2, B_2)$

The Branch On Count instruction will cause a program logic branch to the address referenced by the second operand as long as the value of the first operand register is not zero. Each time this instruction is executed it algebraically decrements the value of the first operand register by "1". Once the value of the first operand register reaches zero, the branch is not taken and the processing logic "falls through" to the next sequential program instruction statement.

The Condition Code setting is not changed by this instruction.

* * *

INSTRUCTION:

BRANCH ON COUNT TO REGISTER

Mnemonic	Hex Code	Operand Format
BCTR	06	R_1,R_2

The Branch On Count To Register instruction will create a branch to the address contained within the second operand register as long as the value of the first operand register is not zero. Each time the processing logic passes through this instruction it will algebraically decrement the value of the first operand register by "1". When the value of that register reaches zero, the branch is not taken and the processing logic "falls through" to the next sequential program instruction.

The Condition Code setting is not changed by this instruction.

* * *

INSTRUCTION:

BRANCH ON INDEX HIGH

Mnemonic	Hex Code	Operand Format
BXH	86	$R_1,R_3,D_2(B_2)$

This instruction requires a trio of *odd-even-odd* registers. The first operand register represents the first odd-numbered general register, the third operand register (R_3) represents the even-numbered register, and the next odd-numbered register is implied. The action of this instruction will add the value of the third operand register (normally a decrementing value such as -1) to the first operand register and then compare that value to the next odd-numbered register that is higher than the assigned third operand register. If the comparison is equal or low, the program processing will fall through to the next sequential program instruction statement; if the comparison is high, the program logic will branch to the address specified by the second operand.

The Condition Code setting is not changed by this instruction.

* * *

INSTRUCTION:

BRANCH ON INDEX LOW OR EQUAL

Mnemonic	Hex Code	Operand Format
BXLE	87	$R_1,R_3,D_2(B_2)$

This instruction, functioning somewhat like the BXH instruction, requires a trio of *odd-even-odd* registers. The instruction will add the value of the third operand register (normally a plus-value increment) to the first operand register and compare that value to the next higher odd-numbered register. If the compare is low or equal, the "branch to" address or symbol contained in the second operand will be the route of the program processing action. Once the comparison results in a "high" condition, the program processing will fall through the BXLE instruction to the next sequential program instruction statement.

The Condition Code setting is not changed by this instruction.

* * *

INSTRUCTION: BRANCH & LINK

Mnemonic	Hex Code	Operand Format
BAL	45	$R_1,D_2(X_2,B_2)$

The Branch & Link instruction first stores the low-order 32 bits of the updated Program Status Word, containing the address of the next sequential program instruction, into the first operand register. It then proceeds to branch to the address specified, or implied, by the second operand.

The Condition Code setting is not changed by this instruction.

* * *

INSTRUCTION:

BRANCH & LINK REGISTERS

Mnemonic	Hex Code	Operand Format
BALR	05	R_1,R_2

The Branch & Link Registers instruction stores the low-order 32 bits of the updated Program Status Word, containing the address of the next sequential program instruction statement, into the first operand register and then branches to the address contained in the register specified by the second operand. If the second operand specifies general register 0, the PSW data is stored but the branch is not taken.

The Condition Code is not changed by this instruction.

* * *

B. THE USE OF BRANCHING LOGIC IN THE PROGRAM

The terms *branch* and *branching* may be defined as "a transfer of the program processing logic from one statement to another within the problem program, but not necessarily in the sequential appearance of those instruction statements. The branch is usually taken as the result of a decision based on the action of a prior instruction." In general, the branch instructions can be grouped into two categories—conditional branches and program linkage branches.

Conditional branches are those that may direct the program logic operations through one or more separate paths, depending on the status of the Condition Code bits or a register value. Program linkage branches are usually established to require the program logic to branch to another routine, subroutine, or module, perform the instructions contained within that section, and then return to the next logical instruction statement following the statement that forced the branch to occur.

1. Conditional Branch Instructions

Before discussing any conditional branch instructions, it would be well to evaluate the factor that determines whether or not a conditional branch instruction statement will reroute the program processing logic. This factor is the Condition Code. It is comprised of two binary bit positions, residing in bit positions 34 and 35 of the Program Status Word (PSW). These two bit positions have a maximum range of four individual unique bit configurations—00, 01, 10, and 11. Most

of the Assembler Language instructions, though not all of them, will result in the setting of the Condition Code bits on completion of the execution of that instruction. Two of the Conditional Branch instructions (Branch On Condition and Branch On Condition To Register) use the first operand of the instruction statement to mask the Condition Code bits for any specific condition or conditions.

The Condition Code bit configurations and their corresponding operand mask values for these instructions are shown below.

Binary Bits 34-35 within the PSW	Equivalent Operand for BC and BCR Instructions
00 (0)	8
01 (1)	4
10 (2)	2
11 (3)	1

The value of the mask operand in a conditional branch instruction may be an aggregate of several values. This capability is discussed in detail further on within this section, under the Branch On Condition instruction.

The use of conditional branches allows the programmer to utilize multiple logic paths and to predetermine program decisions based on factors encountered during the processing of data by his program. For example, if a certain numeric field is zero, he may want to go to a routine to bypass further arithmetic operations; if the field has a plus value in excess of zero, he may wish to take another route of operation; if the field has a negative value less than minus-zero, he may want the program logic to convert that number to a positive value before continuing the sequential logic path.

Some of the conditional branch instructions, such as the Branch On Count and Branch On Index instructions, do not require a mask operand as a part of the instruction statement. This type of branch instruction has a built-in function that performs a compare and a branch on condition as a part of the overall instruction. They compare the content value of an operand to a numeric value and then decide whether or not to branch as a result of that internal comparison.

(a) Branch on Condition (BC). The Branch On Condition instruction statement will create a branch to the address implied by the second operand if the Condition Code in the Program Status Word is properly masked by the first operand in the instruction statement. The mask operand is comprised solely, or as a compounded value, of four basic numeric values—8, 4, 2, and 1. Depending on the nature of the instruction statement that set the Condition Code bits, each of these four basic settings could have variable meanings. As an example of this, instructions that compare data fields for logical contents are normally interpreted as setting the Condition Code bits to a condition wherein the corresponding mask for each setting indicates:

8 Both operands are equal.
4 The first operand has a lower value than the second operand.
2 The first operand has a higher value than the second operand.
1 The '1' value is not used for compare instructions.

Instructions that perform arithmetic operations are generally considered to set the Condition Code wherein the equivalent mask indicates:

8 The answer is zero.
4 The answer is negative (minus-one or less).
2 The answer is positive (plus-one or greater).
1 An arithmetic overflow occurred.

In the event that a branch is to be taken to a particular address if any one of a number of possible conditions exist, the mask operand of the Branch On Condition instruction may be an aggregate of any combination of the 8-4-2-1 mask values. Using the Condition Code interpretations for a logical compare instruction as an example of this, there are a number of valid mask code configurations. Because a mask operand of '8' states "branch on an equal condition,"

it would be permissible to indicate that if the first operand in a previous compare instruction has proved to be low or equal, the branch should be taken on a mask value of "12" within the BC instruction—a value of "8" for the equal condition and a value of "4" for the "lower than" condition. The combination of mask values, assuming a general use, might be defined as shown in Table 8-1.

As stated previously, the exact interpretation for these mixed values will vary among the different instruction statements that set the Condition Code bits. In addition to the foregoing list, a mask value of zero (0) or fifteen (15) may be used as the first operand of the BC instruction statement. When the value of zero is used for the first operand, the branch will not be taken. This is because a zero mask code will never find that condition within the Condition Code setting since it does not exist. This creates an effective *"No Operation"* (NOP) instruction statement. The programmer, however, may have the program later move a valid value into the mask at any time during the processing and that branch condition will then become effective. In order to create a *"forced branch,"* or a branch that will occur under any of the Condition Code settings, the mask operand value of the first operand in a BC statement may be specified as "15". This guarantees a successful branch because the Condition Code must be set equal to one of the values comprising the mask value—$8 + 4 + 2 + 1$.

The following examples contain Compare Logical Character instruction statements followed by a Branch On Condition instruction statement.

Example 1

```
CLC      INPUT,HOLDATA
BC       7,NOGOOD
```

The BC instruction statement in this example specifies that "if the result of the previous compare was an unequal condition, indicating that the first operand of the compare statement was either high or low to the second operand, branch to the address of the instruction labeled NOGOOD."

TABLE 8-1

Value Of Mask Operand	Which Interprets As:	
14	Branch on equal, high, or low	(8 + 4 + 2)
13	Branch on equal, low, or overflow	(8 + 4 + 1)
12	Branch on equal or low	(8 + 4)
11	Branch on equal, high, or overflow	(8 + 2 + 1)
10	Branch on equal or high	(8 + 2)
9	Branch on equal or overflow	(8 + 1)
8	Branch on equal	(8)
7	Branch on unequal (high, low, or overflow)	(4 + 2 + 1)
6	Branch on high or low	(4 + 2)
5	Branch on low or overflow	(4 + 1)
4	Branch on low	(4)
3	Branch on high or overflow	(2 + 1)
2	Branch on high	(2)
1	Branch on overflow	(1)

Example 2

```
CLC     OUTPUT,HOLD1
BC      8,PROCESS
```

The BC instruction statement specifies, "if the two operands of the previous compare statement were equal, branch to the address of a routine that is labeled PROCESS."

Example 3

```
CLC     FLD1,FLD2
BC      8,MOVEIT
BC      4,SUBTR
BC      2,ADDIT
```

This is an example of multiple branching decisions based on the result of a single comparison.

The first BC statement states, "if the operands were equal to each other, branch to a routine labeled MOVEIT." The second instruction statement for a BC states, "if FLD1 was of a lower logical value than FLD2, branch to a routine labeled SUBTR." The third BC instruction statement indicates, "if FLD1 was of a higher logical value than that of FLD2, branch to a routine labeled ADDIT." Because the CLC instruction will set the Condition Code to a value equal to one of the mask operands shown in the BC instruction statements (8, 4, or 2), one

of the branches in this set of instruction statements will be taken.

Example 4

```
BC      15,GOTHERE
```

This instruction statement can be written as shown without regard for the instruction statement that immediately precedes it. It literally states, "regardless of what configuration now exists in the Condition Code bits, branch to the instruction statement or routine that is labeled GOTHERE." This is referred to as a *forced* or an *unconditional* branch.

(b) Branch on Condition to Register (BCR). This instruction is nearly identical to the Branch On Condition instruction except that the branch, if taken, will be to the address contained in the register that is specified by the second operand. The instruction will check the first operand (the mask operand) against the Condition Code bit setting and if the appropriate condition exists, it will effectively cause a branch to occur. All of the general rules and techniques available to the BC instruction also apply here.

In order to illustrate the use of this instruction, several examples are presented in which various packed decimal instruction statements are followed by BCR instruction statements.

Example 1

```
CP      PAKFLD1,PAKFLD2
BCR     10,2
BCR     4,3
```

The first instruction statement is comparing two fields of packed decimal data. The first BCR instruction statement specifies, "if the CP statement indicated that PAKFLD1 was equal to (8), or greater than (2), PAKFLD2, then branch to the address contained in general register 2." The second BCR instruction statement states, "if PAKFLD1 was of a lesser value than PAKFLD2, branch to the address contained within general register 3."

Example 2

```
LA      9,BADADDR
LA      10,ZEROSUM
LA      11,NEGSUM
AP      SUMPK,INPAK
BCR     8,10
BCR     4,11
BCR     1,9
```

The first three instruction statements are loading the addresses of three separate routines into general registers 9, 10, and 11. The Add Packed (AP) instruction statement is adding two fields of packed decimal values together, with the resulting sum residing in the SUMPK field. The first BCR instruction statement indicates, "if the total sum now found in SUMPK is zero, branch to the address contained in general register 10." This is the address of a routine called ZEROSUM, loaded into general register 10 by the second Load Address instruction statement. The second BCR instruction statement indicates that "if the total sum now found in SUMPK is a negative value (less than minus-zero), branch to the address contained within general register 11." This would be the address of the routine called NEGSUM, which was loaded into general register 11 by the third Load Address instruction statement. The third BCR instruction statement

specifies that "if an overflow condition occurred during the addition of these fields, then branch to the address contained within general register 9." This address would be that of a routine labeled BADADDR, which was loaded into general register 9 by the first LA instruction statement. It is also implied here, with this particular set of instructions, that if the result of the packed decimal addition was a positive value in excess of plus-zero, no branch would be taken and the program logic processing would fall through the three branch instruction statements to the next sequential program statement. This can be logically assumed because the branches shown were established to intercept a zero, a negative, or an overflow condition.

Example 3

```
BCR     15,8
```

This instruction statement would cause a forced branch of the program logic to be taken to the address contained within general register 8. The first operand demands a branch, regardless of any particular setting of the Condition Code bits. Prior to this instruction statement, general register 8 should have been loaded with the address of the routine to which the branch was to have been taken. This is one means of returning from a routine which, in turn, was branched to by a Branch & Link instruction that specified general register 8 as the linking register.

(c) **Branch on Count (BCT).** The Branch On Count instruction will branch to the storage address created by the second operand unless the value contained within the first operand register is zero. It is used frequently for table look-ups, loop control, and count control. Each time the program logic encounters this instruction it will result in the following action:

1. The value in the first operand register is decremented by a fixed-point value of 1.

2. The general register is then checked to see if it now equals zero.

3. If the register value is not zero, the instruction statement will cause a branch to be taken to the address specified by the second operand of the statement.

4. If the register contents have been decremented to a zero value, the branch is ignored and the program logic processing falls through to the next sequential program statement.

The programmer may reload the register operand with any value suitable to its reuse, as long as it conforms to his correct program logic.

An impractical but easily understood example of the use of this instruction would be shown in this set of coding:

```
        SR    5,5                001
        LA    5,100              002
LOOP    AP    PAKSUM,=PL1'3'     003
        BCT   5,LOOP             004
        ZAP   BIGSUM,PAKSUM      005
```

This set of statements has functionally performed a multiplication routine that could have been accomplished with one instruction statement. It does, however, present a simple illustration of the use and performance of the Branch On Count instruction.

Statement 001 subtracts general register 5 from itself, effectively clearing that register.

Statement 002 loads the absolute value of 100 into general register 5.

Statement 003 adds a one-byte packed decimal literal value of +3 into a packed decimal accumulator area.

Statement 004 will decrement register 5 by a value of 1 each time that this instruction statement is executed and then branch back to Statement 003.

This action will continue until general register 5 is decremented to zero, at which time the branch to LOOP will not be taken and the processing will fall through to Statement 005. Because the value of +100 was originally loaded into general register 5, the processing program will pass through the LOOP instruction statement 100 times including the initial pass through that statement. Each time the program passes through the LOOP instruction statement, it will add an additional packed decimal value of +3 to the accumulator (PAKSUM). When the BCT instruction is executed for the 100th

time, general register 5 is decremented by 1 to a value of zero and the branch is not taken. PAKSUM would now contain a packed decimal value of +300—100 loop cycles times the value of +3 added during each loop.

(d) Branch on Count to Register (BCTR). The BCTR instruction will force the program logic to branch to the address of the second operand unless the value contained within the first operand register is zero. Whenever the program in operation encounters this instruction the following sequence of events takes place:

1. The value of the contents of the general register specified by the first operand is decremented by a value of 1.

2. The contents of that general register are then compared to a zero value by the instruction.

3. If the contents of the first operand register are not zero, the instruction statement will create an effective branch to the address contained, or implied by, the second operand register.

4. If the contents of the first operand register have been decremented to zero, the branch is not taken and the processing falls through to the next sequential instruction statement following the BCTR statement.

In order to illustrate the basic capabilities of this instruction, an example similar to the "looping" technique that was used to illustrate the BCT instruction is used. However, in this example the "loop within a loop" technique is illustrated (see Fig. 8-1).

In this illustrated set of coding the first four instruction statements, Statement 001 through Statement 004, are zeroing out the contents of the general registers that are to be used for the BCTR instruction statements. The outside loop (LOOPONE) will be controlled by general registers 6 and 8; the inside loop (LOOPTWO) will be controlled by registers 7 and 9.

Statement 005 is loading the absolute value of 50 into general register 6, the loop control register for LOOPONE.

Statement 006 is loading the address of the

IBM IBM System/360 Assembler Coding Form

X28-6509-2 U/M050
Printed in U.S.A.

Name	Operation	Operand	Sequence
*			001
LOOPRTE	SR	6,6	002
	SR	7,7	003
	SR	8,8	004
	SR	9,9	005
	LA	6,50	006
	LA	8,LOOPONE	007
LOOPONE	LA	7,100	008
	LA	9,LOOPTWO	009
LOOPTWO	AP	SMALPAK,=PL1'2'	010
	BCTR	7,9	011
	AP	BIGPAK,SMALPAK	012
	ZAP	SMALPAK,=PL1'0'	013
	BCTR	6,8	014
	BC	15,FINIS	
*			

Figure 8-1

LOOPONE routine into general register 8, the "branch to" address that is referenced by Statement 012. These two instruction statements have now set up the basis for the control of the outer loop, LOOPONE.

Statement 007 is loading the absolute value of 100 into general register 7, the loop control register for LOOPTWO.

Statement 008 is loading the address of LOOPTWO into general register 9, the "branch to" address that is referenced by Statement 010.

Statement 009 is adding a packed decimal literal value of $+2$ into an accumulator area for LOOPTWO.

Statement 010 is the BCTR instruction statement for LOOPTWO. Each time the LOOPTWO routine is entered, it will be executed 100 times before falling through to Statement 011.

Statement 011 is adding the packed decimal contents of the LOOPTWO accumulator, SMALPAK, to the packed decimal accumulator for LOOPONE. Each time this statement is encountered, it will be adding a value of $+200$ to the accumulator BIGPAK, since 100 cycles through LOOPTWO results in SMALPAK being equal to $+200$—100 cycles with a value of $+2$ being added for each cycle equals $+200$.

Statement 012 is using the ZAP instruction to zero-out the accumulated amount in SMALPAK prior to entering a new loop-control cycle.

Statement 013 is the BCTR instruction statement for LOOPONE, the outside loop. Inasmuch as Statement 005 loaded general register 6 with an absolute value of 50, this instruction will be executed 50 times, of which the branch will be taken 49 times before falling through to Statement 014.

Statement 014 is a "forced" branch to a hypothetical routine that will end the program or subroutine.

When the entire series of instructions has been completed, the packed decimal value contained in BIGPAK should be $+10,000$. This can be determined by applying the loop values as:

LOOPONE times
    (LOOPTWO times 2)
        equals BIGPAK

or

50 times (100 times 2) equals 10,000

While considering this example, it is an excellent opportunity to illustrate how the erroneous omission of a single statement can affect the outcome of a desired solution. If the programmer had overlooked the instruction statement that zeros-out the contents of the inside loop accumulator after each 100 cycles (Statement 012), the resulting value of BIGPAK at the completion of the entire routine would have been 255,000. Follow the logic process through, excluding Statement 012, to prove this result.

The BCTR instruction may also be used to decrement the value of a general register without branching by specifying general register 0 as the second operand register. If this type of instruction statement appeared as BCTR 6,0, the instruction would decrement general register 6 by a value of 1, but would not branch regardless of the value remaining within general register 6.

(e)   Branch on Index High (BXH). The BXH instruction utilizes three registers, two of which are expressed as statement operands along with a symbolic or actual address for branching. The basic functions of the three registers are:

1. An accumulator register.
2. An increment or decrement register.
3. A comparison value register.

Each time that the BXH instruction statement is executed, it will perform the following:

1. It will add the value of the contents of the second general register (either as a plus-value increment or as a minus-value decrement) to the contents of the first general register, placing the result of that addition into the first register.

2. It will then compare the new value of the contents of the first general register to the value of the contents of the third general register.

3. If the value of the first register compares high to the third register value, the instruction will effectively branch to the storage operand address.

4. If the value of the first register compares low or equal to the third register value, the branch is not taken and the program logic falls through to the next sequential instruction statement.

For practical application and consistency, it is suggested that a contiguous trio of odd-even-odd general registers be used for this instruction.

In the example that follows, assume that the programmer has a table containing 50 elements, each element having a length of four bytes. This would bring the total table length to 200 bytes. If the first character in each element is a character "A", he desires to insert a character "D" in the second position of that table element; otherwise he will make no change to the table element. The table definition, values, and instruction statements are presented in Fig. 8-2.

Statement 001 loads the address of TABLE incremented by 49 table units (or 196 bytes) into general register 12. This is done because the search of the table is going to commence at the highest core position and decrement downward to the beginning point of the table. Register 12 is to be used as a base register that will point directly at the various elements of TABLE.

Statement 002 loads general register 3 with a fullword value of $+196$, general register 4 with a fullword value of -4, and general register 5 with a fullword value of -4.

Statement 003 performs a Compare Logical Immediate on the first byte of the table element currently addressed by general register 12, comparing it to a character "A".

Statement 004 tests the Condition Code setting that resulted from the CLI instruction in Statement 003. If an unequal condition is indicated by the Condition Code bits, this instruction will create a branch to Statement 006. If the Condition Code indicates that the comparison resulted in an equal condition,

the program logic will fall through to Statement 005, the next sequential program instruction statement.

Statement 005 will perform a Move Immediate (MVI) instruction in order to move a character "D" into the second byte of the table element that is currently addressed by general register 12.

Statement 006 performs an Add Registers (AR) instruction, adding the value of the contents of general register 5 (a -4 value that effectively results in a subtraction of 4) to the current address in general register 12. This action decrements general register 12 by 4 bytes so that the next time the program logic passes through the instruction statement labeled RELOOK, register 12 will then be addressing the next lower table element.

Statement 007 performs the BXH instruction statement. Each time it is executed, general register 3 is decremented by the value of general register 4 and the result is compared to general register 5. If register 3 contains a higher value than register 5, the program logic is branched back to RELOOK. Once the value contained in register 3 is decremented to a value of -4, it is found to be an equal compare to register 5 (which contains a value of -4) and the branch is not taken. The program logic would then fall through to the next sequential instruction statement.

Statement 008 is a forced branch to an assumed routine that would probably terminate this part of the program.

If this example was listed using the actual decimal core storage position addresses, assume that the first byte of TABLE might reside at storage location 15000. TABLE would then occupy bytes 15000 through 15199 or 200 bytes. If these addresses were used, then:

Statement 001 would load the address 15196 into general register 12. This would be the first byte of the last four-byte table element.

Statement 003 would check position 15196 to see if it contained a character "A". If the equal condition was found, Statement 005

IBM System/360 Assembler Coding Form

X28-6509-2 U/M050
Printed in U.S.A.

Name	Operation	Operand				Comments	Identification-Sequence
*							001
SETABLE	LA	12,TABLE+196					002
	LM	3,5,VALUES					003
RELOOK	CLI	0(12),C'A'					004
	BC	7,BYPASS					005
	MVI	1(12),C'D'					006
BYPASS	AR	12,5					007
	BXH	3,4,RELOOK					008
	BC	15,ALLDONE					009
*							010
*							011
*							012
TABLE	DS	50CL4					013
VALUES	DC	F'196'					014
	DC	F'-4'					015
	DC	F'-4'					016
*							017
*							

Figure 8-2

would move a character "D" into position 15197, the second byte of the four-byte table element presently being scanned.

Statement 006 would add −4 (subtracting a value of 4 from 15196) to general register 12, resulting in a value of 15192 now in register 12.

Statement 007, the BXH instruction statement, would add −4 to general register 3 (actually subtracting 4 from 196), compare the new register 3 value of 192 against the register 5 value of −4, and then branch back to RELOOK, Statement 003.

Statement 003 would now be checking storage location 15192 for a character "A". This cycle would continue down through the table elements until general register 3 was equal or low to register 5 at the time the BXH instruction statement was executed.

(f) **Branch on Index Low or Equal (BXLE).** The BXLE instruction statement utilizes the same type of operands as the BXH instruction (i.e., three registers and a symbolic or actual address that is to be branched to). The functions of the registers also perform similarly—the first general register is an accumulator, the second register contains an increment value, and the third register contains a value for the first register to be compared against. It is also suggested here that the three general registers be a contiguous trio of odd-even-odd general registers.

Each time this instruction is executed, it will perform in the following manner.

1. It will sum the value of the second register (the increment register) with the value of the first register, placing the result into the first register.

2. It will then compare the new value of the first register to the value contained within the third register.

3. If the value of the first general register compares low or equal to the third general register, the instruction will effectively branch to the storage operand address.

4. If the value of the first register compares high to the third register the branch is not taken and the program logic falls through to the next sequential program instruction statement.

For the purpose of demonstrating the use of this instruction, assume that the programmer has a 75-byte table, one byte per table element, that he wishes to put into another table area, but in reverse order. The definition of the table storage area, the values that are to be used by the general registers, and the coded instruction statements are shown in Fig. 8-3.

Statement 001 loads the trio of registers via a Load Multiple instruction statement. The LM instruction loads general register 5 with a fullword value of zero, general register 6 with a fullword value of +1 for incrementing, and general register 7 with a fullword value of +74 that will be used as a comparator.

Statement 002 loads the address of TABLE1, incremented by 74 bytes, into general register 8. General register 8 now contains the address of the highest core storage position occupied by TABLE1.

Statement 003 loads the address of TABLE2 into general register 9. This address would be the lowest storage position occupied by TABLE2. Registers 8 and 9 now contain the opposite storage limits for TABLE1 and TABLE2 in order that the sequence of the data contained within TABLE1 can be reversed into TABLE2.

Statement 004 moves one byte of data from TABLE1 (as addressed by general register 8) into one byte of TABLE2 (as addressed by general register 9).

Statement 005 adds the value of the contents of general register 6 (+1) to the contents of general register 9. Register 9 contains the address of the current table element of TABLE2.

Statement 006 subtracts the value of general register 6 (equal to +1) from general register 8. General register 8 contains the current table element address of TABLE1.

Statement 007 activates the BXLE instruction statement. Each time this instruction is executed, general register 5 is incremented by the value in general register 6 and the result is compared to the value in general register 7. If general register 5 compares low or equal to the contents of general register

Name	Operation	Operand	Comments	Identification-Sequence
*				001
MIXTABLE	LM	5,7,REGVALS		002
	LA	8,TABLE1+74		003
	LA	9,TABLE2		004
REPEAT	MVC	0(1,9),0(8)		005
	AR	9,6		006
	SR	8,6		007
	BXLE	5,6,REPEAT		008
	BC	15,MOVEDIT		009
*				010
*				011
*				012
TABLE1	DS	CL75		013
TABLE2	DS	CL75		014
REGVALS	DC	F'0'		015
	DC	F'1'		016
	DC	F'74'		017
*				018
*				

Figure 8-3

157

7, the branch is taken to REPEAT. However, when register 5 is incremented sufficiently to compare high to register 7, the branch is not taken and the program execution falls through to Statement 008.

Statement 008 is a forced branch to another part of the main-line program logic. This exit is to be taken once the subroutine of Statements 001 through 007 have completed their cycles.

In order to more clearly visualize the processing of these instruction statements, assume that the actual decimal storage position addresses have been assigned as:

TABLE1   Storage locations
                32000 through 32074

TABLE2   Storage locations
                32075 through 32149

Using these addresses, the instruction statements for the previous routine would effectively be executed as follows.

Statement 001 would function as previously explained.

Statement 002 would load general register 8 with the address 32074. This value represents the address of TABLE1 (32000) incremented by 74, or the last one-byte element within TABLE1.

Statement 003 would load general register 9 with the address 32075, the address of the first table element of TABLE2.

Statement 004 would move one byte of data from address 32074 to address 32075. This would be from the last element of TABLE1 to the first element of TABLE2.

Statement 005 would add general register 6 (a $+1$ value) to the present contents of general register 9 ($+32075$), resulting in general register 9 now containing $+32076$.

Statement 006 would subtract general register 6 ($+1$) from general register 8 ($+32074$) resulting in general register 8 now containing $+32073$. At the end of the execution of Statement 007, general register 5 would now contain a value of $+1$, general register 6 would be $+1$, and general register 7 would be $+74$. The branch would be taken back to Statement 004, REPEAT.

Statement 004 would now move one byte of data from address 32073 to address 32076, from the next-to-last table element of TABLE1 to the second element of TABLE2.

Statement 005 would increment the address within general register 9 to $+32077$.

Statement 006 would decrement the address within general register 8 to $+32072$.

This action would continue within the cycle from the REPEAT instruction statement through the BXLE instruction statement until general register 5 contained a value of $+75$, an amount that would compare high to $+74$, the value within general register 7. At this point the logic execution of the program would fall through to Statement 008.

2. Branch & Link Instructions

The instructions that fall within this category may be considered to be "forced" branches that provide the problem program with the capability of returning to the next sequential program statement at the discretion of the programmer. They can be used to establish program linkage between routine-to-routine, subroutine to subroutine, module to module, or any combination of this type of linkage. A very frequent use of the Branch & Link instructions is to access a common subroutine from many points of the main-line program logic. This would enable the programmer to write the subroutine just once and then access it at will instead of requiring him to rewrite the same logic statements at many points within his program.

(a) Branch & Link (BAL). The BAL instruction will store the address of the next sequential program instruction statement (as contained within the updated Program Status Word) into the general register that is specified by the first operand of the statement and then branch to the address that is generated by the second operand. Once the routine that was "branched to" has been completed, the programmer can return to the instruction series that immediately follows the BAL instruction statement by coding a forced branch to the address contained within the general register that was used as the first operand in the BAL instruction statement. This is based on the premise that the instruction statements executed by the "branched to" routine did not destroy or alter the contents of the linking register.

Assume that the programmer is required to write a simple packed decimal math routine that will be used numerous places throughout his main-line program logic. The data fields that he has established and the coded instruction statements appear in Fig. 8-4.

The implied sequence of execution of these instruction statements would be:

001, 002, 085, 086, 003, –, 010, 011, 085, 086, 012, –, 017, 018, 085, 086, 019, 020.

Statement 001 would zero the PAKANSR field and add the value of PACK1 into it.

Statement 002 would effect a Branch & Link to Statement 085.

Statement 085 would multiply the contents of PAKANSR (now the same value as PACK1) by PAKMULT (a +5 value in packed decimal form).

Statement 086 would then branch back to Statement 003. The branch is to that address because the BAL instruction loaded the address of Statement 003 into general register 10.

Statement 003 would add the new value of PAKANSR to an accumulator that is labeled CUMULAT.

Statements 004 through 009 are not shown, but are implied to be obtaining data records, additional processing, etc.

Statement 010 would zero the PAKANSR field and add the value contained within PACK2 into it.

Statement 011 would cause a Branch & Link to Statement 085, at the same time loading the address of Statement 012 into general register 10.

Statement 085 would multiply the contents of PAKANSR (now the same value as PACK2) by the value contained in PACK-MULT, a +5 value.

Statement 086 is a forced branch to the address that is contained in general register 10. At this point within the program the address is that of Statement 012.

Statement 012 would add the new value of PAKANSR to the accumulator, CUMU-LAT.

Statements 013 through 016 are implied to be processing additional data, etc.

Statement 017 would zero the PAKANSR field and add the value of PACK3 into it.

Statement 018 would perform the BAL instruction, loading the address of Statement 019 into general register 10 and then branching to Statement 085.

Statement 085 would multiply the contents of PAKANSR (now the same value as PACK3) by PAKMULT, a value of +5.

Statement 086 would branch back to Statement 019 because that is the address that is contained within general register 10.

Statement 019 would add the new value of PAKANSR to the accumulator, CUMU-LAT.

Statement 020 is a forced branch to another section of the main-line portion of the program.

Although the overall function performed by this set of instruction statements may not necessarily be the best means of arriving at the proper answer for these calculations, it sufficiently outlines the use of the Branch & Link instruction and the means of returning to the sequence of instruction statements from where it was issued.

(b)   Branch & Link Registers (BALR). The BALR instruction performs the same basic functions as the BAL instruction except that the branch is to the address contained in the register that is specified by the second operand of the statement. Explicitly, it will store the address of the next sequential program instruction statement into the first operand register and branch to the address contained in the second operand register. Using the same basic instruction statement logic contained in Fig. 8-4 for the BAL instruction, the restated instructions would appear as in Fig. 8-5.

The primary difference between this illus-

IBM

X28-6509-2 U/M080
Printed in U.S.A.

IBM System/360 Assembler Coding Form

PROGRAM				PAGE	OF
PROGRAMMER		DATE		CARD ELECTRO NUMBER	
		PUNCHING INSTRUCTIONS	GRAPHIC		
			PUNCH		

Name	Operation	Operand	Comments	Identification-Sequence
ROUTE1	ZAP	PAKANSR,PACK1		001
	BAL	10,DOMULT		002
	AP	CUMULAT,PAKANSR		003
	- -	- - - - -		- -
	ZAP	PAKANSR,PACK2		010
	BAL	10,DOMULT		011
	AP	CUMULAT,PAKANSR		012
	- -	- - - - -		- -
	ZAP	PAKANSR,PACK3		017
	BAL	10,DOMULT		018
	AP	CUMULAT,PAKANSR		019
	BC	15,DUNCALC		020
*				- -
DOMULT	MP	PAKANSR,PAKMULT		085
	BCR	15,10		086
*				087
*				088
PACK1	DC	PL3'0'		089
PACK2	DC	PL3'0'		090
PACK3	DC	PL3'0'		091
CUMULAT	DC	PL6'0'		092
PAKANSR	DC	PL4'0'		093
PAKMULT	DC	PL1'5'		094
*				095

Figure 8-4

IBM

IBM System/360 Assembler Coding Form

X28-6509-2 U/M050
Printed in U.S.A.

PROGRAM

PROGRAMMER

DATE

PUNCHING INSTRUCTIONS

GRAPHIC

PUNCH

PAGE ___ OF ___

CARD ELECTRO NUMBER

STATEMENT

Name	Operation	Operand / Comments	Identification-Sequence
PRELOAD	LA	11,DOMULT	000
ROUTE1	ZAP	PAKANSR,PACK1	001
	BALR	10,11	002
	AP	CUMULAT,PAKANSR	003
	-	-	-
	ZAP	PAKANSR,PACK2	010
	BALR	10,11	011
	AP	CUMULAT,PAKANSR	012
	-	-	-
	ZAP	PAKANSR,PACK3	017
	BALR	10,11	018
	AP	CUMULAT,PAKANSR	019
	BC	15,DUNCALC	020
*			-
DOMULT	MP	PAKANSR,PAKMULT	085
	BCR	15,10	086
*			
*			

Figure 8-5

161

tration and the similar example for the BAL instruction is the PRELOAD statement in which general register 11 is loaded with the address of DOMULT. Thereafter, the BALR

instruction statements use the address in general register 11 as the "branch to" address, effectively branching to DOMULT.

Review Exercises

1. In general, the "branch" instructions may be grouped into two categories—conditional branches and _Program_ _Linkage_ branches.

2. The only branch instructions that require a mask value as the first operand of the statement are the _BC_ and the _BCR_ instructions.

3. A BC or BCR instruction statement containing a first operand mask value of _15_ is considered to be an unconditional, or _forced_, branch.

4. The four individual mask values that are used singularly or collectively to test the PSW Condition Code are _8_, _4_, _2_, and _1_.

5. Each time that a BCT instruction statement is executed the value contained within the _1st_ operand will be automatically decremented by a value of _1_.

6. For each of the following sets of instruction statements indicate the comparison relationship that would have to exist between the two operands within the first statement in order for the branch to be successfully taken in the second statement. (This should be expressed as "the first operand would be greater than or equal to the second operand," etc.)

a.	COMPA	CL	8,FLWDA
		BC	12,ROUTE1
b.	COMPC	CH	3,HALFWDA
		BC	6,ROUTE2
c.	COMPE	CP	PACKFLDA,=PL3'8952'
		BC	10,ROUTE3
d.	COMPG	CLC	DATAFLD+3(7),INCARD+20
		BC	2,ROUTE4
e.	COMPI	CLI	FIELD6+3,X'40'
		BC	8,BYPASS
f.	COMPK	CLR	10,4
		BC	14,NEWROUTE
g.	COMPM	C	3,FULLWDG
		BC	2,ROUTE5
h.	COMPN	CR	3,13
		BC	4,ROUTE6

7. The maximum value that can be represented by the first operand of a BCT instruction statement is _2,147,483,647_

8. In a BCTR instruction statement the "branch to" address is represented within a _Register_.

9. The BXH and the BXLE instruction statements each utilize a total of _THREE_ registers.

10. In a BCT instruction statement, the processing logic of the program will fail to branch as soon as the value within the first operand register has been decremented to a value of _____.

11. The BAL instruction statement will load the first operand register with the _____ of the next sequential instruction statement.

12. The BALR instruction statement consists of two operands, both of which are _____.

13. An effective "no operation" instruction statement can be created by coding a mask value of _____ as the first operand of a BC or a BCR instruction statement.

14. Assuming that general register 7 contained a fixed-point value of +75 before the execution of the following instruction statement, what would be the fixed-point value contained in register 7 after execution of the statement? _____.

```
LOOPUP      BCTR      7,9
```

15. Assume the following:

Register 5 contains a fixed-point value of +3275
Register 6 contains a fixed-point value of −25
Register 7 contains a fixed-point value of +50

After execution of the following instruction statement register 5 would contain a fixed-point value of _____, register 6 would contain a fixed-point value of _____, and register 7 would contain a fixed-point value of _____.

```
BXH      5,6,RESEEK
```

16. If general register 9 contained a fixed-point value of +32500 prior to execution of the statement labeled BRNCH, what would it contain immediately following the execution of that statement? _____.

```
BRNCH      BAL      9,EXITRTE
BACK       CLI      SWITCH,C'A'
```

17. If general register 10 contains a value of +1 prior to executing the BCT instruction labeled ENDLOOP, the program would proceed to the statement labeled _____ after execution of the BCT instruction.

```
ENDLOOP      BCT      10,RELOOP
CONTIG       CLC      DATA,INPUT
```

18. In each of the following sets of instruction statements, a branch will be taken. Based on the values shown for the fields that are being compared, place a check mark beside the branch that would be successfully taken.

    a. Register 8 contains a fixed-point value of +3598;
       Register 12 contains a fixed-point value of +15,782.

```
COMPARA      CR      8,12
             BC      4,SUBRT1      _____
             BC      8,SUBRT2      _____
             BC      3,SUBRT3      _____
```

b. Register 9 contains a fixed-point value of -783;
FLWD2 contains a fixed-point value of $+6$.

```
COMPARB     CL      9,FLWD2
            BC      4,SUBRT4       _____
            BC      2,SUBRT5       _____
            BC      9,SUBRT6       _____
```

c. PAKFLDA contains a packed decimal value of -0.

```
COMPARF     CP      PAKFLDA,=P'0'
            BC      8,SUBRT7       _____
            BC      7,SUBRT8       _____
```

d. FIELD1 contains the EBCDIC characters S1FA;
FIELD2 contains the EBCDIC characters S12A.

```
COMPARG     CLC     FIELD1,FIELD2
            BC      10,SUBRT9      _____
            BC      4,SUBRT10      _____
            BC      15,SUBRT11     _____
```

e. SETBYTE contains an EBCDIC character X.

```
COMPARH     CLI     SETBYTE,X'40'
            BC      6,SUBRT12A     _____
            BC      8,SUBRT12B     _____
```

f. Register 8 contains a fixed-point value of $+9810516$;
Register 10 contains a fixed-point value of $+5$.

```
COMPARJ     CLR     8,10
            BC      15,SUBRT14     _____
            BC      10,SUBRT15     _____
            BC      4,SUBRT16      _____
```

g. Register 9 contains a fixed-point value of $+3516$;
HAFWORD6 contains a fixed-point value of -3516.

```
COMPARK     CH      9,HAFWORD6
            BC      2,SUBRT17      _____
            BC      8,SUBRT18      _____
            BC      4,SUBRT19      _____
```

MOVING, STORING, AND LOADING DATA

A. THE DATA MOVEMENT INSTRUCTIONS

INSTRUCTION: MOVE IMMEDIATE

Mnemonic	Hex Code	Operand Format
MVI	92	$D_1(B_1),I_2$

This instruction will move one byte of immediate data, defined by the second operand, into the one-byte area that is specified by the first operand. Regardless of the implied length of the first operand, this instruction will move only one byte of data.

The Condition Code setting is not changed by this instruction.

* * *

INSTRUCTION: MOVE CHARACTERS

Mnemonic	Hex Code	Operand Format
MVC	D2	$D_1(L,B_1),D_2(B_2)$

The MVC instruction will move the stor-age data specified by the second operand into the storage area specified by the first operand. The data will be moved one byte at a time, from left to right, for the explicit or implied length of the first operand. The data that is being moved is not changed or altered. Up to 256 bytes of data may be moved with one instruction statement.

The Condition Code setting is not changed by this instruction.

* * *

INSTRUCTION: MOVE NUMERIC

Mnemonic	Hex Code	Operand Format
MVN	D1	$D_1(L,B_1),D_2(B_2)$

The Move Numeric instruction will move only the right-most four bits (the right nibble) of each byte, which in zoned decimal format would be the numeric portion of the byte. It will move the right-most half-byte of each byte of storage data specified by the

165

second operand into the corresponding position of each byte of the storage area that is specified by the first operand. The numeric value of the half-bytes being moved are not checked for numeric validity; therefore, it is possible to move a hex value of 'A', 'B', 'C', 'D', 'E', or 'F' with this instruction. The data is moved from left to right, one nibble at a time, for the explicit length or implied length of the first operand. The left-most four bits of each byte of the first operand receiving field are not altered. The alphanumeric character validity of the bit configuration of the bytes resulting from this instruction are not checked; therefore, the generation of nonprintable characters may occur. The right-most four bits of up to 256 bytes of data may be moved with one instruction statement.

The Condition Code setting is not changed by this instruction.

*   *   *

INSTRUCTION: MOVE ZONE

Mnemonic	Hex Code	Operand Format
MVZ	D3	$D_1(L,B_1),D_2(B_2)$

The MVZ instruction will move only the left-most four bits (the left nibble) of each byte specified, which in zoned character format would be the zone portion of the byte. This does not preclude the movement of numeric values that might be contained within the left nibbles being moved. The instruction will move the left-most four bits of each byte of storage data specified by the second operand into the corresponding left-most four bits of each byte of the storage area specified by the first operand. The data is moved from left to right, one nibble at a time, for the explicit or implied length of the first operand. The right-most four bits (the right nibble) of each byte of the receiving field specified by the first operand are not altered. The left-most four bits of up to 256 bytes of data may be moved with one instruction statement.

The Condition Code setting is not changed by this instruction.

*   *   *

INSTRUCTION: STORE CHARACTER

Mnemonic	Hex Code	Operand Format
STC	42	$R_1,D_2(X_2,B_2)$

The Store Character instruction will take the low-order eight bits (one byte) from the general register that is specified by the first operand and place them in the one-byte storage area specified by the second operand. The eight bits that are stored are not altered from their original configuration.

The Condition Code setting is not changed by this instruction.

*   *   *

INSTRUCTION: STORE HALFWORD

Mnemonic	Hex Code	Operand Format
STH	40	$R_1,D_2(X_2,B_2)$

The STH instruction will take the low-order 16 bits (two bytes) from the general register that is specified by the first operand and place them into the halfword storage location that is specified by the second operand. The configuration of the two bytes that are being stored is not altered. The address generated by the second operand must be on a halfword boundary alignment.

The Condition Code setting is not changed by this instruction.

*   *   *

INSTRUCTION: STORE

Mnemonic	Hex Code	Operand Format
ST	50	$R_1,D_2(X_2,B_2)$

The Store instruction will take the 32-bit contents of the general register specified by the first operand and place them unaltered in the four-byte fullword that is specified by the second operand. The address generated by the second operand must be on a fullword boundary alignment.

The Condition Code is not changed by this instruction.

*   *   *

INSTRUCTION: STORE MULTIPLE

Mnemonic	Hex Code	Operand Format
STM	90	$R_1,R_3,D_2(B_2)$

The STM instruction will store a multiple number of general registers (two, three, four, five, or more) into a contiguous storage area of fullwords. The first operand specifies the beginning register of a multiple register set and the second operand (R_3) specifies the ending register of that set. The storage area addressed by the D_2 operand must be on a fullword boundary alignment and consist of enough fullwords to contain the registers being stored—one fullword for each register. The general registers will be stored in ascending sequence from the register specified by the first operand and will revert back to general register 0 after storing general register 15 if the register specified by the R_3 operand has not been encountered. For example, if the R_1 operand specified register 13 and the R_3 operand specified register 2, this instruction would store general registers 13, 14, 15, 0, 1, and 2, in that order.

The Condition Code setting would not be changed by this instruction.

* * *

INSTRUCTION: INSERT CHARACTER

Mnemonic	Hex Code	Operand Format
IC	43	$R_1,D_2(X_2,B_2)$

The Insert Character instruction will take an eight-bit configuration or character, as addressed by the second operand, and insert it into the low-order eight-bits of the register specified by the first operand. The high-order 24 bits of the first operand register will be left unaltered.

The Condition Code setting will not be changed by this instruction.

* * *

INSTRUCTION: LOAD HALFWORD

Mnemonic	Hex Code	Operand Format
LH	48	$R_1,D_2(X_2,B_2)$

The Load Halfword instruction will first extract the 16-bit halfword stored at the location addressed by the second operand and expand it to a 32-bit fullword by creating 16 additional high-order bits that are identical to the sign-bit of the original halfword. It will then load the expanded 32 bits into

the general register specified by the first operand. The configuration of the original halfword in storage is not altered. The address generated by the second operand must be on a halfword boundary alignment.

The Condition Code setting is not changed by this instruction.

* * *

INSTRUCTION: LOAD

Mnemonic	Hex Code	Operand Format
L	58	$R_1,D_2(X_2,B_2)$

The Load instruction will take the fullword of data stored at the location addressed by the second operand and load all 32 bits into the general register specified by the first operand. Upon completion of the Load instruction, the contents of the first operand will be identical to the second operand. The address generated by the second operand must be on a fullword boundary alignment.

The Condition Code setting is not changed by this instruction.

* * *

INSTRUCTION: LOAD REGISTER

Mnemonic	Hex Code	Operand Format
LR	18	R_1,R_2

The LR instruction places the exact contents of the second operand register into the first operand register. Upon completion of this operation, the contents of both registers are identical.

The Condition Code setting is not changed by this instruction.

* * *

INSTRUCTION: LOAD MULTIPLE

Mnemonic	Hex Code	Operand Format
LM	98	$R_1,R_3,D_2(B_2)$

The Load Multiple instruction loads fullwords of data, beginning at the location specified by the last operand, into the sequence of registers beginning with the first operand and terminating with the R_3 operand register. The sequence of registers to be loaded may go from the high-numbered registers through to the low-numbered registers in contiguous sequence. For example, if the operands specified the R_1 register as register 13 and the R_3 register as register 4, the load sequence would be general registers 13, 14, 15, 0, 1, 2, 3, and 4.

The Condition Code setting is not changed by this instruction.

*   *   *

INSTRUCTION: LOAD ADDRESS

Mnemonic	Hex Code	Operand Format
LA	41	$R_1,D_2(X_2,B_2)$

The Load Address instruction will generate a 24-bit address as specified by the second operand and place that address into the low-order 24 bit positions of the register specified by the first operand. It will also set the high-order eight bits of the first operand register to zero. The second operand may be an absolute decimal value or a symbolic reference to an address, including indexing and displacement.

The Condition Code setting is not changed by this instruction.

*   *   *

INSTRUCTION:

LOAD AND TEST REGISTER

Mnemonic	Hex Code	Operand Format
LTR	12	R_1,R_2

The Load and Test Register instruction takes the contents of the second operand register and places them into the register specified by the first operand, after which the contents of both register operands are identical. The Condition Code setting is determined by the combined value and sign of the data loaded into the first operand register.

CC	BC	Condition
0	8	The first operand register now contains a zero value.
1	4	The first operand register now contains a value less than zero.
2	2	The first operand register now

contains a value greater than zero.

*   *   *

INSTRUCTION:

LOAD COMPLEMENT REGISTER

Mnemonic	Hex Code	Operand Format
LCR	13	R_1,R_2

The Load Complement Register instruction will take the contents of the second operand register, reverse the configuration of those contents to their complement value, and place that complement into the first operand register. The same general register may be specified for both operands in order to reverse the configuration contained within a single register. The complement value that is placed into the first operand register will determine the setting of the Condition Code bits.

CC	BC	Condition
0	8	The first operand register now contains a zero value.
1	4	The first operand register now contains a negative value.
2	2	The first operand register now contains a positive value.
3	1	The complement value placed into the first operand register created an overflow condition.

*   *   *

INSTRUCTION:

LOAD POSITIVE REGISTER

Mnemonic	Hex Code	Operand Format
LPR	10	R_1,R_2

If the second operand register contains a negative value, this instruction will load the positive complement of that value into the first operand register. If the second operand register already contains a positive value, the contents of that register will be placed unaltered into the first operand register. In the event that the complementation of the maximum number occurs, an overflow condition will exist, setting the Condition Code accordingly.

CC	BC	Condition
0	8	The first operand register contains a zero value.
2	2	The first operand register contains a positive value.
3	1	An overflow occurred as a result of this instruction.

*   *   *

INSTRUCTION:

LOAD NEGATIVE REGISTER

Mnemonic	Hex Code	Operand Format
LNR	11	R_1, R_2

If the second operand register contains a positive value, this instruction will load the negative complement of that value into the first operand register. If the second operand register already contains a negative value, the contents of that register will be placed unaltered into the first operand register. If the second operand register contains a value of zero, that value will be placed into the first operand register with a positive sign.

CC	BC	Condition
0	8	The first operand register contains a zero value.
1	4	The first operand register contains a negative value.

*   *   *

INSTRUCTION:

SHIFT LEFT LOGICAL

Mnemonic	Hex Code	Operand Format
SLL	89	$R_1, D_2(B_2)$

This instruction will shift to the left all 32 bits contained within the general register specified by the first operand, for the number of bit positions specified by the second operand. Only the low-order six bits of the address created by the second operand are used to determine the number of bit positions to be shifted. All bits are shifted, including the sign-bit, and any significant-digit bits shifted out of the high-order positions are lost without an overflow condition being indicated. Zero-bits are added to the low-order bit positions to replace bits that were shifted to the left.

The Condition Code setting is not changed by this instruction.

*   *   *

INSTRUCTION:

SHIFT LEFT DOUBLE LOGICAL

Mnemonic	Hex Code	Operand Format
SLDL	8D	$R_1, D_2(B_2)$

The SLDL instruction will shift to the left all 64 bits contained within an even-odd pair of general registers, for the number of bit positions specified by the second operand. The first operand register must address the even-numbered register of the pair of general registers. Only the low-order six bits of the address created by the second operand are used to determine the number of bit positions to be shifted. All bits are shifted and significant-digit bits that might be shifted out of the high-order positions are lost; the overflow condition is not activated when such a loss occurs. Zero-bits are added to the low-order bit positions to replace bits shifted to the left.

The Condition Code setting is not changed by this instruction.

*   *   *

INSTRUCTION:

SHIFT RIGHT LOGICAL

Mnemonic	Hex Code	Operand Format
SRL	88	$R_1, D_2(B_2)$

This instruction will shift to the right all 32 bits contained within the general register specified by the first operand, for the number of bit positions specified by the second operand. Only the low-order six bits of the address created by the second operand are used to determine the number of bit positions comprising the shift quantity. All bits are shifted and any significant-digit bits that are shifted out of the low-order positions are lost; the Condition Code will not reflect the loss of such bits. Zero-bits are supplied to the high-order bit positions to replace bits that were shifted to the right.

The Condition Code setting is not changed by this instruction.

*   *   *

INSTRUCTION:

SHIFT RIGHT DOUBLE LOGICAL

Mnemonic	Hex Code	Operand Format
SRDL	8C	$R_1, D_2(B_2)$

The SRDL instruction will shift to the right all 64 bits contained within an even-odd pair of general registers, for the number of bit positions specified by the second operand. The first operand register must address the even-numbered register of the pair of general registers. Only the low-order six bits of the address created by the second operand are used to determine the number of bit positions representing the shift quantity. All bits are shifted and any significant-digit bits that might be shifted out of the low-order positions are lost; the Condition Code will not reflect the loss of such bits. Zero-bits are supplied to the high-order bit positions to replace bits that were shifted to the right.

The Condition Code setting is not changed by this instruction.

*   *   *

INSTRUCTION:

SHIFT LEFT ALGEBRAICALLY

Mnemonic	Hex Code	Operand Format
SLA	8B	$R_1, D_2(B_2)$

This instruction will shift to the left the 31 integer-bits contained within the general register specified by the first operand, for the number of bit positions specified by the second operand. However, only the low-order six bits of the address created by the second operand are used to determine the shift quantity. The sign-bit of the first operand register is not shifted. Low-order zero-bits are supplied to replace the bits shifted from the low-order bit positions. If a significant-digit bit (one unlike the sign-bit) is shifted out of the high-order integer bit position, the Condition Code will indicate an overflow condition.

CC	BC	Condition
0	8	The first operand register contains a zero value.
1	4	The first operand register contains a negative value.
2	2	The first operand register contains a positive value.
3	1	An overflow condition occurred during the execution of the shift.

*   *   *

INSTRUCTION:

SHIFT LEFT DOUBLE ALGEBRAICALLY

Mnemonic	Hex Code	Operand Format
SLDA	8F	$R_1, D_2(B_2)$

The SLDA instruction will shift to the left the 63 integer-bits of the value contained within an even-odd pair of general registers, for the number of bit positions specified by the second operand of the statement. The first operand register must address the even-numbered register of the pair of registers. Only the low-order six bits of the second operand address are used to determine the shift quantity. The sign-bit of the odd-numbered general register is shifted along with the other bits, but the sign-bit of the even-numbered register is unaffected. Zero-bits are supplied to replace the bits shifted from the low-order bit positions. If a significant-digit bit (one unlike the even-numbered register sign-bit) is shifted out of the high-order integer-bit position, the Condition Code is configured to indicate an overflow condition.

CC	BC	Condition
0	8	The first operand registers contain a zero value.
1	4	The first operand registers contain a negative value.
2	2	The first operand registers contain a positive value.
3	1	An overflow condition occurred during the execution of the shift.

*   *   *

INSTRUCTION:

SHIFT RIGHT ALGEBRAICALLY

Mnemonic	Hex Code	Operand Format
SRA	8A	$R_1, D_2(B_2)$

This instruction will shift to the right the 31 integer-bits contained within the general register specified by the first operand, for the number of bit positions specified by the second operand. Only the low-order six bits of the address created by the second operand are used to determine the shift quantity. Any significant-digit bits shifted out of the low-order bit positions are lost; the Condition Code bit settings will not indicate such a loss. The sign-bit of the first operand register is not affected by the shift, but bits supplied to the high-order bit positions to replace those shifted to the right will be identical to the sign-bit.

CC	BC	Condition
0	8	The first operand register contains a zero value.
1	4	The first operand register contains a negative value.
2	2	The first operand register contains a positive value.

* * *

INSTRUCTION: SHIFT RIGHT DOUBLE ALGEBRAICALLY

Mnemonic	Hex Code	Operand Format
SRDA	8E	$R_1, D_2(B_2)$

The SRDA instruction will shift to the right the 63 integer-bits of the value contained within an even-odd pair of general registers, for the number of bit positions specified by the second operand of the statement. The first operand register must address the even-number register of the pair of registers. Only the low-order six bits of the address created by the second operand are used to determine the shift quantity. Significant-digit bits shifted out of the low-order bit positions of the odd-numbered general register are lost. The sign-bit of the even-numbered register is not affected, but the sign-bit position of the odd-numbered register is shifted along with the other integer-bits. Bits that are supplied to the high-order positions of the pair of registers are of the same value as the sign-bit of the even-numbered general register and are equal in number of bit positions to those shifted out of the low-order bit

positions. An overflow condition does not occur for the loss of a significant-digit bit shifted out of the low-order bit positions.

CC	BC	Condition
0	8	The first operand registers contain a zero value.
1	4	The first operand registers contain a negative value.
2	2	The first operand registers contain a positive value.

B. THE APPLICATION OF THE MOVE, STORE, LOAD, AND SHIFT INSTRUCTIONS

During the design and subsequent coding of the problem program, it is necessary to manipulate and relocate data from one area to another within the problem program. Such relocation and reassignment of data is controlled almost entirely by the various types of move, load, store, and shift instructions. The move instructions perform data relocation from one storage address to another; the load instructions relocate data from storage areas to registers or from register to register; the store instructions perform data relocation from registers to storage areas; the shift instructions manipulate data within general registers. Examples and illustrations of the use and performance of the individual instructions that are represented by these four groups are contained within this section. The presentation of certain instructions will be superficial in some instances because they are discussed in detail within other sections of this text.

Because of the number of individual instructions discussed within this chapter, the review exercises have been arranged into four groups; one each for the Move, Load, Store, and Shift instructions. It is suggested that the reader do the appropriate review exercise group as he completes the respective portion of this chapter.

1. Moving Data Within the Problem Program

Although any data that is transferred from one location to another within the problem program might correctly be assumed to have been "moved," the term "move" is technically representative of the relocation of data between two storage locations only— from one problem program storage address to another. The specific Assembler Language instructions that fall within this category are:

1. MOVE IMMEDIATE (MVI)
2. MOVE CHARACTERS (MVC)
3. MOVE NUMERIC (MVN)
4. MOVE ZONE (MVZ)
5. MOVE WITH OFFSET (MVO)

The latter instruction, Move With Offset, is sufficiently and more appropriately described in "Packed Decimal Arithmetic Operations"; hence, it will not be elaborated on within this section.

As the discussion of these instructions progresses, it will be obvious that the range of data that may be moved will vary from 1 byte to 256 bytes by any single instruction statement. Special attention will be given to the movement of data fields consisting of more than 256 bytes, as well as to the concept of "sliding" a single data byte through a multiple-byte field.

(a) Move Immediate (MVI). The Move Immediate instruction is used as an expedient move of one byte of immediate data into a storage area field. It is considerably faster than moving one byte of data with the Move Characters instruction. The difference in performance speed results from the characteristics of the second operand. In a Move Characters instruction statement, the second operand generates an address at which the character that is to be moved is located. In the Move Immediate instruction statement, the one-byte character that is to be moved is a part of the generated machine-language instruction itself. The operation of the MVI instruction is demonstrated within this illustration:

```
FIELDA     DC    CL5'123D5'
           MVI   FIELDA+3,C'4'
```

FIELDA (Before MVI)

+1	+2	+3	+4
1	2	3	D	5

FIELDA (After MVI)

+1	+2	+3	+4
1	2	3	4	5

The MVI instruction statement shown here would move an EBCDIC numeric character "4" into the fourth byte of the field addressed by the label FIELDA. Because the "4" is constructed as a part of the machine-language instruction itself, it does not require additional core to create a storage byte for that character.

(b) Move Characters (MVC). This instruction, which is used to move full bytes of data from one storage area to another, will move up to 256 bytes of data with one instruction statement. The number of data bytes to be moved will be determined by the implied or explicit length of the area that is addressed by the first operand of the instruction statement.

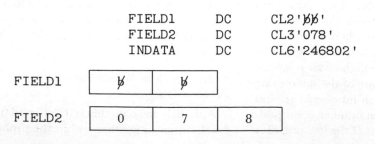

```
FIELD1     DC    CL2'ЬЬ'
FIELD2     DC    CL3'078'
INDATA     DC    CL6'246802'
```

INDATA	2	4	6	8	0	2

```
        MUVIT    MVC    FIELD1,INDATA              001
                 MVC    FIELD2(1),INDATA+2         002
```

Statement 001 instructs the problem program logic to "move data, commencing at the address generated by INDATA, into the area labeled FIELD1 for the number of bytes implied by the actual length attribute of FIELD1." This would then move the first two bytes of INDATA, containing '24', into the two byte length of FIELD1.

Statement 002 specifies, "from the address generated by INDATA+2, move data into the address referenced by the label FIELD2 for a length of one byte as specified in the first operand of this instruction statement." This statement would move the third byte of INDATA, containing a '6', into the first byte of FIELD2.

After the execution of these two instruction statements, the contents of these same fields would be:

FIELD1	2	4

FIELD2	6	7	8

INDATA	2	4	6	8	0	2

The Move Characters instruction is relatively easy to understand. It can be applied to a number of different tasks as long as both operands refer to storage areas.

One of the unique methods of utilizing the MVC instruction is in its application in creating a "sliding" move of a single data byte through a field. Because the movement of data is from left to right, from low to high storage address, the first byte of any given field can be used to set all bytes of that field to an identical configuration. This is not only an expedient means of setting a field to blanks, but it also does away with the necessity of creating a constant that contains the same number of blanks as the field length that is to be cleared. The actual execution of this technique requires two statements—one statement to move a single blank into the first byte of the field that is to be cleared and one statement to start the "sliding" action.

The following set of illustrations contains the definition of a storage area, the contents of that area at the time the program logic encounters the instruction statements, and the instruction statements themselves.

```
BIGFIELD     DS     CL15
```

BIGFIELD	1	R	3	9	5	P	A	R	T	6	5	9	2	2	Z

```
        MVI    BIGFIELD,C'b'                 001
        MVC    BIGFIELD+1(14),BIGFIELD       002
```

Statement 001 will use the Move Immediate instruction to place a valid "blank" configuration (Hex '40') into the first byte of BIGFIELD. At this point BIGFIELD would contain:

BIGFIELD	b	R	3	9	5	P	A	R	T	6	5	9	2	2	Z

Statement 002 would cause the "slide" action of the first byte of BIGFIELD. It indicates that each byte of BIGFIELD, commencing at the first byte of that field, should be moved to the next right-most byte location. The byte-by-byte movement of the data would appear to be:

BIGFIELD

As indicated within Statement 002, the length of the first operand was specified as 14 bytes from a point addressed by BIG-FIELD+1, which effectively placed blanks (Hex '40') into the remaining 14 bytes of BIGFIELD. This same type of application may be used to configurate a field of up to 256 bytes, either with blanks or any other desired configuration.

In some instances, the programmer may need to move data whose field length exceeds the 256-byte allowable maximum of the MVC instruction within a single statement. The movement of such data between over-sized fields can be accomplished by *"chaining"* a series of MVC instruction statements. After the first Move Characters statement is coded for the maximum allowable length, the first and second operands of the next instruction statement will reference an address that is one byte higher in storage than the last byte of the fields addressed by the first and second operands within the previous statement. This can be more easily illustrated than described.

```
DATAFLD     DS      CL750
INPUT       DS      CL890
*
            MVC     DATAFLD(256),INPUT              001
            MVC     DATAFLD+256(256),INPUT+256      002
            MVC     DATAFLD+512(238),INPUT+512      003
```

The data fields described by the Define Storage (DS) statements are considered to contain valid data. The instruction statements coded thereafter are intended to move 750 bytes of data from the INPUT field into the entire area that is defined by DATAFLD.

Statement 001 will move the first 256 bytes (from left to right) out of the INPUT field and place that data into the first 256 bytes of DATAFLD.

Statement 002 will move another 256 bytes of data from INPUT to DATAFLD. The data moved by this statement will be bytes #257 through #512 of the area labeled INPUT. They will be placed into the same relative positions within DATAFLD.

Statement 003 will move bytes #513 through #750 from INPUT into DATAFLD for a total move length of 238 bytes of data. All 750 bytes of data that were to be placed into DATAFLD from INPUT have now been moved—256 bytes by Statement 001 plus 256 bytes by Statement 002 plus 238 bytes by Statement 003 equals 750 bytes.

This type of chained MVC statements can go on for as long as the programmer desires; thousands of bytes of data may be moved if it is practical to do so.

A combination of the "sliding" MVC technique and the "chained" MVC statements may be used in order to identically configurate all bytes of a very large area or data field. This combined application is presented in Fig. 9-1.

Based on the combined logic of the "sliding" and "chained" MVC instructions, these statements would effectively place valid blanks (Hex '40') into all 810 bytes of HOLD-AREA.

Multiple groups, or segments, of data may be relocated into storage areas throughout the program by use of loop controls and MVC instruction statements. This is a technique that is sometimes referred to as a *"sliding table,"* or sometimes as *"elastic indexing."* It basically consists of adding or deleting segments of data from a large block of data segments that are comprised of equal-length segments arranged in a sequential pattern. Although an example of this type of application would be rather lengthy to present here, along with the necessary detailed explanations of the instruction statements themselves, there follows a set of general rules that should enable the programmer to create an example of this technique. Keep in mind that this is a storage-to-storage movement of data that is intended to sequentially insert, or delete, any random segment of data into its appropriate position within a block of data consisting of segments of the same length.

IBM

IBM System/360 Assembler Coding Form

X28-6509-2 U/M050
Printed in U.S.A.

PROGRAM				PAGE	OF
PROGRAMMER		DATE		CARD ELECTRO NUMBER	
	PUNCHING INSTRUCTIONS	GRAPHIC			
		PUNCH			

```
     Name      Operation  Operand                                          Comments        Identification-Sequence
*
MOVELOT  MVI   HOLDAREA,C' '
         MVC   HOLDAREA+1(255),HOLDAREA
         MVC   HOLDAREA+256(256),HOLDAREA+255
         MVC   HOLDAREA+512(256),HOLDAREA+511
         MVC   HOLDAREA+768(42),HOLDAREA+767
         BC    15,BACK
*
*
HOLDAREA DS    CL810
*
```

Figure 9-1

The general rules for this application are given below.

1. The expansion or contraction of the overall data contained within the block must affect only the high end of the block; any expansion must be from lower storage addresses to higher storage addresses; any contraction must be from the higher storage addresses to lower storage addresses. This indicates that the initial starting address of the overall block of data must not change, although the high-storage address of the last segment of valid data *within the block* may vary as necessary.

2. The last valid data segment within the block should be followed by a delimiter segment to indicate this fact, even though the overall length of the block is not occupied by valid segments.

3. The last (highest) available position within the area defined by the block itself should contain a block delimiter segment. If the program is coded properly this would prevent any attempt to move a segment outside of the defined limits of the block area.

In order to insert a data segment into its logical sequential position within the block of data segments, the following steps should be taken.

1. Locate the address of the position within the block where the segment belongs. This can be done by comparing the new segment value to the existing segment values in an ascending search. As soon as the new segment compares low to an existing segment, this is the point where the new segment is to be placed. Store this address in a hold area or load it into a register for retention.

2. Scan the remainder of the block to find the segment delimiter.

3. Create a loop routine that will move each data segment, including the segment delimiter, one segment length higher into the addresses within the block. Each cycle through the loop should decrement the address of both operands in the MVC instruction by the length of one segment.

4. The loop routine should be written so that the loop cycles are terminated once the segment is moved that occupies the area where the new segment is to be placed. On the first move of a data segment, which will be the segment delimiter, a check should be made to see if this action would encounter the block delimiter.

5. The new segment should then be moved into the proper position within the block. When it is moved into that position, it will destroy the copy of the segment that previously existed there, but that is now also located one segment higher within the block.

In order to delete a data segment from the block of data segments and to contract the remaining segments in order to eliminate the space occupied by the deleted segment, the following steps should be coded.

1. Locate the segment that is to be eliminated.

2. Load that address into two general registers, X and Y. Add the length of a table segment to the second register.

3. Create a loop routine containing an MVC instruction statement with an explicit length equal to that of a segment. Use the first general register (X) to create an address for the first operand in the MVC statement; use the second general register (Y) to create an address for the second operand in the MVC statement. The MVC instruction statement should then move each segment downward in the block by the length of one segment. The first time that this statement is encountered, it should move the next higher segment into the position occupied by the segment that is to be deleted.

4. Each time through the loop cycle the logic should increment the values contained in both registers by a value equal to the length of a segment.

5. As each segment is moved downward, the logic should check to see if that segment was in reality a segment delimiter. If so, then the contraction of the segments has been completed.

By using the three sets of general rules

presented here, the programmer should be able to originate the coding required to generate a basic "sliding table" routine. Admittedly, this application might be somewhat complex for a student programmer, but the successful completion of such a routine will add considerably to the understanding and knowledge of data manipulation.

(c) Move Numeric (MVN). The Move Numeric instruction is one of two Assembler Language instructions that will move data in a fragmented manner. Although the data will be moved in an orderly method from one storage area to another, this instruction will move only the right-most half-byte (four bit positions) of each data byte. The composition of EBCDIC alphanumeric characters is so formatted that the right nibble (right-most half-byte) of each byte contains a hexadecimal numeric digit; it is logical then that this instruction should be called the Move Numeric instruction. As indicated, the right nibble of each byte in the sending field is moved to the right nibble of each corresponding byte in the receiving field, for a length implied or specified by the receiving field. The left nibble of each byte in the two fields are not altered in any way. Up to 256 bytes of data may be affected by one MVN instruction statement.

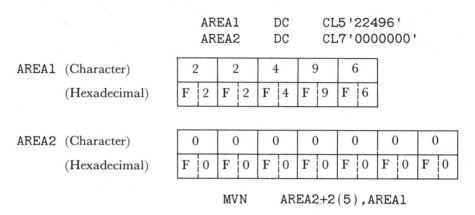

This instruction statement specifies that the right nibble of each byte of AREA1 should be moved into the right nibble of each byte of AREA2+2 (commencing at the third byte of AREA2) for a length of five bytes. This action would appear to be:

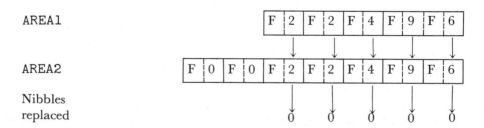

This instruction may also be used in an application that will convert valid EBCDIC alphabetic characters into their respective right nibble numeric values. This is shown in the following illustration.

```
ALPHAFLD    DC      CL6'AKTDNW'
NUMERFLD    DC      CL6'000000'
```

NUMERFLD (Character)	0	0	0	0	0	0
(Hexadecimal)	F 0	F 0	F 0	F 0	F 0	F 0

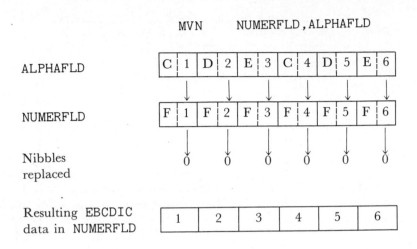

ALPHAFLD (Character)	A		K		T		D		N		W	
(Hexadecimal)	C	1	D	2	E	3	C	4	D	5	E	6

MVN   NUMERFLD,ALPHAFLD

ALPHAFLD

C	1	D	2	E	3	C	4	D	5	E	6

NUMERFLD

F	1	F	2	F	3	F	4	F	5	F	6

Nibbles replaced

0   0   0   0   0   0

Resulting EBCDIC data in NUMERFLD

1	2	3	4	5	6

In this instance, the MVN instruction statement has moved only the right nibble (hexadecimal numeric digit) of each byte of ALPHAFLD to the corresponding right nibble of each byte of NUMERFLD, effectively transforming the EBCDIC alphabetic character data into EBCDIC numeric character data.

One of the applications for the MVN instruction is the formatting of a partially numeric character field to a full numeric character field. This type of situation might occur in an instance where a numeric character field is so comprised that high-order (leading) zeros of the EBCDIC numeric characters have been stated as blanks. This condition could occur through previous editing of the data in another program. Assume that the problem program was expecting a set of EBCDIC numeric characters that might range from 0000001 to 9999999. However, because of previous editing the data is read into the problem program in a format range of from ƀƀƀƀƀƀ1 to 9999999. As a peculiarity of the present program, these numeric characters are to be expressed in their full numeric character form. At any given point within the problem program, the fields and respective action might appear as:

```
DATAFLD     DS     CL7
NUMCONV     DC     CL7'0000000'
*
            MVN    NUMCONV,DATAFLD
```

DATAFLD (Character)	ƀ		ƀ		ƀ		5	9	7	4
(Hex)	4	0	4	0	4	0	F 5	F 9	F 7	F 4

NUMCONV (Character)	0		0		0		0		0		0		0	
(Hex)	F	0	F	0	F	0	F	0	F	0	F	0	F	0

The resulting action would be:

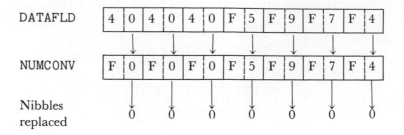

This statement has now changed the data configuration of 'bbb5974' to its full numeric character representation of '0005974'. This same type of transformation can also be accomplished, but by moving the left nibble of each byte instead of the right nibble. This will be described within the analysis of the Move Zone instruction.

(d) Move Zone (MVZ). The Move Zone instruction is the only one other than the Move Numeric instruction that will move data by partial bytes, somewhat in a fragmented mode. It is the opposite of the MVN instruction, however, in that it moves only the left nibble (four bits) of each byte from the sending field to the receiving field. It is generally considered that the left nibble of EBCDIC alphanumeric character data is the "zone" portion of the byte; hence, the Move Zone instruction moves only the left-most four bits of each byte. Up to 256 bytes of data may be affected by one MVZ instruction statement.

The movement of the portions of the data bytes would be in the manner indicated below.

```
DATA1      DC       CL5'PNJLQ'
CONVRT     DC       X'COCOCOCOCO'
   *
           MVZ      DATA1+1(4),CONVRT
```

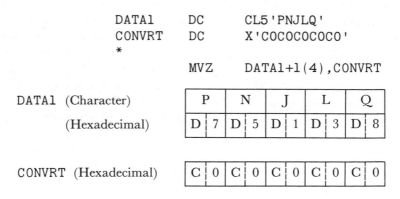

The execution of the instruction statement would result in the following alteration of the fields:

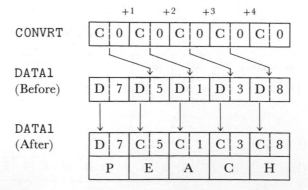

As shown in the illustration, the Move Zone instruction statement has changed the five bytes of data containing 'PNJLQ' so that they now contain 'PEACH'. This was done by altering only the zone portion of each of the last four bytes.

As mentioned within the discussion on the Move Numeric instruction, the Move Zone instruction can be used to expediently con-figurate a field of mixed blanks and numeric characters to a full numeric character field. Because a blank is configurated as a hexadecimal '40', it can be converted to a numeric zero (hex 'F0') by moving a hex digit 'F' into the zone portion of each byte. This is illustrated in the following set of illustrations:

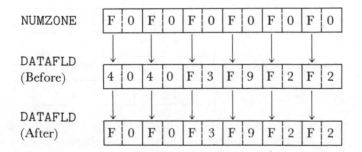

```
DATAFLD      DC      CL6'ØØ3922'
NUMZONE      DC      CL6'000000'
```

DATAFLD (Character)	Ø	Ø	3	9	2	2

(Hex)	4 0	4 0	F 3	F 9	F 2	F 2

NUMZONE (Character)	0	0	0	0	0	0

(Hex)	F 0	F 0	F 0	F 0	F 0	F 0

```
MVZ      DATAFLD,NUMZONE
```

The execution of this instruction statement would cause the following action:

NUMZONE	F 0	F 0	F 0	F 0	F 0	F 0

DATAFLD (Before)	4 0	4 0	F 3	F 9	F 2	F 2

DATAFLD (After)	F 0	F 0	F 3	F 9	F 2	F 2

DATAFLD, which was originally comprised of a set of numeric characters and leading blanks, has now been configurated as a full field of numeric character data. This type of application can be very useful in assuring that an incoming field does not contain a valid blank in the low-order (rightmost) byte prior to a Pack instruction. If a Pack instruction operates on a field that contains a blank in the low-order byte, the resulting packed decimal field will be invalid for packed decimal arithmetic operations. (Refer to Packed Decimal Arithmetic Operations for further details on this.)

In the preceding examples it was assumed that the numeric data being verified was considered to be "unsigned," that is, without a plus or minus zone indicated in the low-order byte other than the standard assumed plus value indicator. For example, when a hex configuration of 'C1' (the character "A") is packed into packed decimal form, it is considered to be a standard value of $+1$; when a hex configuration of 'D1' (the character "J") is packed, it is considered to be an expressed value of -1; a hexadecimal configuration of 'F1' (the numeric character '1') is considered to be a value of $+1$. If all of the numeric character data to be affected by the Move Zone instruction is to be considered as valid "plus" numerics, there will be no adverse action resulting from moving a hexadecimal 'F' digit into the left nibble of the low-order byte of the field. If the low-order byte of the field of numeric data contains a negatively signed numeric character, the MVZ instruction will "strip" that zone and replace it with a positive (plus) zone. This can be avoided by not affecting the low-order byte of the numeric field. This would appear as:

```
NUMERIC     DC      CL5'ᵇ465J'
ZONEIT      DC      CL4'0000'
```

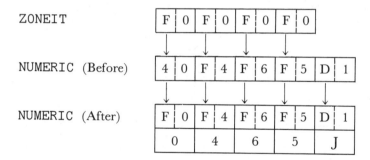

NUMERIC (Character)

ᵇ	4	6	5	J

(Hex)

4	0	F	4	F	6	F	5	D	1

ZONEIT (Character)

0	0	0	0

(Hex)

F	0	F	0	F	0	F	0

```
MVZ     NUMERIC(4),ZONEIT
```

The instruction statement indicates the zone portion (left-most four bits) of each byte of ZONEIT is to be moved into the corresponding position of only the first four bytes of NUMERIC. This would appear to be:

ZONEIT

F	0	F	0	F	0	F	0

NUMERIC (Before)

4	0	F	4	F	6	F	5	D	1

NUMERIC (After)

F	0	F	4	F	6	F	5	D	1
0		4		6		5		J	

The original configuration of NUMERIC represented a set of partially configured numeric character data, of which the low-order numeric was indicated to be a signed zoned decimal character of "J", equal to a value of -1. If the MVZ instruction had moved numeric zones into all bytes of NUMERIC, the hex configuration of the low-order byte would have been 'F1'—equal to a numeric character of "1", which implies a positive value. This would have resulted in a change of the intended sign attached to that numeric character representing a negative zoned decimal.

2. The "Store" Instructions

The Store instructions are used to move all, or part, of the contents of registers into storage areas. There are four such instructions, and between them they will store 1 byte, 2 bytes, 4 bytes, or up to 64 bytes of data. Other than for the storage of one byte of data from a register, the storage of two bytes or more must be to an area of storage that is appropriately boundary-aligned. Two-byte storage areas must be halfword-aligned; four-byte storage areas must be fullword-aligned; multiples of four-byte storage areas must be contiguously fullword-aligned.

These instructions are particularly useful in preserving addresses and values that are currently within a register. This is often necessary, especially when any given general register is to be used for several functions within a single problem program. The data may be stored, held until the required processing logic is completed, and then moved back into the register via any of the Load instructions.

There are four Store instructions—Store,

Store Character, Store Halfword, and Store Multiple. The programmer's decision as to which one of these would be used is entirely dependent on the amount of data that is to be stored.

(a) Store Character (STC). This Store instruction affects only one byte of data of the four bytes that are contained within a general register. It derives its name from the fact that the EBCDIC character is represented by one byte—eight bit positions. When the Store Character instruction statement is executed, it will take the low-order byte of data from the general register that is specified by the first operand and will place that data, unaltered, into the one-byte storage area specified by the second operand.

Although there are many conceivable applications for this instruction, one of its primary uses is to modify the length attribute of an existing instruction statement. For example, assume that a problem program contained this instruction statement:

```
MOVEDATA   MVC    FLD1(6),FLD2
```

This statement indicates that the problem program is to move six bytes of data from FLD2 to FLD1. The hexadecimal configuration of the first two bytes of the machine-language instruction generated by this statement would appear as:

D205

The hex 'D2' is the hexadecimal code for the MVC instruction statement; the hex '05' is the machine-language length attribute of '6'; the machine-language length attribute is always one less than the desired decimal length of the operation. If, at a later point within the problem program, the pro-

grammer desired to change the length attribute of the MOVEDATA instruction statement so that it would move 11 bytes of data, he could code the statements necessary to do this as:

```
LA     8,10
STC    8,MOVEDATA+1
```

In the first instruction statement, a fixed-point value of +10 (equal to a machine-language length attribute that would move 11 bytes of data) is loaded into general register 8. The low-order byte of general register 8 now contains a hexadecimal configuration of '0A'. The second instruction statement stores the low-order byte of general register 8 into the address generated by MOVEDATA+1, or the second byte of the machine-language instruction generated by the statement that is labeled MOVEDATA. That portion of the machine-language instruction (which was previously D205) would now appear as 'D20A', indicating a length attribute of 11 bytes for the fields specified within the remainder of the statement. As indicated by this example, the STC instruction can be easily used to modify other instruction statements at will.

(b) Store Halfword (STH). The Store Halfword instruction will take the contents of the right-most two bytes of the general register specified by the first operand and place them unaltered into the halfword storage location that is addressed by the second operand. This instruction may be used to store values into a storage area for retention purposes. Assume:

General register 4 contains a fixed-point value +3926.

```
HAFWD    DC     H'0'
  *

         STH    4,HAFWD
```

Register 4 (Binary)	0	000	0000	0000	0000	0000	1111	0101	0110

(Hex)	+	0	0	0	0	0	F	5	6

HAFWD (Binary)	0000	0000	0000	0000

(Hex)	0	0	0	0

The register and storage area would be affected in the following way:

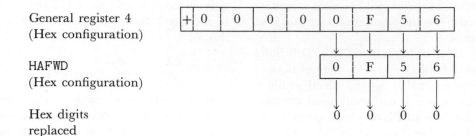

As indicated, the low-order two bytes of general register 4 have replaced the data originally contained within HAFWD. In general, the Store Halfword instruction might be used to extract halfword values from a register or to selectively pull out and retain address increment values, such as positional pointers to table segments.

(c) **Store (ST).** The Store instruction will take the contents of an entire general register and place that data, without change, into a fullword storage location. Because general registers are often used for multiple purposes within a single problem program, it is quite often necessary to temporarily store the contents of a general register, use that register for another application, and then reinstate the register with the original value that was stored from it. This application is useful in arithmetic routines, for holding address increments, and for storing actual addresses for future reference. The Store instruction is one means of retrieving the results of a fixed-point arithmetic routine for further manipulation. For example:

```
AR      8,9
ST      8,FULLWD
```

The first statement adds together the fixed-point contents of registers 8 and 9. The second statement takes the sum that resulted from that operation, residing in general register 8, and places it into a fullword storage location for future reference or use.

Utilizing the Store instruction in order to allow multiple use of a single general register is indicated in the set of instruction statements shown in Fig. 9-2.

Basically these instruction statements are performing two rather elementary table lookups. Statements 001 through 005 are performing the first table search, using general register 9 as the address pointer to the current table segment within the first table, TABLE1. Whenever an equal condition is found in the first table, the program will branch to the second table lookup routine, HITA. HITA, consisting of Statements 006 through 013, also intends to use general register 9 but only as a loop count control register for a BCT instruction. As soon as the HITA subroutine is entered, the problem program stores the address that is contained in register 9 into HOLDR9 because this address may be used after completion of HITA. Once general register 9 is stored, the logic loads general register 9 with a loop count value of 150 and the logic pattern of the second table lookup commences. If an equal condition is found on TABLE2 the program logic branches to HITB, which now wants to use the address of the table segment pointed to in TABLE1 by the address contained within HOLDR9. HOLDR9 is, therefore, loaded into general register 9 by Statement 014. Statement 015 then uses the address in register 10 (representing a segment in TABLE2) to move data into the table segment of TABLE1 that is pointed to by the address within general register 9. It was unnecessary to save the loop control value contained in general register 9 upon exit from the HITA routine since this value is reinstated each time that particular routine is entered.

Each unique problem program may have many of its own peculiar needs for using the Store instruction. The performance of this

IBM

IBM System/360 Assembler Coding Form

X28-6509-2 U/M050
Printed in U.S.A.

Name	Operation	Operand	Comments	Identification-Sequence
*				
LOOKUPS	LA	9,TABLE1		001
LOOP1	CLC	0(3,9),KEY1		002
	BC	8,HITA		003
	AH	9,=H'10'		004
	BC	15,LOOP1		005
*				
HITA	ST	9,HOLDR9		006
	LA	9,150		007
LOOP2	LA	10,TABLE2		008
	CLC	0(3,10),KEY2		009
	BC	8,HITB		010
	AH	10,=H'10'		011
	BCT	9,LOOP2		012
	BC	15,NOHIT		013
*				
HITB	L	9,HOLDR9		014
	MVC	4(3,9),0(10)		015
	BC	15,GETOUT		016
*				
HOLDR9	DC	F'0'		017

Figure 9-2

185

instruction is quite simple, but it may well be used to assist in creating compound, complex routines.

(d) Store Multiple (STM). The STM instruction is used to move the contents of two or more general registers into a corresponding number of contiguous fullword storage locations. The first and last registers that are to be stored are specified as the first two operands of the instruction statement; the last operand specifies the first fullword storage area of the set of fullwords into which the registers are to be stored. A Store Multiple instruction statement may be analyzed as:

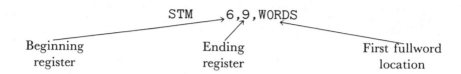

Beginning register	Ending register	First fullword location

Although the general registers are numbered from '0' through '15', it is not necessary that the Store Multiple ending register be of a higher value than the beginning register. The following examples will indicate some of the different ways that a Store Multiple instruction might be reasonably expressed, in each instance using a similar set of fullword storage locations that are defined as:

```
SAVEWDS     DS      16F
```

Example 1

```
STM    8,2,SAVEWDS
```

This statement would store general registers 8, 9, 10, 11, 12, 13, 14, 15, 0, 1, and 2 into the first eleven fullwords (44 bytes) of SAVEWDS in the exact order shown.

Example 2

```
STM    5,7,SAVEWDS
```

This statement would store general registers 5, 6, and 7 into the first three fullwords of SAVEWDS.

Example 3

```
STM    13,0,SAVEWDS+8
```

This statement would store general registers 13, 14, 15, and 0 into the third, fourth, fifth, and sixth fullwords of SAVEWDS.

Example 4

```
STM    9,8,SAVEWDS
```

This statement would store all sixteen general registers into the whole of SAVEWDS. The first register to be stored would be general register 9, the second would be register 10, etc., until all 16 general registers had been stored.

3. The "Load" Instructions

The Load instructions are provided to enable the programmer to insert (or load) data or values into general registers. The amount of data that may be placed into a general register by these instructions ranges from one to four bytes per register. In effect, the Load instructions are the reverse of the Store instructions—data residing within certain types of storage areas, absolute values, addresses, or the contents of other registers may be loaded into one or more general registers.

(a)   Insert Character (IC). Although this particular instruction does not contain the term "load" within its title, it may be considered to be a Load instruction. It is, in effect, a means of extracting one byte of data from a storage location and placing it into the low-order byte of a general register. The insertion of this byte of data into the register does not alter the contents of the three high-order bytes of the register. The IC instruction may be used to alter an address contained within a register, to store or restore a portion of a register to a particular value, and similar other applications. Note the configuration of general register 6 and FIELDA in this illustration:

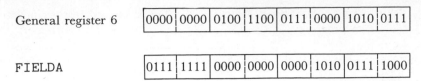

General register 6   0000 0000 0100 1100 0111 0000 1010 0111

FIELDA   0111 1111 0000 0000 0000 1010 0111 1000

The instruction statement and the resulting action are:

IC   6,FIELDA

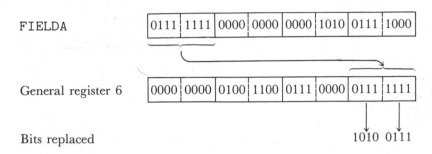

FIELDA   0111 1111 0000 0000 0000 1010 0111 1000

General register 6   0000 0000 0100 1100 0111 0000 0111 1111

Bits replaced   1010 0111

As shown, the instruction statement has caused the first byte of FIELDA to be inserted (or loaded) into the low-order byte of general register 6.

(b) Load Halfword (LH). The Load Halfword instruction is used to insert the contents of two bytes of storage data, aligned on a halfword storage boundary, into a general register. The halfword value is first extracted from its storage location, expanded to a fullword configuration, and then placed into the general register specified by the first operand of the instruction statement. As in the use of the Insert Character instruction, this instruction is often used to reload a register with the value of a constant. This value may represent an address, a loop control count value, or any other practical application developed by the programmer.

By using the same values as shown in the example for the Insert Character instruction, this example will demonstrate the resemblance, and the difference, of the two instructions:

```
FIELDA     DS      F
*
           LH      6,FIELDA
```

General register 6   0000 0000 0100 1100 0111 0000 1010 0111

FIELDA   0111 1111 0000 0000 0000 1010 0111 1000

The halfword value contained within the first two bytes of FIELDA is first extracted and then expanded to a fullword by duplicating the sign-bit throughout 16 additional high-order bit positions.

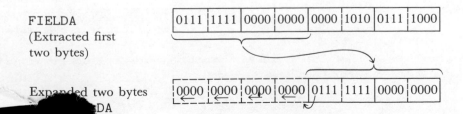

FIELDA
(Extracted first
two bytes)   0111 1111 0000 0000 0000 1010 0111 1000

Expanded two bytes
...DA   0000 0000 0000 0000 0111 1111 0000 0000

The new fullword configuration is then placed into the general register.

General register 6 | 0000 | 0000 | 0000 | 0000 | 0111 | 1111 | 0000 | 0000 |

(c) Load (L). The Load instruction is the reverse of the Store instruction. The four bytes of data (a fullword) that is addressed by the second operand of the instruction statement is loaded in its entirety into the general register that is specified by the first operand. The most commonly used application for this instruction is to initialize a register or to reinstate a general register with an address or value which, at some previous point within the program, had been stored into a fullword until needed. The same values that were used in the examples for Insert Character and Load Halfword will also be used to illustrate this instruction. Compare the action of the example provided here to the action taken by the Insert Character and Load Halfword instructions.

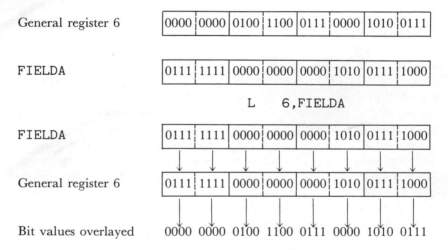

General register 6 | 0000 | 0000 | 0100 | 1100 | 0111 | 0000 | 1010 | 0111 |

FIELDA | 0111 | 1111 | 0000 | 0000 | 0000 | 1010 | 0111 | 1000 |

L   6,FIELDA

FIELDA | 0111 | 1111 | 0000 | 0000 | 0000 | 1010 | 0111 | 1000 |

General register 6 | 0111 | 1111 | 0000 | 0000 | 0000 | 1010 | 0111 | 1000 |

Bit values overlayed   0000 0000 0100 1100 0111 0000 1010 0111

(d) Load Register (LR). The Load Register instruction merely takes the four-byte contents from one general register (specified by the second operand) and places that configuration into the general register specified by the first operand. The data being moved is not altered in any way. The general register from which the data has been moved still contains the original configuration. In a sense, this instruction and all similar move, load, and store instructions may be thought of as a duplication process. Although the data has been placed into another location, the original data configuration remains unchanged.

Suppose that general registers 4 and 8 contains the following bit configuration:

General register 4 | 0000 | 0000 | 0000 | 0000 | 0111 | 0001 | 1111 | 0000 |

General register 8 | 0001 | 1111 | 0101 | 1011 | 0000 | 1100 | 0011 | 1100 |

The instruction statement that is being executed, and the result of the Load Register instruction on those registers, are represented as:

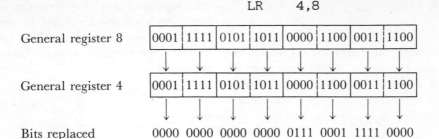

LR   4,8

| General register 8 | 0001 | 1111 | 0101 | 1011 | 0000 | 1100 | 0011 | 1100 |

| General register 4 | 0001 | 1111 | 0101 | 1011 | 0000 | 1100 | 0011 | 1100 |

Bits replaced   0000 0000 0000 0000 0111 0001 1111 0000

(e) Load Multiple (LM). The Load Multiple instruction is used to load two or more fullword values, located in a contiguous set of fullword storage locations, into a corresponding number of contiguous general registers. The number of fullwords loaded is determined by the quantity of registers indicated by the first two operands. The registers are expressed as a range, the first operand indicating the first general register that is to be loaded and the next operand indicating the last general register that is to be loaded. For example, a Load Multiple instruction statement might appear as:

LM   7,10,DATAFWDS

This statement would indicate that general registers 7, 8, 9, and 10 are to be loaded with the values contained in four fullwords that are located beginning at a storage point addressed by the label DATAFWDS.

This application is further illustrated in the following example:

```
FULLWD1      DS      F
FULLWD2      DS      F
FULLWD3      DS      F
FULLWD4      DS      F
FULLWD5      DS      F
FULLWD6      DS      F
*
ROUTINEA     LM      8,13,FULLWD1
```

After execution of this instruction statement, general register 8 would contain the value from FULLWD1, general register 9 would contain the value from FULLWD2, general register 10 would contain the value from FULLWD3, general register 11 would contain the value from FULLWD4, general register 12 would contain the value from FULLWD5, and general register 13 would contain the value from FULLWD6.

The use of this instruction permits the loading of multiple contiguous registers at one time by one instruction statement, if the data to be loaded is located in contiguous fullword storage locations.

(f) Load Address (LA). The Load Address instruction is used to load the address of a specified storage location or an actual value into a general register. The address that is to be loaded, as indicated by the second operand of the statement, may be represented by a symbolic label or an absolute value expressed in decimal form. It should be noted that the value of the second operand, whether it be a generated address or a stated value, is only loaded into the low-order three bytes of the general register. The high-order byte of the register is set to zero.

The following examples illustrate some of the ways in which this instruction might be expressed.

Example 1

LA   11,SUBRTE1

If, at program execution time, the address point generated by SUBRTE1 was at storage address 83,596 (or '1468C' in hexadecimals), then that value would be loaded into general register 11. Register 11 would then be configured as:

Address of SUBRTE1

| Register 11 (Binary) | 0000 | 0000 | 0000 | 0001 | 0100 | 0110 | 1000 | 1100 |
| (Hex) | 0 | 0 | 0 | 1 | 4 | 6 | 8 | C |

Example 2

        LA   8,300

In this instance, the instruction would load a fixed-point value of +300 into general register 8. This is one way that a loop-control value, or any other type of specific value, may be loaded into a general register.

Example 3

        LA   4,2(0,4)

In this example, general register 4 is being loaded with a fixed-point value which is equivalent to the current value of general register 4 plus a decimal value of 2. If, in this instance, register 4 contained a value of +3386 prior to the execution of the instruction statement, subsequently it would contain a value of +3388. This may be expressed as:

Displacement + Index + Prior Register 4
                    equals New Register 4

or

    2 + 0 + 3386 equals 3388

The Load Address instruction may, therefore, be readily used for incrementing (systematically "adding to") a general register value.

(g) **Load & Test Register (LTR).** The execution of this instruction will load the value of the second operand register into the first operand register, at the same time testing that value for a zero, negative, or positive condition. The action of setting the Condition Code bits of the PSW is the only difference between this instruction and the Load Register instruction. Once the Load & Test Register instruction has been executed, it would be expected the program logic would encounter another statement that would test the condition of the Condition Code, and indicate the action that should occur as a result of that comparison.

The general register specified by the first and second operands may be different general registers, or a single register may be tested, by loading it into itself, by specifying that same general register as both operands of the instruction statement. Such a test would be coded as:

        LTR   6,6
        BC   8,ZERORTE
        BC   4,NEGRTE

In this set of instruction statements, general register 6 would first be loaded into itself and the Condition Code bits would be set according to the value then contained in that register. If the register value was zero, then the program logic would branch out to a routine labeled ZERORTE upon execution of the second instruction statement. If the value was not zero, but rather a negative value, the program logic would branch to a routine labeled NEGRTE when executing the third instruction statement. If neither of those conditions existed, implying that the value in register 6 was a nonzero positive value, the processing logic would fall through to the next sequential program instruction statement.

(h) **Load Complement Register (LCR).** The Load Complement Register instruction will take the fixed-point value of the second operand register, convert it to its complement form, and place that complement value into the general register specified by the first operand. If the fixed-point content of the second operand register is a negative value, it will be converted to the true Powers-Of-Two binary notation; if it is a positive value, it will be converted to its complement negative form. This action is illustrated in the following examples.

Example 1

        LCR   4,6

General register 4 contains a fixed-point value of +79,327 and general register 6 contains a fixed-point value of +29,231. Initially, the binary configuration of these registers would appear as:

General register 4 | 0000 | 0000 | 0000 | 0001 | 0011 | 0101 | 1101 | 1111 | +79,327

General register 6 | 0000 | 0000 | 0000 | 0000 | 0111 | 0010 | 0010 | 1111 | +29,231

When the instruction statement is executed, the positive fixed-point value contained in general register 6 would be extracted and converted to its negative complement. This conversion can be assumed to be:

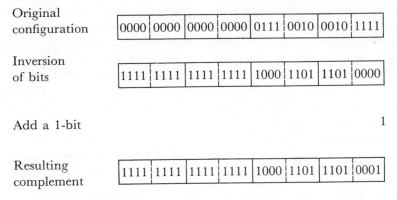

Original configuration

| 0000 | 0000 | 0000 | 0000 | 0111 | 0010 | 0010 | 1111 |

Inversion of bits

| 1111 | 1111 | 1111 | 1111 | 1000 | 1101 | 1101 | 0000 |

Add a 1-bit   1

Resulting complement

| 1111 | 1111 | 1111 | 1111 | 1000 | 1101 | 1101 | 0001 |

The complement configuration of the value of general register 6 would then be placed into general register 4, after which register 4 would appear as:

General register 4 | 1111 | 1111 | 1111 | 1111 | 1000 | 1101 | 1101 | 0001 | −29,231

Example 2

    LCR   9,9

General register 9 contains a fixed-point value of −165,288. The binary negative configuration of this register would be:

General register 9 | 1111 | 1111 | 1111 | 1101 | 0111 | 1010 | 0101 | 1000 | −165,288

The conversion of the contents of register 9 to the complement of the negative value, which is now to be loaded into register 9, may be assumed to be:

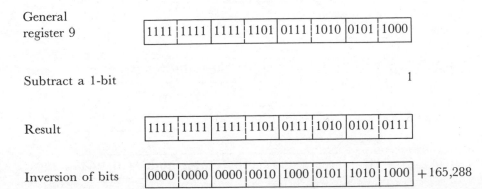

General register 9

| 1111 | 1111 | 1111 | 1101 | 0111 | 1010 | 0101 | 1000 |

Subtract a 1-bit   1

Result

| 1111 | 1111 | 1111 | 1101 | 0111 | 1010 | 0101 | 0111 |

Inversion of bits

| 0000 | 0000 | 0000 | 0010 | 1000 | 0101 | 1010 | 1000 | +165,288

The inverted bit configuration, representing +165,288, would be placed back into general register 9, overlaying the original configuration of −165,288 that resided there prior to the LCR instruction statement.

(i)   Load Positive Register (LPR). The Load Positive Register instruction will take the fixed-point value contained within the general register specified by the second operand of the statement and place a positive representation of that value into the general register specified by the first operand. If the configuration of that value was negative, it is converted to the positive complement, in true Power-Of-Two notation, before it is loaded into the receiving register. If the configuration of the value was already a positive representation prior to encountering the LPR instruction, that configuration is placed unaltered into the receiving register.

A positive configuration of any value contained in a general register can be assured by specifying that register in both operands of a Load Positive Register instruction statement. The performance of this instruction under various conditions can be seen in these examples.

Example 1. In this example the value contained in the second operand register is already a positive configuration. Therefore, when it is loaded into the first operand register it will not be altered by the Load Positive Register instruction. The instruction statement that is to be executed is:

        LPR   6,12

If general register 12 contained a value of +693,221, that value would be unaltered during the load into general register 6.

General register 12
(Second operand)

General register 6   (Binary)
(First operand)

                       (Hex)

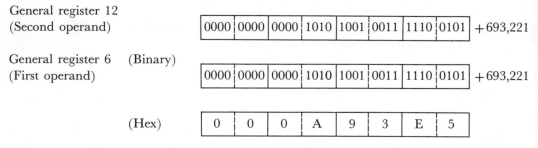

General register 12 (Second operand): 0000 0000 0000 1010 1001 0011 1110 0101   +693,221

General register 6 (Binary) (First operand): 0000 0000 0000 1010 1001 0011 1110 0101   +693,221

(Hex): 0 0 0 A 9 3 E 5

Example 2

        LPR   11,8

This example will indicate the conversion of a negative fixed-point value to a positive value during the execution of the LPR instruction. Assuming that general register 8 had contained a negative fixed-point value of −219,883 at the time of execution of the instruction statement, the LPR instruction would effectively perform this action:

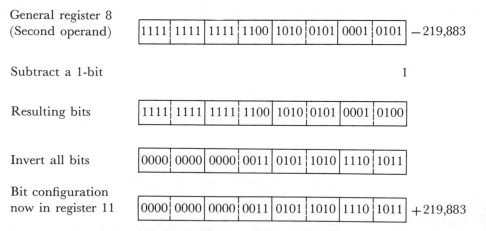

General register 8 (Second operand): 1111 1111 1111 1100 1010 0101 0001 0101   −219,883

Subtract a 1-bit: 1

Resulting bits: 1111 1111 1111 1100 1010 0101 0001 0100

Invert all bits: 0000 0000 0000 0011 0101 1010 1110 1011

Bit configuration now in register 11: 0000 0000 0000 0011 0101 1010 1110 1011   +219,883

Example 3. In this example, a single general register is used for both operands in an LPR instruction statement. This will guarantee that the fixed-point value of that general register will have a positive-value configuration, regardless of its configuration prior to the execution of the LPR instruction statement.

        LPR   4,4

If register 4 had originally contained a value of +36,984, it would now still contain that identical configuration. However, had general register 4 contained a value of −2,675,037, it would now contain the configuration for a fixed-point value of +2,675,037.

(j) Load Negative Register (LNR). This instruction performs the exact opposite function of the Load Positive Register instruction. The LNR instruction will first extract the fixed-point value configuration from the general register specified by the second operand and will examine that value for its positive or negative condition. If the configuration is already a negative value, that same configuration will be placed unaltered into the general register specified by the first operand. However, if the configuration of the second operand contents is of a positive value, the LNR instruction will convert that value to its complement negative configuration before placing it into the first operand register. This action is demonstrated in the following examples.

Example 1

LNR   8,8

Assuming that general register 8 had contained a fixed-point value of +3,965,709 prior to the execution of this instruction statement, the subsequent action of the LNR instruction would be:

General register 8 (Second operand)	`0000` `0000` `0011` `1100` `1000` `0011` `0000` `1011`	+3,965,709
Invert all bits	`1111` `1111` `1100` `0011` `0111` `1100` `1111` `0100`	
Add a 1-bit	1	
Result	`1111` `1111` `1100` `0011` `0111` `1100` `1111` `0101`	
General register 8 (First operand)	`1111` `1111` `1100` `0011` `0111` `1100` `1111` `0101`	−3,965,709

Example 2

LNR   12,2

In this example, it is assumed that general register 2 contains a fixed-point value of −15,299. Since this value already consists of a negative configuration, that configuration will be loaded unchanged into general register 12.

General register 2 (Second operand)	`1111` `1111` `1111` `1111` `1100` `0100` `0011` `1101`	−15,299
General register 12 (First operand)	`1111` `1111` `1111` `1111` `1100` `0100` `0011` `1101`	−15,299

4. *"Shifting" Operations*

The terms "shift" and "shifting" are used to describe the sidewise movement of data bits within one or more consecutive general registers. The movement is accomplished on the basis of the number of individual bit positions specified by the second operand of the shift instruction statement. While it is entirely possible to multiply or divide with some fixed-point values by use of a shift instruction, this practice is generally ignored because the multiplier or divisor may only be a value that is equivalent to an increment of the "Powers-Of-Two" scale—2, 4, 8, 16, 32, 64, 128, etc. The most common use of the shift instructions is to alter, relocate, or isolate certain bit position representations that are contained within one or more general registers. These applications will be discussed further within the descriptions of the individual shift instructions. The illustrations of the concepts of shifting will contain both the binary and hexadecimal configurations of the general registers.

(a) "Logical" Shifting Operations and Instructions. The Assembler Language instructions for shifting that are defined as "logical" shifts will affect all bit positions within the specified register(s) without regard for the sign-bit. Insofar as these instructions are concerned, all bit positions contain a logical configuration of either '0' or '1' and no particular bit position maintains any more significance than another. Therefore, when logical shifting is accomplished, a sign-bit is moved in accordance with the movement of the contents of the other bit positions.

(1) Shift Left Logical (SLL). The Shift Left Logical instruction will perform a logical shift within a single general register for a maximum length of 32 bit positions. The contents of the register specified by the first operand will be moved to the left in a logical

bit-by-bit manner for the number of bit positions specified by the second operand. The significance of the high-order sign-bit is ignored and it is shifted along with the other bits. As the bit configuration of the specified general register is moved to the left, vacated low-order bit positions are supplied with zero-bits. Bits shifted out of the high-order bit positions are lost as they are replaced by the bits being moved from the lower positions. The loss (shifting out) of a high-order significant-digit bit (a bit unlike the left-most bit of the original configuration) does not activate a unique setting of the Condition Code within the PSW.

Example 1. This example will indicate the ability to alter the configuration of a general register in which program interest is expressed as to the hexadecimal contents of that register. Consequently, assume that general register 7 currently contains a bit configuration representing the equivalent of hexadecimal 'FEDCBA21'. This configuration would appear as:

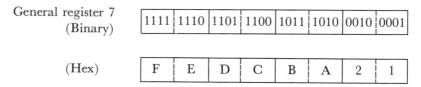

General register 7
(Binary) `1111 1110 1101 1100 1011 1010 0010 0001`

(Hex) `F E D C B A 2 1`

The instruction statement that is to be executed is:

SLL   7,4

This statement instructs that the current bit configuration of general register 7 should be logically moved to the left by four bit positions.

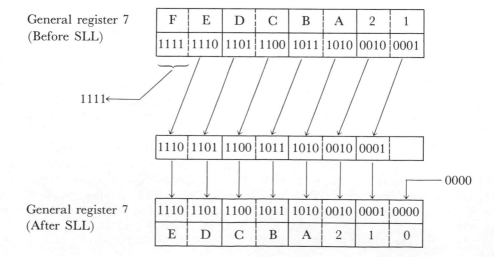

General register 7
(Before SLL) `F E D C B A 2 1`
`1111 1110 1101 1100 1011 1010 0010 0001`

1111←

`1110 1101 1100 1011 1010 0010 0001`

0000

General register 7
(After SLL) `1110 1101 1100 1011 1010 0010 0001 0000`
`E D C B A 2 1 0`

The four high-order bit positions, consisting of bits '1111' (Hex 'F'), have now been lost to general register 7, while the four low-order bit positions have been supplied with zero-bits, comprising a hexadecimal zero (Bits '0000'). The low-order 28 bits have all been moved to the left by four bit positions, so that they now represent the high-order 28 bit positions.

Example 2. In the previous example, the shift was used to move all bit values to the left by four bit positions, the same length as is required to move a single hexadecimal character. Accordingly, each hex digit was merely moved one position higher within the general register, the highest-order hex digit being lost and a new hex digit of zero being supplied to the low-order hex position in the register. This example will show the result of logically shifting the same original value by a number of bit positions that do not preserve the identity of the original hexadecimal digits. The original value of general register 7 will again be X'FEDCBA21'. The instruction statement being executed is:

SLL   7,5

This statement indicates that each bit in general register 7 is to be moved to the left until it occupies the bit position that is five positions higher than the one in which it originally resided. The bits of the five high-order bit positions will be shifted out of the general register and lost; the five low-order bit positions vacated during the shift will be supplied with zero-bits.

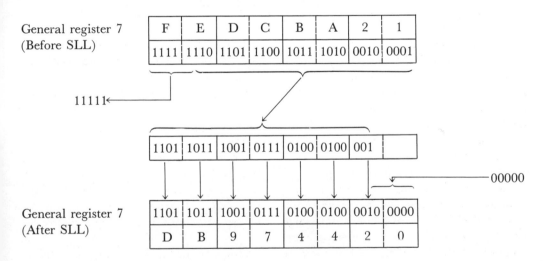

The resulting configuration now bears neither a whole nor a partial resemblance to the original hexadecimal configuration of general register 7. Even so, the programmer could conceivably have many valid reasons within his program for a shift of this type.

Example 3. Although the SLL instruction might likely be used more often to shift character or hexadecimal data within a register, the shifting of fixed-point values may also be accomplished with it. This can be either a poorly applied or a useful application because the logical shift does not regard the high-order sign-bit with any particular significance. This example indicates the problem that might be incurred in shifting a fixed-point value with a logical shift. The fixed-point value in general register 5 is +9,180,679, which would appear to be:

General register 5	0000	0000	1000	1100	0001	0110	0000	0111
	0	0	8	C	1	6	0	7

The programmer, wishing to multiply this value by +256, has coded the instruction   statement as:

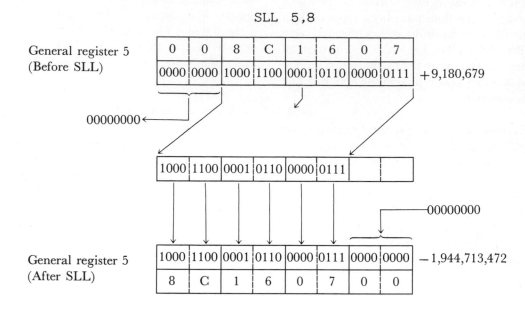

SLL 5,8

General register 5 (Before SLL)

| 0 | 0 | 8 | C | 1 | 6 | 0 | 7 |

| 0000 | 0000 | 1000 | 1100 | 0001 | 0110 | 0000 | 0111 | +9,180,679

00000000 ←

| 1000 | 1100 | 0001 | 0110 | 0000 | 0111 | | |

00000000

General register 5 (After SLL)

| 1000 | 1100 | 0001 | 0110 | 0000 | 0111 | 0000 | 0000 | −1,944,713,472

| 8 | C | 1 | 6 | 0 | 7 | 0 | 0 |

The logical result of the multiplication of +9,180,679 by +256 would be equal to a result of +2,350,253,824. Although no high-order significant-digit bits have been shifted out of the register, the inadvertent use of the logical shift has resulted in a one-bit residing in the high-order bit position. This now indicates that the general register contains a negative fixed-point value, the low-order 31 bit positions comprising the integer of that value. Instead of arriving at the desired result of +2,350,253,824 the SLL instruction statement has created a negative fixed-point value of −1,944,713,472 or a hexadecimal configuration of X'8C160700'. Because a logical shift, instead of an algebraic shift, was used to accomplish this task the programmer would receive no indication that his application had not performed as anticipated. Therefore, it must be noted that logical shifts should not be used for fixed-point arithmetic operations unless the results of such applications are closely verified.

(2) *Shift Left Double Logical (SLDL)*. The SLDL instruction performs with the same principles as the SLL instruction except that two general registers are utilized. These two registers must consist of an *even-odd* pair of consecutive general registers such as 4 & 5,

8 & 9, 12 & 13, 2 & 3, etc. When using this instruction, or any other shift instruction that utilizes a two-register shift, the first operand of the instruction statement must specify the even-numbered register of the even-odd pair of general registers. A double register shift may be used to move a maximum of 64 bits. Data contained within the high-order byte(s) of a register may be isolated through the use of the SLDL instruction and then extracted into a storage area by use of a Store instruction statement.

Example 1. In this illustration, general register 7 will contain data in its high-order byte that is to be isolated for separate use by the program logic. Assuming that general register 6 has been cleared to a +0 value and that general register 7 contains a hexadecimal configuration of 'C30000D3', the process of extracting the high-order byte could be coded with these statements.

```
SLDL    6,8
STC     6,HOLD
```

The first instruction would execute the SLDL instruction, resulting in this shifting of the bits.

General registers 6 & 7 (Before SLDL)

0	0	0	0	0	0	0	0	C	3	0	0	0	0	D	3
0000	0000	0000	0000	0000	0000	0000	0000	1100	0011	0000	0000	0000	0000	1101	0011

0000 ←

| 0000 | 0000 | 0000 | 0000 | 0000 | 0000 | 1100 | 0011 | 0000 | 0000 | 0000 | 0000 | 1101 | 0011 | | |

0000 0000

0000	0000	0000	0000	0000	0000	1100	0011	0000	0000	0000	0000	1101	0011	0000	0000
0	0	0	0	0	0	C	3	0	0	0	0	D	3	0	0

General registers 6 & 7 (After SLDL)

At this point, the high-order byte of general register 7 has been shifted into the low-order byte of general register 6. The second instruction statement, Store Character, will place that byte into a one-byte area labeled HOLD where it may be manipulated or used as the program requires.

Example 2. For all practical purposes, any single byte or groups of bytes contained within a general register may be isolated for extraction through the use of the shift instructions. In this example, it is shown how the middle two bytes of a general register can be isolated by the SLDL instruction and then extracted by the Store Halfword instruction.

```
SLDL    10,24
STH     10,HAFWRD
```

Assume that general register 10 originally contained a hexadecimal configuration of X'003FC1D2' and general register 11 contained a configuration of X'F0F1F2F3'. The SLDL instruction statement would act on these values in this manner:

General registers 10 & 11 (Before SLDL)

0	0	3	F	C	1	D	2	F	0	F	1	F	2	F	3
0000	0000	0011	1111	1100	0001	1101	0010	1111	0000	1111	0001	1111	0010	1111	0011

000000000001111111111000001

| 1101 | 0010 | 1111 | 0000 | 1111 | 0001 | 1111 | 0010 | 1111 | 0011 | | | | | | |

0000000000000000000000000

1101	0010	1111	0000	1111	0001	1111	0010	1111	0011	0000	0000	0000	0000	0000	0000
D	2	F	0	F	1	F	2	F	3	0	0	0	0	0	0

General registers 10 & 11 (After SLDL)

The middle two bytes of general register 11, containing hexadecimal digits 'F1F2', have now been shifted into the low-order two bytes of general register 10. The Store Half-word instruction statement will now take those two bytes and place them in a halfword storage location labeled HAFWRD.

(3)   Shift Right Logical (SRL). The SRL

instruction will perform a logical shift of bits within a general register for a maximum length of 32 bit positions. The bit configuration of the general register specified by the first operand will be moved to the right in a logical bit-by-bit manner for the number of bit positions specified by the second operand. As in the case of all logical shifts, the significance of the high-order sign-bit is ignored and it is shifted along with the other data bits. As the bits of the specified register are moved to the right, vacated high-order bit positions are supplied with zero-bits. Bits shifted out of the low-order end of the general register are lost as they are replaced by the bits being moved in from the high-order bit positions. The Condition Code in the PSW will not reflect the loss (shifting-out) of a significant-digit bit. The SRL instruction has limited use as a "divide" instruction, being restricted to the capability of dividing by positive Powers-Of-Two increment values

only. When it is used in conjunction with an SLL instruction, it can be used to zero-out a low-order byte or bytes of a general register. Some of its applications are examined in these examples.

Example 1. This example will show how the combined application of the SRL and SLL instructions may be used to clear the rightmost three bytes of a general register. This application may also be used to zero-out any number of bits or bytes up to the maximum length of a single register. In this instance, general register 9 contains a hexadecimal configuration of X'C1C2C3C4', representing the EBCDIC characters 'ABCD'. The instruction statements coded will reset the hexadecimal configuration of that register to X'C1000000'.

```
SRL     9,24
SLL     9,24
```

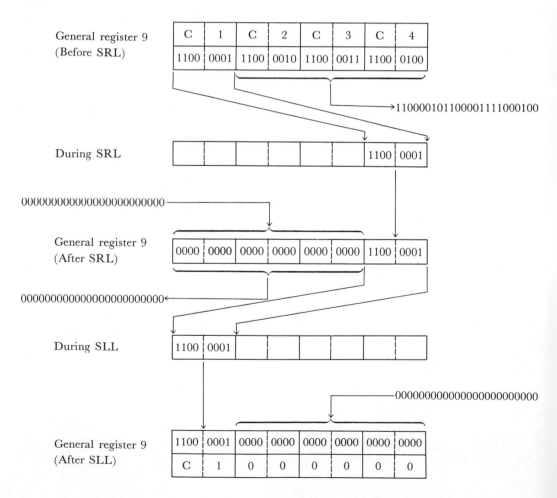

As shown here, the high-order byte of general register 9 (X'C1') was shifted right until it occupied the low-order byte of that register. It was then reshifted left until it occupied its original position, the latter shift supplying zero-bits to the low-order 24 bit positions in lieu of the former configuration that was lost when it was shifted out by the SRL instruction statement.

Example 2. A simple division by a value of eight is shown in this example, being possible only because that value is one of the increment values of the Powers-Of-Two table. This application with a logical shift is also limited to a positive value, resulting from the disregard of this instruction for the significance of the sign-bit. In addition, in a single register logical right shift only the quotient of the division is retained; the remainder is shifted out and is lost. Register 3, upon which the shift is being performed, contains a fixed-point value of +39,875. Since this value is to be divided by +8, the shift is for a length of three bit positions. This is determined by the fact that the third increment in the Powers-Of-Two table of the value of bit positions has a value of 8—that is, 2, 4, 8, 16, 32, etc.

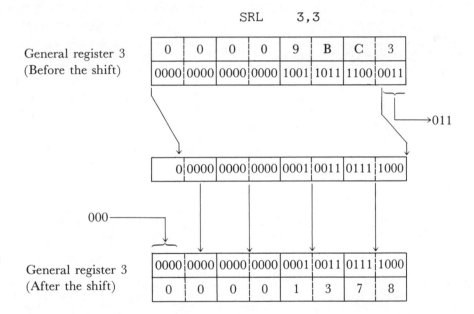

The shift results in general register 3 containing a hexadecimal configuration of significant digits of X'1378', which is equal to 4984—the quotient resulting from the division of +39,875 by +8. You will note that the three bits shifted out of the low-order positions of general register 3 comprise a Powers-Of-Two value of +3; the same amount as would be the remainder in a true arithmetic division problem.

(4) *Shift Right Double Logical (SRDL)*. The principle difference between this instruction and the Shift Right Logical instruction is that the SRDL will shift the contents of two consecutive general registers. These two reg-

isters must consist of an even-odd pair of general registers. The shift is coded by addressing the even-numbered register as the first operand and by specifying the number of bit positions to be shifted as the second operand. The maximum length of a logical double register shift is 64 bit positions. As with the single register logical right shift, this instruction may be used under limited circumstances to accomplish an arithmetic division routine. The value to be divided must be a positive value and the value of the divisor can only be one of the increment values of the Powers-Of-Two table. With this instruction, however, the shift will place the remainder into the odd-numbered register and the quotient into the even-numbered register, conditional that the dividend originated in the even-numbered register. By combining the SRDL instruction in sequence with the other logical shift operations, a great number of variable tasks can be performed within a set of registers. Bytes of data, decimal values, hexadecimal digits and single bit values can be shifted, switched, or altered at will.

Example 1. If the programmer has a particular division to accomplish that meets the qualifications required by the SRDL instruc-

tion, this example will demonstrate the proper means of aligning the remainder. General register 4 contains a fixed-point positive value of +277,169, which is to be divided by a value of +16. Upon completion of the division by shifting, the remainder must be aligned in general register 5. The instruction statements that have been coded to perform this operation are:

```
SRDL    4,4
SRL     5,28
```

The action generated by these statements would appear to be:

General registers 4 & 5 (Before SRDL)

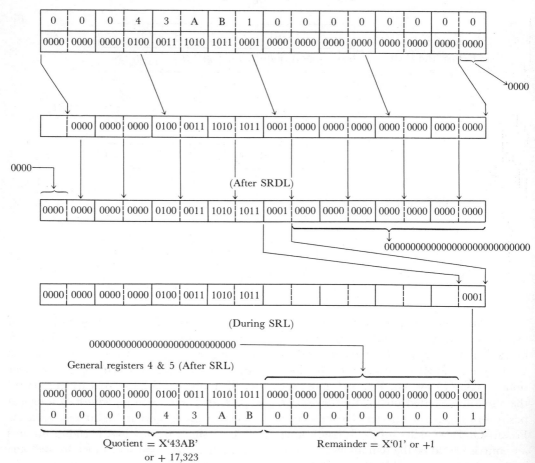

Quotient = X'43AB'
or + 17,323

Remainder = X'01' or +1

The first instruction statement created a logical right shift of all bits for a move of four bit positions in length. The four bits shifted out of general register 5 represent the remainder resulting from the divide operation. In order for these four bits to have a

fixed-point value of their own, they must be right-aligned within register 5. The four bit positions occupied by the remainder are subtracted from the total number of bit positions contained within a general register (32), the resulting difference of 28 being the number of positions that the remainder must be shifted. The second instruction statement performs the single register logical right shift for a move length of 28 bit positions and the remainder has assumed its own identity as a fixed-point value of $+1$.

Example 2. This example is presented only for the purpose of indicating the versatility of the combined use of various shift instructions. It is not suggested for any specific application, although it may well have a unique use in some programmers' logic for

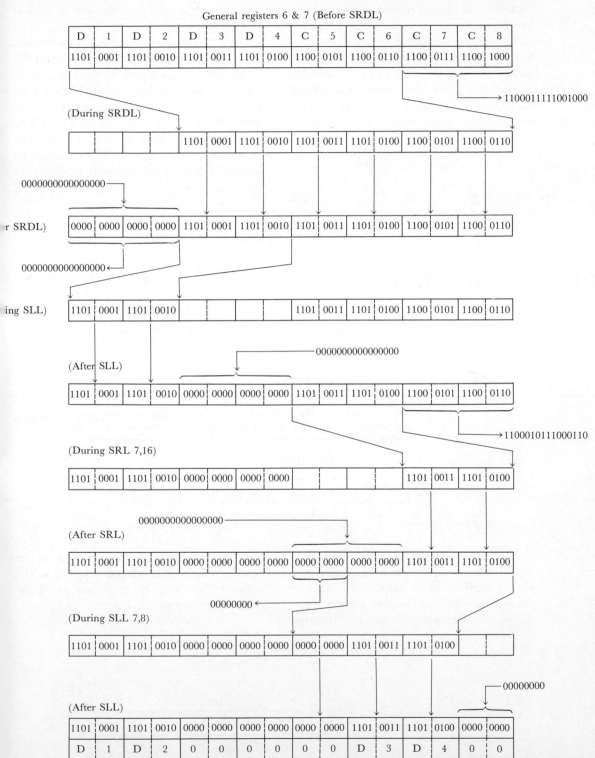

a problem program. In this instance, the pair of general registers (6 and 7) contain X'D1D2D3D4' and X'C5C6C7C8'. The task to be performed is to move the low-order two bytes (X'D3D4') from general register 6, using them to replace the middle two bytes (X'C6C7') of general register 7. The first and last bytes of register 7 should be cleared to X'00' configuration and the low-order two bytes of general register 6 should be cleared to X'0000'. Although this same task could be performed with the various Store, Load and Move instructions, the means of doing it with Shift instructions only would be:

```
SRDL      6,16
SLL       6,16
```

```
SRL       7,16
SLL       7,8
```

See general registers 6 and 7 (Before SRDL) on page 201.

The specifications of the task have now been met through the sole use of logical shifting operations.

(b) "Algebraic" Shifting Operations. While the logical shift instructions consider all bit positions as part of the shift operation, the algebraic shift instructions always consider the left-most (high-order) single bit position as being an unmovable sign-bit. The supplying of bit values to vacated high-order or low-order bit positions differ between the logical and the algebraic shift as shown in this illustration.

Logical shifts

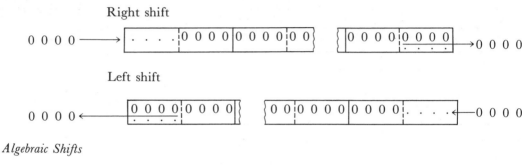

Algebraic Shifts

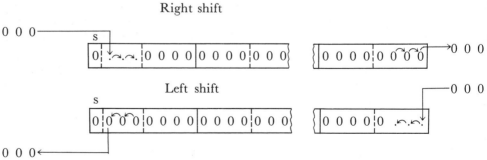

Algebraic shift operations maintain the fixed-point configuration of a general register, regardless of its positive or negative value. This is accomplished by separate functions in the algebraic left shift and the algebraic right shift. In the performance of the algebraic right shift, all bits supplied to the vacated high-order bit positions are of the same value as the sign-bit:

Six bits supplied to a positive value

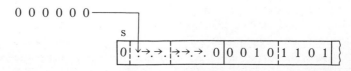

Six bits supplied to a negative value

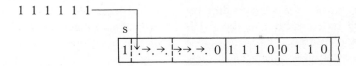

As shown here, the value of the bits supplied to the vacated high-order bit positions are of the same value as the sign-bit.

In the performance of the algebraic left shift, the continuity of the fixed-point value is preserved by "dropping out" the bit values just prior to the sign-bit. At this point, the left algebraic shifts perform another unique function. If a bit-value unlike the value of the sign-bit is shifted out of the high-order end of the integer bits, a fixed-point overflow exception is signaled and a program interrupt will occur. The bit value that is unlike the sign-bit value is considered to be a significant-digit bit; for a positive value, a one-bit is a significant-digit bit; for a negative value, a zero-bit is a significant-digit bit. The conditions wherein a significant-digit bit being shifted out would cause a program interrupt are:

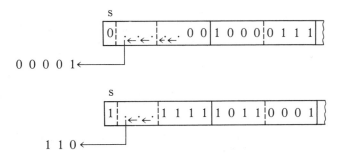

As soon as a significant-digit bit (a bit unlike the sign-bit) is shifted out of the high-order of the integer field, the fixed-point overflow exception occurs. Based on the foregoing information, it is now evident that algebraic shift operations are primarily intended for applications involving fixed point arithmetic operations and functions.

(1) Shift Left Algebraic (SLA). The SLA instruction will shift all 31 integer-bits contained within the general register specified by the first operand by the number of positions specified by the second operand. For applications with this shift, and all other algebraic shifts, the integer-bits are construed to be all bit positions other than the single high-order bit position. In a regular 32-bit general register, the left-most bit position is understood to be the sign-bit, while the remaining 31 bit positions comprise the integer value. In a double register algebraic shift operation, consisting of a total of 64 bit positions, the left-most bit position of the combined length of both registers is considered to be the sign-bit and the remaining 63 bit positions contain the bits to be shifted.

As the Shift Left Algebraic instruction is executing, bits will be shifted to the left for the specified number of positions. Bits being shifted out of the high-order end of the integer portion of the register will be dropped out of the bit position next to the sign-bit. The sign-bit will not be shifted or altered. As low-order bit positions are vacated by bits being shifted to the left, the vacated positions will be supplied with zero bits. In the event that a significant-digit bit is shifted out of the highest-order integer-bit position, a fixed-point overflow exception occurs. The algebraic shift left may be used for multiplication operations with the limiting factor that the value of the desired multiplier may only be one of the increments of the Powers-Of-Two table—2, 4, 8, 16, 32, 128, 256, etc.—and that the multiplicand must be a positive value. If the multiplication operation performed by shifting should happen to result in a product that is too large to be contained within a 31-bit integer, a significant-digit bit will be shifted out, resulting in the fixed-point overflow condition. The performance of the SLA instruction is illustrated in these examples;

Example 1. For this example, general register 3 contains a fixed-point value of +379,518.

By using the SLA instruction, the programmer intends to multiply that value by +32. In order to do so, the coding must indicate an algebraic left shift for a length of five bit positions.

$$SLA \qquad 2,5$$

The execution of this instruction statement would perform as follows:

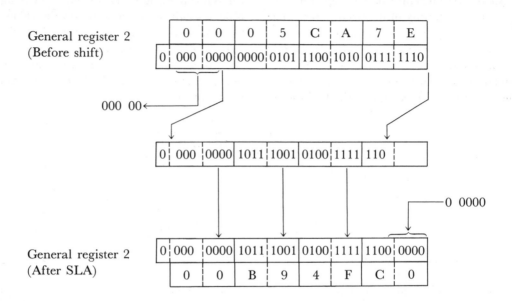

The product resulting from this shift of general register 2 indicates that:

32 times 379,518 equals 12,144,576

The number of bit positions to be shifted was determined by the fact that the fifth increment of the Powers-Of-Two table is a value of 32—2, 4, 8, 16, 32. Hence the shift was indicated to be effective for a move length of five bit positions.

Example 2. In this example, the programmer wishes to find the length of any one of a series of flexible tables contained within his program. There are a set of twelve tables, each table being comprised of four-byte segments. Although each table has a maximum allocated length of 2048 bytes reserved for it (or a maximum of 512 segments), the program logic intends only to use as much of the table as has been loaded with data at program

execution time. The amount of data stored into each table has been counted, by segments, and the programmer desires to use shifting to determine the byte length of usable data within each table. Because the length of each segment is four bytes, the proper answer may be obtained by coding this instruction statement:

$$SLA \qquad 8,2$$

This instruction statement implies that general register 8 contains the number of valid data segments in any given table and will effectively multiply that number of segments by a value of +4, the length of each segment, in order to arrive at the overall byte length of the valid data segments portion of the table. If, in this example, the table segment count in general register 8 was +317, the SLA instruction statement would result in this type of performance:

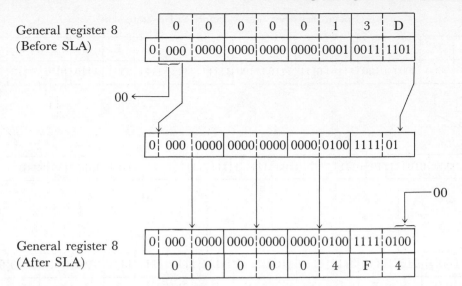

General register 8 (Before SLA)	0	0	0	0	0	1	3	D

General register 8 (After SLA)

| 0 | 0 | 0 | 0 | 0 | 4 | F | 4 |

The SLA instruction has functioned as a multiplication routine—general register 8 now contains a fixed-point value of +1268, the total length of the valid data segments in that particular table.

(*2*) *Shift Left Double Algebraic (SLDA)*. The SLDA instruction, another double register shift, considers the combined length of two general registers as consisting of a single high-order sign-bit and 63 integer-bits. As in the case of other double register shifts, the set of general registers must be an even-odd consecutive pair and the shift instruction statement must address the even-numbered register as the first operand. The length of the shift of the 63 integer-bits is specified by the second operand of the instruction statement. Bits shifted out of the high-order of the even-numbered register are dropped immediately prior to the sign-bit position, each bit being inspected as it is dropped. If a significant-digit bit is shifted out, the fixed-point overflow exception occurs. Bits shifted out of the odd-numbered register, including its assumed sign-bit, are shifted along into the even-numbered register without inspection. If the fixed-point value in the odd-numbered register was a negative value, the high-order one-bit sign-bit of that register would be shifted into the even-numbered register where it would represent the Powers-Of-Two value of the position where it resided upon completion of the shift. Low-order bit positions vacated as a result of the shift are supplied with zero-bits, regardless of the positive or negative configuration contained within either register.

Using the values of +321,516 and −6810 as the contents of general registers 2 and 3, the bit configuration of these registers would be:

General registers 2 and 3

0	0	0	4	E	7	E	C	F	F	F	F	E	5	6	6
0:000	0000	0000	0100	1110	0111	1110	1100	1:111	1111	1111	1111	1110	0101	0110	0110

If each of these general registers were interpreted individually as containing fixed-point values, the high-order bit position would be considered to be the sign-bit. However, if these registers were used in conjunction with an SLDA instruction, only the left-most bit position of the combined registers (the high-order bit of register 2) would be considered to be the sign-bit. An instruction statement such as:

SLDA   2,4

would then shift the entire 63 integer bits in this manner:

General registers 2 and 3 (Before SLDA statement)

0	0	0	4	E	7	E	C	F	F	F	F	E	5	6	6
0 000 0000	0000 0100	1110 0111	1110 1100	1 111 1111	1111 1111	1110 0101	0110 0110

0000←⏝

| 0 000 0000 | 0100 1110 | 0111 1110 | 1100 1111 | 1 111 1111 | 1111 1110 | 0101 0110 | 0110 |

0000

0 000 0000	0100 1110	0111 1110	1100 1111	1 111 1111	1111 1110	0101 0110	0110 0000
0	0	4	E	7	E	C	F	F	F	F	E	5	6	6	0

General registers 2 and 3 (After SLDA statement)

This shift has resulted in the moving of the four high-order one-bits from general register 3 into the four low-order bit positions of general register 2. Register 2 now contains a hexadecimal configuration of X'004E7ECF' that is a fixed-point value of +5,144,271; register 3 contains X'FFFE5660', the fixed-point value of −108,975.

(3) *Shift Right Algebraic (SRA).* The Shift Right Algebraic instruction will shift the 31 integer-bits of the value contained in a general register. The shift will be toward the low-order positions of that general register. The bits are shifted right for the length specified by the second operand of the instruction statement. As with other algebraic shift instructions, the high-order sign-bit is not disturbed by the shift of the integer-bits. Bits shifted out of the low-order positions of the register are lost without inspection for significant-digit bits. As high-order integer-bit positions are vacated, bits of the same value as the sign-bit are supplied to the vacated positions:

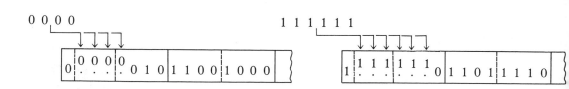

In order to illustrate this action more thoroughly, two examples are presented, one representing the SRA shift of a positive and the other representing the SRA shift of a negative value.

Example 1. General register 9 contains a fixed-point value of −811,574 that is to be shifted to the right algebraically for a length of six bit positions. The instruction statement that should be coded, and the resulting action, are:

SRA   9,6

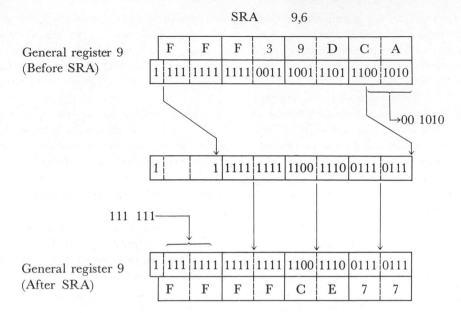

As indicated, the shift has caused the shifting-out of significant-digit bits from the low-order positions of the register without signaling this event. The bits supplied to the vacated high-order integer-bit positions were one-bits—the same as the sign-bit of the original negative value occupying that general register.

Example 2. For this example, general register 10 will contain a fixed-point value of +14,893,275. This shift is to be for a length of 12 bit positions. The coding and the representative action resulting from execution of the instruction statement would be:

SRA   10,12

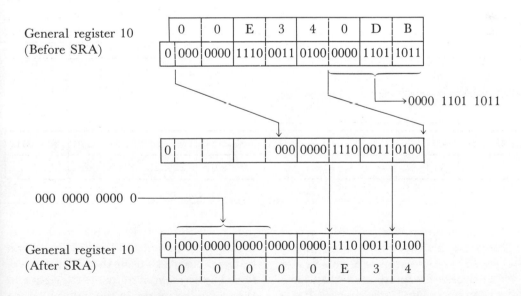

This example has, in effect, divided the original value, as contained in general register 10, by a divisor of 4096. The result contained within register 10 (+3636) represents the unrounded quotient resulting from that divide. The remainder portion of the answer was lost when the low-order integer-bits were shifted out. The value of the divisor was determined by the number of bit positions shifted—a shift of 12 positions representing the twelfth increment in the Powers-Of-Two table—2, 4, 8, 16, 32, 64, 128, 256, 512, 1024, 2048, 4096.

(*4*) *Shift Right Double Algebraic (SRDA).* The SRDA instruction follows the rules of the SRA instruction, except that it performs the shift on an even-odd pair of general registers. Consequently, the maximum shift length of this instruction is the total length of the assumed integer—63 bits. As in all double register shifts, the assumed sign-bit of the odd-numbered register has no significance as a sign-bit. It is considered to be a portion of the overall integer and is shifted along with the other integer-bits. The leftmost bit of the combined registers is construed to be the sign-bit for the entire integer and as such it is not moved or altered by this instruction. All bits shifted out of the low-order positions of the odd-numbered register, regardless of their significance, are considered to be lost. Bits supplied to the vacated high-order bit positions of the integer are of the same configuration as the sign-bit—zero-bits for positive values, one-bits for negative values. A positive fixed-point value contained within an even-numbered register can be shifted in its entirety into the consecutive odd-numbered register, at the same time effectively setting the even-numbered register to +0. Using a fixed-point value of +16,295,799 as the contents of general register 4, the proper instruction statement and its execution might appear as:

$$\text{SRDA} \qquad 4,32$$

General registers 4 and 5 (Before shift)

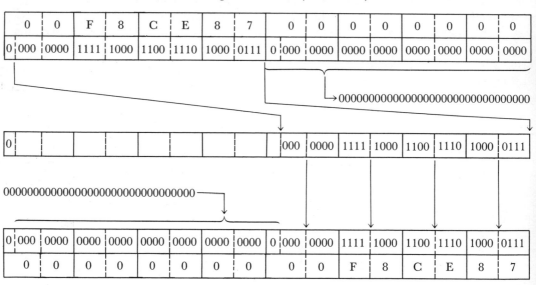

General registers 4 and 5 (After SRDA shift)

The configuration that originally existed in general register 4 has now been effectively transferred to general register 5, with register 4 being cleared for future use by the same instruction statement. If this same result was accomplished through the use of the various Load instructions, it would require two complete instruction statements.

A simple "divide" process of positive values, in which the divisor is one of the increments of the Powers-Of-Two table, can also be accomplished by using the SRDA instruction. The dividend is shifted to the right and the remainder resides in the right-most (the odd-numbered) register after completion of the shift. A logical right shift is then performed on the odd-numbered register for a length that will move the low-order bit of the remainder into the low-order bit position of that register. In processing such a division routine, wherein the value of +93,268 was to be divided by +8, the statement coding would appear as:

SRDA 10,3
SRL 11,29

Although it would make no difference as to the contents of general register 11 at the time these statements were executed, assume that it contained a value of +10. The action of the statements on the contents of the general registers would appear to be:

General register 10 and 11 (Before SRDA)

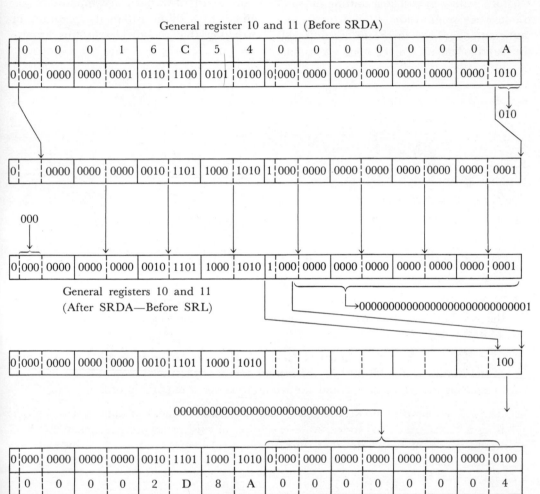

General registers 10 and 11
(After SRDA—Before SRL)

General registers 10 and 11
(After SRL)

The SRDA instruction statement effected the division of "93,268 divided by 8 equals 11,658," with the three bits that were shifted into the high-order of general register 11 comprising the remainder. The SRL instruction statement aligned those three bits into the low-order positions of general register 11, therein creating a valid fixed-point value for representing the division remainder of +4.

Throughout the explanations of the per-formance of the shift instructions and the applicable examples, comments have basic-ally related to the alteration of character or hexadecimal data representation and fixed-point value manipulation. This relationship has been stressed only for the purpose of clarifying the manner in which these in-structions perform, and in no way implies a limitation of their use to this type of func-tion. The various bit positions within one or two general registers can be cleared to zero-bits, set to one-bits, or switched around in many different patterns through the combined use of the logical and algebraic left and right shift instructions. "Bit Switches" contained within a register format could easily be cleared to an "off" condition or to an "on" setting by utilizing shifting instructions. Such applications cannot totally be anticipated; more often, the use of a shift will be found to lend itself to a unique or peculiar task that otherwise might require multiple instruction statements. Depending on the conditions leading up to the placement of the value in the registers, and the eventual disposition of the resulting values, it is probable that any of the arithmetic operations performed in the examples within this section could have been accomplished more efficiently with the arithmetic operations instructions that are provided for this purpose.

Review Exercises

The "Move" Instructions

1. The two format types of "move" instructions are the SS format and the ___*SI*___ format.

2. The Move Numeric instruction will move only the right ___*4*___ bits of each byte of the sending field to each byte of the receiving field.

3. The ___*MVI*___ instruction will move one byte of immediate data, as specified by the second operand of the instruction statement, into the single byte of storage that is addressed by the first operand.

4. The ___*MVZ*___ instruction will move the contents of the left nibble of each byte of the storage area addressed by the second operand into the corresponding left nibble of each byte of the first operand storage address, for a maximum of 256 bytes.

5. The following instruction statement would cause a movement of data that is referred to as a "___*Sliding*___" move. After execution of this instruction statement, FIELD7 would consist of data bytes that were all identical to the ___*first*___ byte of that field.

        SETLIKE   MVC   FIELD7+1(17),FIELD7

6. If BYTEA contained a valid blank, X'40', and BYTEB contained X'F6', the following instruction statement should have a mnemonic op code of ___*MVZ*___ in order for that statement to change the character configuration of BYTEA from a blank to an EBCDIC numeric character of zero.

        ALTERFLD   ____   BYTEA,BYTEB

7. The ___*MVN*___ instruction will move the right nibble of each byte of the storage area addressed by the second operand into the corresponding right nibble of each byte of the first operand storage area, for a length of up to 256 bytes.

8. When an explicit length attribute is not stated within an MVC (Move Characters) instruction statement the length of the move is determined by the implied length of the field addressed by the ___*1st*___ operand.

9. The ___*MVC*___ instruction will move the storage bytes addressed by the second operand into the storage bytes addressed by the first operand, for the length implied or specified by the first operand but not exceeding 256 bytes.

10. If an MVN instruction statement is executed wherein the sending byte contains X'D7' and the receiving field byte originally contains X'F0', the receiving field byte will subsequently contain an EBCDIC numeric character of ___*7*___.

11. Data fields in excess of 256 bytes may be moved from one storage location to another by "___*CHAINING*___" a series of MVC instruction statements.

12. In the following problems, one or more storage areas are defined in the sequence in which they reside in core storage. Examine the contents of the fields and the instruction statement and then fill in the configuration of the receiving field in the blank layout provided. Express the contents of this field in the same format as its original configuration—if it was in hex format before the move, express it as a hex format after the move, etc.

12a. FIELD1

A	3	9

FIELD2

5	6

FIELD3

G	∅	∅	9	6

MVC   FIELD3+1(4),FIELD1

FIELD3

G	A	3	9	5

12b. FLD4

D	A	T	A

MVI   FLD4+3,X'C5'

FLD4

D	A	T	E

12c. DATASET

C	2	4	0	4	0	D	5	C	4	E	8

MVC   DATASET+1(2),=CL2'RA'

DATASET

C	2	D	9	C	1	D	5	C	4	E	8

12d. COUNTFLD

R	H	X	O	N

AUDITFLD

1	2	3	4	5

MVZ   COUNTFLD,AUDITFLD

COUNTFLD

12e. CHEXFLD

F	F	2	0	9	C

MVI   CHEXFLD+2,B'00100000'

CHEXFLD

12*f.* AFLD

A	T

BFLD

E	A	T	S

CFLD

T	R	I	P

```
MVC     CFLD+2(2),BFLD+3
MVC     CFLD(2),AFLD+2
```

CFLD

12*g.* FLD1B

2	4	9	3	8

FLD1G

R	T	Q	C	W	B

```
MVN     FLD1G+1(5),FLD1B
```

FLD1G

12*h.* SET1

H	I	B	R	O	W	S

SET2

H	J	P	G	H

```
MVZ     SET2+1(4),SET1+2
```

SET2

12*i.* SETPAK

0	0	0	0

```
MVI     SETPAK,C'Ø'
MVI     SETPAK+1,B'01011100'
```

SETPAK

12*j.* INFIELD

D	A	T	A	9	9

```
MVI     INFIELD,C'9'
MVC     INFIELD+1(3),INFIELD
```

INFIELD

12*k.* DATAREV

G	L	A	R	E	D

```
MVC     DATAREV(2),DATAREV+3
```

DATAREV

The "Store" Instructions

13. In the following instruction statement the low-order byte of the first operand register must contain a valid EBCDIC character. (True) (False)

$$STC \qquad 6,HOLDBYTE$$

14. The ___STH___ instruction will store the low-order two bytes of the first operand register into the first two bytes of a halfword-aligned storage location.

15. The ___STM___ instruction will store a series of contiguous general registers into an equal quantity of contiguous fullword storage areas.

16. The ___ST___ instruction will store the contents of the first operand register into the four bytes of the fullword-aligned storage area of the second operand.

17. When a Store (ST) instruction statement is executed, only the low-order three bytes of the first operand register are stored into the second operand fullword. (True) (False)

18. The ___STC___ instruction will store the contents of the low-order byte of the first operand register into the single storage byte addressed by the second operand of the instruction statement.

19. If a Store Halfword instruction statement is coded within which the second operand defines a fullword of storage, the low-order ___2___ bytes of the first operand register will be stored into the ___High order___ two bytes of the fullword.

20. There would be a total of ___Nine___ general registers stored into a like number of fullwords by this instruction statement:

$$STM \qquad 12,4,FULLWDS$$

21. In the following set of instruction statements, the statement labeled MODFY would alter the statement labeled MVCHAR so that when MVCHAR was executed it would move a total of _____ bytes. (Register 12 contains a hexadecimal configuration of X'00000009').

```
MODFY     STC     12,MVCHAR+1
MVCHAR    MVC     FIELDREC(5),FIELDSND
```

22. If general register 10 contains a fixed-point value of $-319,771$, then the fullword labeled POSTVFWD will contain a fixed-point value of _____ after execution of this instruction statement:

```
STOREPOS     ST     10,POSTVFWD
```

23. The following instruction statement would store the contents of the specified general registers into a total of _____ contiguous bytes of storage beginning at the point addressed by the label SETWORDS, if that address was on a fullword boundary of storage.

```
DATASET     STM     15,0,SETWORDS
```

24. The following problems define one or more general registers and storage areas. Examine the contents of the specified operands and then fill in the configuration of the receiving field in the blank field layout provided. Express the contents of this field in the same format as it was originally defined—if it was in hex format before the "store" instruction statement, express it in hex format after it has been stored.

24a. Register 5

0	0	0	0	2	5	3	1

FULLWD6

0	0	2	8	0	9	7	D

STH   5,FULLWD6

FULLWD6

24b. Register 6

0	0	0	3	9	5	6	C

Register 7

0	0	0	0	0	F	C	3

Register 8

0	0	6	9	2	1	C	6

Register 9

0	0	0	C	0	7	4	2

SETWD1

0	0	0	0	0	0	0	0

SETWD2

0	0	0	0	0	0	0	0

SETWD3

0	0	F	3	2	6	5	7

SETWD4

0	0	0	0	0	0	7	3

STM   6,9,SETWD1

SETWD1

SETWD2

SETWD3

SETWD4

24c. Register 13

0	0	0	3	0	0	4	C

DAFLD

0	0	0	0	0	0	0	0

STC   13,DAFLD

DAFLD

24d. Register 8

F	F	2	9	0	0	6	C

DATA 8

0	0	0	0	0	5	C	6

F	9	0	3	2	2	0	0

ST   8,DATA8+4

DATA 8

The "Load" Instructions

25. The ___*LH*___ instruction will load two bytes of storage data, as aligned on a halfword boundary, into a general register in the form of a fullword. The two bytes of data are expanded to a fullword by propagation of the sign-bit throughout sixteen additional high-order bit positions.

26. The ___*LA*___ instruction will take the address generated by the second operand, either as an actual address or as one created by symbolic reference, and load it into the low-order three bytes of the first operand register. The high-order byte of the receiving register will be set to zero.

27. The ___*LPR*___ instruction will load the first operand register with a positive configuration of the value contained within the second operand register.

28. The instructions that are classified as "load" instructions can cause from ___*ONE*___ to ___*64*___ bytes of data to be placed into general registers.

29. One of the primary reasons for utilizing the LTR instruction is to test for the _____ or _____ configuration of a register.

30. The ___*L*___ instruction will load the first operand register with the contents of the fullword-aligned four bytes of storage data that are addressed by the second operand.

31. The ___*IC*___ instruction takes the single storage byte addressed by the second operand and loads it into the low-order byte of the general register specified by the first operand.

32. The ___*LNR*___ instruction will load the first operand register with a negative (two's complement) configuration of the value contained within the second operand register.

33. The maximum positive fixed-point value that can be loaded into a register by the Load Halfword instruction is _*32,767*_ .

34. The following instruction statement would load a total of _*32*_ bytes of storage into the specified general registers.

RELOAD   LM   9,0,REGAREAS

35. The ___*LR*___ instruction loads the first operand register with the unaltered contents of the second operand register.

36. The ___*LTR*___ instruction will load the value that is contained within the second operand register into the first operand register and then set the condition code to indicate the negative, positive, or zero condition of that value.

37. After execution of the following instruction statement, the high-order byte of register 12 would contain a hexadecimal configuration of X' _____ '.

LOADADDR   LA   12,FIELDB+255

38. Register 8 originally contains a hexadecimal configuration of X'712400FF'. After execution of the following instruction statement register 8 will contain X' _____ '.

LPR   8,8

39. The _____ instruction will take the fixed-point value contained within the second operand register, convert that value to its complement form, and then load that complement value into the first operand register.

40. The _____ instruction will load two or more contiguous fullwords of storage data, as addressed by the last operand, into the range of contiguous general registers specified by the first two operands.

41. If a halfword of storage, containing the EBCDIC alpha characters "AB," were loaded into general register 8 via the Load Halfword instruction, the hexadecimal contents of register 8 would then be:

Register 8   [| | | | | | |]

42. After execution of the following instruction statement, register 3 contains a hexadecimal configuration of X'03040506'. Therefore, register 7 must contain a hexadecimal configuration of X' _____ '.

FLIPREG   LCR   3,7

43. If general register 9 contained a hexadecimal configuration of X'003D0E46' after execution of the following instruction statement, general register 10 would have contained a hexadecimal configuration of X' _____ ' before execution of the instruction statement.

LTR   9,10

44. The following problems define one or more general registers and storage areas. Examine the contents of the specified operands and the instruction statements and then fill in the blank register layouts provided. Express the results in the same format as the register was originally defined—if it was in hex format before the "load" instruction, define and express it in hex format after it has been loaded, etc.

44a. Register 3   [0 | 0 | 0 | F | 3 | 9 | 2 | 0]

SETFLD   [0 | F | 3 | 9 | 0 | 0]

IC   3,SETFLD+2

Register 3   [| | | | | | |]

44b. Register 11   [0 | 0 | 0 | 0 | 9 | 3 | 2 | C]

LA   11,4095

Register 11   [| | | | | | |]

44c. Register 5 | 0 | 0 | 3 | 5 | 2 | 1 | F | F |

Register 6 | F | F | F | 2 | 0 | 5 | 9 | F |

LNR   5,6

Register 5 | | | | | | | | |

44d. Register 3 | F | F | F | F | 2 | 1 | F | 3 |

LCR   3,3

Register 3 | | | | | | | | |

44e. Register 4 | 0 | 6 | 3 | 9 | 0 | 0 | F | F |

LTR   4,4

Register 4 | | | | | | | | |

44f. Register 6 | 0 | 0 | 0 | 6 | 0 | F | 9 | 7 |

LNR   6,6

Register 6 | | | | | | | | |

44g. Register 8 | 0 | 0 | 0 | 0 | C | 0 | C | 0 |

Register 11 | F | 0 | F | F | 0 | C | 0 | C |

LR   8,11

Register 8 | | | | | | | | |

44h. Register 3 | 0 | 0 | 3 | 9 | 5 | 4 | 2 | D |

Register 4 | F | F | 3 | 9 | 5 | 4 | 2 | D |

LPR   3,4

Register 3 | | | | | | | | |

44i. Register 2 | 0 | 0 | 0 | 0 | 0 | 0 | 0 | 0 |

DATAWD | 0 | 0 | 0 | 6 | 5 | 1 | F | F |

L   2,DATAWD

Register 2 | | | | | | | | |

44j. Register 3

| 0 | 0 | 0 | 0 | 0 | 0 | 0 | 0 |

Register 4

| 0 | 0 | 0 | 0 | 0 | 0 | 0 | 0 |

Register 5

| 0 | 0 | 0 | C | F | D | 1 | B |

FULLWD1

| 0 | 0 | 6 | 9 | 3 | 2 | C | D |

| F | 0 | F | A | C | D | 6 | B |

| F | F | 3 | 9 | F | B | D | F |

| F | F | F | 2 | 9 | A | A | 6 |

LM   3,5,FULLWD1+4

Register 3

| | | | | | | | |

Register 4

| | | | | | | | |

Register 5

| | | | | | | | |

44k. Register 12

| 0 | 0 | C | 8 | 0 | 0 | 0 | 0 |

FULLWD1

| 3 | 2 | 5 | 1 | 7 | 6 | 5 | 4 |

LH   12,FULLWD1+2

Register 12

| | | | | | | | |

44l. Register 12

| F | F | 3 | 9 | 0 | 6 | 2 | 7 |

Register 2

| 0 | 0 | 0 | 0 | 7 | F | F | D |

LCR   12,12

Register 12

| | | | | | | | |

The "Shift" Instructions

45. The _____ operand of all shift instructions defines the number of bit positions that are construed to be the length of the shift.

46. A bit shift to the left for a length of three positions is the same as multiplying the positive value being shifted by _____ .

47. The _____ instruction will shift to the left all bits within a single general register without regard for the significance of the sign-bit.

48. In an algbraic right shift, bits supplied to vacated high-order bit positions will be identical to the _____ .

49. The _____ instruction will shift all integer-bits within a single register to the right for a maximum shift length of 31 bit positions.

50. In a double register algebraic shift all bits are shifted except the sign-bit of the _____-numbered general register.

51. The _____ instruction will shift all bits contains within two contiguous general registers to the left for a maximum of sixty-four bit positions.

52. In a double register shift the first operand of the instruction must address the _____-numbered register of the contiguous pair of general registers.

53. The _____ instruction will shift all bits to the right within a single register, supplying the vacated high-order bit positions with zero-bits.

54. In an algebraic left shift an overflow exception will occur whenever a bit _____ the sign-bit has been shifted out of the high-order integer-bit position.

55. The _____ instruction will shift the 63 integer-bits of a contiguous pair of general registers to the left for a maximum of 63 bit positions.

56. On a double register shift the sign-bit of the _____-numbered register is considered to be only another integer-bit.

57. The _____ instruction will shift to the right all of the 31 integer-bits contained within a single general register.

58. In all left-shift operations _____-bits are supplied to the vacated bit positions.

59. The _____ instruction will shift the entire 64 bits of a pair of contiguous registers to the right for a maximum of 64 bit positions, supplying the vacated high-order bit positions with _____-bits.

60. A shift to the right for a length of 5 bit positions will result in a value that would be the same as a quotient resulting from the division of a positive value by a value of _____ .

61. The _____ instruction will shift the 63 integer-bits of a pair of contiguous registers to the right for a maximum of _____ bit positions.

62. A double register logical shift to the right for a length of 32 bit positions will result in the even-numbered register containing a value of _____ .

63. The following problems define one or more general registers. Examine the contents of the specified operands, study the instruction statements and then express the results in both binary and hexadecimal format.

63a. Register 5

1000	0000	1110	1111	1000	0111	0100	0011

SRA   5,7

Register 5 (Binary)

(Hex)

63b. Registers 2 and 3

| 0000 | 0000 | 0011 | 0110 | 0011 | 1111 | 1110 | 0000 | 0000 | 1111 | 1111 | 1110 | 0101 | 1001 | 1000 | 0100 |

SLDL   2,18

Registers 2 and 3 (In binary and hex)

(Binary)

(Hex)

63c. Register 10

| 0000 | 1000 | 1110 | 0010 | 1011 | 1010 | 0111 | 1011 |

SLL   10,32

Register 10 (Binary)

(Hex)

63d. Register 9

| 1111 | 0100 | 1110 | 0101 | 1101 | 1011 | 1110 | 0111 |

SRL   9,12

Register 9 (Binary)

(Hex)

63e. Registers 6 and 7

| 1111 | 1000 | 0111 | 1011 | 1010 | 0000 | 1110 | 0101 | 0000 | 0000 | 0100 | 1101 | 1001 | 1111 | 0101 | 1011 |

SLDA   6,4

Registers 6 and 7 (Binary and hex)

63f. Registers 10 and 11

| 1000 | 0000 | 0000 | 0000 | 0000 | 0000 | 1000 | 0001 | 0000 | 1111 | 1111 | 0101 | 1011 | 1101 | 0011 | 0000 |

SRDA   10,31

Registers 10 and 11 (Binary and hex)

63g. Register 2

0000	0000	1000	1100	0001	1101	0100	0010

$$\text{SLA} \qquad 2,7$$

Register 2 (Binary)

(Hex)

63h. Registers 8 and 9

0010	1000	0000	1100	1111	1101	0001	1000	0111	1111	0000	0101	1111	1101	0001	1000

$$\text{SLL} \qquad 9,16$$
$$\text{SRDL} \qquad 8,16$$

Registers 8 and 9 (Binary and Hex)

PACKED DECIMAL ARITHMETIC OPERATIONS

A. THE PACKED DECIMAL ARITHMETIC INSTRUCTIONS

INSTRUCTION: PACK

Mnemonic	Hex Code	Operand Format
PACK	F2	$D_1(L_1,B_1),D_2(L_2,B_2)$

The PACK instruction will take the stored data (assumed to be zoned decimals) specified by the second operand and convert it into packed decimal format in the storage address specified by the first operand. The converted data is supplied to the first operand storage area in half-bytes, moving from right to left. The first nibble (half-byte) supplied is the sign of the zone from the rightmost (low-order) byte of the sending field (the second operand). This is placed in the low-order four bit positions of the receiving field, the first operand. The next nibble supplied to the receiving field is the numeric value of the same byte from which the sign-

zone was taken, the right-most byte of the second operand. These two half-bytes have now reversed their position from the sending field and reside within the receiving field with the zone value in the right nibble and the numeric value in the left nibble of the low-order byte. The instruction at this point will now only transfer the right nibble (numeric value) of each byte from the sending field. However, they will be placed in the receiving field in contiguous half-byte positions. If the instruction statement should run out of sending field area data before the receiving field is filled, it will insert hexadecimal zeros in the remaining high-order nibbles. If the first operand field is filled before the second operand field has run out of sending data, the remaining data to be sent is ignored. Since all data is not transmitted between the operands (only one zone-value nibble is moved), it is obvious that the first operand will not require a byte-length attribute equal to that of the second operand. The formula for computing the byte length of the field that is to contain the packed decimal format is:

> Length of second operand plus 1 divided by 2 equals required length for first operand, rounded high for any fractions.

This formula would apply as:

	Example 1	*Example 2*
Length of the second operand field	5	10
Add one byte for the sign-zone	1	1
Sum	6	11
Sum divided by 2	3	5½
Rounded high		6
Required length of first operand	3	6

The maximum explicit, or implied, length for either operand is 16 bytes.

The Condition Code setting is not changed by this instruction.

*   *   *

INSTRUCTION: UNPACK

Mnemonic	*Hex Code*	*Operand Format*
UNPK	F3	$D_1(L_1,B_1),D_2(L_2,B_2)$

The UNPACK instruction will take the storage data specified by the second operand (in packed decimal format) and convert it into zoned decimal format within the storage address specified by the first operand. The data is moved from right to left of the sending field to the receiving field. The sign of the packed field (the low-order four bits) is placed into the left nibble of the low-order byte of the zoned decimal receiving field. The right-most numeric digit associated with this sign within the packed field is moved into the right-most four bit positions of the receiving field to complete the single low-order signed, zoned decimal. Thereafter, the instruction will pick up each contiguous four-bit nibble, expand it to a full byte in zoned decimal format by applying a standard EBCDIC zone (hex digit 'F'), and place

that byte into the first operand field, loading the field from right to left. If the area specified by the first operand is longer than the field or area specified by the second operand, the unfilled high-order bytes of the first operand area are supplied with zoned decimal values of zero. If the second operand is longer than the first operand area, the unused high-order digits of the second operand area are ignored. In the event that the packed field contains a sign in the low-order four bits, the formula for computing the byte length of the field to contain the expanded, unpacked data is as follows:

> Length of the second operand times 2 less 1 equals required length for the first operand.

This may be applied as:

	Example 1	*Example 2*
Length of the second operand area	3	5
Multiplied by 2	×2	× 2
Product	6	10
Less 1 for the packed sign	−1	− 1
Required length for the first operand area	5	9

If the field that is being unpacked is not signed in the low-order four bits, the calculation is "Packed field times 2 equals required length for first operand area."

The maximum implied or explicit length for either operand is 16 bytes.

The Condition Code setting is not changed by the execution of this instruction.

*   *   *

INSTRUCTION: CONVERT TO BINARY

Mnemonic	*Hex Code*	*Operand Format*
CVB	4F	$R_1,D_2(X_2,B_2)$

The Convert To Binary instruction will take the packed decimal contents of the second operand and convert that value into a signed, binary integer in the general register specified by the first operand. The address generated by the second operand must be on a doubleword boundary alignment and consist of eight bytes containing packed decimal data. The sign of the packed decimal (the low-order half-byte) will create the sign-bit of the integer. The maximum packed decimal positive value that may be converted to binary format is 2,147,483,647. Any number greater than this will create a fixed-point division interruption during the conversion and will result in a program termination.

The Condition Code setting is not changed by this instruction.

* * *

INSTRUCTION:

CONVERT TO DECIMAL

Mnemonic	Hex Code	Operand Format
CVD	4E	$R_1,D_2(X_2,B_2)$

The Convert To Decimal instruction will take the 32-bit signed integer that is contained within the general register specified by the first operand and convert it to a packed decimal format within the area specified by the second operand. The address generated by the second operand must be that of eight bytes commencing on a doubleword boundary alignment. The packed decimal field will be signed in the low-order four bits (right-most half-byte) in accordance with packed decimal conventions.

The Condition Code setting is not changed by this instruction.

* * *

INSTRUCTION:

ZERO & ADD PACKED DECIMALS

Mnemonic	Hex Code	Operand Format
ZAP	F8	$D_1(L_1,B_1),D_2(L_2,B_2)$

This instruction will take the packed decimal contents of the second operand and place them into the storage area specified by the first operand, setting any additional high-order half-bytes of the receiving field to zero. This instruction is unique from other packed decimal instructions in that it is only necessary for the second operand to be in validly signed packed decimal format. If the length of the first operand field is greater

than that of the second operand field, the instruction will cause the high-order half-bytes to be filled with zero-digits for the unfilled portion of the first operand field. If the length of the first operand field is shorter than the length of the second operand area, an overflow condition will result. The maximum implied or explicit length for either operand is 16 bytes.

CC	BC	Condition
0	8	The value of the contents of the first operand is zero.
1	4	The first operand contains a value of less than zero (negative).
2	2	The first operand contains a value greater than zero (positive).
3	1	An overflow condition occurred during the execution.

* * *

INSTRUCTION:

ADD PACKED DECIMALS

Mnemonic	Hex Code	Operand Format
AP	FA	$D_1(L_1,B_1),D_2(L_2,B_2)$

This instruction will algebraically add the packed decimal contents of the second operand to the packed decimal contents of the first operand. The resulting sum will be placed within the field of the first operand and will contain an algebraically determined sign in the low-order half-byte. The packed decimal contents of both operands must have a valid packed decimal sign in the low-order half-byte of their area—a hex value of A through F (10 through 15) in the right-most nibble. There are two overflow conditions that might result from the execution of this instruction. They are:

1. If both operand fields are of equal length, a carry-out of a high-order digit might occur, depending entirely upon the values of the operand contents.

2. If the second operand length is greater than the length of the first operand, significant high-order digits in excess of the first operand length will be lost.

If the significant digits of a packed decimal field are less than half of the allowable maximum numeric value for that field, the number may be added to itself by coding the same field identity for both operands.

The maximum implied or explicit length for either operand is 16 bytes.

CC	BC	Condition
0	8	The first operand contains a value of zero.
1	4	The first operand contains a value of less than zero (negative).
2	2	The first operand contains a value greater than zero (positive).
3	0	An overflow exception occurred.

*   *   *

INSTRUCTION:

SUBTRACT PACKED DECIMALS

Mnemonic	*Hex Code*	*Operand Format*
SP	FB	$D_1(L_1,B_1),D_2(L_2,B_2)$

The Subtract Packed instruction will algebraically subtract the packed decimal contents of the second operand from the packed decimal contents of the first operand. The net difference between the two operands will replace the contents of the first operand and will be algebraically signed as the result of the subtraction. The packed decimal contents of both operands must contain a valid sign in the low-order half-byte (right-most four bits) of their data fields. The maximum implied or explicit length for either operand is 16 bytes.

CC	BC	Condition
0	8	The first operand contains a value of zero.
1	4	The first operand contains a value that is less than zero (negative).
2	2	The first operand contains a value greater than zero (positive).
3	1	An overflow condition occurred during execution of the instruction.

*   *   *

INSTRUCTION:

MULTIPLY PACKED DECIMALS

Mnemonic	*Hex Code*	*Operand Format*
MP	FC	$D_1(L_1,B_1),D_2(L_2,B_2)$

This instruction will multiply the packed decimal contents of the second operand (the multiplier) times the packed decimal contents of the first operand (the multiplicand). The packed contents of both operands must have a valid sign in the low-order half-byte of their data fields. The resulting product will occupy the whole of the first operand field. The sign of the product is determined algebraically by the signs of the multiplicand and the multiplier. The length of the multiplier may not exceed eight bytes, nor may the length be equal to, or greater than, the length specified by the first operand. A formula for determining the length of the first operand for a successful MP instruction statement would be:

Length of the Multiplier plus Length of the Multiplicand plus one byte equals the Product Area

	Example 1	*Example 2*
Multiplicand length	9	6
Multiplier length	4	5
Add one more byte	1	1
Product field length should be	14	12

By using this formula, a product overflow cannot occur. Since the definition of this instruction implies that the "multiplier is multiplied against the multiplicand," it should be mentioned that the following would be the normal sequence of consideration when creating an MP instruction statement.

1. The multiplier should be in a storage location.

2. The multiplicand should be in a storage location.

3. Determine the length required for the product and allocate an area or constant for it.

4. Load the multiplicand into the product area with a Zero & Add Packed instruction statement.

5. Code the Multiply Packed instruction statement.

The maximum allowable length of the product area is 16 bytes.

The Condition Code setting is not changed by this instruction.

* * *

INSTRUCTION:

DIVIDE PACKED DECIMALS

Mnemonic	*Hex Code*	*Operand Format*
DP	FD	$D_1(L_1,B_1),D_2(L_2,B_2)$

The Divide Packed instruction will divide the packed decimal contents of the second operand (the divisor) into the packed decimal contents of the first operand which contains the dividend. The contents of both operands must have a valid packed sign in the low-order half-byte of their data fields. The resulting quotient and remainder will replace the dividend in the field of the first operand. The quotient will be in the high-order bytes of the first operand field; its length will be the result of the subtraction of the length of the second operand from the length of the first operand field. The remainder from the divide operation will reside in the low-order bytes of the first operand field and will be the same number of bytes in length as the second operand field, the divisor. The signs of the divisor and dividend algebraically combine to determine the sign of the quotient; the value of the sign of the dividend creates the sign of the remainder. The length of the divisor may not exceed eight bytes, nor may the length of the divisor be equal to, or greater than, the length specified by the first operand.

The Condition Code setting is not changed by the execution of this instruction.

* * *

INSTRUCTION: MOVE WITH OFFSET

Mnemonic	*Hex Code*	*Operand Format*
MVO	F1	$D_1(L_1,B_1),D_2(L_2,B_2)$

The MVO instruction will move data by taking each byte of the storage area specified by the second operand and placing it into the storage area specified by the first operand, but offset to the left of the corresponding byte positions by one-half byte. The movement of the data within the fields is right to left in the transfer. Both the first operand and the second operand have their own length attribute for this instruction, but the offset is in the receiving field only. If the second operand is shorter in length than the first operand, the instruction statement will place hexadecimal zero-digits into the high-order nibbles of the first operand. If the first operand field is shorter in length than the second operand, the instruction will ignore data remaining to be moved once the first operand field is filled.

A maximum length of 16 bytes of data may be moved by this instruction.

The Condition Code setting is not changed by this instruction.

B. PACKED DECIMAL ARITHMETIC OPERATIONS

By utilizing System/360 Assembler Language, the programmer has access to three basic types of arithmetic instruction sets—fixed-point, packed decimal, and floating-point. For the reasons previously mentioned, floating-point features have been intentionally omitted from this text. Therefore, the subject matter of arithmetic operations will be limited to fixed-point and packed decimal instructions.

When referring to a fixed-point numeric (or a binary format decimal) within this text, it is construed to mean an integer value occupying a halfword, a fullword, or a general register in which the left-most (high-order) bit position identifies the sign of the value and the remaining bit positions comprise the whole of the integer. There must be at least one register operand in every fixed-point arithmetic instruction.

Packed decimal values are represented by a field of one or more bytes, in which the individual half-bytes (nibbles) represent a decimal value expressed in hexadecimal digit form. For arithmetic operations, the rightmost nibble of the packed field must contain a valid packed decimal sign. This would consist of a hexadecimal digit within the range of from X'A' through X'F'.

1. *Packed Decimal/Fixed-Point Conversion Processes*

The actual data that is to be used in arithmetic operations of any type often must be converted into the format of the particular type of arithmetic instructions that are to be coded. Accordingly, prior to investigating the use of the arithmetic instructions, the means of converting the data should be thoroughly explained.

Data that is received by the problem program in EBCDIC form may be converted first into packed decimal form and then into fixed-point or binary format. Data in binary or fixed-point format may be converted back to EBCDIC form by a reversal of those steps.

The transition of the data is as follows.

1. Incoming data is received in EBCDIC.
2. It is converted to packed decimals by the Pack instruction.
3. The packed decimal value is converted to binary or fixed-point by the Convert To Binary instruction.

1. The data is in binary or fixed-point format.
2. It is converted into packed decimals by the Convert To Decimal instruction.
3. The packed decimals are converted into EBCDIC character numerics by the Unpack instruction.

(a) The PACK Instruction. The Pack instruction is used to convert EBCDIC numeric character data into packed decimal form. In converting the data, the instruction takes the sign-zone of the low-order byte of the incoming data and places it into the low-order half-byte of the receiving field.

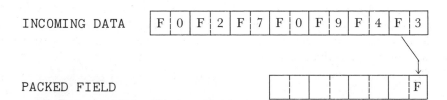

The numeric portion of the low-order byte of the incoming field is then placed into the other half of the low-order byte of the field that is being packed.

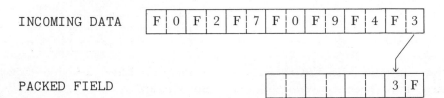

It then proceeds to take the numeric portion of each subsequent higher-order byte and places these hexadecimal digits into the subsequent higher-order half-bytes of the packed decimal receiving field.

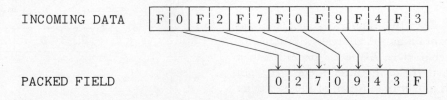

If the EBCDIC field contains more numeric characters than can be accommodated by the packed decimal field, the surplus high-order numeric digits are ignored. This is illustrated as:

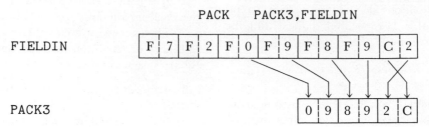

However if the EBCDIC field does not contain sufficient numeric characters to fill the high-order positions of the packed field, the Pack instruction will supply high-order packed decimal zero-digits to those positions.

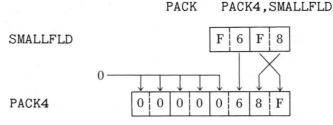

EBCDIC alpha characters could be converted into packed decimal format, but they could never be reconverted back into EBCDIC alpha characters again. The reason for this will be shown in the discussion of the Unpack instruction. There could be a reason, however, for desiring a one-way transformation of EBCDIC alpha characters into a packed decimal value. A transformation of this type would be:

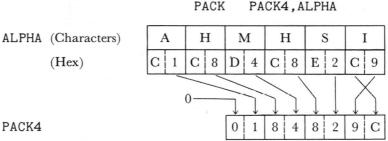

In this illustration, the EBCDIC alpha characters have been converted into a packed decimal value of +184,829.

Further examples of packed decimals are shown in the following illustrations.

Example 1

The EBCDIC numeric zoned decimal field, containing the equivalent of four numeric characters, has been packed into a three-byte field. Because there were not enough numerics to fill all of the half-bytes of the packed field, a high-order zero-digit was supplied.

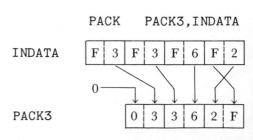

Example 2

PACK   PACK4+1(3),DATA+2(5)

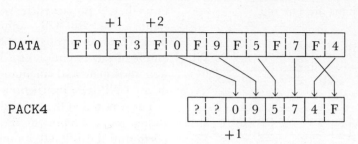

In this example, the low-order five bytes of a seven-byte EBCDIC numeric field have been packed into the low-order three bytes of a four-byte packed field. The contents of the high-order byte of the packed decimal field would remain unchanged from their previous configuration, whatever it was prior to the Pack.

(b)   The UNPACK Instruction. The re-verse process of the Pack instruction is created by the Unpack instruction, converting a packed decimal value into an EBCDIC numeric field. The instruction first takes the low-order half-byte of the packed decimal field and places it into the zone portion of the low-order byte of the receiving field.

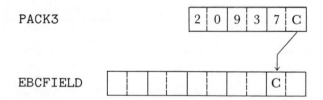

The low-order numeric digit of the packed field is then supplied to the numeric portion of the low-order byte of the receiving field.

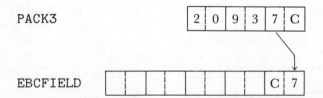

Each successive higher-order packed decimal digit is then inserted into the numeric portion of each successive high-order byte of the EBCDIC receiving field, the zone portion of the bytes being supplied with the standard zone of an EBCDIC numeric character.

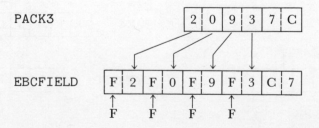

If the packed decimal field contains more numeric digits than the EBCDIC receiving field can accommodate, the surplus high-order packed digits are ignored.

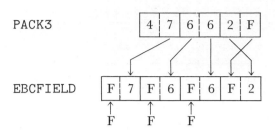

Regardless of the alpha or numeric representation of the data that was used to create a packed decimal field, if that field were immediately unpacked it would inevitably result in an EBCDIC numeric character field. This is illustrated in the following example of the execution of a PACK instruction statement and an immediately subsequent UNPACK instruction statement.

The reason that the low-order byte did not change is that it represents the zoned decimal portion of the EBCDIC numeric field.

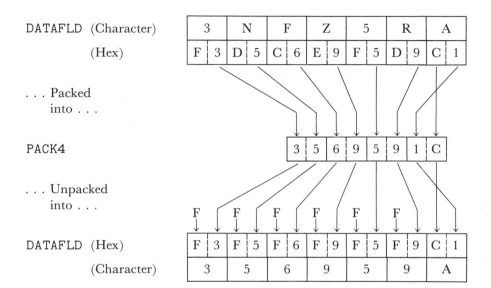

As with many other instructions, an explicit length attribute or address adjusting may be used to modify the portions of the fields that would be affected by the UNPACK instruction. This is illustrated within these examples.

In this example, the three numeric digits of the two-byte packed field were unpacked into the low-order three bytes of a field labeled DATA. The high-order byte of DATA would remain unchanged from what it was before execution of the UNPACK instruction.

Example 1

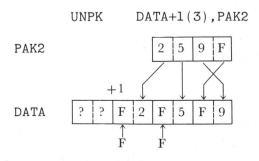

Example 2

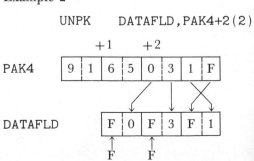

As shown here, the two low-order bytes of a four-byte packed decimal field, containing three numeric digits, are unpacked into a three-byte numeric character field.

(c) Convert to Binary (CVB). The CVB instruction will take a packed decimal value, as contained within an eight-byte doubleword-aligned field, and convert it to a binary-formatted fixed-point value within a general register. The first operand of the instruction statement indicates the register that is to contain the converted value and the second operand addresses the eight-byte field containing the packed decimal value. This is the second instruction that is required to convert an EBCDIC numeric character value to a fixed-point value—the first step is to pack the EBCDIC field. In order to establish the eight-byte doubleword field into which packed values may be placed, the programmer may use either of the following types of statements:

```
BIGDBWDA    DS    D          001
BIGDBWDB    DC    D'0'        002
```

The first statement reserves eight bytes of program storage, aligned on a doubleword boundary, but does not guarantee the contents of that area prior to moving a packed decimal value into it. The second statement creates an eight-byte doubleword, properly aligned, containing a value of +0, or all hexadecimal zero-digits.

In either case, the packed decimal value that is to be converted to binary format should be moved into the doubleword via the Zero & Add Packed (ZAP) instruction. This would guarantee that any previous contents of this doubleword area have been cleared out and the value being moved in will retain a valid packed decimal configuration.

Assume that a packed decimal field of four bytes, LITTLPAK, is to be converted to a binary value. It will first be moved into a field labeled DUBLPAK and then converted to binary-formatted fixed-point within general register 7. The configuration of these areas prior to execution of the instruction statements are:

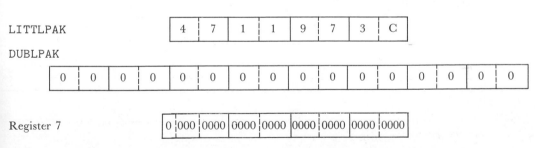

LITTLPAK

DUBLPAK

Register 7

The instruction statements that are to be executed are:

```
ZAP    DUBLPAK,LITTLPAK    001
CVB    7,DUBLPAK           002
```

Statement 001 will effectively place the contents of LITTLPAK into the low-order four bytes of DUBLPAK and reset the four

high-order bytes of DUBLPAK to contain hexadecimal zero-digits.

Statement 002 will take the packed decimal value of +4,711,973 as now contained in DUBLPAK and convert it to its fixed-point equivalent in general register 7. After execution of this statement these three areas will appear as:

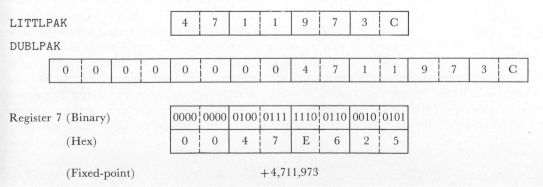

LITTLPAK

DUBLPAK

Register 7 (Binary)

(Hex)

(Fixed-point)   +4,711,973

(d) Convert To Decimal (CVD). The purpose of the CVD instruction is to take a binary-formatted fixed-point value and convert it into its equivalent packed decimal value format. The fixed-point value must reside within a general register and the receiving field must consist of eight bytes aligned on a doubleword boundary. The fixed-point value, contained within the general register specified by the first operand, is converted to packed decimal form and placed into the field that is addressed by the second operand.

Assuming that the fixed-point value resided in general register 5 and the receiving field is labeled PACK8D, the following examples illustrate various fixed-point values and the resulting packed decimal values after execution of a CVD instruction statement.

CVD   5,PACK8D

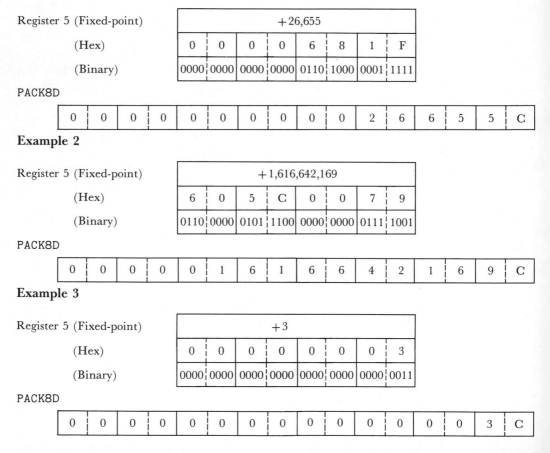

Example 1

Register 5 (Fixed-point): +26,655

(Hex): 0 0 0 0 6 8 1 F

(Binary): 0000 0000 0000 0000 0110 1000 0001 1111

PACK8D: 0 0 0 0 0 0 0 0 0 0 2 6 6 5 5 C

Example 2

Register 5 (Fixed-point): +1,616,642,169

(Hex): 6 0 5 C 0 0 7 9

(Binary): 0110 0000 0101 1100 0000 0000 0111 1001

PACK8D: 0 0 0 0 0 1 6 1 6 6 4 2 1 6 9 C

Example 3

Register 5 (Fixed-point): +3

(Hex): 0 0 0 0 0 0 0 3

(Binary): 0000 0000 0000 0000 0000 0000 0000 0011

PACK8D: 0 0 0 0 0 0 0 0 0 0 0 0 0 0 3 C

C. PERFORMING ARITHMETIC OPERATIONS WITH PACKED DECIMAL VALUES

One of the most frequent decisions made by the programmer results from the question, "Which arithmetic operation mode shall I use—fixed-point or packed decimal?" As might be expected, both types of arithmetic functions have offsetting attributes over the other. One of the key factors in making that decision should be the determination of the use that will be applied to the results of those calculations. A comparison of the performance of individual arithmetic operations between fixed-point and packed decimal instructions (i.e., Add versus Add Packed) will clearly indicate that the fixed-point instructions are considerably faster. However, if the data to be processed is entering the program in character format, or packed decimal format, and is to eventually be printed out or stored in a data set in character or packed decimal format, the wisest decision could be to perform all arithmetic functions in packed decimal mode. The instructions required to convert a packed decimal value to binary fixed-point values (CVB) and back to packed decimal format again (CVD) use considerable time. Any time saved by using fixed-point arithmetic routines may well be more than offset by the Convert To Binary and Convert To Decimal instructions. However, if the data to be processed (1) Enters the program logic in binary fixed-point format, or (2) will be put out or stored in binary fixed-point format, or (3) will be repetitiously used in fixed-point format, then it may be to the programmer's advantage to use fixed-point arithmetic operations. One of the other considerations that must be evaluated is the work area required by each of these types—fixed-point arithmetic operations require the use of *at least* one general register; packed decimal arithmetic operations use storage areas that are set up by the programmer in order for those instructions to perform. With fixed-point instructions, the programmer may find that he has to reuse several registers for many different functions. Providing that core space allocation is not a problem, the packed decimal instructions may be set up to use a separate work area for each set of statements.

General experience has indicated that if data resulting from arithmetic operations is to be printed, displayed, or stored on data sets in character or packed decimal format, it is normally advantageous to perform those arithmetic functions with packed decimal arithmetic instructions. However, there are numerous valid arguments for using either mode.

Before covering the applications of packed decimal arithmetic operations, it is in order to review the configuration and rules governing packed decimal arithmetic fields.

The configuration of a packed decimal value is directly related to the hexadecimal character concept. That is, each digit of a packed decimal value is represented by a hexadecimal character—one digit for every four binary bit positions. The hexadecimal characters or digits of '0' through '9' represent valid packed decimal numeric digits; the hexadecimal characters of 'A' through 'F' represent signs/zones for valid packed decimal arithmetic values. In order for a packed decimal value to be used in an arithmetic operation, it must have a valid sign (Hex 'A' through 'F') in the right-most half-byte of the field. All of the remaining hex digits in that field must have a value of hex '9' or less—hex '0' through '9'. If an attempt is made to process an invalidly packed decimal field, a program interrupt will occur, resulting in an abnormal termination (ABEND) of the task. It should be noted that unlike fixed-point arithmetic instructions, packed decimal arithmetic operations do not require word boundary alignment, nor do these use a general register. Therefore, the programmer may use as little as one byte, or as many as 16 bytes, in setting up the work areas for packed decimal arithmetic operations.

Another unique factor regarding any packed decimal instruction statement is the existence of the length attribute on both operands. This should be carefully noted, because the length attribute does exist for both operands whether it is implied or explicit. The reaction of the individual instructions to a variation of length attributes between operands must be considered when using packed decimal instructions.

Throughout the section dealing with fixed-point operations, all register and data field illustrations will be presented in both binary bit configuration and hexadecimal configuration. This will be done in order that the individual bit positions can be related to their Powers-Of-Two values. For the purpose of illustrating packed decimal fields in this section, however, all graphic presentations will be represented in hexadecimal format only, since this is the only relative association with packed decimals.

1. Zero & Add Packed Decimals (ZAP)

This instruction, often humorously referred to as "The ZAP," can efficiently perform the initialization of a nonformatted area to a formatted packed decimal work area, clear previous data stored in an area and reinitialize an area to zero, or move packed decimal data from a short packed decimal field to a longer packed decimal field without clearing all of the receiving field in advance. It will act on a maximum of 16 bytes of data for either operand. Upon issuance of a ZAP instruction statement, the system will effectively set all nibbles (half-bytes) in the first operand storage location to contain hexadecimal zero-digits if such nibbles were not directly affected by the data moved into the area as specified by the second operand. If the first operand is greater in length than the second operand, hex zero-digits will occupy the unfilled high-order positions of the first operand. If the first operand is not long enough to contain all of the significant hex digits (nonzeros) of the second operand, a program interruption will occur, indicated by a decimal overflow code contained within the Condition Code bits of the PSW. Some examples of the use of this instruction are presented in the following illustrations.

Example 1. The instruction statement to be executed is:

```
ZAP      FIELDA,=PL1'0'
```

Before execution of the statement, FIELDA appears to be:

Byte 1 Byte 2 Byte 3 Byte 4

FIELDA | 0 | 9 | F | 3 | 6 | 4 | B | 0 |

After execution of the ZAP instruction statement, the field will contain:

FIELDA | 0 | 0 | 0 | 0 | 0 | 0 | 0 | C |

Note that although a one-byte literal was specified as the second operand, the entire length of the first operand was configured with hex zero-digits.

Example 2. The instruction statement to be executed is:

```
ZAP      FLD1,FLD2+1(2)
```

Before the ZAP instruction statement is executed, the fields appear as:

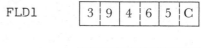

FLD1 | 3 | 9 | 4 | 6 | 5 | C |

FLD2 | 0 | 6 | 9 | 8 | 1 | C |

After the execution of the instruction statement these fields would be configured as:

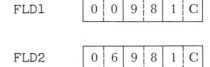

FLD1 | 0 | 0 | 9 | 8 | 1 | C |

FLD2 | 0 | 6 | 9 | 8 | 1 | C |

In this instance, the instruction statement specified that the data to be moved from FLD2 should commence one byte higher than the address of the first byte of FLD2. Therefore, only two bytes of data were transmitted from FLD2 to FLD1, and the unfilled half-bytes of FLD1 were set to hex zero-digits.

Example 3. The instruction statement to be executed is:

```
ZAP      PACKA,PACKB
```

The packed decimal fields to be affected by this statement are:

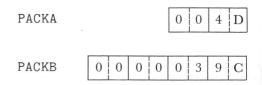

PACKA | 0 | 0 | 4 | D |

PACKB | 0 | 0 | 0 | 0 | 0 | 3 | 9 | C |

After the execution of the instruction statement these fields will appear as:

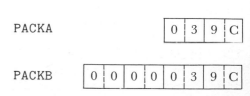

PACKA | 0 | 3 | 9 | C |

PACKB | 0 | 0 | 0 | 0 | 0 | 3 | 9 | C |

Although the field length of the first operand was shorter than that of the second operand, a program interrupt (decimal overflow) would not have occurred because no significant digits (nonzero hex values) were lost in the transmission.

Example 4. The instruction statement that is to be executed is:

```
ZAP     SETFLD,SETFLD+2(1)
```

The configuration of SETFLD before execution of the ZAP instruction statement is:

SETFLD

3	9	4	5	2	C

After execution of the instruction statement, SETFLD would appear as:

SETFLD

0	0	0	0	2	C

In this example, the ZAP instruction has effectively cleared the high-order bytes of a packed decimal field by incrementing the starting point of reference in the second operand, but referring to the same field as the second operand. Note that the explicit length attribute of one byte was used in order to limit the implied length of the second operand.

Example 5. This example is intended to show the use of explicit length attributes that are applicable to both operands in a packed decimal instruction. The instruction statement to be used for this example is:

```
ZAP   PACKER1+1(2),PACKER2+2(2)
```

The configuration of the fields referred to by this instruction are:

PACKER1

2	4	4	3	6	0	0	C

PACKER2

0	1	0	0	3	2	5	C

Once the instruction statement has been performed, the configuration of these fields would appear as:

PACKER1

2	4	3	2	5	C	0	C

PACKER2

0	1	0	0	3	2	5	C

Note that only bytes #2 and #3 of the PACKER1 field have been altered by the instruction statement. As specified by the first operand, the action to be performed on PACKER1 was to commence at one byte beyond the high-order point of that field and was to affect only two bytes of storage. After execution of this instruction statement, any attempt to use the four-byte contents of PACKER1 for arithmetic operations would result in a program interrupt. This is because one hex character position (the sixth half-byte from the left) is a nonnumeric digit residing at a point other than the low-order half-byte. This field could be used for arithmetic operations if the length attribute was specified as three—that is, PACKER1(3)—and only the left-most three bytes of data were acted upon. Even the single right-most byte of this field could be used if it were specified as PACKER1+3(1) in the instruction statement.

2. Add Packed (AP)

This instruction, which adds together two fields of packed decimal data, takes a form that is visually interpreted rather easily by the programmer. In other words, 4C + 6C equals 10C is easier to comprehend than is fixed-point arithmetics wherein F + F equals 1E. With this instruction, the packed decimal value of the second operand is added to the packed decimal value of the first operand and the resulting sum is placed in the first operand location. If the sum of the addition exceeds the length of the first operand location, a decimal overflow will occur, causing a program interruption. This can occur when the fields of both operands are of equal length, or when the length of the second operand field is greater than that of the first operand field and contains significant digits in the locations that are in excess of the length of the first operand field. A validly completed addition resulting in a zero sum will always have a positive (+) sign in the low order nibble. A valid positive sign may be a hex digit 'A', 'C', 'E', or 'F'. A valid negative sign may be either a hex digit 'B' or 'D'.

Example 1. Before the AP instruction is executed, the fields that are to be specified as the operands appear as:

PKFLD1 | 0 | 0 | 3 | 9 | 7 | C |

PKFLD2 | 0 | 0 | 0 | 9 | 9 | C |

The instruction statement that is to be executed is coded as:

    AP   PKFLD1,PKFLD2

After this AP instruction has been executed, the configuration of these fields would be:

PKFLD1 | 0 | 0 | 4 | 9 | 6 | C |

PKFLD2 | 0 | 0 | 0 | 9 | 9 | C |

Note that the data contained in the second operand field is not altered by the execution of the instruction statement. Since this is true in all cases of packed decimal arithmetic operations, any further examples contained in this section will show only the result of the changes to the first operand.

Example 2. The fields to be utilized by this example are:

PKA | 0 | 3 | 2 | 2 | 1 | C |

PKB | 3 | 6 | 4 | 4 | 7 | C |

The instruction statement that is to be executed is:

    AP   PKA,PKB+2(1)

After the instruction statement has been executed, PKA will have the hexadecimal configuration of:

PKA | 0 | 3 | 2 | 2 | 8 | C |

In this instance the second operand specified an address that was two bytes beyond the starting point of the PKB field and specified that only one byte should be added to the first operand. Therefore, the addition that was performed was equivalent to 03221C + 7C = 03228C. The 'C' suffix on each of these values is the packed decimal sign of the values.

Example 3. The configuration of the fields that are to be used by this example are:

PACKA | 0 | 0 | 1 | 0 | 8 | 2 | 1 | 0 | 0 | 0 | 5 | C |

PACKB | 3 | 0 | 0 | 6 | 1 | 1 | 1 | C |

The instruction statement that is to be executed is:

    AP   PACKA,PACKB

After execution of this statement the configuration of PACKA is:

PACKA | 0 | 0 | 1 | 1 | 1 | 2 | 1 | 6 | 1 | 1 | 6 | C |

Example 4. Before the AP instruction statement is to be executed for this example, the fields to be used are configured as:

PKR1

0	8	5	C

PKR2

0	0	0	0	1	5	8	C

The instruction statement is:

> AP   PKR1,PKR2

As a result of the performance of this instruction, PKR1 now contains the packed decimal value configured as:

PKR1

2	4	3	C

This example would not have resulted in a decimal overflow and subsequent program interruption. Although the length of the second operand was greater than that of the first operand, the excess-length bytes did not contain significant hex digits (nonzeros), nor did the significant sum of the two operands exceed the length of the first operand field.

Example 5. The instruction statement to be executed in this example is:

> AP   FIELDR,FIELDS

The hexadecimal configuration of the fields affected by this statement appears as:

FIELDR

0	0	3	7	5	7	2	C

FIELDS

0	0	0	4	9	1	6	D

After the execution of the instruction statement, FIELDR would appear to contain:

FIELDR

0	0	3	2	6	5	6	C

In this example, FIELDS contained a negative value of −4916 as indicated by the hex digit 'D' in the low-order half-byte of that field. By adding this value to the positive value of +37,572 contained in FIELDR, the resulting sum reflects that a subtraction, in effect, has taken place. If the negative value had been greater than the positive value to which it was added, the resulting sum would have been signed as a negative value.

3. Subtract Packed (SP)

The Subtract Packed instruction will subtract the packed decimal contents of the second operand field from the packed decimal contents of the first operand field. The difference is placed in the first operand field. Both fields must contain validly signed packed decimal values. A decimal overflow interrupt will occur under similar circumstances as described for the Add Packed instruction.

Example 1. Before the SP instruction statement is acted upon, the fields that are to be used by that statement appear as:

PACKERA

0	2	2	5	8	C

PACKERB

0	0	9	9	4	C

The instruction statement that has been coded is:

> SP   PACKERA,PACKERB

After the instruction statement has been executed, the first operand field contains:

PACKERA

0	1	2	6	4	C

This example has presented a straightforward subtraction. In effect, it states that 2258C less 994C equals 1264C.

Example 2. The instruction statement to be executed is:

> SP   PKFA,PKFB

The configuration of the fields referred to by this statement are:

PKFA | 0 | 0 | 0 | 3 | 4 | 4 | 7 | C |

PKFB | 0 | 0 | 2 | 1 | 1 | 6 | 2 | D |

As a result of the performance of this statement, the configuration of PKFA would be changed to:

PKFA | 0 | 0 | 2 | 4 | 6 | 0 | 9 | C |

This example reflects the application that subtracting a negative value from a positive value results in a net positive value equal to the sum of the two values if they were unsigned.

Example 3. The configuration of the fields that are to be used for this example are:

ONEPK | 0 | 0 | 0 | 8 | 1 | 7 | 6 | 6 | 2 | C |

TWOPK | 0 | 0 | 0 | 9 | 4 | 4 | 3 | 7 | 5 | C |

The instruction statement that utilizes these fields is coded as:

SP   ONEPK,TWOPK

The execution of this statement affects the configuration of ONEPK as

ONEPK | 0 | 0 | 0 | 1 | 2 | 6 | 7 | 1 | 3 | D |

In this instance, the packed decimal value of the second operand was subtracted from the lesser value of the first operand, resulting in a negative difference.

Example 4. This example is presented to illustrate the type of condition that would cause a decimal overflow program interruption. The configuration of the fields to be used represents their contents prior to execution of the SP instruction statement.

FLDPOS | 6 | 2 | 0 | 0 | 3 | C |

FLDNEG | 3 | 9 | 7 | 7 | 0 | D |

The instruction statement that is being executed is:

SP   FLDPOS,FLDNEG

After the SP instruction statement has been executed, the area occupied by FLDPOS would appear as:

FLDPOS | 0 | 1 | 7 | 7 | 3 | C |

The result of this statement's performance created a value in excess of the length parameter of the first operand field. This condition, called a "carry-out" of the high-order digit position, would have caused a program interruption.

4. Multiply Packed (MP)

This instruction will multiply the packed decimal contents of the first operand (containing the multiplicand) by the packed decimal contents of the second operand (the multiplier), placing the resulting product in the first operand storage location. In establishing the work areas that are to be used by this instruction, there are a number of rules to be followed.

1. The length of the multiplier value cannot exceed eight bytes.

2. A product area should be established into which the multiplicand value is to be moved prior to the MP instruction statement.

3. The length of the product area should be equal to the length of the multiplier plus the length of the multiplicand value.

4. The length of the product area cannot exceed 16 bytes.

5. The length of the multiplier must be at least one byte less than the length of the product area.

6. Once the multiplicand is moved into the product area, the product area must have

at least as many high-order zero-digits as to equal a length the size of the multiplier.

7. Both operands must be validly signed packed decimal values.

If these rules are followed in their entirety, there will be no opportunity for a program interruption to occur as a result of this instructions performance. This does not preclude the possibility, however, of a program interruption occurring during the execution of this instruction for reasons such as using an invalidly signed packed decimal field, etc. If these rules are not followed, a program interruption will most likely occur as a result of a data exception or specification exception.

Inasmuch as the product area will probably be used rather frequently, at least by one set of instruction statements, the best means of getting the multiplicand into the product area is to use the Zero & Add Packed instruction. This will not only right-align the multiplicand into the product area, but it will also clear out any high-order digits that might have contained significant values and set those digit positions to hexadecimal zeros. Upon completion of the Multiply Packed instruction statement, the sign of the product will reside in the right-most nibble of the product field—the low-order half-byte.

The capabilities of using assumed decimal points, and increasing and decreasing decimal point positions for packed decimal arithmetic operations, is discussed within the section entitled "Packed Decimal Logic With Assumed Decimal Points."

The length of the product field may be specified as being shorter than the overall combined length of the multiplier and the multiplicand, but only if the product area contains enough high-order zero-digits to equal the length of the multiplier after the multiplicand has been moved in. By stating this, it is inferred that the programmer knows that the high-order positions of the multiplicand, in its own field, contains at least several zero digits. When the multiplicand is ZAP'd into the product area, there would be more than enough zero-digits on the left (high-order side) of the left-most significant digit of the multiplicand to equal the length of the multiplier. In this instance, the product area could be defined as being reduced by the length of the excess zero-digits. This practice is not recommended for general applications; it requires firm knowledge that the high-order zero-digits as contained within the multiplicand field will never be any value other than zero-digits.

The following examples will point out the means of applying the rules and conditions for utilizing the Multiply Packed instruction.

Example 1. The defined constants and the instruction statements that have been coded for this example are:

```
MPCAND     DC      PL4'23221'
MPLIER     DC      PL3'1176'
PRODUCT    DC      PL7'0'
*
           ZAP     PRODUCT,MPCAND          001
           MP      PRODUCT,MPLIER          002
```

Prior to the execution of these statements, the defined packed decimal areas would contain:

MPCAND

0	0	2	3	2	2	1	C

MPLIER

0	1	1	7	6	C

PRODUCT

0	0	0	0	0	0	0	0	0	0	0	0	0	C

Statement 001 is using the ZAP instruction to place the multiplicand into the low-order bytes of the PRODUCT field. After execution of this statement the contents of PRODUCT will be:

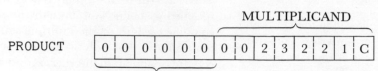

MULTIPLICAND

PRODUCT | 0 | 0 | 0 | 0 | 0 | 0 | 0 | 0 | 2 | 3 | 2 | 2 | 1 | C |

High-order zero-digits equal to the length of the multiplier

Statement 002 will then be executed, performing the MP function, after which PRODUCT will contain:

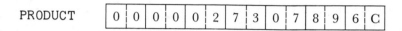

PRODUCT | 0 | 0 | 0 | 0 | 0 | 2 | 7 | 3 | 0 | 7 | 8 | 9 | 6 | C |

In effect this routine has shown that $1176 \times 23{,}221 = 27{,}307{,}896$.

Example 2. The defined areas for this example have been coded as:

```
CASES      DC      PL3'43351'
PERCASE    DC      PL2'144'
PRODT      DC      PL5'0'
```

The configuration of these areas, once they have been defined, appears as:

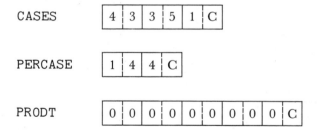

CASES | 4 | 3 | 3 | 5 | 1 | C |

PERCASE | 1 | 4 | 4 | C |

PRODT | 0 | 0 | 0 | 0 | 0 | 0 | 0 | 0 | 0 | C |

The instruction statements that are to be executed have been coded as:

```
ZAP     PRODT,CASES        001
MP      PRODT,PERCASE      002
```

Statement 001 will ZAP the multiplicand into the product area, PRODT, which will then contain:

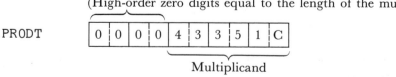

(High-order zero digits equal to the length of the multiplier)

PRODT | 0 | 0 | 0 | 0 | 4 | 3 | 3 | 5 | 1 | C |

Multiplicand

Statement 002 will multiply the multiplier, PERCASE, times the contents of PRODT. PRODT will now contain the product, appearing as:

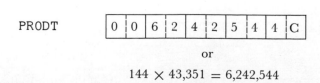

PRODT | 0 | 0 | 6 | 2 | 4 | 2 | 5 | 4 | 4 | C |

or

$$144 \times 43{,}351 = 6{,}242{,}544$$

Note that although all digit positions in both the multiplier and the multiplicand contained significant digits, the resulting product contained two high-order zero digits. One of these zero-digits resulted from the fact that although both operands contained a sign-digit in their low-order nibble, the resulting product contains only one sign-digit even though the length of the product was construed to be the combined length of the multiplier and the multiplicand. The other zero-digit resulted from the fact that the high-order position of the multiplication did not result in a carry. This can be demonstrated by stating that "two single position units multiplied together may or may not equal a value that would occupy two positions." For instance, $2 \times 2 = 4$ and $4 \times 4 = 16$—in either case both the multiplier and the multiplicand were only one-position values, yet the number of positions required by the product had a variance of one position. Therefore, it may be logically concluded that although both the multiplier and the multiplicand fields contain their maximum significant-digit capacity, the resulting product will always contain at least one high-order zero-digit; if the high-order positions of the multiplier and the multiplicand do not combine to create a carry, then the product will contain two high-order zero-digits.

Example 3. The hexadecimal configuration of the packed decimal constants and work areas that are to be used for this example are given below.

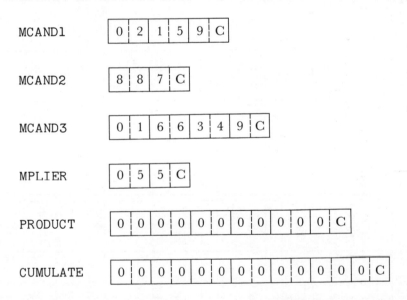

The coded definitions of these areas and the instruction statements to be executed are shown in Fig. 10-1.

The performance of each of the instruction statements are listed below. In each instance, the current configuration of the field that has been affected will be shown.

Statement 001 will ZAP the four-byte multiplicand, MCAND1, into PRODUCT.

PRODUCT | 0 | 0 | 0 | 0 | 0 | 0 | 0 | 2 | 1 | 5 | 9 | C |

Statement 002 will multiply the contents of PRODUCT by the packed decimal contents of MPLIER, resulting in:

PRODUCT | 0 | 0 | 0 | 0 | 0 | 1 | 1 | 8 | 7 | 4 | 5 | C |

IBM

PROGRAM				GRAPHIC		PAGE	OF
PROGRAMMER		DATE	PUNCHING INSTRUCTIONS	PUNCH		CARD ELECTRO NUMBER	

X28-6509-2 U/M050
Printed in U.S.A.

Name	Operation	Operand	Comments	Identification-Sequence
*				
MPSUB	ZAP	PRODUCT,MCAND1		001
	MP	PRODUCT,MPLIER		002
	ZAP	CUMULATE,PRODUCT		003
	ZAP	PRODUCT,MCAND2		004
	MP	PRODUCT,MPLIER		005
	AP	CUMULATE,PRODUCT		006
	ZAP	PRODUCT,MCAND3		007
	MP	PRODUCT,MPLIER		008
	AP	CUMULATE,PRODUCT		009
*				
MCAND1	DC	PL3'2159'		215
MCAND2	DC	PL2'887'		216
MCAND3	DC	PL4'166349'		217
MPLIER	DC	PL2'55'		218
PRODUCT	DC	PL6'0'		219
CUMULATE	DC	PL7'0'		220
*				

Figure 10-1

Statement 003 will use the ZAP instruction to initialize the area labeled CUMU-LATE with the value currently contained within PRODUCT.

CUMULATE | 0 | 0 | 0 | 0 | 0 | 0 | 0 | 1 | 1 | 8 | 7 | 4 | 5 | C |

Statement 004 places the value of the contents of MCAND2 into the low-order bytes of PRODUCT. Note that the previous value contained within PRODUCT has now been entirely overlayed.

PRODUCT | 0 | 0 | 0 | 0 | 0 | 0 | 0 | 0 | 8 | 8 | 7 | C |

Statement 005 multiplies the current value contained in PRODUCT (that of MCAND2) by the value contained within MPLIER. PRODUCT now contains:

PRODUCT | 0 | 0 | 0 | 0 | 0 | 0 | 4 | 8 | 7 | 8 | 5 | C |

Statement 006 adds the new value of PRODUCT (+48,785) to the current value of CUMULATE (+118,745), resulting in a new total of +167,530 in CUMULATE.

CUMULATE (Before AP) | 0 | 0 | 0 | 0 | 0 | 0 | 0 | 1 | 1 | 8 | 7 | 4 | 5 | C |

PRODUCT | 0 | 0 | 0 | 0 | 0 | 0 | 4 | 8 | 7 | 8 | 5 | C |

CUMULATE (After AP) | 0 | 0 | 0 | 0 | 0 | 0 | 0 | 1 | 6 | 7 | 5 | 3 | 0 | C |

Statement 007 now ZAP's the value of MCAND3 into PRODUCT. This represents the movement of the new multiplicand into the low-order bytes of the product area.

PRODUCT | 0 | 0 | 0 | 0 | 0 | 1 | 6 | 6 | 3 | 4 | 9 | C |

Statement 008 uses the MP instruction to multiply the current value of PRODUCT (+166,349, the multiplicand) by the value of MPLIER.

PRODUCT | 0 | 0 | 0 | 0 | 9 | 1 | 4 | 9 | 1 | 9 | 5 | C |

Statement 009 adds the new value of PRODUCT (+9,149,195) to the current value of CUMULATE (+167,530), resulting in a new CUMULATE total of +9,316,725.

CUMULATE (Before AP) | 0 | 0 | 0 | 0 | 0 | 0 | 0 | 1 | 6 | 7 | 5 | 3 | 0 | C |

PRODUCT | 0 | 0 | 0 | 0 | 9 | 1 | 4 | 9 | 1 | 9 | 5 | C |

CUMULATE (After AP) | 0 | 0 | 0 | 0 | 0 | 0 | 9 | 3 | 1 | 6 | 7 | 2 | 5 | C |

This example has performed a set of calculations that verifies the fact that:

$$(55 \times 2159) + (55 \times 887)$$
$$+ (55 \times 166{,}349) = 9{,}316{,}725$$

Although the length of the multiplier was the same for each MP instruction statement in this last example, the length of the multiplicand was different for each. Since the PRODUCT area length was established for the maximum length of any of the multiplier/multiplicand combinations, the logic was always able to use the same product area.

Also note that the CUMULATE field length was one byte larger than the length of the PRODUCT field. If the results of a packed decimal field arithmetic operation are being accumulated into another packed decimal field, the accumulator field should be *at least* one byte larger than the field from which the data is being accumulated in order to prevent the possibility of an overflow condition.

5. *Divide Packed (DP)*

This instruction will divide the packed decimal contents of the first operand (containing the dividend) by the packed decimal contents of the second operand, the divisor. The quotient and remainder will replace the dividend in the whole of the first operand storage location. The signs of the dividend and the divisor will combine algebraically to form thc sign of the quotient; the sign of the remainder will be of the same value as the sign of the dividend.

The following rules should be followed when establishing the divide work areas and in issuing the Divide Packed instruction.

1. The length of the divisor cannot exceed eight bytes.

2. A QUOREM field (Quotient and Remainder) should be established, into which the dividend is to be moved prior to the DP instruction statement.

3. The length of the QUOREM field should be equal to the combined lengths of the dividend and the divisor.

4. The length of the QUOREM area cannot exceed 16 bytes.

5. The length of the divisor must be at least one byte less than the length of the dividend field.

6. The length of the dividend field may not exceed 15 bytes.

7. Both operands must contain validly signed packed decimal data.

Adherence to these rules should prevent any possible program interruptions while executing the Divide Packed instruction. The infraction of any single rule, as specified in the preceding list, will most likely result in a specification exception or decimal divide exception, subsequently followed by a program interruption.

As similarly used with the Multiply Packed instruction, the ZAP (Zero & Add Packed) instruction should be used in this instance to move the dividend into the QUOREM field. This will not only assure that the dividend value is right-aligned into the QUOREM field, but it will also reset the high-order digit positions of the QUOREM field to contain zero-digits.

After execution of the Divide Packed instruction, both the quotient and the remainder will occupy the whole of the quorem field. The quotient will be found in the left-most bytes of the field and will have the length attribute of the dividend in even bytes. The remainder will be found in the right-most bytes of the quorem field and will have the length attribute of the divisor. Both the quotient and the remainder will be signed in the low-order nibble of their share of the quorem field. This can be illustrated as:

```
DIVIDEND     DC      PL4'0'
DIVISOR      DC      PL3'0'
QUOREM       DC      PL7'0'
```

After the execution of a DP instruction referencing these fields, the interpreted format of the resultant QUOREM field would be:

QUOREM | Q | Q | Q | Q | Q | Q | Q | sz | R | R | R | R | R | sz |

wherein:

Q = Quotient (Length of the dividend, including the sign/zone).

R = Remainder (Length of the divisor, including the sign/zone).

sz = Sign/zone for each subfield.

The use of arithmetic division operations often requires the concept of utilizing decimal points. An analysis of that method, as applied to the Divide Packed instruction, can be found within the section titled "Packed Decimal Logic with Assumed Decimal Points."

The step-by-step analysis of the following examples should aid in providing a reasonable understanding of the Divide Packed instruction and the format of the fields associated with it.

Example 1. The contents of the fields and work areas that are to be used by this example contain the following hexadecimal configurations:

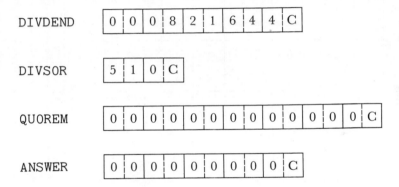

The coding that established these areas and the subsequent instruction statements for this example are presented in Fig. 10-2.

Statement 001 will use the ZAP instruction to place the packed decimal value of DIVDEND into the low-order bytes of QUOREM.

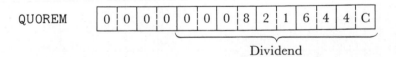

Dividend

Statement 002, the Divide Packed instruction statement, would then be executed, after which the contents of QUOREM would appear to be:

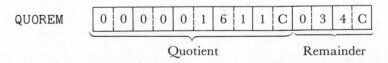

Quotient   Remainder

Notice that since the dividend was construed to have a length attribute of five bytes, the high-order five bytes of the QUOREM field, after the DP instruction statement, is considered to be the quotient. Inasmuch as the length of the divisor was two bytes, the low-order two bytes of the QUOREM field

now contain the remainder.

Statement 003 is moving the quotient out of the QUOREM field via the ZAP instruction and is placing it into the field labeled ANSWER. Because the quotient only occupies the first five bytes of the QUOREM field, the second operand of this instruction

IBM System/360 Assembler Coding Form

PROGRAM			PUNCHING INSTRUCTIONS	GRAPHIC		PAGE	OF
PROGRAMMER		DATE		PUNCH		CARD ELECTRO NUMBER	

X28-6509-2 U/M050
Printed in U.S.A.

Name	Operation	Operand	Comments	Identification-Sequence
*				
DIV.SUB	ZAP	QUOREM,DIVDEND		001
	DP	QUOREM,DIVSOR		002
	ZAP	ANSWER,QUOREM(5)		003
*				
DIVDEND	DC	PL5'821644'		072
DIVSOR	DC	PL2'510'		073
QUOREM	DC	PL7'0'		074
ANSWER	DC	PL5'0'		075
*				

Figure 10-2

statement (indicating the "move from" field address) has been given a specific length of five bytes. If this specific length had not been given, this statement would have attempted to move all seven bytes of the QUOREM field into the ANSWER field. This would have resulted in a program interruption, either because of an overflow or because of the fact that the overall data field would have contained a sign/zone in the low-order half-byte of the fifth byte from the left, which was not the low-order byte of the seven-byte field.

Example 2. This example will use both the quotient and remainder that have resulted from the Divide Packed operation. The contents of the work areas and fields prior to the execution of the statements are:

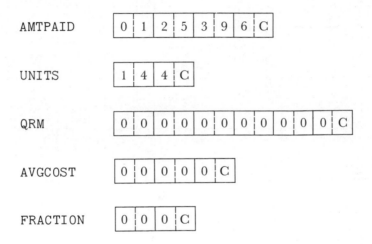

The coded instruction statements are represented in Fig. 10-3.

Statement 001 will use the ZAP instruction to place the dividend (AMTPAID) into the low-order four bytes of the QRM field. The hexadecimal configuration of QRM will then be:

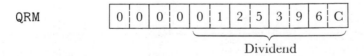

Statement 002 will execute the Divide Packed instruction statement, dividing the packed decimal contents of UNITS into the packed decimal contents of QRM, which represents the dividend. After completion of this operation, the quotient and remainder will be found in QRM in the following form and positions.

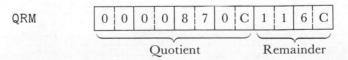

Statement 003 is using the ZAP instruction to move the *low-order three bytes of the quotient* into an answer field labeled AVGCOST. The second operand in this statement has addressed the first byte beyond the address generated by QRM (QRM + 1) and has specified the move length of three bytes of data. The addressing increment points of QRM can be illustrated as:

IBM

IBM System/360 Assembler Coding Form

X28-6509-2 U/M050
Printed in U.S.A.

| PROGRAM | | | PUNCHING INSTRUCTIONS | GRAPHIC | | PAGE | OF |
| PROGRAMMER | | DATE | | PUNCH | | CARD ELECTRO NUMBER | |

Name	Operation	Operand	Comments	Identification-Sequence
*				
DIVRTE	ZAP	QRM,AMTPAID		001
	DP	QRM,UNITS		002
	ZAP	AVGCOST,QRM+1(3)		003
	ZAP	FRACTION,QRM+4(2)		004
*				
AMTPAID	DC	PL4'125396'		341
UNITS	DC	PL2'144'		342
QRM	DC	PL6'0'		343
AVGCOST	DC	PL3'0'		344
FRACTION	DC	PL2'0'		345
*				

Figure 10-3

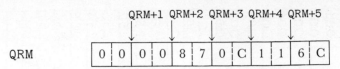

QRM+1 QRM+2 QRM+3 QRM+4 QRM+5

QRM | 0 | 0 | 0 | 0 | 8 | 7 | 0 | C | 1 | 1 | 6 | C |

In this instance the programmer knew that the dividend was being divided by a three-digit divisor; therefore, the quotient was certain to have at least one byte of high-order zero digits. Accordingly, the field that was to contain the stored answer (AVGCOST) was established with a length attribute of one byte less than the dividend. After execution of this instruction, the AVGCOST field would appear as:

AVGCOST | 0 | 0 | 8 | 7 | 0 | C |

Statement 004 is using the ZAP instruction to move the remainder into a storage area. It is assumed that the programmer may have wanted to use this remainder at another point in the program logic. Note the manner in which the remainder is addressed in the second operand of this statement—the starting point of the value of the remainder is

four bytes beyond the beginning of the QRM field, hence it is addressed as QRM+4. The two-byte length of the remainder has also been specified, as opposed to allowing it to be inferred as the number of bytes remaining in that field. The contents of the FRACTION field would now be:

FRACTION | 1 | 1 | 6 | C |

Example 3. This example becomes a bit more involved and would have required close attention by the programmer in his use of specific length attributes and address incrementing. The task being performed is to take a single base value and sequentially divide that number and the subsequent quotients by three different values. The hexadecimal configuration of the areas and fields that are to be used in this example is represented as:

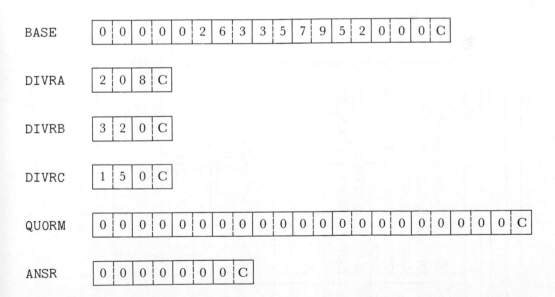

BASE | 0 | 0 | 0 | 0 | 0 | 2 | 6 | 3 | 3 | 5 | 7 | 9 | 5 | 2 | 0 | 0 | 0 | C |

DIVRA | 2 | 0 | 8 | C |

DIVRB | 3 | 2 | 0 | C |

DIVRC | 1 | 5 | 0 | C |

QUORM | 0 | 0 | 0 | 0 | 0 | 0 | 0 | 0 | 0 | 0 | 0 | 0 | 0 | 0 | 0 | 0 | 0 | 0 | 0 | 0 | 0 | 0 | 0 | C |

ANSR | 0 | 0 | 0 | 0 | 0 | 0 | 0 | C |

The coding for this example appears in Fig. 10-4.

Statement 001, STARTUP, will ZAP the packed decimal contents of BASE into the

division work area labeled QUORM. The hexadecimal configuration of QUORM will then appear to be:

IBM System/360 Assembler Coding Form

X28-6509-2 U/M050
Printed in U.S.A.

```
Name      Operation  Operand                          Identification-Sequence

*                                                     001
STARTUP   ZAP        QUORM,BASE                        002
          DP         QUORM,DIVRA                       003
          ZAP        QUORM,QUORM(9)                    004
          DP         QUORM+2(9),DIVRB                  005
          ZAP        QUORM,QUORM+2(7)                  006
          DP         QUORM+4(7),DIVRC                  007
          ZAP        ANSR,QUORM+5(4)                   008

*
*
BASE      DC         PL9'263357952000'                 250
DIVRA     DC         PL2'208'                          251
DIVRB     DC         PL2'320'                          252
DIVRC     DC         PL2'150'                          253
QUORM     DC         PL11'0'                           254
ANSR      DC         PL4'0'                            255
*                                                     256
*                                                     257
```

Figure 10-4

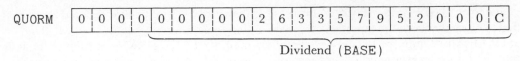

QUORM | 0 | 0 | 0 | 0 | 0 | 0 | 0 | 0 | 0 | 2 | 6 | 3 | 3 | 5 | 7 | 9 | 5 | 2 | 0 | 0 | 0 | C

Dividend (BASE)

Statement 002 will execute a Divide Packed instruction, dividing the contents of QUORM by the packed decimal contents of DIVRA (+208). The quotient and the remainder will then appear in the QUORM field as:

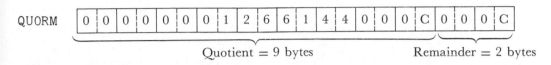

QUORM | 0 | 0 | 0 | 0 | 0 | 0 | 0 | 1 | 2 | 6 | 6 | 1 | 4 | 4 | 0 | 0 | 0 | C | 0 | 0 | 0 | C

Quotient = 9 bytes   Remainder = 2 bytes

Statement 003 is using the ZAP instruction to move the nine-byte quotient into the low-order bytes of the same field, QUORM. Since the next Divide Packed instruction will use this quotient as its dividend, this is an expedient means of getting that value right-aligned into the QUORM field. In order that the ZAP instruction statement would move only the high-order nine bytes (the quotient), the second operand included a specified length of nine bytes. As each DP instruction is encountered during the next several statements, it has been arranged that the assumed length of the QUORM field is decremented by two bytes at a time. Therefore, address adjusting and specific lengths have been assigned to the instruction statements. For the purpose of the problem program at this point, QUORM has now been theoretically reduced to a length of nine bytes and would appear in hexadecimal format as:

Dividend

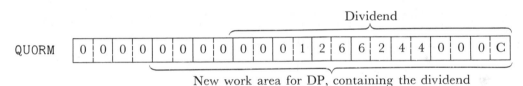

QUORM | 0 | 0 | 0 | 0 | 0 | 0 | 0 | 0 | 0 | 0 | 0 | 1 | 2 | 6 | 6 | 2 | 4 | 4 | 0 | 0 | 0 | C

New work area for DP, containing the dividend

Even though the second operand of the ZAP instruction specified that only nine bytes of data were to be moved, the first operand still reflects the implied length of QUORM, consequently the high-order two bytes of QUORM are also set to hex zero-digits. In this example, they already contained zeros, but had they contained significant-digits the effect of the implied length for the first operand would have been discernable.

Statement 004 now divides the low-order nine bytes of the QUORM field by the two-byte divisor, DIVRB. In order to relate this division to these bytes, the DP instruction addressed the QUORM field as QUORM + 2 for a specified length of nine bytes. Inasmuch as the divisor consists of two bytes and the overall specified length of the portion of the QUORM field being used for this instruction is nine bytes, the implication stands that the dividend consists of only seven bytes. Therefore, the quotient will consist of only seven bytes. After execution of this instruction statement, the assume format of QUORM would be:

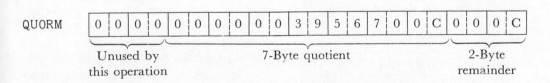

QUORM | 0 | 0 | 0 | 0 | 0 | 0 | 0 | 0 | 0 | 0 | 3 | 9 | 5 | 6 | 7 | 0 | 0 | C | 0 | 0 | 0 | C

Unused by   7-Byte quotient   2-Byte
this operation   remainder

Statement 005 is using the ZAP instruction to move the seven-byte quotient, located at QUORM+2, into the low-order bytes of that field, thus right-aligning it in preparation for the next DP instruction. Because the second operand specifies a length attribute of seven bytes, starting at QUORM+2, only the seven bytes of packed decimal representing the quotient will be moved. The remainder of QUORM, the high-order four bytes, would be set to zero on the basis that the first operand used the implied length (11 bytes) of QUORM. The hexadecimal format of QUORM would now appear as:

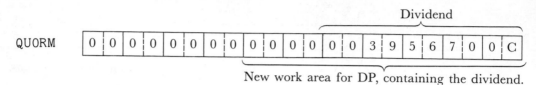

QUORM

New work area for DP, containing the dividend.

Statement 006 will now divide the low-order seven bytes of the QUORM field by the two-byte divisor, DIVRC. The DP instruction statement has addressed this seven-byte work area as QUORM+4 and has specified a length attribute of seven bytes. This will enable the DP instruction statement to perform its operation on that particular part of QUORM, as opposed to utilizing the entire 11 bytes of that field.

Because the programmer has, at this point, construed that the overall specified length of the QUORM field to be used is seven bytes and the divisor should consist of two bytes, it is, therefore, to be implied that the dividend, and consequently the quotient, must consist of only five bytes. Upon completion of this instruction statement, the hexadecimal configuration of QUORM would appear to be:

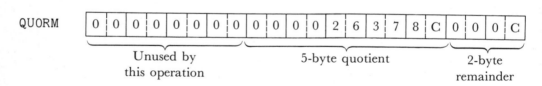

QUORM

Statement 007 is using the ZAP instruction to move the quotient that resulted from the last instruction statement from the QUORM field into a storage area that is addressed by the label ANSR. Although the quotient is understood to be five bytes of data commencing at QUORM+4, it is known in advance that at least one high-order byte of the quotient will contain zero-digits. The programmer, accordingly, has specified the address of the second operand to commence at QUORM+5 for a length of four bytes. This will move the four low-order bytes of the quotient (bytes 6, 7, 8, and 9 of QUORM) into the ANSR field, whose configuration would then appear as:

In coding the instruction statements for this last example, it would not have been necessary to adjust the length attributes of the QUORM field for each successive Divide Packed operation. The programmer could have stipulated that the length of the dividend was always nine bytes and that the divisor always required two bytes, combining to require a work area (QUORM) of 11 bytes for each DP instruction statement. In the format that was used, however, the logic and means of adjusting field lengths and addresses was well demonstrated.

6. Move with Offset (MVO)

Although this instruction does not perform a true arithmetic function, it is used so frequently with arithmetic routines that it should logically be discussed at this time.

This instruction will take the data speci-

ANSR   0 0 2 6 3 7 8 C

fied by the second operand and move it to the location specified by the first operand but offset to the left by $\frac{1}{2}$ byte, four bit positions, of the low-order position of the field addressed by the first operand.

If the length of the first operand field (the receiving field) is longer than the length of the second operand field (the sending field), the high-order nibbles of the first operand field will be set up as zero-digits. If the length of the first operand field is shorter than the second operand field, the excess $\frac{1}{2}$ bytes in the second operand field are ignored.

Data is moved from the sending field to

the receiving field in $\frac{1}{2}$ bytes increments, moving from right to left—low-order to high-order. The offset of $\frac{1}{2}$ byte is in the receiving field only.

A frequent application for this instruction is to remove unwanted decimal point positions in a packed decimal value. This application will be illustrated in the section titled "Packed Decimal Logic With Assumed Decimal Points," which follows within this section.

Example 1. The packed decimal field that is to be manipulated is defined as:

```
PACKFLD5     DC      PL5'32596421'
```

PACKFLD5 | 0 | 3 | 2 | 5 | 9 | 6 | 4 | 2 | 1 | C |

The instruction statement that is to be executed is:

```
MVO      PACKFLD5(5),PACKFLD5(3)
```

The resulting action will be accomplished by this statement in the following manner.

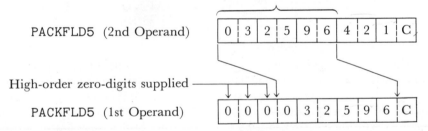

This instruction statement took the first three bytes of PACKFLD5, as specified by the second operand, and moved them into PACKFLD5, right-aligned and offset by $\frac{1}{2}$ bytes. Since the sending field was shorter in length than the receiving field, the high-

order digit positions of the receiving field were supplied with zero-digit values.

Example 2. The packed decimal fields that are to be manipulated in this example are:

```
PKFIELDA     DC      PL5'13376711'
PKFIELDB     DC      PL3'50'
```

PKFIELDA | 0 | 1 | 3 | 3 | 7 | 6 | 7 | 1 | 1 | C |

PKFIELDB | 0 | 0 | 0 | 5 | 0 | C |

The MVO instruction statement to be performed is:

```
MVO      PKFIELDB,PKFIELDA+2(2)
```

The movement of the data as specified by this statement would be accomplished in the following manner.

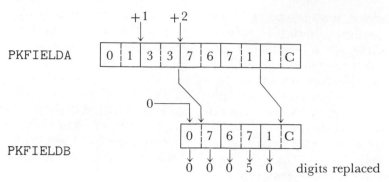

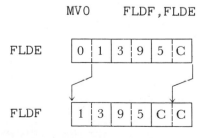

This example has stated that two bytes of packed decimal data within PKFIELDA, commencing at the third byte of that field (PKFIELDA + 2) for a length of two bytes, is to be moved into the whole of PKFIELDB, right-aligned and offset in the low-order position by ½ byte. As requested, the two bytes of data containing the hexadecimal digits '7671' were moved into PKFIELDB, offset to the left by ½ byte. This effectively created a validly signed packed decimal value of +7,671 since the standard plus-sign ('C') in the low-order nibble was not disturbed.

Example 3. This example is intended to show the resulting configuration of the movement of an entire field of packed decimal data (containing a sign-digit) into another packed decimal field that already contains a sign-digit. The data fields that are to be used are:

```
        FLDE    DC      PL3'1395'
        FLDF    DC      PL3'00'
```

The instruction statement that is to be executed, and the resulting action from the performance of that statement, is as follows:

```
        MVO     FLDF,FLDE
```

Because the entire sending field is moved and the low-order nibble of the receiving field is not altered, the result is that FLDF has become invalid for packed decimal arithmetic applications; it now has a hexadecimal digit with a value greater than '9' in a position other than the right-most nibble of the field. The proper means of moving FLDE to FLDF, in this instance, would have been to use the ZAP instruction.

D. PACKED DECIMAL LOGIC WITH ASSUMED DECIMAL POINTS

The majority of programmers will find that they will frequently be required to use decimal point logic in performing packed decimal arithmetic operations. It is reasonably certain, therefore, they will require knowledge of this concept as well as a familiarity with *"rounding"* packed decimal values. As in the case of fixed-point arithmetic operations, extra decimal places can be added or deleted in a packed decimal field by multiplying or dividing by 10, 100, 1000, etc. In working with packed decimal values, it will be noted that the Move With Offset instruction may perform many of these tasks in a more efficient manner.

Whether the programmer desires to add decimal point positions, or to delete them, there are several ways by which duplicate results may be obtained. It must be the responsibility of the individual to determine which method is best suited to his needs, preferably a decision that will be based on the efficiency of the operations, rather than on the likes and dislikes of the user. The examples that follow will present a reasonable comparison of these methods on the basis of the coding required. The efficiency of their performance must be rated by the computer system on which they are applied and the requirements of the problem program.

Example 1. The coding sheet illustration shown in Fig. 10-5 contains the instruction statements that are to be executed and the definition of the field and work areas that are to be used. Wherever applicable, the assumed number of decimal point positions are indicated as a comment on the same line as the field or area.

Statement 001 will use the ZAP instruction to move the value of UNITS into the low-order bytes of WORK. The hexadecimal configuration of WORK would then appear as:

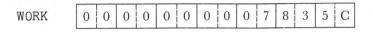

Statement 002 multiplies the value of WORK (containing the multiplicand) by the value of COSTPER, the multiplier. The resulting product would be configurated in WORK as:

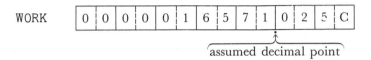

Since the value of COSTPER contains three assumed decimal point positions, the product is assumed to have a similar number of assumed decimal positions. The product, therefore, is construed to have a value of +16,571.025. The desired answer at this point must be rounded off to the nearest cent, which is taken care of by the next instruction statement.

Statement 003 is adding a value of +5 to the low-order of WORK, effectively rounding that value to the nearest cent. WORK would now appear as:

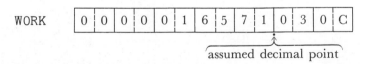

Statement 004 is utilizing the MVO instruction to remove one decimal point position from the value contained in WORK. This is done because that value is to be moved to GROSS by the next instruction statement, and GROSS is set up to accept a value containing only two assumed decimal point positions. The logic of the MVO instruction statement is to move the first seven bytes of WORK into the low-order positions of WORK, offset by ½ bytes. The action can be represented by this illustration:

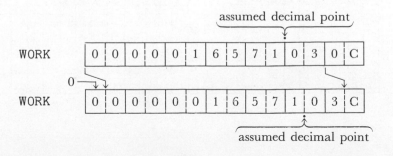

IBM System/360 Assembler Coding Form

Name	Operation	Operand	Comments	Identification-Sequence
*				
UNITS	DC	PL3'7835'	(XXXXX. ASSUMED)	001
COSTPER	DC	PL3'2115'	(X.000 ASSUMED)	002
GROSS	DC	PL4'0'	(XXXXX.00 ASSUMED)	003
DISCOUNT	DC	PL2'95'	(X.00 ASSUMED)	004
NET	DC	PL4'0'	(XXXXX.00 ASSUMED)	005
WORK	DC	PL7'0'		006
ROUND1	DC	PL1'5'		007
ROUND2	DC	PL2'50'		008
*				
*				
STARTER	ZAP	WORK,UNITS		009
	MP	WORK,COSTPER		
	AP	WORK,ROUND1		
	MVO	WORK(7),WORK(6)		
	ZAP	GROSS,WORK+3(4)		
	MP	WORK,DISCOUNT		
	AP	WORK,ROUND2		
	MVO	WORK(7),WORK(6)		
	MVO	WORK(7),WORK(6)		
	ZAP	NET,WORK+3(4)		010
				011

Figure 10-5

Statement 005 is using the ZAP instruction to move the low-order four bytes of WORK, as specified by the operand WORK+3(4), into the field labeled GROSS. The contents of GROSS should then appear to contain:

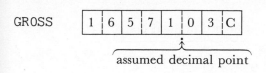

GROSS

| 1 | 6 | 5 | 7 | 1 | 0 | 3 | C |

assumed decimal point

In effect, a 5% discount has been taken against the gross amount (95% of gross) resulting in a net value. This value must now be rounded to the nearest cent and moved to NET.

Statement 006 will multiply the contents of WORK (the same value as is in GROSS) by the value of DISCOUNT. Inasmuch as WORK already contained two assumed decimal point positions and DISCOUNT contains two assumed decimal point positions, the resulting product in WORK must be considered to contain four assumed decimal point positions. Upon completion of the execution of this instruction statement, the hex configuration of WORK would be:

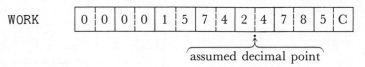

WORK

| 0 | 0 | 0 | 0 | 1 | 5 | 7 | 4 | 2 | 4 | 7 | 8 | 5 | C |

assumed decimal point

Statement 007 is adding +50 to WORK in order to round that value to the nearest cent. WORK would now appear as:

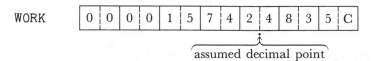

WORK

| 0 | 0 | 0 | 0 | 1 | 5 | 7 | 4 | 2 | 4 | 8 | 3 | 5 | C |

assumed decimal point

Statements 008 and 009 are a duplicate set of Move With Offset instructions. They would cause the following change on WORK as a result of their execution.

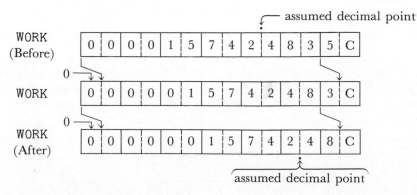

WORK (Before)

| 0 | 0 | 0 | 0 | 1 | 5 | 7 | 4 | 2 | 4 | 8 | 3 | 5 | C |

assumed decimal point

WORK

| 0 | 0 | 0 | 0 | 0 | 1 | 5 | 7 | 4 | 2 | 4 | 8 | 3 | C |

WORK (After)

| 0 | 0 | 0 | 0 | 0 | 0 | 1 | 5 | 7 | 4 | 2 | 4 | 8 | C |

assumed decimal point

It would have been possible to reduce the value of WORK by two decimal point positions by dividing that value by +100. The use of a duplicate MVO instruction was taken in order to show the action of these instruction sets in an instance where an even number of positions are to be removed.

Statement 010 is using the ZAP instruction to move the low-order four bytes of

WORK into an answer field that is labeled NET. The hex configuration of NET would then appear as:

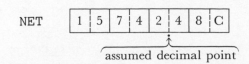

NET

| 1 | 5 | 7 | 4 | 2 | 4 | 8 | C |

assumed decimal point

Example 2. This example is merely a series of MVO instruction statements that are operating on various fields. It will indicate the addressing required to delete low-order decimal point positions in increments of 1, 3, 5, 7, etc, as coded by the instruction statements in Fig. 10-6.

Statement 001 is using the MVO instruction to reduce the value of FLDPKA by one decimal point position as it moves it into RECVA. This move would appear to be accomplished as:

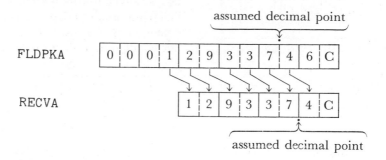

This has now moved the contents of FLDPKA into RECVA and changed the value of its contents from +129,337.46 to +129,337.4.

Statement 002 is reducing the value of FLDPKB by three decimal point positions as it moves it into RECVB. This would appear as:

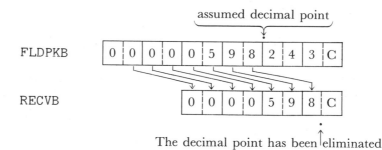

The decimal point has been eliminated

This has moved the packed decimal contents of FLDPKB into RECVB and has changed the value from +598.243 to +598.

Statement 003 is moving the value of FLDPKC into RECVC by using the MVO instruction, but is reducing that value by five decimal point positions as the move is accomplished.

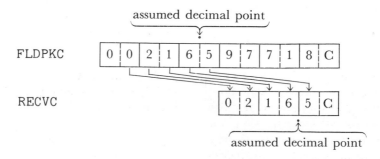

The packed decimal contents of FLDPKC have now been partially moved into RECVC, but in doing so the value of that data has been changed from +216.597718 to +216.5.

Statement 004 is using the MVO instruction to move a portion of the contents of FLDPKD into RECVD, reducing that data by seven decimal point positions during the move. The configuration of the data as it is changed would appear as:

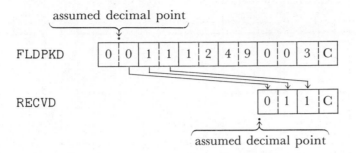

This has effectively reduced the value by seven decimal places during the move from FLDPKD to RECVD, decreasing the expressed value from +.0111249003 to +.011.

Example 3. This example demonstrates the method of reducing a value by an even number of decimal point positions or digits. This can be accomplished by a Divide Packed instruction or by two Move With Offset instructions. Both methods will be illustrated (see Fig. 10-7).

Statement 001 uses the ZAP instruction to move the packed decimal value of AFLD into the low-order bytes of QUORM in preparation for a divide instruction. The hex configuration of QUORM would now be:

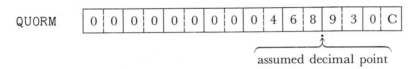

Statement 002 divides the packed decimal value of QUORM by a packed decimal literal value of +100. This action will reduce the value contained in QUORM by the two low-order digit positions. As a result of this instruction the configuration of QUORM will appear to be:

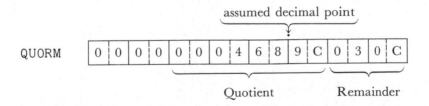

As shown, the original value of the dividend, which is now represented by the quotient, has been reduced from +468.930 to +468.9.

Statement 003 is moving the low-order three bytes of the quotient out of the QUORM field and into the HOLDA field. HOLDA would now contain that data as:

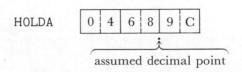

Statement 004 is performing an MVO instruction to reduce the value of BFLD by

IBM

IBM System/360 Assembler Coding Form

X28-6509-2 U/M050
Printed in U.S.A.

| PROGRAM | | | | | PAGE | OF |
| PROGRAMMER | | DATE | PUNCHING INSTRUCTIONS | GRAPHIC / PUNCH | CARD ELECTRO NUMBER | |

```
Name      Operation  Operand                      Identification-Sequence
*
FLDPKA    DC   PL6'12933746'   (XXXXXXX.00 ASSUMED)
FLDPKB    DC   PL6'598243'     (XXXXXX.000 ASSUMED)
FLDPKC    DC   PL6'216597718'  (XXX.000000 ASSUMED)
FLDPKD    DC   PL6'111249003'  (.000000000 ASSUMED)
RECVA     DC   PL4'0'
RECVB     DC   PL4'0'
RECVC     DC   PL3'0'
RECVD     DC   PL2'0'
*
MODRTE    MVO  RECVA,FLDPKA(5)                     001
          MVO  RECVB,FLDPKB(4)                     002
          MVO  RECVC,FLDPKC(3)                     003
          MVO  RECVD,FLDPKD(2)                     004
```

Figure 10-6

IBM System/360 Assembler Coding Form

Name	Operation	Operand		Identification-Sequence
*				
AFLD	DC	PL4'468930'	(XXXX.000 ASSUMED)	
BFLD	DC	PL4'468930'	(XXXX.000 ASSUMED)	
CFLD	DC	PL5'12600521'	(XXX.000000 ASSUMED)	
DFLD	DC	PL5'76599444'	(XXXXXXXXX. ASSUMED)	
QUORM	DC	PL8'0'		
HOLDA	DC	PL3'0'		
HOLDB	DC	PL3'0'		
HOLDC	DC	PL3'0'		
HOLDD	DC	PL2'0'		
*				
SPECRTE	ZAP	QUORM,AFLD		001
	DP	QUORM+2(6),=PL2'100'		002
	ZAP	HOLDA,QUORM+3(3)		003
	MVO	BFLD(4),BFLD(3)		004
	MVO	HOLDB,BFLD(3)		005
	ZAP	QUORM,CFLD		006
	DP	QUORM,=PL3'10000'		007
	ZAP	HOLDC,QUORM+2(3)		008
	MVO	DFLD,DFLD(2)		009
	MVO	HOLDD,DFLD+3(1)		010

Figure 10-7

261

one low-order digit. BFLD will then have a value configuration of +468.93 based on the following action:

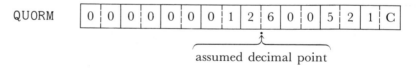

This statement was the first of two steps to delete two low-order digits from the value of BFLD. The deletion of the second digit will be accomplished by the next instruction statement.

Statement 005 is moving the value of BFLD to HOLDB and at the same time is

removing one more low-order digit position.

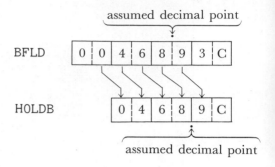

By comparing the results of Statements 004 and 005 to that of Statements 001, 002, and 003 you will note that they created the same final value. Both AFLD and BFLD had the same original value; now HOLDA and HOLDB have identical values.

Statement 006 will ZAP the content value of CFLD into the low-order bytes of QUORM.

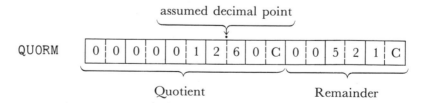

Statement 007 divides QUORM by a packed decimal literal of +10,000 in order to reduce the value in QUORM by four

low-order digits. After execution of this statement, QUORM will appear as:

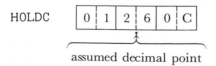

Statement 008 is taking the low-order three bytes of the quotient [QUORM+2(3)] and moving it into HOLDC by using the ZAP instruction. CFLD has now been reduced by four low-order digits, changing its assumed value from +12.600521 to +12.60, and that value now resides in HOLDC.

Statements 009 and 010 are using a pair of MVO instructions to reduce the magnitude of the packed decimal value of DFLD by six low-order digits. In doing so the value is also being moved to HOLDD by Statement 010. The action accomplished by these two statements is represented by the illustration appearing at the top of page 263.

As shown, the low-order six digits of DFLD have been successfully deleted.

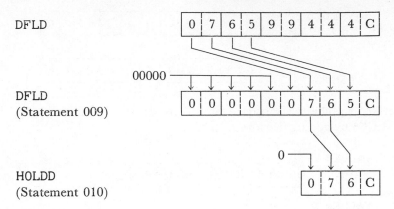

DFLD

DFLD
(Statement 009)

HOLDD
(Statement 010)

Example 4. Supplying additional zero-digits to the low-order positions of a packed decimal value can be easily accomplished using the Multiply Packed instruction. This will be illustrated using the following coding:

```
VALUE1    DC     PL4'2664'
VALUE2    DC     PL6'5983'
VALUE3    DC     PL6'7717'
VALUE4    DC     PL7'4092'
*
RTE1      MP     VALUE1,=PL2'100'         0001
          MP     VALUE2,=PL3'1000'        0002
          MP     VALUE3,=PL3'10000'       0003
          MP     VALUE4,=PL4'100000'      0004
```

Statement 0001 will increase the value of VALUE1 by the increment of two low-order zero-digits. This is accomplished by multiplying its current value by a packed decimal literal of +100. The configuration of the field VALUE1 would appear as:

VALUE1 (Before)

VALUE1 (After)

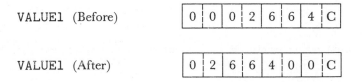

Statement 0002 effectively adds three low-order zero-digits to the value of VALUE2 by multiplying that field with a packed decimal literal of +1000.

VALUE2
(Before)

VALUE2
(After)

Statement 0003 increases the content value of VALUE3 by multiplying it by a packed decimal literal of +10,000. This action has added four low-order zero-digits to the original value.

VALUE3
(Before)

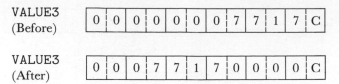

| 0 | 0 | 0 | 0 | 0 | 0 | 0 | 7 | 7 | 1 | 7 | C |

VALUE3
(After)

| 0 | 0 | 0 | 7 | 7 | 1 | 7 | 0 | 0 | 0 | 0 | C |

Statement 0004 will effectively increase the value of VALUE4 by adding five low-order   zero-digits.

VALUE4
(Before)

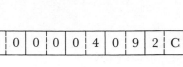

| 0 | 0 | 0 | 0 | 0 | 0 | 0 | 0 | 0 | 4 | 0 | 9 | 2 | C |

VALUE4
(After)

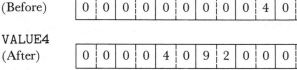

| 0 | 0 | 0 | 0 | 4 | 0 | 9 | 2 | 0 | 0 | 0 | 0 | 0 | C |

The examples shown on these pages should provide the programmer with sufficient material to manipulate any assumed decimal point assignments with packed decimal values. This concept might well be used for general reduction or incrementing of whole values, not necessarily in conjunction with decimal point logic. By utilizing the MP, DP, MVO, and ZAP instructions, packed decimal values can be rearranged and/or configured in any valid manner that might be required by the problem program.

Review Exercises

The following problems are either in the form of questions or instruction statements that are to be executed. For the questions, fill in the missing word or words; for the instruction statements, fill in the field layouts as they would appear after execution of the instruction statement.

1. EBCDIC numeric character data is converted to packed decimal format by the _____ instruction.

2. Fixed-point values are converted to packed decimal values by the _____ instruction.

3. Packed decimal instruction statements are unique in that both operands have either an implied or explicit _Length_ attribute.

4. INFLD

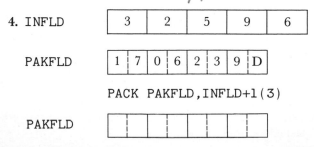

| 3 | 2 | 5 | 9 | 6 |

PAKFLD

| 1 | 7 | 0 | 6 | 2 | 3 | 9 | D |

PACK PAKFLD,INFLD+1(3)

PAKFLD

| | | | | | | | |

5. PAKSET | 2 | 4 | 0 | 0 | 3 | 9 | 6 | C |

   OUTFLD | 0 | 0 | 0 | 0 | 0 | 0 | 0 |

   UNPK OUTFLD,PAKSET+l(3)

   OUTFLD | | | | | | | | | | | | | |

6. PKFA | 6 | 0 | 5 | 5 | 2 | 1 | 9 | C |

   PKFB | 4 | 4 | 7 | C |

   AP   PKFA,PKFB

   PKFA | | | | | | | | |

7. DATAREC | 9 | 1 | 1 | 2 | 3 | C |

   INPACK | 0 | 0 | 0 | 0 | 0 | C |

   PACK   INPACK(3),DATAREC

   INPACK | | | | | |

8. PACKRA | 0 | 0 | 0 | 2 | 9 | 5 | 3 | C |

   PACKSB | 0 | 5 | 3 | 8 | 0 | 0 | 1 | D |

   SP   PACKRA,PACKSB

   PACKRA | | | | | | | | |

9. BIGPACK | 0 | 6 | 5 | 9 | 2 | 3 | 5 | E |

   DATAFLD | F | 5 | F | 9 | F | 2 | F | 0 | F | 0 | F | 1 | F | 6 |

   UNPK   DATAFLD,BIGPACK

   DATAFLD | | | | | | | | |

10. PKSETB | 0 | 0 | 3 | 6 | 5 | 1 | 2 | 4 | 6 | D |

    MVO   PKSETB+l(4),PKSETB+l(3)

    PKSETB | | | | | | | | | |

11. PKFLD | 0 | 0 | 0 | 0 | 0 | 0 | 0 | 0 | 0 | 0 | 0 | C |

MPLIER

0	2	2	1	4	C

MPCAND

0	0	0	3	9	1	1	C

```
MULRTE    ZAP    PKFLD,MPCAND+1(3)
          MP     PKFLD,MPLIER
```

PKFLD

12. The maximum length of the divisor in a DP instruction statement is _____8_____ bytes.

13. If the multiplicand field is 6 bytes in length and the multiplier field is 4 bytes in length, then the product field of the corresponding MP instruction statement should be _____ bytes long.

14. Packed decimal data that is to be converted into a fixed-point value must be contained within an _____ byte field that is _____-aligned.

15. If the EBCDIC alphabetic characters "ABCDEF" are packed and then immediately unpacked they would then be the EBCDIC characters "_____".

16. The work area for a DP instruction, referred to as the "quorem," should be equal in length to the combined lengths of the dividend and the _____.

17. Only the _____ operand in a ZAP instruction statement must represent a validly signed packed decimal field.

18. Fixed-point values may be converted into EBCDIC numeric character form via the combined use of both the _____ and the _____ instructions.

19. If an EBCDIC field that is being packed contains more numeric characters than can be contained within the receiving packed decimal field, then the _____-order numeric digits of the sending field are ignored.

20. The Move With Offset (MVO) instruction will move the contents of the sending field into the receiving field but offset to the _____ by a half-byte within the receiving field.

21. If a signed 3-byte packed decimal field is being unpacked into an 8-byte field, the three high-order bytes of the receiving field will each be supplied with a hexadecimal configuration of X'_____'.

22. PAKFLDA

2	0	4	0	9	3	6	C

PAKFLDB

0	0	1	9	0	6	4	5	1	C

```
SP    PAKFLDA,PAKFLDB
```

PAKFLDA

23. PAKFLDC

0	0	0	0	0	6	0	0	3	C

DATAPAK

6	0	0	5	0	0	0	D

```
        ZAP     DATAPAK+1(3),PAKFLDC+2(3)
```

DATAPAK　| | | | | | | | |

24. DIVRPAK　| 0 | 4 | 0 | C |

DIVNDPAK　| 0 | 4 | 1 | 6 | 2 | 0 | 6 | C |

QUOREM　| 0 | 0 | 0 | 0 | 0 | 0 | 0 | 0 | 0 | 0 | 0 | C |

```
        ZAP     QUOREM,DIVNDPAK
        DP      QUOREM,DIVRPAK
```

QUOREM　| | | | | | | | | | | |

25. SETPAKA　| 0 | 0 | 8 | 9 | 2 | 6 | 0 | 0 | 4 | C |

SETPAKB　| 4 | 6 | 2 | 1 | 3 | 9 | 8 | D |

```
        SP      SETPAKA,SETPAKB
```

SETPAKA　| | | | | | | | | |

26. MULTIPAK　| 0 | 0 | 0 | 0 | 0 | 0 | 6 | 5 | 9 | C |

PLIERPAK　| 0 | 8 | 4 | C |

ANSWER　| 0 | 0 | 0 | 0 | 0 | 0 | 0 | C |

```
        MP      MULTPAK,PLIERPAK
        ZAP     ANSWER,MULTPAK+1(4)
```

MULTPAK　| | | | | | | | | | |

ANSWER　| | | | | | | | |

27. XPANDPAK　| 0 | 9 | 3 | 4 | 6 | C |

PAKONE　| 0 | 6 | 8 | 2 | 1 | C |

PAKTWO　| 2 | 5 | 9 | 6 | 0 | 7 | 8 | C |

```
        MVO     PAKONE(7),XPANDPAK(2)
```

PAKONE　| | | | | |

PAKTWO　| | | | | | | | |

28. DATASFLD

3	B	C	D	5	H

PAKRECV

0	0	0	0	0	0	0	C

```
PACK    PAKRECV,DATASFLD
UNPK    DATASFLD,PAKRECV
```

PAKRECV

DATASFLD

29. QUOREM

0	0	0	0	0	6	2	9	4	C

DIVSOR

0	1	3	C

ANSW

0	0	0	0	0	C

```
DP     QUOREM,DIVSOR
ZAP    ANSW,QUOREM(3)
```

QUOREM

ANSW

30. REPACK

0	7	4	3	9	2	6	0	8	C

```
ZAP    REPACK,REPACK+2(3)
```

REPACK

31. MULTAREA

0	0	0	0	0	0	1	4	9	2	C

MPLR

0	0	3	0	5	C

ANSWR

0	0	0	0	0	0	0	C

```
MP     MULTAREA,MPLR
MVO    ANSWR(4),MULTAREA(3)
```

MULTAREA

ANSWR

FIXED-POINT ARITHMETIC OPERATIONS

A. THE FIXED-POINT ARITHMETIC INSTRUCTIONS

INSTRUCTION: ADD

Mnemonic	Hex Code	Operand Format
A	5A	$R_1, D_2(X_2, B_2)$

This particular Add instruction will add the 32-bit value of the second operand (consisting of a sign-bit and a 31-bit integer) to the value of the contents of the first operand register. The second operand address must be that of a fullword boundary alignment. The sum of the result will reside in the general register specified by the first operand.

CC	BC	Condition
0	8	The first operand register contains a value of zero.
1	4	The first operand register contains a value less than zero.
2	2	The first operand register contains a value greater than zero.
3	1	An overflow condition occurred.

* * *

INSTRUCTION: ADD HALFWORD

Mnemonic	Hex Code	Operand Format
AH	4A	$R_1, D_2(X_2, B_2)$

The Add Halfword instruction will first of all extract the 16-bit value of the second operand and expand it to a 32-bit fullword by creating 16 additional high-order bits, each additional bit having the same value as the sign-bit for the original value of the second operand. It will then add this expanded value to the 32-bit value (1 sign-bit and 31 integer-bits) of the first operand register and place the sum in the first operand register. The second operand must address a location in storage that is aligned on a halfword boundary.

CC	BC	Condition
0	8	The first operand register contains a value of zero.
1	4	The first operand register contains a value that is less than zero.
2	2	The first operand register contains a value that is greater than zero.
3	1	An overflow condition occurred.

*   *   *

INSTRUCTION: ADD REGISTERS

Mnemonic	*Hex Code*	*Operand Format*
AR	1A	R_1,R_2

The Add Register instruction will add the fixed-point value of the second operand register to the fixed-point value of the first operand register, placing the sum of the operation in the first operand. Both general registers contain a value consisting of a sign-bit and a 31-bit integer.

CC	BC	Condition
0	8	The first operand register contains a value of zero.
1	4	The first operand register contains a value less than zero.
2	2	The first operand register contains a value greater than zero.
3	1	An overflow condition occurred.

*   *   *

INSTRUCTION: ADD LOGICAL

Mnemonic	*Hex Code*	*Operand Format*
AL	5E	$R_1,D_2(X_2,B_2)$

This instruction will add the 32-bit representation of the value of the second operand to the 32 bits of the first operand register and place the sum of that addition into the first operand register. All bits, including the sign-bits, are logically added together with no change to the resulting sign-bit. An overflow condition will not cause a program interrupt. The address created by the second operand must be that of a properly aligned fullword. When the Condition Code is set by this instruction, it will indicate whether or not a carry-out of the sign-bit occurred.

CC	BC	Condition
0	8	The first operand contains a zero value; there was no carry-out of the sign-bit.
1	4	The first operand does not contain a zero value; there was no carry-out of the sign-bit.
2	2	The first operand contains a zero value; a carry-out of the sign-bit occurred.
3	1	The first operand does not contain a zero value; a carry-out of the sign-bit occurred.

*   *   *

INSTRUCTION: ADD LOGICAL REGISTERS

Mnemonic	*Hex Code*	*Operand Format*
ALR	1E	R_1,R_2

The Add Logical Registers instruction will add the 32-bit representation of the second operand register to the 32 bits of the first operand register and place the sum into the first operand register. All bits, including the sign-bits, are logically added together with no change to the resulting sign-bit. An overflow condition will not cause a program interrupt. The Condition Code setting will indicate whether or not a carry-out of the sign-bit occurred.

CC	BC	Condition
0	8	The first operand contains a zero value; there was no carry-out of the sign-bit.
1	4	The first operand does not contain a zero value; there was no carry-out of the sign-bit.
2	2	The first operand contains a zero value; a carry-out of the sign-bit occurred.
3	1	The first operand does not contain a zero value; a carry-out of the sign-bit occurred.

* * *

INSTRUCTION: SUBTRACT

Mnemonic	Hex Code	Operand Format
S	5B	$R_1, D_2(X_2, B_2)$

This Subtract instruction will take the fixed-point signed integer value of the full-word specified by the second operand and subtract it from the fixed-point contents of the first operand register. This is done by taking the complement of the second operand contents and summing that complement with the fixed-point value of the first operand. The result is placed into the general register specified by the first operand. If an overflow condition occurs as a result of this instruction, the Condition Code will be set accordingly and a program interruption will normally occur. The address generated by the second operand must be that of a full-word boundary location.

CC	BC	Condition
0	8	The first operand contains a zero value.
1	4	The first operand contains a value of less than zero.
2	2	The first operand contains a value that is greater than zero.
3	1	An overflow condition occurred.

* * *

INSTRUCTION: SUBTRACT HALFWORD

Mnemonic	Hex Code	Operand Format
SH	4B	$R_1, D_2(X_2, B_2)$

This instruction will first extract the 16-bit signed integer halfword from the address specified by the second operand and expand it to a 32-bit signed integer fullword. This is done by creating 16 additional high-order bits of the same value as the sign-bit of the original halfword value. The SH instruction will then subtract the expanded value from the contents of the first operand register. This will be done by complementing the bit configuration value of the expanded value and summing that complement with the value contained in the general register specified by

the first operand. The address generated by the second operand must be that of a half-word boundary alignment. If an overflow condition takes place during the execution of this instruction, the Condition Code is set to its respective configuration and a program interruption would normally occur.

CC	BC	Condition
0	8	The first operand contains a zero value.
1	4	The first operand contains a value of less than zero.
2	2	The first operand contains a value greater than zero.
3	1	An overflow condition occurred.

* * *

INSTRUCTION: SUBTRACT REGISTERS

Mnemonic	Hex Code	Operand Format
SR	1B	R_1, R_2

This instruction subtracts the second operand register value from the value of the first operand register. This is accomplished by summing the complement of the second operand value with actual value contained within the first operand register. The result of this operation is placed into the first operand register. If an overflow condition occurs as a result of this instruction, the overflow condition is reflected by the configuration of the Condition Code bits.

CC	BC	Condition
0	8	The first operand contains a value of zero.
1	4	The first operand contains a value of less than zero.
2	2	The first operand contains a value greater than zero.
3	1	An overflow condition occurred.

* * *

INSTRUCTION: SUBTRACT LOGICAL

Mnemonic	Hex Code	Operand Format
SL	5F	$R_1, D_2(X_2, B_2)$

The Subtract Logical instruction will logically subtract all 32 bits representing the value of the second operand fullword from the 32 bits representing the first operand register value. This is accomplished by summing the complement of the second operand value with the value of the first operand register and placing the total into the first operand register. The instruction uses all 32 bits, including the sign-bit, of each operand. If an overflow condition should occur, representing a carry-out of the sign-bit position, a program interrupt does not take place. Instead, the resulting Condition Code will indicate whether or not a carry-out of the sign-bit did occur during the execution of this instruction.

CC	BC	Condition
1	4	The first operand contains a nonzero value; a carry-out of the sign-bit did not occur.
2	2	The first operand contains a zero value; a carry-out of the sign-bit occurred.
3	1	The first operand contains a nonzero value; a carry-out of the sign-bit occurred.

*   *   *

INSTRUCTION:

SUBTRACT LOGICAL REGISTERS

Mnemonic	*Hex Code*	*Operand Format*
SLR	1F	R_1, R_2

The Subtract Logical Registers instruction will logically subtract all 32 bits representing the value of the contents of the second operand register from the 32 bits representing the contents of the first operand register. This is done by summing the complement of the second operand value with the value of the first operand and placing the total into the first operand register. The instruction uses all 32 bits, including the sign-bit, of each operand as logical digit values. If an overflow condition should occur, representing a carry-out of the sign-bit, a program interrupt will not take place. The Condition Code

settings from this instruction will indicate whether or not a carry-out of the sign-bit did occur.

CC	BC	Condition
1	4	The first operand contains a nonzero value; a carry-out of the sign-bit did not occur.
2	2	The first operand contains a zero value; a carry-out of the sign-bit occurred.
3	1	The first operand contains a nonzero value; a carry-out of the sign-bit occurred.

*   *   *

INSTRUCTION: MULTIPLY

Mnemonic	*Hex Code*	*Operand Format*
M	5C	$R_1, D_2(X_2, B_2)$

In this instruction, the contents of the first operand register (representing the multiplicand residing in an even-odd pair of general registers) is multiplied by the value contained at the address specified by the second operand, the multiplier. Both operands represent 32-bit signed integers, consisting of a sign-bit and a 31-bit integer. The first operand must always reference the even-numbered register of the even-odd pair of general registers. The address of the multiplier created by the second operand must reside on fullword boundary alignment. The resulting product of the multiplication represents a 64-bit signed integer residing in the whole of the even-odd pair of registers referenced by the R_1 operand register. The signs of the multiplier and multiplicand algebraically combine to determine the sign of the product.

The configuration of the Condition Code is not changed by this instruction.

*   *   *

INSTRUCTION:

MULTIPLY REGISTERS

Mnemonic	*Hex Code*	*Operand Format*
MR	1C	R_1, R_2

In the Multiply Registers instruction, the contents of the first operand register (representing the multiplicand residing in an even-odd pair of general registers) is multiplied by the value of the contents of the second operand register, the multiplier. The first operand register must always reference the even-numbered register of the even-odd pair of registers. The product of the multiplication is contained in the whole of the even-odd pair of general registers. The signs of the multiplicand and the multiplier algebraically combine to determine the sign of the product.

The configuration of the Condition Code is not changed by this instruction.

* * *

INSTRUCTION: MULTIPLY HALFWORD

Mnemonic	*Hex Code*	*Operand Format*
MH	4C	$R_1, D_2(X_2, B_2)$

Although the name of this instruction might seem to imply that both the multiplier and the multiplicand are halfword values, the multiplicand may actually be in excess of the maximum value of a halfword if the multiplier is not of a magnitude that would create a true product in excess of a maximum fullword value. The contents of the halfword at the location addressed by the second operand are first extracted and expanded to a 32-bit fullword by creating 16 additional high-order bits of the same configuration as the sign-bit of the original halfword multiplier. It will then take the 32-bit signed integer field of the first operand register (the multiplicand) and multiply that value by the 32-bit expanded multiplier. The product that results from this operation is a 32-bit signed integer residing in the general register specified by the first operand register referral. The signs of the multiplier and the multiplicand combine algebraically to determine the sign of the product. The address created by the second operand must be that of a halfword boundary alignment.

The configuration of the Condition Code is not changed by this instruction.

* * *

INSTRUCTION: DIVIDE

Mnemonic	*Hex Code*	*Operand Format*
D	5D	$R_1, D_2(X_2, B_2)$

The Divide instruction will divide the 32-bit signed integer specified by the second operand into an even-odd pair of general registers that contain the dividend. When the instruction statement is coded, it must always have the first operand register refer to the even-numbered register of the even-odd pair of general registers containing the dividend. The dividend itself resides as a 64-bit signed integer within the even-odd registers. Upon completion of the divide operation, the remainder will be in the even-numbered register and the quotient will be in the odd-numbered register, both of which will appear as 32-bit signed integers. The address created by the second operand must be that of a fullword boundary alignment.

The configuration of the Condition Code is not altered by this instruction.

* * *

INSTRUCTION: DIVIDE REGISTERS

Mnemonic	*Hex Code*	*Operand Format*
DR	1D	R_1, R_2

The Divide Registers instruction will divide the 32-bit signed integer contents of the general register specified by the second operand into an even-odd pair of general registers containing the dividend. When the instruction statement is coded, it must always have the first operand register refer to the even-numbered register of the even-odd pair of general registers containing the dividend. The dividend resides within the pair of registers as a 64-bit signed integer. Upon completion of the divide operation, the remainder will be contained within the even-numbered register and the quotient within the odd-numbered register, both of which will appear as 32-bit signed integers.

The configuration of the Condition Code is not changed by this instruction.

B. PERFORMING ARITHMETIC OPERATIONS WITH FIXED-POINT VALUES

To further clarify the value representation of a fixed-point integer, several more pieces of general information should be stated. Along with these, the configuration of the plus-positive or minus-negative value of a fixed-point value is an essential point to review here.

A positive (+) fixed-point value is represented as consisting of a zero-bit sign-bit in the high-order bit position and the value of the integer represented by the true binary Powers-Of-Two bit configuration in the remaining bit positions. A negative (−) fixed-point value is represented to consist of a one-bit sign-bit in the high-order bit position with the negative value of the integer represented in the two's complement notation in the remaining bit positions. Two of the tables that appear in the back of this text, the Powers-Of-Two Table and the Hexadecimal/Decimal Conversion Table, can be of considerable value in understanding fixed-point values and bit configurations.

In addition to requiring the use of at least one general register per instruction statement, fixed-point arithmetic operations require that data fields of storage containing arithmetic values must be on fullword or halfword boundary alignments, depending on the particular instruction that is to be performed.

The following illustrations present a graphic representation of the bit configurations of positive and negative fixed-point values.

1. A fullword containing a value of +33,974:

Fixed-point	s 0000	0000	0000	0000	1000	0100	1011	0110
Hexadecimal	0	0	0	0	8	4	B	6

2. A halfword containing a value of +29,878:

Fixed-point	s 0111	0100	1011	0110
Hexadecimal	7	4	B	6

3. A halfword containing a value of −987:

Fixed-point	s 1111	1100	0010	0101
Hexadecimal	F	C	2	5

4. A fullword containing a value of +4,593,211:

Fixed-point	s 0000	0000	0100	0110	0001	0110	0011	1011
Hexadecimal	0	0	4	6	1	6	3	B

5. A fullword containing a value of −3,915,228:

Fixed-point	s 1111	1111	1100	0100	0100	0010	0010	0100
Hexadecimal	F	F	C	4	4	2	2	4

6. A halfword containing a value of −1:

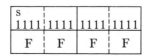

Fixed-point	s 1111	1111	1111	1111
Hexadecimal	F	F	F	F

It should be noted that the representation of a negative fixed-point value does not visually agree with the concept of significant digit-bits comprising the value of the whole number. If the last illustration, that of a halfword value of −1, were interpreted to have the Powers-Of-Two value of all significant 1-bits, exclusive of the sign-bit, the assumed value would be $-32,767$. The correct way to determine the true negative value of a negative fixed-point value is to sum the Powers-Of-Two value of the significant 1-bits and then subtract that amount from the maximum negative value of the particular field length in which the value appears; a halfword has a maximum negative value of $-32,768$, a fullword has a maximum negative value of $-2,147,483,648$. Using the last example shown, the one representing a halfword with a value of -1, the significant 1-bits would sum to a Powers-Of-Two value

of 32,767. By subtracting this amount from the maximum negative value for a halfword, $-32,768$, the difference is a -1 value, the true negative value of that halfword.

The conversion of a value with a true binary notation (a positive value) to a two's complement notation (a negative value) can easily be made by the programmer. Each bit position content in the positive value is reversed; one-bits become zero-bits and zero-bits become one-bits. Upon completion of the reversal of the value of all bits, add a one-bit to the low-order (right-most) bit position and the transition to the two's complement form is completed. For example:

1. Halfword containing $+15,093$ converted to $-15,093$:

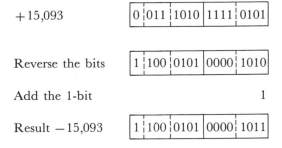

$+15,093$	0 011 1010 1111 0101
Reverse the bits	1 100 0101 0000 1010
Add the 1-bit	1
Result $-15,093$	1 100 0101 0000 1011

2. Halfword containing $+78$ converted to -78:

$+78$	0 000 0000 0100 1110
Reverse the bits	1 111 1111 1011 0001
Add the 1-bit	1
Result -78	1 111 1111 1011 0010

The opposite conversion is accomplished just as easily. The low-order one-bit is first subtracted from the two's complement form and then the bit position values are reversed. This will revert a two's complement notation

back to a positive value in true binary notation. For example:

1. Halfword containing -393 converted to $+393$:

-393	1 111 1110 0111 0111
Subtract the 1-bit	-1
Result	1 111 1110 0111 0110
Reverse all bits ($+393$)	0 000 0001 1000 1001

2. Halfword containing −1716 to +1716:

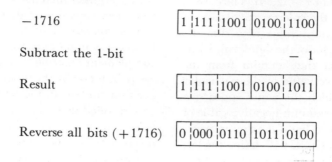

−1716	1 1111 1001 0100 1100
Subtract the 1-bit	− 1
Result	1 1111 1001 0100 1011
Reverse all bits (+1716)	0 0000 0110 1011 0100

These explanations and illustrations should provide enough information on fixed-point numeric formatting to allow the discussions that follow on fixed-point arithmetic instructions to be readily understood.

Throughout the remainder of these discussions of fixed-point arithmetic operations and instructions, the configurations of the storage areas and general registers will be shown as:

0110	0000	1101	0111
6	0	D	7

The '0' and '1' configuration on the upper line will represent the binary bit configuration of the fields, while the '0' through '9' and 'A' through 'F' configurations on the lower line will be the hexadecimal digit rep-

resentation for every four bit positions.

1. *The Fixed-Point "Add" Instructions*

(a) Add (A). This instruction will add the fixed-point value of the contents of a four-byte fullword storage area to the fixed-point value contained within a general register. As the addition is completed, the instruction checks for the occurrence of a fixed-point overflow.

The first operand in the instruction statement must be a general register or a symbol or label that has been equated to a general register. The second operand must represent a fullword and generate an address that is resident at a fullword boundary location of storage. The second operand is added to the first operand, the sum of which is placed into the general register specified by the first operand.

Example 1

A   6,FULLWRD1

Register 6 (Before)	S 0000 0000 0000 1001 0000 1111 0110 1001	+593,769
	0 0 0 9 0 F 6 9	

FULLWRD1	S 0000 0000 0000 0000 0001 0100 1011 0101	+5,301
	0 0 0 0 1 4 B 5	

Sum now in register 6	S 0000 0000 0000 1001 0010 0100 0001 1110	+599,070
	0 0 0 9 2 4 1 E	

This example has added the fixed-point value of FULLWRD1 ($+5301$) to the fixed-point value of general register 6 ($+593,769$), placing the sum of that operation into register 6. The hexadecimal configuration (Base-16) for the operands shown may be interpreted as:

Register 6	$+$ 9 0 F 6 9	or 593,769
FULLWRD1	$+$ 1 4 B 5	or 5,301
Register 6 (Sum)	$+$ 9 2 4 1 E	599,070

By using the Powers-Of-Two table and the Hexadecimal/Decimal Conversion table provided in the back of this text, the binary-formatted contents of these examples can be verified as shown above.

Example 2

$$A \qquad 8,=F'75963'$$

Register 8
(Before)

S							
0000	0000	0000	0000	0000	0000	1111	1111
0	0	0	0	0	0	F	F

$+255$

Literal F'75963'

S							
0000	0000	0000	0001	0010	1000	1011	1011
0	0	0	1	2	8	B	B

$+75,963$

Sum now in register 8

S							
0000	0000	0000	0001	0010	1001	1011	1010
0	0	0	1	2	9	B	A

$+76,218$

In this example, a fullword literal with a fixed-point value of $+75,963$ is being added to general register 8, which contains a fixed-point value of $+255$. The rule that the second operand must consist of a fullword that is boundary aligned is adhered to since the literal is established as a fullword value and the compiler will give it the proper boundary alignment.

The addition of the hexadecimal values for this example would appear as:

Register 8	$+$ F F	or 255
Literal	$+$ 1 2 8 B B	or 75,963
Register 8 (Sum)	$+$ 1 2 9 B A	or 76,218

(b) Add Halfword (AH). The Add Halfword instruction will add the fixed-point value of the contents of a two-byte storage area to the fixed-point value contained in a general register. The first operand in the instruction statement must be a general register or a symbol or label that has been equated to a general register. The second operand must represent a halfword and generate an address that is resident at a halfword boundary location of storage. The initial action taken by this instruction is to extract the value of the halfword operand and expand it to a 32-bit fullword. This is done by propagating 16 additional high-order bits of the same bit value as the sign-bit of the halfword. The fixed-point value is not changed by this expansion, nor are the contents of the halfword storage location changed in any way. The expanded operand value is then added to the value of the register operand, the sum of which is placed into the register. A fixed-point overflow is possible and the instruction statement will check for that condition.

Example 1

AH   3,HAFWRD2

Before the AH instruction statement is executed the contents of HAFWRD2 appeared as:

0000	1011	1100	1100
0	B	C	C

HAFWRD2   +3020

The AH instruction statement extracts this configuration and expands it to a fullword, so that when the addition takes place the operands and the result would appear as:

HAFWRD2 (Expanded)

S							
0000	0000	0000	0000	0000	1011	1100	1100
0	0	0	0	0	B	C	C

+3,020

Register 3 (Before)

S							
0000	0000	0000	0110	1001	0101	0011	0111
0	0	0	6	9	5	3	7

+431,415

Register 3 (Sum)

S							
0000	0000	0000	0110	1010	0001	0000	0011
0	0	0	6	A	1	0	3

+434,435

The addition of the hexadecimal values for this example would be:

HAFWRD2		+	B C C	or	3,020
Register 3	+	6	9 5 3 7	or	431,415
Sum in register 3	+	6	A 1 0 3	or	434,435

Example 2. As in the Add instruction, a literal may be used as the second operand, providing that it meets the halfword alignment specifications that normally apply. This could be coded as:

AH   5,=H'7721'

The literal would be established by the compiler on a halfword boundary alignment as the following configuration:

Literal H'7721'

S			
0001	1110	0010	1001
1	E	2	9

+7721

The value of the literal would then be extracted, expanded to a 32-bit fullword, and

the resulting addition function would result as:

Expanded	S								+7,721
Literal H'7721'	0000	0000	0000	0000	0001	1110	0010	1001	
	0	0	0	0	1	E	2	9	

Register 5	S								+139,852
(Before)	0000	0000	0000	0010	0010	0010	0100	1100	
	0	0	0	2	2	2	4	C	

Sum now in	S								+147,573
register 5	0000	0000	0000	0010	0100	0000	0111	0101	
	0	0	0	2	4	0	7	5	

The addition of the hexadecimal values for this example would be:

Literal H'7721'	+ 1 E 2 9	or	+ 7,721
Register 5	+ 2 2 2 4 C	or	+ 139,852
Sum in register 5	+ 2 4 0 7 5	or	+ 147,573

(c)   Add Registers (AR). This instruction will, as the name implies, add together the fixed-point values contained within two general registers. The value of the contents of the first operand register will be added together with the value of the contents of the second operand register, the sum of which is placed into the first operand register. As the addition is completed, the instruction checks for the occurrence of a fixed-point overflow. Both operands must be general registers, or symbols or labels that have been equated to a general register.

Example 1

General register 7 contains +396
General register 8 contains +4001

The instruction statement that is to be executed is:

    AR   7,8

Register 7	S								+396
(Before)	0000	0000	0000	0000	0000	0001	1000	1100	
	0	0	0	0	0	1	8	C	

Register 8	S								+4001
	0000	0000	0000	0000	0000	1111	1010	0001	
	0	0	0	0	0	F	A	1	

Sum in	S								+4397
register 7	0000	0000	0000	0000	0001	0001	0010	1101	
	0	0	0	0	1	1	2	D	

The addition of the hexadecimal values for this example would be:

General register 7	+	1 8 C	or	+ 396
General register 8	+	F A 1	or	+ 4001
Sum now in register 7	+ 1	1 2 D	or	+ 4397

The value of a general register may be doubled by adding that register to itself using the Add Register instruction, as shown in the following example.

Example 2. The statement that is to be executed is:

$$AR \quad 8,8$$

This would essentially create the following action:

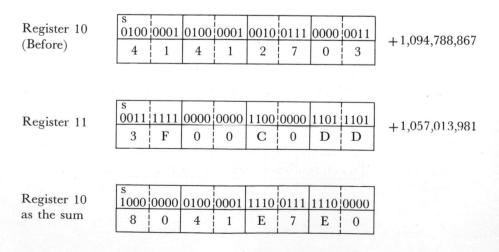

| Register 8 (1st operand) | S 0000 0000 0000 0000 0000 1111 1010 0001 / 0 0 0 0 0 F A 1 | +4001 |

| Register 8 (2nd operand) | S 0000 0000 0000 0000 0000 1111 1010 0001 / 0 0 0 0 0 F A 1 | +4001 |

| Sum in register 8 | S 0000 0000 0000 0000 0001 1111 0100 0010 / 0 0 0 0 1 F 4 2 | +8002 |

The fixed-point value in general register 8 has now been effectively doubled. It is altogether likely that at some time or another the programmer will unintentionally create a fixed-point overflow condition. The following example illustrates, through the use of the AR instruction, how this would occur and what the resulting configuration would be.

Example 3. The instruction statement that is to be executed is:

$$AR \quad 10,11$$

The fixed-point value of register 10 is +1,094,788,867.

The fixed-point value of register 11 is +1,057,013,981.

| Register 10 (Before) | S 0100 0001 0100 0001 0010 0111 0000 0011 / 4 1 4 1 2 7 0 3 | +1,094,788,867 |

| Register 11 | S 0011 1111 0000 0000 1100 0000 1101 1101 / 3 F 0 0 C 0 D D | +1,057,013,981 |

| Register 10 as the sum | S 1000 0000 0100 0001 1110 0111 1110 0000 / 8 0 4 1 E 7 E 0 | |

Note that the total value in general register 10 should have been +2,151,802,848, but the sign-bit in the high-order bit position has been changed to a negative sign. Because the sum of the addition was of a magnitude exceeding the maximum positive fixed-point value for a general register, the high-order overflow of the integer bits changed the value of the sign-bit. This would signal a fixed-point overflow to the system, the Condition Code would be set to indicate this problem, and a fixed-point interrupt would occur as a program exception.

(d) Add Logical (AL). The Add Logical instruction is very similar to the Add instruction, except that the data contained within the operands does not necessarily have to consist of valid fixed-point data consisting of a signed integer. It will logically add the bit configuration of the data specified by the second operand to the bit configuration of the data contained in the general register specified by the first operand. All 32-bits of each operand are added together without consideration for the existence of a sign-bit and the sum is placed into the first operand register. It is necessary that the address generated by the second operand should represent a four-byte area that resides on a full-word boundary alignment. Unlike the Add instruction, however, the Add Logical instruction will not create an exception condition in the event of a fixed-point overflow. The Condition Code settings for this instruction will indicate if a "carry-out" of the sign-bit occurred rather than indicating an overflow condition.

The next example illustrates an Add Logical instruction statement in which the sign-bit is not altered as a result of the addition.

Example 1. The instruction statement to be executed is:

AL   7,FULLWD9

Register 7 (Before)		S 0000	0000	0000	1001	0001	1110	0110	0000	+597,060
		0	0	0	9	1	E	6	0	

FULLWD9		S 0000	0000	0000	0000	0000	0000	1111	1111	+255
		0	0	0	0	0	0	F	F	

Sum now in register 7		S 0000	0000	0000	1001	0001	1111	0101	1111	+597,315
		0	0	0	9	1	F	5	F	

The addition of the hexadecimal values for this example would be:

General register 7	+ 9 1 E 6 0	or	597,060
FULLWD9	+ F F	or	255
Sum in register 7	+ 9 1 F 5 F	or	597,315

As a result of this example, the Condition Code bits would be set to indicate that "the answer is not zero and no carry-out of the sign-bit occurred."

Example 2. This next example will illustrate an Add Logical instruction statement in which a carry-out of the high-order integer-bit occurred, changing the sign-bit of the sum. The instruction statement to be executed:

AL   11,ONEFWRD

Register 11
(Before)

S							
0111	0001	0000	0000	0011	1100	0000	1111
7	1	0	0	3	C	0	F

+1,895,840,783

ONEFWRD

S							
0000	1111	0011	0111	0001	0001	1001	0000
0	F	3	7	1	1	9	0

+255,267,216

Register 11
Sum of AL

S							
1000	0000	0011	0111	0100	1101	1001	1111
8	0	3	7	4	D	9	F

−2,143,859,297

As a result of the addition, the sign-bit has been changed by the overflow of the high-order integer-bit into the sign-bit position. The fixed-point representation created by this overflow is a value of −2,143,859,297. After the execution of this example the Condition Code bits would be configurated to indicate that "the answer is not zero and a carry-out of the sign-bit occurred."

(e) **Add Logical Registers (ALR).** The Add Logical Registers instruction bears the same resemblance to the Add Registers instruction that the Add Logical instruction has to the Add instruction. The bit configuration of the value or data contained within the second operand register is added logically to the bit configuration of the value or data contained within the first operand register. This instruction will not cause an exception interruption in the event of an occurrence that would normally be considered to be a fixed-point overflow. In such an instance, a carry-out of the sign-bit will be indicated by the particular settings of the Condition Code bits. The sum of the addition resulting from this instruction will be placed into the general register specified by the first operand. Both operands must be general registers, or symbols or labels that have been equated to a general register.

Example 1. The instruction statement that is to be executed is:

ALR   2,7

General register 2 contains −3,596.
General register 7 contains −398,541.

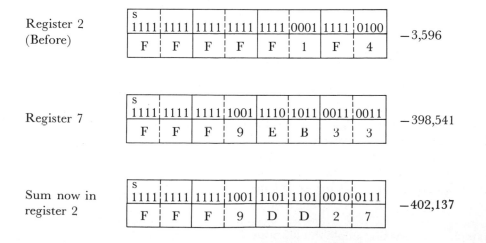

Register 2
(Before)

S							
1111	1111	1111	1111	1111	0001	1111	0100
F	F	F	F	F	1	F	4

−3,596

Register 7

S							
1111	1111	1111	1001	1110	1011	0011	0011
F	F	F	9	E	B	3	3

−398,541

Sum now in
register 2

S							
1111	1111	1111	1001	1101	1101	0010	0111
F	F	F	9	D	D	2	7

−402,137

Note that the bit configuration for the negative fixed-point value is in the two's complement form. Verification of the bit configuration for these negative values can be established by application of the techniques described earlier in this section under the heading of "Performing Arithmetic Operations with Fixed-Point Values."

(f) Summation of Fixed-Point Add Instructions. Although the five fixed-point Add instructions each have one or two individual peculiarities, they generally perform in a similar manner. A reasonable means of comparison may be found in the following example in which each of these five instructions are used at least once. The coding for this example is shown in Fig. 11-1.

Statement 001 subtracts general register 10 from itself by utilizing the Subtract Registers instruction. This effectively configurates general register 10 as a zero value.

Register 10

S								
0000	0000	0000	0000	0000	0000	0000	0000
0	0	0	0	0	0	0	0

+0

Statement 002 loads the contents of FULLWD4 into general register 7, after which that register will contain a fixed-point value of +9000.

Register 7

S								
0000	0000	0000	0000	0010	0011	0010	1000
0	0	0	0	2	3	2	8

+9000

Statement 003 adds general register 7 (+9000) to general register 10 (+0), using the Add Registers (AR) instruction. Register 10 now contains a fixed-point value of +9000 that results from the following action:

Register 10 (Before)

S								
0000	0000	0000	0000	0000	0000	0000	0000
0	0	0	0	0	0	0	0

+0

Register 7

S								
0000	0000	0000	0000	0010	0011	0010	1000
0	0	0	0	2	3	2	8

+9000

Register 10 (After)

S								
0000	0000	0000	0000	0010	0011	0010	1000
0	0	0	0	2	3	2	8

+9000

Statement 004 uses the Add instruction to add FULLWD2 (+75) to general register 10 (+9000). Register 10 now contains +9075.

Register 10 (Before)

S								
0000	0000	0000	0000	0010	0011	0010	1000
0	0	0	0	2	3	2	8

+9000

IBM System/360 Assembler Coding Form

X28-6509-2 U/M050
Printed in U.S.A.

Name	Operation	Operand	Comments	Identification-Sequence
*		CONSTANTS		
*				
FULLWD1	DC	F'256'		001
FULLWD2	DC	F'075'		002
FULLWD3	DC	F'16299'		003
FULLWD4	DC	F'9000'		004
FULLWD5	DC	F'296333'		005
HALFWD1	DC	H'3500'		006
*				
*				
ADDRTE	SR	10,10		007
	L	7,FULLWD4		008
	AR	10,7		009
	A	10,FULLWD2		010
	AL	10,FULLWD1		011
	AH	10,HALFWD1		012
	L	9,FULLWD5		
	L	8,FULLWD3		
	ALR	10,9		
	AR	10,8		
	BC	15,END		
*				
*				

Figure 11-1

FULLWD2

s							
0000	0000	0000	0000	0000	0000	0100	1011
0	0	0	0	0	0	4	B

+75

Register 10
Sum of Add

s							
0000	0000	0000	0000	0010	0011	0111	0011
0	0	0	0	2	3	7	3

+9075

Statement 005 adds FULLWD1 (+256) to general register 10 (+9075) by utilizing the Add Logical (AL) instruction. Because the values were not of a size great enough to affect the sign-bit, this instruction performed as efficiently as a regular Add (A) instruction would have. General register 10 now contains +9331.

Register 10
(Before)

s							
0000	0000	0000	0000	0010	0011	0111	0011
0	0	0	0	2	3	7	3

+9075

FULLWD1

s							
0000	0000	0000	0000	0000	0001	0000	0000
0	0	0	0	0	1	0	0

+256

Sum now in
Register 10

s							
0000	0000	0000	0000	0010	0100	0111	0011
0	0	0	0	2	4	7	3

+9331

Statement 006 uses the Add Halfword (AH) instruction to add HALFWD1 (+3500) to general register 10 (+9331). Register 10 now contains +12,831.

Register 10
(Before)

s							
0000	0000	0000	0000	0010	0100	0111	0011
0	0	0	0	2	4	7	3

+9331

HALFWD1

s							
0000	0000	0000	0000	0000	1101	1010	1100
0	0	0	0	0	D	A	C

+3500

Sum now in
register 10

s							
0000	0000	0000	0000	0011	0010	0001	1111
0	0	0	0	3	2	1	F

+12,831

Statement 007 loads general register 9 with the contents of FULLWD5 ($+296,333$).

Register 9

S 0000	0000	0000	0100	1000	0101	1000	1101	
0	0	0	4	8	5	8	D	$+296,333$

Statement 008 loads general register 8 with the contents of FULLWD3 ($+16,299$).

Register 8

S 0000	0000	0000	0000	0011	1111	1010	1011	
0	0	0	0	3	F	A	B	$+16,299$

Statement 009 adds general register 9 ($+296,333$) to general register 10 ($+12,831$) by using the Add Logical Registers (ALR) instruction. Register 10 now contains a fixed-point value of $+309,164$.

Register 10 (Before)

S 0000	0000	0000	0000	0011	0010	0001	1111	
0	0	0	0	3	2	1	F	$+12,831$

Register 9

S 0000	0000	0000	0100	1000	0101	1000	1101	
0	0	0	4	8	5	8	D	$+296,333$

Register 10 Sum of ALR

S 0000	0000	0000	0100	1011	0111	1010	1100	
0	0	0	4	B	7	A	C	$+309,164$

Statement 010 again uses the Add Registers instruction, this time to add general register 8 ($+16,299$) to general register 10 ($+309,164$). General register 10 now contains a fixed-point value of $+325,463$.

Register 10 (Before)

S 0000	0000	0000	0100	1011	0111	1010	1100	
0	0	0	4	B	7	A	C	$+309,164$

Register 8

S 0000	0000	0000	0000	0011	1111	1010	1011	
0	0	0	0	3	F	A	B	$+16,299$

Sum now in Register 10

S 0000	0000	0000	0100	1111	0111	0101	0111	
0	0	0	4	F	7	5	7	$+325,463$

Statement 011 is a forced branch to a routine that is labeled END.

Although this example illustrates the various fixed-point "add" instructions, it is not the most efficient manner in which to

arrive at the final result. It could have been coded in many ways, some of which would be considerably more efficient both in coding and in speed. For instance, it could have been more efficiently coded as:

```
ADDRTE    LM     6,10,FULLWD1            001
          AR     6,7                    002
          AR     6,8                    003
          AR     6,9                    004
          AR     10,6                   005
          AH     10,HALFWD1             006
          BC     15,END                 007
```

In this coding, Statement 001 would load FULLWD1 into general register 6, FULLWD2 into general register 7, FULLWD3 into general register 8, FULLWD4 into general register 9, and FULLWD5 into general register 10. The rest of the statements are self-explanatory. As shown by the coding, the final answer would still be found in general register 10.

2. *The Fixed-Point "Subtract" Instructions*

(a) Subtract (S). This instruction will subtract the fixed-point value of the contents of the second operand from the fixed-point value contained within the first operand register. The second operand must address a four-byte storage area that is located on fullword boundary alignment. The subtraction is performed by adding together the fixed-point value of the first operand and the complement of the fixed-point value of the second operand. The sum of this operation, representing the difference between the original value representations, is placed into the general register that is specified by the first operand. The Subtract instruction will check for a fixed-point overflow. If such a condition is found, the Condition Code bits are set to indicate that condition and a program interruption will occur.

For the purpose of illustrating this action, assume that general register 8 contains a fixed-point value of $+18,793$ and that a fullword, FXPONE, contains a fixed-point value of $+793$. The statement that is to be executed is:

S   8,FXPONE

Prior to the actual subtraction, the contents of FXPONE would be internally transposed to its two's complement notation. This transposition would appear as:

FXPONE
(True binary notation)
$+793$

S 0000	0000	0000	0000	0000	0011	0001	1001
0	0	0	0	0	3	1	9

FXPONE
(Two's complement)
-793

S 1111	1111	1111	1111	1111	1100	1110	0111
F	F	F	F	F	C	E	7

The subtraction would then be accomplished by adding the value of the contents

general register 8 with the two's complement of FXPONE. This addition would appear as:

Register 8
(Before)

S							
0000	0000	0000	0000	0100	1001	0110	1001
0	0	0	0	4	9	6	9

+18,793

FXPONE
(Complement)

S							
1111	1111	1111	1111	1111	1100	1110	0111
F	F	F	F	F	C	E	7

−793

Sum/difference
in register 8

S							
0000	0000	0000	0000	0100	0110	0101	0000
0	0	0	0	4	6	5	0

+18,000

If one negative fixed-point value was being subtracted from another fixed-point value, the second operand would be converted back to the true binary notation (the two's complement of the negative configuration) and then added to the value of the first operand.

To illustrate this action, assume that general register 5 contains a fixed-point value of −659,236 and that a fullword of storage, referenced by the label FXPTWO, contains a fixed-point value of −38,523. The instruction statement to be executed is:

S   5,FXPTWO

The contents of FXPTWO would be first internally transposed as:

FXPTWO
(Before)
−38,523

S							
1111	1111	1111	1111	0110	1001	1000	0101
F	F	F	F	6	9	8	5

FXPTWO
(Complement)
+38,523

S							
0000	0000	0000	0000	1001	0110	0111	1011
0	0	0	0	9	6	7	B

The subtraction specified by the instruction statement would then be accomplished by adding the contents of FXPTWO to the fixed-point contents of register 5.

Register 5
(Before)

S							
1111	1111	1111	0101	1111	0000	1101	1010
F	F	F	5	F	0	D	A

−659,236

FXPTWO

S							
0000	0000	0000	0000	1001	0110	0111	1011
0	0	0	0	9	6	7	B

+38,523

Sum/difference
in register 5

S							
1111	1111	1111	0110	1000	0111	0101	0101
F	F	F	6	8	7	5	5

−620,713

If the instruction statement should specify the subtraction of a field containing a negative value from a register containing a positive value, the negative value configuration (in two's complement form) would be reversed to the true binary notation and the two positive values would be added together.

(b) Subtract Halfword (SH). The Subtract Halfword instruction will subtract the fixed-point value of the contents of a two-byte halfword storage area from the fixed-point value of the contents of a general register. The first operand in the instruction statement must be a general register, or a label or symbol that has been equated to a general register. The second operand must represent a halfword; a two-byte storage area residing at a halfword boundary alignment. The instruction will first extract the value of the contents of the halfword and expand it to a 32-bit fullword by providing 16 additional high-order bits of the same value as the halfword sign-bit. The fixed-point value is not changed by this expansion and the contents of the halfword storage area are not altered. The subtraction is then performed by adding together the fixed-point value of the general register and the two's complement of the expanded halfword value. The result of this operation is then placed into the general register specified by the first operand. Since a fixed-point overflow is possible, the instruction will check for that condition. If an overflow has occurred, it will be indicated by the Condition Code bit configuration and a program interrupt.

A sample statement using this instruction would be:

$$\text{SH} \quad 2,\text{HAFSUB}$$

In order to illustrate this instruction statement, assume that general register 2 contains a fixed-point value of $+3,972,555$ and a stored halfword, referenced by the label HAFSUB, contains a fixed-point value of $+29,511$. The bit configuration of general register 2, the stored halfword HAFSUB, and the expanded 32-bit configuration of HAFSUB, would appear as:

Register 2							
S 0000	0000	0011	1100	1001	1101	1100	1011
0	0	3	C	9	D	C	B

$+3,972,555$

HAFSUB (Stored)			
S 0111	0011	0100	0111
7	3	4	7

$+29,511$

HAFSUB (Expanded)							
S 0000	0000	0000	0000	0111	0011	0100	0111
0	0	0	0	7	3	4	7

$+29,511$

The two's complement of the value of the expanded HAFSUB, which would occur prior to the arithmetic operation of the Subtract Halfword instruction statement, would appear as:

HAFSUB (Expanded) complement							
S 1111	1111	1111	1111	1000	1100	1011	1001
F	F	F	F	8	C	B	9

$-29,511$

The arithmetic subtraction would then be completed by summing the fixed-point value contained in general register 2 with the complement form of the value of the expanded HAFSUB. This would appear as:

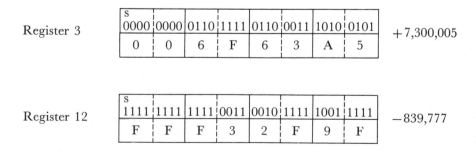

Register 2 (Before)

S 0000	0000	0011	1100	1001	1101	1100	1011
0	0	3	C	9	D	C	B

+3,972,555

HAFSUB (Expanded) complement

S 1111	1111	1111	1111	1000	1100	1011	1001
F	F	F	F	8	C	B	9

−29,511

Sum/difference in register 2

S 0000	0000	0011	1100	0010	1010	1000	0100
0	0	3	C	2	A	8	4

+3,943,044

(c) Subtract Registers (SR). The Subtract Registers instruction will subtract the fixed-point value of the contents of the second operand register from the fixed-point value of the contents of the first operand register. As in the performance of the Subtract and Subtract Halfword instructions, the fixed-point value indicated by the second operand is converted to its complement form and added to the fixed-point value of the first operand. This effectively creates the subtraction, after which the net result is placed into the first operand register. The possibility of a fixed-point overflow occurring is tested and the Condition Code bits are configurated accordingly. In the event of an overflow condition, a program exception interrupt will occur. The original value of the second register operand is always reversed for the arithmetic operation. If it was originally a positive value, it is changed to the two's complement negative form; if it was a negative value, it is changed to the complement of the negative, which would result in the true binary notation of a positive value.

To illustrate this concept, assume that general register 3 contains a value of +7,300,005 and general register 12 contains a value of −839,777. The bit configuration of these registers, prior to the issuance of a Subtract Registers instruction statement, would appear as:

Register 3

S 0000	0000	0110	1111	0110	0011	1010	0101
0	0	6	F	6	3	A	5

+7,300,005

Register 12

S 1111	1111	1111	0011	0010	1111	1001	1111
F	F	F	3	2	F	9	F

−839,777

The instruction statement to be executed is:

```
SR      3,12
```

This statement would first reverse the negative configuration of the value in general register 12 so that it would appear as:

Register 12 (Complemented)		S							

Register 12 (Complemented)	0000	0000	0000	1100	1101	0000	0110	0001	+839,777
	0	0	0	C	D	0	6	1	

It would then add together the value of register 12, as complemented, and the value of register 3, placing the sum of that addition into general register 3. This can be illustrated as:

Register 3 (Before)	0000	0000	0110	1111	0110	0011	1010	0101	+7,300,005
	0	0	6	F	6	3	A	5	

Register 12	0000	0000	0000	1100	1101	0000	0110	0001	+839,777
	0	0	0	C	D	0	6	1	

Sum/difference in register 3	0000	0000	0111	1100	0011	0100	0000	0110	+8,139,782
	0	0	7	C	3	4	0	6	

The Subtract Register instruction is often used to clear the contents of a general register. By subtracting a register from itself all 32 bit positions of that register are set to zero-bits. An example of this can be shown by using the instruction statement coded as:

SR   11,11

The performance of this instruction statement on general register 11 would be:

Register 11 (As 1st operand)	0000	0000	0100	0000	0111	0110	0101	1011	+4,224,603
	0	0	4	0	7	6	5	B	

Register 11 (In complement as 2nd operand)	1111	1111	1011	1111	1000	1001	1010	0101	−4,224,603
	F	F	B	F	8	9	A	5	

Sum now in register 11	0000	0000	0000	0000	0000	0000	0000	0000	+0
	0	0	0	0	0	0	0	0	

Because certain instructions only affect a portion of the bit configuration of a general register, this action would ensure that the high-order bits did not contain a resident value. As in the case of Insert Character, wherein the instruction only changed the low-order byte of the register, the programmer may wish to place a one-byte value into the register and then use that as an actual value. If the high-order bits or bytes are not set to zero, the actual value of the register is not consistent with the value inserted into the low-order byte. This can be prevented by using the Subtract Register instruction and stating the subject general register as both operands.

(d) Subtract Logical (SL). This instruction executes and performs quite similar to the Subtract instruction. It will logically subtract the bit configuration of the value contained within the second operand from the bit configuration of the value contained within the first operand register. The subtraction is actually performed by converting the bit configuration of the second operand value to its complement form and adding this configuration to the fixed-point value bit configuration of the first operand register. The result of this performance is placed into the general register specified by the first operand. The second operand must represent a four-byte area that is resident on a fullword boundary alignment of storage. The Subtract Logical instruction is different from the Subtract instruction in that it logically sub-

tracts all 32 bits of the second operand from that of the first operand; it will not cause a program interrupt if a fixed-point overflow occurs in the form of a carry-out of the sign-bit. Instead the Condition Code settings have unique interpretations to indicate whether or not a carry-out of the sign-bit did occur. Generally, if the execution of the Subtract Logical instruction did not cause the carry-out of the sign-bit it would perform the same function as the Subtract instruction. The only exception would be in interpreting the Condition Code bits.

Assume that general register 9 contains a fixed-point value of $+13,825$ and a fullword of storage, labeled SUBT, contains a fixed-point value of $+13,663$. The configuration of these values within their respective locations would be:

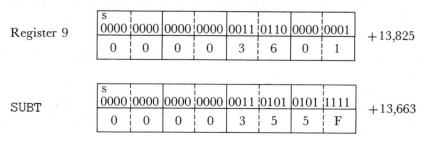

The instruction statement that is to be executed is:

    SL   9,SUBT

The first action to be taken by the instruction statement would be to convert the value of the second operand, SUBT, to its complement form. SUBT would then appear as:

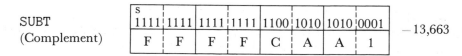

The instruction statement would then add together the bit configuration of the complement of SUBT and the bit configuration

of the contents of general register 9, placing the sum of that addition into register 9. This action would appear to affect these fields as:

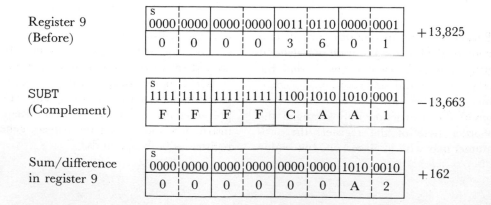

In this instance, the Condition Code bits will be set to indicate that "the difference in general register 9 is not zero and a carry-out of the sign-bit did not occur."

(e) Subtract Logical Registers (SLR). This instruction will logically subtract the bit configuration of the value contained within the second operand register from the bit configuration of the value contained within the first operand register. The actual subtraction is performed in the same manner as the other "subtract" instructions contained within this section; the bit configuration of the second operand is complemented and added to the bit configuration of the contents of the first operand.

The resulting sum is placed into the first operand register. As indicated, both operands must specify general registers, or a symbol or label that has been equated to a general register. The Subtract Logical Registers instruction will not cause a program interrupt if a fixed-point overflow in the form of a carry-out of the sign-bit occurs. The Condition Code bit settings, however, do have unique interpretations to indicate whether or not a carry-out of the sign-bit did occur.

To illustrate this instruction, consider that general register 9 contains a fixed-point value of +2,147,483,600 and general register 12 contains a fixed-point value of −486. The bit configuration of these registers would appear as:

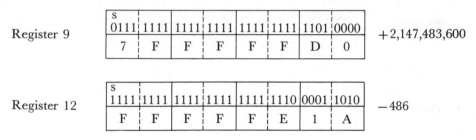

Register 9

s 0111	1111	1111	1111	1111	1111	1101	0000
7	F	F	F	F	F	D	0

+2,147,483,600

Register 12

s 1111	1111	1111	1111	1111	1110	0001	1010
F	F	F	F	F	E	1	A

−486

The instruction statement that is to be executed is:

        SLR   9,12

As with the performance of all fixed-point "subtract" instructions, the first action that is taken would be to convert the bit configuration of the contents of the second operand to its complement form. After doing this, general register 12 would have a bit configuration that appeared as:

Register 12
(Complement)

s 0000	0000	0000	0000	0000	0001	1110	0110
0	0	0	0	0	1	E	6

+486

The remaining action taken by the instruction statement will logically add together the fixed-point bit configuration of register 9 and the complement bit configuration of the value contained in general register 12. This would appear as:

Register 9
(Before)

s 0111	1111	1111	1111	1111	1111	1101	0000
7	F	F	F	F	F	D	0

+2,147,483,600

Register 12
(Complement)

s 0000	0000	0000	0000	0000	0001	1110	0110
0	0	0	0	0	1	E	6

+486

Sum/difference
in register 9

s 1000	0000	0000	0000	0000	0001	1011	0110
8	0	0	0	0	1	B	6

−2,147,483,210

Notice that the resulting sum is not the value to be expected from a normal operation. The operation resulted in a carry-out of the sign-bit, changing the positive/negative value of the answer. In this instance the Condition Code bits would indicate that "the difference is not zero and a carry-out of the sign-bit occurred."

(f) Summation of Fixed-Point Subtract Instructions. Having discussed the action and general use of the five fixed-point subtract instructions, it is in order to present a series of instruction statements that use those instructions. This will assist in demonstrating the peculiarities and similarities of each of the instructions as they are applied to fixed-

point values. The logic path drawn by the sample statements is not necessarily a practical application, but rather is solely intended to graphically offer an application pattern.

The instruction statements for this general example have been coded as shown in Fig. 11-2.

Statement 001 is a Load Multiple instruction statement. It will load the contents of LESS2 (+376) into general register 7 and the contents of LESS3 (−49,377) into general register 8. After the execution of this instruction statement, the fixed-point contents of general registers 7 and 8 will appear as:

Register 7	S 0000	0000	0000	0000	0000	0001	0111	1000	+376
	0	0	0	0	0	1	7	8	

Register 8	S 1111	1111	1111	1111	0011	1111	0001	1111	−49,377
	F	F	F	F	3	F	1	F	

Statement 002 is a Subtract Logical Registers instruction statement that will subtract the value contained within general register 8 (−49,377) from the value that is within general register 7 (+376). The result of the subtraction (+49,753) is placed into general register 7. The content value configuration of general register 8 is first changed to the

complement of its original value and then added to general register 7 to effectively perform the subtraction. The configuration of these registers during the execution of the instruction, at which time general register 8 is in its complement form of the original value, is shown by the following:

Register 7 (Before)	S 0000	0000	0000	0000	0000	0001	0111	1000	+376
	0	0	0	0	0	1	7	8	

Register 8 (Complement)	S 0000	0000	0000	0000	1100	0000	1110	0001	+49,377
	0	0	0	0	C	0	E	1	

Sum/difference in register 7	S 0000	0000	0000	0000	1100	0010	0101	1001	+49,753
	0	0	0	0	C	2	5	9	

IBM IBM System/360 Assembler Coding Form

X28-8509-2 U/M050
Printed in U.S.A.

PROGRAM

PROGRAMMER

DATE

PUNCHING INSTRUCTIONS — GRAPHIC — PUNCH

PAGE — OF — CARD ELECTRO NUMBER

Name	Operation	Operand	Identification-Sequence
*			
LESS1	DC	F'2590'	001
LESS2	DC	F'376'	002
LESS3	DC	F'-49377'	003
HAFSUB	DC	H'-747'	004
LOGWRD	DC	F'20000'	005
WORD	DC	F'32596'	006
*			
*			
SUBTEX	LM	7,8,LESS2	007
	SLR	7,8	
	SR	3,3	
	L	3,WORD	
	S	3,LESS1	
	SR	3,7	
	SH	3,HAFSUB	008
	SL	3,LOGWRD	009
	BC	15,FINSUBT	
*			010

Figure 11-2

295

Statement 003 performs a Subtract Register instruction. It will subtract general register 3 from itself. Upon completion of this statement, register 3 will contain a fixed-point value of +0.

Statement 004 loads general register 3 with the contents of WORD, a value of +32,596 which will be in the fixed-point value format. After execution of this statement, the bit configuration of general register 3 will be:

Register 3

S							
0000	0000	0000	0000	0111	1111	0101	0100
0	0	0	0	7	F	5	4

+32,596

Statement 005 will subtract the fixed-point value of the contents of a fullword labeled LESS1 (+2,590) from the fixed-point contents of general register 3 (+32,596). The fullword value, LESS1, will first be converted to the two's complement of its bit configuration value, after which it will be represented as:

LESS1
(Complement)

S							
1111	1111	1111	1111	1111	0101	1110	0010
F	F	F	F	F	5	E	2

−2,590

This value configuration will then be added to the fixed-point contents of general register 3, constituting the subtraction as requested. The bit configuration of register 3, before and after the execution of the instruction, and the use of the complement of LESS1, can be illustrated as:

Register 3
(Before)

S							
0000	0000	0000	0000	0111	1111	0101	0100
0	0	0	0	7	F	5	4

+32,596

LESS1
(Complement)

S							
1111	1111	1111	1111	1111	0101	1110	0010
F	F	F	F	F	5	E	2

−2,590

Result in
register 3

S							
0000	0000	0000	0000	0111	0101	0011	0110
0	0	0	0	7	5	3	6

+30,006

Statement 006, a Subtract Registers instruction statement, will subtract the fixed-point value of the contents of general register 7 (+49,753) from the fixed-point value of the contents of general register 3. The bit configurations shown below are for the value of general register 3 before and after the execution of this statement, and for the complement configuration of general register 7 as it is used by the SR instruction.

Register 3
(Before)

s 0000	0000	0000	0000	0111	0101	0011	0110
0	0	0	0	7	5	3	6

+30,006

Register 7
(Complement)

s 1111	1111	1111	1111	0011	1101	1010	0111
F	F	F	F	3	D	A	7

−49,753

Register 3
(Result)

s 1111	1111	1111	1111	1011	0010	1101	1101
F	F	F	F	B	2	D	D

−19,747

Statement 007 subtracts the fixed-point value of HAFSUB (a stored Halfword) from the fixed-point value contents of general register 3 (−19,747). After its expansion to a 32-bit fullword, the bit configuration of HAFSUB is converted to its complement form and is then added to the value of general register 3, as shown in the following illustration.

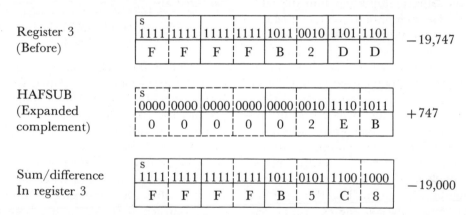

Register 3
(Before)

s 1111	1111	1111	1111	1011	0010	1101	1101
F	F	F	F	B	2	D	D

−19,747

HAFSUB
(Expanded complement)

s 0000	0000	0000	0000	0000	0010	1110	1011
0	0	0	0	0	2	E	B

+747

Sum/difference
In register 3

s 1111	1111	1111	1111	1011	0101	1100	1000
F	F	F	F	B	5	C	8

−19,000

Statement 008, a Subtract Logical instruction statement, will subtract the fixed-point value contained within the fullword LOGWRD (−20,000) from the fixed-point value of the contents of general register 3 (−19,000). The effect of the statement on general register 3 when it is added to the complement of LOGWRD, can be shown as:

Register 3
(Before)

s 1111	1111	1111	1111	1011	0101	1100	1000
F	F	F	F	B	5	C	8

−19,000

LOGWRD
(Complement)

s 0000	0000	0000	0000	0100	1110	0010	0000
0	0	0	0	4	E	2	0

+20,000

Register 3
(Result)

s 0000	0000	0000	0000	0000	0011	1110	1000
0	0	0	0	0	3	E	8

+1,000

Statement 009 is a forced branch to a routine that is referenced by the label FINSUBT.

After performing all of the instruction statements listed within this subroutine, the fixed-point value of the contents of general register 3 would be $+1000$. Unless the values of the fullword constants were changed prior to each time that the subroutine was entered, these instructions would always return the same answer, making it a useless calculation.

3. The Fixed-Point "Multiply" Instructions

(a) **Multiply (M).** The Multiply instruction requires an even-odd contiguous pair of general registers that are to be used as a work area and product field. The programmer must load the multiplicand into the odd-numbered register prior to issuing the Multiply instruction. When the Multiply instruction statement is executed, it will multiply the fixed-point value contained in the even-odd register pair by the fixed-point value of the multiplier, a fullword value in storage. The resulting product will reside in the combined even-odd pair of registers as a 64-bit signed integer (1 sign-bit, 63 integer-bits) with the units position of the answer occupying the low-order position of the odd-numbered register. The first operand register must always address the even-numbered register of the pair, otherwise a specification error interrupt will occur. If the product is known to be small enough to be contained within a single general register, the product may be extracted from the odd-numbered register only; otherwise it must be extracted from the combined length of the even-odd register pair.

To illustrate the performance of this instruction and its effect on the registers that are used as the operand work areas, the following examples are presented.

Example 1. The fixed-point values that are to be used for this Multiply example are contained in two fullwords of storage. They are:

```
FULLWD1     DC      F'32973'
FULLWD2     DC      F'7851'
```

The instruction statements that are to be executed are:

```
L       9,FULLWD1                   001
M       8,FULLWD2                   002
```

Statement 001 loads general register 9 with the fixed-point value that is specified by the label FULLWD1. Although the entire product area is comprised of general registers 8 and 9, the loading of the multiplicand into the odd-numbered register affects that general register only. Register 8 has not yet been affected at this point and its contents are unpredictable and unspecified. After the Load instruction statement has been executed, the configuration of the general registers used in this example will be:

General register 8   General register 9 $(+32,973)$

?	?	?	?	?	?	?	?	S 0000	0000	0000	0000	1000	0000	1100	1101
								0	0	0	0	8	0	C	D

Statement 002 will multiply the fixed-point value of the multiplicand (assumed to be residing in general register 9) by the fixed-point value of FULLWD2, the multiplier. The resulting product will be found in the combined length of general registers 8 and 9, residing as a 64-bit signed integer. The bit configuration of the multiplicand, multiplier and product would be:

Multiplicand (Before the Multiply instruction statement)

General register 8   General register 9

?	?	?	?	?	?	?	?	S 0000	0000	0000	0000	1000	0000	1100	1101
								0	0	0	0	8	0	C	D

Multiplier   FULLWD2   (+7,851)

S							
0000	0000	0000	0000	0001	1110	1010	1011
0	0	0	0	1	E	A	B

Product

General register 8   (+258,871,023)   General register 9

S															
0000	0000	0000	0000	0000	0000	0000	0000	0000	1111	0110	1110	0000	1110	1110	1111
0	0	0	0	0	0	0	0	0	F	6	E	0	E	E	F

In this instance, the product did not exceed the length of the odd-numbered register. Therefore, the answer (the product) could be moved out for retention in another area by storing the contents of general register 9 into a fullword storage location. The sign-bit in register 9 is the same as the sign-bit in general register 8. This is because once the multiplication function is completed, the algebraically determined sign-bit is expanded toward the right until the first significant-digit of the product is encountered. In a positive value, the first significant-digit of the product would be a one-bit; in a negative value it would be a zero-bit. This interpretation could be stated as: "A significant product digit is a bit that is unlike (or the opposite of) the sign-bit of the product."

Example 2. This example will show the result of a multiplication in which the product exceeds the length of the odd-numbered general register. The values that are to be used are stated as:

```
MPCAN     DC     F'75968322'
MPLIER    DC     F'59312'
ANSWER    DS     D
```

The instruction statements that are to be executed are:

```
L      3,MPCAN          001
M      2,MPLIER         002
STM    2,3,ANSWER       003
```

Statement 001 loads general register 3 with the fixed-point value of MPCAN, equal to +75,968,322. The bit configuration of general register 3 should then appear to be:

Register 3

S							
0000	0100	0111	0111	1110	1101	0000	0010
0	4	7	7	E	D	0	2

+75,968,322

Statement 002 will multiply the fixed-point value contained in general register 3 by the fixed-point value of MPLIER, placing the resulting product into the whole of general registers 2 and 3. The bit configuration of the registers affected by the execution of Statement 002 would be:

Multiplicand (Before the Multiply statement)

General register 3   (+75,968,322)

?	?	?	?	?	?	?	?	S							
								0000	0100	0111	0111	1110	1101	0000	0010
									0	4	7	7	E	D	0	2

Multiplier (MPLIER)

(+59,312)

s							
0000 0000	0000 0000	1110 0111	1011 0000				

0	0	0	0	E	7	B	0

Product

General register 2   (+4,505,833,114,464)   General register 3

s															
0000 0000	0000 0000	0000 0100	0001 1001	0001 1000	1001 0101	0000 1011	0110 0000								

0	0	0	0	0	4	1	9	1	8	9	5	0	B	6	0

Notice that the product that resulted from the execution of Statement 002 exceeded the limit of general register 3 and extended into the two low-order bytes of general register 2.

Statement 003 loads the multiple combination of registers 2 and 3 into a doubleword (ANSWER) field of storage. Because the product value exceeded the length of one general register, the storage area for the answer was required to be a doubleword in length.

(b) Multiply Registers (MR). The Multiply Registers instruction is identical to the Multiply instruction with the single exception that the second operand of the statement must refer to a general register. The MR instruction requires an even-odd contiguous pair of registers for the product area. Normally the multiplicand should be loaded into the odd-numbered general register of the pair of registers and the multiplier should be loaded into another general register. An exception to this rule is discussed later in this analysis. When the Multiply Registers instruction statement is executed, it will multiply the fixed-point value contained within the odd-numbered register of the pair by the fixed-point value of the contents of the second operand register. The product will reside in the whole of the even-odd pair of registers as a 64-bit signed integer; a sign-bit, and a 63-bit integer value. The units position of the product will occupy the low-order bit posi-

tions of the odd-numbered general register. The first operand register must always address the even-numbered register of the pair, otherwise a specification interrupt will occur. If it is known that the product value will be small enough to be contained within one register, the answer may be extracted from the odd-numbered register only; otherwise the answer must be moved out of the entire pair of registers.

Example 1. The fixed-point values, as contained within fullword storage locations, are:

```
POINTA      DC        F'3276'
POINTB      DC        F'991'
ANSR        DC        F'0'
```

The instruction statements that will be executed are:

```
LM      5,6,POINTA              001
MR      4,6                     002
ST      5,ANSR                  003
```

Statement 001 is a Load Multiple statement. It loads the fixed-point value of POINTA into general register 5 first and then loads the fixed-point value of the contents of POINTB into general register 6. Register 5, as the odd-numbered register of the pair of registers 4 and 5, will now contain the multiplicand. The value now contained in general register 6 is considered to be the multiplier for this example. At this point, the bit configuration of the three registers would be:

General register 4   General register 5   (+3276)

?	?	?	?	?	?	?	?	S 0000¦0000	0000¦0000	0000¦1100	1100¦1100
								0 ¦ 0	0 ¦ 0	0 ¦ C	C ¦ C

General register 6   (+991)

S 0000¦0000	0000¦0000	0000¦0011	1101¦1111
0 ¦ 0	0 ¦ 0	0 ¦ 3	D ¦ F

As indicated above, general register 4 contains unpredictable data prior to the execution of the Multiply Registers instruction.

Statement 002 will perform the Multiply Registers instruction statement. The fixed-point value of the contents of general register 6 will be used as the multiplier against the fixed-point value contained in general register 5. The product will reside in the whole of general registers 4 and 5. The bit configuration of the product will appear as:

General register 4   General register 5

S 0000¦0000	0000¦0000	0000¦0000	0000¦0000	0000¦0000	0011¦0001	1000¦1001	1011¦0100
0 ¦ 0	0 ¦ 0	0 ¦ 0	0 ¦ 0	0 ¦ 0	3 ¦ 1	8 ¦ 9	B ¦ 4

(+3,246,516)

Statement 003 will store the fixed-point value contained in general register 5 into a fullword storage area labeled ANSR. It is assumed that the programmer was aware that the fixed-point value of the product would not exceed the maximum value content of a single general register. After the Store instruction was executed, the bit configuration of ANSR would be:

ANSR

S 0000¦0000	0011¦0001	1000¦1001	1011¦0100
0 ¦ 0	3 ¦ 1	8 ¦ 9	B ¦ 4

+3,246,516

Example 2. The multiply function of the Multiply Registers instruction can also be used to square a number (i.e., multiply a fixed-point value times itself). This is done by loading the value into the odd-numbered register of an even-odd pair of registers and then issuing the Multiply Registers instruction using the even-numbered register as the first operand and the odd-numbered register as the second operand. Assume that the fixed-point value of +1006 is to be squared by the following instruction statement coding:

```
SQRIT    DC     F'1006'
*
RTE      L      3,SQRIT          001
         MR     2,3              002
```

Statement 001 loads the fixed-point value of +1006 into general register 3. The bit configuration of general registers 2 and 3 would now appear as:

General register 2   General register 3   (+1006)

?	?	?	?	?	?	?	?	S 0000	0000	0000	0000	0000	0011	1110	1110
								0	0	0	0	0	3	E	E

Statement 002 specifies that the instruction should "multiply the fixed-point contents of general register 3 (by addressing general register 2 as the first operand) by the contents of general register 3." This effectively squares the fixed-point value contained in register 3, placing the product in the whole of general registers 2 and 3. After execution of this instruction statement, general registers 2 and 3 would have a bit configuration of:

General register 2   (+1,012,036)   General register 3

S 0000	0000	0000	0000	0000	0000	0000	0000	0000	0000	0000	1111	0111	0001	0100	0100
0	0	0	0	0	0	0	0	0	0	0	F	7	1	4	4

Example 3. By using an application similar to Example 2, the programmer can load both the multiplier and the multiplicand into the product area and multiply them together. Assume that the following fields have been defined:

```
LM   6,7,QUANTITY    001
MR   6,6             002
ST   7,ANSWER        003
```

```
QUANTITY     DC     F'395'
UNITCOST     DC     F'75'
ANSWER       DC     F'0'
```

The instruction statements would then be:

Statement 001 will perform a Load Multiple instruction, during which the contents of QUANTITY will be loaded into general register 6 and the contents of UNITCOST will be loaded into general register 7. At the completion of this statement the contents of these registers will be:

General register 6   (+395)   General register 7   (+75)

S 0000	0000	0000	0000	0000	0001	1000	1011	S 0000	0000	0000	0000	0000	0000	0100	1011
0	0	0	0	0	1	8	B	0	0	0	0	0	0	4	B

Statement 002 will multiply the contents of general register 6 against the contents of general register 7, even though the operands both refer to general register 6.

Statement 003 is storing the result of the multiplication operation into a fullword storage area labeled ANSWER. It is presumed, in this example, that the result of the multiplication will not exceed the maximum value of one general register.

(c) **Multiply Halfword (MH).** This instruction may be used to multiply a halfword fixed-point value times a fixed-point value contained within a general register. In this instruction, the product area required consists of only one general register. The value that is to be multiplied is first loaded into the product register and is then multiplied by the halfword value that resides in storage. The result will reside in the whole of the product register. An overflow condition might occur, but a program interrupt will not take place in such an instance. Care should be taken to assure that the values being used will not create an overflow condition because this could alter the sign-bit of the product from its true value.

Example 1. The fixed-point values, contained within storage locations, are:

```
MPLIER      DC      H'352'
MPCAND      DC      F'49365'
PRODANS     DC      F'0'
```

The instruction statements have been coded as:

```
L    6,MPCAND              001
MH   6,MPLIER              002
ST   6,PRODANS             003
```

Statement 001 loads the fixed-point value contained in MPCAND into general register 6. At this point the bit configuration of general register 6 would appear as:

Register 6

S							
0000	0000	0000	0000	1100	0000	1101	0101
0	0	0	0	C	0	D	5

+49,365

Statement 002 multiplies the fixed-point value contained in general register 6 (+49,365) by the fixed-point value contained in MPLIER (+352). The halfword value of MPLIER is first extracted and expanded to a 32-bit fullword format. The general register is then multiplied by this expanded halfword, with the resulting product residing in the whole of the general register. The bit configuration of MPLIER, before and after expansion, and the product value in general register 6 resulting from the multiplication, are as follows:

Register 6
(Before)

S							
0000	0000	0000	0000	1100	0000	1101	0101
0	0	0	0	C	0	D	5

+49,365

MPLIER
(Before)

S			
0000	0001	0110	0000
0	1	6	0

+352

MPLIER
(Expanded)

S							
0000	0000	0000	0000	0000	0001	0110	0000
0	0	0	0	0	1	6	0

+352

Register 6
(Product)

S							
0000	0001	0000	1001	0010	0100	1110	0000
0	1	0	9	2	4	E	0

+17,376,480

Statement 003 stores the fixed-point value contents of general register 6 into a fullword storage area labeled PRODANS.

Example 2. This example illustrates the multiplication of two halfword fixed-point values by using the Multiply Halfword instruction. For this example the values to be used are defined as:

```
HAF1     DC      H'4392'
HAF2     DC      H'68'
ANSW     DC      F'0'
```

The instruction statements have been coded as:

```
LH    7,HAF1               001
MH    7,HAF2               002
ST    7,ANSW               003
```

Statement 001 loads the fixed-point half-word value from HAF1 into general register 7. In doing so, the instruction statement will expand the halfword configuration to a 32-bit fullword configuration by adding 16 additional high-order bits of the same bit value as the original sign-bit of the halfword. Therefore, it is not necessary to clear general register 7 to a zero value before loading HAF1 into general register 7. The bit configuration of general register 7 now appears as:

S 0000	0000	0000	0000	0001	0001	0010	1000
0	0	0	0	1	1	2	8

Register 7   +4392

Statement 002 multiplies the value contained in general register 7 by the fixed-point value contained in HAF2. HAF2 is expanded to a 32-bit fullword configuration, after which the multiplication occurs. The bit configuration of the expanded value of HAF2 and the product in general register 7 after the multiplication, would be:

HAF2 (Expanded)

S 0000	0000	0000	0000	0000	0000	0100	0100
0	0	0	0	0	0	4	4

+68

Register 7 (Product)

S 0000	0000	0000	0100	1000	1110	1010	0000
0	0	0	4	8	E	A	0

+298,656

Statement 003 stores the fixed-point value contained in general register 7 into a full-word storage area that is referenced by the label ANSW. If it were definitely known that the product contained within general register 7 would never exceed the maximum value of a halfword, then Statement 003 could have been a Store Halfword instruction—from general register 7 into a halfword storage location.

(d)   Summation of Fixed-Point "Multiply" Instructions. In learning about the three fixed-point multiply instructions it was probably apparent that the concept of the operations performed by these instructions varied quite little. The use of any of these would depend largely on the requirements of the data to be processed, its magnitude and, if all of these considerations were equal, the programmers personal preference for instruction use.

In order to illustrate these instructions, the following example is presented. Assume that the programmer wishes to determine the total number of rivets used to assemble bulk quantities of various pieces of equipment. Although it would not be practical to use a series of multiply instructions such as this, it is shown here in that manner in order to relate the similarity of the fixed-point multiply instructions. Normally, the quantity of rivets used and the quantities of the assemblies would be variable factors dependent on the particular assembly to be completed. Assume that at the point in time that the processing is passing through this particular logic part of the problem program that the data fields will contain the values indicated. The coding created for this example is shown in Fig. 11-3.

Statement 001 sets the contents of general register 11 to zero by subtracting it from itself. Register 11 is to be used as an accumulator to hold the total sum of the rivets required as calculated by the multiply statements that are coded.

Statement 002 loads general register 3

IBM System/360 Assembler Coding Form

X28-6509-2 U/M050
Printed in U.S.A.

PROGRAM					PUNCHING INSTRUCTIONS	GRAPHIC			PAGE	OF	
PROGRAMMER			DATE			PUNCH			CARD ELECTRO NUMBER		

Name	Operation	Operand	Comments	Identification-Sequence
*				
ITEM1QTY	DC	F'593'		001
RIVET1	DC	F'15'		002
ITEM2QTY	DC	F'278'		003
RIVET2	DC	F'38'		004
ITEM3QTY	DC	F'899'		005
RIVET3	DC	H'9'		006
TOTALRVT	DC	F'0'		007
*				
GOCALC	SR	11,11		008
	L	3,ITEM1QTY		
	M	2,RIVET1		
	AR	11,3		009
	LM	5,6,ITEM2QTY		
	MR	4,6		
	AR	11,5		010
	L	8,ITEM3QTY		
	MH	8,RIVET3		011
	AR	11,8		
	ST	11,TOTALRVT		012
*				

Figure 11-3

with the fixed-point value from the stored fullword ITEM1QTY (+593). Because general register 3 is part of a pair of even-odd general registers that are construed to be the product area, the bit configuration of the product area would now appear as:

General register 2

General register 3   (+593)

?	?	?	?	?	?	?	?	s 0000	0000	0000	0000	0000	0010	0101	0001
								0	0	0	0	0	2	5	1

Statement 003 multiplies the multiplicand content (+593) of general registers 2 and 3 by the fixed-point value contained within RIVET1 (+15), resulting in a product of +8895, a figure small enough to be contained within general register 3 although the product is construed to be in the whole of general registers 2 and 3. The bit configuration of registers 2 and 3 would now be:

General register 2   (+8895)   General register 3

s 0000	0000	0000	0000	0000	0000	0000	0000	0000	0000	0000	0000	0010	0010	1011	1111
0	0	0	0	0	0	0	0	0	0	0	0	2	2	B	F

Statement 004 adds the fixed-point value that is contained within general register 3 (+8895) to the fixed-point value currently residing within general register 11 (+0), resulting in a new value of +8895 for general register 11.

Statement 005 executes a Load Multiple instruction statement that will take the value from ITEM2QTY and load it into general register 5 and will also load the value of RIVET2 into general register 6. In effect, this is loading the multiplicand into general registers 4 and 5, and the multiplier into general register 6. After this instruction is executed, the fixed-point value within those registers will be:

General register 4

General register 5   (+278)

?	?	?	?	?	?	?	?	s 0000	0000	0000	0000	0000	0001	0001	0110
								0	0	0	0	0	1	1	6

Register 6

s 0000	0000	0000	0000	0000	0000	0010	0110
0	0	0	0	0	0	2	6

+38

Statement 006 multiplies the fixed-point contents of general register 5 (+278) by the fixed-point contents of general register 6 (+38), resulting in the product residing in the whole of general registers 4 and 5 (+10,564). This product would have a bit configuration of:

General register 4   General register 5   (+10,564)

s 0000	0000	0000	0000	0000	0000	0000	0000	0000	0000	0000	0000	0010	1001	0100	0100
0	0	0	0	0	0	0	0	0	0	0	0	2	9	4	4

Statement 007 adds the fixed-point value of the contents of register 5 (+10,564) to the value of the contents of general register 11

(+8895). Register 11 would then contain a new fixed-point value of +19,459, which would appear as:

	S							
Register 11	0000	0000	0000	0000	0100	1100	0000	0011
	0	0	0	0	4	C	0	3

+19,459

Statement 008 loads the fixed-point value of the contents of ITEM3QTY (+899) into general register 8. Because the next instruction statement is to be a Multiply Halfword statement, it is only necessary to load that

value into a single register, which may be either even-numbered or odd-numbered. Register 8 would then contain a bit configuration of:

	S							
Register 8	0000	0000	0000	0000	0000	0011	1000	0011
	0	0	0	0	0	3	8	3

+899

Statement 009 will execute the Multiply Halfword instruction. This will multiply the value of the contents of general register 8

(+899) by the value of the contents of RIVET3 (+9). After this operation register 8 will contain a value of +8091.

	S							
Register 8	0000	0000	0000	0000	0001	1111	1001	1011
	0	0	0	0	1	F	9	B

+8091

Statement 010 performs another Add Registers instruction, adding together the values contained in general register 8

(+8091) and register 11 (+19,459); the resulting sum appearing in general register 11 as:

	S							
Register 11	0000	0000	0000	0000	0110	1011	1001	1110
	0	0	0	0	6	B	9	E

+27,550

Statement 011 will store the fixed-point value of the contents of general register 11 into a fullword of storage that is referred to by the label TOTALRVT.

The program routine has now determined, via a series of multiply routines, that the bulk quantities of rivets required for the various part assemblies will total 27,550.

4. The Fixed-Point "Divide" Instructions

(a) Divide (D). The Divide instruction,

like the Multiply instruction, also requires an even-odd contiguous pair of general registers that are to be used as the area for the dividend, quotient, and the remainder. The dividend must first be loaded into this pair of registers. The instruction statement that loads the dividend may address the odd-numbered register of the pair unless the programmer intends to manipulate the sign of the dividend by shifting. If the dividend is loaded directly into the odd-numbered register, the content of the even-numbered register is unpredictable, but the odd-numbered register will contain the fixed-point value of the dividend. The dividend may be loaded from a fullword in storage or from another general register. When the Divide instruction is executed it will divide the fixed-point value contained within the odd-numbered general register by the fixed-point value of the divisor operand. After completion of the divide operation, the quotient will be found in the odd-numbered register in fixed-point format. The remainder will be contained within the even-numbered register and will have the sign of the dividend. The sign of the quotient is algebraically determined. Inasmuch as the dividend is considered to consist of an even-odd pair of registers once it has been moved into the divide work area as a 64-bit signed integer, it is suggested that the even-numbered register be guaranteed the sign of the odd-numbered register. This may be accomplished in several different ways as will be shown. Several examples of the use and function of the Divide instruction follow.

Example 1. The fixed-point values to be used in this example are represented by:

```
DIVDEND     DC          F'48933'
DIVSOR      DC          F'37'
QUOTNT      DC          F'0'
REMNDR      DC          F'0'
```

The instruction statements that are to be executed are:

```
ROUTE1      SR    8,8              001
            L     9,DIVDEND        002
            D     8,DIVSOR         003
            ST    8,REMNDR         004
            ST    9,QUOTNT         005
```

Statement 001 is subtracting general register 8 from itself, guaranteeing a +0 value for that register. In this instance, it is known that all dividends will be a positive value, so this action will assure the 64-bit dividend of a sign of the same configuration as will be loaded into the low-order 32 bit positions.

Statement 002 is loading the fixed-point value of DIVDEND into general register 9, the odd-numbered register of the even-odd pair of registers. After completion of this instruction statement, those registers will appear as:

General register 8   General register 9   (+48,933)

s 0000	0000	0000	0000	0000	0000	0000	0000	0000	0000	0000	0000	1011	1111	0010	0101
0	0	0	0	0	0	0	0	0	0	0	0	B	F	2	5

Statement 003 will divide the contents of general registers 8 and 9 (+48,933) by the fixed-point value contained in DIVSOR (+37). After execution of this instruction statement, the quotient may be found in general register 9 and the remainder, if any, may be found in register 8. The contents of these two registers would be configured as:

General register 8 (Remainder—+19)   General register 9 (Quotient—+1322)

s 0000	0000	0000	0000	0000	0000	0001	0011	s 0000	0000	0000	0000	0000	0101	0010	1010
0	0	0	0	0	0	1	3	0	0	0	0	0	5	2	A

Statement 004 will store the remainder of +19, as found in general register 8, into a fullword storage area labeled REMNDR.

Statement 005 will store the quotient of +1322, as found in general register 9, into a fullword storage area labeled QUOTNT.

Example 2. This example will take the gross amount of dollars paid for a quantity of items and divide that amount by the number of pieces purchased in order to determine the average dollar cost per piece.

The statements have been coded as:

```
AMTPD        DC      F'3927869'
UNITS        DC      F'8346'
REMAINDR     DC      F'0'
AVGCOST      DC      F'0'
*
DIVRTE       L       4,AMTPD              001
             SRDA    4,32                 002
             D       4,UNITS              003
             STM     4,5,REMAINDR         004
```

Statement 001 is loading general register 4 with the fixed-point value contained in AMTPD. This represents the gross dollars paid for the entire quantity of units. After this instruction statement is completed, the configuration of general registers 4 and 5 will appear as:

General register 4   General register 5

S 0000	0000	0011	1011	1110	1111	0011	1101	?	?	?	?	?	?	?	?
0	0	3	B	E	F	3	D								

Statement 002 is a Shift Right Double Algebraic instruction with a shift length of 32 bit positions. This will shift the entire contents of general register 4 into general register 5 and replace the bits shifted out of register 4 with the same value of bits as the sign-bit of general register 4. This has now assured that the sign-bit of the 64-bit signed integer, considered to be comprised of registers 4 and 5, has the same sign-bit as that of the original dividend, AMTPD. After the shift the configuration of general registers 4 and 5 will appear as:

General register 4   General register 5

S 0000	0000	0000	0000	0000	0000	0000	0000	0000	0000	0011	1011	1110	1111	0011	1101
0	0	0	0	0	0	0	0	0	0	3	B	E	F	3	D

Statement 003 divides the contents of registers 4 and 5 (+3,927,869) by the total number of units purchased, which is represented by the fixed-point value contained in UNITS (+8346). After this statement has been executed, general register 4 will contain the remainder and general register 5 will contain the quotient, the quotient representing the average gross dollar price per unit. The configuration of these will appear to be:

General register 4 (Remainder—+5249)   General register 5 (Quotient—+470)

S 0000	0000	0000	0000	0001	0100	1000	0001	S 0000	0000	0000	0000	0000	0001	1101	0110
0	0	0	0	1	4	8	1	0	0	0	0	0	1	D	6

Statement 004 is performing a Store Multiple operation. It will store the contents of general register 4 (Remainder—+5249) into a fullword of storage labeled remainder by the identity REMAINDR and also store the contents of general register 5 (Quotient—+470) into a fullword of storage labeled AVGCOST.

(b) Divide Registers (DR). The Divide Registers instruction performs identically to the Divide instruction with the single exception that the divisor operand must address a general register rather than a fullword storage location. It too uses a pair of even-odd contiguous general registers as the division work area for the dividend.

Example 1. The values that are to be used in this example and the instruction statements that are to be performed have been coded as:

```
SETSIGN   DC    F'0'
DIVDEN    DC    F'72833117'
DIVSR     DC    F'442'
REMDR     DC    F'0'
ANSR      DC    F'0'
*
BEGINDV   LM    6,8,SETSIGN    001
          DR    6,8            002
          STM   6,7,REMDR      003
```

Statement 001 is performing a Load Multiple instruction statement. It will load the fixed-point value of SETSIGN into general register 6, the value of DIVDEN into general register 7, and the value of DIVSR into general register 8. This program has assumed that all dividends are to be positive values. Therefore, the loading of a +0 value (SETSIGN) into register 6 has assured that the 64-bit signed integer (representing the whole of general registers 6 and 7) will have the same sign-bit configuration as the dividend (DIVDEN) that was loaded into register 7. At the same time that the forced sign-bits and the dividend were loaded into registers 6 and 7, this statement has also loaded the divisor (DIVSR) into general register 8. This single instruction statement has effectively replaced three possible individual Load instruction statements. Upon completion of the execution of this statement the configuration of general registers 6, 7, and 8 would appear to be:

General register 6   (+72,833,117)   General register 7

s															
0000	0000	0000	0000	0000	0000	0000	0000	0000	0100	0101	0111	0101	1000	0101	1101
0	0	0	0	0	0	0	0	0	4	5	7	5	8	5	D

Register 8 (Divisor)

s							
0000	0000	0000	0000	0000	0001	1011	1010
0	0	0	0	0	1	B	A

(+442)

Statement 002 will execute the Divide Registers instruction. In this instance, it will divide the fixed-point value of general register 8 into the fixed-point 64-bit signed integer represented by general registers 6 and 7. After the execution of this statement, the bit configuration of registers 6 and 7 will be:

Register 6 (Remainder—+357)   Register 7 (Quotient—+164,780)

s								s							
0000	0000	0000	0000	0000	0001	0110	0101	0000	0000	0000	0010	1000	0011	1010	1100
0	0	0	0	0	1	6	5	0	0	0	2	8	3	A	C

Statement 003 is a Store Multiple instruction statement. It will store the fixed-point value of the contents of register 6 (the remainder) into a fullword storage area labeled REMDR and will also then store the fixed-point value of register 7 (the quotient or answer) into a fullword of storage that is addressed by the label ANSR.

Because there are only two fixed-point "divide" instructions, it is not considered necessary to have a summary of their performance included at this point. It is intended that the section that follows, dealing with the application of decimal point concepts in fixed-point math routines, will suffice for a generalization of the use of the Divide and Divide Registers instructions.

C. FIXED-POINT LOGIC APPLICATIONS WITH ASSUMED DECIMAL POINTS

The task of applying decimal point logic to fixed-point math routines is quite easily accomplished. Basically, it is merely the interim step of multiplying or dividing the various fixed-point values by increments of 10, 100, 1000, 10,000, etc. To increase the value of a whole number so that it retains its whole number value plus two assumed decimal places, it is only necessary to multiply that number by 100. To remove unwanted assumed decimal places from a mixed number containing two decimal places, it would only require the division of that number by 100 in order to reduce it to a whole number configuration. "Rounding off" of decimal point values and subsequent reduction to a whole number is similarly accomplished.

For example, assume that the programmer desires to multiply a given quantity of units by an even-dollar per unit cost and to arrive at a total cost that includes two decimal places. Using the base data constants stated within the following coding, this could be accomplished by at least two different methods.

```
UNITCOST   DC     F'95'        (xxxx. assumed format)
UNITQTY    DC     F'863'       (xxxx. assumed format)
TOTLCOST   DC     F'0'         (xxxxxxxx.00 assumed format)
XPANDIT    DC     F'100'       (x.00 assumed format)
*
DORTE      SR     4,4                                          001
           L      5,UNITCOST                                   002
           M      4,XPANDIT                                    003
           M      4,UNITQTY                                    004
           ST     5,TOTLCOST                                   005
```

Statement 001 clears general register 4 to a +0 value by subtracting it from itself.

Statement 002 loads general register 5 with the fixed-point value contained in UNITCOST. In this instance it is considered to be +$95. The configuration of general registers 4 and 5 would now be:

General register 4   (+0)   General register 5   (+95)

S								S							
0000 0000	0000 0000	0000 0000	0000 0000	0000 0000	0000 0000	0000 0000	0101 1111
0 0	0 0	0 0	0 0	0 0	0 0	0 0	5 F

Statement 003 multiplies the contents of general registers 4 and 5 by a value of +100, the value contained in the fullword storage location, XPANDIT. This action would change the configuration of registers 4 and 5 to:

General register 4   (+9500)   General register 5

S								S							
0000 0000	0000 0000	0000 0000	0000 0000	0000 0000	0000 0000	0010 0101	0001 1100
0 0	0 0	0 0	0 0	0 0	0 0	2 5	1 C

Statement 004 multiplies general registers 4 and 5 by the total number of units (+863), the value contained in UNITQTY. These registers would now have a configuration of:

General register 4   General register 5
(+8,198,500—assumed to $81,985.00)

S 0000	0000	0000	0000	0000	0000	0000	0000	0000	0000	0111	1101	0001	1001	0110	0100
0	0	0	0	0	0	0	0	0	0	7	D	1	9	6	4

Statement 005 stores the value of general register 5 into a fullword storage area labeled TOTLCOST. For the intent and purpose of the programmer, the data being stored there has a format of 81,985.00, even though the physical decimal point does not exist. It is the programmer's responsibility to remember this assumed decimal point if he should perform any further operations with this value.

The same results could have been accomplished by this series of coded instruction statements:

```
DORTE    SR    4,4           001
         L     5,UNITCOST    002
         M     4,UNITQTY     003
         M     4,XPANDIT     004
         ST    5,TOTLCOST    005
```

In this instance the unit cost and the unit quantity are first multiplied together and the resulting product of that action is then multiplied by +100. The configuration of the registers for the first four instruction statements would then be:

After Statements 001 and 002:

General register 4   (+0)   General register 5   (+95)

S 0000	0000	0000	0000	0000	0000	0000	0000	0000	0000	0000	0000	0000	0000	0101	1111
0	0	0	0	0	0	0	0	0	0	0	0	0	0	5	F

After Statement 003:

General register 4   (+81,985)   General register 5

S 0000	0000	0000	0000	0000	0000	0000	0000	0000	0000	0000	0001	0100	0000	0100	0001
0	0	0	0	0	0	0	0	0	0	0	1	4	0	4	1

After Statement 004

General register 4   General register 5
(+8,198,500—assumed to be $81,985.00)

S 0000	0000	0000	0000	0000	0000	0000	0000	0000	0000	0111	1101	0001	1001	0110	0100
0	0	0	0	0	0	0	0	0	0	7	D	1	9	6	4

Statement 005 is performing exactly the same function in this instruction statement set as it did in the previous set of statements.

Another frequent use of this method of adding decimal points to a whole number is to increase the magnitude of a value that is to be divided by a similar value, or by a larger value, in order to determine a percentage ratio. This is demonstrated in the following set of coding.

```
SQUARES   DC     F'893'      (xxxx. assumed format)
CIRCLES   DC     F'995'      (xxxx. assumed format)
MULT      DC     F'1000'     (x.000 assumed format)
RATIO     DC     F'0'        (xxxx.0% assumed format)
*
PCTRTE    SR     6,6                                    001
          L      7,SQUARES                              002
          M      6,MULT                                 003
          D      6,CIRCLES                              004
          ST     7,RATIO                                005
```

Statement 001 sets general register 6 to a +0 value by subtracting it from itself.

Statement 002 loads general register 7 with the fixed-point value of the contents of SQUARES. The bit configuration of general registers 6 and 7 would then appear to be:

General register 6   (+893)   General register 7

S															
0000	0000	0000	0000	0000	0000	0000	0000	0000	0000	0000	0000	0000	0011	0111	1101
0	0	0	0	0	0	0	0	0	0	0	0	0	3	7	D

Statement 003 will multiply the contents of general registers 6 and 7 (+893) by +1000, the fixed-point value contained in MULT. This has now effectively added three assumed decimal places to the value in general register 7. The configuration of these registers would now be:

General register 6   General register 7
(+893,000—assumed to be 893.000)

S															
0000	0000	0000	0000	0000	0000	0000	0000	0000	0000	0000	1101	1010	0000	0100	1000
0	0	0	0	0	0	0	0	0	0	0	D	A	0	4	8

Statement 004 will divide the contents of general registers 6 and 7 (+893,000) by the fixed-point value contained within the stored fullword CIRCLES (+995). After execution of this instruction the configuration of these registers would be:

General register 6   General register 7 (Quotient—+897)
(Remainder—+485)   (Assumed to be .897 or 89.7%)

S								S							
0000	0000	0000	0000	0000	0001	1110	0101	0000	0000	0000	0000	0000	0011	1000	0001
0	0	0	0	0	1	E	5	0	0	0	0	0	3	8	1

Statement 005 is storing the fixed-point contents of general register 7 into a stored fullword labeled RATIO. The programmer has assumed that the configuration of the data at this point is .897 or 89.7%, whichever way he may wish to express the ratio or percentage.

"Rounding off" of decimal places to the nearest whole number value, or to a lesser number of decimal places, is performed in a similar manner. The following two examples, a multiply routine and a divide routine, will illustrate the common concept of "rounding off."

Example 1. This example will multiply together several "mixed" values (whole numbers and decimal places) and then "round off" the product to the nearest whole number unit. That is, if the first decimal point position is equal to, or greater than, a value of five, the unit position of the whole number will be increased by a value of +1.

The values to be used in this example and the instruction statements that have been coded are shown in Fig. 11-4.

Statement 001 is setting general register 2 to a zero balance by subtracting it from itself.

Statement 002 is loading the fixed-point value of CASES into general register 3. Registers 2 and 3 would now appear to be:

General register 2   (+4331)   General register 3

S 0000	0000	0000	0000	0000	0000	0000	0000	0000	0000	0000	0000	0001	0000	1110	1011
0	0	0	0	0	0	0	0	0	0	0	0	1	0	E	C

Statement 003 is multiplying the contents of general register 2 (+4331) by the fixed-point value of UNITS. Although the visual value of UNITS is +293, for the programmer's application it has an assumed value of .293. After execution of the Multiply instruction, the general registers will contain:

General register 2   General register 3

S 0000	0000	0000	0000	0000	0000	0000	0000	0000	0000	0001	0011	0101	1100	1111	0111
0	0	0	0	0	0	0	0	0	0	1	3	5	C	F	7

+1,268,983   (Assumed to be +1,268.983)

Statement 004 is adding the fixed-point value of +500, contained within ROUNDER, to the value contained within general register 3. The logic of the program has intended that if the first digit to the right of the assumed decimal point is equal to, or greater than, a value of five, then the units position of the whole number should be increased by +1. In adding .500 to the digits to the right of the assumed decimal point, this will automatically increase the units position of the whole number by one if the first decimal value to the right of the decimal point is five or greater. After execution of this statement the configuration of the registers will be:

General register 2   General register 3

S 0000	0000	0000	0000	0000	0000	0000	0000	0000	0000	0001	0011	0101	1110	1110	1011
0	0	0	0	0	0	0	0	0	0	1	3	5	E	E	B

+1,269,483   (Assumed to be +1,269.483)

IBM System/360 Assembler Coding Form

| PROGRAM | | | | PAGE | OF |
| PROGRAMMER | | DATE | | CARD ELECTRO NUMBER | |

PUNCHING INSTRUCTIONS — GRAPHIC | PUNCH

X28-6509-2 U/M050
Printed in U.S.A.

STATEMENT

Name	Operation	Operand	Comments	Identification-Sequence
*				
*				
CASES	DC	F'4331'	(xxxx. ASSUMED FORMAT)	001
UNITS	DC	F'293'	(.000 ASSUMED FORMAT)	002
ROUNDER	DC	F'500'	(.000 ASSUMED FORMAT)	003
REDUCE	DC	F'1000'	(x.000 ASSUMED FORMAT)	004
ANSWER	DC	F'0'	(xxxxxx. ASSUMED FORMAT)	005
*				
*				
SAMPRTE	SR	2,2		006
	L	3,CASES		
	M	2,UNITS		
	A	3,ROUNDER		
	D	2,REDUCE		
	ST	3,ANSWER		

Figure 11-4

Statement 005 will divide the value of REDUCE (+1000) into the value contained within general registers 2 and 3. In doing this, it effectively reduces the dividend to an assumed whole number value. Because the three assumed decimal point positions had a power of 1000ths, the division of this value by 1000 eliminates all digits to the right of the assumed decimal point. The configuration of the registers would now be:

General register 2

S							
0000	0000	0000	0000	0000	0001	1110	0011
0	0	0	0	0	1	E	3

(Remainder— +483)

General register 3

S							
0000	0000	0000	0000	0000	0100	1111	0101
0	0	0	0	0	4	F	5

(Quotient— +1269)

Statement 006 is storing the value of general register 3 (+1269) into a fullword of storage labeled ANSWER.

Example 2. This example intends to find a percentage ratio between two values, carried out to an assumed value expression of 0.0000 or 000.00%. This value will then be rounded to an assumed value expression of 0.000 or 000.0% and then stored into a receiving area. The values to be used and the instruction statements that have been coded are shown in Fig. 11-5.

Statement 001 is setting the contents of general register 8 to a zero value by subtracting that register from itself.

Statement 002 is loading the fixed-point value of RECEIPTS (+2395) into general register 9. The configuration of registers 8 and 9 would now appear as:

General register 8   (+2395)   General register 9

S															
0000	0000	0000	0000	0000	0000	0000	0000	0000	0000	0000	0000	0000	1001	0101	1011
0	0	0	0	0	0	0	0	0	0	0	0	0	9	5	C

Statement 003 will multiply the value of these registers by 10,000, the value contained within XPAND. The configuration of the new values now found in these registers is:

General register 8   General register 9

S															
0000	0000	0000	0000	0000	0000	0000	0000	0000	0001	0110	1101	0111	0010	1011	0000
0	0	0	0	0	0	0	0	0	1	6	D	7	2	B	0

+23,950,000   (Assumed to be 2,395.0000)

Statement 004 will divide the contents of general registers 8 and 9 by the value of SALES. The resulting quotient in register 9 is construed to have the format of an unexpressed percentage (0.0000). The registers would now appear in a configuration of:

General register 8

S							
0000	0000	0000	0000	0000	1100	0010	1000
0	0	0	0	0	C	2	8

(Remainder— +3112)

General register 9

S							
0000	0000	0000	0000	0001	0110	1011	1010
0	0	0	0	1	6	B	A

(Quotient— +5818)
(Assumed to be .5818 or 58.18%)

IBM IBM System/360 Assembler Coding Form

X28-6509-2 U/M050
Printed in U.S.A.

| PROGRAM | | | GRAPHIC | | PAGE | OF |
| PROGRAMMER | | DATE | PUNCHING INSTRUCTIONS | PUNCH | CARD ELECTRO NUMBER | |

Name	Operation	Operand		Comments		Identification-Sequence
*						
RECEIPTS	DC	F'2395'		(xxxx. ASSUMED FORMAT)		001
SALES	DC	F'4116'		(xxxx. ASSUMED FORMAT)		002
XPAND	DC	F'10000'		(x.0000 ASSUMED FORMAT)		003
ROUND	DC	F'5'		(.0000 ASSUMED FORMAT)		004
CUTOFF	DC	F'10'		(x.0 ASSUMED FORMAT)		005
HOLDIT	DC	F'0'		(xxx.0% ASSUMED FORMAT)		006
*						
*						
NOWRTE	SR	8,8				
	L	9,RECEIPTS				
	M	8,XPAND				
	D	8,SALES				
	A	9,ROUND				
	SR	8,8				
	D	8,CUTOFF				007
	ST	9,HOLDIT				008

Figure 11-5

317

Statement 005 is adding a value of +5 (assumed to be .0005 or .05%) to general register 9 in order to round off the percentage to the nearest .0% value. After execution of this instruction statement the configuration of general registers 8 and 9 will be:

General register 8		General register 9	

s								s							
0000	0000	0000	0000	0000	1100	0010	1000	0000	0000	0000	0000	0001	0110	1011	1111
0	0	0	0	0	C	2	8	0	0	0	0	1	6	B	F

(+3112)   (+5823—assumed to be .5823 or 58.23%)

Statement 006 sets register 8 to zero in preparation for the Divide instruction statement that immediately follows. The registers would now appear to contain:

General register 8		General register 9	

s								s							
0000	0000	0000	0000	0000	0000	0000	0000	0000	0000	0000	0000	0001	0110	1011	1111
0	0	0	0	0	0	0	0	0	0	0	0	1	6	B	F

(+0)   (+5823—assumed to be .5823 or 58.23%)

Statement 007 divides general registers 8 and 9 by the value contained within CUT-OFF (+10). This effectively reduces the value in general register 9 by one decimal point position. The configuration of the registers now is:

General register 8		General register 9	

s								s							
0000	0000	0000	0000	0000	0000	0000	0011	0000	0000	0000	0000	0000	0010	0100	0110
0	0	0	0	0	0	0	3	0	0	0	0	0	2	4	6

(Remainder—+3)   (Quotient—+582)
                                    (Assumed to be .582 or 58.2%)

Statement 008 will store the fixed-point contents of general register 9 into a fullword storage location that is referenced by the label HOLDIT. The value of +582, which is being stored, has been assigned an assumed identity of 58.2% by the programmer and will be recognized as this format at any other point within the program.

The foregoing illustrations and examples should have presented a reasonable basis for understanding the application and manipulation of assumed decimal point locations. In general, to remove unwanted decimal point positions, it is only necessary to divide by 10, 100, 1000, 10,000, 100,000, etc. In order to add a required number of decimal point positions, it is only necessary to multiply by 10, 100, 1000, 10,000, 100,000, etc. A combination of both of these concepts may be used by the programmer at his discretion to manipulate decimal point concepts in fixed-point arithmetic routines.

Review Exercises

1. When an Add Halfword instruction statement is executed, the stored two-byte halfword specified by the second operand is added to the low-order two bytes of general register specified by the first operand register. (True) (False)

2. SLR is the mnemonic op code for the Assembler Language instruction *Subtract Logical Registers*.

3. In fixed-point arithmetic instructions, the PSW Condition Code is not altered by the execution of any one of the *Multiply* or *Divide* instructions.

4. A negative fixed-point value will always have a single sign-bit that is comprised of a *ONE*-bit.

5. During the execution of a fixed-point Subtract instruction statement, the value of the content of the second operand is *Complemented* and that new configuration is then algebraically *ADDED* to the value of the content of the first operand.

6. When coding a Multiply or Multiply Registers instruction statement, the first operand of the statement must always specify the *EVEN*-numbered register of a contiguous pair of even-odd registers.

7. If a Subtract Registers instruction statement was executed in which the first operand register contained a fixed-point value of +2048 and the second operand register contained a fixed-point value of −2048, the first operand register would subsequently contain a fixed-point value of *+4096*.

8. An odd-numbered general register may be validly addressed by the first operand in a Multiply Halfword instruction statement. (True) (False)

9. In an Add Registers (AR) instruction statement the sum of the addition will be placed into the (first) (second) operand register.

10. If a storage halfword, containing a fixed-point value of −32,768, was to be added to a general register via the Add Halfword instruction, the expanded fullword version of that halfword during execution of the statement could be represented in hexadecimal form as:

F	F	F	F	8	0	0	0

11. A fixed-point Multiply (M) instruction statement can validly generate a fixed-point value that is greater than the capacity of a single register. (True) (False)

12. In a fixed-point Add *Logical* instruction statement all bits of the fullword storage area will be added to all bits of the general register specified by the first operand without regard for sign-bit significance.

13. Although only a single register is specified as the first operand in a Multiply Halfword instruction statement, it is not possible for a fixed-point overflow to occur as a result of execution of an MH instruction statement. (True) (False)

Using the values defined as residing within the specified general register and storage areas for the following problems, complete both the binary and hexadecimal configurations of the fields as they would appear upon completion of the execution of the instruction statement.

14. Register 3 . . . contains $+23,975$
Register 9 . . . contains $-14,210$

ADDFLDS   AR   3,9

Register 3 (Hex)

(Binary)

15. Register 11 . . . contains $+392,417$
HAFWD . . . contains $+32,519$

SETADDRT   AH   11,HAFWD

Register 11 (Hex)

(Binary)

16. Register 7 . . . contains 32,416,817
FWD9 . . . contains $-27,941$

LOGADD   AL   7,FWD9

Register 7 (Hex)

(Binary)

17. Register 3 . . . contains $+31,965,423$
Register 9 . . . contains $+7,592,087$

CALCADD   ALR   9,3

Register 9 (Hex)

(Binary)

18. Register 10 . . . contains $+159,375$
Register 9 . . . contains $+2,899$

SUBRTE   SLR   10,9

Register 10 (Hex)

(Binary)

19. Register 4 . . . contains $-39,541,782$

SUBRT2   SR   4,4

Register 4 (Hex)

(Binary)

20. Register 12 . . . contains $-389,510$
FULLWD6 . . . contains $+426,877$

SUMRTE   A   12,FULLWD6

Register 12 (Hex)

(Binary)

21. Register 7 . . . contains +319,586
HALFWDB . . . contains −7,853

                           J0BRTE7   SH   7,HALFWDB

Register 7 (Hex)

        (Binary)

22. Register 10 . . . contains +21,583,910
FULLWRDX . . . contains +30,009

                           CLRTE5   SL   10,FULLWRDX

Register 10 (Hex)

        (Binary)

23. Register 3 . . . contains +325,198
FWORD . . . contains −2,768,447

                           SETCALC   S   3,FWORD

Register 3 (Hex)

        (Binary)

24. Register 2 . . . contains +83,915
Register 3 . . . contains −5,176,933
Register 4 . . . contains +213,847
FVALUE1 . . . contains +15,006
FVALUE2 . . . contains +8,092

                           SETVALS   SR   2,2
                                           LM   3,4,FVALUE1
                                         MR   2,4

Register 2 (Hex)

        (Binary)

Register 3 (Hex)

        (Binary)

25. Register 4 . . . contains +3,975
Register 5 . . . contains +17,842,931
FULLWORD . . . contains +800,216
FWMP . . . contains +83

                           MULTRTE   L   4,FULLWORD
                                       SRDL   4,32
                                       M   4,FWMP

Register 4 (Hex)

        (Binary)

Register 5 (Hex)

        (Binary)

26. Register 6 . . . contains +0
Register 7 . . . contains +385,910
HAFWD9 . . . contains +16,694

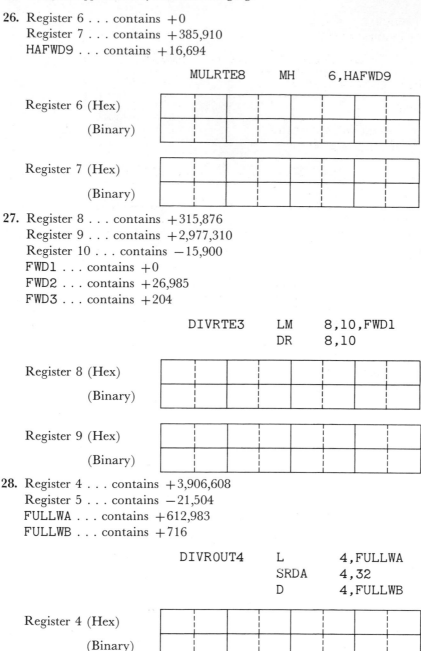

MULRTE8   MH   6,HAFWD9

Register 6 (Hex)

(Binary)

Register 7 (Hex)

(Binary)

27. Register 8 . . . contains +315,876
Register 9 . . . contains +2,977,310
Register 10 . . . contains −15,900
FWD1 . . . contains +0
FWD2 . . . contains +26,985
FWD3 . . . contains +204

DIVRTE3   LM   8,10,FWD1
             DR   8,10

Register 8 (Hex)

(Binary)

Register 9 (Hex)

(Binary)

28. Register 4 . . . contains +3,906,608
Register 5 . . . contains −21,504
FULLWA . . . contains +612,983
FULLWB . . . contains +716

DIVROUT4   L   4,FULLWA
             SRDA   4,32
             D   4,FULLWB

Register 4 (Hex)

(Binary)

Register 5 (Hex)

(Binary)

Additional Review Exercises for Chapters 3 through 11

This review consists of instruction statements that may or may not be valid. The errors will include incorrect formatting of statements, incorrect operands, and invalid length and register specifications. Place a checkmark before the incorrect statements.

1. _____	DATARTE	CLI	DATA3+9,Z'6'
2. _____		AP	DATPAK(5),7(4,5)
3. _____	BIN4SET	DC	63BL1'11000001'
4. _____	LOADEM	L	2,ADCON1
5. _____		MVC	BIGFLD+1500(6),PADDATA
6. _____	LOADSET	LM	13,2,4(8)
7. _____		SL	5,15(0,8)
8. _____	BRANCHA	BALR	3,6
9. _____	SETLARGE	DC	6000XL2'4040'
10. _____		M	10,0(0,3)
11. _____		D	3,FULLWORD
12. _____	PUTTEM	STM	10,9,8(7)
13. _____		AP	DATAPAK,=XL3'004593'
14. _____		C	DATA1(6),DATA2
15. _____	MULTEM	MH	3,=H'328'
16. _____		SH	11,=H'1'
17. _____		LH	10,FULLWRD9
18. _____	ADDUP	A	6,=H'12396'
19. _____	COMPRTE	CLC	0+260(260,3),0(4)
20. _____		AR	6(4),8
21. _____		SLDA	5,12
22. _____		CLC	DATA1+900(15),INDATA(15,5)
23. _____		LCR	10,10
24. _____	CONVRTER	CVB	DUBLPAK,6
25. _____	ODDSET	DS	0CL393
26. _____		MVI	DATAFLD+56(4,4),C'DATE'
27. _____		SR	10,1
28. _____		SP	0+19(15,12),0+45(12,8)
29. _____		SL	3,4,FULLWORDS
30. _____	CALCIT	AP	0+5(3,9),8(2,10)
31. _____		MH	5,HAFWRD1
32. _____		L	6,8,FULWD3
33. _____	REROUTE	A	10,FLWD(0,9)
34. _____	SETCHAR	STC	5,ONEBYTE
35. _____		S	3,F'820015916'

36. _____	DIVREG	DR	10,4
37. _____		ALR	4,=F'9831'
38. _____	NULLAREA	DC	0CL6'123123'
39. _____	LTROUTE	LTR	9,0(10)
40. _____	SETTLERTE	SR	10,9
41. _____		M	7,=F'99210'
42. _____		MVZ	B8(17),CONST1
43. _____	S3468F	MVC	G,A(2)
44. _____		SP	DATAPAK(3),LONGPACK(4)
45. _____		CP	PACKBYTE(1),PL1'4'
46. _____		AR	5,5(5)
47. _____	CHEXIT	CH	4,=H'15002'
48. _____		MVC	DATA+1(255),DATA
49. _____		SH	6(2),=H'32765'
50. _____		SRA	8,8
51. _____		SP	7(7,8),DATA3+2(1)
52. _____		A	11,4(3,5)
53. _____	PAKITUP	PACK	PAKIT(9),0+400(12,5)
54. _____		MVC	0+256(256),0(8)
55. _____		DP	QUOREM(7),=P'51'
56. _____		MR	6,5
57. _____		SRL	4,1
58. _____	CLEARIT	SR	11,11
59. _____		BAL	8,GOBACK
60. _____		SH	H'523',HAFWRD
61. _____		LA	6,6
62. _____	LEFTITE	SLDL	8,60
63. _____		ST	6,FULLWORDS
64. _____		SR	5,5
65. _____	DIVIT	D	7,11
66. _____		BC	5,NEWLOOP
67. _____		M	3,FULLWRD7
68. _____		L	FULLWD,9
69. _____		SRDR	8,32

70. _____		LM	5,WORD1,WORD2
71. _____	SUMUP	AH	9,2(8,9)
72. _____		DR	6,5
73. _____		ST	11,FULLWORDS
74. _____	TOTALS	AL	6,=F'392566'
75. _____		S	9,10(0,4)
76. _____		LH	3,HAFWRDA
77. _____		MVZ	DATAHOLD(3,5),CHANGE(3,6)
78. _____		AR	3,=F'5932'
79. _____	LEFTMUV	SLL	2,2
80. _____		LTR	8,8
81. _____		MH	5,0(0,5)
82. _____	DIVQRM	DR	3,8
83. _____		C	6,4(0,9)
84. _____	VALCONST	DC	PL10'+15356983.333'
85. _____		MR	8,10
86. _____		BXLE	9,10,12
87. _____	OUTRTE	BCT	7,RELOOP
88. _____		L	8,DUBLWD
89. _____		D	6,FULLWRD9
90. _____		AL	8,FULLWD1
91. _____	SETTAB	CLI	FIELDA(6,1),=CL1'X'
92. _____		M	11,0(0,8)
93. _____		SH	HAFWORD,2
94. _____		UNPK	DATAFLD(20),PACKFLD+20(8)
95. _____		AL	2,36(1,11)
96. _____		D	12,14(0,8)
97. _____		LM	6,15,WORDS
98. _____	SAVE	STH	3,FULLSWT
99. _____		A	8,5,(6,8)
100. _____		SRDA	11,48
101. _____		MR	10,=F'939'
102. _____		CL	DATAFIELD,=F'155220'
103. _____	SETPAK	PACK	PACKER(18),DATA(18)

104. _____	BCTEXIT	BCT	10,0(0,8)
105. _____		C	10,FULLWD5
106. _____		IC	6,6(6,12)
107. _____		LNR	13,13
108. _____		MP	MULTPAK(12),MPLIER(10)
109. _____		BC	0,NEXTRTE
110. _____		CH	HAFWRD1,HAFWRD2
111. _____		ST	FULLWD,7
112. _____		MVC	DATASET+8(1),=C'A'
113. _____		CVD	10,PACK8
114. _____		BCTR	8,8
115. _____	MATCH	CR	9,10
116. _____		LM	FULLWORD,6,9
117. _____		STC	DATABYTE,=CL1'X'
118. _____		BAL	6,3,NEWROUTE
119. _____		AP	DPACK(12),EPACK(11)
120. _____		CLR	10,0(3,4)
121. _____		LA	7,1932659
122. _____		BXH	5,9,10(11)
123. _____	VALCONS	DS	8CL2'00'
124. _____	SETREDY	DC	CL9'IN && OUT'
125. _____	H	DH	8,HALFWRD

BOOLEAN LOGIC APPLICATIONS

A. THE BOOLEAN ALGEBRA LOGIC INSTRUCTIONS

INSTRUCTION: AND IMMEDIATE

Mnemonic	Hex Code	Operand Format
NI	94	$D_1(B_1),I_2$

The And Immediate instruction (a binary logic "times" instruction) uses the one byte of immediate data, as defined by the second operand, to mask one byte of data specified by the first operand. The operation of this instruction affects the bits in the following manner:

Bit Values

Second Operand	First Operand		Result in First Operand
1	1	equals	1
1	0	equals	0
0	0	equals	0
0	1	equals	0

As indicated, the result of the operation is placed into the first operand location.

This instruction will act upon only 1 byte of data.

CC	BC	Condition
0	8	The first operand is zero (all zero-bits).
1	4	The first operand is not zero (one or more one-bits).

*   *   *

INSTRUCTION: AND

Mnemonic	Hex Code	Operand Format
N	54	$R_1,D_2(X_2,B_2)$

This And instruction (a binary logic "times" instruction) uses the contents of the second operand to mask the contents of the first operand register. The effect of this instruction on the contents of the first operand register are:

327

Bit Values

Second Operand	First Operand		Result in First Operand
1	1	equals	1
1	0	equals	0
0	0	equals	0
0	1	equals	0

The result of the operation is placed into the first operand register. The address created by the second operand must reside on a fullword boundary alignment.

Both operands must be of the same length, four bytes.

CC	BC	Condition
0	8	The first operand register contains zero (all zero-bits).
1	4	The first operand register does not contain zero (one or more one-bits).

*   *   *

INSTRUCTION: AND

Mnemonic	Hex Code	Operand Format
NC	D4	$D_1(L,B_1),D_2(B_2)$

This particular And instruction (a binary logic "times" instruction) uses the storage data specified by the second operand to mask the storage data specified by the first operand. The resulting operation affects the bits of the first operand in the following manner:

Bit Values

Second Operand	First Operand		Result In First Operand
1	1	equals	1
1	0	equals	0
0	0	equals	0
0	1	equals	0

The result of the masking operation is placed into the first operand storage area. This particular And instruction may be used to mask up to 256 bytes of data in one operation.

CC	BC	Condition
0	8	The contents of the first oper-

and are zero (all zero-bits).

1	4	The contents of the first operand are not zero (one or more one-bits).

*   *   *

INSTRUCTION: AND

Mnemonic	Hex Code	Operand Format
NR	14	R_1,R_2

This instruction (a binary logic "times" instruction) uses the contents of the second operand register to mask the contents of the first operand register. The results of this action are:

Bit Values

Second Operand	First Operand		Result in First Operand
1	1	equals	1
1	0	equals	0
0	0	equals	0
0	1	equals	0

The result of the performance of this instruction is placed into the first operand register. As indicated, both operands must be general registers.

CC	BC	Condition
0	8	The first operand register contains zero (all zero-bits).
1	4	The first operand register does not contain zero (one or more one-bits).

*   *   *

INSTRUCTION: OR IMMEDIATE

Mnemonic	Hex Code	Operand Format
OI	96	$D_1(B_1),I_2$

The Or Immediate instruction (a binary logic "add" instruction) uses the one byte of immediate data, as defined by the second operand, to mask the single byte of data that is specified by the first operand. The resulting operations affect the bits of the first operand as follows:

Bit Values			
Second Operand	First Operand		Result in First Operand
1	1	equals	1
1	0	equals	1
0	1	equals	1
0	0	equals	0

The result of the execution of the instruction is available in the first operand location.

This instruction will act upon only one byte of data.

CC	BC	Condition
0	8	The first operand contains zero (all zero-bits).
1	4	The first operand does not contain zero (one or more one-bits).

*   *   *

INSTRUCTION: OR

Mnemonic	Hex Code	Operand Format
O	56	$R_1, D_2(X_2, B_2)$

This Or instruction (a binary logic "add" instruction) uses the fullword contents of the second operand to mask the contents of the first operand register, wherein the results of the operation are:

Bit Values			
Second Operand	First Operand		Result in First Operand
1	1	equals	1
1	0	equals	1
0	1	equals	1
0	0	equals	0

The result of the operation is placed into the general register specified by the first operand. The address generated by the second operand must be located on a fullword boundary alignment.

CC	BC	Condition
0	8	The first operand contains zero (all zero-bits).

1	4	The first operand does not contain zero (one or more one-bits).

*   *   *

INSTRUCTION: OR

Mnemonic	Hex Code	Operand Format
OC	D6	$D_1(L, B_1), D_2(B_2)$

This Or instruction (a binary logic "add" instruction) uses the storage data specified by the second operand to mask the storage data specified by the first operand. The action of this instruction modifies the bits of the first operand field as follows:

Bit Values			
Second Operand	First Operand		Result in First Operand
1	1	equals	1
1	0	equals	1
0	1	equals	1
0	0	equals	0

The result of this operation is placed in the first operand location. Up to 256 bytes of data may be masked with a single instruction statement of this type.

CC	BC	Condition
0	8	The first operand contains zero (all zero-bits).
1	4	The first operand does not contain zero (one or more one-bits).

*   *   *

INSTRUCTION: OR

Mnemonic	Hex Code	Operand Format
OR	16	R_1, R_2

This particular Or instruction (a binary logic "add" instruction) uses the contents of the second operand register to mask the contents of the first operand register. The action of this instruction upon the bits would be:

Bit Values

Second Operand	First Operand		Result in First Operand
1	1	equals	1
1	0	equals	1
0	1	equals	1
0	0	equals	0

The result of the operation is placed into the general register specified by the first operand. Both operands must refer to general registers.

CC	BC	Condition
0	8	The first operand register contains zero (all zero-bits).
1	4	The first operand register does not contain zero (one or more one-bits).

* * *

INSTRUCTION:

EXCLUSIVE OR IMMEDIATE

Mnemonic	Hex Code	Operand Format
XI	97	$D_1(B_1), I_2$

The Exclusive Or Immediate instruction (a binary logic "modified add" instruction) uses one byte of immediate data, defined by the second operand, to mask a single byte of storage data as specified by the first operand. The resulting operation affects the first operand bits as follows:

Bit Values

Second Operand	First Operand		Result in First Operand
1	1	equals	0
1	0	equals	1
0	0	equals	0
0	1	equals	1

The results of the operation of this instruction is placed into the first operand location.

This instruction will act on only one byte of storage data.

CC	BC	Condition
0	8	The first operand contains zero (all zero bits).
1	4	The second operand does not contain zero (one or more one-bits).

* * *

INSTRUCTION: EXCLUSIVE OR

Mnemonic	Hex Code	Operand Format
X	57	$R_1, D_2(X_2, B_2)$

This Exclusive Or instruction (a binary logic "modified add" instruction) uses the contents of the fullword specified by the second operand to mask the contents of the first operand register. The results of the operation of this instruction would be as follows:

Bit Values

Second Operand	First Operand		Result In First Operand
1	1	equals	0
1	0	equals	1
0	0	equals	0
0	1	equals	1

The result of the operation is placed into the general register specified by the first operand. The address generated by the second operand must be that of an aligned fullword boundary.

CC	BC	Condition
0	8	The first operand contains zero (all zero-bits).
1	4	The first operand does not contain zero (one or more one-bits).

* * *

INSTRUCTION: EXCLUSIVE OR

Mnemonic	Hex Code	Operand Format
XC	D7	$D_1(L, B_1), D_2(B_2)$

This instruction (a binary logic "modified add" instruction) uses the storage data specified by the second operand to mask the storage data specified by the first operand. The resulting action modifies the first operand bit configuration as follows:

Bit Values

Second Operand	First Operand		Result in First Operand
1	1	equals	0
1	0	equals	1
0	0	equals	0
0	1	equals	1

The result of the operation is placed into the storage area addressed by the first operand.

Up to 256 bytes of data may be masked with one instruction statement.

CC	BC	Condition
0	8	The first operand contains zero (all zero-bits).
1	4	The first operand does not contain zero (one or more one-bits).

* * *

INSTRUCTION: EXCLUSIVE OR

Mnemonic	Hex Code	Operand Format
XR	17	R_1, R_2

This particular Exclusive Or instruction (a binary logic "modified add" instruction) uses the contents of the second operand register to mask the contents of the first operand register. The execution of this instruction results in the following action on the bits:

Bit Values

Second Operand	First Operand		Result in First Operand
1	1	equals	0
1	0	equals	1
0	0	equals	0
0	1	equals	1

The result of this operation is placed into the general register specified by the first operand. Both operands in the statement coded with this instruction must be general registers.

CC	BC	Condition
0	8	The first operand contains zero (all zero-bits).
1	4	The first operand does not contain zero (one or more one-bits).

B. UTILIZING THE BOOLEAN BINARY LOGIC INSTRUCTIONS

Boolean logic, or Boolean binary logic, consists of a set of instructions that will manipulate individual bits or groups of bits. The data that is processed by these instructions would not normally be thought of as consisting of character configurations. There are three unique classes of Boolean logic instructions in System/360 Assembler Language—the AND, the OR, and the EXCLUSIVE OR. Within each of these groups are several instructions, all of which perform the same type of function but depend on different types and lengths of data fields.

All of these instructions have one common factor in that each uses a "mask" to determine which bit positions in the source field are to be manipulated or altered. This mask may be logically thought of as a bit position pattern, wherein each unique pattern would cause a correspondingly unique reaction on a similar source field. There is no standard configuration for the mask pattern inasmuch as this would depend entirely on the interpretation of the meaning of the individual bit positions and whether or not any action was to be taken against them individually or collectively.

The instruction statements are coded by specifying the source field as the first operand and the mask as the second operand. The actual bit configuration of the source field will be altered if the mask creates any resulting action at all—which does not necessarily occur.

1. The "And" Instructions

The set of And instructions function as a logical "times" (multiplication) instruction. The logic applied here is that "any value times zero equals zero" or "zero times any value equals zero." Because the Boolean instructions are associated only with bits, the understanding is generated that the multiplication of each bit of the source field by each corresponding bit in the mask must, therefore, be limited to "0 × 1," "0 × 0," "1 × 0," or "1 × 1"; zero and one being the maximum range of any single bit. The resulting configuration of the source field, based on its original content and the content of the mask, would be as follows.

Mask Bit		Corresponding Source Field Bit		Resulting Source Field Bit
1	times (×)	1	equals	1
1	times (×)	0	equals	0
0	times (×)	0	equals	0
0	times (×)	1	equals	0

As a result of the execution of any of the And instructions, the PSW Condition Code will be set to one of two conditions—the indication will be that the source field is now zero (consisting of all zero-bits) or it is not zero (containing one or more one-bits).

Condition Code Value	Corresponding Test Value	Condition Indicated
0	8	The result was zero.
1	4	The result was not zero.

The And instructions have a very definite application in being used to turn "bit switches" to an "off" condition.

Three of the four And instructions have an identical name; they do have different mnemonic codes, however, which relate to the type of data fields that they are to be used with.

(a) And Immediate (NI). The And Immediate instruction uses a one-byte "immediate character" mask to act on a one-byte area of storage. For clarity, it is a good practice to express the "immediate character" in hexadecimal form, thereby making the bit configuration of that character easily identifiable. As with all of the And instructions, the NI instruction is quite useful for setting bit switches to an "off" condition. This particular instruction would mask a single byte, representing eight bit switches if so desired, and for every zero-bit in the mask it would set every corresponding bit in the source field byte to a zero-bit value. For any bit positions in the source field byte that were not to be altered, a one-bit should be constructed in the mask prior to executing the NI instruction statement.

If a single byte of storage data, addressed by the label CHEXBITS, is used as a set of bit switches the logical concept of the switches would be:

One Byte

CHEXBITS	0	0	0	0	0	0	0	0
Switch number	1	2	3	4	5	6	7	8

Using the concept that the one-bit equals an "on" condition and a zero-bit equals an "off" condition, a value of X'B6' in CHEXBITS would indicate the following switch conditions:

One Byte

CHEXBITS	1	0	1	1	0	1	1	0

Switch number	1	2	3	4	5	6	7	8
Switch status	On	Off	On	On	Off	On	On	Off

In the following examples, this configuration (X'B6') will be used as the source byte field, which will be altered by various "immediate character" masks.

Example 1. The logic of this program routine intends to reset bit-switches 1, 4, 5, and 8 to an "off" condition prior to reentry to a certain routine. In order to set these bits "off" and leave all other bits unaltered, it is necessary to construct a mask in which bit positions 1, 4, 5, and 8 contain a zero-bit and all other positions contain a one-bit. This mask would be configurated as:

One Byte

0	1	1	0	0	1	1	0	Equals X'66'

Bit-switch position	1	2	3	4	5	6	7	8

Using the source field byte CHEXBITS, the instruction statement and the resulting action would be:

```
NI     CHEXBITS,X'66'
```

One Byte

CHEXBITS (Before)	1	0	1	1	0	1	1	0	X'B6'

X'66'(Mask)	0	1	1	0	0	1	1	0	X'66'

CHEXBITS (Result)	0	0	1	0	0	1	1	0	X'26'

Switch number	1	2	3	4	5	6	7	8
Switch status	Off	Off	On	Off	Off	On	On	Off

As requested by the program task, switches 1, 4, 5, and 8 have been reset, or remain, in an "off" condition. Switches 2, 3, 6, and 7 remain as they were, regardless of their previous condition.

Example 2. The program now requires that all bit switches contained in CHEXBITS be set to an "off" condition. According to the performance of the NI instruction, a zero-bit in the mask will guarantee a zero-bit in the corresponding position of the source byte. Therefore, the mask should be all zero-bits, or X'00', to assure the program of all zero-bits in CHEXBITS.

NI   CHEXBITS,X'00'

CHEXBITS (Before)	1	0	1	1	0	1	1	0

X'00' (Mask)	0	0	0	0	0	0	0	0

CHEXBITS (After)	0	0	0	0	0	0	0	0

Switch number	1	2	3	4	5	6	7	8
Switch status	Off	Off	Off	Off	Off	Off	Off	Off

All switches contained within CHEXBITS have now been set to, or remain in, an "off" condition.

Example 3. In this example, a destructive test of certain bit positions is being made. The program logic intends to determine whether or not bit switches 5, 6, 7, and 8 are in an "off" status. If they are all "off," the program logic should branch to a subroutine labeled AUDIT; if one or more are "on," the branch will be to a subroutine labeled ERROR. Because switches 1, 2, 3, and 4 are not to be tested and the program logic prefers that they be reset to a zero-bit configuration at this time, the mask that will be used is:

	0	0	0	0	1	1	1	1	X'OF'

Bit-switch position	1	2	3	4	5	6	7	8

This mask will turn off bit-switches 1, 2, 3, and 4 if they are "on" and at the same time will leave bit-switches 5, 6, 7, and 8 "on" if they are not "off." The Condition Code will indicate whether the result of the operation was zero or not zero. A zero condition would indicate that none of the last four switches were on; a nonzero condition would indicate that one or more of switches 5, 6, 7, or 8 were on. The coding of the instruction statements for this example would be:

```
NI   CHEXBITS,X'OF'   001
BC   8,AUDIT          002
BC   4,ERROR          003
```

CHEXBITS (Before)	1	0	1	1	0	1	1	0	X'B6'

X'OF'	0	0	0	0	1	1	1	1	X'OF'

CHEXBITS (After)	0	0	0	0	0	1	1	0	X'06'

Switch number	1	2	3	4	5	6	7	8
Switch status	Off	Off	Off	Off	Off	On	On	Off

Statement 001 would execute the And Immediate instruction statement, giving the results shown in the field "CHEXBITS (After)."

Statement 002 specifies, "if the result was a totally zero configuration, branch to the subroutine AUDIT." This branch would not have been taken in this example.

Statement 003 indicates, "if the result was not zero, branch to the subroutine labeled ERROR." In this example the branch would have been made at this point.

These examples have illustrated the type of action that is generated by all And instructions. Just as the And Immediate is used to mask only one storage byte with an immediate character, the other And instructions each have individual requirements regarding the source field and mask.

(b) And (N). This particular And instruction, the mnemonic code of which is 'N', will use a fullword of storage as a mask to audit the bit contents of a general register. The length of the operation is fixed at 32 bit positions. The mask must reside on a fullword boundary location of program storage and the source field must be specified in the first operand of the instruction statement as a general register, either directly or symbolically.

This instruction may be used in a bit-switch application similar to those shown in the examples for the And Immediate instruction. It may also be used to set bits or bytes of a general register to zero.

To illustrate this particular type of And instruction, assume that the following conditions are to be programmed.

1. General register 8 contains a value in the low-order three bytes and a code character in the high-order byte.

2. The high-order byte is to be cleared by using the 'N' version of the And instruction.

3. The value contained within the low-order three bytes of the register must be an "even" number; if it is an odd number it is to be reduced by one to the next lower even number.

At the time of execution of the following instruction statements, general register 8 contains a value of +15,391 and a code character of "D" in the high-order byte.

The fullword mask that is to be used and the instruction statement that is to be executed are:

```
            DS    0F
MASKl       DC    X'00FFFFFE'
   *
            N     8,MASKl
```

The bit manipulation generated by this statement would appear to be:

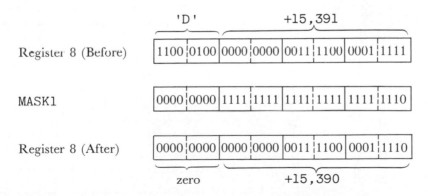

The high-order byte of the mask (X'00') has cleared the high-order byte of general register 8 to all zero-bits. The single low-order zero-bit in the mask has guaranteed that a low-order one-bit in the register would be changed to a zero-bit, therefore assuring

the program logic that general register 8 now contains an even number.

Note that wherever a one-bit appeared in the mask, the corresponding bit position in general register 8 was not altered; wherever a zero-bit appeared in the mask, a zero-bit was forced into the corresponding bit position in general register 8.

(c) And (NC). The NC version of the And instruction utilizes a program storage mask to inspect and alter a similar-length program storage source field. The mask, and the corresponding general storage source field, may each be up to 256 bytes in length. Both operands of the instruction statement may be represented by either symbolic or actual storage addresses.

A unique application for this instruction would be to convert all EBCDIC alpha characters to a range of 'A' through 'I'. Because of the configuration of the high-order four bits of EBCDIC character alphabetics this conversion is possible.

The similarity between these matched character sets may be found by examining the EBCDIC Character Table.

Source Alphabetics		Converted Alphabetics
A or J	equals	A or X'C1'
B or K or S	equals	B or X'C2'
C or L or T	equals	C or X'C3'
D or M or U	equals	D or X'C4'
E or N or V	equals	E or X'C5'
F or O or W	equals	F or X'C6'
G or P or X	equals	G or X'C7'
H or Q or Y	equals	H or X'C8'
I or R or Z	equals	I or X'C9'

The data field that is to be converted (where necessary) is a five-byte storage area (DATAFLD) that presently contains the EBCDIC characters 'RAQWS'. The mask that would be used to accomplish the specified conversion of such a five-byte source field is defined as a five-byte constant labeled BIGMASK. Its bit configuration is:

```
BIGMASK        DC        XL5'CFCFCFCFCF'
```

or

BIGMASK	1100 1111	1100 1111	1100 1111	1100 1111	1100 1111

The instruction statement that is to be executed is:

```
NC     DATAFLD,BIGMASK
```

The execution of this statement would result in the following conversion of the data in DATAFLD.

DATAFLD (Character)	R		A		Q		W		S	
(Hex)	D	9	C	1	D	8	E	6	E	2
(Binary)	1101	1001	1100	0001	1101	1000	1110	0110	1110	0010

BIGMASK	1100 1111	1100 1111	1100 1111	1100 1111	1100 1111

DATAFLD Result (Binary)	1100 1001	1100 0001	1100 1000	1100 0110	1100 0010
(Hex)	C 9	C 1	C 8	C 6	C 2
(Character)	I	A	H	F	B

As shown here the conversion was accomplished as specified by the task. The same mask would be used to perform the conversion regardless of what characters were contained in DATAFLD, as long as these characters were valid EBCDIC alphabetic representations.

(d) And (NR). This instruction is the

register version of the And instruction—both the mask and the source field must be contained within general registers. Accordingly, the execution of this instruction will affect exactly 32 bits, four bytes—the length of a general register. Any of the applications illustrated within the examples shown for the other And instructions may be applied to this one, providing that the length restrictions of registers are observed.

An interesting concept that might be applied to illustrate this instruction would be to use the NR to create a mask for subsequent use by the result register with a third register. This would be to And (NR) general register 'X' (the mask) with general register 'Y', then subsequently And (NR) general register 'Y' (the mask) with general register 'Z'. The logic behind such a technique might be:

1. The data content of general register 'Y' has been created through a set of program subroutines that have configured the bits of that register as switches. Any critical bit switches are assumed to be "on."

2. Register 'Z' has also been partially configurated by program subroutines. The program intends to compare the portion of register 'Z' containing critical bit switches to comparable bit positions in general register 'Y'. The resulting logic would depend on whether or not the comparable critical bit positions were all of opposing conditions prior to the And'ing.

In the example that follows the bit-switches of general register 'Z' are only the even-numbered bit positions, assuming that the positions are numbered from left to right, from 1 to 32. Consequently, the mask in general register 'X' must delete any one-bits that might appear in the odd-numbered bit positions of general register 'Y' inasmuch as register 'Y' will be used as the mask when it is And'ed with general register 'Z'. Instead of a hypothetical assignment of registers as 'X', 'Y', and 'Z', general registers 6, 7, and 8 will be used. Prior to the execution of any of the And (NR) instructions, the configuration of these general registers are:

Register 6	0101	0101	0101	0101	0101	0101	0101	0101	X'55555555'

Register 7	1101	1111	0010	1101	1111	0111	0101	0011	X'DF2DF753'

Register 8	0000	0000	0000	0100	0000	0000	0100	0000	X'00040040'

The instruction statements have been coded as:

```
NROUTE    NR    7,6              001
          NR    8,7              002
          BC    4,BADMATCH       003
          BC    8,VALID          004
```

Statement 001 will And the contents of register 6 with register 7, placing the result of that operation into register 7. All one-bits occupying odd-numbered bit positions in general register 7 will be replaced with zero-bits. Any remaining one-bits will occupy even-numbered bit positions and these will be used as the significant mask digits in Statement 002.

Statement 002 uses the new configuration of general register 7 as the mask for the And with general register 8. Only those bit positions within register 7 that contain one-bits will test the corresponding positions within register 8. All other bit positions in general register 8 are considered as not participating and are supplied with zero-bits.

Statement 003 is testing the Condition Code that resulted from the execution of Statement 002. If one or more one-bits remained in general register 8 after the And was completed, the Condition Code would indicate that the result was not zero and the program would branch out of Statement 003 to a subroutine labeled BADMATCH.

Statement 004 assumes that if the branch in Statement 003 was not taken, then the result of the And must have been zero—the only other alternative. Accordingly, this statement is testing the Condition and branching to a subroutine labeled VALID. Because there would be only two possible conditions resulting from Statement 002, either zero or nonzero, Statement 004 could have been coded as a forced branch (i.e., BC 15,VALID).

The configuration of the general registers as they existed through the two And statements would have been:

Statement 001

Register 7 (Before)

| 1101 | 1111 | 0010 | 1101 | 1111 | 0111 | 0101 | 0011 |

Register 6 (Mask)

| 0101 | 0101 | 0101 | 0101 | 0101 | 0101 | 0101 | 0101 |

Register 7 (After)

| 0101 | 0101 | 0000 | 0101 | 0101 | 0101 | 0101 | 0001 |

Statement 002

Register 8 (Before)

| 0000 | 0000 | 0000 | 0100 | 0000 | 0000 | 0100 | 0000 |

Register 7 (Mask)

| 0101 | 0101 | 0000 | 0101 | 0101 | 0101 | 0101 | 0001 |

Register 8 (After)

| 0000 | 0000 | 0000 | 0100 | 0000 | 0000 | 0100 | 0000 |

It is not necessary that the reader be able to find, or completely understand, an application for the technique just illustrated. What is important is that he fully understands the use of the significant and nonsignificant digits in the And mask.

2. The "Or" Instructions

Comprising a "matched set" similar to the And instructions, there are four comparable Or instructions. The Or instructions perform as an "add" function, adding together the bits of the mask and the corresponding bits of the source field. Each bit position is treated as a separate add function in binary form and a carry-over from one bit position to the next is ignored. This can be more clearly explained by stating that within this unique function "one plus zero equals one," "zero plus one equals one," "one plus one equals one," and "zero plus zero equals zero." Based on the original configuration of the source field and the bit content of the mask, the Or would affect the source field as follows:

Mask Bit		Corresponding Source Field Bit		Resulting Source Field Bit
1	plus (+)	1	equals	1
1	plus (+)	0	equals	1
0	plus (+)	1	equals	1
0	plus (+)	0	equals	0

Note carefully that "1 + 1 equals 1," with no carry-over to the next higher bit position.

Upon completion of an Or instruction statement, the PSW Condition Code bits will

Condition Code Value	Corresponding Test Value	Condition Indicated
0	8	The result was zero
1	4	The result was not zero

While the And instructions were used to set bit-switches to an "off" condition, the Or instructions are used to set bit-switches to an "on" condition. If a source field bit position is considered to be "on" (containing a one-bit) either a one-bit or a zero-bit in the corresponding mask position will leave that source bit on. If the source field bit position is "off" (containing a zero-bit), a one-bit in the mask will turn it "on," a zero-bit in the mask will leave it "off." Only one of the Or instructions has a unique name (OR IM-MEDIATE), although each of the four instructions do have unique mnemonic codes. The use of any one particular Or instruction is directly related to the type of data fields (either storage or register) that are to be used for the source field and the mask.

(a) Or Immediate (OI). The Or Immediate instruction will act upon a one-byte source field of storage by using the immediate character specified as the second operand of the instruction statement as the mask. Each bit of the eight-bit mask is Or'ed with each corresponding bit of the single-byte storage area specified by the first operand of the instruction statement. The sum of the bits represents the result of the Or statement. The PSW Condition Code will reflect the status of the sum—zero or not zero.

The configuration of the mask is determined by evaluating the action that is to be

indicate one of two possible conditions: (1) the source field is zero (containing all zero-bits) or (2) the source field is not zero (containing one or more one-bits).

taken on the source field byte. A zero-bit in the mask will not alter the configuration of the corresponding source field bit; a one-bit in the mask will guarantee that the corresponding bit position in the source field will contain a one-bit.

To illustrate this instruction, assume that a one-byte storage area (BITSET) contains all zero-bits at the beginning of the program subroutine. During the first cycle through the program logic two Or Immediate instructions are encountered. Each of these instruction statements will set a separate bit-switch to an "on" condition. Although these two statements appear relatively close together here, in the program source statements they are separated by a considerable number of instruction statements.

```
— —   — — — — — —

OI      BITSET,X'20'              0011

— —   — — — — — —


— —   — — — — — —

OI      BITSET,X'08'              0132

— —   — — — — — —
```

Statement 0011 will Or the bit configuration of the immediate character X'20' with the bit content of BITSET. At this point within the program BITSET contains a configuration of X'00'.

One Byte

BITSET (Before)	0	0	0	0	0	0	0	0

X'20' (Mask)	0	0	1	0	0	0	0	0

BITSET (After)	0	0	1	0	0	0	0	0

Statement 0132 will Or an immediate character mask of X'08' with the current configuration of BITSET.

One Byte

BITSET (Before)

0	0	1	0	0	0	0	0

X'08' (Mask)

0	0	0	0	1	0	0	0

BITSET (After)

0	0	1	0	1	0	0	0

Thinking of BITSET as an eight-switch byte, it could be stated that switches 3 and 5 are now "on."

BITSET

0	0	1	0	1	0	0	0

Switch number	1	2	3	4	5	6	7	8
Switch status	Off	Off	On	Off	On	Off	Off	Off

The Or Immediate instruction may be used for any application that requires one or more bit positions filled with one-bits.

(b) Or (O). The 'O' version of the Or instruction will Or a fullword storage mask with a general register source field. All 32 bits of the four-byte mask are used to determine the resulting status of the register bits. The instruction statement is written with the first operand specifying, or referring to, a general register and the second operand consists of the actual or symbolic address of the full-word storage location.

As an example of this instruction, the programmer has designed a modular program that consists of eight subroutine modules and a control module. In each of the various subroutines, the program logic loads an address value, in fixed-point form, into the low-order three bytes of general register 10. Once the processing returns to the control module, it is necessary to know which subroutine was responsible for loading general register 10 with the value that now resides there. This problem could be easily solved by considering the eight high-order bits of general register 10 as bit-switches. After any one of the subroutine modules perform the task of loading register 10 that module can immediately set a bit-switch

"on" to correspond to the module identity —such as module 6 could turn "on" bit-switch 6. Then when the address value in general register 10 was passed back to the control module that register would also contain the identity of the sub-module from which it was passed. The instruction statements that follow are assumed to be a part of the coding within subroutine 6:

```
- -  - - - - - -
L    10,NEWVALUE        010
O    10,MASK6           011
BC   15,CONTROL         012
```

In this instance MASK6 is a fullword constant containing a hexadecimal configuration of X'04000000'.

Statement 010 loads general register 10 with the address value that is contained in NEWVALUE. Assume that this value is +385,911.

Statement 011 will Or the fullword at MASK6 with general register 10. Inasmuch as the low-order three bytes of MASK6 do not contain any significant digits, the address value in general register 10 will not be affected. The execution of Statement 011 would appear to affect general register 10 as:

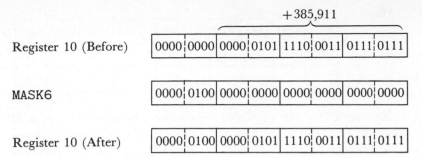

$$+385,911$$

| Register 10 (Before) | 0000 0000 | 0000 0101 | 1110 0011 | 0111 0111 |

| MASK6 | 0000 0100 | 0000 0000 | 0000 0000 | 0000 0000 |

| Register 10 (After) | 0000 0100 | 0000 0101 | 1110 0011 | 0111 0111 |

Register 10 now contains the address value in the low-order three bytes and an indicator (bit-switch) in the single high-order byte that will tell the control module which subroutine module was responsible for loading that address.

Statement 012 is a forced (unconditional) branch back to the control module.

(c) **Or (OC).** The storage-to-storage version of the Or instruction uses the mnemonic 'OC' as its op code. Both the mask and the source field are located in program-defined storage fields and each may be up to 256 bytes in length. The areas that are addressed by the first and second operands of the instruction statement must have equal length characteristics, whether specified or implied, if the mask is to affect all of the area specified by the first operand.

The example for the 'NC' instruction illustrated the means of converting certain

EBCDIC alphabetic character representation into an alphabetic range of from A to I. In order to demonstrate the performance of the 'OC' instruction, the example to be presented will show how to convert any EBCDIC alphabetic character into its comparable EBCDIC numeric character representation. Because every valid EBCDIC alpha character contains a hexadecimal numeric digit in its low-order four bit positions, it is an excellent application for the OC instruction to change the four high-order bits of each character to one-bits, thus converting the alpha character to an EBCDIC numeric character.

This example uses a six-byte storage area labeled CONVRSN as the source field and a six-byte mask that is referred to by the label NUMASK. The data contained within CONVRSN at the time of execution of this example is:

CONVRSN (Character)	N		U		M		B		E		R	
(Hexadecimal)	D	5	E	4	D	4	C	2	C	5	D	9
(Binary)	1101	0101	1110	0100	1101	0100	1100	0010	1100	0101	1101	1001

The instruction statement that is to be executed is:

```
OC    CONVRSN(6),NUMASK
```

Assuming that NUMASK consisted of a

hexadecimal format configuration of X'F0F0F0F0F0F0', the action generated by the instruction statement would appear to be:

| CONVRSN (Before) | 1101 0101 | 1110 0100 | 1101 0100 | 1100 0010 | 1100 0101 | 1101 1001 |

| NUMASK | 1111 0000 | 1111 0000 | 1111 0000 | 1111 0000 | 1111 0000 | 1111 0000 |

CONVRSN (After)
(Binary)

1111 0101	1111 0100	1111 0100	1111 0010	1111 0101	1111 1001

(Hexadecimal)

F	5	F	4	F	4	F	2	F	5	F	9

(Character)

5	4	4	2	5	9

By Or'ing a mask of X'F0' with any valid EBCDIC alphabetic character, that character representation becomes a valid EBCDIC numeric of the same numeric value as the right-most hex digit of the original alphabetic character.

(d) Or (OR). This instruction is coincidentally mnemonically coded the same as its functional name. The instruction name Or states the group of Boolean instructions to which it belongs; the mnemonic OR specifies that it is an "Or Register" instruction op code.

Inasmuch as both operands of the instruction statement (the source field and the mask) must refer symbolically or directly to general registers, it is understood that a length of four bytes, 32 bits, will be Or'ed.

The logic that is to be applied in the example for this instruction is that the programmer needs to assure the next subroutine within the problem program that general register 9 contains a minimum fixed-point value of +65,535. Any sum larger than +65,535 will be modified by the insertion of one-bits into any of the 16 low-order bit positions of the source field that contain zero-bits. Because this required minimum value (+65,535) has a configuration of X'FFFF', the programmer may Or that configuration with the low-order two bytes of general register 9. It should also be noted that because general register 9 might contain a negative value the programmer must first guarantee a positive value. At the time of execution of the coded statements general register 9 contains a value of +48,373 and the mask is located within general register 2. The instruction statements to be executed are:

– – – – – – – –

```
LPR    9,9                          061
OR     9,2                          062
```

Statement 061 is a Load Positive Register instruction statement. This would force the value contained within general register 9 into a positive configuration if it did not already consist of one.

Statement 062 has set the low-order 16 bits of general register 9 to all one-bits. Register 9 now contains the *minimum* positive value of +65,535 as required by the program logic.

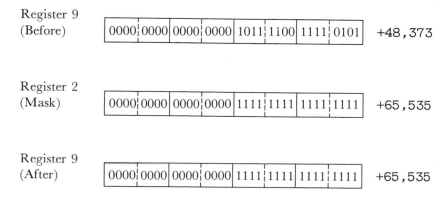

Register 9
(Before)

| 0000 0000 0000 0000 | 1011 1100 1111 0101 | +48,373
|---|---|

Register 2
(Mask)

| 0000 0000 0000 0000 | 1111 1111 1111 1111 | +65,535
|---|---|

Register 9
(After)

| 0000 0000 0000 0000 | 1111 1111 1111 1111 | +65,535
|---|---|

Because the logic of this application is not necessarily obvious, it should be explained further in order that it might be referenced for possible use. The program in question contains a routine that will take the value contained within general register 9 and assign blocks of core storage in increments of +65,536 until register 9 has been decremented to less than one block size. At that point, one more block of storage minus one byte (65,536 less 1 equals 65,535) will be assigned. The storage location byte immediately following the short (65,535) block will be filled with a delimiter character to indicate that this is the final storage block assigned. If the value in register 9 at this point was less than +65,535 it will be increased by the Or statement to that minimum value. The resulting block of storage will be the only block, and also the short block, with a delimiter character immediately following it. The Or statement has guaranteed that the last, or only, block will contain exactly 65,535 bytes.

3. The "Exclusive Or" Instructions

The Exclusive Or instruction set is comprised of four comparable instructions, each of which perform identical functions but using different types of data storage area. The action created by any one of the Exclusive Or variations takes the form of a "modified add" function. The basic logic of the "modified add" is that "two similar bits result in a zero-bit" and "two unlike bits result in a one-bit." The specific results of every possible combined configuration of the source field and the mask would be:

Mask Bit		Corresponding Source Field Bit		Resulting Source Field Bit
1	plus (m+)	1	equals	0
1	plus (m+)	0	equals	1
0	plus (m+)	0	equals	0
0	plus (m+)	1	equals	1

Because each bit position is treated as a separate and complete entity, there is no carry-over from the modified addition of "1 + 1 equals 0."

The PSW Condition Code bit settings that result from the execution of an Exclusive Or are identical to those of the other Boolean logic instructions—"the result was zero" or "the result was not zero."

Condition Code Value	Corresponding Test Value	Condition Indicated
0	8	The result was zero.
1	4	The result was not zero.

The Exclusive Or instruction has several practical applications, one of which is the reversing of the status of bit-switches. If a bit-switch is "on" the Exclusive Or can turn it "off"; if it is "off" the Exclusive Or can turn it "on." The explanation of these instructions may be more aptly defined by stating that a one-bit in the mask will reverse the corresponding bit of the source field—a zero-bit in the mask will not affect the source field bit.

(a) Exclusive Or Immediate (XI). The "XI" version of the Exclusive Or will use a one-byte "immediate character" mask to alter the contents of a one-byte storage area. Each significant bit (one-bit) of the mask will reverse the configuration of the corresponding bit in the source field byte. A zero-bit in the mask will not alter the corresponding bit in the source field.

Relating once again to the application of bit-switches, assume that a storage byte, labeled BITTS, contains the hexadecimal configuration of X'7D'.

BITTS (1 Byte)	0	1	1	1	1	1	0	1	X'7D'

Switch number	1	2	3	4	5	6	7	8
Switch status	Off	On	On	On	On	On	Off	On

An Exclusive Or instruction, with an immediate character of X'FF', is to be applied against BITTS and the resulting Condition Code is to be tested to see whether or not the bit-switches are now all in an "off" status.

```
XI        BITTS,X'FF'                001
```

```
BC        8,ALLOFF                   002
BC        15,NOTOFF                  003
```

Statement 001 is the Exclusive Or Immediate instruction statement, applying the X'FF' mask against BITTS. The performance of this statement would appear to be:

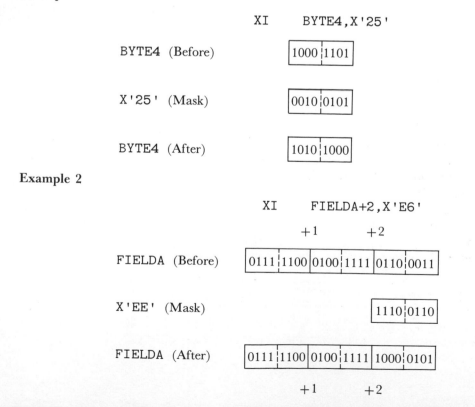

One Byte

BITTS (Before)	0 1 1 1 1 1 0 1
X'FF' (Mask)	1 1 1 1 1 1 1 1
BITTS (After)	1 0 0 0 0 0 1 0

The Condition Code would now contain a bit configuration indicating that the result of the operation was not zero.

Statement 002 indicates that if the Condition Code happened to indicate that BITTS is now all zero-bits, the branch should be taken to a subroutine labeled ALLOFF. However, in this particular example the branch would not be taken at this point.

Statement 003 is a forced branch to a subroutine labeled NOTOFF. Because the branch in Statement 002 was not taken the Condition Code result of the XI statement must have been that the result was not zero. An instruction statement of BC 4,NOTOFF would have caused the same branch to take place.

The following examples, presented without detail logic, are for the purpose of illustrating the "modified add" effect of the Exclusive Or Immediate instruction.

Example 1

```
XI        BYTE4,X'25'
```

BYTE4 (Before)	1000 1101
X'25' (Mask)	0010 0101
BYTE4 (After)	1010 1000

Example 2

```
XI        FIELDA+2,X'E6'
```

| | +1 | +2 |

FIELDA (Before)	0111 1100	0100 1111	0110 0011
X'EE' (Mask)			1110 0110
FIELDA (After)	0111 1100	0100 1111	1000 0101

| | +1 | +2 |

Example 3

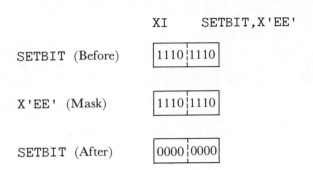

```
            XI    SETBIT,X'EE'
```

SETBIT (Before)   1110 1110

X'EE' (Mask)   1110 1110

SETBIT (After)   0000 0000

(b) Exclusive Or (X). The single mnemonic character 'X' represents the op code for this Exclusive Or instruction. The instruction statement for the 'X' should specify a general register as the first operand and the address of a fullword storage area (either symbolic or actual address) as the second operand. The second operand fullword is expected to contain the mask that will be Exclusive Or'ed to the contents of the first operand general register. The operation length of this Exclusive Or instruction is fixed at 32 bit positions—equal to the length of the register source field and the fullword mask.

A fullword mask, residing at an address labeled FULLMASK, contains a hexadecimal configuration of X'FF000000'. The Exclusive Or instruction is to apply this mask against general register 3. At the time of execution of this example, general register 3 was configured as X'EE783D01'. The execution of the instruction statement, and the coded statement itself, would be:

```
            X     3,FULLMASK
```

Register 3 (Before) | 1110 1110 | 0111 1000 | 0011 1101 | 0000 0001 |

FULLMASK | 1111 1111 | 0000 0000 | 0000 0000 | 0000 0000 |

Register 3 (After) | 0001 0001 | 0111 1000 | 0011 1101 | 0000 0001 |

As indicated, the significant one-bits in the high-order byte of the mask reversed the configuration of all of the corresponding bits in general register 3. The zero-bits in the mask had no effect on the relative bits of general register 3.

(c) Exclusive Or (XC). The 'XC' version of the Exclusive Or is a storage-to-storage type of operation. Both the mask and the data field are program storage areas with a maximum length of 256 bytes; both operands must have the same implied or explicit length attribute.

The example that is to be used to demonstrate the performance of this instruction is an EBCDIC alphanumeric conversion routine. Any alphabetic character from 'A' to 'I' will be changed to a numeric character from '1' to '9'—or any EBCDIC numeric character of from '1' to '9' will be converted to an alpha character of from 'A' to 'I'.

The conversion table would be:

From A to 1	or	From 1 to A	From J to 'blank' (X'E1')		
From B to 2	or	From 2 to B	From K to S	or	From S to K
From C to 3	or	From 3 to C	From L to T	or	From T to L
From D to 4	or	From 4 to D	From M to U	or	From U to M
From E to 5	or	From 5 to E	From N to V	or	From V to N
From F to 6	or	From 6 to F	From O to W	or	From W to O
From G to 7	or	From 7 to G	From P to X	or	From X to P
From H to 8	or	From 8 to H	From Q to Y	or	From Y to Q
From I to 9	or	From 9 to I	From R to Z	or	From Z to R

If an invalid alpha character or special character (one other than 'A' through 'I') is encountered, it will be converted as follows:

The mask that is to be used for the conversion is stored in a six-byte storage area labeled **KEYBITS**, and contains a configuration of X'303030303030'

KEYBITS	0011	0000	0011	0000	0011	0000	0011	0000	0011	0000	0011	0000

The data that is to be converted by this example consists of two six-byte fields labeled **TRANSA** and **TRANSB**. . . .

TRANSA	A	H	I	J	2	5

TRANSB	1	3	8	J	K	L

The instruction statements that are to be executed have been coded as:

```
XC      TRANSA,KEYBITS
XC      TRANSB,KEYBITS
```

The 'XC' instruction statements would translate/convert the source field data in the following manner.

TRANSA (Character) (Before)

A		H		I		J		2		5	

(Hcx)

C	1	C	8	C	9	D	1	F	2	F	5

(Binary)

1100	0001	1100	1000	1100	1001	1101	0001	1111	0010	1111	0101

KEYBITS (Mask)

0011	0000	0011	0000	0011	0000	0011	0000	0011	0000	0011	0000

TRANSA (Binary) (After)

1111	0001	1111	1000	1111	1001	1110	0001	1100	0010	1100	0101
F	1	F	8	F	9	E	1	C	2	C	5

(Hex)

1		8		9		'blank'		B		E	

(Character)

TRANSB (Character) (Before)

1		3		8		J		K		L	

(Hex)

F	1	F	3	F	8	D	1	D	2	D	3

(Binary)

1111	0001	1111	0011	1111	1000	1101	0001	1101	0010	1101	0011

KEYBITS (Mask)	0011┆0000	0011┆0000	0011┆0000	0011┆0000	0011┆0000	0011┆0000

TRANSB (Binary) (After)	1100┆0001	1100┆0011	1100┆1000	1110┆0001	1110┆0010	1110┆0011
(Hex)	C ┆ 1	C ┆ 3	C ┆ 8	E ┆ 1	E ┆ 2	E ┆ 3
(Character)	A	C	H	'blank'	S	T

If the two data fields, TRANSA and TRANSB, were now concatenated, their combined data content would appear to be:

1 ┆ 8	9 ┆ ƀ	B ┆ E	A ┆ C	H ┆ ƀ	S ┆ T

Many corporations and organizations have data files that are classified as confidential. Various schemes are devised, ranging from very complex to extremely simple, to "scramble" and code the data contained within these files. If unauthorized personnel inadvertently gained access to these files, the information would be useless masses of data bytes unless the proper "key" was supplied with which to unscramble them. The example just presented could be utilized for this type of application—not only was the third and fourth bit of each byte reversed, but also the logical data fields were segmented and placed into separate storage locations.

(d) Exclusive Or (XR). The register-to-register version of the Exclusive Or instruction uses 'XR' as the instruction statement op code. All 32 bits of a general register mask are Or'ed with all 32 bits of a general register source field. The source field data bits are altered whenever the corresponding bit position within the mask contains a one-bit. Both operands of the instruction statement must refer specifically or symbolically to a general register.

In the following illustration of this particular instruction, general register 8 contains a hexadecimal configuration of X'007A91BF', representing the source field; general register 12 contains X'96969696', representing the mask.

The instruction statement to be executed is:

$$\text{XR} \qquad 8,12$$

Register 8 (Before)	(Hex)	0 ┆ 0	7 ┆ A	9 ┆ 1	B ┆ F
	(Binary)	0000┆0000	0111┆1010	1001┆0001	1011┆1111

Register 12 (Mask)	1001┆0110	1001┆0110	1001┆0110	1001┆0110

Register 8 (After)	(Binary)	1001┆0110	1110┆1100	0000┆0111	0010┆1001
	(Hex)	9 ┆ 6	E ┆ C	0 ┆ 7	2 ┆ 9

C. BOOLEAN LOGIC INSTRUCTIONS IN DATA SEARCHES

As industry, government, and various other organizations attempt to computerize mass information and store it for selective search criteria, the problem of which media to use to store this data becomes increasingly critical. Even within industry the storage space required to record the background and employment information on one employee may consume thousands of bytes. It has long been an accepted practice to store data in EBCDIC character form, each section of information being assigned to a particular field that is identified as to the type of information it contains. Some fields could contain a single character that would represent the explicit information. For example, a one-byte field used to determine "Marital Status"

could contain an 'M' for married or an 'S' for single. Even this abbreviated form of coded data requires considerable data storage space.

The ability to manipulate data bits via Boolean instructions presents a challenge to both the system analyst and the programmer. Information that previously required a single byte, or even more, of storage area on a magnetic tape or disk drive can now be reflected within a single bit position. As many as 16 separate conditions, or answers, may be contained within a single eight-bit data byte.

To illustrate this capability, an information query-byte is utilized in the following examples. Within the data record for each individual that is employed by Company 'K', there is a single byte of data that contains the following information:

Bit Position	Information	One-Bit Implies	Zero-Bit Implies
1	Sex	Male	Female
2	Marital status	Married	Single
3	Age group	25 or over	Under 25
4	High school	Graduated	Did not graduate
5	College (4 Year)	Degree	Nondegreed
6	Driver's license	Yes	No
7	Home owner	Yes	No
8	Citizenship	Native-born	Naturalized

If a search were to be made of this file for certain personnel matching multiple selective criteria, it could be accomplished in an absolute minimum of time as compared to a character search of multiple fields on each personnel record. Not only is the minimum length field (one byte) being used, but the real advantage is that multiple conditions may be audited within that single byte via one instruction statement. The type of information provided by the simple query byte illustrated here is very general; this could be refined and expanded to meet the need and scope of almost any type of data inquiry system.

Each example presented in this section is looking for a matching set of data conditions. Each match would either be noted and ex-

tracted along with other pertinent data or it would be used to accumulate a tally-count for an analytical survey. Because the Boolean instructions will destructively analyze the query byte, that byte is first moved to a work-area byte before the Boolean instruction statement is applied against it.

Example 1. The management of company 'K' requires a list of all male personnel who are 25 years of age or over and have graduated from high school but who do not have college degrees. The company plans to use this listing to advise such personnel of a new college tuitional aid program being made available. The bit conditions that are to be searched for are as follows:

Bit 1	1-bit equals . . . Male	
Bit 3	1-bit equals . . . 25 years of age or over	
Bit 4	1-bit equals . . . High school graduate	
Bit 5	0-bit equals . . . No college degree	

The instruction statements for this example have been coded as:

MVC	HOLDBYTE(1),DATA+3	001
NI	HOLDBYTE,X'B8'	002
XI	HOLDBYTE,X'B0'	003

BC	8,HIT	004
BC	15,MISS	005

To illustrate the effect of these statements, assume that the byte that is being checked contains the following bit configuration:

One Byte

HOLDBYTE	1	1	1	1	1	1	0	1
Bit Position	1	2	3	4	5	6	7	8

These bit conditions indicate the following about the individual:

Bit 1	1-bit equals . . . Male
Bit 2	1-bit equals . . . Married
Bit 3	1-bit equals . . . 25 years old or over
Bit 4	1-bit equals . . . High School graduate
Bit 5	1-bit equals . . . College Degree
Bit 6	1-bit equals . . . Has a driver's license
Bit 7	0-bit equals . . . Does not own his home
Bit 8	1-bit equals . . . Is a native-born citizen

Statement 001 moves the query-byte from the data record into the one-byte work area labeled HOLDBYTE.

Statement 002 executes an And Immediate instruction. The mask contains a one-bit in the bit positions that correspond with the bit positions of the query-byte that are to be audited.

One Byte

HOLDBYTE (Before)	1	1	1	1	1	1	0	1
X'B8' (Mask)	1	0	1	1	1	0	0	0
HOLDBYTE (After)	1	0	1	1	1	0	0	0
Bit position number	1	2	3	4	5	6	7	8

This instruction statement has forced zero-bits into all of the bit positions in which the inquiry is not interested. The X'B8' mask has stated, "maintain the status of the bits of the source field for which there is a corresponding one-bit in the mask."

Statement 003 is executing an Exclusive Or Immediate instruction, using a mask of X'B0'.

One Byte

HOLDBYTE (Before)	1	0	1	1	1	0	0	0

X'B0' (Mask)	1	0	1	1	0	0	0	0

HOLDBYTE (After)	0	0	0	0	1	0	0	0

Bit position number   1   2   3   4   5   6   7   8

The mask of X'B0' will cause the result to be zero if the proper bit-settings were present in HOLDBYTE prior to the 'XI' instruction statement. The analysis of this would be based on the following assumptions:

Bit Position	Should Be	Indicating	Mask	Desired Result After 'XI'
1	1-bit	Male	1-bit	0-bit
3	1-bit	25 or over	1-bit	0-bit
4	1-bit	High school graduate	1-bit	0-bit
5	0-bit	No college degree	0-bit	0-bit

In this example, however, the result was not zero—the individual whose record was being checked had received a college degree. Therefore, when bit position 5 of HOLDBYTE was Exclusive Or'ed with the corresponding zero-bit of the mask, the result was a one-bit.

Statement 004 is testing the PSW Condition Code that resulted from the Exclusive Or Immediate. If the result contained within HOLDBYTE was zero, the branch would be taken at this statement.

Statement 005 is a forced branch to a subroutine labeled MISS, implying that the personnel record for this particular employee did not meet the search criteria.

Example 2. In this file search, the management of company 'K' have asked to be provided with a count of all unmarried native-born employees under 25 years of age who are not high school graduates. These combined characteristics would have required a search for the following bit conditions:

Bit 2   0-bit equals . . . Unmarried
Bit 3   0-bit equals . . . Under 25 years old
Bit 4   0-bit equals . . . Not a high school graduate
Bit 8   1-bit equals . . . A native-born citizen

The instruction statements have been coded as:

```
              MVC      HOLDBYTE(1),DATA+3              001
              NI       HOLDBYTE,X'71'                 002
              XI       HOLDBYTE,X'01'                 003
              BC       4,EXIT                         004
              AP       COUNT,=PL1'1'                  005
     EXIT     BC       15,NEXTCHEK                    006
```

For this example, the byte that will be moved into HOLDBYTE is:

One Byte

HOLDBYTE	1	0	0	0	0	1	0	1

Bit position   1   2   3   4   5   6   7   8

Statement 001 is moving the query byte out of the fourth byte position of DATA and into the HOLDBYTE work area.

Statement 002 is the And Immediate instruction statement. The configuration of the mask will place zero-bits into bit positions 1, 5, 6, and 7 of the source field but will not alter the bits that reside in positions 2, 3, 4, and 8.

HOLDBYTE (Before)	1	0	0	0	0	1	0	1

X'71' (Mask)	0	1	1	1	0	0	0	1

HOLDBYTE (After)	0	0	0	0	0	0	0	1

Bit position   1   2   3   4   5   6   7   8

Statement 003 is the Exclusive Or Immediate instruction statement. The mask of X'01' will create the following action:

One Byte

HOLDBYTE (Before)	0	0	0	0	0	0	0	1

X'01' (Mask)	0	0	0	0	0	0	0	1

HOLDBYTE (After)	0	0	0	0	0	0	0	0

Bit position   1   2   3   4   5   6   7   8

The program logic was searching for a zero-bit in bit positions 2, 3, and 4. In order to confirm this condition, a zero-bit was placed in the mask in these positions. If any one of those positions had contained a one-bit in the source field, the one-bit would have carried through to the result. Because the logic was checking for a one-bit in the eighth position bit of HOLDBYTE, a one-bit was also used in the mask at this position. If the one-bit did exist in the source byte the execution of the Exclusive Or would have placed a zero-bit there in the result. Upon completion of the 'XI' instruction statement, HOLDBYTE contains all zero-bits, indicating that the necessary conditions were found for including this record in the count analysis.

Statement 004 is a conditional branch instruction statement. It specifies, "if the result field does not contain a zero value, branch to the instruction labeled EXIT."

The result field was zero in this example and the branch from this statement is not taken.

Statement 005 assumes that because the program logic is passing through to it and did not branch out of Statement 004, then the value in HOLDBYTE must be zero. This is a valid assumption. The Add Packed instruction statement is, therefore, adding a packed decimal literal of +1 to the counter to indicate that a selected record has been found.

Statement 006 is a forced branch to a point within the program labeled NEXT-CHEX. That routine would probably bring in another data record and pass through Statements 001 to 006 again. The program logic has arrived at Statement 006 by one of two ways—either the branch was taken from Statement 004 directly to Statement 006 in which case the value of +1 would not have been added to COUNT; or the processing logic fell through Statements 004 and 005 in sequence.

The examples for this application could go on and on, almost endlessly. Two bytes, three bytes, four bytes, or many bytes could be utilized to contain information in the bit-indicator form. Consider the effective savings of stored data space when four bytes (32 bit positions) can supply as much information as can be supplied by 32 bytes—a savings of 28 bytes per individual record. Compound this savings by 15,000 employees (28 times 15,000) and the overall result is a savings of 420,000 bytes of data storage—on only one file. Even though some mediums and methods of storing data are relatively inexpensive, computer time is not. Actual processing time saved by the examples shown is approximately a "1 to n" ratio, wherein "n" represents the number of compare statements necessary to accomplish the same task via EBCDIC character data comparisons.

Review Exercises

1. The Boolean Logic instructions are generally considered to be useful in manipulating individual ___*bits*___ or groups of ___*bits*___.

2. The ___*And*___ instructions are useful in setting or forcing bit-switches to an "off" condition.

3. The Or series of Boolean instructions perform an "___*Add*___" function wherein "one plus zero or one plus one equals one."

4. The performance of the Exclusive Or instructions generates results in which similar bits in corresponding bit positions in the mask and the source field combine to create a ___*zero*___-bit; unlike bits in corresponding bit positions in the mask and the source field combine to create a ___*one*___-bit.

5. Up to 2048 bit positions can be altered by the ___*XC*___ mnemonic op code version of the Exclusive Or instructions.

6. In all Boolean Logic instruction statements, the content of the second operand is considered to be a "___*mask*___," whether it is represented by an immediate character, a register, or a storage field.

7. When executing any one of the Or instructions, a one-bit in the resulting source field may be guaranteed by coding a ___*one*___-bit in the corresponding bit position of the mask as represented by the second operand.

8. A mnemonic op code of X, as contained in a valid instruction statement, will cause action against all of the ___*32*___ bit positions represented by the first operand.

9. When executing an And instruction statement, a one-bit in the mask and a corresponding one-bit in the source field will result in a ___*ONE*___-bit in the source field; a zero-bit in the mask and a corresponding one-bit in the source field will result in a ___*ZERO*___-bit.

10. The O version of the Boolean Logic Or instructions requires that the first operand of the statement in which it is used be specified as a ___*Register*___ and that the second operand represent a valid-aligned ___*full word*___ storage location.

11. A coded instruction statement containing the mnemonic op code of XI indicates that the first operand addresses a single byte of storage and that the second operand is represented by an ___*immediate*___ character.

12. The And instructions function on the data bits as a logical "___*times*___" or ___*Multiplication*___ instruction.

13. The NC version of the Boolean Logic series of ___*AND*___ instructions utilizes defined storage areas as both operands of the statement, and may affect from 1 to ___*256*___ bytes of source field data.

14. The NR instruction statement is considered to be a ___*Register*___-to-register operation.

15. The mnemonic op code of OR indicates that the first operand of the instruction statement should be a ___*Register*___, and the second operand of the instruction statement should be a ___*Register*___.

16. The Boolean Logic Or instructions are useful in bit-switch applications inasmuch as they may be used to guarantee that any single bit position, or bit-switch, is set to an/a "___*on*___" condition.

17. When utilizing an Or instruction to perform an operation, a ___*zero*___-bit in the mask (the second operand) is used to guarantee that the corresponding bit position of the source field is not altered.

18. Upon execution of an Exclusive Or instruction statement, any ___*one*___-bit in the second operand mask will result in the reversal of the content of the corresponding bit position of the source field; a one-bit will be changed to a zero-bit, a zero-bit will be changed to a one-bit.

In each of the following problems there will be one or more source fields and a masking value defined. Apply the mask against the source field(s) using the Boolean instruction indicated, and supply both the hexadecimal configuration and bit configuration of the source field(s) as they would be after execution of the statement(s).

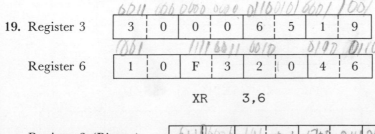

19. Register 3

3	0	0	0	6	5	1	9

Register 6

1	0	F	3	2	0	4	6

XR   3,6

Register 3 (Binary)

(Hex)

20. Register 8

0	F	3	9	2	F	F	F

FULLWRD3

1	1	3	1	0	0	6	C

FULLWRD4

0	0	4	2	7	7	D	3

```
L    8,FULLWRD4
O    8,FULLWRD3
```

Register 8 (Binary)

(Hex)

21. DATAFLD

D	1	D	2	E	3

```
NI   DATAFLD+1,X'CF'
```

DATAFLD (Binary)

(Hex)

22. DATATEST

D	C	E	7	E	0	3	C	E	9

MASK22

4	0	2	4	1	8	1	4	2	4

```
XC    DATATEST(3),MASK22+2
```

DATATEST (Binary)

(Hex)

23. Register 12

0	0	C	3	5	6	9	8

WORDTWO

0	0	0	4	0	4	0	4

```
O    12,WORDTWO
```

Register 12 (Binary)

(Hex)

24. DATASET

C	7	C	8	D	7	D	9	C	1

MASK1

0	2	0	2	0	2

```
NC    DATASET+2(3),MASK1
```

DATASET (Binary)

(Hex)

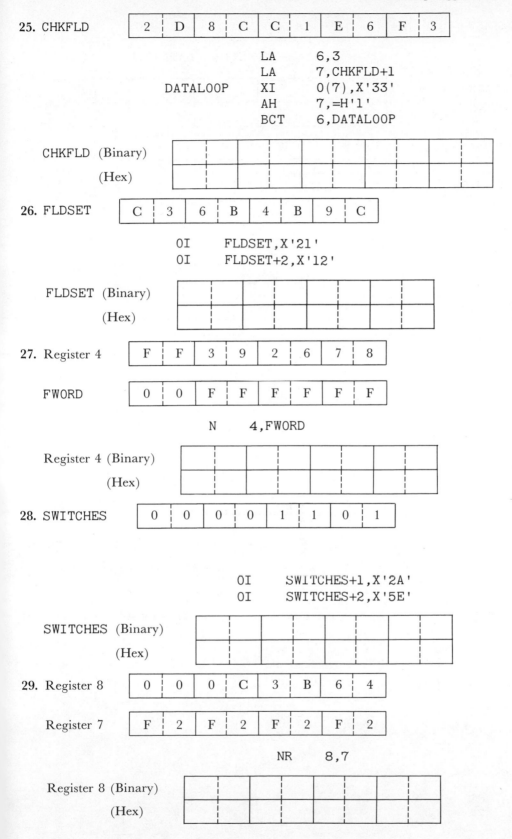

25. CHKFLD

2	D	8	C	C	1	E	6	F	3

```
                  LA       6,3
                  LA       7,CHKFLD+1
      DATALOOP    XI       0(7),X'33'
                  AH       7,=H'1'
                  BCT      6,DATALOOP
```

CHKFLD (Binary)

(Hex)

26. FLDSET

C	3	6	B	4	B	9	C

```
      OI       FLDSET,X'21'
      OI       FLDSET+2,X'12'
```

FLDSET (Binary)

(Hex)

27. Register 4

F	F	3	9	2	6	7	8

FWORD

0	0	F	F	F	F	F	F

```
      N       4,FWORD
```

Register 4 (Binary)

(Hex)

28. SWITCHES

0	0	0	0	1	1	0	1

```
      OI       SWITCHES+1,X'2A'
      OI       SWITCHES+2,X'5E'
```

SWITCHES (Binary)

(Hex)

29. Register 8

0	0	0	C	3	B	6	4

Register 7

F	2	F	2	F	2	F	2

```
      NR       8,7
```

Register 8 (Binary)

(Hex)

30. DATASW

0	4	4	0	8	2	A	3	C	6

OC   DATASW(2),DATASW+2

DATASW (Binary)

(Hex)

31. WORDBASE

F	3	F	5	D	4	D	1	D	7

SETCHNGE

F	F	C	D	C	3

NC   WORDBASE+2(2),SETCHNGE+1

WORDBASE (Binary)

(Hex)

32. Register 6

8	2	8	7	8	5	8	8

Register 10

4	0	4	0	4	0	4	0

OR   6,10

Register 6 (Binary)

(Hex)

33. Register 5

F	F	F	F	F	F	F	3

FULLWD3

F	F	F	F	F	F	F	F

X   5,FULLWD3

Register 5 (Binary)

(Hex)

USING SWITCHES AND INDICATORS FOR PROGRAM LOGIC CONTROL

A. THE TEST UNDER MASK INSTRUCTION

INSTRUCTION: TEST UNDER MASK

Mnemonic	*Hex Code*	*Operand Format*
TM	91	$D_1(B_1)$,I_2

This instruction will take the single byte of immediate data, defined by the second operand, and use it to test the bit configuration of the single byte of data addressed by the first operand. The execution of this instruction will not change the bit configuration of the data that is being tested. The second operand, which is considered to be the mask, is constructed by the programmer as follows:

1. For each bit that is to be tested in the data, the corresponding bit within the mask should be a one-bit.

2. For each bit that is to be ignored within the data-byte, the corresponding bit within the mask should be a zero-bit.

The instruction will then test only the bits in the data field that have corresponding one-bits in the mask. When the actual test is performed the instruction creates a work-byte in the image of the data-byte that has been addressed. Each mask-bit that is a one-bit will test for a one-bit in the corresponding position of the data/work-byte; if a corresponding one-bit is found, a similar one-bit is placed, or remains, in the work-byte. If a corresponding one-bit is not found, a zero-bit is placed into the work-byte. At the end of the test operation, the instruction reviews the contents of the result and sets a Condition Code based on the contents. This instruction will allow the programmer to test the "on/off" condition of any single bit-switch,

357

or the bit configuration of an entire byte of data, without altering that bit configuration.

CC	BC	Condition
0	8	The result-bits were all zero-bits.
1	4	The result-bits were both zero-bits and one-bits.
3	1	The result-bits were all one-bits.

B. THE CONCEPTS OF SWITCHES AND INDICATORS

In the computer equipment existing prior to the Third Generation systems, any reference to a switch or indicator might well have been understood to pertain to a physical device or signal unit. Certain problem program functions could relate to the requirement of altering a physical switch on the computer console panel in order for the program to perform its functions. Physical switches do exist in System/360, but these are more often related to the performance of peripheral equipment, such as a two-channel switch on a direct access device or tape drive control unit. This type of a switch is normally not under problem program control or even directly related to the performance of the problem program insofar as knowledge of its status is concerned.

The switches and indicators to be discussed herein may be thought of as existing in the form of stored data or characters. The condition of these switches may be considered to signal many variations of status, such as "yes" or "no," "on" or "off," "branch" or "fall through," and as many other decisions as there are questions requiring such an answer.

Unfortunately, there is often a lot of pro-and-con controversy about the practice of using switches within the program logic. Improper manipulation of logic switches can create havoc with any problem program, and is too often of such magnitude that it is extremely difficult to pinpoint the errant or omitted instruction. The omission of a single instruction statement to turn a switch to "on" or "off" at the proper logic point can result in a complete reversal of the intended logic pattern. On the other hand, by following a set of proper programming conventions and by adequate flow-charting, a single switch is often all that is needed to replace an entire subroutine of logic or data interpretation.

Setting a switch to an "on" condition, or turning it "off," does not in itself create any resulting action by the problem program. The condition of the switch is merely established for subsequent testing of that condition and a logic decision based on the result of that test. The application of setting and testing a switch or indicator will be thoroughly discussed and illustrated within this section.

As a rule, there are two types of switches and indicators—the character-switch and the bit-switch. Each have their own peculiar characteristics and functions, although the applications for which they are used can often be interchangeable. For the purpose of this text, each type will be reviewed in relationship to the environment in which they are most frequently used. The similarity of use will point out their interchangeability without discussing that factor in detail.

1. Character-Switches and Indicators

A character-switch or indicator is construed to consist of one byte of data; therefore, it may also be referred to as a byte-switch. Inasmuch as one byte of data may be any one of 256 unique bit configurations, it is conceivable that a byte-switch, or character-switch, could be considered to represent 256 unique conditions. For all practical purposes, however, the usual application is that a byte-switch be considered to have only two conditions. This is not meant to imply that it is not good logic to have a switch represent multiple conditions, but the main reason usually justifying the existence of a switch will normally be found to be an "on" or "off" condition.

Because character-switches inherently consist of one byte of data, it is logical to use an instruction that processes only one byte in order to set or test the switch. These are referred to as the "immediate" type of instructions. For the purpose of setting a byte-switch to a desired condition, the Move Immediate (MVI) instruction is ideally suited; for the purpose of testing a byte-switch, the Compare Logical Immediate (CLI) instruction holds precedent. Both of these instructions, the MVI and the CLI, are far more expedient than a regular "move" or "compare" instruction. In each instance, the second operand is a self-defining character value and the overall performance of these instructions is considerably faster than if the second operand generated an address which, in turn, contained a character.

A common means of using a switch is to first establish a constant labeled by a unique name. Because the original value of the switch, before it is ever used, should be a null value, it is good practice to create the switch as a one-byte constant containing a valid blank. This might be expressed as:

```
SWITCH1        DC       CL1'ϕ'
```

or

```
SWITCH1        DC       XL1'40'
```

The symbol 'ϕ' as used here, and in other places within this text, is considered to represent a legitimate blank, configurated as hexadecimal '40'.

Assuming that this particular switch is to be used to represent an "on" or "off" condition, it has been arbitrarily decided that an "X" will indicate that the switch is on and a blank will represent that it is off. In order to alter the setting of the switch at will, two instruction statements will be applied:

```
MVI          SWITCH1,C'X'
```

or

```
MVI          SWITCH1,C'ϕ'
```

The first instruction statement is moving a character "X" into the one-byte field labeled SWITCH1. This is considered to be turning the switch on. The second instruction statement is moving a valid blank (hex '40') into SWITCH1, turning the switch off.

The routine shown in Fig. 13-1 demonstrates the application of a byte-switch.

This routine, although not a practical application in itself, illustrates setting the switch on, testing the condition of the switch, and turning the switch off. The assumed logic here appears to be that the switch is first set to an "on" condition, followed by an unspecified number of instruction statements and then the switch is tested to see if it is still on. If it is on, a branch is taken to a subroutine to check the accumulated value of a particular packed decimal field. If that packed decimal value is equal to +2999, the logic falls through to OFFIT. At this point, the switch is turned off, the logic branches back to REPEAT, processes, checks the switch at ONOFF and finds that it is off (not equal to "X"), so the logic falls through to the branch to END. In this particular example, the switch concept could have been eliminated and the Compare Packed instruction statement labeled CHECKIT could have replaced the ONOFF instruction statement, eliminating the need for the entire CHECKIT subroutine. This example would then appear as:

```
REPEAT     AP     FIELD,=PL1'1'
    _ _     _ _ _ _ _ _
    _ _     _ _ _ _ _ _
    _ _     _ _ _ _ _ _
           CP     FIELD,=PL3'3000'
           BC     7,REPEAT
           BC     15,END
```

As previously mentioned, a byte-switch may represent more than two conditions. Consider an instance in which the problem program has three types of record input—a type-1 record, a type-2 record, and a type-3 record. As the problem program brings each new record into storage, a switch is set by inserting either a 1, 2, or 3 into it. Further on in the program logic it is necessary to check again for the type of record being processed, and to branch to one of three subroutines based on the value contained within the switch. One compare instruction statement would test the switch, as shown following:

IBM

IBM System/360 Assembler Coding Form

PROGRAM						PAGE	OF
PROGRAMMER		DATE				CARD ELECTRO NUMBER	
		PUNCHING INSTRUCTIONS	GRAPHIC				
			PUNCH				

X28-6509-2 U/M050
Printed in U.S.A.

Name	Operation	Operand	Comments	Identification-Sequence
*				
TURNON	MVI	SWITCH1,C'X'		0040
REPEAT	AP	FIELD,=PL1'1'		0041
ONOFF	CLI	SWITCH1,C'X'		0063
EQUALB	BC	8,CHECKIT		0064
	BC	15,END		0065
*				
**				
*				
CHECKIT	CP	FIELD,=PL3'2999'		0066
	BC	7,REPEAT		0067
OFFIT	MVI	SWITCH1,C'Ø'		0068
	BC	15,REPEAT		0069
*				
**				

Figure 13-1

Name	Operation	Operand		Comments	Identification-Sequence
*					
READCON	GET	CARDER,CARD			001
	CLI	CARD+4,C'X'			002
	BC	7,PASS1			003
	MVI	SWTAPE,C'T'			004
PASS1	CLI	CARD+5,C'X'			005
	BC	7,PASS2			006
	MVI	SWPUNCH,C'P'			007
PASS2	CLI	CARD+6,C'X'			008
	BC	7,PASS3			009
	MVI	SWPRINT,C'W'			010
PASS3					011

Figure 13-2

361

IBM

IBM System/360 Assembler Coding Form

X28-6509-2 U/M050
Printed in U.S.A.

| PROGRAM | | | | | PAGE | OF |
| PROGRAMMER | | DATE | | PUNCHING INSTRUCTIONS / GRAPHIC / PUNCH | CARD ELECTRO NUMBER | |

Name	Operation	Operand	Comments	Identification-Sequence
*				
WHATOUT	CLI	SWTAPE,C'T'		001
	BC	7,SKIP1		002
	BAL	10,MAGTAPE		003
SKIP1	CLI	SWPUNCH,C'P'		004
	BC	7,SKIP2		005
	BAL	10,PUNCHER		006
SKIP2	CLI	SWPRINT,C'W'		007
	BC	7,SKIP3		008
	BAL	10,PRINTER		009
SKIP3	- -	- - - -		010
	- -	- - - -		011

Figure 13-3

```
            CLI       SWITCH,C'2'
            BC        4,RECORD1        (Switch low)
            BC        2,RECORD3        (Switch high)
RECORD2     MVC       FLDB,FLDA        (Switch equal to '2')
```

The first instruction statement compares the one-byte character content of SWITCH to a character '2'. The next instruction will cause a branch to RECORD1 subroutine if SWITCH compared low to the '2'. The next instruction will cause a branch to the REC-ORD3 subroutine if SWITCH compared high to '2'. If a branch was not taken via the second or third statements, then the comparison must have been equal (SWITCH contains '2'), so the processing falls through to the RECORD2 routine.

Another application for switches is in a multipurpose program that gives the user a choice of output options. For this example, assume that the problem program will create output to any, or all, of three output devices—a magnetic tape drive, a card punch unit, and/or an output printer unit. At the time that the problem program is read into the computer, the user must supply a control card indicating which output types he desires. The control card should have an "X" in card column 5 for the magnetic tape output option, an "X" in card column 6 for the punched card output option, and/or an "X" in card column 7 for the printed output option. One of the very first routines in the program is to read the control card and set the output switches that are indicated by the user. This routine could appear as shown in Fig. 13-2.

Statement 001 is a standard QSAM macroinstruction that will read in the control card into a data area labeled CARD.

Statement 002 is checking card position 5 of the input (CARD + 4) for an "X". If it does not contain an "X", then Statement 003 will cause a branch around the next statement, Statement 004.

Statement 004 will set a switch that will indicate that magnetic tape output is desired.

Statement 005 is checking card position 6 of the input (CARD + 5) for an "X". If it does not contain an "X", Statement 006 will

cause a branch around Statement 007.

Statement 007 will set a switch to indicate that punched card output is desired.

Statement 008 is checking card position 7 of the input (CARD + 6) for an "X". If it does not contain an "X", then Statement 009 will cause a branch around Statement 010.

Statement 010 will set a switch to indicate that printed output is desired.

Now that the switches are set, the program logic continues on until it is time to create the output. The instruction statements for testing the switches and branching to the output routines as required could appear as illustrated in Fig. 13-3.

Statements 001, 004, and 007 are testing the three switches so as to determine what form of output is to be created. If the switch is not set to the "on" condition, the subsequent instruction statement causes a branch to the next switch-test statement. The branch decision is expressed as:

```
            BC        7, . . .
```

which states, "if the preceding compare instruction statement resulted in an unequal comparison, branch to . . . ." If the CLI instruction statement resulted in an equal comparison, indicating that the switch was on for that output method, the program logic would fall through the BC instruction statement to the BAL (Branch & Link) instruction statement. The BAL instruction would, in turn, force a branch back to the next sequential instruction statement following the BAL.

Another means of loading, or setting, switches of this type is to move the contents of the control card directly into the switches. Assume that as in the previous example, columns 5, 6, and 7 of the control card were to contain any mixture of X's or blanks in order to specify the output mode. Accordingly, the three switches were established in storage in a contiguous manner such as:

```
SWTAPE    DC    CL1'∅'
SWPUNCH   DC    CL1'∅'
SWPRINT   DC    CL1'∅'
```

The instruction statements required to set the switches to "on," or to leave them "off," according to the contents of the control card, would be:

```
READCON  GET   CARDER,CARD
         MVC   SWTAPE(3),CARD+4
```

The second statement would move the contents of card columns 5, 6, and 7 (either an "X" or a blank in each) into SWTAPE, SWPUNCH and SWPRINT. Notice that this has been accomplished in two instruction statements as compared to the ten statements required to set the switches in the previous example. The only other difference would be that when the routine that tested the switches was entered, each test would be for an "X" rather than for a unique character for each switch.

As the programmer becomes more proficient in his techniques he will discover the many additional ways to utilize byte-switches. Perhaps the greatest failing by programmers attempting to use "switch" techniques is the lack of care in clearing, or turning off, switches at the proper time and logic point.

2. Bit-Switches and Indicators

While character-switches utilize a full byte of data and may contain many condition signals, a bit-switch consists of only one binary bit position and can represent a maximum of two conditions. On the other hand, a single byte of data can contain eight individual bit-switches—one for each bit position.

These switches are of particular value when the program logic depends on a set of information as can be provided by a group of switches or indicators. For example, one byte of detail can contain a string of switches that would answer eight conditional tests, individually or collectively, such as:

(yes or no) and/or (yes or no) and/or
(yes or no) and/or (yes or no) and/or

(yes or no) and/or (yes or no) and/or
(yes or no) and/or (yes or no)

A sample test of the yes/no or the on/off condition of the eight bit-switches might possibly follow the logic of:

"If bit-1 is yes and bit-2 is yes/or bit-3 is no, then . . . ."

Establishing the single byte of data that is to contain from one to eight switches is accomplished in a similar manner as for a byte-switch. The exception, however, is that the defined value of the field being established for bit-switches should contain a fixed-point value of zero instead of a blank. A one-byte fixed-point value of zero will create eight zero-bits (00000000); a blank (Hex '40') will create a bit configuration of '01000000'. The constant used to create the bit-switch would appear as:

```
SWITCHES DC      X'00'
```

For manipulating the configuration of the bit-switches, it is expedient to use the Boolean logic instruction statements. For turning bit-switches "on" in a single byte of data, the Or Immediate Logical (OI) instruction may be used. For turning bit-switches "off" in a single byte of data, the And Immediate Logical (NI) instruction is used. By utilizing these two instructions, the programmer has the capability of setting any one bit position, or combination of positions, to an "on" or an "off" condition. The condition of one or more bit-switches may be tested by using the Test Under Mask (TM) instruction. This instruction will test selective bit positions without altering the configuration of those positions. The means of using these three instructions will be pointed out and illustrated in the paragraphs that follow.

As stated, the Or Immediate Logical instruction is used to set bit-switches to an "on" condition; that is, to insert a one-bit in the particular bit position representing that switch. Using a one-byte storage area labeled CHEX, it could be interpreted that the eight bit positions of that area would each constitute a bit-switch. Graphically this would appear as:

SW-1 SW-2 SW-3 SW-4 SW-5 SW-6 SW-7 SW-8

CHEX

| 0 | 0 | 0 | 0 | 0 | 0 | 0 | 0 |

One Byte

Each bit position would represent an individual switch, capable of indicating a yes/no condition—'0' for no, '1' for yes. By using the Or Immediate Logical instruction, any one or multiple bit positions can be set to a "yes" condition. A few examples of this application follow.

Example 1. Set switch 5 (SW-5) to a yes (or on) condition.

The first task to be accomplished is to establish the mask for the OI instruction. This can be done by visualizing the switch positions.

The mask that is to be used for this example can, therefore, be construed to be configurated as bits of 0-0-0-0-1-0-0-0. This configuration represents a hexadecimal value of X'08', so the mask to be used with the OI instruction should be coded as X'08'. The

Switch Number	*Is It To Be Turned On?* $0 = No$ *or do not change* $1 = Yes$	
SW-1	0	... No
SW-2	0	... No
SW-3	0	... No
SW-4	0	... No
SW-5	1	... Yes
SW-6	0	... No
SW-7	0	... No
SW-8	0	... No

instruction statement to be performed would be:

OI   CHEX,X'08'

The execution of this instruction statement would act on CHEX in the following manner:

SW-1 SW-2 SW-3 SW-4 SW-5 SW-6 SW-7 SW-8

CHEX (Before)

| 0 | 0 | 0 | 0 | 0 | 0 | 0 | 0 |

X'08' (Mask)

| 0 | 0 | 0 | 0 | 1 | 0 | 0 | 0 |

CHEX (After)

| 0 | 0 | 0 | 0 | 1 | 0 | 0 | 0 |

Switch 5 has now been successfully set to a "yes" or an on condition.

Example 2. The task is to "turn on" SW-2, SW-4, and SW-8. The mask for this example would be determined as follows:

Switch Number	*Is It to Be Turned On?* $0 = No$ *or do no change* $1 = Yes$	
SW-1	0	... No
SW-2	1	... Yes
SW-3	0	... No
SW-4	1	... Yes
SW-5	0	... No
SW-6	0	... No
SW-7	0	... No
SW-8	1	... Yes

This indicates that the mask should be coded as a set of bits consisting of 0-1-0-1-0-0-0-1, or hexadecimal '51'. The instruction statement itself would be written:

OI   CHEX,X'51'

	SW-1	SW-2	SW-3	SW-4	SW-5	SW-6	SW-7	SW-8
CHEX (Before)	0	0	0	0	0	0	0	0
X'51' (Mask)	0	1	0	1	0	0	0	1
CHEX (After)	0	1	0	1	0	0	0	1

Example 3. The problem in this instance is to assure the program that SW-1, SW-2, SW-6, SW-7, and SW-8 are set to a "yes" condition. If they are off, turn them on; if they are already on, leave them in that condition. In presenting this example, it shall be assumed that SW-1 and SW-8 are already in an "on" condition. When setting up the mask, however, this fact is not known so the provision for activating all of these switches must be taken. The mask will be comprised of a bit configuration of 1-1-0-0-0-1-1-1 or X'C7' and the instruction statement will be:

OI   CHEX,X'C7'

	SW-1	SW-2	SW-3	SW-4	SW-5	SW-6	SW-7	SW-8
CHEX (Before)	1	0	1	0	0	0	0	1
X'C7' (Mask)	1	1	0	0	0	1	1	1
CHEX (After)	1	1	1	0	0	1	1	1

Two reactions have occurred in this example which had not been illustrated in the previous examples. First, whenever a one-bit in the mask encountered a one-bit in the switch position the resulting condition was a one-bit. This follows the request to assure that it would be set to an "on" condition even if the switch was already indicating that condition. Second, when a zero-bit in the mask encountered a one-bit in the switch position, the one-bit was not altered. This follows the request that "if the switch is already on, leave it that way." This action was shown by the condition of SW-3—it was on before the instruction statement was executed and it was left on after a zero-bit in the mask was matched to it.

Conversely, the And Immediate Logical (NI) is used to "turn off" switches, or to set them to a "no" condition. The basis for establishing the mask to be used with the NI instruction is also the opposite of the OI instruction usage. If a bit-switch is to be turned off, then a zero-bit must be placed in the corresponding position in the mask; if a switch is to be left unaltered, whether it is on or off, then a one-bit is placed in the corresponding position in the mask. The examples that follow will demonstrate this activity.

Example 1. The task for the instruction is to turn off SW-3. The mask for this example would be created from the following logic:

Switch Number	Is It to Be Turned Off? 0 = yes 1 = no or do not change	
SW-1	1	... No
SW-2	1	... No
SW-3	0	... Yes
SW-4	1	... No
SW-5	1	... No
SW-6	1	... No
SW-7	1	... No
SW-8	1	... No

This would determine that the mask should be configured as 1-1-0-1-1-1-1-1 or hex 'DF'. The instruction statement would be coded as:

$$\text{NI} \quad \text{CHEX,X'DF'}$$

If SW-3 was the only switch that was currently on, the resulting action from this instruction statement would be:

	SW-1	SW-2	SW-3	SW-4	SW-5	SW-6	SW-7	SW-8
CHEX (Before)	0	0	1	0	0	0	0	0
X'DF' (Mask)	1	1	0	1	1	1	1	1
CHEX (After)	0	0	0	0	0	0	0	0

Example 2. Regardless of whether they are currently on or off, SW-2, SW-5, and SW-7 are to be set to an "off" condition. The mask for this example would, therefore, be a set of bits appearing as 1-0-1-1-0-1-0-1 or a hexadecimal value of 'B5'. The instruction statement is coded as:

$$\text{NI} \quad \text{CHEX,X'B5'}$$

If, in this instance, SW-2 and SW-5 were on, the operation would be:

	SW-1	SW-2	SW-3	SW-4	SW-5	SW-6	SW-7	SW-8
CHEX (Before)	0	1	0	0	1	0	0	0
X'B5'	1	0	1	1	0	1	0	1
CHEX (After)	0	0	0	0	0	0	0	0

SW-2 and SW-5 have been now set to an "off" condition as requested. Since SW-7 was already off, the corresponding zero-bit in the mask did not alter that condition.

Example 3. The task is to assure the program that SW-1, SW-3, SW-4, and SW-6 are off, or in a "no" condition. If they are off, they should remain that way; if they are on, turn them off. Do not alter the configuration of any of the other switches. For this request, the mask would be a set of bits consisting of 0-1-0-0-1-0-1-1 or X'4B'. The instruction statement would be:

$$\text{NI} \quad \text{CHEX,X'4B'}$$

	SW-1	SW-2	SW-3	SW-4	SW-5	SW-6	SW-7	SW-8
CHEX (Before)	1	1	0	1	0	1	0	1

X'4B' (Mask)	0	1	0	0	1	0	1	1

CHEX (After)	0	1	0	0	0	0	0	1

As requested by the program requirements, this instruction statement has successfully warranted that SW-1, SW-3, SW-4, and SW-6 are now in an "off" condition. SW-2 and SW-8, which were "on" before execution of this statement, remain as they were because the corresponding one-bit in the mask specified that they were to stand unaltered.

Now that the means of setting bit-switches to an "on" or "off" condition has been presented, there remains the method of checking the condition of each switch—testing the value of any or all bit positions via the use of the Test Under Mask instruction. As in the instructions that are used to set the bit-switches on and off, a mask is used as a part of the TM instruction. Because that instruction will perform on only one byte of data, the mask is established as a one-byte self-defining immediate character. Bit positions in the data-byte representing the bit-switches that are to be tested are correspondingly indicated by a one-bit in the mask. That is, for each bit-switch to be tested, the mask will contain a one-bit for that indicated position; for bit-switches that are not to be tested, or are to be ignored, the mask will contain a zero-bit in the corresponding bit position. During the execution of the TM instruction statement a zero-bit in the mask will not cause a result indication. A one-bit in the mask will cause the Condition Code bits to be set in accordance with the result of the match of that bit to its corresponding bit-switch. If a one-bit in the mask detects a one-bit in the bit-switch, a one-bit result is stored; if it detects a zero-bit in the bit-switch, a zero-bit result is stored. After all one-bits in the mask have tested all corresponding bit-switches, the Condition Code will indicate any one of three possible conditions. These conditions may be construed to be as follows:

CC	BC	Condition
0	8	All result-bits were zero-bits.
1	4	Result-bits were both one-bits and zero-bits.
3	1	All result-bits were one-bits.

The first condition states that all bit-switches tested were off; the second condition states that some were off and some were on; the third states that all bit-switches were on.

The criteria for determining the hexadecimal value of the mask is similar to creating a mask for the OI instruction. If, for example, a TM instruction statement was to be executed for the purpose of testing SW-3, SW-5, and SW-8 the mask would be arrived at by:

Switch Number	Mask 0 = Do not test 1 = Test this switch	
SW-1	0	. . . No
SW-2	0	. . . No
SW-3	1	. . . Yes
SW-4	0	. . . No
SW-5	1	. . . Yes
SW-6	0	. . . No
SW-7	0	. . . No
SW-8	1	. . . Yes

This represents a mask of 0-0-1-0-1-0-0-1 or hex '29'. If the instruction statement were to be subsequently issued as:

TM   CHEX,X'29'

then only SW-3, SW-5 and SW-8 would be tested. The result of the test of these three bit-switches, and only these three, would determine the status of the Condition Code bits.

Example 1. The data-byte to be tested contains eight bit-switches. The current value of these switches, in their respective "on/off" conditions, represents a hexadecimal value of '9D'. In this example, only switches SW-3 and SW-7 are to be tested, requiring a mask value of X'22'. The instruction statement could be coded as:

TM   BITSWIT,X'22'

The resulting performance of this instruction statement would appear as:

	SW-1	SW-2	SW-3	SW-4	SW-5	SW-6	SW-7	SW-8
BITSWIT (Before)	1	0	0	1	1	1	0	1
X'22' (Mask)	0	0	1	0	0	0	1	0
Result bits			0				0	

Note that although several switches were equal to an "on" condition, there were only result-bits for the particular switches tested by the one-bits within the mask. For this example, the Condition Code would have indicated that "all result bits were zero-bits."

Example 2. The byte of bit-switches that is to be tested has a value of hexadecimal 'FF'. The individual switches that are to be tested are SW-1, SW-2, and SW-4.

TM   BITSWITB,X'DO'

	SW-1	SW-2	SW-3	SW-4	SW-5	SW-6	SW-7	SW-8
BITSWITB (Before)	1	1	1	1	1	1	1	1
X'DO' (Mask)	1	1	0	1	0	0	0	0
Result bits	1	1		1				

The resulting Condition Code for this example would indicate that "all result bits were one-bits." This would signal that all three switches tested were of a configuration that represented an "on" condition.

Example 3. The byte of data that is to be tested within this example has a hexadecimal value of '27'. The instruction statement is to test for an "on" condition of SW-2, SW-3, SW-5, and SW-8.

TM   BITSWITC,X'69'

	SW-1	SW-2	SW-3	SW-4	SW-5	SW-6	SW-7	SW-8
BITSWITC (Before)	0	0	1	0	0	1	1	1
X'69' (Mask)	0	1	1	0	1	0	0	1
Result bits		0	1		0			1

After execution of the instruction statement, the PSW Condition Code bits would be interpreted as stating, "the result bits are both one-bits and zero-bits."

C. GENERAL APPLICATIONS OF SWITCHES

The particular circumstances under which character-switches or bit-switches may be effectively applied are innumerable. They do, however, fall within major groupings, each of which might have many variations based on the logic of the individual problem program. A detailed listing of some of these major groupings of switch applications appear in the following paragraphs.

1. End-of-File-Routine Multiple Conditions

A program that utilizes parallel multireel magnetic tape input and output quite often presents a logic problem in the closing routines when those multiple reels represent different sets of data. This would be exemplified by a sizable merge or update routine wherein several separate tape data sets are being simultaneously merged into a master tape file. In this type of situation, it is usually not known which tape will reach an EOF (End-Of-File) condition first; therefore, some type of indicator or switch is quite often utilized in order to allow the program to check if certain tapes have already been closed out. For example, if TAPE1, TAPE2, and TAPE3 are to be sequentially merged with MASTER1, the program logic would require knowledge of whether MASTER1 reached the end of its data first, or if any one or all of the updating tapes were the first to be exhausted. If TAPE2 reached an EOF condition prior to any of the other three tapes, the program should continue merging TAPE1 and TAPE3 with MASTER1, ignoring or bypassing the existence of TAPE2. Any further attempts to read TAPE2 would now result in a program interrupt by the system, so the possible application of a switch would be evident. Upon the completion of TAPE2, an EOF routine could be entered, within which the program logic could set a switch to indicate that TAPE2 had been depleted. Any further attempts to read TAPE2 could be deterred by a test of that switch immediately prior to the "read" routine. This same logic is applicable to "clos-ing" routines. Peculiar program logic could present the condition that one or more of these tape data sets might possibly be closed during the execution of the main-line logic. When the entire program has been completed, it would be necessary to know if this condition had occurred, and which particular tape data sets it had affected. If a tape data set was closed during the execution of the main-line logic, it would have been a simple application for the programmer to set a switch indicating this fact. Then, at the completion of the program and within the final closing routines, the logic could test an individual switch for each tape data set used by the program—if the switch was "on," the logic would know that this data set had already been closed and it would bypass further action; if the switch was "off," the logic would know that the tape data set was still "open" and could issue the necessary macroinstructions required to close it. Although this application has been used in reference to tape data sets, it applies equally well to any type of data set, whether it resides on a disk, drum, or any other type of storage device.

2. Has a Routine Been Completed?

Any given routine, or subroutine, may consist of stages of execution utilizing a common logic module. The performance of this module might well vary in accordance with the completion, or partial completion, of the controlling routine. By setting a variable switch at unique points within the control routine and then testing that switch for various conditions within the common module, many variations can be applied to the execution of the common module.

3. What Subroutine or Routine Passed Control?

This type of application is similar to the one just described. A common module may be used from many different logic points in the problem program, each one accessing it by a Branch & Link instruction statement. Each exit point in the main logic may require one or more unique functions within the common module, but not to such a point as to require a separate module. Prior to exiting from the main logic by the BAL instruction, a single switch can be given a unique setting so as to identify the exit point from which the common module was entered. That module, in turn, can test this switch and establish the criteria demanded by that unique condition.

4. Special Conditions During Processing

There are so many possibilities within this group that it precludes mentioning even a general application; however, one example that may give some indication of this type of use is the previously mentioned application of updating master files. When the update is in process, it might be assumed that input data will match to a currently existing master record. If this is so, then certain functions might be bypassed since the control data already exists on the master record. If a record of input data is encountered for which there is no master record, certain additional functions that are located noncontiguously throughout the program logic could be required to create a master record. Once again here is a logical task for a switch. At the time that the comparison of the input record to the master file has determined that no master records exist for this data, a switch can be set, indicating this exception.

As sequential logic is performed, this switch is tested at critical points—if the switch is off, certain additional routines are bypassed by branches; if the switch is on, the branches are not taken and the logic falls through in order to build the additional data required to create the master record.

5. Embedded Switches Within Data Records

The use of embedded switches is often a major factor in the maintenance of data files that are time-dependent. In this type of maintenance, the records themselves are "flagged" by the setting of a switch embedded in the data as a part of the record. One concept of this is that the record is flagged and a subsequent listing of flagged records is produced. If no action is taken to reinstate the "keep" status of these records prior to the next update, all such records are deleted from the data file.

6. Multiple Conditions

This application, primarily using bit-switches, depends on the status of two or more switch conditions in order to make a decision. If the bit-switches were set whenever a record of data was input to the problem program (in this instance a Purchase Order System), some of the switches might represent:

		Switch Settings	
		Yes	*No*
SW-1	Has the material been received?	1	0
SW-2	Has the material been back-ordered?	1	0
SW-3	Back-ordered for more than 60 days?	1	0
SW-4	Has an invoice been received?	1	0
SW-5	Was there more than a 5% price variance from the P.O.?	1	0
SW-6	Was it a partial shipment?	1	0
SW-7	Any defects found during Purchase Material Inspection?	1	0
SW-8	Should invoice payment be withheld?	1	0

Based on the contents of these switches for each data record, certain records might be extracted for special use. For example, an Accounts Payable Department might wish to obtain a listing of all records for which switches SW-1, SW-4, SW-5, and SW-8 were set to an "on" condition. These would be the records that indicated that the material has been received, an invoice for the material had been received from the vendor, the vendor price varied more than 5% from the quoted price on the purchase order, and payment of this invoice was to be withheld at this time. It is true that each of these conditions could have been tested individually from embedded switches or indicators within the record. In a system of this type, however, many phases of logical extracts test for similar conditions. By setting a series of bit-switches in the input routines, each phase can test for the particular conditions it is interested in, merely by using one TM (Test Under Mask) instruction statement. In the example described for the Accounts Payable Department extract, a mask of X'99' would have given a satisfactory test for the questioned conditions.

Review Exercises

1. Using the concept of bit-switches, a single byte of storage can represent a total of _____ unique switches or indicators.

2. When it is necessary to compare the contents of a character-switch to a particular configuration, the _____ _____ _____ instruction will prove to be the most expedient method of doing so.

3. Nondestructive testing of the condition of bit-switches can be accomplished by the use of the _____ _____ _____ instruction.

4. A byte-switch may also be referred to as a _____ switch.

5. A single bit position of a source byte can be tested by coding a _____-bit in the corresponding bit position of the mask operand within a Test Under Mask instruction statement.

6. The Assembler Language instruction that would be the most efficient for setting the configuration of a byte-switch or character-switch is the _____ _____.

7. A character-switch could be configurated so as to represent _____ different switch conditions.

In each of the following problems, a one-byte set of switches is defined. Logical action to be taken against each byte is defined in terms of the bit positions, numbered from left to right as bit-switch 1 through bit-switch 8. Fill in the appropriate Boolean Logic instruction mnemonic op code and the hexadecimal configuration of the mask that would be required to perform the task as requested, assuming that the contents of the source byte is not known prior to the execution of the instruction statement. Then complete the blank field representing the source byte as it would appear after execution of the instruction statement.

8. ABITS | 0 1 1 0 | 0 0 1 0 |

   Task: Turn on switches 1, 3, and 5:

                       _____ ABITS,X'_____'

   ABITS | | |

9. KBITS | 0 1 1 0 | 1 0 0 1 |

Task: Define KBITS after execution of the following statements:

$$
\begin{array}{ll}
\text{NI} & \text{KBITS,X'C3'} \\
\text{XI} & \text{KBITS,X'17'} \\
\text{OI} & \text{KBITS,X'4D'} \\
\text{NI} & \text{KBITS,X'A0'}
\end{array}
$$

KBITS | | |

10. HBITS | 0 0 1 1 | 0 1 1 1 |

Task: Turn off all switches except switch 4:

_____ HBITS,X'_____'

HBITS | | |

11. BBITS | 1 0 0 1 | 0 0 1 1 |

Task: Turn on switches 1, 4, 6, 7, and 8:

_____ BBITS,X'_____'

BBITS | | |

12. EBITS | 0 0 1 0 | 1 0 1 1 |

Task: Turn off switches 1, 3, and 8; turn on switches 2 and 5:

_____ EBITS,X'_____'
_____ EBITS,X'_____'

EBITS | | |

13. CBITS | 0 1 0 0 | 1 1 0 1 |

Task: Turn off switches 2, 4, and 6:

_____ CBITS,X'_____'

CBITS | | |

14. FBITS | 1 0 0 1 | 1 1 1 1 |

Task: Reverse the individual conditions of switches 3, 4, 5, and 7. If they are on, turn them off; if they are off, turn them on.

_____ FBITS,X'_____'

FBITS | | |

15. GBITS | 0 1 1 0 | 0 0 0 1 |

Task: Non-destructively test the conditions of switches 2, 5, 7, and 8.

TM   GBITS,X'_____'

GBITS | | |

16. DBITS | 1 1 1 0 | 1 0 1 1 |

Task: Turn off switches 1, 2, 6, 7, and 8:

_____ DBITS,X'_____'

DBITS | | |

LOOP CONTROLS AND TABLE LOOK-UPS

This chapter will provide a basis for applying index and/or table look-up logic utilizing loop control techniques and direct addressing manipulation. In essence, look-up techniques generally involve incremental addressing through a contiguous field or block of data under the control of a loop count value or conditional compare. In some instances it is possible to manipulate the key value of the segment being sought and create the actual address of that segment as it resides within the parent table or index. Prior to a detailed discussion of the actual look-up techniques, it is essential that the means of utilizing loop controls be thoroughly understood.

A. LOOP CONTROLS

The controlling of the quantity of cycles through any given loop pattern may be ac-

complished by utilizing any of the "Branch On Count" or "Branch On Condition" type of instructions. Most often, the instructions that are to be used are the Branch On Count, Branch On Count To Register, Branch On Condition, and Branch On Condition To Register instructions. Less frequently used, but equally effective, are the Branch On Index High and Branch On Index Low Or Equal instructions. Because of the similarity and general applications of all of these instructions, this discussion will utilize only the Branch On Count and Branch On Condition instructions for demonstrating and reviewing loop control functions. Any of the other instructions mentioned may be suitably applied to these functions, as a review of their capabilities would indicate.

If the total length of a field, table, or index is fixed and unvariable, the loop cycle control may be assumed to be a constant value that should not be exceeded. In this instance,

375

a Branch On Count instruction may be used to terminate a complete set of cycles through that field, table, or index. If the length of the area to be scanned is a variable, changing from time to time, a Branch On Condition instruction may be more practical to apply. The common logic for this application would be to insert a number of unique characters, or an entire table segment of unique characters, at the end of the data and then check for the occurence of those characters each time the area address is incremented. When those characters are encountered, the program logic should signal that the entire area has been scanned without finding the original argument for which the search was being made.

B. SEQUENTIAL LOOK-UPS AND SCANS

Sequential look-up or scanning is construed to mean the sequential checking of contiguous data elements, whether or not those elements are in a logically sequential value arrangement. Such groups of elements may be organized in either a sequential or random pattern of the value of the identifier (key) field. The term sequential, as used in "sequential look-up," means that the elements of the table or index will be looked at in a physically element-by-element pattern regardless of whether or not their values correspond to that arrangement. A physically sequential table array, arranged in a logically sequential mode would be:

/001/002/003/005/006/007
/009/010/012/013/017/018
/019/020/021/023/025/026

A physically sequential table array, arranged in a random value pattern, would be:

/006/005/047/001/012/017
/075/065/066/063/014/019
/003/008/010/009/088/027

Sequential look-up processing may be applied to either format. In some instances, however, it might be considerably more expedient to use another type of look-up for a table or index that is both physically and logically sequential; perhaps a binary or a sectoring look-up.

The performance of a sequential look-up is based on a series of loop cycles, each cycle containing a comparison of the present table segment being addressed, a decision based on that comparison, and an instruction statement to increment the current table address setting to the next segment. In this type of scan, or look-up, the search is normally initialized at the beginning point of the table and increments its way through the table by one segment at a time. Many variations of this scheme are possible—the search may start at the end of the table and decrement downward one segment at a time; or the search may proceed in both directions at the same time. Several of these variations will be shown in the examples that follow.

Example 1. This routine consists of a table look-up that will convert a three-byte EBCDIC numeric to a one-byte EBCDIC alphabetic character. The organization of the table is physically sequential and logically random. Each table segment consists of four bytes—a three-byte numeric and a one-byte character. The table consists of 50 segments plus an end-of-table delimiter. If a "hit" is encountered, the logic branches to a subroutine to pick up the character from the table segment; if a "hit" is not encountered the entire table is scanned and the logic then falls through to the next statement.

The coded instructions shown in Fig. 14-1*a* and *b* may be defined as performing in the manner described in these following statements.

Statement 0101 is a Branch & Link to an assumed routine that will read a card into the CARDIN area.

Statement 0102 moves the third, fourth, and fifth characters from CARDIN (assumed to be containing a three-byte numeric key) to HOLDKEY. HOLDKEY now contains the three-byte code (argument) that is to be used to search the table.

Statement 0103 loads the address of the first byte of TABLE into general register 6.

IBM

PROGRAM: TABLE LOOK-UP ROUTINE

```
Name     Operation  Operand                            Comments
*
*                   PROGRAM WORK AREAS
*
CARDIN   DC   CL80' '                                  -CARD INPUT AREA
HOLDKEY  DC   CL3' '                                   -HOLD AREA FOR RECORD KEY
CONVKEY  DC   CL1' '                                   -HOLD AREA FOR 1-BYTE CHARACTER
*
**
*                   TABLE
*
*
TABLE    DC   CL28'010A015D020E031B045A048C242C'
         DC   CL28'026B053G056A096B100C177D316G'
         DC   CL28'049A098E072C039D176E134A410F'
         DC   CL28'092C121B165H073A016F265C259H'
         DC   CL28'071D041A083F030A088B085G047F'
         DC   CL28'110E378D059A237B103A025A196H'
         DC   CL28'051F283B075E066A217C291D019J'
         DC   CL8'035C999X'
*
```

Figure 14-1a

377

IBM

IBM System/360 Assembler Coding Form

X28-6500-2 U/M050
Printed in U.S.A.

PROGRAM	TABLE LOOK-UP ROUTINE		PUNCHING INSTRUCTIONS		GRAPHIC			PAGE 2 OF 2
PROGRAMMER		DATE			PUNCH			CARD ELECTRO NUMBER

STATEMENT

Name	Operation	Operand	Comments	Identification-Sequence
*		ROUTINE LOGIC		
*				
GO	BAL	8,GETCARD		0101
	MVC	HOLDKEY(3),CARDIN+3		0102
	LA	6,TABLE		0103
	LA	7,50		0104
LOOP	CLC	HOLDKEY(3),0(6)		0105
	BC	8,FOUND		0106
	AH	6,=H'4'		0107
	BCT	7,LOOP		0108
	BC	15,GO		0109
*				
**				
FOUND	MVC	CONVKEY(1),0+3(6)		0110
	BAL	8,PUTDATA		0111
	BC	15,GO		0112
*				
**				
*				

Figure 14-1b

This value (address) can now be incremented for "stepping" through the table in a sequential manner.

Statement 0104 is using the Load Address instruction to place a value of +50 into general register 7. Register 7 will be the Branch On Count register for loop control. Because there are only 50 valid segments in the table, the value of +50 in general register 7 will allow a maximum of 50 increments to the table starting-point address.

Statement 0105 is the initial statement within LOOP. It will compare the three bytes of HOLDKEY to the data located at the current address in general register 6. Each time that general register 6 is incremented, this instruction will be comparing HOLDKEY to a new table segment—the one that is pointed to by register 6.

Statement 0106 is a Branch On Condition instruction statement, specifying that if HOLDKEY is equal to the table segment being addressed by register 6, then the problem program logic should branch to the FOUND routine.

Statement 0107 is adding a value of +4 to general register 6. Because the branch in Statement 0106 was not taken, the logic knows that an equal condition was not found in the compare between HOLDKEY and the current table segment pointed to by the address contained in register 6. Therefore, the address in register 6 is increased by one table segment (four bytes) so that if Statement 0105 is encountered again it will be comparing HOLDKEY to the next higher table segment.

Statement 0108 is the Branch On Count loop control statement. Each time that this statement is encountered, the value in general register 7 is reduced by a value of +1. As long as general register 7 is greater than zero the branch to LOOP will be taken. As soon as register 7 is decremented to zero, indicating that the entire table has been scanned, the branch will not be taken and the program execution will fall through to Statement 0109.

Statement 0109 is a forced branch back to GO. Because the key held in HOLDKEY was not found, the program is designed to branch back to GO, get a new card, move in the new key value, reset the loop controls, reset the pointer to the beginning of TABLE, and then enter LOOP to see if that new key is within the TABLE.

Statement 0110 is the beginning of the subroutine that is branched to if a "hit" is made against the table. It will move the fourth byte of the current TABLE segment into a one-byte area labeled CONVKEY. This segment is pointed to by the address contained in general register 6 and the one-byte of data is accessed by incrementing that address by +3—pointing to the fourth byte in that segment.

Statement 0111 is a Branch & Link to an assumed routine to perform an output operation using the character that was moved into CONVKEY.

Statement 0112 is a forced branch to GO that will start through the series of instruction statements again, getting a new input card, moving in the look-up argument, re-initializing the loop control, etc.

In this example, the BCT instruction was used to determine when the entire table had been checked. Because there were 50 valid table segments, the value of +50 was loaded into the BCT register. In reality, the table consists of 51 segments, the last segment being a table delimiter segment. In the set of instruction statements just explained, it would have been assumed that the table would always consist of 50 valid segments. By utilizing the table delimiter segment, it would make no difference what the length of the overall table would be. Compare the instruction statements in Fig. 14-2 to the first set of statements of the preceding example.

This set of coding gives no consideration to the number of segments in the table. It will continue incrementing through the table and will terminate the look-up only when a "hit" has occurred or when Statement 0107 encounters the table delimiter segment. As soon as Statement 0107 creates an equal comparison, Statement 0108 knows that the entire table has been scanned without a "hit" and the processing logic will fall through to

IBM

IBM System/360 Assembler Coding Form

X28-6509-2 U/M050
Printed in U.S.A.

Name	Operation	Operand		Comments		Identification-Sequence
*						
*						
GO	BAL	8,GETCARD				0101
	MVC	HOLDKEY(3),CARDIN+3				0102
	LA	6,TABLE				0103
LOOP	CLC	HOLDKEY(3),0(6)				0104
	BC	8,FOUND				0105
	AH	6,=H'4'				0106
	CLC	0(3,6),=CL3'999'				0107
	BC	7,LOOP				0108
	BC	15,GO				0109
*						
*						

Figure 14-2

Statement 0110. Although Statements 0107 and 0108 have been added to this set of instructions, Statements 0104 and 0108 have been eliminated from the previous set of instructions, resulting in exactly the same number of statements to perform the task. Either method is logically correct to use, but the latter method has definite merit if the overall length of the table might possibly vary from time to time.

In many instances the table that is to be used by a problem program exists only as a defined area within that program and actually contains no data. The data that belongs within the table is not supplied until execution time of the program. It will exist as a supplement to the program object module, or as an input data set, and will be loaded into the table area by the problem program itself. This is generally referred to as a "loadable" table. For example, if the problem program is being input to the CPU via the card reader, the data to be supplied to the table could be a set of additional card data that follows the object module delimiter card. The problem program begins execution and as one of its first tasks it commences reading-in the table data cards and placing their data into the defined table area. Once again, a table delimiter segment may be used, but this time for two purposes. As the cards are being read in, this card will signify the end of the table input; when the table is actually being searched, the delimiter card will signal that the end of the table has been reached. This is also an excellent use of the application of a variable-length table concept. When loading the card data into the table, both the check for the table delimiter segment card and the Branch On Count loop control functions may be used. The compare for the table delimiter segment will indicate when the last card of the input has been read—the Branch On Count loop control will make sure that the number of table segment data cards do not exceed the maximum overall length of the table area. If the defined area for the table within the problem program allowed for a maximum of 500 table segments and the program encounters a table delimiter segment card on the 400th

read, only 400 table segments would be loaded—and only that many would be utilized in subsequent searches if the search compare was looking for a table delimiter segment. If the problem program tried to read 510 table segments into the storage area, the Branch On Count loop control instruction would not allow the branch to be taken once the 500th segment had been read. The program logic could fall through to the next sequential instruction, one which might well be a message to the computer operator advising him that the table capacity had been exceeded. The following example presents a set of data as described for this type of an application.

Example 2. The instruction statements and defined areas have been coded as shown in Fig. 14-3.

Statement 0041 defines a label of CARDIN that is to reference the 80 bytes of storage defined following this statement. The zero preceding the 'CL' indicates that no storage area is to be reserved by this define-statement. The card data to be placed in the next 80 bytes of storage may be referenced by this label or by the labels sub-defined by the DC statements for Statements 0042 and 0043.

Statement 0042 actually reserves four bytes of storage, tagged with the label IDNO. This represents the first four bytes of each of the table cards that are to be read in, these bytes containing the unique identification number of an employee record that is to be part of the data loaded into the table.

Statement 0043 reserves 76 more bytes of storage, completing the area of 80 bytes referenced by CARDIN. Only the first 16 bytes of this field are important because they contain the name that is to be loaded into the table along with the associated identification number field of four bytes that immediately precedes this field.

Statement 0044 reserves a total of 16,000 bytes of storage, labeled TABLE, for the "Employee I.D. and Name" table. It is estimated that the table will consist of a maxi-

IBM

IBM System/360 Assembler Coding Form

PROGRAM						PUNCHING INSTRUCTIONS	GRAPHIC				PAGE	OF
PROGRAMMER			DATE				PUNCH				CARD ELECTRO NUMBER	

X28-6509-2 U/M050
Printed in U.S.A.

Name	Operation	Operand	Comments	Identification-Sequence
*				
CARDIN	DS	0CL80		0041
IDNO	DC	CL4' '		0042
MISC	DC	CL76' '		0043
TABLE	DC	800CL20' '		0044
*				
*				
STARTIN	LA	6,TABLE		0051
	LA	7,800		0052
GETDATA	BAL	5,CARDGET		0053
	MVC	0(20,6),CARDIN		0054
	CLC	IDNO,=CL4'9999'		0055
	BC	8,ALLIN		0056
	AH	6,=H'20'		0057
	BCT	7,GETDATA		0058
	WTO	'ID TABLE EXCEEDED - ABEND'		0059
	ABEND	400		0060
*				
*				
ALLIN				

Figure 14-3

mum of 800 segments of 20 bytes each—4 bytes for the I.D. number and 16 bytes for the name associated with that number. Any quantity of table segments within the range of 1 to 800, including the table delimiter segment, may be loaded into this table. As the number of employees varies from week to week, the table will accept these variances.

The remaining statements of this particular illustration are those that control the loading of the table segments from card form into the problem program table area.

Statement 0051 loads the address of the first byte of the TABLE area (16,000 bytes long) into general register 6.

Statement 0052 loads a value of +800 into general register 7, this value to be used for loop control in the BCT instruction in Statement 0058. This assures that a maximum of 800 table segments are all that can be loaded into TABLE.

Statement 0053 is a Branch & Link instruction statement to an assumed data access routine that will read a card into the area addressed by CARDIN. Once this data has been read in, it may be referenced in whole by CARDIN or in part by IDNO or MISC.

Statement 0054 moves the first 20 bytes of the CARDIN field into the current table segment that is pointed to by general register 6. These 20 bytes contain a 4-byte I.D. number and a 16-byte employee name, comprising one table segment. When the first card is read, register 6 points to the address generated by TABLE+0, on the second card it points to TABLE+20, on the third to TABLE+40, on the fourth to TABLE+60, etc.

Statement 0055 compares the first four bytes of CARDIN (as subdefined by the label IDNO), the same four bytes that have just been moved into the table, to a four-byte literal constant of '9999'. This particular program is using a card containing '9999' as its combined input delimiter and table delimiter segment value. Because the logic wants this end-of-table delimiter indicator to be a part of the table, the comparison looking for the input delimiter card is not made until the data has been moved into the table.

Statement 0056 is a Branch On Condition statement that will cause a branch to be taken if the comparison in Statement 0055 created an "equal" condition setting of the Condition Code bits. If the condition was "equal," the branch will be taken to a routine that will begin additional problem program processing on the assumption that all current table segments have been loaded.

Statement 0057 adds a halfword value of +20 to general register 6 if the preceding statement, Statement 0056, did not cause a branch to be taken. This is incrementing general register 6 so that it points to the next logical table segment that is to be loaded with data.

Statement 0058 is the Branch On Count loop control. Because general register 7, the first operand in this statement, was loaded with a value of +800, this instruction statement will allow up to 800 table segments to be loaded before dropping through to Statement 0059. If less than 800 segments are loaded, the input card delimiter will be encountered and the branch in Statement 0056 will be taken before general register 7 can be decremented to zero.

Statement 0059 is an OS (Operating System) macroinstruction, referred to as the "Write To Operator" (WTO) macro. It will cause the system data management routines to type out the message, as contained within quotes, onto the computer console typewriter. In this case, the message is advising the computer operator that the number of table segments have exceeded 800 and that the program is unable to process further.

Statement 0060 is an ABEND macroinstruction that advises the system to terminate the current problem program with an ABnormal END condition, using a termination condition code of '400'. The program will be terminated and the related data remaining in the job input stream will be "flushed," or passed through the card reader without further action.

Now that the table has been loaded with an "X" amount of segments, the problem program can search it by using the second version of logic as shown under Example 1 in this section. That is, instead of using a Branch On Count instruction to signal the problem program when the entire table has been searched, a compare statement should be issued that will look for the '9999' code, indicating the end of the active table segments.

Whenever programming a sequential look-up on a table or index that is arranged with the data in a logically sequential identity pattern, another shortcut in processing time is available. This option is a Branch On Condition instruction statement that will cause a branch whenever the argument (the data being compared to the table) compares "low" to the current table segment. In effect, such a condition indicates that the table segments have been sequentially scanned to a point where the logical value of the table key is now greater than that of the argument key, indicating that the table did not contain a segment comparable to the argument. It would then be appropriate to branch out of the table look-up loop inasmuch as any further scanning of the table would be useless— all remaining table keys being even greater than the one for which the search is being made. This technique is illustrated in the next example.

Example 3. The logic to be applied within this routine is that KEYCHEX is compared to the index to seek an address contained within the last four bytes of each INDEX table segment. If a "hit" occurs, the routine will move the corresponding address from INDEX into the ADDRESS field. If a "hit" is not encountered, the table look-up loop will be terminated as soon as KEYCHEX compares "low" to INDEX or when the table delimiter segment of '999' is encountered. The routine assumes that the table has already been loaded with an unspecified number of index table segments arranged in ascending sequential order of the value of the first three bytes of each segment. (See Fig. 14-4)

Statement 0061 is a Branch & Link instruction, branching to an assumed subroutine for the purpose of accessing a tape data

set and placing the incoming data records into the field labeled TAPEIN.

Statement 0062 loads the address of the first byte of INDEX into general register 10. That register will be used as the pointer register for incrementing through the seven-byte segments of INDEX.

Statement 0063 will move three bytes of data from TAPEIN into the KEYCHEX field. This data is assumed to be the three-byte key that will be compared to the contents of the INDEX segment keys.

Statement 0064 is the first statement within the table look-up loop. It is comparing the three bytes of data in KEYCHEX to the first three bytes in the single INDEX segment that is currently pointed to by general register 10. As a result of this comparison, the Condition Code bits in the PSW will be set so as to indicate the existing condition—high, low, or equal.

Statement 0065 indicates that if Statement 0064 resulted in an "equal" compare, then the program logic should branch to an assumed subroutine that will move the last four bytes of the current table segment into ADDRESS. Otherwise, the logic will "fall through" Statement 0065 and the branch will not be taken.

Statement 0066 specifies that if the comparison in Statement 0064 indicated that KEYCHEX was of a lower logical value than the current INDEX segment referenced by general register 10, then the program should branch back to GONOW. This condition would indicate that since the current table segment key was of a higher logical value than KEYCHEX, the portion of the INDEX where a corresponding key to KEYCHEX would have been found had already been passed. Therefore, it is concluded that no match to KEYCHEX existed within INDEX and there is no reason to search that table any further. If the branch is not taken, the logic will "fall through" to the next instruction statement.

Statement 0067 adds a halfword value of +7 to general register 10. This will increment general register 10 so that the address contained therein points to the next INDEX

Name	Operation	Operand	Comments	Identification-Sequence
*				
*				
GONOW	BAL	5,GETAPE		0061
	LA	10,INDEX		0062
	MVC	KEYCHEX(3),TAPEIN+14		0063
LOOPCHEX	CLC	KEYCHEX(3),0(10)		0064
	BC	8,GOTADDR		0065
	BC	4,GONOW		0066
	AH	10,=H'7'		0067
	CLC	0(3,10),=CL3'999'		0068
	BC	7,LOOPCHEX		0069
NOHIT	BC	15,GONOW		0070
*				
*				
*				
TAPEIN	DC	CL25' '		0071
KEYCHEX	DC	CL3' '		0072
INDEX	DC	300CL7' '		0073
ADDRESS	DC	CL4' '		0074
*				
*				

Figure 14-4

segment that is higher than the one just checked.

Statement 0068 is comparing the first three bytes of the table segment now addressed by general register 10 to a three-byte character literal to see if the end of INDEX has been reached. The last segment of INDEX would be the table delimiter segment containing '999' in its first three bytes.

Statement 0069 indicates that as long as Statement 0068 did not create an "equal" setting of the Condition Code bits, then the logic should branch back to the first instruction in the loop cycle, LOOPCHEX. If Statement 0068 did result in an equal compare, the program logic would fall through to Statement 0070 on the assumption that the entire table had been searched.

Statement 0070 is a forced branch to GONOW. Because a match to the current value in KEYCHEX was not found in the table, the logic of this particular routine wishes to now bypass that record and get a new key field value from the next tape record.

As mentioned previously, this particular type of look-up routine, utilizing an exiting branch when the argument is of a lower value than the corresponding table value, is applicable *only* when the table is organized in the ascending or descending sequential order of the value of the table segment keys.

C. SECTORED LOOK-UP TECHNIQUES

The concept of a sectored look-up routine, or sectoring the table by search arguments, is based on the technique of arranging a table into logical sections, each section containing approximately an equal number of segments. The overall contents of the table, however, should be arranged in a logical sequence of values. When activating a look-up of this type of file table, the inquiry may start at any sector point within that table, based on the subsequent program logic that follows it. In explaining this technique further, Table 14-1 will be used to reference the types of sectoring logic.

This table consists of 250 segments of four bytes each, a total of 1000 bytes. It is broken down into five primary sectors, each sector having a unique name and each containing 50 individual table segments. For example, the segments within sector PTA may be addressed as PTA+0, PTA+4, PTA+8, PTA+12, etc., through to PTA+196. The table segment that follows PTA+196 is the first segment within sector PTB; it could, however, also be addressed as PTA+200. Note that the first segment in sector PTA (0000) and the last segment in sector PTE (9999) represent the maximum low and high limits of the segment keys. By initializing the table with '0000' and ending it with '9999', the table may now be scanned in ascending or descending sequence without overrunning the table boundaries. This statement is made with the assumption that the programmer will issue the proper comparative statements to these values to prevent such an overrun. If the table is being checked in ascending sequence a comparison should be made to branch out if the KEY compares less than '9999', or equal to '9999', once it reaches that segment. If the table is being checked in descending sequence, a comparison should be made to branch out if the KEY compares equal to or higher than '0000' once it reaches that segment. The degree of detail used in any sectoring technique is dependent on the programmer's skill as well as the size of the file table that is being scanned.

In order to understand the basic idea of sectored look-ups, apply the following cases of simple sectoring to Table 14-1. In each case, the argument is referred to as KEY and the table segment sectors are referred to as PTA, PTB, PTC, PTD, and PTE, respectively. The reference to these diagrams (Type 1, Type 2, etc.) is merely to relate to these techniques during subsequent discussions.

Type 1

In this type of sectoring technique (Fig. 14-5), the sector segments are sequentially checked in their logical ascending order. PTA+0 is not checked since it is already known that the value of its KEY contents

TABLE 14-1. Logical Arrangement of a Sectored Table

	+4	+8	+12	+16	+20	+24	+28	+32	+36
PTA →	0000	0008	0010	0012	0014	0018	0023	0024	0025	0027
+40	0029	0030	0033	004i	0042	0043	0045	0046	0047	0049
+80	0051	0060	0061	0062	0065	0066	0067	0068	0069	0070
+120	0072	0074	0076	0078	0079	0080	0082	0083	0085	0086
+160	0087	0088	0092	0094	0095	0096	0097	0100	0101	0103
PTB →	0105	0106	0107	0109	0110	0112	0114	0116	0117	0118
+40	0119	0120	0122	0123	0124	0127	0128	0129	0130	0132
+80	0133	0134	0135	0136	0137	0138	0139	0140	0144	0146
+120	0147	0149	0150	0151	0152	0153	0154	0155	0156	0157
+160	0158	0159	0160	0161	0162	0163	0164	0165	0166	0168
PTC →	0169	0170	0171	0172	0173	0174	0175	0176	0177	0178
+40	0180	0181	0182	0183	0184	0185	0186	0187	0189	0191
+80	0192	0193	0194	0195	0196	0197	0198	0200	0202	0203
+120	0204	0205	0206	0207	0208	0210	0211	0212	0213	0214
+160	0215	0216	0217	0218	0219	0220	0221	0222	0224	0225
PTD →	0226	0228	0230	0235	0237	0238	0239	0240	0241	0242
+40	0245	0246	0247	0248	0250	0252	0254	0256	0257	0259
+80	0260	0261	0263	0264	0265	0266	0267	0268	0269	0270
+120	0271	0272	0273	0274	0275	0276	0279	0280	0282	0284
+160	0295	0310	0311	0312	0315	0317	0321	0322	0330	0331
PTE →	0332	0335	0336	0337	0338	0339	0340	0341	0342	0343
+40	0344	0350	0351	0352	0353	0354	0355	0356	0357	0358
+80	0360	0362	0364	0365	0366	0380	0384	0385	0387	0390
+120	0391	0392	0393	0394	0395	0402	0403	0405	0407	0410
+160	0411	0412	0413	0414	0424	0425	0426	0429	0431	9999

+164 +168 +172 +176 +180 +184 +188 +192 +196

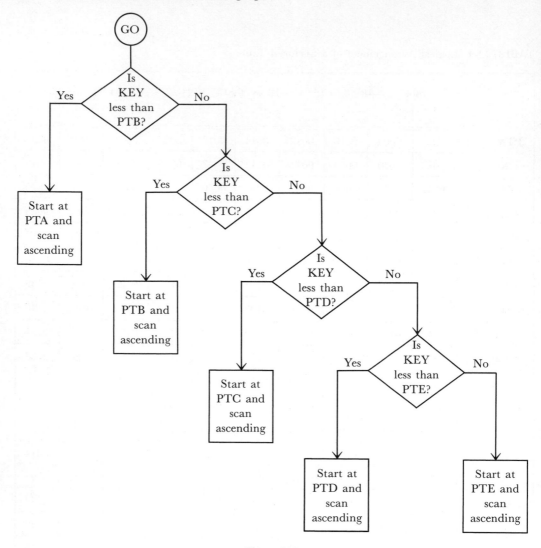

Figure 14-5

is '0000'. Under the worst possible conditions this particular sectoring technique, as applied to this table, would require a maximum of 54 comparisons—one compare each for PTB, PTC, PTD, and PTE, and one compare for each segment within the PTE sector.

Type 2

This type of sectored look-up (Fig. 14-6), starting at the approximate middle of the table, would require a maximum of 53 comparisons during the search for the data within Table 14-1. Depending on the num-

ber of defined sectors within a table, as well as the size of the table itself, this type of look-up could reduce search time by a considerable amount.

Type 3. This particular logic pattern (Fig. 14-7) is an expansion on the Type 2 sectoring lookup.

Pick any number at random and follow this logic through to find that number on the table. Using the logic pattern shown for this particular sectored look-up, a maximum of 29 comparisons would be made to find any given table key, although this number

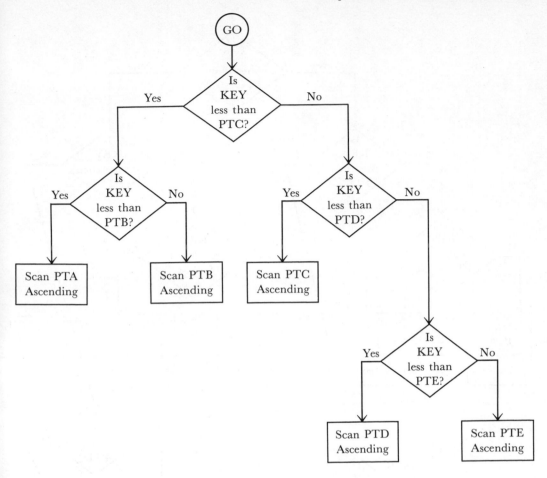

Figure 14-6

would occur only under the optimum adverse conditions. Note that the logic flow of these graphs of sectoring techniques does not provide for an equal condition during one of the indicated comparisons. Even though an equal condition does not appear thereon, the programmer would have to check after each comparison for such a condition and arrange his program logic to accept that condition as a "hit."

The three preceding types of sectoring techniques are noncomplex in nature and are intended only to start the programmer thinking about the many variations on this theme. Literally dozens of sectoring schemes might be developed to expedite search time, the design of which would be *relatively dependent* on the size and format of the table to be

searched and *quite dependent* on the ingenuity and ability of the programmer.

Once the logic pattern for any given sectoring technique has been developed, the coding of the instruction statements merely follows the logic path for that technique. Referring to Table 14-1, the following program coding contains the statements necessary to define those table segments and sectors. The subroutines contained in this example represent the typical statements for a Type 1 sectoring technique. Assume that the program in which these routines are coded has already accessed a data record and placed a four-byte set of numeric characters into the field labeled KEY. (See Fig. 14-8*a* and *b*.)

Statement 0201 compares the characters in KEY to the table segment addressed by

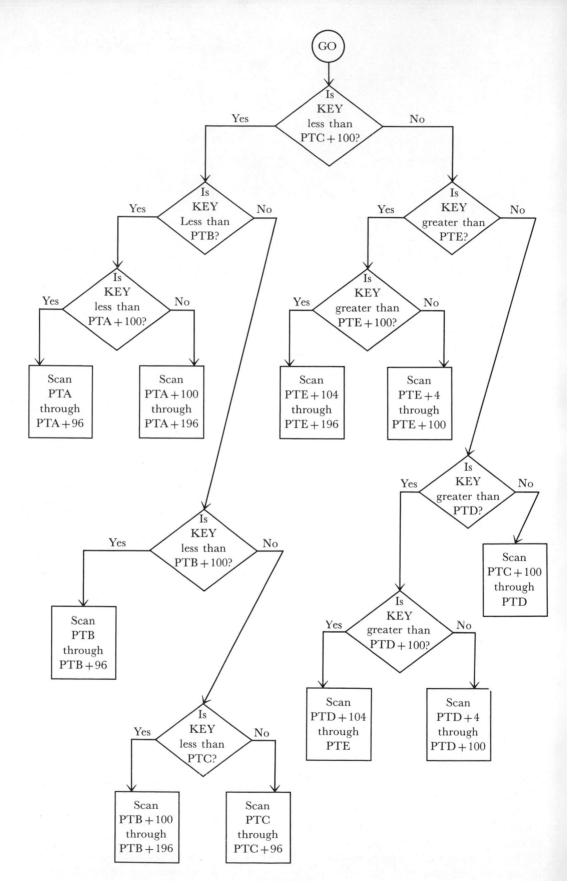

Figure 14-7

IBM System/360 Assembler Coding Form

PROGRAM TYPE #1 SECTORING TECHNIQUE

PROGRAMMER

PUNCHING INSTRUCTIONS   GRAPHIC

PUNCH

DATE

PAGE 1 OF 2

CARD ELECTRO NUMBER

X28-6509-2 U/M050
Printed In U.S.A.

Name	Operation	Operand	Comments	Identification-Sequence
*				
TABLE	DS	0CL2000		0094
PTA	DC	50CL4' '		0095
PTB	DC	50CL4' '		0096
PTC	DC	50CL4' '		0097
PTD	DC	50CL4' '		0098
PTE	DC	50CL4' '		0099
*				0100
KEY	DC	CL4' '		0101
*				
*				
GOTDATA	CLC	KEY(4),PTB		0201
	BC	2,SKIP1		0202
	LA	10,PTA		0203
	BC	15,SCANITA		0204
*				
SKIP1	CLC	KEY(4),PTC		0205
	BC	2,SKIP2		0206
	LA	10,PTB		0207
	BC	15,SCANITA		0208
*				
*				

Figure 14-8a

IBM

IBM System/360 Assembler Coding Form

PROGRAM	Type #1 Sectoring Technique		PUNCHING INSTRUCTIONS	GRAPHIC		PAGE 2 OF 2	X28-6509-2 U/M050 Printed in U.S.A.
PROGRAMMER		DATE		PUNCH		CARD ELECTRO NUMBER	

STATEMENT

Name 1	8	Operation 10	14	16	20	Operand 25	30	35	40	45	50	Comments 55	60	65	71	73	Identification-Sequence 80
SKIP2		CLC		KEY(4),PTD													0209
		BC		2,SKIP3													0210
		LA		10,PTC													0211
		BC		15,SCANITA													0212
*																	
*																	
SKIP3		CLC		KEY(4),PTE													0213
		BC		2,SKIP4													0214
		LA		10,PTD													0215
		BC		15,SCANITA													0216
*																	
*																	
SKIP4		LA		10,PTE													0217
		BC		15,SCANITA													0218
*																	
*																	
SCANITA		LA		11,50													0219
SCANIT		CLC		KEY(4),0(10)													0220
		BC		8,HITKEY													0221
		BC		4,NOGO													0222
		AH		10,=H'4'													0223
		BC		15,SCANIT													0224
*																	

Figure 14-8b

the label PTB. In this case, using the contents of the sectored table (Table 14-1), PTB would be referring to the four bytes of storage containing '0105'.

Statement 0202 specifies, "if KEY compared high to PTB, branch to Statement 0205." This result would indicate that the corresponding value to KEY was not contained in the table segments from PTA to PTB. However, if KEY had compared low to PTB, this would indicate that a corresponding value to KEY would fall within the table segments between PTA and PTB. In the latter condition, the branch would not be taken and the program processing would fall through to Statement 0203.

Statement 0203 will load the address of the first byte of PTA into general register 10. This address is to be used by a common subroutine labeled SCANITA.

Statement 0204 is a forced branch to SCANITA, the subroutine that will check the table segments of the sector pointed to by the address in general register 10.

Statement 0205, SKIP1, is entered if the branch in Statement 0202 was taken. This statement compares KEY to the first four-byte table segment address by PTC—the segment containing '0169'.

Statement 0206 states, "if KEY compared high to PTC, branch to Statement 0209." If the branch is taken it would indicate that the range of value that would correspond to KEY was not within the table segments from PTB to PTC, but was at a higher table segment location. If the branch is not taken, the program logic will fall through to Statement 0207, indicating that the comparable value range of KEY is to be found somewhere between PTB and PTC. This can be proved by noting that in order to get to Statement 0205, KEY had to compare high or equal to PTB, and in order to get to Statement 0207, KEY had to compare low to PTC.

Statement 0207 loads the address of the first byte of PTB into general register 10. This address will be used by SCANITA to check the table segments from PTB to PTC for a match to KEY.

Statement 0208 is a forced branch to SCANITA, the subroutine that will check the table segments of the sector pointed to by the address within general register 10.

Statement 0209, SKIP2, is entered if the branch in Statement 0206 was taken. This statement compares KEY to '0226', the first four bytes addressed by PTD.

Statement 0210 will cause a branch to be taken to Statement 0213 if the value of KEY compared high to PTD in Statement 0209. By taking the branch, the program would indicate that KEY was of a value equal to, or greater than, PTD. If the branch was not taken, this would indicate that the table value range comparable to KEY was somewhere between PTC and PTD. Statement 0205 and the branch from Statement 0206 to Statement 0209 has already indicated that KEY was higher than PTC; because the compare in Statement 0209 did not result in a branch in Statement 0210, KEY must have a value that fits the table range between PTC and PTD.

Statement 0211 will load the address of the first byte of the table segment pointed to by PTC. General register 10 will be used as the address pointer register in the SCANITA subroutine.

Statement 0212 is a forced branch to SCANITA. If entered from this point, SCANIT will check the table segments from PTC to PTD in an attempt to find a match for KEY.

Statement 0213, SKIP 3, would be entered only if the branch in Statement 0210 was taken. This would indicate that KEY was of a higher value than the table segment addressed by PTD. This statement will now compare KEY to the table segment addressed by PTE.

Statement 0214 will cause a branch to Statement 0217 if KEY compared high to PTE in Statement 0213. If KEY compared low to PTE, indicating that the table values comparable to KEY are between PTD and PTE, the processing logic will fall through this statement to Statement 0215.

Statement 0215 will load the address of PTD into general register 10, pointing to the first byte of the table segment referenced by

PTD. Register 10 will be used as the pointer register in SCANIT.

Statement 0216 is a forced branch to SCANITA. If SCANIT is entered from this point, it will check the table segments from PTD to PTE for a matching value to KEY.

Statement 0217 loads the address of PTE into general register 10. This statement is entered only if the branch in Statement 0214 was taken, indicating that KEY contained a logical value equal to, or greater than, PTE. Because PTE is the last sector of the segments in the table, the logic assumes that the corresponding value range for KEY is somewhere between PTE and the end of the table. General register 10, now containing the address of the first byte of the table segment referenced by PTE, will be used by the SCANIT subroutine.

Statement 0218 is a forced branch to Statement 0219, SCANITA. When SCANIT is entered from this point, it will check the table segments from PTE to the end of the table.

Statement 0220 is the second statement in the SCANITA subroutine. The preceding statement loaded the Branch On Count register for this subroutine with the maximum number of items within a single table sector. This statement will now compare KEY to the table segment pointed to by the address in general register 10, for a length of four bytes. When this instruction statement is first entered at the beginning of a loop cycle, general register 10 will point to sector:

1. PTA, if SCANITA was branched to from Statement 0204.
2. PTB, if SCANITA was branched to from Statement 0208.
3. PTC, if SCANITA was branched to from Statement 0212.
4. PTD, if SCANITA was branched to from Statement 0216.
5. PTE, if SCANITA was branched to from Statement 0218.

Each time this statement is entered from Statement 0223, the address in general register 10 will be incremented in order to step through the table segments of the table sector

being scanned. This subroutine, SCANITA, is therefore an effective "common" set of instruction statements that will be shared by five different logic points of the main-line logic, the five forced branches represented by Statements 0204, 0208, 0212, 0216, and 0218.

Statement 0221 is a test for an equal condition as a result of the comparison (in Statement 0219) of KEY to the table segment pointed to by general register 10. If the equal status is indicated by the Condition Code bits, this statement will cause a branch to an assumed routine, HITKEY. HITKEY will proceed with whatever logic the programmer intended to accomplish once a "hit" was made against the table. If the Condition Code indicates that the comparison was not equal, the processing action will fall through to Statement 0222.

Statement 0222 tests the current setting of the Condition Code bits for an indication that KEY was of a lower logical value than the table segment that it was compared to in Statement 0220. If this condition exists, indicating that an exact match for KEY does not exist within the table, this instruction statement will cause a branch to NOGO. NOGO is assumed to be a routine that will tell the program logic that the value of KEY was not found and that it is to proceed with whatever corresponding action the programmer intended to take under such circumstances. If KEY did not compare low to the current table segment, the branch is not taken here and the processing logic falls through to Statement 0223.

Statement 0223 increments the address contained in general register 10 by a halfword value of +4. This has now pointed general register 10 to the next table segment beyond the one just tested by Statement 0220.

Statement 0224 is a forced branch back to Statement 0220, SCANIT, for the purpose of comparing KEY to the new table segment pointed to by register 10.

In order to visually follow the logic pattern of these instruction statements as the table is scanned for a particular value, trace the action represented by the search for these values. The keys that are to be sought are assumed to be on Table 14-1.

(a) The key to be found is . . . 0185.
(b) The sequence of the instruction statements performed would be . . .
0201, 0202, 0205, 0206, 0209, 0210, 0211, 0212, 0219, 0220, 0221, 0222, 0223, 0224, 0220, 0221, 0222, 0223, 0224, 0220, 0221, 0222, 0223, 0224, 0220, 0221, 0222, 0223, 0224, 0220, 0221, 0222, 0223, 0224, 0220, 0221, 0222, 0223, 0224, 0220, 0221, 0222, 0223, 0224, 0220, 0221, 0222, 0223, 0224, 0220, 0221, 0222, 0223, 0224, 0220, 0221, 0222, 0223, 0224, 0220, 0221, 0222, 0223, 0224, 0220, 0221, 0222, 0223, 0224, 0220, 0221, HITKEY.

(a) The key to be found is . . . 0107.
(b) The sequence of the statements executed would be . . .
0201, 0202, 0205, 0206, 0207, 0208, 0219, 0220, 0221, 0222, 0223, 0224, 0220, 0221, 0222, 0223, 0224, 0220, 0221, HITKEY.

(a) The key to be found is . . . 0236.
(b) The sequence of the statements executed are . . .
0201, 0202, 0205, 0206, 0209, 0210, 0213, 0214, 0215, 0216, 0219, 0220, 0221, 0222, 0223, 0224, 0220, 0221, 0222, 0223, 0224, 0220, 0221, 0222, 0223, 0224, 0220, 0221, 0222, 0223, 0224, 0220, 0221, 0222, NOGO.

(a) The key to be found is . . . 0332.
(b) The sequence of the statements would be . . .
0201, 0202, 0205, 0206, 0209, 0210, 0213, 0214, 0217, 0218, 0219, 0220, 0221, HITKEY.

Utilizing these same field descriptions and the values shown in Table 14-1, the instruction statements that could be used to code the Type 2 sectoring technique might appear as shown in Fig. 14-9a and b.
The performance of these statements

should be similar enough to the previous set of instruction statements so as to be easily understood. To prove the logic of these instruction statements, follow these value keys as the routine searches the table for their corresponding match.

(a) The value of the key to be found is . . . 0014.
(b) The sequence of the statements executed in this search would be . . .
0301, 0302, 0303, 0304, 0305, 0306, 0319, 0320, 0321, 0322, 0323, 0319, 0320, 0321, 0322, 0323, 0319, 0320, 0321, 0322, 0323, 0319, 0320, 0321, 0322, 0323, 0319, 0320, HITKEY.

(a) The key to be found is . . . 0333.
(b) The sequence of the statements executed would be . . .
0301, 0302, 0309, 0310, 0313, 0314, 0317, 0318, 0319, 0320, 0321, 0322, 0323, 0319, 0320, 0321, NOGO.

(a) The key to be found is . . . 0226.
(b) The search sequence would be . . .
0301, 0302, 0309, 0310, 0313, 0314, 0315, 0316, 0319, 0320, HITKEY.

(a) The value of KEY is . . . 0112.
(b) The sequence of the instructions executed during the lookup are . . .
0301, 0302, 0303, 0304, 0307, 0308, 0319, 0320, 0321, 0322, 0323, 0319, 0320, 0321, 0322, 0323, 0319, 0320, 0321, 0322, 0323, 0319, 0320, 0321, 0322, 0323, 0319, 0320, 0321, 0322, 0323, 0319, 0320, HITKEY.

The instruction statement coding for the sectoring technique referred to within this section as a Type 3 application becomes somewhat more involved. The more complex the task becomes, the more variation that can be applied to the coding of that task. Therefore, the following instruction statements are only one way of performing the logic pattern for the Type 3 sectoring technique. Note that the field definitions and values are the same as used in the examples for the Type 1 and Type 2 sectoring applications, but that address adjusting has been implemented in some of the instruction statements. (See Fig. 14-10a, b, and c.)

IBM

Type #2 Sectoring Technique

Name	Operation	Operand	Comments	Identification-Sequence
*				
GOTDATA	CLC	KEY(4),PTC		0301
	BC	10,PASS1		0302
	CLC	KEY(4),PTB		0303
	BC	10,SKIP1		0304
	LA	10,PTA		0305
	BC	15,SCANIT		0306
*				
*				
SKIP1	LA	10,PTB		0307
	BC	15,SCANIT		0308
*				
*				
PASS1	CLC	KEY(4),PTD		0309
	BC	10,PASS2		0310
	LA	10,PTC		0311
	BC	15,SCANIT		0312
*				
*				
PASS2	CLC	KEY(4),PTE		0313
	BC	10,PASS3		0314
	LA	10,PTD		0315
	BC	15,SCANIT		0316
*				

Figure 14-9a

IBM

IBM System/360 Assembler Coding Form

PROGRAM			PUNCHING INSTRUCTIONS	GRAPHIC			PAGE 2 OF 2	X28-6509-2 U/M050 Printed in U.S.A.
PROGRAMMER		DATE		PUNCH			CARD ELECTRO NUMBER	

Type #2 Sectoring Technique

Name	Operation	Operand	Comments	Identification-Sequence
1 8	10 14	16 20 25 30 35 40 45 50 55 60 65 71		73 80
*				
PASS3	LA	10,PTE		0317
	BC	15,SCANIT		0318
*				
*				
SCANIT	CLC	KEY(4),0(10)		0319
	BC	8,HITKEY		0320
	BC	4,NOGO		0321
	AH	10,=H'4'		0322
	BC	15,SCANIT		0323
*				
*				
*				

Figure 14-9b

397

IBM System/360 Assembler Coding Form

X28-6509-2 U/M050
Printed in U.S.A.

PROGRAM TYPE #3 SECTORING TECHNIQUE **PAGE** 1 **OF** 3

Name	Operation	Operand	Identification-Sequence
GOTDATA	CLC	KEY(4),PTC+100	0401
	BC	10,SECTB	0402
	CLC	KEY(4),PTB	0403
	BC	10,SECTA	0404
	CLC	KEY(4),PTA+100	0405
	BC	10,SECTC	0406
	LA	10,PTA	0407
	BC	15,SCANIT	0408
*			
*			
SECTC	LA	10,PTA+100	0409
	BC	15,SCANIT	0410
*			
*			
SECTA	CLC	KEY(4),PTB+100	0411
	BC	10,SECTD	0412
	LA	10,PTB	0413
	BC	15,SCANIT	0414
*			
*			
SECTD	CLC	KEY(4),PTC	0415
	BC	10,SECTE	0416
	LA	10,PTB+100	0417
	BC	15,SCANIT	0418

Figure 14-10a

398

PROGRAM Type #3 Sectoring Technique

```
Name    Operation  Operand              Identification-Sequence
*
*
SECTE   LA    10,PTC                    0419
        BC    15,SCANIT                 0420
*
*
SECTB   CLC   KEY(4),PTE                0421
        BC    4,SECTF                   0422
        CLC   KEY(4),PTE+100            0423
        BC    4,SECTG                   0424
        LA    10,PTE+100                0425
        BC    15,SCANIT                 0426
*
*
SECTG   LA    10,PTE                    0427
        BC    15,SCANIT                 0428
*
*
SECTF   CLC   KEY(4),PTD                0429
        BC    4,SECTH                   0430
        CLC   KEY(4),PTD+100            0431
        BC    4,SECTI                   0432
        LA    10,PTD+100                0433
        BC    15,SCANIT                 0434
```

Figure 14-10b

IBM

| PROGRAM | TYPE #3 SECTORING TECHNIQUE | | | PUNCHING INSTRUCTIONS | GRAPHIC | | |
| PROGRAMMER | | DATE | | | PUNCH | | |

Name	Operation	Operand	Comments	Identification-Sequence
*				
*				
SECTI	LA	10,PTD		0435
	BC	15,SCANIT		0436
*				
*				
SECTH	LA	10,PTC+100		0437
	BC	15,SCANIT		0438
*				
*				
SCANIT	CLC	KEY(4),0(10)		0439
	BC	8,HITKEY		0440
	BC	4,NOGO		0441
	AH	10,=H'4'		0442
	BC	15,SCANIT		0443
*				
*				

X28-6509-2 U/M050
Printed in U.S.A.

400

Figure 14-10c

At this point in the text, the performance and action of these instruction statements should require little or no explanation. Each step and subroutine generated by these statements is directly related to the logic pattern of the logic flow-chart for the Type 3 sectoring technique. A series of values and the logic flow required to find those values during a table look-up is listed below. Trace the sequence of operation through the instruction statements to verify the search for this data.

(a) The value of KEY is . . . 0205.
(b) The search sequence of instructions would be . . .
0401, 0402, 0421, 0422, 0429, 0430, 0437, 0438, 0439, 0440, 0441, 0442, 0443, 0439, 0440, 0441, 0442, 0443, 0439, 0440, 0441, 0442, 0443, 0439, 0440, 0441, 0442, 0443, 0439, 0440, 0441, 0442, 0443, 0439, 0440, 0441, 0442, 0443, 0439, 0440, HITKEY.

(a) The value of the key to be found is . . . 0066.
(b) The sequence of the instructions executed would be . . .
0401, 0402, 0403, 0404, 0405, 0406, 0409, 0410, 0439, 0440, HITKEY.

(a) The value of KEY is . . . 0108.
(b) The Search sequence would be . . .
0401, 0402, 0403, 0404, 0411, 0412, 0413, 0414, 0439, 0440, 0441, 0442, 0443, 0439, 0440, 0441, 0442, 0443, 0439, 0440, 0441, 0442, 0443, 0439, 0440, 0441, NOGO.

(a) The value of KEY is . . . 0385.
(b) The sequence of instructions for the search would be . . .
0401, 0402, 0421, 0422, 0423, 0424, 0425, 0426, 0439, 0440, 0441, 0442, 0443, 0439, 0440, 0441, 0442, 0443, 0439, 0440, HITKEY.

Even though this example followed the logic flow-chart for the Type 3 sectoring technique almost to the instruction symbol, the same basic task could have been coded in considerably fewer statements. The set of instruction statements shown in Fig. 14-11a and b are not conforming entirely to the flow-chart of logic for the Type 3 sectoring technique but they are, however, providing a search pattern on a very similar level.

In order to compare this reduced set of coding statements to the previous example, wherein a total of 43 instruction statements were used, look-up sequences are provided here with the same values as those for the previous look-ups.

(a) The value of KEY is . . . 0205.
(b) The search sequence of instruction statements would be . . .
0501, 0502, 0503, 0513, 0514, 0515, 0507, 0508, 0509, 0510, 0507, 0508, 0509, 0510, 0507, 0508, 0509, 0510, 0507, 0508, 0509, 0510, 0507, 0508, 0509, 0510, 0507, 0508, 0509, 0510, 0507, 0508, 0509, 0510, 0507, 0508, 0509, 0510, 0507, 0508, 0509, 0518, 0519, 0520, 0521, 0522, 0518, 0519, HITKEY.

(a) The value of KEY is . . . 0066.
(b) The sequence of statements would be . . .
0501, 0502, 0503, 0504, 0505, 0506, 0507, 0508, 0509, 0510, 0507, 0508, 0509, 0510, 0507, 0508, 0509, 0510, 0507, 0508, 0509, 0510, 0507, 0508, 0509, 0510, 0507, 0508, 0509, 0510, 0507, 0508, 0509, 0510, 0507, 0508, 0509, 0510, 0507, 0508, 0509, 0518, 0519, HITKEY.

(a) The value of the key is . . . 0108.
(b) The search sequence of the executed statements would be . . .
0501, 0502, 0503, 0504, 0505, 0506, 0507, 0508, 0509, 0510, 0507, 0508, 0509, 0510, 0507, 0508, 0509, 0510, 0507, 0508, 0509, 0510, 0507, 0508, 0509, 0518, 0519, 0520, 0521, 0522, 0518, 0519, 0520, 0521, 0522, 0518, 0519, 0520, 0521, 0522, 0518, 0519, 0520, NOGO.

(a) The value of KEY is . . . 0385.
(b) The sequence of instruction statements for the search would be . . .
0501, 0502, 0503, 0513, 0514, 0515, 0516, 0517, 0507, 0508, 0509, 0510, 0507, 0508, 0509, 0510, 0507, 0508, 0509, 0510, 0507, 0508, 0509, 0510,

IBM

IBM System/360 Assembler Coding Form

X28-6509-2 U/M050
Printed in U.S.A.

Name	Operation	Operand	Identification-Sequence
*			
GOTDATA	LA	10,PTC+100	0501
	CLC	KEY(4),0(10)	0502
	BC	10,SECTA	0503
	SH	10,=H'200'	0504
	CLC	KEY(4),0(10)	0505
	BC	10,SECTB	0506
DOWN20	SH	10,=H'20'	0507
	CLC	KEY(4),0(10)	0508
	BC	10,SCANIT	0509
	BC	4,DOWN20	0510
*			
*			
SECTB	AH	10,=H'200'	0511
	BC	15,DOWN20	0512
*			
*			
SECTA	AH	10,=H'200'	0513
	CLC	KEY(4),0(10)	0514
	BC	12,DOWN20	0515
	LA	10,PTE+196	0516
	BC	15,DOWN20	0517
*			
*			

Figure 14-11a

IBM IBM System/360 Assembler Coding Form

X28-6509-2 U/M050
Printed in U.S.A.

PROGRAM		PUNCHING INSTRUCTIONS	GRAPHIC	PAGE 2 OF 2
PROGRAMMER	DATE		PUNCH	CARD ELECTRO NUMBER

STATEMENT

Name (1–8)	Operation (10–14)	Operand (16–) / Comments (–71)	Identification-Sequence (73–80)
*			
SCANIT	CLC	KEY(4),0(10)	0518
	BC	8,HITKEY	0519
	BC	4,NOGO	0520
	AH	10,=H'4'	0521
	BC	15,SCANIT	0522
*			
*			

Figure 14-11*b*

0507, 0508, 0518, 0519, 0520, 0521, 0522, 0518, 0519, 0520, 0521, 0522, 0518, 0519, HITKEY.

Although this latter set of instruction statements was comprised of fewer statements, the actual search for the table value took more statement executions to accomplish; consequently, the routine would have used more computer time. In this instance, the first set of instructions for a Type 3 sectoring technique would have been considerably more efficient in machine utilization, although it required more coding on the part of the programmer. This is quite often the case—the programmer may spend considerable time devising compact little subroutines only to find in the end that a straight-line approach to the problem would have been more efficient.

It must be explained that the references to the Types 1, 2, and 3 sectoring techniques are intended only to group these techniques by a degree of complexity for the purpose of this section of the text. These references in no way imply a professionally accepted grouping of techniques or an accepted measurement standard of their complexity. Almost needless to say, there are probably more variations of sectoring look-ups than one person could conceive of and, consequently, any attempt to validly group such techniques would be presumptuous.

D. DIRECT ADDRESSING OF TABLE SEGMENTS

The concept of direct addressing techniques for table look-ups has a number of variations ranging from simple "add" functions to extremely complex numerical conversion schemes. For the purpose of this text, only the basic method of directly addressing a table segment will be reviewed. This method is generally applicable in a table that contains a consecutive, contiguous arrangement of key values in ascending sequence. In the discussion that follows, it will be assumed that the table to be used is arranged in such a format. The creation of the table

itself must be considered so that a table segment must be created for each consecutive value in the numbering sequence to be used, whether or not that value does exist for use within the table. For example, if the values 001, 002, 003, 005, 006, 008, and 009 were valid table arguments, then the table would have to contain segments available for 001, 002, 003, 004, 005, 006, 007, 008, and 009. The values of 004 and 007 would have to be provided in the table in order to "balance" it for the direct addressing technique that was to be applied. Table 14-2 represents a table of data that is to be accessed via direct addressing. Notice that all table segments do not contain valid data. The table addresses shown are in decimal format, rather than the normal hexadecimal representation in order that the logic might be more easily followed.

When developing the routine for directly addressing the table segments, the length of the segments themselves must be considered. Multiplication of the key value of the table segment by the number of bytes in each segment is a common way of obtaining a direct address increment.

The illustrated table look-up routine (Fig. 14-12a and b) uses a "shift" instruction to calculate the table segment address from the segment key. The format of PRETAB and TABLE have been established in accordance with the table just illustrated. For the purpose of this example, it is assumed that at problem program execution time PRETAB will be at core position address 32,404 and TABLE will be at 32,420. Normally, the key of the table segment to be located would be brought in through some type of I/O device in a random pattern. For this example, they have been established as constants in order to illustrate their conversion to a direct address.

The explanation of the instruction statements will be given in the order in which they will be executed.

Statement 0601, GOSEEK, will pack the value of KEYA (+12) into DUBPAK. DUBPAK will then appear to be:

TABLE 14-2 A Sequentially Organized Table for Direct Addressing Access

Table Segment Number	Relative Address	Label	Table Segment 16 Bytes	Assumed Binary Address
		PRETAB	Dummy Record	32,404
1	PRETAB+16	TABLE	D049586746384556	32,420
2	+32		D837465847465837	32,436
3	+48		D002838883746554	32,452
4	+64		D922264537394058	32,468
5	+80		b bbbbbbbbbbbbbbb	32,484
6	+96		D847263949555836	32,500
7	+112		D933650003645572	32,516
8	+128		D003232505926266	32,532
9	+144		D225242829254836	32,548
10	+160		D110584711365934	32,564
11	+176		D004619375137473	32,580
12	+192		D199257364563930	32,596
13	+208		D887423641593211	32,612
14	+224		D613800342746513	32,628
15	+240		D222746143804950	32,644
16	+256		D741109384125135	32,660
17	+272		b bbbbbbbbbbbbbbb	32,676
18	+288		D001145848547522	32,692
19	+304		D011466648347436	32,708
20	+320		b bbbbbbbbbbbbbbb	32,724
21	+336		D391004216756481	32,740
22	+352		D190011458374629	32,756
23	+368		D700121232998414	32,772
24	+384		D774038374157193	32,788
25	+400		D283938474911584	32,804
26	+416		D459941374620293	32,820
27	+432		D120290485650481	32,836
28	+448		b bbbbbbbbbbbbbbb	32,852
29	+464		D696870285630575	32,868
30	+480		D113931146577764	32,884
31	+496		D773000395877392	32,900
32	+512		D033472274635443	32,916
33	+528		D373747485930491	32,932
34	+544		D400113843932114	32,948
35	+560		b bbbbbbbbbbbbbbb	32,964
36	+576		b bbbbbbbbbbbbbbb	32,980
37	+592		D110021137894911	32,996
38	+608		D885693847513394	33,012
39	+624		D775648886978411	33,028
40	+640		D103478576849932	33,044
41	+656		D488576829427836	33,060
42	+672		D774638375856342	33,076
43	+688		D933140405768113	33,092
44	+704		b bbbbbbbbbbbbbbb	33,108
45	+720		D559045551438813	33,124
46	+736		D399993374157738	33,140
47	+752		b bbbbbbbbbbbbbbb	33,156
48	+768		D669484857611332	33,172
49	+784		D390046574847339	33,188
50	+800		D110200678511225	33,204

Name	Operation	Operand	Comments	Identification-Sequence
*				
GOSEEK	PACK	DUBPAK,KEYA		0601
	CVB	6,DUBPAK		0602
	SLA	6,4		0603
	BAL	3,LOOKUP		0604
	PACK	DUBPAK,KEYB		0605
	CVB	6,DUBPAK		0606
	SLA	6,4		0607
	BAL	3,LOOKUP		0608
	PACK	DUBPAK,KEYC		0609
	CVB	6,DUBPAK		0610
	SLA	6,4		0611
	BAL	3,LOOKUP		0612
	BC	15,END		0613
*				
*				
LOOKUP	LA	8,PRETAB		0614
	AR	8,6		0615
	CLI	0(8),C'D'		0616
	BC	7,NODATA		0617
	MVC	OUTDATA(16),0(8)		0618
	BAL	5,PUTDATA		0619
NODATA	BCR	15,3		0620
*				

Figure 14-12a

406

IBM System/360 Assembler Coding Form

Name	Operation	Operand
*		
PRETAB	DC	CL16' '
TABLE	DC	50CL16' '
KEYA	DC	CL2'12'
KEYB	DC	CL2'24'
KEYC	DC	CL2'44'
DUBPAK	DC	D'0'
OUTDATA	DC	CL16' '

Figure 14-12b

DUBPAK

Statement 0602 converts the packed decimal value of the contents of DUBPAK into fixed-point format in general register 6. KEYA was packed into a doubleword area in Statement 0601 because the second oper-

and in a CVB instruction statement must be a packed decimal value in a doubleword storage location. General register 6 would now have a configuration of:

Register 6 | 0 | 000 | 0000 | 0000 | 0000 | 0000 | 0000 | 0000 | 1100 | $= +12$

Statement 0603 performs a Shift Left Algebraic instruction statement. The relative address of KEYA (which is $+12$) is the 12th 16-byte table segment. By shifting left algebraic for four bit positions, the value in gen-

eral register 6 is being multiplied by 16, resulting in the relative table address for KEYA; 12 times 16 equals 192. The SLA instruction statement would affect general register 6 in the following manner:

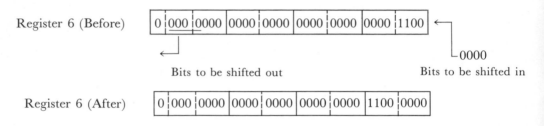

Register 6 (Before)

Bits to be shifted out   Bits to be shifted in

Register 6 (After) | 0 | 000 | 0000 | 0000 | 0000 | 0000 | 0000 | 1100 | 0000 |

Statement 0604 is a Branch & Link to LOOKUP. At the time the branch is accomplished, general register 3 will contain the address of Statement 0605.

Statement 0614, LOOKUP, is loading the

address of PRETAB into general register 8. Because this example has assumed that the address of PRETAB at program execution time will be 32,404, general register 8 will now appear as:

Register 8 (Binary) | 0 | 000 | 0000 | 0000 | 0000 | 0111 | 1110 | 1001 | 0100 |

(Hex) | 0 | 0 | 0 | 0 | 7 | E | 9 | 4 |

Statement 0615 is adding general register 6 to general register 8, with the sum of this addition then residing in general register 8. Register 6 contains the relative address of table segment 12 and register 8 contains the

execution-time address of PRETAB, the resulting sum being the direct actual address of table segment 12. The configuration of general register 8 after the addition would be:

Register 8 | 0 | 000 | 0000 | 0000 | 0000 | 0111 | 1111 | 0101 | 0100 | $= +32,596$

Statement 0616 is comparing the first byte of table segment 12 to see if it contains valid data. A valid table segment must contain a

character 'D' in the first position for the purposes of this example.

Statement 0617 tests the Condition Code

that resulted from the "compare" in Statement 0616. If the compare resulted in an equal condition, the program logic falls through to Statement 0618. If the compare was unequal, the branch is taken to NO-DATA in order to avoid attempting to process the table segment. In this particular instance, the compare would have been equal and the branch would not have been taken.

Statement 0618 moves the table segment that is addressed by general register 8 into a field labeled OUTDATA.

Statement 0619 is a Branch & Link to an assumed sub-routine that will process the data contained in OUTDATA. When that sub-routine is completed the program logic processing should return to Statement 0620.

Statement 0620 is a forced branch to the address contained in register 3. At this point of the program, general register 3 contains the address of Statement 0605.

Statement 0605, the next statement to be executed, will pack the contents of KEYB (+24) into DUBPAK. DUBPAK will then appear as:

DUBPAK

0	0	0	0	0	0	0	0	0	0	0	0	0	2	4	C

Statement 0606 will take the value of DUBPAK and convert it to a fixed-point value in general register 6. Register 6 would then appear to contain:

Register 6 (Binary)

0	000	0000	0000	0000	0000	0000	0001	1000	$= +24$

(Hex)

	0	0	0	0	0	0	1	8

Statement 0607 will shift the integer-bits of general register 6 toward the left for a total algebraic shift of four bit positions. This will effectively multiply the value in register 6 by 16, or 24 times 16 equals 384.

Register 6 (Binary)

0	000	0000	0000	0000	0000	0001	1000	0000	$= +384$

(Hex)

	0	0	0	0	0	1	8	0

Statement 0608 is a Branch & Link to Statement 0614, LOOKUP, with the return address of Statement 0609 being placed into general register 3.

Statement 0614 will load the address of PRETAB into general register 8.

Statement 0615 will add the relative address of the current table segment (+384), which is contained in register 6, to the actual current address of PRETAB (+32,404) as contained in register 8—the resulting sum residing in register 8. General register 8 now contains the actual direct address of table segment 24.

Statements 0616 through 0619 perform the processing logic as explained previously.

Statement 0620 is a forced branch to the address contained in general register 3, which at this point in the program will be the address of Statement 0609.

Statement 0609 packs the contents of KEYC into DUBPAK. KEYC contained "44," representing the pointer key to table segment 44. DUBPAK would now appear to contain:

DUBPAK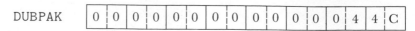

Statement 0610 is converting the packed decimal value of DUBPAK to a binary- fixed-point value in register 6.

Register 6 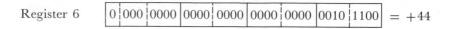 $= +44$

Statement 0611 shifts the binary contents of general register 6 toward the left algebraically for a length of four bit positions. This action represents 44 times 16 equals 704, creating the relative address of table segment 44.

Statement 0612 is a Branch & Link to Statement 0614, at the same time placing the address of Statement 0613 into general register 3.

Statement 0614 loads the actual address of PRETAB ($+32,404$) into general register 8.

Statement 0615 adds general register 6 to general register 8, with the sum residing in register 8. This has added together the actual address of PRETAB ($+32,404$) and the relative address of table segment 44 ($+704$) to create the actual direct address for that table segment ($+33,108$).

Statements 0616 through 0619 are the logic statements that process the data. The branch out of Statement 0617 into Statement 0620 will be taken in this instance because table segment 44 does not contain valid data.

Statement 0620 will branch to Statement 0613, the address contained in general register 3.

Statement 0613 is a forced branch to an assumed routine, representing the end of this module.

Not all table segment direct addressing computations will be able to be accomplished with shifting techniques. Assuming that general register 6 contains the binary value of a table segment, in this instance segment 5, Table 14-3 shows the values obtainable by shifting. The factor by which the table segment number is being multiplied implies the byte-length of each individual table segment.

TABLE 14-3

Table Segment Length (Bytes)	Instruction Statement	Resulting Relative Address in Register 6	The Shift Routine is Equal to:
2 bytes	SLA 6,1	10	5×2 equals 10
4	SLA 6,2	20	5×4 equals 20
8	SLA 6,3	40	5×8 equals 40
16	SLA 6,4	80	5×16 equals 80
32	SLA 6,5	160	5×32 equals 160
64	SLA 6,6	320	5×64 equals 320
128	SLA 6,7	640	5×128 equals 640
256	SLA 6,8	1280	5×256 equals 1280
512	SLA 6,9	2560	5×512 equals 2560
Etc. . . .			

If the table segment length is not one of those specified in this list, a common multi- ply routine, either fixed-point or packed decimal, may be used to determine the relative address of the table segment. Assuming that the table segment length is 17 bytes and the programmer wishes to compute the relative address of table segment 19, the packed decimal multiply routine could be coded as:

```
PACK      DUBPAK,KEY              0001
```

```
MP        DUBPAK,=PL2'17'         0002
CVB       6,DUBPAK                0003
```

Statement 0001 converts the data contents of KEY (the table segment number, now equal to 19) by packing it into DUBPAK. DUBPAK now appears as:

DUBPAK

0	0	0	0	0	0	0	0	0	0	0	0	0	1	9	C

Statement 0002 multiplies the contents of DUBPAK by a packed decimal literal of $+17$, representing the byte-length of each

table segment. DUBPAK now contains $+323$, the relative address of table segment 19.

DUBPAK

0	0	0	0	0	0	0	0	0	0	0	0	3	2	3	C

Statement 0003 performs a Convert To Binary (CVB) instruction statement, taking the packed decimal value of DUBPAK and

placing it into general register 6 in fixed-point format.

Register 6

0	000	0000	0000	0000	0000	0001	0100	0011	$+323$
	0	0	0	0	0	1	4	3	

The fixed-point multiplication routine to accomplish this same process could be coded as:

```
PACK      DUBPAK,KEY              0001
CVB       6,DUBPAK                0002
MH        6,=H'17'                0003
```

Statement 0001 packs KEY into DUBPAK; DUBPAK now would contain a value of $+19$.

Statement 0002 converts the value of DUBPAK ($+19$) into a fixed-point format value in general register 6.

Register 6

0	000	0000	0000	0000	0000	0000	0001	0011	$+19$
	0	0	0	0	0	0	1	3	

Statement 0003 multiplies general register 6 by a halfword literal value of $+17$, the latter value representing the length of the

table segments. General register 6 now would contain a fixed-point value of $+323$, the relative address of table segment 19.

Register 6

0	000	0000	0000	0000	0000	0001	0100	0011	$+323$
	0	0	0	0	0	1	4	3	

Both the fixed-point multiply routine and the packed decimal multiply routine have

efficiently determined the relative address of table segment 19. It should be carefully noted, however, that this is only the *relative* address of the table segment. This value must be added to an *actual* address available during program execution, to combine to create the *actual direct* address of the table segment.

The actual address of the beginning point of the table can be obtained in several ways. In Table 14-2, the programmer has established a "dummy" field of the same length as a table segment, placing that field imme-

diately prior to the table itself. By doing this, he could multiply the table key by the number of bytes in each segment and arrive at a relative address to be added to the address of PRETAB. If he had added the relative address of the key to the actual address of TABLE, the resulting direct address would have been 16 bytes higher in the table than the address desired; for example:

$$\frac{\text{Table Segment Key}}{(4)} \text{ times } \frac{\text{Segment Length}}{(16)} \text{ plus } \frac{\text{Address of Table}}{(32,420)} \text{ equals } 32,484$$

The total address of 32,484 points to the beginning of table segment 5, not table segment 4. If the programmer does not want

to set up a "dummy" area for preaddressing of the table, he may arrive at the proper direct address by the following type of calculation:

$$\frac{\text{Table Segment Key}}{(4)} \text{ less 1 times } \frac{\text{Segment Length}}{(16)} \text{ plus } \frac{\text{Address of Table}}{(32,420)} \text{ equals } 32,468$$

or by

$$\frac{\text{Table Segment Key}}{(4)} \text{ times } \frac{\text{Segment Length}}{(16)} \text{ less } \frac{\text{Segment Length}}{(16)} \text{ plus } \frac{\text{Address of Table}}{(32,420)}$$

equals 32,468

The values shown in these calculations should be replaced by the actual values of the table segment length and address in each unique table to be created. These examples contain the values relevant to the illustrated table of directly addressed data for the purpose of this presentation only.

If the table segment length was 21 bytes, the two calculations just referred to could have been coded as:

```
PACK    DUBPAK,KEY
SP      DUBPAK,=PL1'1'
MP      DUBPAK,=PL2'21'
CVB     6,DUBPAK
LA      7,TABLE
AR      7,6
```

or as:

```
PACK    DUBPAK,KEY
MP      DUBPAK,=PL2'21'
```

```
SP      DUBPAK,=PL2'21'
CVB     6,DUBPAK
LA      7,TABLE
AR      7,6
```

E. TABLES CONTAINING MIXED DATA

It is most likely that the average table to be established by a programmer will contain EBCDIC character-formatted data. However, a table may be comprised of data that is recognized in hexadecimal format, binary format, fixed-point arithmetic format, packed decimal format, or any combination of these. The mixed formatting of the table can be organized by the DC statements or by program execution.

For the purpose of defining the logic of this concept, the desired content of the table should first be described. A typical table might be constructed of the following data.

Table   250 segments
One Segment 4 fields
    Field 1   3 bytes of character data.
    Field 2   4 bytes of fixed-point values on fullword boundary alignment.
    Field 3   6 bytes of packed decimal data.
    Field 4   3 bytes of character data.

This table will be initialized in the following way:

1. The table key values, occupying the first three bytes of each table segment, will be loaded by the problem program. These three bytes should be initialized as blanks prior to the loading of the key values.

2. Field 2, representing a fullword containing a fixed-point value, should be initialized as a fixed-point value of +0. Fixed-point values may be added to the value of this field and stored there for subsequent use. In some instances it will not be known if a valid fixed-point value has already been entered into the field prior to attempting a fixed-point "add" of this field to another value. This is the reason for initializing the field to a +0 fixed-point value.

3. Field 3, to be used as a six-byte packed decimal field, should be initialized with a packed decimal value of +0 for the same reason that Field 2 was initialized. Packed decimal data may, or may not, be accumulated in the field and the program logic may attempt to use this field for arithmetic operations prior to the insertion into it of any tangible value.

4. Field 4 will contain character data in most table segments, but not in all. This data will be placed in the table during program execution. This field should be initialized as blanks.

A relatively easy way to meet the requirements of the formatting necessary for this table would be to use hexadecimal formatting when stating the DC (Define Constant). Keep in mind that the first byte of the second field in each segment must always be aligned on a fullword boundary alignment.

```
ALIGN    DC      F'0'
FILL1    DC      CL1'ᛚ'
TABLE    DC      250X'4040400000000000000000000000C404040'
                      Field 1    Field 2    Field 3    Field 4
```

The DC for ALIGN sets that address on a fullword boundary alignment; therefore, every fourth byte after this label will be on a fullword boundary. Because it is required that Field 2 be on fullword alignment and Field 1 is only three bytes long, the one-byte constant FILL1 has been used to move the beginning point of TABLE one byte further in core. TABLE will now start three bytes short of being on the next fullword boundary. Because the first three bytes of TABLE will use up this shortage, Field 2 will start on a fullword aligned location. Inasmuch as each table segment is a total of 16 bytes long (equivalent to four fullwords), all subsequent table segments will also have Field 2 on a fullword boundary alignment.

In looking at the DC statement for TABLE, you will note that all fields have now been initialized in accordance with the table requirements.

1. Field 1 (three bytes equals six hex digits) is initialized with blanks, represented by '404040'.

2. Field 2 (four bytes equals eight hex digits) contains a fixed-point +0 value, X'00000000'.

3. Field 3 (six bytes equals twelve hex digits) contains a valid packed decimal value of +0, X'00000000000C'—the low-order 'C' representing the plus sign for the field.

4. Field 4 (three bytes equals six hex digits) is also set as blanks, X'404040'.

As shown, all fields are initialized and the DC statement has specified a total table length of 250 of these segments, all formatted identically. The table is now ready to be loaded and utilized.

During the use of this table by the problem program, certain fields may be utilized as limited accumulators. For example, assume that the six-byte packed decimal field in each table segment is to be used as an accumulator until a certain condition occurs. When that event takes place, the packed decimal value in Field 3 of each table segment will be extracted and that field should be reinitialized to a +0 value. Assuming that the values have already been extracted, the subroutine to reinitialize Field 3 in each segment could be coded as:

```
RESETF3     LA      10,TABLE+7              00001
            LA      9,250                  00002
LOOPSET     ZAP     0(6,10),PL1'0'         00003
            AH      10,H'16'               00004
            BCT     9,LOOPSET              00005
            BC      15,ALLSET              00006
```

Statement 00001 loads the address of TABLE + 7 into general register 10. The address generated by TABLE + 7 operand will point to the first byte of the packed decimal field in the first table segment.

Statement 00002 uses the Load Address instruction to place the value of +250 into general register 9. Register 9 will be the Branch On Count (BCT) loop control register, and once loaded with this value it will allow 250 cycles through the LOOPSET routine.

Statement 00003 is using the ZAP instruction to reset to zero the packed decimal field of the table segment currently pointed to by general register 10. Although a one-byte literal is used as the second operand, the first operand specifies a byte length of six bytes for the statement. The ZAP will reset all six bytes of hcx digits to zero with the exception of the low-order nibble, which will contain a valid packed decimal sign of 'C'.

Statement 00004 is incrementing general register 10 by a count of 16 bytes in order to point to the packed field of the next table segment.

Statement 00005 is the Branch On Count instruction for loop control. Until general register 9 in decremented to zero the branch to LOOPSET will continue to be taken.

Statement 00006 is a forced branch to an assumed subroutine, indicating that the packed decimal field of the table have all been reset to +0.

As mentioned throughout this entire section on tables and look-up routines, there are many variations and techniques for accomplishing these concepts in actual application. Table formatting and the subsequent searches of the table must be tailored to the needs of the problem program. Even at this, the programmer is given the challenge of discovering, or designing, the most efficient technique for his application.

EDITING DATA

A. THE EDITING INSTRUCTIONS

INSTRUCTION: EDIT

Mnemonic	Hex Code	Operand Format
ED	DE	$D_1(L,B_1),D_2(B_2)$

This instruction will modify the contents of the second operand by converting it from packed decimal format to zoned decimal format. The converted data, in zoned decimal, is then further modified by the functional control of the edit pattern. The functional address of the edit pattern is specified by the first operand of the statement.

The processing of data occurs from left to right; one byte at a time is processed for the length specified, or implied, by the first operand.

More definitive information on editing capabilities of this instruction is covered within this chapter.

CC	BC	Condition
0	8	The edit resulted in a zero field.
1	4	The edit resulted in a field value of less than zero $(-)$.
2	2	The edit resulted in a field value greater than zero $(+)$.

*   *   *

INSTRUCTION: EDIT AND MARK

Mnemonic	Hex Code	Operand Format
EDMK	DF	$D_1(L,B_1),D_2(B_2)$

This instruction basically performs the same function as the EDIT instruction. In addition, however, a special audit is made during the time that the second operand source data is being modified under the control of the edit pattern specified by the first operand. This audit consists of a scan in which the instruction, during its left to right modification of the data, looks for the encounter of the first significant character (nonzero resulting character) placed into the edit pattern prior to finding a "significant start" character in the edit pattern itself. If such an encounter occurs, the instruction places the address of that byte (the first significant character) into general register 1. If an edit pattern "significant start" character is encountered prior to when a significant character is first inserted into the pattern, the storage of the address into general register 1 is not accomplished. Considerably more information and detail regarding the use of this instruction is presented in the subsequent portions of this chapter.

CC	BC	Condition
0	8	The edit resulted in a zero field.
1	4	The edit resulted in a field value of less than zero ($-$).
2	2	The edit resulted in a field value of more than zero ($+$).

B. THE APPLICATION OF THE EDITING INSTRUCTIONS

1. The Necessity of Editing

The internal configuration of data and fixed-point or decimal values can alternately, or selectively, be thought of as consisting of binary, hexadecimal, or character representations.

These representations, however, cannot always be visually reproduced on a graphic output device in that same form without some manipulation of the configuration. For the purpose of this discussion, a graphic output device shall be interpreted as being any output unit on which data representation appears in a visual character form. This would include printer units, console typewriters, cathode-ray display units, and similar equipment. Regular EBCDIC character representations may be reproduced directly on such devices without any additional alteration of their configuration structure. Fixed-point and packed decimal values, however, require a certain amount of transformation prior to being transmitted to the output unit. Some of this transformation is accomplished by the use of the editing instructions and some is converted by the applications of various instructions, depending on the type of data to be presented. Because the edit instructions require that the data to

be edited be in packed decimal form, numeric character representation is the only type of data that can be edited with these instructions. During the editing itself, however, alphabetic and special characters may be inserted into various sections of the edited field as a part of that function.

Several common types of editing are:

1. Suppression of leading zeros in a numeric field.

2. Insertion of punctuation in a numeric field.

3. Identifying positive and negative values by inserting such descriptives as—CR $-$ $+$ etc.

4. Addition of dollar-signs ($) to monetary values, either in a fixed position or with a "floating" capability.

In order to relate these applications to actual practice, Table 15-1 shows the general content of data that is to be edited and the various output forms that the data may assume through editing.

The means of accomplishing these editing routines are discussed in detail in subsequent paragraphs. At this point, however, it is important to understand the necessity of presenting numeric data in a format that is not only easy to read and evaluate, but in a form that also relates to the association of that numeric to its representation. This would mean, for example, that if a numeric field is used to express the quantity of square inches in different sizes of floor space, it would be illogical to present that field as $268.93; the presentation of such a value in the form of "26,893 SQ.IN." would be considerably more proper in addition to being self-descriptive. In many instances, data of this type would be in columnar form; therefore, column headings may be used to describe the representation of the numeric values. This might appear as:

SQUARE INCHES

26,893

426

5,830

TABLE 15-1

Data Field Content	Edited Output Data

| 0 | 0 | 3 | 9 | 5 | 6 | 1 | C |

395.61

| 0 | 0 | 3 | 9 | 5 | 6 | 1 | F |

395.61 +

| 0 | 0 | 3 | 9 | 5 | 6 | 1 | F |

$ 395.61

| 0 | 0 | 3 | 9 | 5 | 6 | 1 | C |

$395.61

| 2 | 5 | 7 | 8 | 8 | 1 | 4 | D |

25,788.14 −

| 2 | 5 | 7 | 8 | 8 | 1 | 4 | D |

25788.14CR

| 2 | 5 | 7 | 8 | 8 | 1 | 4 | D |

(25,788.14)

| 0 | 0 | 0 | 0 | 0 | 0 | 6 | F |

6

| 0 | 0 | 0 | 0 | 0 | 0 | 6 | F |

.06

| 0 | 0 | 0 | 0 | 0 | 0 | 6 | F |

6¢

Here, the values are correctly expressed and the columnar heading describes their representation. When formatting data to an output device that creates visual information, it is of prime importance for that data to be self-communicating. It must be visually easy to read, logically presented, and bear a descriptive relationship to the overall meaning of what it represents. Proper editing and presentation formatting can accomplish all of these goals. Compare the two sample listings and note the self-descriptive style of the second as compared to the general presentation used in the first listing.

#	LENGTH	WIDTH	WEIGHT	$
0039658	368	36	36–5	95.00
0078621	52	22	3–11	7.00
0113965	89	48	12	25.00

PRODUCT NUMBER	LENGTH (FEET)	WIDTH (INCHES)	WEIGHT PER LINEAR FOOT	COST PER MEASURED UNIT
39658	368'	36"	36# 5 oz	$95.00 lin. ft
78621	52'	22"	3# 11 oz	$ 7.00 lb
113965	89'	48"	12#	$25.00 ea.

In the second listing, the descriptive representation is often presented in both the columnar heading and with the data under that heading; the "length" heading indicates the representation of the values is "quantity of feet" and the numeric value itself is followed by the standard symbol (an apostrophe) for "feet." The printed, or displayed, data that is generated by any single program is normally expected to be used by numerous personnel who are concerned with the overall system. To meet the comprehension level of all personnel, which would normally vary quite considerably, the output data should be in the most logical, explicit form.

2. *The Composition of the Edit Instruction Statements*

The actual editing function is performed by either one of two instructions: the Edit instruction or the Edit & Mark instruction. Because both of these perform relatively similar functions, it is intended that a detailed description of the makeup of the edit functions be described in detail before approaching the instructions themselves. The components that are active during the execution of an editing routine might well be considered to be separate little instructions in themselves; there are many editing variations made possible by merely using a different combination of these optional components. In general, then, the Edit instruction and the Edit instruction statement consist of the following items.

1. The Source Field
2. The Edit Pattern
   a. Insertion Characters
   b. Digit Select Characters
   c. Significant Start Characters
   d. Field Separation Characters
3. Significant Trigger (S-Trigger)

Each of these items have a number of different rules and variations that determine the manner in which the edit instruction will perform.

(a)   The Source Field. The source field is the originating data storage area that contains the numeric value that is to be edited. It may consist of enough data to fill 255 bytes of edited output, under the stipulation that the overall editing process will not involve more than a maximum length of 256 bytes including the length of the edit pattern. The data contained within the source field must be in packed decimal form. The packed value contained within the source field does not have to be a "signed" value, but if it is, then the sign must exist in the right-most half-byte of the field. All other half-bytes within the field must contain valid decimal digits—hexadecimal numeric digits of '0' through '9'. If the edit is to be performed on a source field that contains multiple packed decimal values, each value may contain a "sign" in the right-most nibble (half-byte).

Single Value Source Field

0	0	0	6	3	5	9	C

Multiple Value Source Field

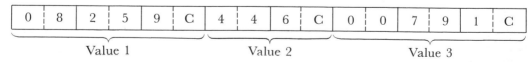

	Value 1				Value 2			Value 3			
0	8	2	5	9	C	4	4	6	C	0	0	7	9	1	C

The source field is edited into the Edit Pattern which would usually exist in a storage area that is to be used as the output location.

(b)   The Edit Pattern. The Edit Pattern contains the specifications of what type of editing functions are to be performed. Unlike the source field, each byte of the Pattern must be in unpacked, zoned format. The Pattern is considered to consist of:

1. Fill Characters (Insertion Characters)

2. Digit Select Character(s)

3. Significant Start Character(s)

4. Field Separator Character(s)—only in a multiple field edit.

5. Any character(s) that is/are to be placed unaltered into the edited output field.

These configurations, some of which do not represent existing printable characters, each participate in their own way to control the editing process. A general description of each of these is offered here. The overall function that they perform is covered in the discussion of Functional Characteristics of Editing.

1. Fill Character—this is also referred to as an insertion character. It may be any valid character including a blank, $, *, (,), #, etc. The Fill Character is used to replace leading nonsignificant digits that exist in the source field.

2. Digit Select Character—this character consists of a hex configuration of X'20', an unprintable character. It is used to indicate a position within the Edit Pattern that is to be filled with a numeric digit from the source field if one is available. The Digit Select Character is always replaced by either the Fill Character of the Edit Pattern or a numeric digit from the source field.

3. Significant Start Character—an unprintable hexadecimal configuration of X'21'. It is used to signal to the editing function that all remaining (low-order) numeric digits in the source field are to be considered to be significant and that suppression of leading zeros is to terminate at this point.

4. Field Separator Character—a hexadecimal configuration (unprintable) of X'22'. This character is only used when the edit process is to act on a source field containing multiple numeric values. It effectively separates the multiple values by appearing as a blank between each of the individual values.

5. In addition, any valid character that is required within the final edited output may be inserted within the Edit Pattern.

(c) **The Significant Trigger (S-Trigger).**

The Significant Trigger is actually a "switch," or condition setting, that is inspected during the editing process in order to determine various processing decisions. The S-Trigger has two conditions—OFF, which is equal to '0', and ON, which is equal to '1'. During the process of editing, the S-Trigger may be alternately switched ON-/OFF several times, depending entirely on the configuration of the Edit Pattern and the contents of the source field that is being edited. The conditions that turn the S-Trigger ON are:

1. The encounter of a Significant Start Character in the Pattern.

2. The insertion into the Edit Pattern of a significant numeric digit from the source field prior to encountering a Significant Start Character in the Pattern.

The conditions that would turn the S-Trigger OFF (assuming it was in an ON status) are:

1. Encountering a Field Separator Character in the Edit Pattern.

2. Detection of a plus sign ($+$) digit in the low-order nibble (half-byte) of a value in the source field.

3. At the initialization of each edit operation.

In addition, the edit operation uses the status of the S-Trigger to determine the setting of the PSW Condition Code at the end of each edit function. If a multiple field edit has been performed in which values of both positive and negative amounts were present, the resulting Condition Code would indicate only the status of the last value that was edited.

Up to this point, the description of the functions and components of editing operations have been limited considerably to the individual structure of each. This in itself does not tend to present a lucid interpretation of editing characteristics. It was necessary, however, to describe these items merely for the purpose of becoming familiar with the terms and nomenclature that will be used to explain the overall performance of Edit instructions. It is recommended that as the remaining portion of this chapter is presented, an occasional reference and review be made of the preceding paragraphs. This should aid the reader in comprehending the many facets and variations possible in editing.

3. Functional Characteristics of Editing

Now that the basic components and their individual actions in an edit instruction statement have been described, it is time to put them all together in order to examine the interaction between them under various circumstances. A preface to the examination should be a brief description of the normal functions of these components. This may be considered to be the general rules of operation for an edit statement and is presented, as follows, in numbered form.

1. The source field (the "sending" field) is changed from packed decimal format to zoned decimal format (EBCDIC) as each numeric digit is edited under control of the Edit Pattern.

2. The editing scan, and the inspection of the Edit Pattern, moves from left to right (high-order to low-order) for the length specified or implied by the length of the Pattern.

3. The edited source field, including any additional characters inserted by the Pattern, replaces the Edit Pattern in its entirety.

4. In order to edit another source field into the same location at a subsequent time, the Edit Pattern must be completely reinitialized.

Because certain characters within the Edit Pattern do not have a printable representation, pseudo-characters will be used at certain points within this text to represent them. These are:

1. ƀ A valid blank; X'40'
2. đ Digit Select Character; X'20'
3. Ş Significant Start Character; X'21'
4. Ƒ Field Separator Character; X'22'

A practical way to prepare for an edit function is to establish the Edit Pattern as a constant. It may then be moved into the output field area before each edit instruction statement, reinitializing that area with the Pattern as required. It is suggested that the Edit Pattern constant be defined in hexadecimal configuration, thus eliminating the need of finding a substitute pseudo-character to represent the nonprintable editing components. A constant of this type might appear as:

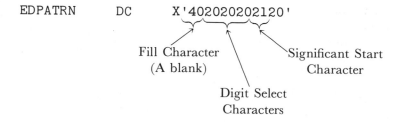

EDPATRN   DC   X'402020202120'

Fill Character
(A blank)

Digit Select
Characters

Significant Start
Character

In pseudo-character representation this same pattern would be coded as:

    EDPATRN   DC   C'ƀđđđŞđ'

When the source program has been compiled, however, and the source listing of the program has been printed, this constant (if coded in pseudo-character form) would appear as:

    EDPATRN   DC   C'   '

Because the constant was expressed as being in character form, the Pattern itself appears as blanks. This is because there is no printable character representation for those components of the Pattern. It is much more practical, therefore, to define the Edit Pattern constant as hexadecimal form in order for the source program listing to contain a printable representation of that Pattern.

Once the Edit Pattern has been moved

into the output field, the Edit instruction is coded and these events occur:

The left-most (high-order) byte of the Edit Pattern is evaluated as the "Fill" Character. Source field digits (half-bytes) are then passed to the Edit Pattern one at a time, from left to right. The Fill Character will be used to replace nonsignificant numeric digits (hex zero digits) from the source field until the first significant (nonzero) digit from the source field is passed to the Pattern, or until a Significant Start Character is encountered within the Pattern, whichever might occur first. If a significant digit from the source field is passed to the edit prior to encountering a Significant Start Character in the Edit Pattern, that digit, and all remaining source field digits for that particular value, will replace the remaining Digit Select Characters in that portion of the Pattern. Inasmuch as the passing of the significant digit to the Edit Pattern has now turned the S-Trigger ON, any subsequent Significant Start Characters within this portion of the Pattern will be ignored. If a Significant Start Character is encountered in the Pattern prior to the time when the source field passes a significant digit, the S-Trigger will be set to an ON condition and all remaining digits in the current value will replace existing Digit Select Characters remaining within this portion of the Edit Pattern.

These last few statements have been rather lengthy, and quite probably confusing, so a closer, descriptive examination of how this would perform is in order at this time.

Assume that an Edit Pattern exists as a constant, coded in hex format as:

```
EDITPAT    DC    X'402020212020'
```

or

```
EDITPAT    DC    C' b̸dd̸$dd̸'
```

Using this Edit Pattern as the base, the following illustrations will show the editing of two numeric values into this Pattern—one in which the Significant Start Character is encountered prior to a significant digit being passed from the source field; the other in which a significant digit is passed from the source field prior to encountering the Significant Start Character.

Example 1

Step 1

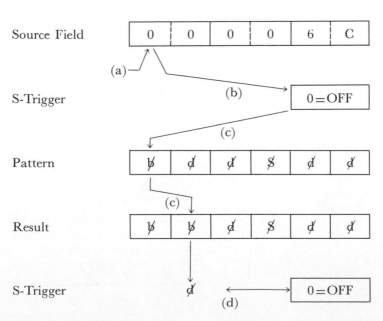

(a) The first digit of the source field is examined to see if it is a significant digit.

(b) Because it is not, the S-Trigger is inspected for an ON condition.

(c) The S-Trigger is OFF, consequently the Fill Character replaces the first Digit Select Character in the Pattern.

(d) The character replaced in the Pattern is inspected to see if it was a Significant Start Character. It was not, so the S-Trigger remains OFF.

Step 2

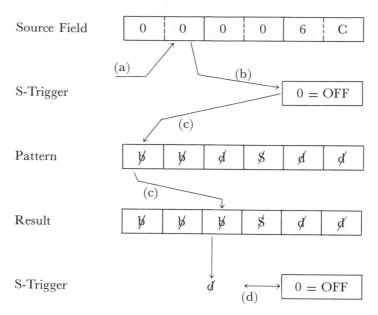

(a) The second digit of the source field is inspected.

(b) It is not a significant digit, so the S-Trigger is checked.

(c) It is OFF, resulting in the Fill Character being used to replace the second Digit Select Character in the Pattern.

(d) The character replaced by the Fill Character is not a Significant Start Character; therefore, the S-Trigger remains OFF.

Step 3

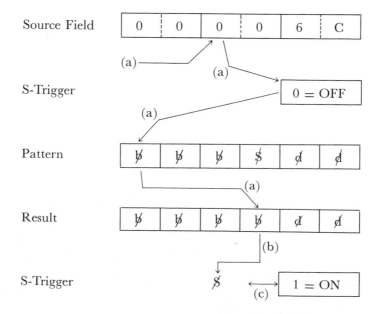

(a) The third digit of the source field is not a significant digit and the S-Trigger is not ON, so the Fill Character is used to replace the next available editing character in the Pattern.

(b) The character replaced by the Fill Character is inspected to see if it was a Significant Start Character.

(c) It was, so the S-Trigger is set to an ON condition. This indicates that remaining digits of the source field, whether significant or nonsignificant, will be placed into the Edit Pattern.

Step 4

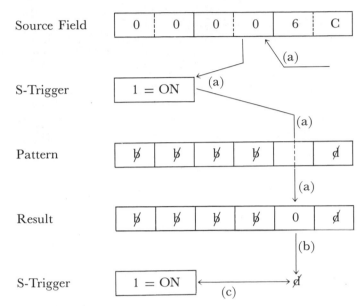

(a) The fourth digit of the source field is found to be nonsignificant, but because the S-Trigger is ON, that digit is sent to the Edit Pattern to replace the next available Digit Select Character.

(b) The character in the Pattern that was replaced by the source field digit is inspected to see if it was a Field Separator Character.

(c) Because it was not, the S-Trigger remains ON.

Step 5

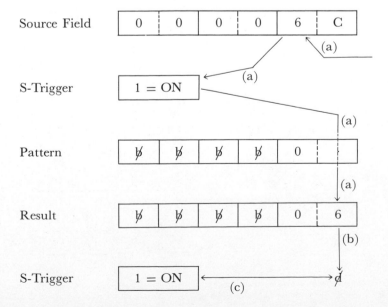

(a) The fifth digit of the source field is sent to replace the next available Digit Select Character in the Edit Pattern. This was done because either: (1) the source field digit was a significant digit, and/or (2) the S-Trigger was ON.

(b) The operation then inspected the character from the Pattern that was replaced by the source field digit to determine if it was a Field Separator Character.

(c) It was not, so the S-Trigger was not altered.

At this point the edit terminated, having completed the length that was assumed to be specified for this statement. If this Pattern was now printed or displayed on an output device it would appear as . . . 06. Had the edit been specified to include one more byte of the source field, the encounter of a valid plus sign would have caused the editing operation to set the S-Trigger to an OFF condition.

Example 2

Step 1

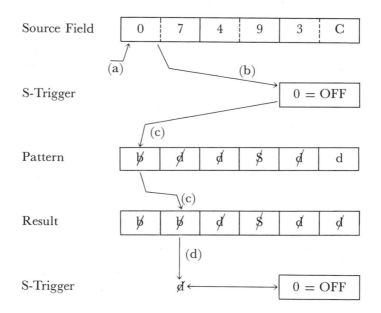

(a) As in the previous example, the first digit of the source field is inspected to see if it is a significant digit.

(b) It is not, so the S-Trigger is checked to see if it is ON.

(c) Because the S-Trigger is OFF, the non-significant digit in the source field is suppressed and the Fill Character is used to

replace the first Digit Select Character in the Edit Pattern.

(d) The character from the Pattern that was replaced by the Fill Character is inspected and found not to be a Significant Start Character, so the S-Trigger is not affected.

Step 2

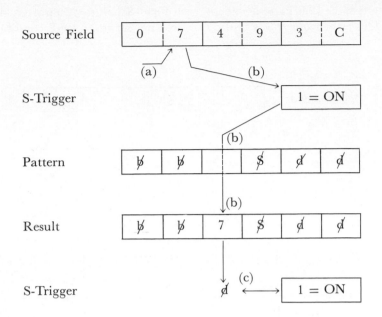

(a) The second character of the source field is inspected and found to be a significant digit.

(b) The S-Trigger is set to an ON condition and the significant source field digit is passed to the Edit Pattern, replacing the next Digit Select Character.

(c) That character, as it is replaced, is examined to determine if it is a Field Separator Character. Because it was not, the S-Trigger is not altered.

Step 3

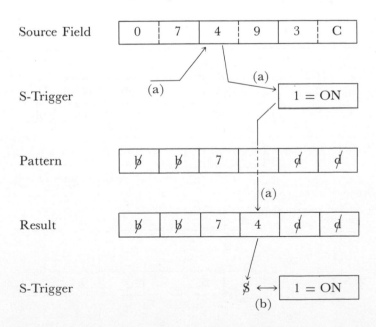

(a) The third character of the source field is passed to the Edit Pattern on the basis that the S-Trigger is ON and the character being passed was a significant digit.

(b) The Significant Start Character that was bumped out of the Edit Pattern will not affect the S-Trigger because it was already ON. Because the replaced character was not a Field Separator Character, the S-Trigger was not set to an OFF condition.

Step 4

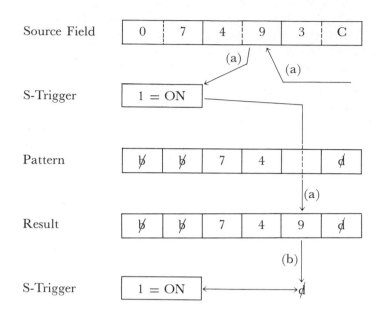

(a) In this step the fourth source field digit is sent to replace the corresponding Digit Select Character in the Edit Pattern; it is a significant digit and the S-Trigger is ON.

(b) The character replaced by the source field digit within the Edit Pattern is tested and found not to be a Field Separator Character. Accordingly, the S-Trigger setting is not changed.

Step 5

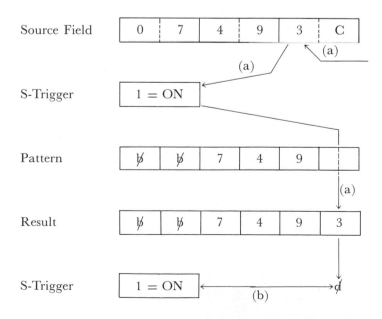

(a) At this point the fifth source field digit is sent to replace the last Digit Select Character in the Edit Pattern. That source field digit is a significant digit and the S-Trigger is ON.

(b) The character that was within the Pattern but was replaced by the source field digit is tested and noted as not being a Field Separator Character. On this basis the S-Trigger setting is not changed.

The length of the edit, as implied by the Pattern length, has been entirely scanned and the editing process terminates. The data residing in the Pattern, if displayed on an output device, would appear as:

7493

To avoid confusion, it should be explained that the foregoing examples and illustrations are presented in a logical manner that is intended to communicate the process of the editing function. They do not include all of the technical functions performed by the edit, but they are sufficiently accurate and complete to fulfill the concepts required to understand those functions. A more technical discourse on these examples would have required considerably more space without really providing the reader with a better understanding.

At this point it has now been explained how the S-Trigger, Significant Start Character, and the Digit Select Character create interacting processes within the editing functions. In effect, the examples so far have demonstrated the simple application of "zero suppression," or suppressing leading nonsignificant digits in a numeric value. Another option that is available, and frequently used, is the insertion of punctuation or characters within the value that is being edited. This would be a process such as converting a number from '03952867' to '39,528.67'. The Edit Pattern would be initialized containing the hexadecimal representation of the punctuation in the proper positions. An Edit Pattern of this type could be defined as a constant, in hexadecimal form, such as:

```
EDPATRN     DC      X'40206B2020214B2020'
```

or

```
EDPATRN     DC      C'b¢,¢¢$.¢¢'
```

In this Edit Pattern, the source field value is implied to consist of a maximum value of +999999, which would be edited as 9,999.99. If the value edited into this Pattern was less than the maximum, all leading nonsignificant digits would be suppressed until either a significant digit was passed from the source field or until after the Significant Start Character in the sixth byte of the Pattern had been encountered. If the first digit of the source field was a nonsignificant digit, the third byte of the Pattern, the comma, would be replaced by the Fill Character. Shown below are a quantity of source field values and the manner in which they would be edited into this Edit Pattern. It may be of help to review the rules regarding the S-Trigger conditions, the Significant Start Character, and the passing of a significant digit, prior to studying these examples.

Example 1

Pattern	b	¢	,	¢	¢	$	.	¢	¢
Source Field				0	0	3	6	7	5
Edited result	b	b	b	b	3	6	.	7	5

Display output   36.75

Example 2

Pattern	
⌿b	⌿d	,	⌿d	⌿d	$	.	⌿d	⌿d

Source Field	
0	0	0	0	0	1

Edited result	
⌿b	⌿b	⌿b	⌿b	⌿b	⌿b	.	0	1

Display output   .01

Example 3

Pattern	
⌿b	⌿d	,	⌿d	⌿d	$	.	⌿d	⌿d

Source Field	
4	7	1	1	6	9

Edited result	
⌿b	4	,	7	1	1	.	6	9

Display output   4,711.69

Example 4

Pattern	
⌿b	⌿d	,	⌿d	⌿d	$	.	⌿d	⌿d

Source Field	
0	8	3	3	5	7

Edited result	
⌿b	⌿b	⌿b	8	3	3	.	5	7

Display output   833.57

In many instances, especially when listing monetary values, the program may require a visible distinction between positive and negative values such as debits and credits or plus and minus amounts. As stated before, the S-Trigger will be turned OFF whenever the edit process encounters a positive/plus sign indication in the low-order half-byte of a packed decimal value. By utilizing this capability, it is now possible to identify all negative values edited. To apply such an edit, an Edit Pattern could be defined as:

```
EDITPT    DC    X'402020214B202040C3D94B'
```

or

```
EDITPT    DC    C'⌿b⌿d⌿d$.⌿d⌿d⌿bCR.'
```

If, when using this Pattern, the edit encounters a valid plus sign in the source field, the S-Trigger will be turned OFF after processing the last numeric digit transmitted from the source field. If the sign is other than a plus sign, the S-Trigger will remain ON and the suffix of '⌿bCR.' will appear immediately following the actual value.

The following packed decimal source fields are shown as they would be transformed into printed or displayed output when using this Edit Pattern.

Example 1

Pattern										
ƀ	ɗ	ɗ	$	.	ɗ	ɗ	ƀ	C	R	.

Source Field					
0	3	4	5	0	C

Edited result										
ƀ	ƀ	3	4	.	5	0	ƀ	ƀ	ƀ	ƀ

Output   34.50

Example 2

Pattern										
ƀ	ɗ	ɗ	$	.	ɗ	ɗ	ƀ	C	R	.

Source Field					
1	3	8	5	3	D

Edited result										
ƀ	1	3	8	.	5	3	ƀ	C	R	.

Output   138.53 CR.

Example 3

Pattern										
ƀ	ɗ	ɗ	$	.	ɗ	ɗ	ƀ	C	R	.

Source Field					
0	0	6	0	0	B

Edited result										
ƀ	ƀ	ƀ	6	.	0	0	ƀ	C	R	.

Output   6.00 CR.

Example 4

Pattern										
ƀ	ɗ	ɗ	$	.	ɗ	ɗ	ƀ	C	R	.

Source Field					
0	0	0	2	9	C

Edited result										
ƀ	ƀ	ƀ	ƀ	.	2	9	ƀ	ƀ	ƀ	ƀ

Output   .29

Example 5

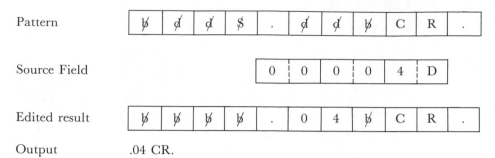

Pattern

Source Field

Edited result

Output   .04 CR.

When using a computer system to create negotiable documents, such as payroll checks, it is desirable to print monetary values in such a way that the suppressed non-significant digits are replaced with a char-acter other than a blank. One application of this type is to use an asterisk (*) as a Fill Character. An Edit Pattern using this char-acter could appear as:

```
        EDITPAY    DC    X'5C20206B2020214B2020'
```

or

```
        EDITPAY    DC    C'*ȼȼ,ȼȼ$.ȼȼ'
```

In actual use, this Pattern would perform as:

Example 1

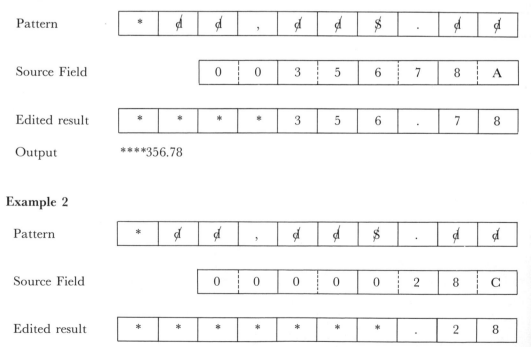

Pattern

Source Field

Edited result

Output   ****356.78

Example 2

Pattern

Source Field

Edited result

Output   *******.28

Example 3

Pattern	*	¢	¢	,	¢	¢	$	.	¢	¢

Source Field			0	1	0	0	4	5	0	C

Edited result	*	*	1	,	0	0	4	.	5	0

Output   **1,004.50

Example 4

Pattern	*	¢	¢	,	¢	¢	$	.	¢	¢

Source Field			2	3	0	0	0	0	0	F

Edited result	*	2	3	,	0	0	0	.	0	0

Output   *23,000.00

In each instance, the asterisks have been inserted up to the first significant digit or to the point where the S-Trigger was set ON by a Significant Start Character. The general purpose of this type of application is to discourage the alteration of monetary amounts on negotiable documents by not allowing any blanks to appear in the high-order positions of the printed value.

Multiple-field editing is accomplished through the use of the Field Separator Character. It is this character that guarantees that the S-Trigger is set to an OFF condition between each successive value encountered during a multiple-field edit. If, for example, an Edit Pattern was established for the purpose of editing three contiguous unsigned numeric fields, the Field Separator Character could be used to assure that zero-suppression was applied to each of the three fields.

When creating the Edit Pattern for a multifield edit, it should be remembered that it is necessary to specify the Fill Character once—as the first (high-order) character of the Pattern.

The multiple fields that are to be edited, assuming that they are in adjacent program storage areas, and the Edit Pattern that is to be used to create the edited output, are shown below.

FIELD1	0	2	6	5

FIELD2	3	9	5	4	2	7

FIELD3	0	0

```
    EDITMF      DC      X'4020202120222020202014B2020222120'
```

or as

```
    EDITMF      DC      C'ƀđđ$đꟻđđ$.đđꟻ$đ'
```

The passing of the digits into the Edit Pattern, and the resulting edited Pattern and source fields, can be shown as follows.

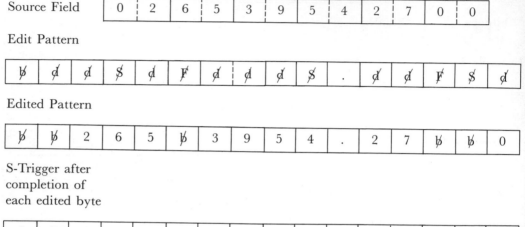

If printed, the edited data would appear as:

265 3954.27　0

The following list shows the manner in which this edit was accomplished.

1. At the initialization of the edit, the S-Trigger is OFF.

2. During the process of editing the value contained in FIELD1, the S-Trigger is turned ON when it encounters the significant digit '2'. As a result, at the completion of the third byte in the Edit Pattern, the S-Trigger is now ON.

3. In processing the sixth byte of the Edit Pattern, a Field Separator Character is detected and the S-Trigger is turned OFF. Zero-suppression is once again effected in the event that the next value to be edited contains leading nonsignificant digits. The Field Separator Character retains its position in the Edit Pattern in the form of a blank.

4. The first digit of FIELD2 happens to be a significant digit; therefore, it is passed directly to the seventh byte of the Pattern, at the same time setting the S-Trigger to an ON condition.

5. Because the S-Trigger is on, the remaining digits are passed to the Edit Pattern, replacing the Digit Select Characters in bytes 7, 8, 9, 10, 12, and 13.

6. Another Field Separator Character is encountered, this time in byte 14 of the Pattern, and once again the S-Trigger is placed in an OFF condition. The Field Separator Character is an effective blank in this position.

7. Byte 15 is a Significant Start Character that sets the S-Trigger ON for subsequent editing of FIELD3.

8. Although the last digit of the source field is a nonsignificant digit, the ON condition of the S-Trigger causes the edit to pass the '0' source digit to byte 16 of the Pattern.

9. After completion of the 16th byte of processing, the operation is terminated, assuming that the implied length of the Edit Pattern was not given as any other specific length.

Having described the components and functions of the editing instructions, it is time to review the instructions themselves and how they are used in an instruction statement.

(a) Edit. The Edit instruction, coded as the mnemonic ED, is used to cause the initialization of any, or all, of the editing functions described in the preceding paragraphs. It performs in accordance with all of the editing rules heretofore specified. Although the variable functions have been suitably described, the entire means of editing a field of data to an output area in storage have not been detailed.

In many, or at least most, instances wherein data is to be transmitted to an output device, an output area of program storage has been defined by the programmer. This is usually coded in the form of a Define Storage (DS) statement or a Define Constant (DC) statement. For the purpose of general practice and good housekeeping, one area may be defined to accommodate each output device. Each defined area is usually stated with a length attribute sufficiently large to accommodate the largest single string of data that is to be sent to that device. For example,

a standard output printer unit is considered to have a line length of 132 printable characters; cathode-ray display devices have varying screen size capabilities, some of which utilize 240, 480, or 960 characters; most card punch units are construed to consist of an 80-byte character line. Although each of these devices could have a "storage output" area specifically designated for its maximum data length, the entire length of those areas need not be transmitted to the output unit. Inasmuch as the actual length of the data sent to the device is more likely dependent on the coding of the access method macroinstructions and DCB statements, which in turn may vary between the different types of operating systems, the means of specifying the length of the data to be transmitted will not be discussed here. It is sufficient to know, at this time, that data sent from a given storage output area to an output device may vary in length. Assume, then, that the programmer has defined an output area labeled PRTLINE, and has then established an Edit Pattern as a constant labeled EDITPRT. Because he intends to edit a field of data into PRTLINE, print it, edit another value into PRTLINE where the previous data was edited, print that new value, etc., it is necessary to move the Edit Pattern into PRTLINE each time before issuing the EDIT instruction. The Edit Pattern that is to be used is stated as:

```
EDITPRT      DC      X'4020206B2020214B2020'
```

or as

```
EDITPRT      DC      CL10'ϸϸϸ,ϸϸ$.ϸϸ'
```

The storage area from which the source data is to be extracted for editing is a packed decimal field that has been defined as:

```
VALUEFLD     DC      PL4'0'
```

The logic of this program example is that the processing will read a data record from tape, pack a particular field from that record into VALUEFLD, edit VALUEFLD into an

output area, and then print the output area onto a printer unit. The GET and PUT macros used in this example are standard OS move-mode Q.S.A.M. (Queued Sequential Access Method) macros, which generate the necessary action to access the tape file and display the necessary print line. The coding itself could be stated as:

```
BACK      GET      TAPEIN,INAREA                0001
          PACK     VALUEFLD,INAREA+25(7)        0002
          MVC      PRTLINE+10(10),EDITPRT       0003
          ED       PRTLINE+10(10),VALUEFLD      0004
          PUT      PRTR,PRTLINE                 0005
          BC       15,BACK                      0006
```

Statement 0001 is the coding of the OS Q.S.A.M. GET macro. It will read the file named TAPEIN and place a logical record unit into an area defined as INAREA. A warning should be made that all of the names (labels) used by the operands in these coding statements have been originated by the programmer and in no way represent established naming convention. The file TAPEIN must be defined elsewhere in the program by a DCB macroinstruction and the field INAREA must have been defined by a DS or DC statement.

Statement 0002 is packing a hypothetical seven-byte EBCDIC numeric field into the four-byte area VALUEFLD. The data field that is to be packed is located at a starting point of the 26th byte within the record residing in INAREA. It is, therefore, referred to as INAREA + 25 in lieu of subdefining INAREA into labeled fields.

Statement 0003 is a Move Character instruction statement that is used to move the Edit Pattern constant into the output area that is to be used by the printer DCB. This output area, labeled PRTLINE, consists of 132 bytes of storage containing additional data other than the value that is to be edited. Because the edited value is to be located starting at the 11th byte of PRTLINE, the Edit Pattern has been moved into the address of PRTLINE + 10. Because the MVC instruction performs a move for the length implied by the first operand, or the length specified within that operand, a length attribute of ten bytes has been specified in order that only the ten bytes representing

EDITPRT will be moved.

Statement 0004 is the Edit instruction statement. Once again, the explicit length attribute is used in the first operand to define the length of the operation. The packed decimal source field, VALUEFLD, will be edited into the Edit Pattern, which now exists in PRTLINE + 10.

Statement 0005 is a conventional OS Q.S.A.M. PUT macro. It will take the output area PRTLINE and generate the necessary input/output task to place that data onto the output unit defined by a DCB macro labeled PRTR.

Statement 0006 is a forced (unconditional) branch back to the instruction statement defined by the label BACK.

The entire set of statements would then be executed again—read a tape record, pack the value, move the Edit Pattern to the output area, edit the packed value into the output area, put out the print line, branch to BACK, etc. This cycle would continue until an end-of-file (EOF) condition was encountered on the input tape, signaling that the source of input data had been exhausted. This example has made no provisions for line counting, page numbering, etc., all of which has been described within the section "Printing Data Listings."

After the completion of an EDIT instruction statement, the PSW Condition Code bits will contain an indication as to the value of the source field just edited. The bits are set as follows:

PSW Bit Setting	Comparable BC Condition	Condition Represented
00	8	A zero-value source field was edited.
01	4	A negative-value source field was edited.
10	2	A positive-value source field was edited.

It is possible that the programmer might intend to make a logic decision based on the Condition Code setting. It should be noted that the Condition Code is set to its resulting configuration based on the last value edited—in a multiple-field edit, this would

be the right-most value in the multiple field; in a single-value edit this would be that value alone.

As noted previously, the first operand in an Edit instruction statement determines the length of the editing process. A length attribute is not implied, or allowed to be explicitly stated, for the source field value represented by the second operand of the statement. It is suggested, therefore, that a specific length attribute, equal to the length of the Edit Pattern, be included as a part of the first operand in the Edit statement.

(b) Edit & Mark. The EDMK performs all of the functions of the regular Edit instruction. In addition, however, it will note the address of the point in the Edit Pattern to which the first significant digit was loaded from the source field, if that digit was passed prior to encountering a Significant Start Character within the Edit Pattern. The address that is noted is returned to the program in general register 1.

This instruction can be used to load "floating" symbols, such as a dollar sign, into an output print area or display device array that is to be edited. By using this instruction in a subroutine, the programmer can always arrange to print a dollar sign, or any other symbol, within a given range of bytes in the edited data. A listing such as this could appear to be:

$$\$2.56$$
$$\$3,918.10$$
$$\$.06$$
$$\$715.75$$
$$\$.28$$

Because the address of the first significant digit to be passed from the source field is not always loaded into general register 1, as in the instance when a Significant Start Character is encountered first, the address of the decimal point may be loaded into register 1 before the Edit & Mark instruction statement is executed. This guarantees that the address in register 1 will never be at a point in the Edit Pattern to the right of the decimal point. The overall logic of this process is:

1. Use the Move Character (MVC) instruction to move the Edit Pattern into the output print area.

2. Load general register 1 with the address of the right-most position plus one-byte within the output area Edit Pattern beyond which the dollar sign should not be placed.

3. Code the Edit & Mark instruction statement, addressing the pattern that resides in the output print area as the first operand and the source field as the second operand.

4. Code a statement that will subtract a value of +1 from the address contained in general register 1.

5. Use a Move Immediate (MVI) instruction statement to move a dollar sign into the address pointed to by general register 1.

Assume that the Edit Pattern that is to be used has been moved into an output area at a point identified as PRTOUT + 25. If the first byte of PRTOUT resided at program storage address of 23,516, the first byte of the Edit Pattern would be at address 23,541.

PRTOUT+25

b̸	d̸	,	d̸	d̸	S̸	.	d̸	d̸

Storage address

| 23,541 | 23,542 | 23,543 | 23,544 | 23,545 | 23,546 | 23,547 | 23,548 | 23,549 |

The data that was being passed to the Edit Pattern shown here would determine whether or not general register 1 was reset.

In describing the coding pertaining to this particular Edit Pattern, it must first be determined that the programmer would want the dollar sign to appear somewhere to the left of the decimal point that immediately follows the Significant Start Character. Because the coding will later subtract a value of +1 from the address contained in general register 1, the address of the decimal point is loaded into general register 1.

```
LA      1,PRTOUT+31
```

Register 1 will now contain a fixed-point value of +23,547, representing the storage address of the decimal point at PRTOUT +31.

The source field that is to be edited into the Pattern that commences at PRTOUT +25 is a three-byte unsigned packed field labeled PACKAMT. The instruction statement to Edit & Mark this field is:

```
EDMK    PRTOUT+25(9),PACKAMT
```

This instruction statement would perform the editing function and at the same time might alter the address contained in general register 1. The determining factor as to whether or not register 1 (+23,547) would be changed is the significance of the numeric digits passed from the source field. If a significant digit was edited from the source field into the Edit Pattern between bytes 23,541 and 23,547 (not including these addresses), the Edit & Mark instruction would load into register 1 the address of the Pattern byte into which that significant digit was placed. If no significant digit was passed to the Edit Pattern prior to storage byte 23,547, the address contained in general register 1 would not be changed.

When the Edit & Mark instruction statement has completed its execution, register 1 contains an address that points to a significant digit or a significant character—the decimal point. Regardless of which address is in register 1, a value of +1 should be subtracted from that address in order that it would point to the first available "blank" immediately preceding the significant digit or character. This could be properly coded using the Subtract Halfword (SH) instruc-

tion or a Branch On Count To Register (BCTR) instruction. These two means of reducing the address in general register 1 by a value of +1 could be coded as:

```
SH      1,=H'1'
```

or as

```
BCTR    1,0
```

The Subtract Halfword instruction statement will subtract a halfword literal of +1 from general register 1. The BCTR instruction statement will also decrement the value in general register 1 by +1, but the branch will not be taken—the second operand of "zero" in a BCTR instruction statement will not allow a branch to take place.

Now that general register 1 points to the storage position where the dollar sign is to be inserted into the edited field, a Move Immediate instruction statement is written as:

```
MVI     0(1),C'$'
```

This statement specifies, "move a one-byte immediate character, consisting of a dollar sign, into storage address zero incremented by the address in general register 1."

The accumulated set of coding statements used to complete this task can be summarized as:

```
MVC     PRTOUT+25(9),EDITPTRN
LA      1,PRTOUT+31
EDMK    PRTOUT+25(9),PACKAMT
SH      1,=H'1'
MVI     0(1),C'$'
```

The placement of the dollar sign into the edited data under various circumstances as caused by different values is illustrated in these examples.

Example 1

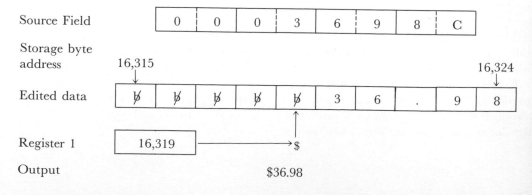

Example 2

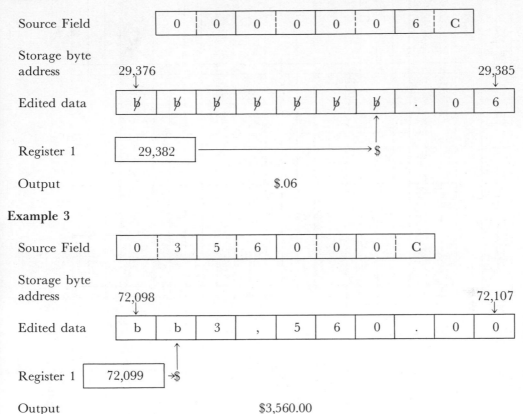

Source Field

0	0	0	0	0	0	6	C

Storage byte address   29,376   29,385

Edited data

⌀	⌀	⌀	⌀	⌀	⌀	⌀	.	0	6

Register 1   29,382 ⟶ $

Output $.06

Example 3

Source Field

0	3	5	6	0	0	0	C

Storage byte address   72,098   72,107

Edited data

b	b	3	,	5	6	0	.	0	0

Register 1   72,099   → $

Output $3,560.00

It is possible to substitute any valid symbol, character, or characters, in place of the dollar sign. A minus sign could be used to indicate credit or negative values in front of the amount instead of after it. This would be done by testing the Condition Code resulting from the execution of the EDMK instruction statement. If the value edited was negative, the program could move a hyphen (-) into the address contained in general register 1; if the value was positive, the MVI instruction could move a plus sign (+) into that address, or move nothing at all. Printed output of this type might appear as:

$$-395.06 \qquad 2,519.78 \qquad -.99$$
$$+.04 \qquad -71.63 \qquad +15,921.88$$

Using this same basic idea, sets of characters such as 'DR.' and 'CR.' could be inserted into the high-order portion of the edited data field. Because the data field might contain its full complement of data, an application of this type should be structured so that the several storage bytes immediately preceding the data field area are blank—and must be reset to blanks after each edit. The only difference between a set of instructions for this EDMK routine and the one shown previously would be the amount of the value subtracted from general register 1, the movement of "blanks" to the bytes preceding the edited data field, and the logic for the insertion of the characters by an MVC instruction rather than an MVI instruction. The coding could be stated as shown in Fig. 15-1.

Statement 0701 moves the Edit Pattern constant into the data field output area.

Statement 0702 moves blanks into the three bytes immediately preceding the data field edit pattern.

Statement 0703 loads the address of the

IBM System/360 Assembler Coding Form

X28-6509-2 U/M050
Printed in U.S.A.

PROGRAM _____ PUNCHING INSTRUCTIONS: GRAPHIC ___ PAGE 1 OF 1

PROGRAMMER _____ DATE ___ PUNCH ___ CARD ELECTRO NUMBER ___

Name	Operation	Operand	Identification-Sequence
*			0000
DOEDIT	MVC	PRTOUT+25(9),EDITPTRN	0701
	MVC	PRTOUT+22(3),=CL3' '	0702
	LA	1,PRTOUT+31	0703
	EDMK	PRTOUT+25(9),PACKAMT	0704
	BC	8,BYALL	0705
	BC	4,NEGTV	0706
	SH	1,=H'4'	0707
	MVC	0(3,1),=CL3'DR.'	0708
	BC	15,BYALL	0709
*			
NEGTV	SH	1,=H'4'	0710
	MVC	0(3,1),=CL3'CR.'	0711
BYALL	BC	15,ANYWHERE	0712
*			
*			

Figure 15-1

438

decimal point of the Edit Pattern into general register 1.

Statement 0704 executes the Edit and Mark instruction statement. The PSW Condition Code will be set after completion of this statement.

Statement 0705 is a "branch if the value edited was zero." The program will go to Statement 0712 if this condition exists, consequently neither 'DR.' nor 'CR.' will be moved into the edited data field.

Statement 0706 is a "branch if the value edited was negative," taking the logic to Statement 0710 if that condition was noted.

Statement 0707 assumes that the value edited was neither negative nor zero, so it is subtracting +4 from the address contained in general register 1.

Statement 0708 moves the characters 'DR.' into the three high-order bytes of the four bytes immediately preceding the first significant digit or character in the edited data field.

Statement 0709 is a forced branch to Statement 0712.

Statement 0710 assumes that the value edited was negative if the logic passes through this statement, so it subtracts a value of +4 from general register 1. If the value edited was either greater than +0 (a positive value) or less than −0 (a negative value), either Statement 0707 or Statement 0710 would be executed, but not both.

Statement 0711 moves the characters 'CR.' into the three high-order bytes of the four bytes immediately preceding the first significant digit or character in the edited data field.

Statement 0712, which is arrived at via a branch from Statement 0705, Statement 0708, or by falling through from Statement 0711, is a forced branch back to an assumed point in the program logic.

Data edited with this routine would probably appear as:

DR. 277.07	.00	CR. 3,984.41
CR. .06	DR. 75.14	DR. 23,109.88

Given the capabilities provided by the Edit instruction and the Edit & Mark instruction, the programmer has considerable versatility in the formatting and presentation of numeric data.

Review Exercises

1. Define the proper segment names for the edit pattern characters pointed to in the following pattern.

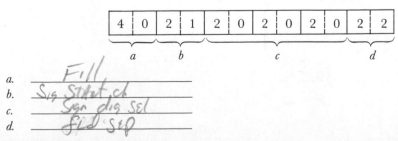

a. _____ Fill _____

b. _____ Sig Start ch _____

c. _____ Sign dig sel _____

d. _____ fld sep _____

2. Which general register is sometimes used by the Edit & Mark instruction as a part of its regular operation? ____1____ .

3. The _Trigger_ _Switch_ is considered to be a switch or condition setting that is inspected during the editing in order for the Edit instruction to make certain processing decisions.

4. The hexadecimal configuration for the edit pattern Significant Start character is X'_21_'.

5. If the editing function detects a _+_-sign in the low-order half-byte of the source field, the S-Trigger will be set to an "off" condition.

6. Even though the source field may contain significant digits, the Edit & Mark instruction will not return the address of the first significant digit if that operation first encounters a _Significant_ _Start_ character within the edit pattern.

7. Data that is to be edited must be in _packed_ _decimal_ form at the time that the Edit instruction is issued.

8. If a source field of four bytes, containing a packed decimal value of +0, were to be edited into the following edit pattern, the total number of zero-digits remaining in the result field after the edit would be _5_ .

4	0	2	0	2	1	2	0	2	0	2	0	2	0	2	0

9. The hexadecimal configuration for the edit pattern Digit Select character is X'_20_'.

10. The _Significant_ _Start_ character is used to signal the editing functions that zero-suppression is to terminate at this point, provided that the edit has not passed any significant digits from the source field.

11. The direction of the editing scan, during the execution of an Edit or an Edit & Mark instruction, is from _Left_ to _Right_ .

12. The hexadecimal configuration for the edit pattern Field Separator character is X'_22_'.

13. If the Edit & Mark instruction encounters the proper conditions to cause it to load register 1 with an address, that address will point to a byte within the particular _Edit_ _Pattern_ being utilized by that statement.

14. Upon encountering a _Fld_ _Sep_ character in an edit pattern, the Edit instruction will set the Significant Trigger (S-Trigger) to an "off" condition.

15. The first (high-order) character in an edit pattern is considered to be the _fill_ _Char._ .

16. A _digit_ _select_ character is used to indicate a position within the edit pattern that is to be filled with a numeric digit from the source field or by the fill character of the pattern.

17. Upon completion of an edit, the Edit operation will set the PSW Condition Code based on the status of the _Trigger_ _Sw_ .

18. The _Fld_ _Sep._ character is generally used in editing a source field containing multiple values.

19. The _fill_ _Char_ is used to replace leading nonsignificant digits of the source field whenever zero-suppression is indicated.

Each of the following problems contain an edit pattern, a source field, an output field in which the editing is to take place, and one or more instruction statements. Analyze the fields and statement(s) and complete the character and hexadecimal format of the output field as it would appear after execution of the statement(s).

20. EDPATA

4 0	2 0	2 0	2 1	2 0	2 0

SOURCEA

0 0	0 0	9 C

RESULTA

C 1	C 2	4 0	4 0	4 0	4 0	4 0

      MVC   RESULTA+1(6),EDPATA
      ED   RESULTA+1(6),SOURCEA

RESULTA (Hex)

(Character)

21. EDPATB

4 0	2 0	2 1	2 0

SOURCEB

3 8	7 C

RESULTB

D 1	F 9	F 9	F 6	F 6	F 8

      .MVC   RESULTB+1(4),EDPATB
      ED   RESULTB+1(4),SOURCEB

RESULTB (Hex)

(Character)

22. EDPATC

4 0	2 1	2 0	2 0	4 B	2 0	2 0

SOURCEC

0 0	0 2	5 8

RESULTC

4 0	4 0	4 0	4 0	4 0	4 0	4 0

      MVC   RESULTC(7),EDPATC
      ED   RESULTC(7),SOURCEC
      MVI   RESULTC,X'5B'

RESULTC (Hex)

(Character)

23. EDPATD | 4 | 0 | 2 | 0 | 2 | 0 | 2 | 0 | 4 | 0 | C | 3 | D | 9

SOURCED | 0 | 8 | 0 | 3 | 6 | C

RESULTD | F | 0 | F | 0 | F | 0 | F | 0 | 4 | 0 | C | 3 | D | 9

```
MVC     RESULTD,EDPATD
ED      RESULTD,SOURCED+1
```

RESULTD (Hex)
(Character)

24. EDPATE | 4 | 0 | 2 | 1 | 4 | B | 2 | 0 | 2 | 0 | C | 3 | D | 9

SOURCEE | 7 | 4 | 8 | D

RESULTE | 4 | 0 | 4 | 0 | 4 | 0 | 4 | 0 | 4 | 0 | C | 4 | D | 9

```
MVC     RESULTE,EDPATE
ED      RESULTE,SOURCEE
```

RESULTE (Hex)
(Character)

25. EDPATF | 5 | C | 2 | 0 | 2 | 1 | 2 | 0 | 2 | 0 | 2 | 0 | 6 | 0

SOURCEF | 0 | 0 | 6 | 2 | 9 | D

RESULTF | 4 | 0 | 4 | 0 | 4 | 0 | 4 | 0 | 4 | 0 | 4 | 0 | 4 | 0

```
MVC     RESULTF,EDPATF
ED      RESULTF,SOURCEF
```

RESULTF (Hex)
(Character)

26. EDPATG | 4 | 0 | 2 | 0 | 2 | 0 | 2 | 1 | 4 | B | 2 | 0 | 2 | 0

SOURCEG | 0 | 6 | 1 | 1 | 7 | D

RESULTG | C | 1 | C | 2 | C | 1 | C | 2 | C | 1 | C | 2 | C | 1

```
LA    1,RESULTG+4
MVC   RESULTG(7),EDPATG
EDMK  RESULTG(7),SOURCEG
SH    1,=H'1'
MVI   0(1),C'$'
```

SULTG (Hex)

(Character)

27. EDPATH

4	0	2	0	2	0	2	1	4	B	2	0	2	0

SOURCEH

0	0	0	3	3	C

RESULTH

4	0	4	0	4	0	4	0	4	0	4	0	4	0

```
LA    1,RESULTH+4
MVC   RESULTH(7),EDPATH
EDMK  RESULTH(7),SOURCEH
SH    1,=H'1'
MVI   0(1),X'5B'
```

SULTH (Hex)

(Character)

PRINTING DATA LISTINGS

In order that the applications explained within this text might be tested under actual computer operating conditions, the general specifications for creating printed output should be discussed at this point. This will enable the programmer to code instruction statements and, if he so desires, print out listings of the data that has been generated by his program.

Some of the routines used in this section will employ the use of Operating System macroinstructions for input/output functions. It must be noted that these macros are applicable only with the Operating System in their expressed form. If the programmer is using any system other than the full Operating System, he will have to be provided with the proper input/output control statements.

A. DEFINING THE OUTPUT AREAS

Data that is to be printed or displayed on an output device is usually arranged and formatted in a program-controlled section of storage that may be referred to as an *output area*. Although various devices are capable of accepting data records of different maximum lengths, this discussion shall relate to a standard printer unit capable of printing up to 132 characters per line. In defining the output area from which the I/O instructions will extract and transmit the data that is to be printed, it will be assumed that this area will consist of 132 bytes of contiguous program storage area.

There are several ways in which the programmer might define the output area. It can be defined as a single 132-byte field or it can be subdefined as a group of smaller fields.

```
          PRTRA      DC      CL132'ƀ'
or as
          PRTRB      DS      OCL132
          FIELD1     DC      CL15'ƀ'
          FIELD2     DC      CL25'ƀ'
          FIELD3     DC      CL10'ƀ'
          FIELD4     DC      CL63'ƀ'
          FIELD5     DC      CL19'ƀ'
```

Data that was to be moved into the PRTRA output area could be located at different places within PRTRA by address-adjusting the first operand of the move statement. This might be coded as:

```
MVC    PRTRA+10(16),DATA1    0001
MVC    PRTRA+35(8),DATA2     0002
MVC    PRTRA+88(12),DATA3    0003
```

Statement 0001 would move 16 bytes of data from the field DATA1 into PRTRA +10, or into the 11th through the 26th bytes of PRTRA.

Statement 0002 would move DATA2 into PRTRA for a length of eight bytes commencing at the 36th byte of PRTRA.

Statement 0003 would move DATA3 into the 88th through the 99th bytes of PRTRA.

Data that was to be moved into the PRTRB output area could either be moved into the subdefined field labels or into the address-adjusted positions of PRTRB. Each of the instruction statements within the following pairs of statements refers to the same address.

```
MVC        FIELD1,AREA1
MVC        PRTRB(15),AREA1

MVC        FIELD3,AREA2
MVC        PRTRB+40(10),AREA2

MVC        FIELD5,AREA3
MVC        PRTRB+113(19),AREA3
```

Quite often, the programmer will find it to his advantage to define the output area as a single constant. This way, he can readily move the data to different locations for each subsequent print line without becoming confused by the subfield descriptions of the labels. On the other hand, a printed listing that follows one or several distinct formats throughout may be more easily understood and manipulated if the output area is defined by specific subfields. A multiple-defined output area can be established as shown in Fig. 16-1.

With the output area PRTROUT defined in this fashion, data can be moved into either type of printed line format as necessary. When the output area is actually printed, it will appear to be in the format into which the data was moved.

Although the output storage area itself has now been explained, it must be noted that a Data Control Block (DCB) macro (or its equivalent) must be coded somewhere within the problem program in order to define the printer output as a data set. The means by which the data set is described varies between the different operating systems—Basic Operating System, Tape Operating System, Disk Operating System, or the full Operating System. For OS, the data set is described by coding a Data Control Block (DCB) macro. This macro contains numerous parameter specifications which, when completed, combine to define most of the information relevent to the type of output data set being utilized. It specifies the length of the records, the record form, the macroinstructions for input/output control that are to be utilized, the input/output options to be used, and many other codes that would be totally unfamiliar to the programmer unless completely analyzed and described. Unfortunately, it is impossible, within the scope of this text, to describe the various macroinstructions used by each of the operating systems. It is assumed that the programmers or students who are studying this text will be divided between the various operating systems. The schools, universities, and industrial locations at which the reader might be located may conceivably have any one, or more, of the four operating systems on their computers. It is, therefore, necessary that any knowledge of the operating systems I/O macros and functional macros be obtained directly from the installation to which the reader is assigned.

For the purpose of identifying an I/O (input/output) macro statement to an output printer device, the OS PUT macro will be used. This macro generates a Queued Sequential Access Method I/O task. An I/O statement of this type would be:

```
PUT     PRTR,PRTAREA
```

The PUT macro defines the I/O task as being initiated to write out a data set (PRTR) using the data contained within the

IBM System/360 Assembler Coding Form

IBM

| PROGRAM | | | | PAGE 1 OF 1 |
| PROGRAMMER | | DATE | | CARD ELECTRO NUMBER |

PUNCHING INSTRUCTIONS — GRAPHIC / PUNCH

X28-6509-2 U/M050
Printed in U.S.A.

```
Name      Operation  Operand
*
PRTROUT   DS         0CL132
AFLD1     DS         CL25
AFLD2     DS         CL10
AFLD3     DS         CL40
AFLD4     DS         CL5
AFLD5     DS         CL42
*
          ORG        PRTROUT
BFLD1     DC         CL12' '
BFLD2     DC         CL38' '
BFLD3     DC         CL9' '
BFLD4     DC         CL38' '
BFLD5     DC         CL15' '
BFLD6     DC         CL20' '
*
*
```

Figure 16-1

storage area PRTAREA. This is a very brief description of this process, but it is intended that full information regarding the operating system macros that are available to the reader will be supplied by the computer center with which he is associated.

B. LINE SPACING AND LINE CONTROL

Another of the features available to the programmer is the ability to control the number of spaces, or blank lines, appearing between the printed lines of his output listing. Printed lines may be single-spaced, double-spaced, triple-spaced, suppressed spacing, or started on a new page. The printed output line spacing can be controlled by a single character representation known as a Carriage Control Symbol. In order for the system to recognize this symbol (when coding under the Operating System), it is

necessary to include the code letter 'A' in the RECFM (Record Form) parameter of the DCB macro. A commonly expressed RECFM parameter used for printer files is:

RECFM=FSA

The code letter 'F' states that the records are fixed length; the 'S' indicates that there should be no "short" blocks or records; the 'A' indicates that Carriage Control Symbols are to be used as part of the output area print line. Once again, it must be stated that the means of advising the system that this type of line space control is to be used will differ among the different operating systems.

If the Carriage Control Symbol is to be used to control line spacing, it must appear in the single byte position immediately preceding the first byte of the data of the record that is to be printed. The character representation of each of the effective Carriage Control Symbols and the resulting action of each are listed as:

Carriage Control Symbol			*Instructs the Printer Carriage to:*
ƀ	(Blank)	X'40'	Space one line before printing data (single-spaced)
0	(Zero)	X'F0'	Space two lines before printing data (double-spaced)
-	(Hyphen)	X'60'	Space three lines before printing data (triple-spaced)
+	(Plus)	X'4E'	Do not space before printing (suppressed spacing)
1	(One)	X'F1'	Go to the beginning of new page before printing the data (page-skip)

Although there are a quantity of other Carriage Control Symbols available, the five listed above are more than sufficient for the use of the text and the novice programmer.

Previously within this section, it was mentioned that the standard-length print line would be considered to consist of a maximum of 132 bytes of data. Accordingly, the output data area was shown as being defined as a 132-byte constant. When using a Carriage Control Symbol, however, the first byte of the defined output area is considered to be that symbol. To allow for 132 bytes of printed data, the output storage area should now be defined as 133 bytes in length—a one-byte Carriage Control Symbol followed by 132 printable data bytes. Here again, the thought of subdefining output data fields becomes applicable. For example:

```
OUTAREA    DS    OCL133
CCSYMB     DC    CL1'ƀ'
DATA       DC    CL132'ƀ'
```

The input/output macro to be used to print out this field of data could be coded as:

```
PUT    PRTR,OUTAREA
```

Even though OUTAREA was specified as the location containing the output data, consisting of 133 bytes, the system has been told, via the RECFM parameter of the DCB, that a Carriage Control Symbol is to be used for printed output. Accordingly, the first byte of OUTAREA (the same as CCSYMB) is interpreted to be the Carriage Control Symbol and the remaining 132 bytes (DATA) are assumed to contain the data that is to be printed.

If the program required an alteration of the line spacing during the printing of a listing, the programmer would only need to code an MVI instruction statement that would move the appropriate symbol into the Carriage Control Symbol byte at the beginning of the print line. To illustrate this, the next example will reflect the effect of altering the Carriage Control Symbol to create different spacings between lines.

The output area is defined as:

```
PRTOUT      DS      0CL133
SYMBOL      DC      CL1'ɸ'
MESSG       DC      CL132'ɸ'
```

In order to represent some printed output data, the message "THIS IS THE WAY DATA LINES ARE SPACED" will be considered as occupying the first 37 bytes of the subfield MESSG. The I/O will be via a standard OS PUT macro referring to an output DCB labeled DEVICE. The instruction statements are:

```
PUT     DEVICE,PRTOUT      00001
PUT     DEVICE,PRTOUT      00002
MVI     SYMBOL,C'0'        00003
PUT     DEVICE,PRTOUT      00004
MVI     SYMBOL,C'-'        00005
PUT     DEVICE,PRTOUT      00006
```

The resulting printed output would appear as:

```
Statement 00001          THIS IS THE WAY DATA LINES ARE SPACED
Statement 00002          THIS IS THE WAY DATA LINES ARE SPACED

Statement 00004          THIS IS THE WAY DATA LINES ARE SPACED


Statement 00006          THIS IS THE WAY DATA LINES ARE SPACED
```

In Statements 00001 and 00002, the Carriage Control Symbol byte contained a valid "blank" so the lines of printed data were single-spaced with no blank lines between them.

Statement 00003 moved a zero into the Carriage Control Symbol byte.

Statement 00004 causes the printer to space two spaces before printing the data line. This double-space created a blank line between the current printed line of data and the one previously printed.

Statement 00005 used the MVI instruction to move a hyphen into the Carriage Control Symbol byte.

Statement 00006, when executed, causes the printer to space three lines before printing the data line.

The "suppress space" Carriage Control Symbol can be used to enable the program to print twice on the same print line. Although this capability may not have many obvious applications, there are occasions when this function can be useful. Double-character configurations, underscoring, and creating of special characters can be accomplished with the "suppress space" feature. Some of these might appear as:

$$\emptyset \quad \theta \quad \div \quad \underline{AB} \quad + \quad +$$

The "page-skip" Carriage Control Symbol is used to start the line of printed data on a new page. There are several ways and equivalent conditions for which this symbol can be applied. It is good program housekeeping to print a title or descriptor data at the top of each page of printed output. If a listing were printed in unbroken sequence, the printed lines would continue across the perforations of the page separations, page after page. It is desirable, therefore, for the program logic to keep count of the number of lines printed per page. By doing this, it can determine when it is time to space forward to the beginning of a new page, print any necessary headings or title lines, and then continue on with the data print lines.

C. PAGE CONTROL

As just indicated in the preceding paragraph, page control is important in producing logical, legible data listings. This is a comparatively easy routine to code, requiring only a knowledge of the size of the printer paper that is to be used for the data listing and the spacing that is to be used for the print lines. The general rules in controlling the number of lines per page are given below:

1. Establish a "counter" into which you can accumulate the number of lines used on each page.

2. After each data line is printed, add the appropriate number to the line counter.

3. Compare the value in the line counter to a constant value that is equal to the maximum number of lines to be printed on each page.

4. If the counter is equal to or greater than the constant, branch to a routine to space to a new page.

5. Otherwise continue processing on that page.

The following set of instruction statements establish a subroutine of this type.

```
LISTING    PUT    PRTR1,OUTAREA          00001
           AP     LINECTR,=PL1'2'        00002
           CP     LINECTR,=PL2'56'       00003
           BC     10,NEWPAGE             00004
LISTDONE   BC     15,GO                  00005
```

Statement 00001 is the PUT macroinstruction statement that will cause the data line to be printed.

Statement 00002 is adding a packed decimal value of +2, expressed as a literal, to the packed decimal line counter. The increment value of +2 is used because this particular report is being printed in double-spaced format, so for every data line printed, a blank line has also been passed.

Statement 00003 is comparing the accumulated count of lines for the current page, as contained in LINECTR, to a packed decimal literal value of +56. This implies that the desired number of lines per page for this program is 56. As a result of this comparison, the PSW Condition Code bits will be set to reflect an "equal," "less than," or "greater than" condition.

Statement 00004 is a conditional branch statement. If the value in LINECTR was equal to or greater than a value +56, a branch would be generated to a subroutine labeled NEWPAGE. Although it is not shown here, the function of the NEWPAGE subroutine would be to:

(a) Space to the beginning of a new page,

(b) Reset the LINECTR to zero,

(c) Print any necessary headings or title lines,

(d) Branch back to LISTDONE.

Statement 00005 is an unconditional branch to another section of the program.

Page control does not necessarily need to be based solely on the number of lines used (either printed or spaced) on a single page. Logical page breaks are just as often the prime reason for skipping ahead to the beginning of a new page. For example, assume that the listing being created by the program represents the purchase orders placed by a quantity of customers. The vendor wishes to start the analysis for each unique customer on a new page so that he may separate the listing by customer number identity and forward a copy of that customer's orders to him for confirmation. The average number of orders placed by each customer is ten; therefore, it would be the rule that the listing for each customer would normally require less than one-half page of printed data. The logic required to properly handle the vendor's request would be that each time a new "customer #" is encountered, the program would branch to a subroutine that skipped ahead to the beginning of a new page and performed whatever headings and title lines were required. The customer's data would be listed until another "customer #" was encountered, at which time the program would branch to the new-page routine, etc.

D. FORMATTING TITLES, HEADINGS, AND SUBHEADINGS

When the program is printing data lists, it is almost always desirable to have each title page begin with a title line that identifies the contents of the listing, the data to which the listing refers, and a page number. Second in priority is the insertion of headings, which may or may not identify the data on that page as being different in classification than data on other pages, but yet falling within the scope of the title of the overall listing. Subheadings are used whenever data lines create columns of items that can be identified by placing a printed explanation at the top of each column.

The formatting and data content of the titles and headings can be widely varied. The decision of how to arrange these items is usually the responsibility of the analysts who have designed the system for which the program is to be written. If prior requirements have not been specified, the programmer is sometimes given the responsibility of the design of the printed output. In this instance, the programmer must strive to create a logical, well-defined listing that will not require cross-referencing to other information sources in order to be understood. The following paragraphs, which describe title lines and headings, are general in nature yet specific enough to create reasonable guidelines for the programmer to follow. There is no "magic formula" to follow—common sense and logic can arrive at a practical data list format.

1. The Title

The title line for any printed listing should be self-explanatory in content. The actual title itself should contain the name of the listing and the name of the system or program to which the report belongs. This might also include the identification number of the program that generates the report if such a number is applicable. For all practical purposes, the name or actual title portion of the title line should be centered in such a way that it will be easily distinguished at first glance. If a 132-byte print line is being used, the midpoint of a corresponding report title line would be the 66th byte. Count the number of characters in the title name, divide that number by '2', then use the quotient as the number of spaces to back-off from the center (the 66th byte) to a point where the title name should begin.

For example:

> Title name equals . . . 38 bytes.
> ½ of name length equals . . . 19 bytes.
> 66th byte less 19 bytes equals . . . 47th byte.
> The title name should begin at the 47th byte of the output field of the title line.

The title line should also contain two other small fields—one for the page number and one for the effective date of the listing. These may be used to "balance" the title name itself (one on either side of it) or they may both be placed on the right-hand side of the page. General systems practices have advocated that both the date and the page number should appear in the top right corner of the report. This has apparently been determined through system studies as being the most obvious point where the average reader will look for that information. These can be arranged as:

DATE: PAGE

In order to supply the page number for each page of a listing, the programmer can maintain another counter or accumulator. Each time that the program logic branches to the "new page" routine, it can add a value of $+1$ to the page counter, edit that value into the title line immediately following the PAGE # field, and then proceed to print the title line.

The date information can be provided from many sources, depending considerably on the programming logic. Some means of obtaining the date are:

1. By control card input at the time that the object program is executed. The program logic should include a routine to read in the control card, extract the date from it, and then move the date into the title line output area.

2. By console typewriter entry to/from the computer operator. The program logic would include a "Write To Operator" message that would request him to supply a date via the console typewriter. The date portion of his reply would be inserted into the title line output area.

3. By extracting the current system date from the computer operating system itself. In most operating systems it is possible for the program logic to interrogate the "supervisor" of the system control program and receive the current system date in reply. This action is all accomplished internally, with no external reference to the task. The only objection to this method is that many data lists contain an effective date other than the date on which the listing was produced.

Although the loading of a date into the title line output area would appear to be a very minor item, it is often necessary to use a date conversion routine to meet the requirements of the personnel using the listing. Sometimes a "Gregorian/Julian" date conversion is necessary; other such conversions are "month/day/year" to "production day," etc. Such dates may appear as:

Month/day/year	November 18, 1969
Month/day/year	11-18-69 or 11/18/69
Year and day-of-year	69-322
Year and production day	69-209
Day/month/year (military)	18 November 1969

Now that the components of the title line have been explained, it would be of assistance to know of a convenient means of establishing that data as a program constant. It is suggested that the title line output area be created as a 133-byte constant, including the Carriage Control Symbol, with each byte of the constant set up in its intended form. The coding statement for this type of constant is shown in Fig. 16-2.

Note that the first byte of the output field is a Carriage Control Symbol of '1', indicating that the printer is to skip to the beginning of a new page before printing the title. This enables the program to skip to a new page by just issuing an I/O instruction to print the title. One of the other advantages of establishing a title line output area as a separate constant from the data output area is that the PUT macro, or its equivalent, can directly reference the TITLE1 area, such as:

```
PUT       PRTR1,TITLE1
```

It is not necessary, therefore, to move the title line information into the data output area in order to print it.

Using the information supplied thus far, the following set of statements are typical of a subroutine to initialize the beginning of a new page.

```
NEWPAGE        AP       PAGECTR,=PL1'1'                    0001
               MVC      TITLE1+126(4),PAGEDIT              0002
               ED       TITLE1+126(4),PAGECTR             0003
               PUT      PRTR1,TITLE1                       0004
               BCR      15,6                              0005
```

This subroutine assumes that the data has already been moved into the TITLE1 field at the initialization of the program and that the program has logically branched to the address of NEWPAGE at this point in order to print the title line for a new page of data.

Statement 0001 is adding a packed decimal literal of +1 to the page count accumulator, the sum of which will be the new page number in packed decimal form.

Statement 0002 is moving an Edit Pattern into the four bytes of TITLE1 that immediately follows the "PAGE #". Information on this editing is provided in the section "Editing Data".

Statement 0003 is editing the packed decimal value from PAGECTR, representing the page number, into the Edit Pattern that was moved into TITLE1 by Statement 0002.

Statement 0004 is the OS PUT macro

IBM

IBM System/360 Assembler Coding Form

| PROGRAM | | | | GRAPHIC | | PAGE 1 OF 1 |
| PROGRAMMER | | DATE | PUNCHING INSTRUCTIONS | PUNCH | | CARD ELECTRO NUMBER |

X28-6509-2 U/M050
Printed in U.S.A.

STATEMENT

Name	Operation	Operand	Comments	Identification-Sequence
*				
*				
TITLE1	DC	CL133'1	PAGE #	title information *
			,	DATE *

Figure 16-2

statement that will transfer the data contents of the title output area labeled TITLE1 to the output printer defined as PRTR1. When this macro-instruction is executed, the printer will skip to the beginning of a new physical page before actually printing the title line.

Statement 0005 is a "Branch On Condition To Register" instruction statement that will cause a forced branch to the address contained in general register 6. That address should be the address of the next instruction following the one that branched to NEW-PAGE.

2. Headings and Subheadings

The distinction between headings and subheadings is a very slight matter of interpretation. What would be considered to be a heading in one listing could also be properly defined as a subheading in another listing. It would not be incorrect to state that "a subheading is a secondary level of heading that further defines the subject matter associated with the primary headings." Because this appears to be a rather ambiguous statement, the following examples of headings and subheadings are used to clarify its intended meaning.

```
Line 1          J.D.S.S.G. MANUFACTURING CO.—PAYROLL ANALYSIS REPORT      PAGE 16

Line 2      EMPLOYEE  1049         EMPLOYEE NAME:    NANCY HUNT

Line 3          PAY PERIOD       HOURS          GROSS          DEDUCTIONS        NET AMOUNT

Line 4              1            40.0         $120.00          $33.15            $86.85
Line 5              2            36.0         $108.00          $21.62            $86.38
Line 6              3            40.0         $120.00          $27.87            $92.13
```

Line 1 is the title line. It indicates the name of the company for whom the report is being created and the type of analysis that the report is listing.

Line 2 may be defined as the heading line. It implies that the report is created with a section or page for each employee. The employee identification number and name are printed as a heading in order to indicate

which employee the subsequent data is related to.

Line 3 is a subheading line, consisting of columnar headings that are used to define that data which appears for the employee named in the heading.

Lines 4, 5, and 6 are the data lines, representing the actual data for the employee.

```
Line 1          J.D.S.S.G. MANUFACTURING CO.—PAYROLL ANALYSIS REPORT

Line 2   EMP. #       NAME      PERIOD    HOURS     GROSS     DEDUCTIONS    NET PAY

Line 3   1049    Nancy Hunt       1       40.0     $120.00     $33.15      $ 86.85
Line 4                            2       36.0     $108.00     $21.62      $ 86.38
Line 5                            3       40.0     $120.00     $27.87      $ 92.13

Line 6   1052    James Warren     1       40.0     $140.00     $26.15      $113.85
Line 7                            2       40.0     $140.00     $20.02      $119.98
Line 8                            3       20.0     $ 70.00     $14.80      $ 55.20
```

In this second example, there appears only one set of headings in addition to the title line. Rather than necessarily starting a new page and a new set of headings each time another employee number is encountered, this listing format has combined the headings and subheadings of Example 1 into a single set of headings. The identity number

and name of the employee is listed only once, at the point where the first line of information for that employee is printed. Line 2 can, therefore, be considered to be a heading or a subheading, depending on the programmer's interpretation of these terms. Generally, a heading can be assumed to be the first definitive print line that follows the

IBM System/360 Assembler Coding Form

X28-6509-2 U/M050
Printed in U.S.A.

PROGRAM _____

PROGRAMMER _____ DATE _____

PUNCHING INSTRUCTIONS GRAPHIC _____ PUNCH _____

```
Name    Operation  Operand / Comments                                          73-80
*
*             DEFINE PRINT-LINE CONSTANTS
*
*
TITLE   DC    CL133'1                              J.D.S.S.G.  MA *
                   NUFACTURING CO. - PAYROLL ANALYSIS REPORT
                   PAGE #'                                       *
*
*
*
HEADING DC    CL133'0      EMPLOYEE #              EMPLOYEE NA *
              ME'                                              *
*
*
*
SUBHEAD DC    CL133'0   PAY PERIOD   HOURS        GROSS        *
                   DEDUCTIONS    NET PAY'                      *
*
*
```

Figure 16-3

title line, and subheadings may be defined as any subsequent lines that further define preceding headings or subheadings. A number of subheading lines may be used if necessary to establish the analysis and identification of the report data lines. This is shown in the next example.

Example 3. This example uses the third line of Example 1 and relates the association of a subheading line to subsequent subheadings.

	PAY PERIOD	HOURS	GROSS	DEDUCTIONS			NET PAY
Line 3	PAY PERIOD	HOURS	GROSS	DEDUCTIONS			NET PAY
Line 4				F.I.C.A.	WITHHOLDING TAX	OTHER	
Line 5	1	40.0	$120.00	5.55	22.15	5.45	$86.85
Line 6	2	36.0	$108.00	5.00	16.62	.00	$86.38

In this example, the columnar heading "Deductions" has been further broken down into additional subheadings.

Regardless of the programmer's interpretation or definition of headings and subheadings, they may be established as fixed or variable constants in the same manner as the title lines are originated. A 133-byte constant is coded for each heading line that is to be printed, leaving blanks wherever variable heading data is to be inserted. Using the title line, heading, and subheading illustrated for the "J.D.S.S.G. Manufacturing Co." in Example 1, the coding of the Define Constant (DC) statements could be illustrated as shown in Fig. 16-3.

The spacing of the headings represented by these DC statements is not identical to those shown in Example 1. However, all three types of definitive lines have been effectively created by these statements and each may be directly specified as an output area associated with an output device Data Control Block. If only one output area had been designated for the listing it would be necessary to move each set of data into that output area prior to issuing the PUT macro to print that line. By establishing the three output areas for the title and headings, the data may be listed by issuing three consecutive PUT statements.

```
PUT    PRTDEV,TITLE          00001
PUT    PRTDEV,HEADING        00002
PUT    PRTDEV,SUBHEAD        00003
```

Statement 00001 will print the title line. Because the first byte of the constant TITLE is a '1', the printer unit will skip to the beginning of a new page prior to printing.

Statement 00002 will space two lines and will then print the data contained within the constant HEADING.

Statement 00003 will space two lines and then print the constant SUBHEAD.

Although it was not shown as a part of these statements, the programmer would also have coded the necessary instruction statements to move a page number into the TITLE constant and to move the employee number and employee name into the HEADING constant prior to printing those lines.

The practice of creating more than one output area constant for any given output device applies equally well whenever it is needed. It is not limited in its application to the data list titles and headings as shown herein. Separations between logical groups of printed data can be emphasized by inserting a print line consisting of asterisks or hyphens. Larger gaps of blank lines within a single page can be created by the repeated issuance of a PUT instruction that references a print line of blanks, the Carriage Control Symbol consisting of a hyphen, indicating the request to skip three lines before printing.

In much the same manner, multiple display screen formats for a cathode-ray display device may be established as individual output areas. Each output area is called on as the screen format of data contained within it is required.

The design capabilities and common sense of the programmer are often thoroughly tested when the formatting of printed or displayed data lists are entirely his responsibility.

DATA VALIDATION

INSTRUCTION: TRANSLATE

Mnemonic	Hex Code	Operand Format
TR	DC	$D_1(L,B_1),D_2(B_2)$

This instruction can be used to convert from one bit configuration code to another bit configuration code. This is applicable as long as both codes refer to a configuration of eight bits or less. It can be used to translate ASCII codes, EBCDIC, paper tape transmission codes, or any code application required by the user, just as long as the configuration requirements are met. The first operand of the statement specifies the location of the data to be translated and the second operand specifies the beginning location of a translate table.

A translate table would normally consist of 256 contiguous bytes of storage containing the "translated to" data. Provision should be made to allow for all of the 256 possible eight-bit hexadecimal configurations—X'00' through X'FF'. The table would be estab-lished by the user to conform to the particular code that he wishes to convert his data to. The sequence of the table would be arranged in the hex value of the character that he is translating *from*, but that table position would contain the bit configuration of the coded character that he is translating *to*.

This instruction will then take the beginning address of the translate table, increment the low-order bits of that address by the hexadecimal value of the character to be translated, go to the total incremented address, pick up the one-byte configuration of the translated code and replace the original character bit configuration with the one that it has just picked up from the translate table.

The movement of the translate is from left to right, one byte at a time, through the data field specified by the first operand for the implied, or specified, length of that field.

The Condition Code setting is not altered by this instruction.

* * *

INSTRUCTION:

TRANSLATE AND TEST

Mnemonic	Hex Code	Operand Format
TRT	DD	$D_1(L,B_1),D_2(B_2)$

This instruction performs similarly to the TRANSLATE instruction except that it terminates operation once a byte in the translate table is scanned that does not contain a value of hexadecimal '00' configuration. The instruction is used primarily to scan a set of data for special characters and to return information to the user when such a character is encountered. The field containing the data to be scanned is specified by the first operand and the translate table beginning address is specified by the second operand.

Referring to the characters in the first operand as the "check" characters, the translate table should be arranged in the hexadecimal sequence of those characters. Provision should be made to allow for all of the 256 possible eight-bit hexadecimal configurations—X'00' through X'FF'. For the characters that are not to be flagged, a hexadecimal value of '00' should be built into the table segment that is addressed by that character. Each character that is to be flagged should have a unique eight-bit configuration built into the table segment that is addressed by that character. The TRT instruction will then begin checking each character (from left to right) of the data field specified by the first operand, against the translate table. If the table segment for that character contains a X'00' value, the instruction will continue on to check the next character, etc. However, once the instruction statement checks a character and finds that the appropriate table segment is not a X'00' value, the instruction discontinues the scan. It will then insert the low-order 24 bits of the address of the "check character" into general register 1 and insert the contents of the unique table segment for that character into the low-order eight bits (one byte) of general register 2. The Condition Code is then set and the instruction terminates.

CC	BC	Condition
0	8	All of the table segments encountered were X'00'.
1	4	A nonzero table segment was encountered prior to the last "check character" in the first operand of the statement.
2	2	The last check character in the first operand of the statement had a nonzero table segment.

A. DATA VALIDATION

Almost every commercial program, in one way or another, requires that a certain amount of auditing and certification of data be accomplished. This can range from a single "compare" statement to a very complex auditing subroutine certifying data as a numeric value or as to its character contents. Auditing and validation of this type is required for many reasons, some of which are given below.

1. To inspect input data as to its category, such as when there are several classes of input and each class has its own unique processing routines.

2. To audit numeric values for valid configurations. This might include checking for the positive or negative configuration of a value or determining its magnitude to confirm that it exceeds or fails to meet a minimum value.

3. Auditing for special characters. One such application would be to ascertain that an EBCDIC numeric field does not contain any blanks prior to a pack operation.

4. Searching for certain characters which, if found, are to be converted into another character or set of characters or, in some instances, are to be eliminated altogether.

There are probably hundreds of reasons for unique auditing and validation of data, and an equal or greater number of ways to accomplish those tasks within Assembler Language programming. This section of the text will strive to point out a few of the applicable techniques that might be used to accomplish this and to establish the general groundwork that could provide the programmer with some ideas for developing auditing and validation techniques of his own. It must be mentioned once again that there is more than one "correct" programming answer to every problem that is to be solved—and the configuration of the computer system and available core storage is often the limiting factor as to the efficiency of that answer.

1. Validation of Numeric Values

The validation of numeric or decimal value representation might take many variable forms. Rather than attempting to define these possibilities through many sentences of explanations and descriptions, examples of

```
CHECKAMT     DC        F'0'
*
AUDIT        CLI       CHECKAMT,X'80'      0001
             BC        4,POSVALUE          0002
             MVC       CHECKAMT,=F'0'      0003
POSVALUE     - -       - - - - - - -       0004
             - -       - - - - - - -
```

Statement 0001 is the first instruction statement in the audit subroutine and is addressed by reference to the symbolic label AUDIT. The Compare Logical Immediate (CLI) instruction statement will determine whether or not the left-most bit of the high-order byte (the sign-bit) is a one-bit or a zero-bit. The immediate character of the second operand of this statement represents a bit configuration of '1000 0000'. Because a negative fixed-point value will contain a one-bit sign-bit, this comparison will result in the PSW Condition Code defining that status of the fullword value. If CHECKAMT is a negative value the Condition Code will be set to indicate an "equal" or "greater than" condition.

Statement 0002 is a test of the Condition Code and a branch to POSVALUE if the Condition Code indicates that the first byte of CHECKAMT was less than X'80'. If the first byte of CHECKAMT was not less than X'80', indicating that CHECKAMT contained a negative value, the branch would not be taken and the processing logic would

several types of decimal value validation tasks are to be presented. In each instance the reason for the auditing will be explained, sets of instruction statements will be illustrated, and an explanation of the action generated by the coding will be offered.

Task 1. A fullword value, supplied by another portion of the problem program, is to be tested for a negative value configuration. If the fullword is a positive value, it is acceptable; if the fullword is a negative value, it must be deleted and replaced with a plus-zero value. The first item in the coding, CHECKAMT, is a fullword defined constant that will be supplied with a fixed-point value by the program prior to entering the audit routine.

fall through to Statement 0003.

Statement 0003 assumes that because the processing logic has entered this instruction statement, CHECKAMT must contain a negative value. According to the requirements of the task, a negative value must be deleted and replaced with a plus-zero value. The Move Character instruction will move a four-byte fullword, containing a plus-zero value, into CHECKAMT.

Statement 0004, addressed by the symbolic label POSVALUE, would contain whatever instruction was the next step in the program logic. If CHECKAMT contained a positive value, this statement would have been entered via the branch from Statement 0002.

Task 2. In this program logic, a value has previously been loaded into general register 6. The audit subroutine is to reverse the positive/negative configuration of that value if the integer portion is greater than 32,768; otherwise, the configuration of the value is to remain unaltered.

CHEXRTE	LPR	5,6	0001
	C	5,=F'32768'	0002
	BC	12,NOTGREAT	0003
	LCR	6,6	0004
NOTGREAT	– –	– – – – –	0005
	– –	– – – – –	

Statement 0001 is the opening instruction of this subroutine. It will take the value that is contained in general register 6, regardless of its configuration, and load it in its positive form into general register 5. This will allow the integer portion of that value to be tested with a single compare statement.

Statement 0002 is comparing the value contained in general register 5 to a fullword fixed-point value literal of +32,768. The PSW Condition Code will reflect the high, low or equal result of this comparison.

Statement 0003 tests the result of the comparison made within Statement 0002 by requesting that a branch to NOTGREAT be made if general register 5 contained a value that was equal to or less than 32,768. If register 5 contained a value that was greater than 32,768, the processing would fall through to Statement 0004.

Statement 0004 assumes that the integer value in general register 6, regardless of its positive or negative configuration, is greater than 32,768. In accordance with the task logic, the Load Complement Register (LCR) instruction statement will load the current value contained within general register 6 back into register 6 in its complemented form. If the value was originally positive, it will be reloaded as a negative configuration; if it was originally a negative configuration, it will be loaded in its positive complement.

Statement 0005 represents the next logic step that is to be executed by the program. This statement would have been entered by the branch from Statement 0003 or by natural sequence through Statement 0004.

Task 3. This subroutine is to be passed a series of packed decimal values, each of which may vary in length from two to four bytes, and may or may not contain a valid packed decimal sign in the right-most half-byte. Two objectives are to be accomplished:

1. All values are to be expanded to a five-byte packed decimal without altering the decimal value itself;
2. Any unsigned values are to be supplied with a hexadecimal 'C' in the right-most half-byte, representing a packed decimal positive sign.

At the time that this subroutine receives the incoming packed decimals they have already been left-aligned into a four-byte field that is referred to by the symbolic label INFIELD and the byte-length of the value has been placed into general register 8 in fixed-point form. (See Fig. 17-1*a* and *b*.)

The general logic of this set of statements accomplishes the task as requested, but requires an application that modifies the length and displacement parameters within an instruction statement.

Statement 0901, SIGNCHEX, is using the Load Address instruction to place a fixed-point value of +4 into general register 9. Because the length of the packed decimal value that is to be passed is contained in general register 8, that value will be subtracted from register 9 in order to determine the displacement factor for moving the packed decimal into its receiving field.

Statement 0902 is subtracting the length of the packed decimal value, that length being contained in general register 8, from the maximum possible length of four as contained in general register 9. The result of this subtraction will provide a displacement increment if the length of the packed decimal value is less than four.

Statement 0903 will subtract the halfword fixed-point literal of +1 from the value in general register 8. This is preparing that value for insertion as a machine-language length into the instruction statement that will move the incoming packed decimal field into its receiving field.

IBM

IBM System/360 Assembler Coding Form

X28-6509-2 U/M050
Printed in U.S.A.

| PROGRAM | | | | GRAPHIC | | PAGE 1 OF 2 |
| PROGRAMMER | | DATE | | PUNCH | | CARD ELECTRO NUMBER |

PUNCHING INSTRUCTIONS

Name	Operation	Operand / Comments	Identification-Sequence
*			0880
*			0881
*		DEFINED WORK AREAS	0882
			0883
			0884
LENGTH	DC	XL1'00'	0885
PACK5	DC	PL5'0'	0886
PACK1	DC	PL1'0'	0887
SIGNTEST	DC	XL1'00'	0888
OUTPACK	DC	PL5'0'	0889
			0890
*			0891
*		AUDIT SUBROUTINE	0892
*			0893
*			0900
SIGNCHEX	LA	9,4	0901
	SR	9,8	0902
	SH	8,=H'1'	0903
	STC	8,LENGTH	0904
	ZAP	PACK5(5),=PL1'0'	0906
	LA	10,PACK5+1	0907
	MVC	LOADVAL+1(1),LENGTH	0908
	AR	10,9	0909
LOADVAL	MVC	0(1,10),INFIELD	0910

Figure 17-1a

460

IBM

IBM System/360 Assembler Coding Form

PROGRAM

PROGRAMMER DATE

PUNCHING INSTRUCTIONS | GRAPHIC | | PUNCH

PAGE 2 OF 2

CARD ELECTRO NUMBER

X28-6509-2 U/M050
Printed in U.S.A.

Name	Operation	Operand / Comments	Identification-Sequence
	MVN	SIGNTEST(1),PACK5+4	0911
	CLI	SIGNTEST,X'09'	0912
	BC	12,NOTVALID	0913
	ZAP	OUTPACK(5),PACK5	0914
	BC	15,VALID	0915
NOTVALID	MVI	PACK1,X'0C'	0916
	MVO	PACK5(6),PACK5(5)	0917
	ZAP	OUTPACK(5),PACK5+1	0918
VALID	BC	15,COMPLETE	0919
*			0920
*			0921
*			0922

Figure 17-1b

461

Statement 0904 is storing the low-order byte of general register 8, containing the machine-language length of the packed decimal field, into a one-byte storage area labeled LENGTH.

Statement 0906 clears the five-byte packed decimal field to a value of +0 each time this subroutine is entered. This will assure that all high-order bytes of this receiving field are zero-digits.

Statement 0907 loads the address of the second byte of the packed decimal receiving field into general register 10. This address, plus the displacement increment contained in register 9, should properly align the packed decimal value that is to be moved into the PACK5 field.

Statement 0908 will move the machine-language length of the incoming packed decimal value from its storage byte into the second byte of the instruction statement that actually moves the value into PACK5.

Statement 0909 adds register 9, containing the displacement increment, to the contents of general register 10. Register 10 now addresses the byte of the PACK5 field that is to receive the value from INFIELD.

Statement 0910, having been modified by Statements 0908 and 0909, will move the proper number of left-aligned packed decimal bytes from INFIELD into the proper right-aligned bytes of PACK5. The correct number of bytes was inserted from the LENGTH field in Statement 0908—the alignment was adjusted by adding in the displacement increment from register 9 by Statement 0909.

Statement 0911 is utilizing a Move Numeric instruction statement to move the right-most half-byte of PACK5 into a storage work area.

Statement 0912 is comparing a one-byte area, containing a high-order hex digit of '0' and a low-order hex digit consisting of the half-byte passed to this field in Statement 0911, to a hexadecimal literal of X'09'. This comparison is made to determine whether or not the packed decimal value in PACK5 contains a sign-digit in the low-order half-byte.

Statement 0913 requests that a branch be taken to NOTVALID if the comparison in Statement 0912 indicated that the low-order half-byte of PACK5 contained a hex digit of X'9' or less. That condition would indicate that it was not a packed decimal sign-digit. If that digit was a valid sign-digit the processing logic would fall through to Statement 0914.

Statement 0914 will Zero & Add Packed (ZAP) all five bytes of PACK5 into the outgoing packed decimal field. Regardless of the byte length of the value when it was moved into PACK5 by Statement 0910, it will be put out as a five-byte field containing high-order packed decimal zero-digits.

Statement 0915 is a forced branch to the exit statement for this subroutine.

Statement 0916, NOTVALID, is entered if the branch in Statement 0913 was taken. This would indicate that the packed decimal value in PACK5 does not contain a valid sign in the low-order half-byte. The statement itself is moving a hex value of X'0C' into the single byte that immediately follows PACK5 in order to reinitialize that byte each time this routine is entered. The hex 'C' digit will supply the standard packed decimal positive sign to the value in PACK5.

Statement 0917 is using the Move With Offset (MVO) instruction to literally shift the packed decimal value that is in PACK5 to the right by one-half byte and into the high-order half-byte of PACK1. This places that value immediately in conjunction with the hex 'C' digit residing in the low-order half-byte of PACK1, effectively creating a validly signed packed decimal value that now ranges from PACK5+1 through PACK1.

Statement 0918 uses the Zero & Add Packed (ZAP) instruction to move the right-most five bytes of the combined six-byte length of PACK5 and PACK1 into the outgoing five-byte packed decimal field.

Statement 0919, VALID, is the exit from this entire subroutine. It consists of an unconditional branch to an assumed routine that is labeled COMPLETE.

It is suggested that the reader originate several packed decimal values of varying lengths of from one to four bytes, both signed and unsigned, and follow the process of that data through this subroutine.

Task 4. In this task, the subroutine will be passed a validly signed six-byte packed deci-mal number. If the passed value contains any low-order zero-digits, they are to be deleted by shifting all other high-order digits to the right one-half byte at a time until a signifi-cant digit shares the low-order byte with the sign-digit. For example, if the incoming field contained a packed decimal configuration of:

0	0	6	0	4	5	0	9	0	0	0	C

it should pass through the subroutine and be modified so that its configuration is:

0	0	0	0	0	6	0	4	5	0	9	C

The field is collapsed in half-byte incre-ments until the first significant hex digit is placed adjacent to the sign-digit. If the re-sulting field is a zero-value, the program logic is to go to a special routine labeled ZEROVALU.

The instruction statements comprising this routine are:

```
TESTPACK    DC      PL6'0'                          04000
*
TESTRTE     ZAP     TESTPACK,INFIELD                04001
            LA      4,11                            04002
LOOPIN      TM      TESTPACK+5,X'F0'                04003
            BC      5,TESTDONE                      04004
            MVO     TESTPACK(6),TESTPACK(5)         04005
            BCT     4,LOOPIN                        04006
            BC      15,ZEROVALU                     04007
```

Statement 04001, the entry statement into this subroutine, uses the Zero & Add Packed instruction to move the incoming packed decimal value into the work area labeled TESTPACK.

Statement 04002 is utilizing the Load Address instruction to place a fixed-point value of $+11$ into general register 4. Register 4 will be the loop control counter register for the BCT instruction in Statement 04006.

Statement 04003 will test the left-most four bits of the low-order byte of TEST-PACK. The X'F0' operand of the Test Under Mask instruction statement will only cause a one-bit result-bit if any of the left-most four bit positions of the right-most byte of TESTPACK have a corresponding one-bit.

Statement 04004 is a conditional branch instruction. It states that if the result of the TM instruction in Statement 04003 indi-cated that one or more one-bits were found in the left-most four bit positions of TEST-PACK+5, the program logic would branch out of this statement to TESTDONE. This would indicate that the packed decimal digit currently residing immediately to the left of the sign-digit was a value other than a zero-digit.

Statement 04005 will perform a Move With Offset instruction. All half-bytes within TESTPACK will be effectively moved to the right by one-half byte except for the low-order byte. The digit immediately to the left of the sign-digit will be replaced by the digit to its left and so on, up through the length of TESTPACK. The vacated high-order digit position of the field will be supplied with a zero-digit.

Statement 04006 is the Branch On Count (BCT) instruction that creates the loop control back to the LOOPIN statement. General register 4 was loaded with a value of $+11$, equal to the number of numeric digits in the six-byte packed decimal field of TEST-PACK. Each time the processing logic passes through this statement, the BCT instruction would reduce general register 4 by a value of $+1$. If general register 4 became decremented to zero, the processing logic would not branch, but would fall through to Statement 04007. This would indicate that all eleven numeric digit positions of TEST-PACK were inspected without encountering a significant digit.

Statement 04007 is a forced branch to a routine labeled ZEROVAL. In order to get to this instruction statement, the processing logic had to fall through the BCT instruction statement. This would indicate that the original value in TESTPACK was, and still is, a total of zero.

Carefully inspect the following set of instruction statements and evaluate what difference they could have in performing the same task as the foregoing statements.

```
TESTRTE    ZAP    TESTPACK,INFIELD           05001
           CP     TESTPACK,=PL6'0'           05002
           BC     8,ZEROVALU                 05003
LOOPIN     TM     TESTPACK+5,X'F0'           05004
           BC     5,TESTDONE                 05005
           MVO    TESTPACK(6),TESTPACK(5)    05006
           BC     15,LOOPIN
```

This set of instruction statements are equal in quantity to the previous set of statements, but would probably result in less processing time if any input values of zero were encountered. The logic contained in Statements 05002 and 05003 would detect any overall zero values before entering the test loop, rather than processing through the test loop eleven times before concluding that TEST-PACK contained a zero value. The Load Address (LA) and Branch On Count (BCT) instruction statements are no longer necessary inasmuch as it is known that if a value enters the testing loop, at least one digit position of that value contains a significant digit.

2. Auditing for Special Characters or Conditions

Because of the wide range of potential applications for this type of task, it would be impractical to give any typical examples. The tasks illustrated within this subject are merely a means of familiarizing the reader with the overall scope of such routines.

In most instances, a routine calling for special auditing techniques is aimed at transforming or converting one form of existing data into another representation or form. An example of this could be that a unique data file contains a number of different unprintable characters that are necessary for the interpretation of the data on that file when it is listed in printed form. Unless these unprintable configuration were interpreted into some type of printable character, or combination of printable characters, each one would appear as a blank position on a printed listing.

If the problem program logic for auditing data also requires a conversion of invalid characters to valid characters, the Translate instruction provides an exceptional service.

(a) **Translate.** The Translate instruction utilizes a table consisting of 256 bytes, each byte representing one of the 256 hexadecimal configurations that are available in System/360. Each table byte is considered to be an individual table segment whose displacement from the beginning of the table is addressed by the binary value of its hexadecimal representation. For example, if the translate table started at core location 32,000, then X'00' would represent the first table segment (32000), X'01' would represent the second table segment (32001), X'02' would represent the third table segment (32002), X'03' would represent the fourth (32003), X'04' would represent the fifth (32004), etc. Each byte (segment) of this table, however, does not necessarily contain the same hexadecimal configuration as the configuration implied by its relative location to the beginning of the table.

In effect the Translate instruction does the following:

1. Takes a byte of data specified by the first operand of the instruction statement.

2. Adds the binary value of that byte to the address of the translate table, which is referred to by the second operand.

3. Goes to the table segment referenced by this incremented address.

4. Extracts the resident character from that segment and places it into the first op-

erand field in the byte that was used to find the relative table segment position.

The first operand field may consist of multiple bytes, in which case each byte will be used to address a table segment in order to extract the byte representation from that segment.

In order to illustrate the use of this instruction, assume that a program is to be written that will delete all punctuation and symbols from data fields by replacing such characters with a slash or diagonal bar. This would mean that any bytes of the table whose relative position to the beginning of the table generated a hex value synonomous to a valid EBCDIC punctuation symbol or character symbol should contain the hexadecimal configuration for a diagonal. The standard EBCDIC configuration for this character is X'61'. Accordingly, the following relative bytes of the table would contain a hexadeci-

Hex Configuration for EBCDIC Punctuation Symbol or Character Symbol	Character Represented by that Configuration		Relative Byte Position of the Table that Will Contain X'61'
4A	Cent sign	¢	4A
4B	Period	.	4B
4C	Less than	<	4C
4D	Left parenthesis	(	4D
4E	Plus sign	+	4E
4F	Concatenate symbol			4F
50	Ampersand	&	50
5A	Exclamation	!	5A
5B	Dollar sign	$	5B
5C	Asterisk	*	5C
5D	Right parenthesis	)	5D
5E	Semicolon	;	5E
5F	Not sign	⌐	5F
60	Dash	–	60
61	Diagonal	/	61
6B	Comma	,	6B
6C	Percent	%	6C
6D	Bar	—	6D
6E	Greater than	>	6E
6F	Question mark	?	6F
7A	Colon	:	7A
7B	Pound sign	#	7B
7C	At sign	@	7C
7D	Apostrophe	'	7D
7E	Equal sign	=	7E
7F	Quote sign	"	7F

mal configuration of X'61'.

All other segments of the table would contain the standard EBCDIC character representations. There are three tables illustrated for the purpose of explaining this concept.

Translate Table 1 (Table 17-1) represents the 256 individual segments used within the table. The hex values shown within each segment represents the binary value of the relative position of that segment to the beginning of the table. The implied decimal representation of that binary value is also included in each segment.

Translate Table 2 (Table 17-2), representing the same 256 segments, illustrates the contents of the table if each segment contained the hexadecimal configuration that is implied by the relative position of the segment to the beginning of the table. In this instance the EBCDIC character representations have been included where applicable.

Translate Table 3 (Table 17-3) represents the modified table that the programmer would establish for this particular application. Note that the contents of the EBCDIC punctuation symbols and symbol character segments have now been established to contain a value of X'61'—a diagonal.

In the coding statements shown in Fig. 17-2a and b, there will be four fields of data processed through the Translate instruction

TABLE 17-1. Translate Table 1

X'00'a 0b	X'01' 1	X'02' 2	X'03' 3	X'04' 4	X'05' 5	X'06' 6	X'07' 7	X'08' 8	X'09' 9	X'0A' 10	X'0B' 11	X'0C' 12	X'0D' 13	X'0E' 14	X'0F' 15
X'10' 16·	X'11' 17	X'12' 18	X'13' 19	X'14' 20	X'15' 21	X'16' 22	X'17' 23	X'18' 24	X'19' 25	X'1A' 26	X'1B' 27	X'1C' 28	X'1D' 29	X'1E' 30	X'1F' 31
X'20' 32	X'21' 33	X'22' 34	X'23' 35	X'24' 36	X'25' 37	X'26' 38	X'27' 39	X'28' 40	X'29' 41	X'2A' 42	X'2B' 43	X'2C' 44	X'2D' 45	X'2E' 46	X'2F' 47
X'30' 48	X'31' 49	X'32' 50	X'33' 51	X'34' 52	X'35' 53	X'36' 54	X'37' 55	X'38' 56	X'39' 57	X'3A' 58	X'3B' 59	X'3C' 60	X'3D' 61	X'3E' 62	X'3F' 63
X'40' 64	X'41' 65	X'42' 66	X'43' 67	X'44' 68	X'45' 69	X'46' 70	X'47' 71	X'48' 72	X'49' 73	X'4A' 74	X'4B' 75	X'4C' 76	X'4D' 77	X'4E' 78	X4F' 79
X'50' 80	X'51' 81	X'52' 82	X'53' 83	X'54' 84	X'55' 85	X'56' 86	X'57' 87	X'58' 88	X'59' 89	X'5A' 90	X'5B' 91	X'5C' 92	X'5D' 93	X'5E' 94	X'5F' 95
X'60' 96	X'61' 97	X'62' 98	X'63' 99	X'64' 100	X'65' 101	X'66' 102	X'67' 103	X'68' 104	X'69' 105	X'6A' 106	X'6B' 107	X'6C' 108	X'6D' 109	X'6E' 110	X'6F' 111
X'70' 112	X'71' 113	X'72' 114	X'73' 115	X'74' 116	X'75' 117	X'76' 118	X'77' 119	X'78' 120	X'79' 121	X'7A' 122	X'7B' 123	X'7C' 124	X'7D' 125	X'7E' 126	X'7F' 127
X'80' 128	X'81' 129	X'82' 130	X'83' 131	X'84' 132	X'85' 133	X'86' 134	X'87' 135	X'88' 136	X'89' 137	X'8A' 138	X'8B' 139	X'8C' 140	X'8D' 141	X'8E' 142	X'8F' 143
X'90' 144	X'91' 145	X'92' 146	X'93' 147	X'94' 148	X'95' 149	X'96' 150	X'97' 151	X'98' 152	X'99' 153	X'9A' 154	X'9B' 155	X'9C' 156	X'9D' 157	X'9E' 158	X'9F' 159
X'A0' 160	X'A1' 161	X'A2' 162	X'A3' 163	X'A4' 164	X'A5' 165	X'A6' 166	X'A7' 167	X'A8' 168	X'A9' 169	X'AA' 170	X'AB' 171	X'AC' 172	X'AD' 173	X'AE' 174	X'AF' 175
X'B0' 176	X'B1' 177	X'B2' 178	X'B3' 179	X'B4' 180	X'B5' 181	X'B6' 182	X'B7' 183	X'B8' 184	X'B9' 185	X'BA' 186	X'BB' 187	X'BC' 188	X'BD' 189	X'BE' 190	X'BF' 191
X'C0' 192	X'C1' 193	X'C2' 194	X'C3' 195	X'C4' 196	X'C5' 197	X'C6' 198	X'C7' 199	X'C8' 200	X'C9' 201	X'CA' 202	X'CB' 203	X'CC' 204	X'CD' 205	X'CE' 206	X'CF' 207
X'D0' 208	X'D1' 209	X'D2' 210	X'D3' 211	X'D4' 212	X'D5' 213	X'D6' 214	X'D7' 215	X'D8' 216	X'D9' 217	X'DA' 218	X'DB' 219	X'DC' 220	X'DD' 221	X'DE' 222	X'DF' 223
X'E0' 224	X'E1' 225	X'E2' 226	X'E3' 227	X'E4' 228	X'E5' 229	X'E6' 230	X'E7' 231	X'E8' 232	X'E9' 233	X'EA' 234	X'EB' 235	X'EC' 236	X'ED' 237	X'EE' 238	X'EF' 239
X'F0' 240	X'F1' 241	X'F2' 242	X'F3' 243	X'F4' 244	X'F5' 245	X'F6' 246	X'F7' 247	X'F8' 248	X'F9' 249	X'FA' 250	X'FB' 251	X'FC' 252	X'FD' 253	X'FE' 254	X'FF' 255

a Relative position of segment in hex.
b Binary equivalent in decimal.

TABLE 17-2. Translate Table 2—Standard Hexadecimal Configurations and Corresponding EBCDIC Representation.

X'00'[a]	X'01'	X'02'	X'03'	X'04'	X'05'	X'06'	X'07'	X'08'	X'09'	X'0A'	X'0B'	X'0C'	X'0D'	X'0E'	X'0F'
X'10'	X'11'	X'12'	X'13'	X'14'	X'15'	X'16'	X'17'	X'18'	X'19'	X'1A'	X'1B'	X'1C'	X'1D'	X'1E'	X'1F'
X'20'	X'21'	X'22'	X'23'	X'24'	X'25'	X'26'	X'27'	X'28'	X'29'	X'2A'	X'2B'	X'2C'	X'2D'	X'2E'	X'2F'
X'30'	X'31'	X'32'	X'33'	X'34'	X'35'	X'36'	X'37'	X'38'	X'39'	X'3A'	X'3B'	X'3C'	X'3D'	X'3E'	X'3F'
X'40' b[b]	X'41'	X'42'	X'43'	X'44'	X'45'	X'46'	X'47'	X'48'	X'49'	X'4A' ¢	X'4B' .	X'4C' <	X'4D' (	X'4E' +	X'4F' |
X'50' &	X'51'	X'52'	X'53'	X'54'	X'55'	X'56'	X'57'	X'58'	X'59'	X'5A' !	X'5B' $	X'5C' *	X'5D')	X'5E' ;	X'5F' →
X'60' -	X'61' /	X'62'	X'63'	X'64'	X'65'	X'66'	X'67'	X'68'	X'69'	X'6A'	X'6B' ,	X'6C' %	X'6D' —	X'6E' >	X'6F' ?
X'70'	X'71'	X'72'	X'73'	X'74'	X'75'	X'76'	X'77'	X'78'	X'79'	X'7A' :	X'7B' #	X'7C' @	X'7D' '	X'7E' =	X'7F' "
X'80'	X'81' a	X'82' b	X'83' c	X'84' d	X'85' e	X'86' f	X'87' g	X'88' h	X'89' i	X'8A'	X'8B'	X'8C'	X'8D'	X'8E'	X'8F'
X'90'	X'91' j	X'92' k	X'93' l	X'94' m	X'95' n	X'96' o	X'97' p	X'98' q	X'99' r	X'9A'	X'9B'	X'9C'	X'9D'	X'9E'	X'9F'
X'A0'	X'A1'	X'A2' s	X'A3' t	X'A4' u	X'A5' v	X'A6' w	X'A7' x	X'A8' y	X'A9' z	X'AA'	X'AB'	X'AC'	X'AD'	X'AE'	X'AF'
X'B0'	X'B1'	X'B2'	X'B3'	X'B4'	X'B5'	X'B6'	X'B7'	X'B8'	X'B9'	X'BA'	X'BB'	X'BC'	X'BD'	X'BE'	X'BF'
X'C0'	X'C1' A	X'C2' B	X'C3' C	X'C4' D	X'C5' E	X'C6' F	X'C7' G	X'C8' H	X'C9' I	X'CA'	X'CB'	X'CC'	X'CD'	X'CE'	X'CF'
X'D0'	X'D1' J	X'D2' K	X'D3' L	X'D4' M	X'D5' N	X'D6' O	X'D7' P	X'D8' Q	X'D9' R	X'DA'	X'DB'	X'DC'	X'DD'	X'DE'	X'DF'
X'E0'	X'E1'	X'E2' S	X'E3' T	X'E4' U	X'E5' V	X'E6' W	X'E7' X	X'E8' Y	X'E9' Z	X'EA'	X'EB'	X'EC'	X'ED'	X'EE'	X'EF'
X'F0' 0	X'F1' 1	X'F2' 2	X'F3' 3	X'F4' 4	X'F5' 5	X'F6' 6	X'F7' 7	X'F8' 8	X'F9' 9	X'FA'	X'FB'	X'FC'	X'FD'	X'FE'	X'FF'

[a] Hex contents of each segment.
[b] EBCDIC representation.

using the illustration of Translate Table 3 (Table 17-3). These four fields are FIELDA, FIELDB, FIELDC, and FIELDD. For the purpose of this example, these fields have been defined as constants. In a real application, however, the data to be audited would be continually replenished into a work area.

Statement 04001, TRANSOUT, loads general register 6 with a value of +4. This amount in register 6 will be used as a loop control count for the BCT instruction in Statement 04009.

Statement 04002 loads the address of the translate table, TRANSTAB, into general register 7. For the purpose of this example,

assume that at program execution time TRANSTAB resides at core storage location 53,200. General register 7 would now contain a fixed-point value of +53,200 in the low-order three bytes.

Statement 04003 loads the address of the first of the four data fields into general register 8.

Statement 04004 loads the address of OUTFLDA into general register 9. As each of the input data fields are audited, the translate data will be moved into a corresponding output field. OUTFLDA will receive the audited data from FIELDA, OUTFLDB will receive the audited data

TABLE 17-3. Translate Table 3—(with segments representing EBCDIC punctuation and symbols all changed to contain diagonals).

X'00'[a]	X'01'	X'02'	X'03'	X'04'	X'05'	X'06'	X'07'	X'08'	X'09'	X'0A'	X'0B'	X'0C'	X'0D'	X'0E'	X'0F'
X'10'	X'11'	X'12'	X'13'	X'14'	X'15'	X'16'	X'17'	X'18'	X'19'	X'1A'	X'1B'	X'1C'	X'1D'	X'1E'	X'1F'
X'20'	X'21'	X'22'	X'23'	X'24'	X'25'	X'26'	X'27'	X'28'	X'29'	X'2A'	X'2B'	X'2C'	X'2D'	X'2E'	X'2F'
X'30'	X'31'	X'32'	X'33'	X'34'	X'35'	X'36'	X'37'	X'38'	X'39'	X'3A'	X'3B'	X'3C'	X'3D'	X'3E'	X'3F'
X'40' ᵇ[b]	X'41'	X'42'	X'43'	X'44'	X'45'	X'46'	X'47'	X'48'	X'49'	X'61' /	X'61' /	X'61' /	X'61' /	X'61' /	X'61' /
X'61' /	X'51'	X'52'	X'53'	X'54'	X'55'	X'56'	X'57'	X'58'	X'59'	X'61' /	X'61' /	X'61' /	X'61' /	X'61' /	X'61' /
X'61' /	X'61' /	X'62'	X'63'	X'64'	X'65'	X'66'	X'67'	X'68'	X'69'	X'6A'	X'61' /	X'61' /	X'61' /	X'61' /	X'61' /
X'70'	X'71'	X'72'	X'73'	X'74'	X'75'	X'76'	X'77'	X'78'	X'79'	X'61' /	X'61' /	X'61' /	X'61' /	X'61' /	X'61' /
X'80'	X'81' a	X'82' b	X'83' c	X'84' d	X'85' e	X'86' f	X'87' g	X'88' h	X'89' i	X'8A'	X'8B'	X'8C'	X'8D'	X'8E'	X'8F'
X'90'	X'91' j	X'92' k	X'93' l	X'94' m	X'95' n	X'96' o	X'97' p	X'98' q	X'99' r	X'9A'	X'9B'	X'9C'	X'9D'	X'9E'	X'9F'
X'A0'	X'A1'	X'A2' s	X'A3' t	X'A4' u	X'A5' v	X'A6' w	X'A7' x	X'A8' y	X'A9' z	X'AA'	X'AB'	X'AC'	X'AD'	X'AE'	X'AF'
X'B0'	X'B1'	X'B2'	X'B3'	X'B4'	X'B5'	X'B6'	X'B7'	X'B8'	X'B9'	X'BA'	X'BB'	X'BC'	X'BD'	X'BE'	X'BF'
X'C0'	X'C1' A	X'C2' B	X'C3' C	X'C4' D	X'C5' E	X'C6' F	X'C7' G	X'C8' H	X'C9' I	X'CA'	X'CB'	X'CC'	X'CD'	X'CE'	X'CF'
X'D0'	X'D1' J	X'D2' K	X'D3' L	X'D4' M	X'D5' N	X'D6' O	X'D7' P	X'D8' Q	X'D9' R	X'DA'	X'DB'	X'DC'	X'DD'	X'DE'	X'DF'
X'E0'	X'E1'	X'E2' S	X'E3' T	X'E4' U	X'E5' V	X'E6' W	X'E7' X	X'E8' Y	X'E9' Z	X'EA'	X'EB'	X'EC'	X'ED'	X'EE'	X'EF'
X'F0' 0	X'F1' 1	X'F2' 2	X'F3' 3	X'F4' 4	X'F5' 5	X'F6' 6	X'F7' 7	X'F8' 8	X'F9' 9	X'FA'	X'FB'	X'FC'	X'FD'	X'FE'	X'FF'

[a] Hex contents of each segment.
[b] EBCDIC representation.

from FIELDB, OUTFLDC will receive FIELDC, and OUTFLDD will receive FIELDD.

Statement 04005 is the Translate instruction. It will audit the data field addressed by the contents of general register 8 for a length of 15 bytes. The first time through this instruction general register 8 will contain the address of FIELDA as loaded by Statement 04003. The contents of register 8 will then be incremented by a fixed-point value of +15 in Statement 04007 so that the second time through this statement register 8 will be addressing FIELDB. Each subsequent pass through the instruction set will incre-

ment register 8 so that it will point to FIELDC and FIELDD respectively.

Statement 04006 takes the audited data, as addressed by general register 8, and moves it into the field that is pointed to by the address in general register 9. On the first pass through this statement register 9 addresses OUTFLDA. On each subsequent pass through the instruction set register 9 will be incremented to point to OUTFLDB, OUT-FLDC, and OUTFLDD, in that order.

Statement 04007 adds a halfword fixed-point literal value of +15 to general register 8, incrementing the address within that register to point to the next input data field.

IBM

IBM System/360 Assembler Coding Form

PROGRAM

PROGRAMMER

DATE

PUNCHING INSTRUCTIONS — GRAPHIC / PUNCH

PAGE 1 OF 2

CARD ELECTRO NUMBER

X28-6509-2 U/M050
Printed in U.S.A.

Name	Operation	Operand	Comments	Identification-Sequence
*				03900
*		* DEFINING THE TRANSLATE TABLE *		03901
TRANSTAB	DS	0CL256		03902
	DC	XL16'000102030405060708090A0B0C0D0E0F'		03903
	DC	XL16'101112131415161718191A1B1C1D1E1F'		03904
	DC	XL16'202122232425262728292A2B2C2D2E2F'		03905
	DC	XL16'303132333435363738393A3B3C3D3E3F'		03906
	DC	XL16'404142434445464748496161616161616'		03907
	DC	XL16'615152535455565758596161616161616'		03908
	DC	XL16'616162636465666768696A616161616161'		03909
	DC	XL16'707172737475767778796161616161616'		03910
	DC	XL16'808182838485868788898A8B8C8D8E8F'		03911
	DC	XL16'909192939495969798999A9B9C9D9E9F'		03912
	DC	XL16'A0A1A2A3A4A5A6A7A8A9AAABACADAEAF'		03913
	DC	XL16'B0B1B2B3B4B5B6B7B8B9BABBBCBDBEBF'		03914
	DC	XL16'C0C1C2C3C4C5C6C7C8C9CACBCCCDCECF'		03915
	DC	XL16'D0D1D2D3D4D5D6D7D8D9DADBDCDDDEDF'		03916
	DC	XL16'E0E1E2E3E4E5E6E7E8E9EAEBECEDEEEF'		03917
	DC	XL16'F0F1F2F3F4F5F6F7F8F9FAFBFCFDFEFF'		03918
				03919
*				03920
*				

Figure 17-2a

IBM

PROGRAM			
PROGRAMMER		DATE	

PUNCHING INSTRUCTIONS — GRAPHIC / PUNCH

CARD ELECTRO NUMBER

```
Name      Operation  Operand                          Identification-Sequence
*                                                      03921
*                                                      03922
FIELDA    DC  CL15'AMT.    $15  PER'                   03923
FIELDB    DC  CL15'ID IS 23-A65-76'                    03924
FIELDC    DC  CL15'RATIO 15%PCT EA'                    03925
FIELDD    DC  CL15'DATE:  7-15-69'                     03926
*                                                      03927
OUTFLDA   DC  CL15' '                                  03928
OUTFLDB   DC  CL15' '                                  03929
OUTFLDC   DC  CL15' '                                  03930
OUTFLDD   DC  CL15' '                                  03931
*                                                      03932
TRANSOUT  LA  6,4                                      04001
          LA  7,TRANSTAB                               04002
          LA  8,FIELDA                                 04003
          LA  9,OUTFLDA                                04004
NEXTRAN   TR  0(15,8),0(7)                             04005
          MVC 0(15,9),0(8)                             04006
          AH  8,=H'15'                                 04007
          AH  9,=H'15'                                 04008
          BCT 6,NEXTRAN                                04009
          BC  15,DONE                                  04010
*                                                      04011
```

Figure 17-2b

470

Statement 04008 adds a halfword fixed-point literal value of +15 to general register 9, incrementing the address within that register to point to the next output data field.

Statement 04009 is the Branch On Count loop control statement. Because Statement 04001 loaded general register 6 with a value of +4, the processing will branch back to NEXTRAN three times. On the fourth time through this instruction, general register 6 will be decremented to zero and the processing logic will fall through to Statement 04010.

Statement 04010 is a forced branch to an assumed end-of-job routine. That routine might possibly extract the data from the four output fields, place new data into the pre-audit input fields and then branch back to TRANSOUT.

Whenever the TRANSLATE instruction is executed on each of the four input data fields, it will replace all punctuation symbols and character symbols with the replacement character of a diagonal. In accordance with the assumption that the first byte of TRANS-TAB resides at storage location 53,200 at program execution time, each subsequent segment of TRANSTAB would have an address of "53,200 plus the binary value of the bits that represent the relative position of that segment within the table." For example, the segment with a relative position of X'09' would be at an address of "53,200 plus 9" or 53,209.

The action taken by the Translate instruction on FIELDA is shown in Table 17-4.

TABLE 17-4

FIELDA Character			Sum of the Value of the Character Added to the Address of	Character Contained at this Segment of TRANSTAB		Character Placed into FIELDA by the Translate
Character	Hex	Binary Value	TRANSTAB (53,200)	Hex	Character	Instruction
A	C1	193	53,393	C1	A	A
M	D4	212	53,412	D4	M	M
T	E3	227	53,427	E3	T	T
.	4B	75	53,275	61	/	/
ƀ	40	64	53,264	40	ƀ	ƀ
ƀ	40	64	53,264	40	ƀ	ƀ
ƀ	40	64	53,264	40	ƀ	ƀ
$	5B	91	53,291	61	/	/
1	F1	241	53,441	F1	1	1
5	F5	245	53,445	F5	5	5
ƀ	40	64	53,264	40	ƀ	ƀ
ƀ	40	64	53,264	40	ƀ	ƀ
P	D7	215	53,415	D7	P	P
E	C5	197	53,397	C5	E	E
R	D9	217	53,417	D9	R	R

After FIELDA is moved to OUTFLDA, OUTFLDA would contain:

A	M	T	/	ƀ	ƀ	ƀ	/	1	5	ƀ	ƀ	P	E	R

The action then taken by the Translate instruction on FIELDB is shown in Table 17-5.

TABLE 17-5

FIELDB Character			Sum of the Value of the Character Added to the Address of TRANSTAB (53,200)	Character Contained at this Segment of TRANSTAB		Character Placed into FIELDB by the Translate Instruction
Character	Hex	Binary Value		Hex	Character	
I	C9	201	53,401	C9	I	I
D	C4	196	53,396	C4	D	D
⌿	40	64	53,264	40	⌿	⌿
I	C9	201	53,401	C9	I	I
S	E2	226	53,426	E2	S	S
⌿	40	64	53,264	40	⌿	⌿
2	F2	242	53,442	F2	2	2
3	F3	243	53,443	F3	3	3
–	60	96	53,296	61	/	/
A	C1	193	53,393	C1	A	A
6	F6	246	53,446	F6	6	6
5	F5	245	53,445	F5	5	5
–	60	96	53,296	61	/	/
7	F7	247	53,447	F7	7	7
6	F6	246	53,446	F6	6	6

After FIELDB has been moved to OUTFLDB, OUTFLDB will contain:

I	D	⌿	I	S	⌿	2	3	/	A	6	5	/	7	6

The action taken on FIELDC by the Translate instruction is shown in Table 17-6.

The action taken on FIELDD by the Translate instruction is shown in Table 17-7.

The programmer may load the translate table segments with any one-byte hex configurations that he desires. The contents of each segment will then replace any data being translated that generates the address of that segment.

(b) Translate & Test. The Translate and Test instruction uses the same addressing scheme for the scan-table as used by the Translate instruction. That is, the binary value of the hex configuration of the data byte to be checked is used as an incremental value to the address of the first byte of the Translate table. Unlike the Translate instruction, however, the Translate & Test instruction *does not alter* the configuration of the data field being tested.

The TRT instruction statement takes each byte of the data field of the first operand, generates the unique translate table segment address and inspects that segment. If the contents of that segment are X'00', the TRT instruction continues processing, checking each byte of the data field against the table. If a segment is inspected and found to contain a configuration other than X'00', the scan is terminated. At this point, the TRT instruction loads, into general register 1, the address of the data byte of the first operand that it was checking at the time the exception occurred. It will also take the hex contents of the exception segment from the translate table and place that configuration into general register 2.

A practical application for this instruction would be to locate delimiter or separator characters within variable length fields, records, or messages. For example, assume that a series of records have been completed and

TABLE 17-6

FIELDC Character			Sum of the Value of the Character Added to the Address of TRANSTAB (53,200)	Character Contained at this Segment of TRANSTAB		Character Placed into FIELDC by the Translate Instruction
Character	Hex	Binary Value		Hex	Character	
R	D9	217	53,417	D9	R	R
A	C1	193	53,393	C1	A	A
T	E3	227	53,427	E3	T	T
I	C9	201	53,401	C9	I	I
O	D6	214	53,414	D6	O	O
ƀ	40	64	53,264	40	ƀ	ƀ
1	F1	241	53,441	F1	1	1
5	F5	245	53,445	F5	5	5
%	6C	108	53,308	61	/	/
P	D7	215	53,415	D7	P	P
C	C3	195	53,395	C3	C	C
T	E3	227	53,427	E3	T	T
ƀ	40	64	53,264	40	ƀ	ƀ
E	C5	197	53,397	C5	E	E
A	C1	193	53,393	C1	A	A

After OUTFLDC has received the translated data from FIELDC, OUTFLDC will contain:

R	A	T	I	O	ƀ	1	5	/	P	C	T	ƀ	E	A

TABLE 17-7

FIELDD Character			Sum of the Value of the Character Added to the Address of TRANSTAB (53,200)	Character Contained at this Segment of TRANSTAB		Character Placed into FIELDD by the Translate Instruction
Character	Hex	Binary Value		Hex	Character	
D	C4	196	53,396	C4	D	D
A	C1	193	53,393	C1	A	A
T	E3	227	53,427	E3	T	T
E	C5	197	53,397	C5	E	E
:	7A	122	53,322	61	/	/
ƀ	40	64	53,264	40	ƀ	ƀ
ƀ	40	64	53,264	40	ƀ	ƀ
7	F7	247	53,447	F7	7	7
–	60	96	53,296	61	/	/
1	F1	241	53,441	F1	1	1
5	F5	245	53,445	F5	5	5
–	60	96	53,296	61	/	/
6	F6	246	53,446	F6	6	6
9	F9	249	53,449	F9	9	9
ƀ	40	64	53,264	40	ƀ	ƀ

After the data has been moved from FIELDD, OUTFLDD would contain:

D	A	T	E	/	ƀ	ƀ	7	/	1	5	/	6	9	ƀ

created, each record containing several variable length messages. As each record was created, a one-byte configuration of X'01' was placed between each individual message and also immediately following the last message. These records are now being transmitted to another location and it will be the task of the receiving location to extract the messages, one at a time, from each of the records. In this instance the location that was programming to receive the message transmission would find it convenient and expedient to use the Translate & Test instruction to find the logical "break" between messages within a record. Because the "break code" used to separate messages is a hexadecimal '01' configuration, the programmer would create a translate table in which all segments contain X'00' except the segment that would be addressed by a relative value of X'01'. As indicated in the previous illustrations, this would be the second physical segment of the table. In the illustration of a translate table for this particular application (Table 17-8), the programmer has chosen to load the exception segment with the same hexadecimal configuration as the one that will be used to address that segment—X'01'.

The coding for this particular application has been created as shown in Fig. 17-3.

Statement 06001 is the Define Constant (DC) that creates a 256-byte translate table consisting of X'00' bytes. In this instance, the programmer has found it convenient to create the entire table in this manner and then move the X'01' code into the exception segment via an instruction statement.

Statement 06008, INITL, uses the Move Immediate (MVI) instruction to place a hexadecimal configuration of '01' into the second segment, the exception segment, of the translate table.

Statement 06009 is a Branch & Link instruction to a subroutine that is to supply the main-line program logic with records containing the messages. The "branched to" subroutine will use blanks to clear out an area labeled RECAREA, place the incoming record into that area, and then return to the main-line logic via Statement 06010.

Statement 06010 loads general register 7 with the address of the first byte of TRANSTAB, the translate table.

TABLE 17-8. Translate Table for "TRANSLATE & TEST" Instruction

X'00'	X'01'[a]	X'00'	X'00'	X'00'	X'00'	X'00'	X'00'	X'00'	X'00'	X'00'	X'00'	X'00'	X'00'	X'00'	X'00'
X'00'	X'00'	X'00'	X'00'	X'00'	X'00'	X'00'	X'00'	X'00'	X'00'	X'00'	X'00'	X'00'	X'00'	X'00'	X'00'
X'00'	X'00'	X'00'	X'00'	X'00'	X'00'	X'00'	X'00'	X'00'	X'00'	X'00'	X'00'	X'00'	X'00'	X'00'	X'00'
X'00'	X'00'	X'00'	X'00'	X'00'	X'00'	X'00'	X'00'	X'00'	X'00'	X'00'	X'00'	X'00'	X'00'	X'00'	X'00'
X'00'	X'00'	X'00'	X'00'	X'00'	X'00'	X'00'	X'00'	X'00'	X'00'	X'00'	X'00'	X'00'	X'00'	X'00'	X'00'
X'00'	X'00'	X'00'	X'00'	X'00'	X'00'	X'00'	X'00'	X'00'	X'00'	X'00'	X'00'	X'00'	X'00'	X'00'	X'00'
X'00'	X'00'	X'00'	X'00'	X'00'	X'00'	X'00'	X'00'	X'00'	X'00'	X'00'	X'00'	X'00'	X'00'	X'00'	X'00'
X'00'	X'00'	X'00'	X'00'	X'00'	X'00'	X'00'	X'00'	X'00'	X'00'	X'00'	X'00'	X'00'	X'00'	X'00'	X'00'
X'00'	X'00'	X'00'	X'00'	X'00'	X'00'	X'00'	X'00'	X'00'	X'00'	X'00'	X'00'	X'00'	X'00'	X'00'	X'00'
X'00'	X'00'	X'00'	X'00'	X'00'	X'00'	X'00'	X'00'	X'00'	X'00'	X'00'	X'00'	X'00'	X'00'	X'00'	X'00'
X'00'	X'00'	X'00'	X'00'	X'00'	X'00'	X'00'	X'00'	X'00'	X'00'	X'00'	X'00'	X'00'	X'00'	X'00'	X'00'
X'00'	X'00'	X'00'	X'00'	X'00'	X'00'	X'00'	X'00'	X'00'	X'00'	X'00'	X'00'	X'00'	X'00'	X'00'	X'00'
X'00'	X'00'	X'00'	X'00'	X'00'	X'00'	X'00'	X'00'	X'00'	X'00'	X'00'	X'00'	X'00'	X'00'	X'00'	X'00'
X'00'	X'00'	X'00'	X'00'	X'00'	X'00'	X'00'	X'00'	X'00'	X'00'	X'00'	X'00'	X'00'	X'00'	X'00'	X'00'
X'00'	X'00'	X'00'	X'00'	X'00'	X'00'	X'00'	X'00'	X'00'	X'00'	X'00'	X'00'	X'00'	X'00'	X'00'	X'00'
X'00'	X'00'	X'00'	X'00'	X'00'	X'00'	X'00'	X'00'	X'00'	X'00'	X'00'	X'00'	X'00'	X'00'	X'00'	X'00'

[a] Showing a single exception segment.

PROGRAM

PROGRAMMER

DATE

PUNCHING INSTRUCTIONS

GRAPHIC

PUNCH

CARD ELECTRO NUMBER

Name	Operation	Operand / Comments	Identification-Sequence
*			06000
TRANSTAB	DC	256XL1'00'	06001
RECAREA	DC	CL80' '	06002
DUMMY	DC	CL80' '	06003
LENGTH	DC	CL1' '	06004
MSGLENG	DC	CL1' '	06005
MSG	DC	CL80' '	06006
*			06007
INITL	MVI	TRANSTAB+1,X'01'	06008
NEWONE	BAL	6,GETRECD	06009
	LA	7,TRANSTAB	06010
	LA	8,RECAREA	06011
NEXTMSG	TRT	0(80,8),0(7)	06012
	BC	8,NEWONE	06013
	LR	10,1	06014
	SR	10,8	06015
	SH	10,=H'1'	06016
	STC	10,LENGTH	06017
	MVC	MOVER+1(1),LENGTH	06018
MOVER	MVC	MSG(1),0(8)	06019
	BAL	6,ROUTINEB	06020
	LA	8,1(1)	06021
	BC	15,NEXTMSG	06022
*			06023

Figure 17-3

Statement 06011 loads general register 8 with the address of the first byte of the input record work area. This address should also be that of the first byte of the first message within that record. As the routine is processed, general register 8 will be incremented to point to the subsequent messages within the record. However, each time a new record is supplied to the routine this statement will be executed and general register 8 will be reinitialized to the beginning of the record work area.

Statement 06012 is the Translate & Test instruction. As specified by the first operand, it will commence processing at the address stated in general register 8 and will terminate after testing 80 bytes or when encountering a byte that translates into a table segment that is nonzero. The second operand addresses the translate table that contains the translation segments for the test of the data bytes. As a result of the execution of this statement, the Condition Code will be set to indicate whether or not an exception segment was encountered. Rather than keeping track of the number of bytes already processed within the record area, the programmer has set up an additional dummy area that is located immediately following the record work area. In doing this, he has arranged that it will not be necessary to check to see if the previous message processed was the last one in the current record. Once the last message in the record has been processed, the TRT instruction statement will be executed again. At this time there will be no exception segments encountered because general register 8 will be addressing an 80-byte field of blanks. Consequently, the programmer has provided a branch back to the routine that gets a complete new record of messages whenever the Condition Code indicates that no exception segments were encountered during the TRT.

Statement 06013 is the branch just referred to. Whenever the TRT has tested 80 bytes without encountering an exception segment in the translate table, this branch will be taken in order to obtain a new set of messages. If a data byte was tested that resulted in the encounter of an exception segment in the table, the branch would not be taken and the processing logic would fall through to Statement 06014.

Statement 06014 is loading the contents of general register 1 into general register 10. At this time, because the TRT must have terminated on an exception segment, general register 1 will contain the address of the data byte that caused the encounter of an exception segment. This address will now be contained within both register 1 and register 10.

Statement 06015 will subtract general register 8 from general register 10 the resulting difference remaining in register 10. The purpose of this instruction statement is to determine the number of bytes residing between the address where the TRT commenced, as represented by the address in register 8, and the address at which it terminated, as represented by the address in register 10. The resulting difference is the total number of valid data bytes that comprise the current message that is to be extracted, excluding the message delimiter of X'01'.

Statement 06016 is subtracting a halfword fixed-point literal value of $+1$ from the contents of general register 10. The purpose of this statement is to reduce the specified byte-length of the current message to be extracted, that length being contained in register 10. General register 10 now contains the length of that message expressed in machine-language, or one byte less than the true physical length.

Statement 06017 stores the low-order byte of general register 10 into a single storage byte. The byte labeled LENGTH now contains the machine-language length of the current message unit that is going to be extracted from the record.

Statement 06018 will move the machine-language length of the current message unit, as contained in LENGTH, into Statement 06019, modifying the length of the move specified by the MVC instruction contained therein.

Statement 06019 will extract the current message segment as pointed to by register 8 in the second operand and move it into the storage area labeled MSG. The number of data bytes to be moved will depend on the length attribute inserted into this statement by Statement 06018.

Statement 06020 is a Branch & Link to another subroutine. It is assumed that this particular subroutine will do some type of processing with the message unit extracted in Statement 06019 and then return to the main-line logic via Statement 06021.

Statement 06021 loads a value of $+1$ plus the content value of general register 1 into general register 8. Assuming that the contents of register 1 were not altered or destroyed by the subroutine ROUTINEB, that register should be pointing to the message delimiter byte flagged during the preceding TRT instruction. In order to address the next message data byte following that delimiter, it is necessary to increment the value in general register 1 by $+1$. This statement performs that function, resulting in register 8 now containing the address of the storage byte immediately following the last message delimiter encountered.

Statement 06022 is a forced branch back to the statement labeled NEXTMSG. The processing logic will perform the TRT instruction and then as a result of that action:

1. Will encounter another message unit delimiter and continue processing through Statement 06022 again, or
2. Will not encounter a message delimiter within the 80 bytes addressed by register 8, so the logic will branch out to Statement 06009 in order to get a new record.

The Translate & Test instruction will create a unique Condition Code configuration if the last byte specified by the length attribute resulted in an exception segment being noted in the translate table. In this preceding example, however, the length of the data contained within the records was variable, so the programmer created logic to circumvent this problem as explained in Statement 06012.

Aside from the use of the Translate instructions, another real-life example of an auditing technique involves a routine that inspects a rather lengthy field consisting of nearly every conceivable alphanumeric and special character. The requirement for the routine is that upon completion of the audit this field would consist solely of alphanumerics and hyphens, but the hyphens are allowed to exist only if they separate two numeric characters. On the initial phase of the routine, each byte has to be individually scanned—if it contains anything other than an alphanumeric character, a hyphen, or an "at sign" (@), that byte is to be changed to a hyphen. The next phase is to scan the entire field again, one byte at a time and delete any hyphens that do not separate two numeric characters. As hyphens are deleted, the data field is to be collapsed to the left, keeping the data left-aligned within the field by overlaying the deleted hyphen and subsequent bytes with the data that appeared one byte to the right. When the retention or deletion of the existing hyphens has been determined, and the data record has been collapsed to a left-alignment wherever necessary, the next phase is to scan the field for the '@' symbols. It is necessary, in this phase, to maintain a count of the maximum number of data byte that may occupy this field, as well as the number of data bytes, left-aligned, which do occupy it. Whenever an '@' is found within the field, the number of existing data bytes is compared to the allowable maximum number of data bytes in order to determine if the field is full. If the field is not full, all bytes to the right of the '@' are moved one byte to the right. The '@' and the next byte to its right are then replaced with the alpha characters 'AT'. The actual number of bytes occupying the field is incremented by $+1$ and the scan continues through the field looking for any additional '@' characters. In the event that an '@' is found and the field contains the maximum number of data bytes, no change takes place.

Although the routine just described may sound somewhat imaginary, it is one that has actually been programmed and utilized for a particular application. In reality, the overall audit contained several more phases that were not included within this description because of their complexity. The task examples that are to be used in the remainder of this section will not be as complex, but they should indicate some of the audit techniques that may be used for data validation and transformation other than through the use of the Translate instructions.

Task 1. In this task, the subroutine is being passed a field of 200 bytes of mixed data. The subroutine is supposed to check every eighth byte of this data, starting with the first byte, and ascertain whether that byte is a valid EBCDIC alpha character within the range of "A" through "I". If an invalid character is found, that character is to be replaced with an EBCDIC alpha "Z" character. (See Fig. 17-4.)

Statement 02406 will move 200 bytes of data from INFIELD to a 200-byte work area labeled AUDITFLD.

Statement 02407 uses the Load Address instruction to place a fixed-point value of +25 into general register 5. Register 5 is the loop control register for the process of incrementing through AUDITFLD; the field is 200 bytes long and, therefore, contains 25 eight-byte segments.

Statement 02408 is loading the address of the first byte of AUDITFLD into general register 6. Register 6 will be used as the base register for incrementing through AUDITFLD.

Statement 02409 is the first instruction statement within BIGLOOP. It is loading a fixed-point value of +9 into general register 7. Register 7 will be the loop control register for passing through the nine bytes of ALPHAS. The loop BIGLOOP is considered to be all of the instruction statements from Statement 02409 through 02417.

Statement 02410 is loading general register 8 with the address of the first byte of ALPHAS. Register 8 will be used as the base register for incrementing through the nine bytes of ALPHAS, one byte at a time.

Statement 02411 is comparing a single byte of ALPHAS to a single byte of AUDITFLD. Each time the processing enters this instruction statement from State-

ment 02410, the address generated by 0(1,6) will point to the first character in the ALPHAS table. Each time the processing enters this instruction as a result of the branch taken from Statement 02414, the address generated by 0(1,6) will point to the EBCDIC character of ALPHAS that is to the right of the one previously tested. The loop LITTLOOP is considered to be all of the instruction statements from Statement 02411 through Statement 02414.

Statement 02412 is a conditional branch instruction statement. It specifies that if the single byte of AUDITFLD, as pointed to by register 6, contained the same character as the single byte of ALPHAS pointed to by register 8, the program logic should branch to OKALPHA. If the two bytes did not contain identical characters, the program logic should fall through to Statement 02413.

Statement 02413 increases the address in general register 8 by adding a fixed-point halfword literal of +1 to it. General register 8 should now point to the next byte of ALPHAS that is higher than the one tested by Statement 02411. If this loop should be processed all nine times, the last time through the loop general register 8 will point one byte beyond the right end of ALPHAS. This does not matter because the logic will drop through Statement 02414 and a comparison will never be made using that address.

Statement 02414 is the Branch On Count loop control statement for LITTLOOP. The branch to LITTLOOP will be taken until general register 7 is decremented to zero or until the conditional branch in Statement 02412 is taken.

Statement 02415 utilizes a Move Immediate instruction to move an EBCDIC alpha 'Z' character into the address within AUDITFLD that is pointed to by general register 6. The fact that the processing logic entered this statement indicates that the single byte of AUDITFLD currently being checked does not contain one of the EBCDIC alpha characters that comprise the constant ALPHAS.

Statement 02416 adds a halfword fixed-

IBM System/360 Assembler Coding Form

X28-6509-2 U/M050
Printed in U.S.A.

PROGRAM

PROGRAMMER

DATE

PUNCHING INSTRUCTIONS | GRAPHIC | PUNCH

PAGE 1 OF 1

CARD ELECTRO NUMBER

Name	Operation	Operand	Identification-Sequence
*			02400
AUDITFLD	DC	CL200' '	02401
ALPHAS	DC	CL9'ABCDEFGHI'	02402
*			02403
*			02404
*			02405
AUDIT8	MVC	AUDITFLD,INFIELD	02406
	LA	5,25	02407
	LA	6,AUDITFLD	02408
BIGLOOP	LA	7,9	02409
	LA	8,ALPHAS	02410
LITTLOOP	CLC	0(1,6),0(8)	02411
	BC	8,OKALPHA	02412
	AH	8,=H'1'	02413
	BCT	7,LITTLOOP	02414
	MVI	0(6),C'Z'	02415
OKALPHA	AH	6,=H'8'	02416
	BCT	5,BIGLOOP	02417
	BC	15,GETDATA	02418
*			02419
*			02420

Figure 17-4

479

point literal value of +8 to the current address contained in general register 6. Register 6 will now contain an address that points to the next byte of AUDITFLD that is to be tested. This statement may be entered either through Statement 02415 or via the branch from Statement 02412.

Statement 02417 is the Branch On Count loop control statement for BIGLOOP. The branch to BIGLOOP will be taken until general register 5 is decremented to zero, after which the logic execution will fall through to Statement 02418.

Statement 02418 is a forced branch to a routine labeled GETDATA, which, although it does not exist within the example itself, is assumed to consist of the necessary instruction statements to obtain a new set of data and re-enter the AUDIT8 routine.

Whenever a new set of 200 bytes of data is ready to be audited, the AUDIT8 subroutine will be entered. BIGLOOP will check every eighth byte of the 200-byte field, AUDITFLD. For each byte of AUDITFLD that is to be audited, LITTLOOP will be entered. Each time the logic passes through LITTLOOP, it will compare the current byte of AUDITFLD against a table of valid alpha characters, looking for a match. The processing will leave the LITTLOOP routine whenever a character has been found in ALPHAS that correspond to the current byte of AUDITFLD or if the entire ALPHAS table has been scanned without finding a match. In the latter instance, this would indicate that the current character in AUDITFLD is invalid and the program logic will replace it with a character 'Z'.

Task 2. This particular task requests that the program finds several special hex representations within a continuing source of input. The input to the program is passed to the routine, as requested, by a remote terminal application that transmits the data in 80-byte sections from a storage device. Throughout this data there will be two special one-byte hex representations—X'37' and X'26'. The hex '26' byte is an END OF BLOCK symbolic; the hex '37' is an END OF TASK

indicator. Although the data is passed to the problem program in 80-byte increments, that same data will be accumulated in a continuous stream until a X'26' byte is encountered. At that point, the program will pass the accumulated stream of data to an output routine that will place the variable length records on a direct access storage device. The program must count the number of bytes in each output record and pass that value along in the high-order two bytes of a four-byte field that immediately precedes the record itself. If an X'37' byte is encountered, it indicates that all available data has now been supplied to the program and this subroutine may be terminated. The implication of this routine is that variable-length records of data, stored at another location, are being transmitted in 80-byte segments and that any one segment may contain the logical end of one record and the beginning of the next.

Before analyzing this routine, it should be mentioned that this does not necessarily represent the optimum method of accomplishing the required task. It does, however, provide some insight into the logic process of an audit of this type.

The instruction statements for the subroutines comprising this task and the definitions of the fields are given in Fig. 17-5*a, b, c,* and *d.*

Statement 03004, PRESET, would only be entered once during each execution of the program. The functions of Statements 03004 and 03005 are subsequently accomplished by Statements 03204 and 03205 in the BLOCKEND subroutine. This statement loads the address of the first byte of the data portion of the output record area into general register 3. Note that general register 3 has been referred to as R3—this is possible inasmuch as Statements 05003 to 05007 have set up symbolic references for some of the general registers.

Statement 03005 uses the Load Address instruction to set register 7 to a +0 value. This could also have been accomplished by coding—SR 7,7.

Statement 03006, NEWSEGMT, is a Branch & Link to a subroutine that will accomplish the I/O task necessary to supply

IBM System/360 Assembler Coding Form

PROGRAM

PROGRAMMER

PUNCHING INSTRUCTIONS — GRAPHIC / PUNCH

PAGE 1 OF 4

CARD ELECTRO NUMBER

X28-6509-2 U/M050
Printed in U.S.A.

Name	Operation	Operand	Comments	Identification-Sequence
*				03001
*		* MAIN-LINE AUDITING LOGIC *	*	03002
*				03003
PRESET	LA	R3,OUTRECRD		03004
	LA	R7,0		03005
NEWSEGMT	BAL	R6,GETSEGMT		03006
	LA	R4,80		03007
	LA	R5,SEGFIELD		03008
SEGLOOP	CLI	0(5),X'26'		03009
	BC	8,BLOCKEND		03010
	CLI	0(5),X'37'		03011
	BC	8,ALLDONE		03012
	MVC	0(1,3),0(5)		03013
	AH	R5,=H'1'		03014
	AH	R3,=H'1'		03015
	AH	R7,=H'1'		03016
	C	R7,=F'500'		03017
	BC	2,ERROR		03018
	BCT	R4,SEGLOOP		03019
	BC	15,NEWSEGMT		03020
*				03021
*				03022

Figure 17-5a

481

IBM

PROGRAM		
PROGRAMMER	DATE	

PUNCHING INSTRUCTIONS	GRAPHIC	
	PUNCH	

CARD ELECTRO NUMBER

Name	Operation	Operand	Comments	Identification-Sequence
*		ROUTINE FOR END-OF-OUTPUT-BLOCK CONDITION		03200
*				03201
BLOCKEND	STH	R7,PREREC		03202
	BAL	R6,PUTRECRD		03203
	LA	R3,OUTRECRD		03204
	LA	R7,0		03205
	AH	R5,=H'1'		03206
	BCT	R4,SEGLOOP		03207
	BC	15,NEWSEGMT		03208
*				03209
*				03400
ALLDONE	- - -	- - -		03401
	- - -	- - -		03402
	- - -	- - -		03403
*				03404
*			(ASSUMED TO CONTAIN THE	03405
*			CLOSING ROUTINES OF THE	03600
GETSEGMT	- - -	- - -	PROBLEM PROGRAM.)	03601
	- - -	- - -	(ASSUMED TO CONTAIN THE	03602
	- - -	- - -	STATEMENTS NECESSARY TO	03603
	- - -	- - -	BRING IN A NEW 80-BYTE	03604
		- - -	DATA SEGMENT)	03605
	BCR	15,R6		03606
*				03607

Figure 17-5b

IBM

IBM System/360 Assembler Coding Form

PROGRAM

PROGRAMMER

PUNCHING INSTRUCTIONS GRAPHIC PUNCH

DATE

PAGE 3 OF 4

CARD ELECTRO NUMBER

X28-6509-2 U/M050
Printed in U.S.A.

Name	Operation	Operand	Comments	Identification-Sequence
*				03800
*				03801
PUTRECRD			(ASSUMED TO CONTAIN THE	03802
			STATEMENTS NECESSARY TO WRITE	03803
			OUT THE CURRENT VARIABLE-LENGTH	03804
			OUTPUT RECORD JUST COMPLETED.)	03805
	BCR	15,R6		03806
*				03807
*				03808
*				04000
ERROR			(ASSUMED TO CONTAIN THE STATEMENTS	04001
			NECESSARY TO ADVISE THE PROGRAMMER	04002
			THAT AN OUTPUT RECORD IN EXCESS OF	04003
			500 BYTES WAS RECEIVED VIA THE	04004
	BC	15,BLOCKEND	80-BYTE SEGMENTS.)	04005
*				04006
*				05000
*		*	*	05001
*		* CONSTANTS AND WORK AREAS	*	05002
*		*	*	05003
R3	EQU	3		05004
R4	EQU	4		05005
R5	EQU	5		05005
R6	EQU	6		05006
R7	EQU	7		05007

Figure 17-5c

483

IBM

IBM System/360 Assembler Coding Form

PROGRAM

PROGRAMMER

PUNCHING INSTRUCTIONS

GRAPHIC

PUNCH

DATE

PAGE 4 OF 4

CARD ELECTRO NUMBER

X28-6509-2 U/M050
Printed in U.S.A.

Name	Operation	Operand	Comments	Identification-Sequence
*				05008
*				05009
SEGFIELD	DC	CL80' '		05010
PREREC	DC	H'0'		05011
PRESYS	DC	H'0'		05012
OUTRECRD	DC	2CL250' '		05013
*				05014
*				05015

Figure 17-5d

484

SEGFIELD with 80 bytes of incoming data. When the data is received, the program logic should return to continue processing at Statement 03007 because this statement has loaded that address into general register 6 before branching to GETSEGMT. This statement is reentered from Statement 03020 each time the current 80-byte segment has been exhausted.

Statement 03007 loads general register 4 with a fixed-point value of +80. Register 4 will be the loop control register for stepping through the 80-byte segment one byte at a time.

Statement 03008 will load the address of the first byte of SEGFIELD into general register 5. Each time that a new segment is obtained, this address will be reset to the first byte.

Statement 03009 is comparing a single byte within SEGFIELD, as pointed to by the address in general register 5, to a hexadecimal literal of X'26'. This is checking for an EOB (End-Of-Block) indicator.

Statement 03010 is a conditional branch. If Statement 03009 resulted in an "equal" condition, a branch would be generated from this statement to the BLOCKEND routine.

Statement 03011 compares the single byte of SEGFIELD that is addressed by general register 5 to a hexadecimal literal of X'37' —an EOT (End-Of-Task) indicator.

Statement 03012 will cause a branch to ALLDONE if Statement 03011 resulted in an equal condition, indicating that all available data has been received from the sending operations.

Statement 03013 will move a single byte of data from the incoming segment to the output record build-area. This byte is moved because it was determined not to be an EOB or an EOT indicator byte. General register 5 points to an address within SEGFIELD and general register 3 points to an address within OUTRECRD.

Statement 03014 adds a fixed-point value of +1 to the address contained in general register 5. That address will now point to the next sequential byte in SEGFIELD.

Statement 03015 adds a fixed-point value of +1 to the address in general register 3. That address will now point to the next byte in OUTRECRD that is to receive a data byte from SEGFIELD.

Statement 03016 adds a fixed-point value of +1 to the value in general register 7. This value represents the number of bytes of data that have been moved to the output record that is being built in OUTRECRD.

Statement 03017 compares the fixed-point value in general register 7 to a fullword fixed-point literal of +500. This is to determine whether or not 500 bytes of data (the maximum allowable size) have been supplied to OUTRECRD without encountering an EOB condition.

Statement 03018 indicates that as a result of the preceding comparison, the program logic should branch to a routine labeled ERROR if general register 7 contained a value greater than +500. This condition would indicate that the maximum length of OUTRECRD, 500 bytes, has already been filled.

Statement 03019 is the loop control Branch On Count instruction. It will reduce the value contained in general register 4 by one each time the BCT is executed and will branch to SEGLOOP each time until general register 4 is reduced to zero. At that time, the branch will not be taken and the processing will fall through to Statement 03020. This instruction statement controls the reentry to SEGLOOP to a maximum of 80 times—the number of bytes in each segment of data.

Statement 03020 is a forced branch back to NEWSEGMT. If this statement is entered, it indicates that the preceding BCT instruction has signified that all bytes of the current segment have been processed; it is now time to request another segment of data.

Statement 03202, BLOCKEND, is the first instruction within the subroutine that is to handle the output of a completed variable-length record. The statement itself will store the length count of the record, accumulated in the low-order two bytes of general register 7, into the first of two halfwords that immediately precede the OUTRECRD field.

Statement 03203 is a Branch & Link instruction to the subroutine that will actually generate the I/O task for writing the output record, OUTRECRD. It will place the address of Statement 03204 into general register 6 and then branch to PUTRECRD. After completion of the I/O task subroutine, the processing logic should return to Statement 03204.

Statement 03204 is reinitializing the address pointer in general register 3 so that it will once again point to the first byte of OUTRECRD in preparation for building a new output record.

Statement 03205 is reinitializing general register 7 to a zero value. Register 7 is used to keep count of the total number of bytes supplied to the record being built in OUTRECRD.

Statement 03206 is adding a value of $+1$ to the address contained in general register 5. When this set of instructions was entered, register 5 was pointing to a byte containing X'26' within SEGFIELD. Because the processing will leave this subroutine and go directly to either NEWSEGMT or SEGLOOP without passing through Statement 03014, it is necessary to adjust the address pointer to the byte immediately following the EOB byte containing X'26'.

Statement 03207 is a Branch On Count instruction using the same register and logic as used in Statement 03019. This is done because the processing logic will not pass directly through Statement 03019 after leaving this subroutine, and it is necessary to reduce the value in general register 4 to determine whether or not all 80 bytes in the current segment have been processed. If the byte containing a X'26', which brought the processing into this subroutine, was the 80th byte of the current segment, this instruction will result in general register 4 being reduced to zero and the processing will fall through to Statement 03208 rather than branching at this point.

Statement 03208 is a forced branch to NEWSEGMT. If this statement is entered, it indicates that the current segment of data has been exhausted and the processing should go to the statement that will arrange to bring a new segment into storage.

Statement 03401, ALLDONE, would be the first instruction of a set of statements that close the files and perform any other functions necessary to complete the normal program termination.

Statement 03601, GETSEGMT, would be the opening instruction of a set of statements that create the input I/O task and actually receive the data record from the terminal operation.

Statement 03606 is a forced branch to the address contained in general register 6. In this phase of the program, that address should point to Statement 03007, the instruction statement immediately following the BAL that routed the processing logic to the GETSEGMT subroutine.

Statement 03802 is the initial instruction in the subroutine that creates the I/O task for writing out the output record created in OUTRECRD. Because these are considered to be variable-length records, the I/O task would have to specify that the output record was 504 bytes in length—the 500-byte data record preceded by the two halfword areas.

Statement 03806 is a forced branch to the address contained within general register 6. This address should point to Statement 03204, the one immediately following the BAL that brought the processing logic into Statement 03802.

Statement 04001 is the initial statement in a subroutine that must make a decision as to what action is to be taken as a result of the output record area being filled without encountering an EOB indicator. The program logic might include the instruction statements necessary to write a message on the console typewriter for reference by the programmer or the computer operator. On the other hand, it might only want to keep a count of how many records of this type were received by the program. The logic of this program is that since the output record area is now full, write out the completed record by branching to the BLOCKEND routine and then continue processing any remaining bytes as an entirely new record.

Statement 04005 is the forced branch to take the processing logic to the BLOCKEND routine just described.

Statements 05003 through 05007 are equating certain general registers to symbolic references. Any of these five general registers may, therefore, be referred to by their symbolic reference (such as R4) or by their actual representation (4).

Statement 05010 is a Define Constant statement that will create an 80-byte field of blanks. As each 80-byte data segment is requested by the program, that segment will be placed into this area by the I/O tasks.

Statements 05011 through 05013 define the maximum area (500 bytes preceded by a four-byte count area) for the variable-length output record.

Statement 05011 creates a halfword constant containing a fixed-point value of zero. The length of each completed record will be stored into this halfword from general register 7, as shown in Statement 03202.

Statement 05012 creates a second halfword constant of zero. This represents the two bytes used by the system when creating variable-length output records.

Statement 05013 creates a 500-byte string of blanks by specifying a duplication factor of two for a 250-byte constant. This constant constitutes the output record field.

This particular set of routines has indicated more of the "housekeeping" tasks than represented in most of the previous examples. Many other instructions that would be required to make this a complete program are not shown. The omitted statements would be the base register assignments, opening the data sets, I/O task macroinstructions for obtaining the input records, I/O tasks for the output records, closing the data sets, the beginning and ending program housekeeping functions, and many others. These have been intentionally omitted because of the wide variance available in the expression of this type of item between the various operating systems. Once again, it will have to be the responsibility of the computer installation with which the programmer is working to provide him with the proper education on these items. If an OS system is being used, there is an example of creating many of these functions within the section entitled "Basic Program Initialization."

Although the latter two tasks within this particular section did not employ either of the Translate instructions, it would have been entirely possible and practical to use them in solving these tasks. It would be merely a matter of choice on the part of the programmer as to which way he would prefer to code the statements. Hopefully, he would have chosen the way that represented the most expedient processing of the data, regardless of the amount of coding effort that this required on his part.

Review Exercises

1. A single byte within a translate table is accessed by adding the binary value of the hexadecimal contents of the source field byte to the address of the beginning of the _____ _____ .

2. A translate table would normally consist of a total of _____ bytes.

3. Whenever the Translate & Test instruction encounters an "exception byte" in the translate table, it loads general register _____ with the address of the source data byte that pointed to the exception byte.

4. When the same type of exception occurs as was specified in the preceding statement, the TRT statement will load the hexadecimal contents of the translate table exception byte into the low-order byte of general register _____ .

5. The contents of the individual translate table segment pointed to by a source byte is used to replace the contents of the _____ _____ .

6. The programmer may configure the contents of the translate table in any manner that meets the logic requirements of the individual program. (True) (False)

7. In the Translate & Test instruction processing, the binary value of the hexadecimal configuration of the source data byte is used as an _____ value to the address of the _____ byte of the translate table.

8. In a Translate instruction statement the second operand represents the address of the _____ _____ .

9. The Translate & Test instruction does not alter the configuration of the data field being tested. (True) (False)

10. The _____ operand of the Translate instruction statement represents the field of data that is to be translated.

11. When executing the Translate & Test instruction, the processing of that instruction will terminate if a translate table segment is encountered whose contents are other than X'_____'.

Translate Table—Indicating the Hex Contents of Each Byte Segment

ADDRESS RANGE	_0	_1	_2	_3	_4	_5	_6	_7	_8	_9	_A	_B	_C	_D	_E	_F
0_	00	01	02	03	04	05	06	07	08	09	0A	0B	0C	0D	0E	0F
1_	10	11	12	13	14	15	16	17	18	19	1A	1B	1C	1D	1E	1F
2_	20	21	22	23	24	25	26	27	28	29	2A	2B	2C	2D	2E	2F
3_	30	31	32	33	34	35	36	37	38	39	3A	3B	3C	3D	3E	3F
4_	40	41	42	43	44	45	46	47	48	49	4A	4B	4C	4D	4E	4F
5_	50	51	52	53	54	55	56	57	58	59	5A	5B	5C	5D	5E	5F
6_	60	61	62	63	64	65	66	67	68	69	6A	6B	6C	6D	6E	6F
7_	70	71	72	73	74	75	76	77	78	79	7A	7B	7C	7D	7E	7F
8_	80	81	82	83	84	85	86	87	88	89	8A	8B	8C	8D	8E	8F
9_	90	91	92	93	94	95	96	97	98	99	9A	9B	9C	9D	9E	9F
A_	A0	A1	A2	A3	A4	A5	A6	A7	A8	A9	AA	AB	AC	AD	AE	AF
B_	B0	B1	B2	B3	B4	B5	B6	B7	B8	B9	BA	BB	BC	BD	BE	BF
C_	C0	C7	D6	C2	E9	D4	E3	C9	E4	D7	CA	CB	CC	CD	CE	CF
D_	D0	D9	F6	C4	F0	F5	C8	F2	C3	C5	DA	DB	DC	DD	DE	DF
E_	E0	E1	D3	F3	F1	D1	E2	E5	D8	D2	EA	EB	EC	ED	EE	EF
F_	F4	D5	C6	F7	E6	F8	C1	E8	F9	E7	FA	FB	FC	FD	FE	FF

The remainder of the problems within this review will relate specifically to the translation of data using the Translate instruction. Using the following translate table, apply the coded instruction statement in each problem against the original source field configuration. Then supply the character and hexadecimal configuration of each byte of the translated version of the source field as it would appear after execution of the Translate statement. Remember that the translate table, as shown here, indicates the contents of each of the segment bytes; the hexadecimal contents of each of those segment bytes do not necessarily represent the hex configuration that will represent the address of those same bytes. The translate table is assumed to be defined by the label TRANTABL.

12. DATAFLDA

(Character)	F	H	E	C	S	R
(Hex)	C6	C8	C5	C3	E2	D9

```
        TRANSA    TR      DATAFLDA(6),TRANTABL
```

DATAFLDA

(Hex)						
(Character)						

13. DATAFLDB

(Character)	P	J	B	C	S	R	M
(Hex)	D7	D1	C2	C3	E2	D9	D4

```
          TRANSB    TR      DATAFLDB+1(5),TRANTABL
```

DATAFLDB

(Hex)							
(Character)							

14. DATAFLDC

(Character)	S	B	1	A	V	B	C
(Hex)	E2	C2	F1	C1	E5	C2	C3

```
            TRANSC    LA      8,TRANTABL
                      TR      DATAFLDC(7),0(8)
```

DATAFLDC

(Hex)								
(Character)								

15. DATAFLDD

(Character)	J	G	A	0	F
(Hex)	D1	C7	C1	D6	C6

```
          LA      11,TRANTABL
          TR      DATAFLDD(5),0(11)
```

DATAFLDD

(Hex)					
(Character)					

16. DATAFLDE

(Character)	U	K	(Blank)	4	R	W	F
(Hex)	E 4	D 2	4 0	F 4	D 9	E 6	C

```
                TRANSE     TR      DATAFLDE(7),TRANTABL
```

DATAFLDE

(Hex)							
(Character)							

17. DATAFLDF

(Character)	A	P	A	U	A	4
(Hex)	C 1	D 7	C 1	E 4	C 1	F 4

DATAFLDG

(Character)	6	F	9	Z	R
(Hex)	F 6	C 6	F 9	E 9	D 9

```
        TRANSRTE      LA      5,TRANTABL
                      TR      DATAFLDF(6),0(5)
                      MVC     DATAFLDG(5),DATAFLDF+1
                      TR      DATAFLDG(5),0(5)
```

DATAFLDF

(Hex)						
(Character)						

DATAFLDG

(Hex)					
(Character)					

18

INTERPRETING
HEXADECIMAL CORE DUMPS

Each operating system, and even the various control programs within any one system, creates a core dump listing that is unique in some way from all others. Because of this fact, the entire process of problem program interpretation and debugging within a core dump cannot be completely defined within this text. Technical manuals relative to the exact operating system being used should be utilized by the programmer in order to determine the error condition pointers available to him. As an alternative to this exact information, this section will attempt to aid the programmer in his efforts to interpret the data fields contained within the problem program portion of the core dump listing.

To begin with, the hexadecimal data of a core dump listing is not self-descriptive as to the format interpretation of the data that it is intended to represent. Hexadecimal representation is the highest level of common expression for any type of data; binary-expressed data shares equal commonality but is considerably more cumbersome to interpret. Therefore, it is necessary that the programmer knows the intended representation of the hex digits comprising the core data bytes that he is looking at. In order for him to know the intended representation, he must relate the listed core position addresses to the portion of the problem program source listing that it represents.

Most listings of core storage are printed out in lines of data such as:

```
007B20     D5C3C540 E6C9E3C8 40E3C8C5 C9D940D9 C5E2D7C5 C3E3C9E5 C540D5E4 D4C5D9C9
```

The left-most six hex digits represent the beginning address of the storage bytes listed within this line of data:

007B20   D5C3C540 E6C9E3C8 40E3C8C5 C9D940D9 C5E2D7C5 C3E3C9E5 C540D5E4 D4C5D9C9
↑
Address, in hex,
of this storage byte

Because the system cannot determine the intended representation of each storage byte, each byte is printed out as a two-digit hexadecimal configuration. Every pair of hexa-decimal digits has a core storage address that is one byte (+1) greater than the address of the preceding pair of hexadecimal digits.

Hex address of
the first byte
↓

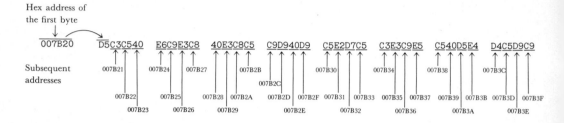

In the illustrations of hexadecimal core dump listings used here, there are 32 one-byte core positions represented on each line, or a total of 64 hexadecimal digits of core storage representation. The hex digits are in groups of eight, equal to four bytes per group. The address of any byte-aligned pair of hex digits can easily be determined by incrementing (in hex) from the address of the first pair of hex digits on the core listing.

In order to become familiar with the hexadecimal formatting of different types of data fields, study Fig. 18-1, an illustration of a partial core dump listing that contains the lines with the addresses 007A20 through 007CA0. The first portion of this listing has been interpreted into the character representation of the hexadecimal digits. Note that a hex configuration of X'40' is a valid "blank"; therefore, there is no character representation indicated for such bytes.

Starting at address 007B80, there are nine arithmetic fields that will be subsequently defined. Addresses 007BA0 through 007C11 contain more character data. Addresses 007C12 through 007C51 contain program instruction statements in machine-language form. The remaining portion of the listing contains additional character-interpreted data.

Assume that the arithmetic fields in this illustration have been defined by the programmer as shown within the following statements. At the time that the hexadecimal core dump has taken place, these fields have not yet been altered.

```
FIELD1      DC      PL6'14539'
FIELD2      DC      H'19'
FIELD3      DC      F'243621'
FIELD4      DC      PL4'−25'
FIELD5      DC      PL8'213116478'
FIELD6      DC      PL1'5'
FIELD7      DC      PL3'0'
FIELD8      DC      H'1365'
FIELD9      DC      H'−1'
```

The interpretation of the arithmetic fields would be as follows:

FIELD1—Address 007B80 through 007B85. This field contains a six-byte packed decimal value of +14,539. The hex 'C' in the right-most half-byte of this field indicates that this amount is a positive value and the remaining high-order hex numeric digits indicate the value itself.

FIELD2—Address 007B86 through 007B87. This is a fixed-point two-byte halfword value of +19. In the instance of fixed-point and binary values, the hex digits themselves are not self-defining as to the assumed decimal value of the field. By using the Hexadecimal/Decimal Conversion Table, you can determine that the hex digit '3' has a value of +3 and the hex digit '1' to its left has a value of +16—or

```
           T H I S     I S     T H E     W A Y     T H A T     A     C O R E     D U M P
007A20     E3C8C9E2  40C9E240  E3C8C540  E6C1E840     E3C8C1E3  40C140C3  D6D9C540  C4E4D4D7

           M I G H T     A P P E A R     I N       H E X A D E C I M A L     F O R
007A40     40D4C9C7  C8E340C1  D7D7C5C1  D940C9D5     40C8C5E7  C1C4C5C3  C9D4C1D3  40C6D6D9

           M A T .       D A T A     A P P E     A R I N G     I N     S T R A I G H
007A60     D4C1E34B  404040C4  C1E3C140  C1D7D7C5     C1D9C9D5  C740C9D5  40E2E3D9  C1C9C7C8

           T     E B C D I C     C H A R A C T     E R     F O R M     C O U L D     B E
007A80     E340C5C2  C3C4C9C3  40C3C8C1  D9C1C3E3     C5D940C6  D6D9D440  C3D6E4D3  C440C2C5

             I N T E R P R E T E D     I N     T H E     S A M E     M A N N E R
007AA0     40C9D5E3  C5D9D7D9  C5E3C5C4  40C9D540     E3C8C540  E2C1D4C5  40D4C1D5  D5C5D940

           A S     T H I S     L I N E     Y O U     A R E     R E A D I N G .
007AC0     C1E240E3  C8C9E240  E3C9D5C5  40E8D6E4     40C1D9C5  40D9C5C1  C4C9D5C7  4B404040

           F I X E D - P O I N T     A N D     P A C K E D     D E C I M A L     V
007AE0     C6C9E7C5  C460D7D6  C9D5E340  C1D5C440     D7C1C3D2  C5C440C4  C5C3C9D4  C1D340E5

           A L U E S     A R E     I N T E R P     R E T E D     I N     A C C O R D A
007B00     C1D3E4C5  E240C1D9  C540C9D5  E3C5D9D7     D9C5E3C5  C440C9D5  40C1C3C3  D6D9C4C1

           N C E     W I T H     T H E I R     R     E S P E C T I V E     N U M E R I
007B20     D5C3C540  E6C9E3C8  40E3C8C5  C9D940D9     C5E2D7C5  C3E3C9E5  C540D5E4  D4C5D9C9

           C     R E P R E S E N T A T I O N     A S     I N D I C A T E D     W I
007B40     C340D9C5  D7D9C5E2  C5D5E3C1  E3C9D6D5     40C1E240  C9D5C4C9  C3C1E3C5  C440E6C9

           T H I N     T H E     F O L L O W I     N G     F I E L D S .
007B60     E3C8C9D5  40E3C8C5  40C6D6D3  D3D6E6C9     D5C740C6  C9C5D3C4  E24B4040  40404040
```

```
                #1          #2          #3          #4              #5          #6  #7      #8    #9
007B80     00000014  539C0013  0003B7A5  0000025D     00000021  3116478C  5C00000C  0555FFFF
```

```
           P R O G R A M     I N S T R U C T     I O N     S T A T E M E N T S     A
007BA0     D7D9D6C7  D9C1D440  C9D5E2E3  D9E4C3E3     C9D6D540  E3E3C1E3  C5D4C5D5  E3E240C1

           R E     S H O W N     I N     M A C H     I N E     L A N G U A G E     F O R
007BC0     D9C540E2  C8D6E6D5  40C9D540  D4C1C3C8     C9D5C540  D3C1D5C7  E4C1C7C5  40C6D6D9

           M A T     A S     R E P R E S E N T     E D     B Y     T H E     F O L L O W
007BE0     D4C1E340  C1E240D9  C5D7D9C5  E2C5D5E3     C5C440C2  E840E3C8  C540C6D6  D3D3D6E6

           I N G     E X A M P L E S .                 #1          #2          #3
007C00     C9D5C740  C5E7C1D4  D7D3C5E2  4B404040     4040D20D  A0056E4B  4AA0568A  58806C98
```

```
                #4          #5          #6              #7          #8          #9          #10
007C20     58906C9C  FA106CB0  56BFF911  6CB0568C     4770449C  95E76CB3  47804462  92E76CB3
```

```
                #11         #12         #13         #14
007C40     41A07B01  4AA0568E  F8106CB0  56BA47F0     449C4040  40404040  40404040  40404040
```

```
           E A C H     2     H E X     D I G I T     S     A P P E A R I N G     I N     T
007C60     C5C1C3C8  40F240C8  C5E740C4  C9C7C9E3     E240C1D7  D7C5C1D9  C9D5C740  C9D540E3

           H E     C O R E     D U M P     R E P     R E S E N T S     1     B Y T E     O
007C80     C8C540C3  D6D9C540  C4E4D4D7  40D9C5D7     D9C5E2C5  D5E3E240  F140C2E8  E3C540D6

           F     C O R E     S T O R A G E .
007CA0     C640C3D6  D9C540E2  E3D6D9C1  C7C54B40     40404040  40404040  40404040  40404040
```

Figure 18-1

+16 plus +3 equals +19. The overall value is considered to be a positive (+) value because the left-most bit position of

the two-byte field contains a zero-digit. This position is the high-order bit position of the left-most hex '0' digit of the field.

If this field were represented in bit-format it would appear as:

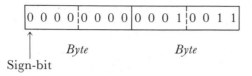

This field could be considered to be an unsigned binary value. Because it resides on a halfword address boundary (any address that is divisible by two) it is also a valid signed fixed-point halfword value.

FIELD3—Address 007B88 through 007B8B. This field is intended as a signed fixed-point fullword value of +243,261. It is aligned on a fullword boundary (an address divisible by four). It could also be interpreted as an unsigned binary value. The bit representation of this field would be:

Byte		Byte		Byte		Byte	
0000	0000	0000	0011	1011	0111	1010	0101

↑
Sign-bit

If this field were interpreted as a fixed-point fullword it would be defined as a positive value—the sign-bit position contains a zero-bit.

FIELD4—Address 007B8C through 007B8F. Although this field could be interpreted as a fixed-point fullword (because it is on a fullword boundary) containing a value of +605, assume that the programmer has defined it as a four-byte packed decimal field. Therefore, the contents of this field must be interpreted as a packed decimal value of −25. The negative condition of the value is indicated by the hex 'D' digit in the right-most half-byte of the field.

FIELD5—Address 007B90 through 007B97. This field contains an eight-byte packed decimal value of +213,116,478. The right-most hex digit of 'C' within this field has defined the positive (+) characteristic of the value.

FIELD6—Address 007B98. This is a one-byte packed decimal value of +5. If the programmer had not declared this single byte as a packed decimal field, this particular configuration could have been interpreted as a character-byte. In the latter instance, the hex configuration of X'5C' represents a valid EBCDIC character of an asterisk (*).

FIELD7—Address 007B99 through 007B9B. This field has been defined as a packed decimal field by the programmer. As such it may be interpreted as a packed decimal value of +0.

FIELD8—Address 007B9C and 007B9D. Because the programmer has defined this field as a fixed-point halfword value, it is interpreted here as containing an integer value of +1365. The bit configuration of this field would be:

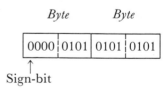

The high-order sign-bit, consisting of a zero-bit, assigns a positive representation to the integer value. The assigned value of this field, +1365, can be verified by summing the "Powers-Of-Two" values of the bit positions containing one-bits, or by converting the hexadecimal configuration of X'0555' through the use of the Hexadecimal/Decimal Conversion Table.

FIELD9—Address 007B9E and 007B9F. This field has also been defined by the programmer as a fixed-point halfword value. In this instance, the value content of the halfword is −1. The bit configuration of this field would appear to be:

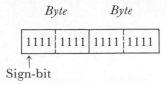

1111	1111	1111	1111

↑
Sign-bit

The one-bit sign-bit indicates that this fixed-point value has a negative representation—in two's complement form. If the programmer inadvertently interpreted this field as a binary value, rather than as a fixed-point value, it would be considered to be an unsigned integer value of 65,535.

The instruction statements shown within this core dump listing, beginning at address 007C12, have been coded within the problem program as:

```
MVC    0+5(14,10),BOLE       001
AH     R10,=H'133'           002
L      R8,HOLDP8             003
L      R9,HOLDP9             004
AP     PECON,=PL1'1'         005
```

```
CP     PECON,=PL2'030'       006
BC     7,NOTWANTA            007
CLI    MINT2,C'X'            008
BC     8,TAP60               009
MVI    MINT2,C'X'            010
LA     R10,PAVE1             011
AH     R10,=H'66'            012
ZAP    PECON,=PL1'0'         013
BC     15,NOTWANTA           014
```

While reviewing these statements, it must be assumed that elsewhere within the program there has been coding created to equate some registers to symbolic labels—register 8 equated to R8, register 9 equated to R9, etc.

The fields of data and the labels referenced by these instruction statements are not shown within this particular portion of the core dump listing. However, the machine-language format of these statements may be interpreted by their hexadecimal representation as follows:

Statement 001—Address 007C12 through 007C17.

Instruction code	D2 or MVC (Move Characters)
Length of move	0D or 13 (machine-language code for 14 bytes)
First operand address	A005

    A states that register 10 is the base register.
    005 is the displacement from that address.

Second operand address	6E4B

    6 states that register 6 is the base register.
    E4B is the displacement from that address.

This statement specifies: "Move 14 bytes of data from the field addressed by the label BOLE into an area that is addressed by the contents of general register 10 plus five bytes." The address of BOLE is the contents of general register 6 plus the decimal value of X'E4B', the displacement.

Statement 002—Address 007C18 through 007C1B.

Instruction code	4A or AH (Add Halfword)
First operand	A or general register 10
Second operand address	0568A

    0 is the indexing register; a zero value.
    5 is the base register.
    68A is the displacement.

The statement is: "Take the fixed-point value of the halfword literal constant (located at the address generated by the sum of the contents of general register 5 plus a displacement of X'68A') and add it to the contents of general register 10."

Statement 003—Address 007C1C through 007C1F.

Instruction code	58 or L (Load)
First operand	8 or general register 8

Second operand address   06C98

    0 is the indexing register; a zero value.

    6 is the base register.

    C98 is the displacement.

The statement is: "Take the contents of the fullword HOLDP8 (located at the address generated by the sum of the contents of general register 6 plus a displacement of X'C98') and load those four bytes into general register 8."

Statement 004—Address 007C20 through 007C23.

Instruction code	58 or L (Load)
First operand	9 or general register 9
Second operand address	06C9C

    0 is the indexing register; a zero value.

    6 is the base register.

    C9C is the displacement.

The statement is: "Take the contents of the fullword HOLDP9 (located at the address generated by the sum of the contents of general register 6 added to a displacement of X'C9C') and load those four bytes into general register 9."

Statement 005—Address 007C24 through 007C29.

Instruction code	FA or AP (Add Packed)
Length of first operand	1 (machine-language code for two bytes)
Length of second operand	0 (machine-language code for one byte)
First operand address	6CB0

    6 is the base register.

    CB0 is the displacement.

Second operand address   56BF

    5 is the base register.

    6BF is the displacement.

The statement is: "Take the packed decimal value of the one-byte literal constant (located at the address generated by the sum of the contents of general register 5 added to a displacement of X'6BF') and add it to the two-byte packed decimal field PECON (located at the address generated by the sum of the contents of general register 6 added to the displacement of X'CB0')."

Statement 006—Address 007C2A through 007C2F.

Instruction code	F9 or CP (Compare Packed)
Length of first operand	1 (machine-language code for two bytes)
Length of second operand	1 (machine-language code for two bytes)
First operand address	6CB0

    6 is the base register.

    CB0 is the displacement.

Second operand address   568C

    5 is the base register.

    68C is the displacement.

The statement is: "Take the packed decimal value of the two-byte literal constant (located at the address generated by the sum of the contents of general register 5 added to a displacement of X'68C') and compare that to the two-byte packed decimal field PECON (located at the address generated by the sum of the contents of general register 6 added to a displacement of X'CB0')."

Statement 007—Address 007C30 through 007C33.

Instruction code   47 or BC (Branch On Condition)
Mask value for condition code   7
Second operand address   0449C
   0 is the indexing register; a zero value.
   4 is the base register.
   49C is the displacement.

This statement specifies: "Take the mask value of the first operand and use it to test the configuration of the Condition Code bits within the Program Status Word for an 'unequal' condition. If the Condition Code reflects an unequal condition setting as a result of Statement 006, then branch to NOTWANTA (located at the address generated by the sum of the contents of general register 4 plus a displacement of X'49C')."

Statement 008—Address 007C34 through 007C37.

Instruction code   95 or CLI (Compare Logical Immediate)
Immediate character   E7 or alpha character 'X'
First operand address   6CB3
   6 is the base register.
   CB3 is the displacement.

The statement is: "Take the single eight-bit character that is contained in the second byte of this machine-language statement and compare it to the single byte of data located at MINT2 (the address generated by the sum of the contents of general register 6 added to a displacement of X'CB3')."

Statement 009—Address 007C38 through 007C3B.

Instruction code   47 or BC (Branch On Condition)
Mask value for condition code   8
Second operand address   04462
   0 is the indexing register; a zero value.
   4 is the base register.
   462 is the displacement.

This statement indicates: "Use the mask value of the first operand to test the configuration of the Condition Code bits within the Program Status Word for an 'equal' condition. If the Condition Code reflects an equal comparison setting as a result of Statement 008, then branch to TAP60 (located at the address generated by the sum of the contents of general register 4 added to the displacement of X'462')."

Statement 010—Address 007C3C through 007C3F.

Instruction code   92 or MVI (Move Immediate)
Immediate character   E7 or alpha character 'X'
First operand address   6CB3
   6 is the base register.
   CB3 is the displacement.

This statement specifies: "Take the single eight-bit character that is contained in the second byte of the machine-language statement and move it into the single storage byte that is addressed by the label MINT2 (the address generated by the sum of the contents of general register 6 plus a displacement of X'CB3')."

Statement 011—Address 007C40 through 007C43.

Instruction code   41 or LA (Load Address)
First operand   A or general register 10.
Second operand address   07B01

0 is the indexing register; a zero value.

7 is the base register.

B01 is the displacement.

The statement is: "Take the address of PAVE1 and load it into general register 10." (The address of PAVE1 is the sum generated by adding the displacement of X'B01' to the address contained in general register 7.)

Statement 012—Address 007C44 through 007C47.

Instruction code	4A or AH (Add Halfword)
First operand	A or general register 10.
Second operand address	0568E

0 is the indexing register; a zero value.

5 is the base register.

68E is the displacement.

The statement specifies: "Take the fixed-point value of the halfword literal value constant (located at the address generated by the sum of the contents of general register 5 added to the displacement of X'68E') and add it to the contents of general register 10."

Statement 013—Address 007C48 through 007C4D.

Instruction code	F8 or ZAP (Zero and Add Packed)
Length of first operand	1 (machine-language code for two bytes)
Length of second operand	0 (machine-language code for one byte)
First operand address	6CB0

6 is the base register.

CB0 is the displacement.

Second operand address   56BA

5 is the base register.

6BA is the displacement.

The statement is: "Set the first operand field, PECON, to a zero content and then add the second operand, a packed decimal literal constant to PECON. PECON is located at the address generated by adding together the displacement of X'CB0' and the contents of general register 6. The packed decimal literal is addressed by the sum of the addition of the displacement of X'6BA' and the contents of general register 5."

Statement 014—Address 007C4E through 007C51.

Instruction code	47 or BC (Branch On Condition)
Mask value for condition code	F or 15
Second operand address	0449C

0 is the indexing register; a zero value.

4 is the base register.

49C is the displacement.

This statement forces the program logic to branch. It states: "Use the mask value of the first operand to test the configuration of the Condition Code bits. Because this mask encompasses all conceivable Condition Code settings, the program logic will branch to NOTWANTA (located at the address generated by the addition of the displacement X'49C' to the address contained in general register 4)."

If the entire core dump listing was presented as an illustration, you would be able to find all of the addresses indicated by these statements.

Although the core dump listing will contain the complete coding statements of the problem program, the addresses of these statements, constants, and areas will no longer be the same as the addresses indicated on the program source code listing. The problem program, as it resides within core storage of the computer, will be offset from the beginning address of zero by some quantity of bytes. This offset could be 10,000, 45,000, 300,000 bytes, or any amount within the range of the available core storage capacity of the computer. The number of bytes comprising this offset not only varies between the different types of operating systems, but also between similar computer systems. This latter variance would be created by the difference between the options specified at system generation time for each individual computer system.

Although there generally is not a predetermined core storage starting point of the problem program that is necessarily consistent between the different systems, the core dump listing does provide an address pointer to the first byte of the program. Once again, unfortunately, this is another item that cannot be completely defined at this time—the core dumps generated by different versions of the various operating systems are not alike in format. For now, it will be sufficient to say that the core dump listing will provide the programmer with the means of locating the problem program coding.

The offset of the problem program from the beginning address of core storage is referred to as a *relocation* factor. For example, assume that a particular problem program actually resided in core storage beginning at an address of X'0035A6'. If the programmer wanted to check the core storage contents of a field of data that resided at a source listing address of X'124', he would add that address to the relocation factor of X'0035A6'— X'124' plus X'0035A6' equals X'0036CA'. The field that was to be analyzed would be located within the core dump listing at address X'0036CA'.

In the previous illustration of a core dump listing, it indicated that instruction statements are contained in machine-language form, generally referencing storage addresses as a "base register and displacement" combination. Most core dump listings will provide the programmer with special analysis

of the contents of the general registers at the time that the dump function was invoked. The programmer can refer to the contents of a base register, add the desired displacement and use the sum of that addition to find the point within the problem program that was referenced by the statement that he is examining. For example, assume that the instruction statement—BC 8,GOTO—appeared within the core dump listing in machine-language format as:

$$47806390$$

In this instance:

47 is the machine instruction code for BC.

8 is the mask value for testing the Condition Code.

0 is the indexing value.

6 is the base register.

390 is the displacement.

If, at this point, general register 6 contained a value of X'0000380D' the actual relocated address of GOTO within the core dump listing could be determined by adding X'390' (the displacement) to X'0000380D' (the base register contents), the sum of which would be X'00003B9D'. This sum would be the address at which GOTO would be found within the core dump listing.

In Fig. 18-2, another illustration of a core dump listing, there are constants of varying lengths and configurations. These represent tables, work areas, switches, and general types of constants. The contents of some of these areas have been altered from the configuration they had when the problem program was loaded; other areas still contain their original values. The instruction statements represented in this core dump listing were coded within the problem program as:

WORKAREA	DC	CL55'b'
BYTESWIT	DC	CL1'b'
TABLE4	DC	30PL3'0'
FULLWD	DC	F'10'
HAFWD1	DC	H'0'
HAFWD2	DC	H'20'
BITSWIT	DC	X'00'
TABLE5	DC	16F'0'

	WORKAREA							
010F60	40404040 40404040 40404040 40404040				40404040 40404040 40404040 40404040			

						TABLE 4		
	WORKAREA				BYTESWIT	S1	S2	S3
010F80	40404040 40404040 40404040 40404040			40404040	404040E7	00000C00	000C0000	

					TABLE 4					
	S4	S5	S6	S7	S8	S9	S10	S11	S12	S13
010FA0	0C00073C	00000C00	568C0000	0C07394D	00000C00	000C0512	4C00006C	00001C00		

				TABLE 4						
	S14	S15	S16	S17	S18	S19	S20	S21	S22	S23	S24
010FC0	000C0700	0C00009C	00220C00	000C6003	2C00000C	00000C00	000C0113	0C00000C		

		TABLE 4						HAFWD1 BITSWIT		
	S25	S26	S27	S28	S29	S30	FILL	FULLWD	↑HAFWD2 ↑	FILL
010FE0	04034C00	003D0000	0C00819C	00007D00	004D0000	0000000A	00000014	08000000		

				TABLE 5			
	F1	F2	F3	F4	F5	F6	F7	F8
011000	00000000	00000009	00000000	0000002A	00000000	00000052	00000000	00000000

				TABLE 5			
	F9	F10	F11	F12	F13	F14	F15	F16
011020	00000080	00000000	00000021	00000000	11111111	0000000C	00000000	0000003D

					LETTERS							SWITCHNO	
	COUNTER1	S1	S2	S3	S4	S5	S6	S7	S8	S9	S10	S11	S12	S13	S14 ↑
011040	00008C00	0C000C00	0C000C00	0C000C00	0C000C00	0C000C00	0C000C00	0C000C00	0C000C40						

Figure 18-2

```
COUNTER1    DC      PL3'0'
LETTERS     DC      14XL2'0C'
SWITCHNO    DC      CL1'b'
```

The contents of this portion of the core dump listing are arranged in the same sequence as the DC statements shown preceding it.

WORKAREA—Core addresses 010F60 through 010F96.

This field consists of 55 bytes, each byte containing the hexadecimal configuration of a valid blank (X'40'). Even though the constant indicated only one blank (which would appear in the first position of the field), the remaining bytes of the field to the right of the first byte were also supplied with the configuration of a blank. This results from the fact that if a character constant is given a length attribute that is greater than the number of characters specified as the constant, then all bytes remaining to the right will be supplied with the X'40' configuration of a blank.

BYTESWIT—Core address 010F97.

This is a one-byte character constant that now contains the hex configuration of an alpha 'X' character. It would be implied that the program logic had moved the 'X' into this byte some time between the point at which the program was initialized and the time when the dump was invoked.

TABLE4—Core address 010F98 through 010FF1.

This area was originally defined as a table consisting of 30 three-byte packed decimal segments, each segment containing a packed decimal value of +0. Once the program began executing, some of the table segments were supplied with packed decimal values. The current contents of the segments are:

Segment Number	Address	Value	Segment Number	Address	Value
S1	010F98	+0	S16	010FC5	+9
S2	010F9B	+0	S17	010FC8	+220
S3	010F9E	+0	S18	010FCB	+0
S4	010FA1	+73	S19	010FCE	+60,032
S5	010FA4	+0	S20	010FD1	+0
S6	010FA7	+568	S21	010FD4	+0
S7	010FAA	+0	S22	010FD7	+0
S8	010FAD	−7,394	S23	010FDA	+1,130
S9	010FB0	+0	S24	010FDD	+0
S10	010FB3	+0	S25	010FE0	+4,034
S11	010FB6	+5,124	S26	010FE3	−3
S12	010FB9	+6	S27	010FE6	+0
S13	010FBC	+1	S28	010FE9	+819
S14	010FBF	+0	S29	010FEC	−7
S15	010FC2	+7,000	S30	010FEF	−4

FULLWD—Core addresses 010FF4 through 010FF7.

This is a fullword fixed-point constant containing a value of +10. Because the DC statement that created this field specified it as a fullword, the first byte was aligned on the next available fullword boundary. As a result of this alignment, there are two unused storage byte locations between the last byte of the previous constant and the first byte of this one.

HAFWD1—Core addresses 010FF8 through 010FF9.

This is a halfword fixed-point constant containing a value of +0. It was not necessary to skip any storage bytes inasmuch as the next available byte was on a halfword boundary.

HAFWD2—Core addresses 010FFA through 010FFB.

This halfword fixed-point constant contains a value of +20. It is aligned properly immediately adjacent to the preceding halfword.

BITSWIT—Core address 010FFC.

This one-byte storage is assumed to consist of eight bit-switches. Although this byte was initialized as all zero-bits, it now contains a one-bit in the fifth bit position from the left. The programmer would be able to determine the implied logic conditions based on the setting of these switches.

TABLE5—Core addresses 011000 through 01103F.

This table consists of 16 fixed-point four-byte segments. As specified by the DC statement that created this table, each segment is aligned on a fullword boundary. In order to align the first fullword segment of the table, it was necessary for the compiler to skip the three bytes immediately following the preceding constant. Originally, each table segment contained a value of +0. During the execution of the program, several of the segments received fixed-point values. The current contents of the segments are shown in detail at the top of page 502.

Fullword Segment Number	Address	Value
F1	011000	+0
F2	011004	+9
F3	011008	+0
F4	01100C	+42
F5	011010	+0
F6	011014	+82
F7	011018	+0
F8	01101C	+0

Fullword Segment Number	Address	Value
F9	011020	+128
F10	011024	+0
F11	011028	+33
F12	01102C	+0
F13	011030	−1
F14	011034	+12
F15	011038	+0
F16	01103C	+61

COUNTER1—Core addresses 011040 through 011042.

As implied by the label, this three-byte packed decimal field is used as a counter by the programmer. Although it was originally defined as containing a value of +0, it now contains a value of +8. Whatever event, or item, was being counted, that situation has occurred eight times before the core dump listing was obtained.

LETTERS—Core addresses 011043 through 01105E.

This area has been defined as consisting of 14 two-byte segments. In the DC statement, however, only the actual contents of one byte (two hex digits) for each segment has been defined. Because the characteristics of the constant have been stated as being in hexadecimal form, the Assembler Language compiler placed the single byte of specific constant into the low-order position of each segment and has supplied hex zero-digits to the remaining portion of each segment. There is no absolute indication of the intended use of these segments, but the total 28 storage bytes allocated to this constant have the acceptable form of 14 two-byte fields, each containing a packed decimal value of +0.

SWITCHNO—Core address 01105F.

This is a one-byte constant containing a valid blank. This particular constant could be used to reset the byte-switch referred to by the label BYTESWIT.

The material presented in this chapter is only a portion of the overall knowledge required to fully interpret a core dump listing. It will provide the programmer with the necessary concepts for interpreting problem data. In addition, it will be necessary for the programmer to obtain the exact format of the core dump listings provided by the particular system that he is working with and to study the technical manuals available for that system.

PART IV

ACCESS METHODS AND DATA SET FORMATS

19

DATA SETS AND
DATA SET RECORD FORMATS

A *data set* is a collection of logical data records. The format and data content of these records consist of an organization and information required to provide input data to one or more specific tasks. In this context a data set is considered to reside on a magnetic tape file, a direct access volume, or a similar storage device. The data records comprising the data set may each be similar in form, size, and data content, or they may vary from record to record. Each record is generally considered to be unique from other records, containing one or more data fields that will create the unique identity of that record. For example, a personnel department would probably maintain a data set that consisted of one or more records for each employee. Within each record there would be data regarding the employee's name, address, age, dependents, job classification, pay grade, and countless other items. Assuming that in this instance there was one record per employee, each record would be considered

to be unique on the basis of the Employee Number contained within that record. In a large corporation or organization, there are many similar or identical proper names—hence the necessity to identify the employee by a unique number rather than by name.

A number of data sets may exist in which the same type of record identifiers are used, but the records within each data set contain a different type of information than that of the other data sets. Referring once again to personnel files, several data sets might exist, in all of which the Employee Number is used to distinguish unique records. One data set could consist of records containing historical or background information for each employee; a second data set might have records containing current year payroll information for each employee, such as gross earnings, withholding taxes, Social Security deductions, net earnings, etc.; a third data set would possibly be comprised of records containing a history of the supervisor's evalua-

505

tion of the employee's performance over certain periods of time. Each of these data sets contain records that may be uniquely identified by the Employee Number, yet each is considered to be a separate collection of records due to the different type of data contained within them.

The manner in which each data set is organized is referred to as the *file organization.* For example:

1. A data set that consists of records that are recorded in a sequential manner, either logically and/or physically sequential, without any built-in or external referencing indexes, is considered to be a sequential data set.

2. A data set that has been created by the data management routines of the Indexed Sequential Access Method is referred to as an indexed sequential data set. This type of data set organization has several levels of internal indexing created by the Access Method. The index structure is used as a reference to the identity key field of the records contained in the data set.

3. A data set that is considered to be formatted in a direct organization mode may have a number of different physical attributes. The records themselves may appear within the data set in a logical sequential order, in a physically sequential by random logical order, or in a "spaced" logically sequential order in which dummy records appear between records whose identity field keys are not of a contiguous sequence. The sequence of records for this latter type might appear as, for example, 1, 2, 3, D, D, 6, D, 8, 9, 10, D, 12, etc. A dummy record resides where a data record with a logical key of 4, 5, 7, and 11 should be inasmuch as no data records with those actual identities exist.

4. A partitioned data set consists of groups of logically sequential records, each group appearing anywhere within the data set where space is available for its records. In this organization, each group of records is called a *member,* and for each member there is an entry within the *directory* of the partitioned data set. The directory consists of a series of entries, one for each member in the data set. The directory entry contains a name for the member and a *pointer* (an address) to the location where the first record of the member may be found.

Of these various types of data set organizations, all types may be applied to direct access devices. Magnetic tape, however, is generally restricted to a sequential data set organization.

A. RECORD FORMATS

A record is considered to be a logical set of data fields that provide information directly related to a unique identifier. The identifier provides the ability to distinguish that set of data fields from other sets of data fields, or other records. Depending on the type of data contained within the records, or on the logic of the problem program, the records do not absolutely require an identifier—in the greater number of data sets, however, a record identifier or key is present.

When the records are actually recorded, or *written,* on the data set, they may be written in a single record configuration or as a group of records recorded in one Input/Output operation. This latter method is referred to as *blocking,* or creating *blocked* records. To the device that contains the data, there is no difference between a single record or a block of records—either one is treated by the hardware as a logical block of data. It is the data management routines of certain access methods that decide whether or not a *read* or *write* operation results in manipulating data consisting of a single record or a group of records. In order to distinguish the beginning and end of logical data blocks, regardless of whether they are single records or blocks of multiple records, the data storage device skips a certain amount of usable recording space between each block of data. Although this is technically referred to as an *Inter-Record Gap* (IRG), it could be more properly referred to as an inter-block gap—it physically exists between blocks of data. Note the slight difference in terminology here, which might be somewhat confusing—

the storage device considers every section of data passed to it by an I/O task to be a block of data; the program logic or access method that passed the data to the device may interpret it as a block of records or as a single record. In other words, either a single record or a block of records will be treated identically by the storage device—as a logical block of data.

To provide a graphic concept of a record and the elements that comprise it, it is necessary to visualize what the same information would appear to be like if it were printed out on a roll of paper tape. For example, the following illustration might represent a portion of a typical personnel record in an Employee Record data set.

Employee Number	Employee Name			S e x	A g e	M or S	D e p	Ins. Class	Etc.	
	Last Name	First Name	MI							

One Record

The fields within the record cannot be independently identified by the data management routines, access methods, or operating system. These fields have significance only to the problem program(s) that might utilize the records. The major fields shown within this record are:

Employee Number
Employee Name
Sex
Age

M or S (Marital Status)
Dep (Dependents)
Ins Class (Insurance Classification)

and any other field that might appear in the remainder of the record. Within the Employee Name field there are subfields to define the length limitations of Last Name, First Name, and MI (Middle Initial). These subfields, like the major fields, are known only to the problem program. The small blocks shown under each field and subfield represent the variable byte area allocated for the data that is to be contained within that field. The layout of this record is for visual representation only—when the record is either written or read, only the actual data bytes themselves exist. The descriptions of the fields, or the field titles, do not exist within the record on the storage device.

Assuming that the terms "record," "block of records," and "data block" or "block of data" are now understood, it is time to interpret the physical structure of these items as they would be considered to exist on a storage device. Single unblocked records would appear to be located on the recording surface of a storage device as:

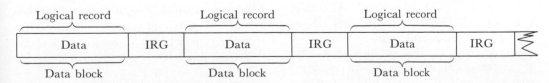

To the storage device, the data contained between two IRG's is a data block; to the problem program, this same data is considered to consist of one logical record.

When the data is formatted in "blocked record" mode, it is considered to appear on the storage device in the following manner:

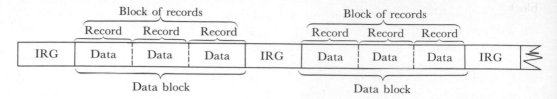

Once again, the storage device interprets the data contained between two IRG's as a data block. However, either the problem program or a portion of the data management routines (if they have been advised accordingly), or perhaps both, will interpret the same data as being comprised of three unique data records per block. These illustrations are a general interpretation of the appearance of data on a storage device; there are some differences in the manner in which this data would appear on either a magnetic tape or a direct access storage device.

Whenever an access method is utilized that handles the blocking and unblocking of blocked data records, the program does not need to be concerned when a new block of records has become filled and ready to be physically written onto a data set. The program merely gives an I/O macroinstruction for each record and proceeds with its normal processing. These I/O requests are intercepted by the access method macroinstructions and the records are placed into the block one at a time. When sufficient records have been completed to fill a block, the access method processes the I/O command to write that completed block onto the data set. It then proceeds to start all over again to fill the block with the next set of records as they are passed from the program. If the records are being read from a storage device, the access method routines work in almost the exact opposite manner. An entire block of records is first brought into core and then, as the problem program issues each I/O request for a read operation, the access method passes a record from that block to the program, one record at a time. When that block has been emptied, another block of records is provided to the access method for it to pass

those records to the problem program.

The individual records may consist of one of three forms—fixed-length, variable-length, or undefined records. Each of these three record forms are described in the subsequent paragraphs.

1. Fixed-Length Records

When the record form of a data set is described as containing fixed-length records, it is specifying that every individual record consists of exactly the same number of bytes of data. For example, if a data set is described as consisting of fixed-length 300-byte records, every record in that data set will be exactly 300 bytes in length. Although the record length is fixed, the interpretation of the data fields within the records does not need to be. The access method data management routines are primarily concerned with the arrangement and the form of the records themselves—the problem program is concerned with the arrangement of the data within the records. Consequently, a data set containing fixed-length records may actually consist of a number of different types of records, or records containing different types of data. The problem program would then be responsible for determining the type of record that it was processing. This can be illustrated by simulating a data set that contains records related to a purchase order reporting system. The data set might contain four types of records, such as:

Type 1   A Requisition Record
Type 2   A Purchase Order Record
Type 3   A Receiving Report Record
Type 4   An Accounts Payable Record

The internal format of each of these types of records might be:

Type 1—Requisition Record

P. O. #	R C	REQN. #	Reqn. Date			Dept.	Expense #	Qty.	etc.	
			Mo.	Day	Year					
	1									

Type 2—Purchase Order Record

P. O. #	R C	REQN. #	Reqn. Date			Vendor Code	Buyer Code	Item #	etc.	
			Mo.	Day	Year					
	2									

Type 3—Receiving Report Record

P. O. #	R C	Vendor Code	Date Recd.			Order Quantity	Quantity Received	Description	
			Mo.	Day	Year				
	3								

Type 4—Accounts Payable Record

P. O. #	R C	Vendor Code	Terms	Cost Per Unit		Quantity	Invoice Amount		
				$	¢		$	¢	
	4								

These examples display the beginning portion of each of the various types of records within the data set. The access method that was used to create the data set or to retrieve the records would not distinguish the difference between the various internal configurations; the fixed-length record attribute of the data set would only require the system data management routines to assure that each record was the correct length. It would probably be a function of the problem program to look at the RC (Record Code) byte of each record in order to determine the type of record configuration applied to that set of data, and then to execute the logic applicable to that type of data.

When the problem program logic calls for sequential processing of data set records, it will be a definite advantage to block the records. The size of the blocks should be as large as are convenient and practical with the system configuration and storage available to the problem program. Each time that a physical read/write operation is performed, it will process an entire block of data—regardless of whether or not that data consists of a single record or a block of fifteen records. As can be assumed, it takes considerably less time to read or write a block of data containing fifteen records than it does to accomplish fifteen read or write operations of one record each.

When blocked records are used to create a data set containing fixed-length records, all blocks will be the same length with the possible exception of the last block on the file. If the number of records remaining that are to constitute the final block are not sufficient to create a full block, they will be written as a *short block*. The operating system automatically checks for short blocks and makes allowance for them.

2. Variable-Length Records

Variable-length records may be comprised of different amounts of data and types of data fields. Each record may be any minimum valid length allowable by the device on which it is stored, and may be as long as the maximum-size record specified for the data set. In order for the operating system to determine the length of any single record, whether blocked or unblocked, each record must include a four-byte prefix that will supply the length of the record to which it is attached. This four-byte prefix consists of two low-order bytes that are used by the operating system and two high-order bytes that contain the binary-expressed length of the record. When the data set is being created, the problem program must provide this length for each record. Whenever the record is being retrieved or accessed from the data set, the system uses the existing record length information for length-checking procedures and deblocking functions when applicable.

A single variable-length data record extracted from a data set would appear as:

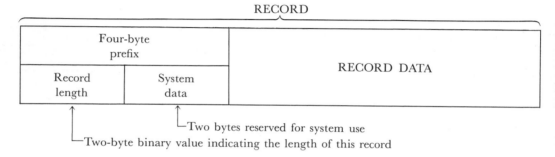

Each and every variable-length record must have the four-byte prefix containing the length specification.

In addition, every block of data that is to be read or written using variable-length records must have a similar four-byte prefix. The block prefix must be present regardless of whether the data block consists of a single record or whether it consists of multiple records. As in the application of the record prefix, the block prefix contains a high-order two-byte binary value and a two-byte field reserved for the use of the operating system.

If the access method that is being used to create a data set provides automatic record blocking, the system will compute the length of the block of records and place that value, in binary form, into the high-order two bytes of the block prefix. If the problem program that is creating a file handles the blocking functions within its own logic, then it must also calculate the block length and supply that value to the prefix of the block.

Blocked variable-length records would appear as:

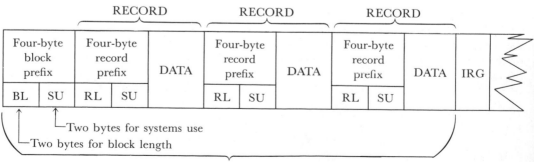

Unblocked variable-length records require a four-byte block count field even though the data block consists of only one record. These would appear as:

	RECORD					RECORD					RECORD		

Block prefix	Record prefix	DATA	IRG	Block prefix	Record prefix	DATA	IRG	Block prefix	Record prefix	DATA
BL | SU	RL | SU			BL | SU	RL | SU			BL | SU	RL | SU	
BLOCK				BLOCK				BLOCK		

In the latter illustration, the system considers each record to also be a data block, therefore requiring the use of the four-byte block descriptor prefix in addition to the four-byte record descriptor prefix.

3. Undefined Records

Undefined records are described in some technical manuals as being records that do not conform to the fixed-length or variable-length form. This description does not properly imply the application for interpreting undefined records. If a program is going to create data records, the programmer would have a choice of all records being the same length or being of varying lengths—both types being classified by either fixed-length or variable-length forms. What is an undefined record then? The practical explanation of an undefined record, and its application, is that it is "any block of data that is to be read from an existing data set, wherein the record form and length is not known." The system treats each logical block of data as a single record, regardless of whether or not that block actually consists of fixed-length or variable-length records, blocked or unblocked. If the programmer does not specify a block size large enough to contain the full length of an undefined record, the system will only read in as much data as space has been provided for.

The appearance of an undefined record on a storage device, regardless of its real organization, is interpreted by the operating system as:

RECORD/BLOCK	IRG	RECORD/BLOCK	IRG	RECORD/BLOCK	IRG

Data will be read into storage until an IRG (Inter-Record Gap) is sensed, or until the programmed data storage area is filled, whichever occurs first. The data records are treated much the same as unblocked variable-length records except that the block prefix and record prefix are not necessarily in evidence with undefined records. If true variable-length records have been read into the problem program, the two four-byte prefixes will be treated as a part of the data record.

B. PRINTED, PUNCHED, OR DISPLAYED RECORDS

In some instances, a general reference to the term "data set" is used to indicate sets of records that are directed to a nonstorage type of output device such as a printer, card punch unit, or display unit. The correctness of this use of the term "data set" is a matter of interpretation by the user's installation. As a rule, however, a data set is construed to consist of records stored on an Input/Output device that allows the data to remain there for an indefinite period and to be retrieved, altered, or added to.

The data that is transmitted to these nonstorage types of devices is properly defined as consisting of records. These records may be either blocked or unblocked as allowed by the system and data management routines under which the data is being processed. The reference is made to this type of data at this point only for the purpose of defining the use of a system function that allows the inclusion of a record *Control Character*. The Control Character referred to in this instance is not a part of the general processing logic of the problem program, although it is the responsibility of the problem program to create that character and place it in the outbound records. If a control character of this type is to be used, the programmer must advise the system of this fact through a specific Data Control Block (DCB) parameter. The one-byte character will appear as the first byte of the data record; therefore, the logical record length must be specified as the logical data length plus one byte.

The purpose of the control character is:

1. If the output data is to be punched, the control character specifies the punched card output bin that is to be selected.

2. If the output data is to be printed, the control character specifies the line spacing that is to be in effect for each line of printed output.

In the event that the programmer has indicated to the system that a control character is to be included within the output record and then he does not provide for one, the system considers the first byte of the data record to be the control character. Conversely, if the programmer creates a control character within the first byte of each record and then does not advise the system that it should look for that character, that single byte is considered to be a part of the data fields comprising the length of the record.

If a record that contains a control character is transmitted to a device that does not utilize, nor recognize, the function of that character, the single byte will again be considered to be a part of the data fields comprising the overall record.

C. MAGNETIC TAPE DATA SETS

Data sets recorded on magnetic tape are stored on reels that are referred to by the system as *volumes*. Each volume, or reel of tape, usually has been assigned a unique serial number that is indicated on the external surface of the reel itself. Magnetic tape internal labeling procedures, when used, will also create an internal label containing the volume serial number. Data sets may then be readily located by both the computer operator and the operating system—the operator using the external serial number for reference, the system using the internal label serial number for reference. One magnetic tape volume may contain a single data set or multiple data sets; a single data set may reside on a series of volumes.

A specific analysis of the construction of the internal magnetic tape labels will not be presented within this text due to the variations employed by different computer installations and operating systems. In general, however, a magnetic tape volume label will contain a label identifier, a label-type number, the volume serial number, and other system data. In addition to the volume label, each data set on a magnetic tape may have its own set of labels—system header labels, "users'" labels, and system trailer labels. The system header labels and trailer labels contain information regarding the data set; such as record format, block length, record length, tape density, and other information necessary for the system to process the data contained within that data set. Standard users' labels are generally formatted according to the procedures set by the individual computer installation. They are normally used to provide additional information to the program that will utilize those data sets.

When a magnetic tape data set occupies more than one reel of tape, the standard trailer labels will advise the operating system whether or not there are subsequent volumes to be processed as a part of this data set. This is accomplished by indicating an EOV (End Of Volume) condition in the trailer label. When an EOV condition is encountered, it advises the system that the physical end of the recorded portion of the tape has been reached, but that the data set itself is continued on a successive volume or volumes. In order that the system knows when all data contained within a data set has been passed, the trailer label contains an EOF (End Of

File) indication.

Admittedly, this has been a brief explanation of what could be a rather extensive subject. It is recommended that each programmer determine the types of labels and label processing utilized by his computer installation and then familiarize himself with those label types by referring to the manufacturers' technical manuals.

D. DIRECT ACCESS DATA SETS

Direct access devices, such as disks and drums, utilize the "volume" concept in much the same manner as magnetic tape volumes. Each pack, in the instance of removable disk packs, is identified externally and internally with a unique volume serial number. This identification is on an internal label called a volume label, usually appearing on the first track of the first cylinder. Unlike magnetic tape, however, direct access volumes maintain a special small data set that provides an indexing service to the operating system. This special data set is referred to as a Volume Table Of Contents (VTOC). It is comprised of a series of reference entries referred to as Data Set Control Blocks (DSCB's), which are created one at a time as new data sets are added to the volume. The DSCB's contain information relative to each existing data set such as the location address, name, and general description, as well as information that is relevant to the volume itself— remaining space available on the volume, space occupied by the VTOC, and other information of this nature.

The initialization of the direct access volume and the creation of a VTOC data set is not an automatic function of the operating system. For example, a new disk pack for a 2314 DASF unit cannot be unpackaged, mounted, and immediately used to store regular data. It must first be initialized through the use of a utility program; under the full Operating System this utility is called DASDI—Direct Access Storage Device Initialization. The utility program, and the action that it generates on the volume, differs between the various operating systems. The general functions of a DASDI-type utility program are given below.

1. Create the volume label and the identity of the volume itself.

2. Create the VTOC data set based on the information supplied on control card statements regarding such variables as quantity of tracks to be supplied to the VTOC and the beginning location of the VTOC.

3. To do a surface analysis of all standard recording tracks that normally can be addressed by the programmer. In the event that a defective recording surface is found, the DASDI will assign an alternate track from one of the spare tracks on the volume. This is done in such a manner that the programmer does not even need to know that the replacement track has been assigned. A pointer is set within the volume so that any reference to the defective track will automatically be directed to the alternate track.

During the life-span of direct access device recording surfaces, one or more tracks might become defective because of deterioration of the oxide recording surface. In such an event the existing data sets may all be recopied to another device and that volume can be reinitialized by the DASDI program. After the defective tracks have been analyzed and the alternate tracks assigned as their replacements, the volume may once again be loaded with data. Direct access device volumes such as disks and drums have unique physical limitations that are not existent in magnetic tape volumes. Recording tracks for certain direct access storage devices are often defined as being capable of containing a maximum number of bytes of data. The real utilization of this available storage space depends almost entirely on the programmer's specification of the data set format parameters. For example, 100 unblocked records of 30 bytes each would require considerably more storage space than a single data block consisting of 100 30-byte records. This results from the presence of the inter-record gap (IRG) between each logical data block. Although the inter-record gap that is created on a magnetic tape is always of the same length for each record, regardless of the record length, the inter-record gaps on a direct access device are variable, although reasonably predictable, in length. There is a formula for calculating the inter-record gap that will follow any data block on a direct access device, but it will suffice to say that the length of the inter-record gap will vary according to the length of the data block just written. The greater the length of the written data block, the greater the length of the inter-record gap. The exception to this rule is that if a data block is recorded up to or near the exact physical end of a recording track, then it is not necessary for an inter-record gap to exist at all. For example, if a record is written that would normally create an inter-record gap of 160 bytes, but is recorded so near the end of a physical track that only enough space for five bytes of inter-record gap exist on that track, the system will accept this condition.

Certain direct access devices contain special features, or have optional features available, that will permit a data block to begin on one logical track and continue for one or more successive tracks without interruption. This is generally referred to as a "track overflow" or "cylinder overflow" feature, depending on the hardware configuration and the operating system that is used. What this means to the programmer is that he is no longer restricted to a record length or block length that is less than or equal to the maximum byte length of a single recording track. The standard byte capacity of a single track on the disk pack for an IBM 2314 DASF is 7294 bytes—but by utilizing the track overflow feature available with this equipment, the problem program could write a 20,000 byte data block without concern for the physical limitations of a single track. Assuming that such a data block began in the first byte of any single track, the system would record 7294 bytes on that track, another 7294 bytes on the following track, and finally 5412 bytes on the third successive track. It should be noted that the track overflow feature will function only when the data set consists entirely of a contiguous quantity of assigned tracks. Any attempt to write a record that would be re-

quired to overflow to a noncontiguous track, or to overflow to another volume, will create an error condition.

The allocation of space on a direct access device is provided at the time that a data set is created. Under the full Operating System this service is performed by the Job Control Language and the respective job control cards. The request for a certain amount of space, expressed in quantities of tracks, cylinders, or blocks, is coded with the "SPACE=" parameter of the Job Control Language on the Data Definition (DD) card. Whenever space is requested, one of the options provided to the programmer is the ability to request an initial amount of space and then to indicate an increment of additional quantities of storage space to be provided in the event that the initial allocation is not sufficient to contain the entire data set. In this type of allocation, whenever the space that was requested by the initial space parameter request has been exhausted, whether during the creation of the data set or during subsequent additions to the data set, the system will allocate additional space to the data set in quantities equal to the secondary increments requested. The areas allocated under these conditions are referred to as secondary extents; the original space provided is referred to as the primary extent. Unless specifically stated within the Job Control Language, the secondary extents are not necessarily assigned contiguously with the primary extents or even with each other. The address of each of the extents of a data set is contained within the DSCB (Data Set Control Block) entries in the volume VTOC.

The information provided within this section has been considerably general in nature because variations occur between the different operating systems. It will be necessary for the programmer to obtain copies of the technical manuals that pertain to the type of operating system that he will be working with and review them in their entirety. In addition, there are numerous educational courses available through commercial training centers and computer manufacturers educational centers on these subjects.

THE OPERATING SYSTEM (OS) ACCESS METHODS

This portion of the text is provided for those readers who wish to become somewhat more involved with the concepts of data set organization and the data management routines that create and access data sets. It is written in relation to the full Operating System (OS) because this is the most powerful and versatile of all of the available operating systems at this time. The data contained within this section is being presented as an overview of the various access methods and the optional variations that are available. It is intended to provide a general overall concept of the relationship of the access methods to the file organizations systems and input/output devices without requiring the detailed study of the individual logic modules and macroinstructions of the Operating System. However, this data *is not* intended as sufficient educational material to provide the proficiency and knowledge required to apply these concepts, but rather should allow the programmer to grasp the fundamentals of access methods and file organization systems.

As implied, and in some instances specified, throughout this section the decision of which access method to use is based on the following considerations.

1. The I/O devices to be utilized.
2. The logical format of the data sets involved.
3. The requirements of the problem program.

The access method utilized by the problem program need not be restricted to one particular method. Multiple access methods, or versions of a single method, may be used by the problem program in order to perform its required functions in an orderly, efficient manner.

A. GENERAL TERMINOLOGY AND DESCRIPTIONS

An access method may be literally defined as ". . . a group, or groups of macroinstructions that will interface for the computer Central Processing Unit (CPU) to a particular device, or devices, in order to accomplish input/output tasks for a problem program." In many instances this includes the I/O completion-checking functions, error handling, data formatting, validity checking, seeking and locating data records, etc. Because of the extensive range of device peculiarities, as well as the unlimited scope of uniqueness in problem programs, it is logical that a number of different access methods have been made available to the programmer. This will allow him the choice of the access method best suited to the task and the execution of that task with a minimum of parameter coding.

At "systems generation" time, the systems analyst has the option of specifying whether or not he may wish to include resident access method load modules in the system nucleus each time this system is loading into the CPU. If he does specify that the resident access method option is to be included within his system, the computer operator is given a choice of three options at IPL (Initial Program Load) time. These options are listed below.

1. The computer operator may advise the operating system, via the console typewriter, that no access method load modules are to be made resident at this time. This would normally provide additional core storage for the problem programs to operate within.

2. He may allow the system to extract, and make resident, a specified list of access method modules. This list would be contained within the "procedure library" of the operating system. That list may be created or altered at any time by the systems analyst responsible for that particular computer operating system. Because of the core allocations required for these resident modules, discretion and experienced judgment must be used in determining which modules would

be on the "resident list" and which ones would not. The systems analyst who is responsible for creating the list of access method load modules to be made resident must analyze them in order to determine their priority to be made resident. This would be based on core size requirements, frequency of usage, time to be saved in having them resident, and similar considerations.

3. The third option available to the computer operator is to enter the name of an alternate list, or lists, of access method load modules that are to be made resident for a special system run or test. An example of this could be related to the testing of telecommunications techniques. During normal system operation, it might not be advantageous to have any telecommunications access method modules resident. However, if a special, lengthy telecommunications test was to be made, it would be correct for the operator to reinitialize the system and make resident only the telecommunications access method modules along with any other modules required by this test.

The access methods that will be generally discussed herein are:

BDAM	Basic Direct Access Method
BISAM	Basic Indexed Sequential Access Method
BPAM	Basic Partitioned Access Method
BSAM	Basic Sequential Access Method
BTAM	Basic Telecommunications Access Method
QISAM	Queued Indexed Sequential Access Method
QSAM	Queued Sequential Access Method
QTAM	Queued Telecommunications Access Method
GAM	Graphics Access Method
EXCP	Execute Channel Program

The last method on this list, EXCP, will not be covered except to recognize its inclusion here. It is indeed an access method, but one that would not normally be used by regular programming personnel. As a rule, the EXCP macroinstruction should only be used by systems analysts and systems programmers who are thoroughly familiar with the internal structure of the Operating System and who have a peculiar task to perform in which they must relay on the "manual" interrogation and manipulation of the I/O devices and channels.

The decision regarding what particular version of which access method to use is often, although not always, a compromise. In many instances a preestablished standard or existing data base will dictate the use of a particular access method. If this is not the case, then the compromise is entered into, based partially on the knowledge and capability of the programmer. It is entirely possible that an experienced programmer can manipulate a basic access method more efficiently than the performance of a queued access method version. The additional effort of detailed instruction and macro coding expended to obtain this control is rewarded by increased efficiency. Consequently, someone who is not as thoroughly experienced in the dictates of a basic access method could find it to his advantage to use a queued access method wherever possible. Inefficient use of an access method, or the use of an access method that is poorly matched to the task, can result in excessive degradation of the performance of the problem program.

B. BASIC VERSUS QUEUED ACCESS METHODS

A graphic comparison between the basic and queued versions of access methods would be the action of preparing a cup of coffee, brewed to your particular liking, adding the measured ingredients, and stirring (Basic) —as opposed to pushing a button on a vending machine and having a prepared cup of coffee poured for you (Queued). The results may be coincidentally the same, but this is not likely the case.

In the one instance (Basic), it is the programmer's responsibility to determine that all of the necessary parameters are supplied and functions performed in order to achieve the desired result; in the other instance (Queued), many of the detail functions are performed for the programmer, leaving him the responsibility of controlling the major parameter functions only.

The five "manual versus automatic" functional differences between basic and queued access methods are the I/O Overlap Synchronization, Anticipatory Buffering, Blocking and Unblocking of Records, I/O Completion Checking, and Error Analysis and Exits. A comparison of these items follows.

1. I/O Overlap Synchronization

A. Basic: Each time that the problem program issues an I/O request, that request is passed on to the system to await execution. However, control is returned to the problem program immediately. If it is logically necessary for the physical I/O task to be completed before additional processing may take place, the program is required to wait for the termination of that I/O event and to test for its successful completion. It is conceivably possible for the programmer to anticipate the need for an I/O request and to consequently issue such a request prior to that point in his program where the logic would depend on completion of that I/O event. If the I/O request is dependent on the result of the logic to determine which record should be retrieved or created next, or which device should be accessed next, this technique would be impractical.

B. Queued: The issuance of an I/O request does not necessarily result in a processing delay at the time that the request was issued by the problem program, as will be explained in the discussion of Anticipatory Buffering. However, if an I/O request should happen to result in an immediate physical I/O task, control is not returned to the problem program until all functions of the task have been completed.

2. Anticipatory Buffering

A. Basic: Because the Operating System (OS) cannot predict the sequence in which records are to be processed under a basic access method, automatic buffering is not accomplished. The programmer does, however, have macroinstructions available to aid him in manipulating buffer control. Buffers are filled, or emptied, in their entirety each time the problem program initiates an I/O request.

B. Queued: Buffer processing is controlled by the Operating System in such a manner that an I/O request by the problem program need not result in a physical I/O task at that time. If it does, an entire buffer of data may be filled, or emptied by the one physical I/O task, deferring the need for a separate physical I/O task each time the problem program requires another single unit of data. The status and location of the next selective buffer of data to be processed is automatically controlled.

3. Blocking and Unblocking

A. Basic: The basic access method macros process blocks of data only. Therefore, a block of data that consists of more than one logical record must be blocked or unblocked by the responsible problem program.

B. Queued: The macroinstructions provided with the queued access methods automatically manipulate the blocking and unblocking of records. This action is based on parameters specified in the problem program DCB (Data Control Block) or from data supplied by the Job Control Language or data set labels. The problem program needs only to request a record for processing, upon which request the combined operating system/access method will provide it with the next logically sequential record that should be processed. The programmer never needs to be concerned with which block, or even which buffer, has passed the record to him; or whether or not a physical I/O task was performed at that time. The reverse action is appropriate when the problem program is creating records to place onto an output data set. The created records are passed to the access method data management routines and thereafter it is the responsibility of those routines to determine when an actual physical I/O task is to be accomplished in order to place those records on the data set.

4. I/O Operation Completion and Error Exits

A. Basic: In order to be assured of proper I/O completion, the problem program may issue a CHECK macroinstruction that, in turn, will:

1. Cause the problem program to enter a "wait" condition until the physical I/O task is ended.
2. Test the Event Control Block for successful I/O completion.
3. Return control to the problem program if the I/O was successfully completed; or,
4. Reroute control to an error analysis routine if the I/O completion was not normal.

In lieu of the CHECK macroinstruction, the problem program may issue its own WAIT macroinstruction and then test the condition of the Event Control Block in order to determine the status of the condition codes returned as a result of the I/O task.

B. Queued: The access method data management routines will automatically handle all functions of completion status checking, error conditions and error routine routing, end-of-file conditions, and end-of-volume conditions. Control will not be returned to the problem program until these functions have been completed.

It should be noted at this point that there is not a queued access method counterpart for each of the basic access methods. Although the basic access methods include direct, indexed sequential, partitioned, sequential, and telecommunications, the queued access methods include only indexed sequential, sequential, and telecommunications. The direct and partitioned access methods contain inherent variables that preclude the use of a queued access method. For example, as discussed previously within this section, the anticipatory buffering provided by a queued access method depends on a predictable sequence of record accessing. This predictable sequence does not exist in a Direct or Partitioned access method, hence they have no queued versions at this time.

C. DIRECT ACCESS METHODS

As implied by the title, a direct access method is used to access or create data sets residing on a direct access storage device. Some devices that would fall into this category are the IBM 2311 DASD, the 2314 DASF, the 2301 or 2303 Drums, and the 2321 Data Cell.

The intent and purpose of direct addressing via direct accessing techniques is to be able to locate randomly organized records within the data set without reading or writing through multiple records that might precede, or follow, the record position that is being sought. This objective can be obtained with reasonably little overhead by using one of three addressing methods—direct addressing, direct addressing via the use of cross-reference tables, and indirect addressing with a randomizing/numerical conversion base. In utilizing these methods, identification of any particular record can be expressed in a number of ways: by relative record number, by relative record and actual identity key, by relative track and actual record number, by relative track and actual identity key, and by an actual address that consists of the unit, cylinder, track, and record numbers. In addition, there is an extended search option that will scan a specified number of records or tracks in an effort to locate the desired record position. Three of these methods of specifying the address of a record should be further defined as follows.

1. Relative Record Number—This type of addressing indicates the relative location of the record within the entire data set; relative to the point immediately prior to the first record within the data set. The access method will then compute the actual track and record position based on the physical number of records per track. This reference is applicable only when used with fixed-length unblocked records.

2. Relative Track and Actual Key—The addressing here is the relative location of the track containing the record (in relationship to the beginning of the data set) and an address of a core storage area containing the value of the identity key that represents the identification of the record to be located. The system computes the actual track address and then searches that track for the record with the matching key value.

3. Relative Track and Actual Record Number—This type of address represents the relative location of the track containing the record (in relationship to the beginning of the data set) and the actual record number on that track. The system computes the actual track address and then goes to the actual record number on that track.

Direct addressing utilizes the principal that each record, record identifier, or key will reflect a sequential/contiguous numbering system that represents the relationship of that record to its relative position within the data set. This is the technique utilized by Relative Record addressing. One example of this might be that if a set of data records contained embedded keys whose values ranged contiguously from 1 to 500, a record with a key of 236 would be construed to be the 236th record within that data set.

When the access method data management routines receive a request for accessing a record via a relative record number, the routines compute the actual track and record number and then directs the I/O function to that address. This concept can be applied only to type "F" (fixed-length) records.

Direct address via the use of a cross-reference table may be interpreted as a form of indexing. In utilizing this technique, it is necessary to create a table containing the actual address (or a relative track and record number) at the time at which the data record is written and stored on the device. The building of that table is the responsibility of the problem program. When attempting to access the data records, it is then necessary for the problem program to search the table for the identifier of this record, find the actual or relative address associated with it, and then use that information to direct the I/O request to the data record desired. Under normal considerations, this scheme of direct addressing would appear to be prohibitive for any large-volume files. However, it is entirely possible to utilize subtables for records containing identifiers with similar attribute groupings, somewhat in the same manner as the index levels of a dictionary might be arranged. For example, if the record identifiers consisted of alphabetic characters, a set of subtables could be organized for the letters from A to F, from G to K, from L to Q, from R to U, and from V to Z. Consideration should be given to the possibility of frequency grouping of certain characters or values. That is, the majority of records may possibly be grouped under a relatively small percentage of the identifier characters, resulting in extremely unbalanced subtables.

Indirect addressing via randomizing or numerical conversion can become quite complex. Generally, it is performed by a mathematical manipulation of the record key in such a manner as to create a unique identifier that will relate to the address of the track containing the record. There are many such randomizing/conversion procedures that may have considerable merit. The majority of technical manuals make no attempt to completely define or to recommend a particular procedure of this type because of the quantity of different types of techniques that are available. It is the user's option to select the one that is most adaptable to his needs.

In essence, then, a direct access method is used to address and access any position within a data set that is comprised of records that may appear in a nonsequential, noncontiguous identity pattern.

D. SEQUENTIAL ACCESS METHODS

Sequential access methods have the widest range of device-independent applications of any of the access methods. They can be applied to magnetic tape, paper tape devices, printers, card reader/punches, and direct access devices. It is this latitude of performance that allows the sequential access methods to increase computer facility capabilities through the concept of *device independence.*

Sequential file organization is the common link between data sets and device independence. The problem program itself may omit all reference to device-dependent characteristics. At execution time, such references may be inserted via the job stream or by computer operator intervention. If the problem program is requesting 80-character data records, it can be designed to accept such records from any device capable of passing them to it—card reader, magnetic tape, or direct access device. This can prove to be a valuable aid in efficient computer scheduling and utilization.

Although it might be normal to assume that a sequential access method is used only to process sequentially-organized data sets, this is not a factual assumption. A data set residing on a direct access device can be processed sequentially, regardless of the data set organization pattern. Generally, however, the realistic interpretation of a sequential access method is to *sequentially access* a stream of data (one block or record of data following another) in a contiguous manner, whether or not the data is in a logically sequential order of value or identity.

Conversely, a sequential data set is usually considered to be in a logical sequential order based on the criteria of a particular identity or value arranged in an ascending or descending sequence. In addition, data sets with a format of other than sequential organization may be created by a sequential access method and later interrogated by an altogether different access method, depending on the format in which it was arranged.

When the Queued Sequential Access Method (QSAM) is used in conjunction with multiple buffering, the most efficient use of processing overlap with I/O tasks is realized. If a problem program specified three buffer areas, each of which would contain a block of data consisting of 20 data records, a physical I/O task would be accomplished for every 20 data records processed—each time all of the data in a single buffer area was utilized. This would mean that the problem program would still have data records to be processed, during which time a physical I/O task could be completed and the recently emptied buffer(s) could be replenished with data and requeued for usage. It must be pointed out however, that each buffer occupies core within the problem program partition of the Central Processing Unit— three 2000-byte buffers would occupy 6000 bytes of core. The decision must be made as to which factor is the more important— process time or core availability.

E. INDEXED SEQUENTIAL ACCESS METHODS

The indexed sequential data set format is arranged in a logical order, based on the criteria of sequence of a particular value or identity related to each record. As each block of records or record is written, the system precedes that block of data with an identity key. This key contains the identity value of the highest-value record within that block. In a logical sequence mode, this would be the value of the last record within a block of records—if the records were unblocked, this would be the key of the single, unblocked record.

In order to easily find a particular record, up to three unique levels of index are created by the data management routines at the time that the data set is generated. These are the track index, the cylinder index, and the master index. Depending on the size of the data set, it is often practical to use only two of these index levels—the track index and the cylinder index. The master index level appears to be practical only when the data set is exceptionally large. Through the use of parameters of Job Control Language, any index other than the track index can be positioned in chosen areas—embedded in the middle of the data set, embedded at the beginning or end of the data set, or assigned to an entirely different volume.

For the purpose of further definition of an indexed sequential data set, assume that the following discussion will relate to a data set that contains a "parts-list" master file. The file has been organized in ascending sequential order, from the lowest-value part-number record to the highest-value part-number record. During the creation of the data set, as each block of part-number records was written, the system initialized a key containing the high-value part-number for that data block and then wrote that key immediately preceding that particular block of data.

For each cylinder of data that is created, the system access method generates a *track index* on the first track of that cylinder. The track index is comprised of one entry for every track of data within that cylinder. In this instance, then, there would be an entry for each track, each entry containing the highest-value part-number key on that track along with the address of the referenced track. If this data set had been created on a 2314 DASF, which contains 20 tracks per cylinder, there would be 19 tracks of part-number data records and one track for the track index. The track index would normally contain 19 track entries—one for each of the data tracks.

For each track index created (referencing the data records in one complete cylinder), the system creates an entry for a *cylinder index*. The cylinder index will contain one entry for each cylinder occupied by the data set. This entry would contain the address of the track index for a cylinder (the cylinder number and track number zero) and the highest-value part-number contained on that track index. Consequently, if the data set physically occupied 50 cylinders, the cylinder index would contain 50 entries—each entry containing the address of a track index and the highest-value part-number related to that index.

If the data set is sufficiently large enough to create numerous tracks of cylinder index entries, the programmer has the option of creating a master index level. In line with the step-by-step scheme demonstrated by the lower-level index structures, the master index may contain an entry for each track of cylinder index entries created—giving the address of each of the cylinder index tracks and the high-value part-number contained on that track. The master index level itself may also consist of three levels of index if the data set is large enough and the programmer deems this to be necessary. Each level of master index can create entries for the next higher level of master index, for a maximum total of three levels.

In describing the procedure that takes place in retrieving a data record, assume that a data record was to be accessed for part-number 32967. From the master index down to the part-number record desired, the action could be represented as follows.

1. Scan the master index (from low value to high value) for the cylinder index address whose highest part-number is greater than or equal to 32967.

2. Go to that cylinder index track and scan it (from low value to high value) for the track index entry whose highest value part-number is greater than or equal to 32967.

3. Go to that track index track and scan it (from low value to high value) for the address of the data track whose highest value part-number is greater than or equal to 32967.

4. Access that data track and scan the block keys (from low value to high value) for the block of data whose highest value part-number is greater than or equal to 32967.

5. Access and extract that block of data records and find the single data record for part-number 32967.

Although this chain of action taken to locate a single record might seem rather lengthy, it performs rather expediently. This type of file accessing is of particular value when used in an environment wherein a particular "header record" is to be located and then a subsequent series of sequential "trailer records" are to be accessed.

Among the various capabilities of the indexed sequential access method are the following:

1. The data set can be read or written sequentially or randomly.

2. Individual records may be processed in any order.

3. Records can be deleted.

4. New records can be added.

5. Automatic logical positioning of new records within the data set.

6. Automatic handling of overflow conditions for new records inserted into the area in which they belong, when such an insertion expands that area beyond the track capacity.

The queued and basic versions of the Indexed Sequential Access Method (QISAM and BISAM) are used interactively for overall performance. Their particular responsibilities are:

1. Create the data set—QISAM only
2. Process or update new data records—QISAM or BISAM
3. Insert new records—BISAM only

Continual insertions of new records are likely to cause the use of numerous overflow areas, resulting in a slowdown of record retrieval speeds. For this reason, the indexed sequential data set should be reorganized periodically, depending on the size and activity of the file.

F. PARTITIONED ACCESS METHOD

This access method, applicable only in conjunction with direct access devices, is used to create and access a partitioned data set. It is necessary, therefore, to understand the format concept of a partitioned data set and its general applications.

The partitioned data set has the general characteristics of both the indexed sequential and the sequentially organized data sets, although it is logically sequential and physically random. It is frequently used to store groups of programs similar to, and often referred to as, a "library." The two basic sections of a partitioned data set are the *directory* and the data area occupied by the *members* of the data set.

A. The Members: A member is a sequentially organized set of records that are referred to within the data set by a symbolic label or name. One or more members, in addition to the directory, comprise the partitioned data set. Although the records within a member are considered to be sequentially arranged, the location of the members themselves (within the overall data set) is random. In order to readily locate a particular member by its given name, the system builds a directory that is quite similar to simple indexing. By referencing the directory, which appears at the very beginning of the data set, the system is able to locate any member within its data set boundaries. A member may be added, deleted, or updated in its entirety. However, when a member is deleted from the data set, only the directory entry is actually removed. The space used by that member is not made available for reuse and cannot be utilized again until the data set is completely reorganized.

B. *The Directory:* The directory itself consists of a series of 256-byte blocks. Each block is made up of variable-length directory records, which may be considered to be entries similar to an index. Of the 256 bytes allocated for a directory block, up to 254 bytes may be utilized by the directory records. Each block is immediately preceded by an eight-byte field that contains the name of the last member record entry within that block. Each 256-byte block of directory records (entries) contains (for each entry):

1. A field containing the name of the member that it is referencing.
2. A three-byte field containing the address of the first record in that member. This address is in the form of a relative track number (relative to the beginning of the data set) and a relative block number within that track.
3. A one-byte field, in binary format, containing information regarding:
   (a) A code to indicate if the data in the name field is an "alias" for this member.
   (b) The number of halfwords of user data within this entry.
   (c) Whether one or more user pointers reference this particular member.

4. Up to 62 bytes of user data, in halfword increments, pertaining to the additional entry pointers for this member.

Because of the unique characteristics of a partitioned data set the Operating System provides special macroinstructions for manipulating the members and directory entries. These macros are:

BLDL—used to construct an entry list for the directory.

FIND—will find the starting address of a specified member and place that address into the Data Control Block so that a subsequent READ operation will access that member.

STOW—to add an entry for a member to an existing directory; or to delete, replace, or change a member name within a directory entry.

Members of a partitioned data set may be retrieved by the QSAM, BSAM, or BPAM access methods.

G. GRAPHICS ACCESS METHOD

The Graphics Access Method consists of a series of macroinstructions and control routines that coordinate the interface activities between the Operating System, a control unit, and cathode-ray display devices. Such devices would include the IBM 2250 Display Unit and the 2260 Display Station.

In effect, these display devices are merely another category of I/O devices that are to be used as a part of a computer system configuration. They are unique, however, inasmuch as both input data and output data can be processed by visual control with reasonably brief CPU lock-up. Data can be entered, retrieved, processed, and/or manipulated in a multiprogramming environment in such a way as to create minimum degradation to programs functioning through normal processing partitions.

In order to maintain a visual display on a CRT (cathode-ray tube) screen without CPU activity, a technique known as *delay-line buffering* is utilized. Data processed through the display unit keyboard, or data passed to the control unit from the CPU, is held in a defined sequence of buffers within the control unit, or control section, of the display device. The contents of these buffers are continually rewritten (or "repainted") across the face of the cathode-ray tube at intervals frequent enough to prevent a "fadeout and regeneration" flicker. The data being displayed will remain constant until it is erased or altered via the device keyboard or by program control.

These activities rquire a unique method of manipulation and control—hence, the Graphics Access Method. In a sense, however, the Graphics Access Method is not truly an access method for interrogation and creation of data sets in the manner normally associated with an access method. Instead, it may be thought of more realistically as a means of accessing a unique device, which in turn can access different data sets via program control.

The three principle functions of the Graphics Access Method are Graphic Data Management, I/O Control, and Attention Handling insofar as each are related to display devices.

The Graphic Data Management includes the performing of buffer management and storing graphic orders and data into user-specified output areas. It is responsible for maintaining the assignment and release of buffer storage areas, delay-line buffer contents and buffered-data positioning.

The I/O Control functions consist of performing "open" and "close" activities and initializing data transmissions as requested by the various read and write macroinstructions peculiar to graphic display devices. This action involves the construction and initialization of control blocks, data fields, and storage areas that are required for the interface of data transmission between the CPU and graphic display devices. The organizing of channel command words and the construction of channel programs is also within the jurisdiction of the I/O Control functions.

The Attention Handling routines are sub-divided into two types—basic and express. The prime purpose of attention handling is to determine which display device is requesting the attention of the CPU in order to transmit a display of data, or to enter a query for a reply.

A reasonable comparison of the performance of the two types of Attention Handling routines would be the similarity to the basic and queued access methods. When using express attention handling, much of the error checking, data analyzing, and control functions are performed by the system, parallel to the manner in which these functions are supervised by the queued access methods. Basic attention handling requires more manipulation and direct control of these functions by the problem program, similar to the effort required in a basic access method. However, this is not meant to infer that express attention handling should be used at all times in order to relieve the problem program of additional responsibilities. The problem program may require peculiar logic performance that necessitates the use of a direct manner of attention handling, in which case the basic attention handling routines should be used.

The capabilities of the Graphics Access Method macroinstructions and control routines provide a wide, flexible base for problem program concepts. Many variations of reading and displaying data are made possible by parameter options within the macroinstructions. As an example, the GREAD macroinstruction contains the option of six differently functioning read operations. The application of the variations of these macros and the control routines would depend entirely on the requirements of the problem program and the configuration/mode of the display units and computer.

It must be noted at this point that display devices are not always directly controlled by graphics macros through the problem program. Some display devices, such as the IBM 2260 Display Station, can be well utilized as a "remote" terminal. The remote application consists of data transmission between the display device and the computer via data line transmission (i.e., telephone lines) as opposed to the local mode in which the device/control unit communicates directly through a channel (cable) with the computer. Although the display device may present similar end results under both the local and remote modes, the intermediate data transmission and interfacing are controlled by telecommunications access methods when the device is operated in a remote status.

H. TELECOMMUNICATIONS ACCESS METHODS

Because of the extensive number of characteristics, logic modules, macroinstructions, and control modules directly comprising the Telecommunications Access Method, this analysis must be presented in a very general nature. It will, however, attempt to review the normal services performed without becoming too detailed into the variations of these functions.

Telecommunications, as related to computer applications, may be interpreted as the exchange and transmission of data, via communication lines, between a remote terminal and the CPU of a computer system. The Telecommunications Access Methods of the System/360 Operating System are used to control the transfer of data in such an environment. Some of the remote terminal devices supported by this access method are the IBM 1030 Data Collection System, the IBM 2848/2260 Display Station Complex and the IBM 2740 Communications Terminal. These devices must be linked to the computer CPU via a Data Adapter Unit or a Transmission Control unit.

Similar to other access methods, the Telecommunications Access Method has both a basic and a queued version. The comparison between these two versions is parallel to the same comparison for other access methods— that is, the queued version performs many functional routines automatically, whereas the basic version requires problem program control of similar functions.

The major role of the Telecommunications Access Method is to control transmission, reception and analysis of units of work, these units being referred to as "messages." In fulfilling this role, it must necessarily be able to interpret problems and conditions arising from transmission line interference, device busy/not available indications, and invalid transmissions in general. These are in addition to its normal functions of I/O Control, Buffer Management, Read/Write Routines, Polling, Addressing, and Message Processing, which are supplemented by an extensive list of macroinstructions.

One of the unique tasks performed by the Telecommunications Access Method is *polling*. This is a periodic sequence of action, taken by the CPU or control terminal and responded to by the remote terminals in order to determine whether or not any terminal is waiting to transmit data. The concept of polling is for the controlling unit to periodically transmit several selective characters whose peculiar identity directs that transmission to a particular remote terminal and its components. If that device has a message to transmit to the control unit, it responds with a coded "yes"; if not, it responds with a "no." In this mode of operation the control unit mandates the periodic and systematic selection of terminals that may transmit, and does so in an orderly fashion. The opposing mode of transmission operations is one in which a terminal will attempt to obtain exclusive control of a transmission line whenever it has data prepared for transmission. This latter mode, known as "contention," could conceivably create undue delay of transmission from any one terminal if its contention for transmission line control was consistently "beat out" by other terminals.

A control unit or terminal may implement another version of polling known as "addressing." In this instance, which is control unit-to-terminal or terminal-to-terminal, the first unit transmits several selective characters identifying the terminal being called and advising that terminal that the sending unit has a message to transmit. The receiving terminal, in turn, will then respond as to whether or not it is available to receive the message at this time.

It is evident that the Telecommunications

Access Methods are necessarily more complex and expansive than the data set access methods usually associated with a computer system. However, proper control and performance of these functions can establish an efficient network of "satellites" capable of remote data entry, data inquiry/response, scheduling, and communication, and a functional means of remote job processing known as remote job entry.

TABLES AND GLOSSARY

A. Table of Contiguous Bit Position Values and Respective "Powers-of-Two" Values

Bit Position	'2' to the Nth Power	Decimal Value of Bit Position
1	0	1
2	1	2
3	2	4
4	3	8
5	4	16
6	5	32
7	6	64
8	7	128
9	8	256
10	9	512
11	10	1,024
12	11	2,048
13	12	4,096
14	13	8,192
15	14	16,384
16	15	32,768
17	16	65,536
18	17	131,072
19	18	262,144
20	19	524,288
21	20	1,048,576
22	21	2,097,152
23	22	4,194,304
24	23	8,388,608
25	24	16,777,216
26	25	33,554,432
27	26	67,108,864
28	27	134,217,728
29	28	268,435,456
30	29	536,870,912
31	30	1,073,741,824
32	31	2,147,483,648

The implied bit positions are considered to be numbered from right to left, from low-order to high-order.

The "Powers-of-Two" value of any given bit position is not considered to be effective unless it is occupied by a one-bit.

B. Hexadecimal/Decimal Conversion Table

FOUR-BYTE FULLWORD

	HALFWORD #1							HALFWORD #2							
	BYTE 1				BYTE 2				BYTE 3				BYTE 4		
HALF-BYTE 1		HALF-BYTE 2		HALF-BYTE 3		HALF-BYTE 4		HALF-BYTE 5		HALF-BYTE 6		HALF-BYTE 7		HALF-BYTE 8	
Hex	Decimal	Hex	Decimal	Hex	Decimal	Hex	Decimal	Hex	Decimal	Hex	Decimal	Hex	Decimal	Hex	Decimal
0	0	0	0	0	0	0	0	0	0	0	0	0	0	0	0
1	1	1	16	1	256	1	4,096	1	65,536	1	1,048,576	1	16,777,216	1	268,435,456
2	2	2	32	2	512	2	8,192	2	131,072	2	2,097,152	2	33,554,432	2	536,870,912
3	3	3	48	3	768	3	12,288	3	196,608	3	3,145,728	3	50,331,648	3	805,306,368
4	4	4	64	4	1,024	4	16,384	4	262,144	4	4,194,304	4	67,108,864	4	1,073,741,824
5	5	5	80	5	1,280	5	20,480	5	327,680	5	5,242,880	5	83,886,080	5	1,342,177,280
6	6	6	96	6	1,536	6	24,576	6	393,216	6	6,291,456	6	100,663,296	6	1,610,612,736
7	7	7	112	7	1,792	7	28,672	7	458,752	7	7,340,032	7	117,440,512	7	1,879,048,192
8	8	8	128	8	2,048	8	32,768	8	524,288	8	8,388,608	8	134,217,728	8	2,147,483,648
9	9	9	144	9	2,304	9	36,864	9	589,824	9	9,437,184	9	150,994,944	9	2,415,919,104
A	10	A	160	A	2,560	A	40,960	A	655,360	A	10,485,760	A	167,772,160	A	2,684,354,560
B	11	B	176	B	2,816	B	45,056	B	720,896	B	11,534,336	B	184,549,376	B	2,952,790,016
C	12	C	192	C	3,072	C	49,152	C	786,432	C	12,582,912	C	201,326,592	C	3,221,225,472
D	13	D	208	D	3,328	D	53,248	D	851,968	D	13,631,488	D	218,103,808	D	3,489,660,928
E	14	E	224	E	3,584	E	57,344	E	917,504	E	14,680,064	E	234,881,024	E	3,758,096,384
F	15	F	240	F	3,840	F	61,440	F	983,040	F	15,728,640	F	251,658,240	F	4,026,531,840

C. Table of Condition Code Settings

This table contains the various Condition Code settings that might occur as a result of the execution of the Assembler Language instructions. The headings over each of the result columns represent the mask value that would agree with the configuration of the PSW Condition Code bits. This mask value is the one that would be used within the instruction statement, i.e., BC 8,LABEL. The condition indicated relates to the result within the first operand or the condition of the first operand as compared to the second operand.

Instruction	Op Code	8 = Mask	4 = Mask	2 = Mask	1 = Mask
ADD	A	Zero	Negative	Positive	Overflow
ADD REGISTERS	AR	Zero	Negative	Positive	Overflow
ADD PACKED	AP	Zero	Negative	Positive	Overflow
ADD HALFWORD	AH	Zero	Negative	Positive	Overflow
ADD LOGICAL	AL	Zero, no carry	Not zero, no carry	Zero, carry	Not zero, carry
AND LOGICAL	N	Zero	Not zero	—	—
AND LOGICAL	NC	Zero	Not zero	—	—
AND LOGICAL	NR	Zero	Not zero	—	—
AND LOGICAL IMMEDIATE	NI	Zero	Not zero	—	—
COMPARE	C	Equal	Low	High	—
COMPARE REGISTERS	CR	Equal	Low	High	—
COMPARE PACKED	CP	Equal	Low	High	—
COMPARE HALFWORD	CH	Equal	Low	High	—
COMPARE LOGICAL	CL	Equal	Low	High	—
COMPARE LOGICAL CHARACTERS	CLC	Equal	Low	High	—
COMPARE LOGICAL REGISTERS	CLR	Equal	Low	High	—
COMPARE LOGICAL IMMEDIATE	CLI	Equal	Low	High	—
EDIT	ED	Zero	Negative	Positive	—
EDIT & MARK	EDMK	Zero	Negative	Positive	—
EXCLUSIVE OR	X	Zero	Not zero	—	—
EXCLUSIVE OR	XC	Zero	Not zero	—	—
EXCLUSIVE OR	XR	Zero	Not zero	—	—
EXCLUSIVE OR IMMEDIATE	XI	Zero	Not zero	—	—
LOAD & TEST REGISTER	LTR	Zero	Negative	Positive	—
LOAD COMPLEMENT REGISTER	LCR	Zero	Negative	Positive	Overflow
LOAD NEGATIVE REGISTER	LNR	Zero	Negative	—	—
LOAD POSITIVE REGISTER	LPR	Zero	—	Positive	Overflow
OR LOGICAL	O	Zero	Not zero	—	—
OR LOGICAL	OC	Zero	Not zero	—	—
OR LOGICAL	OR	Zero	Not zero	—	—
OR LOGICAL IMMEDIATE	OI	Zero	Not zero	—	—
SHIFT LEFT DOUBLE ALGEB.	SLDA	Zero	Negative	Positive	Overflow
SHIFT LEFT ALGEBAICALLY	SLA	Zero	Negative	Positive	Overflow
SHIFT RIGHT DOUBLE ALGEB.	SRDA	Zero	Negative	Positive	—
SHIFT RIGHT ALGEBRAICALLY	SRA	Zero	Negative	Positive	—
SUBTRACT	S	Zero	Negative	Positive	—
SUBTRACT REGISTERS	SR	Zero	Negative	Positive	Overflow
SUBTRACT PACKED	SP	Zero	Negative	Positive	Overflow
SUBTRACT HALFWORD	SH	Zero	Negative	Positive	Overflow
SUBTRACT LOGICAL	SL	—	Not zero, no carry	Zero, carry	Not zero, carry
SUBTRACT LOGICAL REGISTERS	SLR	—	Not zero, no carry	Zero, carry	Not zero, carry
TEST UNDER MASK	TM	All zero-bits	Mixed bits	—	All one-bits
TRANSLATE & TEST	TRT	Zero	Incomplete	Complete	—
ZERO & ADD PACKED	ZAP	Zero	Negative	Positive	Overflow

D. Table of Program Interrupt Conditions

Instruction	OP CODE	Possible Program Interruptions					
		ADDR	SPEC	OVFL	PROT	OPERN	OTHER
ADD	A	X	X	F			
ADD HALFWORD	AH	X	X	F			
ADD LOGICAL	AL	X	X				
ADD PACKED	AP	X		D	X	X	DATA
ADD REGISTERS	AR		F				
AND	N	X	X				
AND	NC	X			X		
AND IMMEDIATE	NI	X			X		
COMPARE	C	X	X				
COMPARE HALFWORD	CH	X	X				
COMPARE LOGICAL	CL	X	X				
COMPARE LOGICAL CHARACTERS	CLC	X	X				
COMPARE LOGICAL IMMEDIATE	CLI	X					
COMPARE LOGICAL REGISTERS	CLR	X					
COMPARE PACKED	CP	X				X	DATA
CONVERT TO BINARY	CVB	X	X				DATA, F
CONVERT TO DECIMAL	CVD	X	X		X		DATA, F
DIVIDE	D	X	X				F
DIVIDE PACKED	DP	X	X		X	X	DATA, D
DIVIDE REGISTERS	DR		X				F
EDIT	ED	X			X	X	DATA
EDIT & MARK	EDMK	X			X	X	DATA
EXCLUSIVE OR	X	X	X				
EXCLUSIVE OR	XC	X			X		
EXCLUSIVE OR IMMEDIATE	XI	X			X		
INSERT CHARACTER	IC	X					
LOAD	L	X	X				
LOAD COMPLEMENT REGISTER	LCR			F			
LOAD HALFWORD	LH	X	X				
LOAD MULTIPLE	LM	X	X				
LOAD POSITIVE REGISTER	LPR			F			
MOVE CHARACTERS	MVC	X			X		
MOVE IMMEDIATE	MVI	X			X		
MOVE NUMERIC	MVN	X			X		
MOVE WITH OFFSET	MVO	X			X		
MOVE ZONE	MVZ	X			X		
MULTIPLY	M	X	X				
MULTIPLY HALFWORD	MH	X	X				
MULTIPLY PACKED	MP	X	X		X	X	DATA
MULTIPLY REGISTERS	MR		X				
OR	O	X	X				
OR	OC	X			X		
OR IMMEDIATE	OI	X			X		
PACK	PACK	X			X		
SHIFT LEFT ALGEBRAICALLY	SLA			F			
SHIFT LEFT DOUBLE ALGEB.	SLDA		X	F			
SHIFT LEFT DOUBLE LOGICAL	SLDL		X				
SHIFT RIGHT DOUBLE ALGEB.	SRDA		X				
SHIFT RIGHT DOUBLE LOGICAL	SRDL		X				
STORE	ST	X	X		X		
STORE CHARACTER	STC	X			X		
STORE HALFWORD	STH	X	X		X		
STORE MULTIPLE	STM	X	X		X		

Table of Program Interrupt Conditions (Continued)

Instruction	OP CODE	ADDR	SPEC	OVFL	PROT	OPERN	OTHER
				Possible Program Interruptions			
SUBTRACT	S	X	X	F			
SUBTRACT HALFWORD	SH	X	X	F			
SUBTRACT LOGICAL	SL	X	X	F			
SUBTRACT PACKED	SP	X		D	X	X	DATA
SUBTRACT REGISTERS	SR			F			
TEST UNDER MASK	TM	X					
TRANSLATE	TR	X			X		
TRANSLATE & TEST	TRT	X			X		
UNPACK	UNPK	X			X		
ZERO & ADD PACKED	ZAP	X		D	X	X	DATA

Explanation of Interruption Codes

ADDR	Addressing	OVFL	Overflow:	PROT	Protection
SPEC	Specification		D—Decimal	OPERN	Operation
			E—Exponent	OTHER	D—Decimal divide
			F—Fixed-point		F—Fixed-point divide

E. EBCDIC Character Table

This table contains the graphic representations of alphabetics, numerics, and symbols that are available as an EBCDIC character set. The lowercase alphabetics are not standard characters, but are available as special characters on printer units and other graphic devices.

Hex	Graphic	Bit Config.	Hex	Graphic	Bit Config.	Hex	Graphic	Bit Config.
40	(Blank)	0100 0000	84	d	1000 0100	C8	H	1100 1000
4A	¢	0100 1010	85	e	1000 0101	C9	I	1100 1001
4B	.	0100 1011	86	f	1000 0110	D1	J	1101 0001
4C	<	0100 1100	87	g	1000 0111	D2	K	1101 0010
4D	(	0100 1101	88	h	1000 1000	D3	L	1101 0011
4E	+	0100 1110	89	i	1000 1001	D4	M	1101 0100
4F	|	0100 1111	91	j	1001 0001	D5	N	1101 0101
50	&	0101 0000	92	k	1001 0010	D6	O	1101 0110
5A	!	0101 1010	93	l	1001 0011	D7	P	1101 0111
5B	$	0101 1011	94	m	1001 0100	D8	Q	1101 1000
5C	*	0101 1100	95	n	1001 0101	D9	R	1101 1001
5D	)	0101 1101	96	o	1001 0110	E2	S	1110 0010
5E	;	0101 1110	97	p	1001 0111	E3	T	1110 0011
5F	→	0101 1111	98	q	1001 1000	E4	U	1110 0100
60	-	0110 0000	99	r	1001 1001	E5	V	1110 0101
61	/	0110 0001	A2	s	1010 0010	E6	W	1110 0110
6B	,	0110 1011	A3	t	1010 0011	E7	X	1110 0111
6C	%	0110 1100	A4	u	1010 0100	E8	Y	1110 1000
6D	—	0110 1101	A5	v	1010 0101	E9	Z	1110 1001
6E	>	0110 1110	A6	w	1010 0110	F0	0	1111 0000
6F	?	0110 1111	A7	x	1010 0111	F1	1	1111 0001
7A	:	0111 1010	A8	y	1010 1000	F2	2	1111 0010
7B	#	0111 1011	A9	z	1010 1001	F3	3	1111 0011
7C	@	0111 1100	C1	A	1100 0001	F4	4	1111 0100
7D	'	0111 1101	C2	B	1100 0010	F5	5	1111 0101
7E	=	0111 1110	C3	C	1100 0011	F6	6	1111 0110
7F	''	0111 1111	C4	D	1100 0100	F7	7	1111 0111
81	a	1000 0001	C5	E	1100 0101	F8	8	1111 1000
82	b	1000 0010	C6	F	1100 0110	F9	9	1111 1001
83	c	1000 0011	C7	G	1100 0111			

F. Table of Assembler Language Instructions by Hexadecimal Code

Hex Code	Mnemonic	Instruction
05	BALR	Branch & Link Registers
06	BCTR	Branch On Count To Register
07	BCR	Branch On Condition To Register
10	LPR	Load Positive Register
11	LNR	Load Negative Register
12	LTR	Load & Test Register
13	LCR	Load Complement Register
14	NR	And (RR Format)
15	CLR	Compare Logical Registers
16	OR	Or Logical (RR Format)
17	XR	Exclusive Or (RR Format)
18	LR	Load Register
19	CR	Compare Registers
1A	AR	Add Registers
1B	SR	Subtract Registers
1C	MR	Multiply Registers
1D	DR	Divide Registers
40	STH	Store Halfword
41	LA	Load Address
42	STC	Store Character
43	IC	Insert Character
45	BAL	Branch & Link
46	BCT	Branch On Count
47	BC	Branch On Condition
48	LH	Load Halfword
49	CH	Compare Halfword
4A	AH	Add Halfword
4B	SH	Subtract Halfword
4C	MH	Multiply Halfword
4E	CVD	Convert To Decimal
4F	CVB	Convert to Binary
50	ST	Store
54	N	And (RX Format)
55	CL	Compare Logical
56	O	Or (RX Format)
57	X	Exclusive Or (RX Format)
58	L	Load
59	C	Compare
5A	A	Add
5B	S	Subtract
5C	M	Multiply
5D	D	Divide
5E	AL	Add Logical
5F	SL	Subtract Logical
86	BXH	Branch On Index High
87	BXLE	Branch On Index Low or Equal
88	SRL	Shift Right Logical
89	SLL	Shift Left Logical
8A	SRA	Shift Right Algebraically
8B	SLA	Shift Left Algebraically
8C	SRDL	Shift Right Double Logical
8D	SLDL	Shift Left Double Logical
8E	SRDA	Shift Right Double Algebraically
8F	SLDA	Shift Left Double Algebraically

Table of Assembler Language Instructions by Hexadecimal Code (Continued)

Hex Code	Mnemonic	Instruction
90	STM	Store Multiple
91	TM	Test Under Mask
92	MVI	Move Immediate
94	NI	And Immediate (SI Format)
95	CLI	Compare Logical Immediate
96	OI	Or Immediate (SI Format)
97	XI	Exclusive Or Immediate (SI Format)
98	LM	Load Multiple
D1	MVN	Move Numeric
D2	MVC	Move Characters
D3	MVZ	Move Zone
D4	NC	And (SS Format)
D5	CLC	Compare Logical Characters
D6	OC	Or (SS Format)
D7	XC	Exclusive Or (SS Format)
DC	TR	Translate
DD	TRT	Translate & Test
DE	ED	Edit
DF	EDMK	Edit & Mark
F1	MVO	Move With Offset
F2	PACK	Pack
F3	UNPK	Unpack
F8	ZAP	Zero & Add Packed
F9	CP	Compare Packed
FA	AP	Add Packed
FB	SP	Subtract Packed
FC	MP	Multiply Packed
FD	DP	Divide Packed

ANSWERS TO
REVIEW EXERCISES

CHAPTER 3

1. Zero and One (0 and 1)
2. Sign-bit   Integer
3. Thirty-one (31)
4. Hexadecimal
5. Eight (8)
6. Twelve (12)
7. Hexadecimal
8. Zoned decimal

9a.

0000	0000	1011	1110	0111	1011		

9b.

0000	0000	0000	0011	0101	1001	0100	1001

9c.

0000	0000	0010	1101	0010	0101		

10a. $+28,781$

10b. $+2,216,797$

10c. $+2,686$

10d. $+10,438,659$

10e. $-7,659$

10f. $-277,522$

11a.

S				
0	110	1000	0101	1011

11b.

S				
1	101	1101	0011	1011

11c.

S							
0	000	0000	1101	1000	1101	1001	1101	0000

11d.

S							
1	111	1111	1111	1001	1110	1101	1111	1101

12a. 9,552,023

12b. 65,535

12c. 22,764

12d. 6,784,601

13a. Hex . . . 5CCA   Decimal . . . 23,754

13b. Hex . . . 3621   Decimal . . . 13,857

13c. Hex . . . DAAC   Decimal . . . 55,980

13d. Hex . . . D1F4   Decimal . . . 53,748

13e. Hex . . . 65F2   Decimal . . . 26,098

13f. Hex . . . BB8A   Decimal . . . 48,010

13g. Hex . . . 76D6   Decimal . . . 30,422

13h. Hex . . . 5010   Decimal . . . 20,496

14a.

0011	1111	1010	0110	1100	0001

14b.

0000	0000	1101	0101	1000	0111

14c.

0000	1111	0011	0100	0111	1110

14d.

0001	1000	1001	1100	0100	1011

15a. Hex . . . F25F   Decimal . . . 62,047

15b. Hex . . . 2EF3   Decimal . . . 12,019

15c. Hex . . . 70EA   Decimal . . . 28,906

15d. Hex . . . 38C6E   Decimal . . . 232,558

16a. +400

16b. −30,970

16c. +65,002

16d. −8,700

16e. 10,786,039 (assumed to be positive value)

17a. −3,022,570,649

17b. −7,034

17c. +5,581

17d. −40,067,997

CHAPTER 4

1. Four (4)   Fullword

2. Statement

3. Label, tag, or symbol

4. Sixteen (16)

5. Alphabetic

6. 0, 1, 2, 3, 4, 5, 6, 7, 8, 9, 10, 11, 12, 13, 14, and 15

7. Eight (8)

8. Op code

9. Hexadecimal

10. Positive

11. Four (4)

12. Operands

13. Positive   Negative

14. Two (2)

15. One (1)

16. +32,767   −32,768

17. Four (4)

18. Asterisk (*)

19. Explicit

20. DC (Define Constant)
    DS (Define Storage)

21. Register

22. Does not

23. True

24. False (The label will only address the first 50-byte field. Subsequent fields of 50 bytes must be accessed by address adjusting.)

25. Sixty (60) bytes

26. Fullword

27a. Eighteen (18)

27b. Sixty (60)

27c. Zero (0)

28. SETDATA1   R6SET
    DC   Y

    FLDA1   Z32MSG
    G   ORG

29. 256

30. Three (3)

31. X'40'

32. Thirteen (13)

33.

S	T	A	R	T	ƀ	ƀ	ƀ

34. Zero (The label contains 9 bytes and is therefore invalid)

35.

0	0	5	C	0	0	5	C	0	0	5	C

36.

0001	0001	0001	0001	0001	0001

37.

3	E	7	F

38. Sixteen (16)

39.

0	0	0	1	5	C	0	0	0	1	5	C

CHAPTER 6

1. Character format

A	B	C	X	Y	Z

Hex format

C	1	C	2	C	3	E	7	E	8	E	9

2. Character

7	8	9

Hex

F	7	F	8	F	9

3. Character

7	8	I	7	8	I	7	8	I

Hex

F	7	F	8	C	9	F	7	F	8	C	9	F	7	F	8	C	9

4. Character

$	.	.	/	/

Hex

5	B	4	B	4	B	6	1	6	1

5. Character

b̸	b̸

Hex

4	0	4	0

6. Character

$	6	1	0	$	6	1	0

Hex

5	B	F	6	F	1	F	0	5	B	F	6	F	1	F	0

7. Character

A	B	C

Hex

C	1	C	2	C	3

8. Character

9	9	9	9	9

Hex

F	9	F	9	F	9	F	9	F	9

9. Character

A	b̸	B	b̸	A	b̸	B	b̸

Hex

C	1	4	0	C	2	4	0	C	1	4	0	C	2	4	0

10. Character

$	-

Hex

5	B	6	0

11. Character

A	D	H	L	P	T

Hex

C	1	C	4	C	8	D	3	D	7	E	3

12.

Character	1		3		1		3		1		3		1		3	
Hex	F	1	F	3	F	1	F	3	F	1	F	3	F	1	F	3

13.

Character	ƀ	ƀ	ƀ	ƀ	ƀ

Character	ƀ	ƀ	ƀ	ƀ	ƀ

Character	ƀ	ƀ	ƀ	ƀ	ƀ

Hex	4	0	4	0	4	0	4	0	4	0

Hex	4	0	4	0	4	0	4	0	4	0

Hex	4	0	4	0	4	0	4	0	4	0	-

14.

Hex	2	2	5	C	2	2	5	C	2	2	5	C	2	2	5	C

15.

Hex	0	0	0	0	0	0	5	1	9	8	3	D

16.

Hex	0	0	6	1	0	C

17.

Hex	1	5	9	8	7	6	2	C	1	5	9	8	7	6	2	C

18.

Hex	9	D	9	D	9	D	9	D	9	D

19.

Hex	5	9	8	7	7	C	5	9	8	7	7	C

20.

Character	0		0		2		1		5		Q	
Hex	F	0	F	0	F	2	F	1	F	5	D	8

21.

Character	7		8		I		7		8		I	
Hex	F	7	F	8	C	9	F	7	F	8	C	9

22.

Character	0		0		3		3		C	
Hex	F	0	F	0	F	3	F	3	C	3

23.

Character	0		N		0		N		0		N	
Hex	F	0	D	5	F	0	D	5	F	0	D	5

24.

Character	4		1		7		B	
Hex	F	4	F	1	F	7	C	2

25.

Character	0		8		5		9		1		G	
Hex	F	0	F	8	F	5	F	9	F	1	C	7

26.

Hex	4	0	4	0	4	0	4	0
Binary	0100	0000	0100	0000	0100	0000	0100	0000

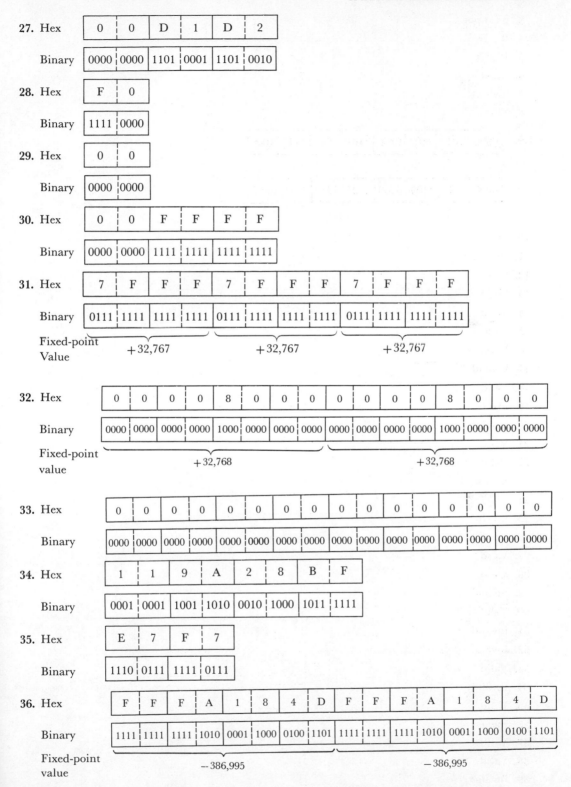

27. Hex

| 0 | 0 | D | 1 | D | 2 |

Binary

| 0000 | 0000 | 1101 | 0001 | 1101 | 0010 |

28. Hex

| F | 0 |

Binary

| 1111 | 0000 |

29. Hex

| 0 | 0 |

Binary

| 0000 | 0000 |

30. Hex

| 0 | 0 | F | F | F | F |

Binary

| 0000 | 0000 | 1111 | 1111 | 1111 | 1111 |

31. Hex

| 7 | F | F | F | 7 | F | F | F | 7 | F | F | F |

Binary

| 0111 | 1111 | 1111 | 1111 | 0111 | 1111 | 1111 | 1111 | 0111 | 1111 | 1111 | 1111 |

Fixed-point Value   +32,767   +32,767   +32,767

32. Hex

| 0 | 0 | 0 | 0 | 8 | 0 | 0 | 0 | 0 | 0 | 0 | 0 | 8 | 0 | 0 | 0 |

Binary

| 0000 | 0000 | 0000 | 0000 | 1000 | 0000 | 0000 | 0000 | 0000 | 0000 | 0000 | 0000 | 1000 | 0000 | 0000 | 0000 |

Fixed-point value   +32,768   +32,768

33. Hex

| 0 | 0 | 0 | 0 | 0 | 0 | 0 | 0 | 0 | 0 | 0 | 0 | 0 | 0 | 0 | 0 |

Binary

| 0000 | 0000 | 0000 | 0000 | 0000 | 0000 | 0000 | 0000 | 0000 | 0000 | 0000 | 0000 | 0000 | 0000 | 0000 | 0000 |

34. Hex

| 1 | 1 | 9 | A | 2 | 8 | B | F |

Binary

| 0001 | 0001 | 1001 | 1010 | 0010 | 1000 | 1011 | 1111 |

35. Hex

| E | 7 | F | 7 |

Binary

| 1110 | 0111 | 1111 | 0111 |

36. Hex

| F | F | F | A | 1 | 8 | 4 | D | F | F | F | A | 1 | 8 | 4 | D |

Binary

| 1111 | 1111 | 1111 | 1010 | 0001 | 1000 | 0100 | 1101 | 1111 | 1111 | 1111 | 1010 | 0001 | 1000 | 0100 | 1101 |

Fixed-point value   −386,995   −386,995

CHAPTER 7

1. High   Low   Bit

2. "immediate"

3. fixed-point

4. B   D

5. 16 bytes

6. equal

7. high

8. 256

9.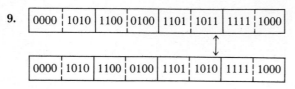

10. equal

11. less than

12. False

13. Valid

14. Valid

15. Valid

16. Valid

17. Invalid

18. Valid

19. Invalid

20. Invalid

21. Valid

22. Valid

23. Invalid

24. Valid

25. Invalid

26. Invalid

27. Valid

28. Valid

29. Invalid

30. Valid

31. Invalid

32. Invalid

33. Valid

34. Invalid

35. Valid

36. Invalid

37. Valid

38. Valid

39. Invalid

40. Invalid

41. Invalid

42. Invalid

43. Valid

44. Valid

45. Invalid

46. Invalid

47. Valid

48. Invalid

49. Valid

50. Invalid

51. Valid

52. Valid

53. Valid

CHAPTER 8

1. Program linkage

2. Branch On Condition (BC)   Branch On Condition to Register (BCR)

3. 15   forced

4. 8   4   2   1

5. 1st   +1

6a. The first operand would be less than or equal to the second operand.

6b. The first operand would not be equal to the second operand; or: The first operand would be greater than or less than the second operand.

6c. The first operand would be greater than or equal to the second operand.

6d. The first operand would be greater than the second operand.

6e. The first operand would be equal to the second operand.

6f. The first operand would be less than, equal to, or greater than the second operand.

6g. The first operand would be greater than the second operand.

6h. The first operand would be less than the second operand.

7. +2,147,483,647

8. register

9. three

10. zero

11. address

12. registers

13. 0 (zero)

14. 74 (seventy-four)

15. $+3,250$ -25 $+50$

16. The address of the statement labeled BACK.

17. CONTIG

18a. BC   4,SUBRT1

18b. BC   2,SUBRT5

18c. BC   8,SUBRT7

18d. BC   4,SUBRT10

18e. BC   6,SUBRT12A

18f. BC   15,SUBRT14

18g. BC   2,SUBRT17

CHAPTER 9

The "Move" Instructions

1. SI
2. 4
3. MVI (Move Immediate)
4. MVZ (Move Zone)
5. "sliding" first
6. MVZ
7. MVN (Move Numeric)
8. first
9. MVC (Move Characters)
10. 7
11. "chaining"

12a. FIELD3

G	A	3	9	5

12b. FLD4

D	A	T	E

12c. DATASET

C	2	D	9	C	1	D	5	C	4	E	8

12d. COUNTFLD

9	8	7	6	5

12e. CHEXFLD

F	F	2	0	2	0

12f. CFLD

E	A	S	T

12g. FLD1G

R	S	M	I	T	H

12h. SET2

H	A	P	P	Y

12i. SETPAK

4	0	5	C

12j. INFIELD

9	9	9	9	9	9

12k. DATAREV

R	E	A	R	E	D

The "Store" Instructions

13. False

14. STH   (Store Halfword)

15. STM   (Store Multiple)

16. ST   (Store)

17. False

18. STC   (Store Character)

19. Two   high-order

20. Nine

21. Ten

22. −319,771

23. eight

24*a*. FULLWD6

2	5	3	1	0	9	7	D

24*b*. SETWD1

0	0	0	3	9	5	6	C

SETWD2

0	0	0	0	0	F	C	3

SETWD3

0	0	6	9	2	1	C	6

SETWD4

0	0	0	C	0	7	4	2

24*c*. DAFLD

4	C	0	0	0	0	0	0

24*d*. DATA8

0	0	0	0	0	5	C	6
F	F	2	9	0	0	6	C

The "Load" Instructions

25. LH   (Load Halfword)

26. LA   (Load Address)

27. LPR (Load Positive Register)

28. one   sixty-four

29. positive   negative

30. L(Load)

31. IC   (Insert Character)

32. LNR   (Load Negative Register)

33. +32,767

34. thirty-two   (32)

35. LR   (Load Register)

36. LTR   (Load & Test Register)

37. X'00'

38. X'712400FF'

39. LCR   (Load Complement Register)

40. LM   (Load Multiple)

41. Register 8

F	F	F	F	C	1	C	2

42. X'FCFBFAFA'

43. X'003D0E46'

44a. Register 3

0	0	0	F	3	9	0	0

44b. Register 11

0	0	0	0	0	F	F	F

44c. Register 5

F	F	F	2	0	5	9	F

44d. Register 3

0	0	0	0	D	E	0	D

44e. Register 4

0	6	3	9	0	0	F	F

44f. Register 6

F	F	F	9	F	0	6	9

44g. Register 8

F	0	F	F	0	C	0	C

44h. Register 3

0	0	C	6	A	B	D	3

44i. Register 2

0	0	0	6	5	1	F	F

44j. Register 3

F	0	F	A	C	D	6	B

Register 4

F	F	3	9	F	B	D	F

Register 5

F	F	F	2	9	A	A	6

44k. Register 12

0	0	0	0	7	6	5	4

44l. Register 12

0	0	C	6	F	9	D	9

The "Shift" Instructions

45. 2nd

46. eight

47. SLL   (Shift Left Logical)

48. Sign-bit

49. SRA   (Shift Right Algebraic)

50. even-numbered

51. SLDL   (Shift Left Double Logical)

52. even-numbered

53. SRL   (Shift Right Logical)

54. Unlike

55. SLDA   (Shift Left Double Algebraic)

56. odd-numbered

57. SRA   (Shift Right Algebraic)

58. zero-bits

59. SRDL   (Shift Right Double Logical)
zero-bits

60. thirty-two   (32)

61. SRDA   (Shift Right Double Algebraic)
sixty-three

62. zero

63a. Register 5 (Binary)

1111	1111	0000	0001	1101	1111	0000	1110

(Hex)

F	F	0	1	D	F	0	E

63b. Registers 2 and 3 (In binary and hex)

1111	1111	1000	0000	0011	1111	1111	1001	0110	0110	0001	0000	0000	0000	0000	0000
F	F	8	0	3	F	F	9	6	6	1	0	0	0	0	0

63c. Register 10 (Binary)

0000	0000	0000	0000	0000	0000	0000	0000

(Hex)

0	0	0	0	0	0	0	0

63d. Register 9 (Binary)

0000	0000	0000	1111	0100	1110	0101	1101

(Hex)

0	0	0	F	4	E	5	D

63e. Registers 6 and 7 (binary and hex)

1000	0111	1011	1010	0000	1110	0101	0000	0000	0100	1101	1001	1111	0101	1011	0000
8	7	B	A	0	E	5	0	0	4	D	9	F	5	B	0

63f. Registers 10 and 11 (binary and hex)

1111	1111	1111	1111	1111	1111	1111	1111	0000	0000	0000	0000	0000	0001	0000	0010
F	F	F	F	F	F	F	F	0	0	0	0	0	1	0	2

63g. Register 2 (Binary)

0100	0110	0000	1110	1010	0001	0000	0000

(Hex)

4	6	0	E	A	1	0	0

63h. Registers 8 and 9 (binary and hex)

0000	0000	0000	0000	0010	1000	0000	1100	1111	1101	0001	1000	1111	1101	0001	1000
0	0	0	0	2	8	0	C	F	D	1	8	F	D	1	8

CHAPTER 10

1. PACK

2. CVD (Convert to Decimal)

3. length

4. PAKFLD

0	0	0	0	2	5	9	F

5. OUTFLD

F	0	F	0	F	0	F	0	F	3	F	9	C	6

6. PKFA

6	0	5	5	6	6	6	C

7. INPACK

1	1	2	3	3	C

8. PACKRA

0	5	4	0	9	5	4	C

9. DATAFLD

0	6	5	9	2	3	V

10. PKSETB

0	0	0	3	6	5	1	2	4	D

11. PKFLD

0	0	0	0	8	6	5	8	9	5	4	C

12. eight (8)

13. ten (10)

14. eight   doubleword

15. "12345F"

16. divisor

17. second

18. CVD   (Convert To Decimal) UNPACK

19. high-order

20. left

21. X'F0'

22. PAKFLDA

0	1	3	4	4	8	5	C

23. DATAPAK

6	0	0	6	0	0	3	C

24. QUOREM

0	0	1	0	4	0	5	C	0	0	6	C

25. SETPAKA

0	1	3	5	4	7	4	0	2	C

26. MULTPAK

0	0	0	0	5	5	3	5	6	C

ANSWER

0	0	5	5	3	5	6	C

27. PAKONE

0	0	0	0	0	0

PAKTWO

0	0	0	0	9	3	4	C

28. PAKRECV

0	3	2	3	4	5	8	C

DATASFLD

3	2	3	4	5	H

29. QUOREM

0	0	4	8	4	C	0	0	2	C

ANSW

0	0	4	8	4	C

30. REPACK

0	0	0	0	9	2	6	0	8	C

31. MULTAREA

0	0	0	4	5	5	0	6	0	C

ANSWR

0	0	0	0	4	5	5	C

CHAPTER 11

1. False
2. Subtract Logical Registers (SLR)
3. Multiply   Divide
4. one-bit
5. complemented   added
6. even-numbered
7. +4096
8. True
9. first

10.

F	F	F	F	8	0	0	0

11. True
12. Logical
13. False

14. Register 3 (Hex)

0	0	0	0	2	6	2	5

    (Binary)

0000	0000	0000	0000	0010	0110	0010	0101

15. Register 11 (Hex)

0	0	0	6	7	B	E	8

    (Binary)

0000	0000	0000	0110	0111	1011	1110	1000

16. Register 7 (Hex)

0	1	E	E	3	7	0	C

    (Binary)

0000	0001	1110	1110	0011	0111	0000	1100

17. Register 9 (Hex)

0	2	5	B	9	9	8	6

    (Binary)

0000	0010	0101	1011	1001	1001	1000	0110

18. Register 10 (Hex)

0	0	0	2	6	3	3	C

    (Binary)

0000	0000	0000	0010	0110	0011	0011	1100

19. Register 4 (Hex)

0	0	0	0	0	0	0	0

    (Binary)

0000	0000	0000	0000	0000	0000	0000	0000

20. Register 12 (Hex)

0	0	0	0	9	1	F	7

    (Binary)

0000	0000	0000	0000	1001	0001	1111	0111

21. Register 7 (Hex)

0	0	0	4	F	F	0	F

    (Binary)

0000	0000	0000	0100	1111	1111	0000	1111

22. Register 10 (Hex)

0	1	4	8	E	2	E	D

    (Binary)

0000	0001	0100	1000	1110	0010	1110	1101

23. Register 3 (Hex)

0	0	2	F	3	4	8	D

(Binary)

0000	0000	0010	1111	0011	0100	1000	1101

24. Register 2 (Hex)

0	0	0	0	0	0	0	0

(Binary)

0000	0000	0000	0000	0000	0000	0000	0000

Register 3 (Hex)

0	7	3	C	D	A	4	8

(Binary)

0000	0111	0011	1100	1101	1010	0100	1000

25. Register 4 (Hex)

0	0	0	0	0	0	0	0

(Binary)

0000	0000	0000	0000	0000	0000	0000	0000

Register 5 (Hex)

0	3	F	5	7	5	0	8

(Binary)

0000	0011	1111	0101	0111	0101	0000	1000

26. Register 6 (Hex)

0	0	0	0	0	0	0	0

(Binary)

0000	0000	0000	0000	0000	0000	0000	0000

Register 7 (Hex)

0	0	0	5	E	3	7	6

(Binary)

0000	0000	0000	0101	1110	0011	0111	0110

27. Register 8 (Hex)

0	0	0	0	0	0	3	9

(Binary)

0000	0000	0000	0000	0000	0000	0011	1001

Register 9 (Hex)

0	0	0	0	0	0	8	4

(Binary)

0000	0000	0000	0000	0000	0000	1000	0100

28. Register 4 (Hex)

0	0	0	0	0	0	5	7

(Binary)

0000	0000	0000	0000	0000	0000	0101	0111

Register 5 (Hex)

0	0	0	0	0	3	5	8

(Binary)

0000	0000	0000	0000	0000	0011	0101	1000

CHAPTERS 3–11—ADDITIONAL REVIEW

1. Correct
2. Correct
3. Correct
4. Correct
5. Correct
6. Correct
7. Correct
8. Correct
9. Correct
10. Correct
11. Incorrect
12. Correct
13. Incorrect
14. Incorrect
15. Correct
16. Correct
17. Correct
18. Incorrect
19. Incorrect
20. Incorrect
21. Incorrect
22. Incorrect
23. Correct
24. Incorrect
25. Correct
26. Incorrect
27. Correct
28. Correct
29. Incorrect
30. Correct
31. Correct
32. Incorrect

33. Correct
34. Correct
35. Incorrect
36. Correct
37. Incorrect
38. Incorrect
39. Incorrect
40. Incorrect
41. Incorrect
42. Correct
43. Correct
44. Correct
45. Incorrect
46. Incorrect
47. Correct
48. Correct
49. Incorrect
50. Correct
51. Correct
52. Correct
53. Correct
54. Correct
55. Correct
56. Correct
57. Correct
58. Correct
59. Correct
60. Incorrect
61. Correct
62. Correct
63. Incorrect
64. Correct

65. Incorrect
66. Correct
67. Incorrect
68. Incorrect
69. Incorrect
70. Incorrect
71. Correct
72. Correct
73. Incorrect
74. Correct
75. Correct
76. Correct
77. Incorrect
78. Incorrect
79. Correct
80. Correct
81. Correct
82. Incorrect
83. Correct
84. Correct
85. Correct
86. Incorrect
87. Correct
88. Correct
89. Correct
90. Correct
91. Incorrect
92. Incorrect
93. Incorrect
94. Incorrect
95. Correct
96. Correct

97. Correct
98. Correct
99. Incorrect
100. Incorrect
101. Incorrect
102. Incorrect
103. Incorrect
104. Correct
105. Correct
106. Correct
107. Correct
108. Incorrect
109. Correct
110. Incorrect
111. Incorrect
112. Correct
113. Correct
114. Correct
115. Correct
116. Incorrect
117. Incorrect
118. Incorrect
119. Correct
120. Incorrect
121. Incorrect
122. Incorrect
123. Incorrect
124. Correct
125. Incorrect

CHAPTER 12

1. bits   bits
2. And
3. "add"
4. zero-bit   one-bit
5. XC
6. "mask"
7. one-bit
8. 32
9. one-bit   zero-bit

10. register   fullword

11. immediate

12. "times"   multiplication

13. And   256

14. Register

15. Register   register

16. "on" (or) "yes"

17. zero-bit

18. one-bits

19. Register 3 (Binary)

0010	0000	1111	0011	0100	0101	0101	1111

(Hex)

2	0	F	3	4	5	5	F

20. Register 8 (Binary)

0001	0001	0111	0011	0111	0111	1111	1111

(Hex)

1	1	7	3	7	7	F	F

21. DATAFLD (Binary)

1101	0001	1100	0010	1110	0011

(Hex)

D	1	C	2	E	3

22. DATATEST (Binary)

1100	0100	1111	0011	1100	0100	0011	1100	1110	1001

(Hex)

C	4	F	3	C	4	3	C	E	9

23. Register 12 (Binary)

0000	0000	1100	0111	0101	0110	1001	1100

(Hex)

0	0	C	7	5	6	9	C

24. DATASET (Binary)

1100	0111	1100	1000	0000	0010	0000	0000	0000	0000

(Hex)

C	7	C	8	0	2	0	0	0	0

25. CHKFLD (Binary)

0010	1101	1011	1111	1111	0010	1101	0101	1111	0011

(Hex)

2	D	B	F	F	2	D	5	F	3

26. FLDSET (Binary)

1110	0011	0110	1011	0101	1011	1001	1100

(Hex)

E	3	6	B	5	B	9	C

27. Register 4 (Binary)

0000	0000	0011	1001	0010	0110	0111	1000

(Hex)

0	0	3	9	2	6	7	8

28. SWITCHES (Binary)

0000	0000	0010	1010	0101	1111	0000	0001

(Hex)

0	0	2	A	5	F	0	1

29. Register 8 (Binary)

0000	0000	0000	0000	0011	0010	0110	0000

(Hex)

0	0	0	0	3	2	6	0

30. DATASW (Binary)

1000	0110	1110	0011	1000	0010	1010	0011	1100	0110

(Hex)

8	6	E	3	8	2	A	3	C	6

31. WORDBASE (Binary)

1111	0011	1111	0101	1100	0100	1100	0001	1101	0111

(Hex)

F	3	F	5	C	4	C	1	D	7

32. Register 6 (Binary)

1100	0010	1100	0111	1100	0101	1100	1000

(Hex)

C	2	C	7	C	5	C	8

33. Register 5 (Binary)

0000	0000	0000	0000	0000	0000	0000	1100

(Hex)

0	0	0	0	0	0	0	C

CHAPTER 13

1. eight
2. Compare Logical Immediate   (CLI)
3. Test Under Mask   (TM)
4. Character
5. one-bit
6. Move Immediate   (MVI)
7. 256
8. ABITS `1 1 1 0 1 0 1 0`   OI   ABITS,X'A8'
9. KBITS `0 0 0 0 0 0 0 0`
10. HBITS `0 0 0 1 0 0 0 0`   NI   HBITS,X'10'
11. BBITS `1 0 0 1 0 1 1 1`   OI   BBITS,X'97'
12. EBITS `0 1 0 0 1 0 1 0`   NI   EBITS,X'5E'
                                   OI   EBITS,X'48'
13. CBITS `0 0 0 0 1 0 0 1`   NI   CBITS,X'AB'
14. FBITS `1 0 1 0 0 1 0 1`   XI   FBITS,X'3A'
15. GBITS `0 1 1 0 0 0 0 1`   TM   GBITS,X'4B'
16. DBITS `0 0 1 0 1 0 0 0`   NI   DBITS,X'38'

CHAPTER 15

1. *a.* fill character
   b. Significant Start Character
   c. Digit Select character
   d. Field Separator character
2. register 1
3. Significant Trigger   (or)   S-Trigger
4. X'21'
5. plus-sign
6. Significant Start
7. packed decimal
8. five

9. X'20'
10. Significant Start
11. left to right   (or)   high-order to low-order
12. X'22'
13. edit pattern
14. Field Separator
15. fill character   (or)   insertion character
16. digit select
17. Significant Trigger   (or)   S-Trigger
18. Field Separator
19. fill character   (or)   insertion character

20. RESULTA (Hex)

C 1	4 0	4 0	4 0	4 0	F 0	F 9
A	(blank)	(blank)	(blank)	(blank)	0	9

21. RESULTB (Hex)

D 1	4 0	F 3	F 8	F 7	F 8
J	(blank)	3	8	7	8

22. RESULTC (Hex)

5 B	4 0	F 0	F 0	4 B	F 2	F 5
$	(blank)	0	0	.	2	5

23. RESULTD (Hex)

4 0	4 0	F 3	F 6	4 0	4 0	4 0
(blank)	(blank)	3	6	(blank)	(blank)	(blank)

24. RESULTE (Hex)

4 0	F 7	4 B	F 4	F 8	C 3	D 9
(blank)	7	.	4	8	C	R

25. RESULTF (Hex)

5 C	5 C	5 C	F 6	F 2	F 9	6 0
*	*	*	6	2	9	—

26. RESULTG (Hex)

4 0	5 B	F 6	F 1	4 B	F 1	F 7
(blank)	$	6	1	.	1	7

27. RESULTH (Hex)

4 0	4 0	4 0	5 B	4 B	F 3	F 3
(blank)	(blank)	(blank)	$	.	3	3

CHAPTER 17

1. translate table
2. 256
3. general register 1
4. general register 2
5. source byte
6. True
7. increment   first

8. translate table

9. True

10. first

11. X'00'

12. DATAFLDA (Hex)

E 3	E 4	D 4	C 2	D 3	C 5

(Character)

T	U	M	B	L	E

13. DATAFLDB (Hex)

D 7	D 9	D 6	C 2	D 3	C 5	D 4

(Character)

P	R	O	B	L	E	M

14. DATAFLDC (Hex)

D 3	D 6	D 5	C 7	D 1	D 6	C 2

(Character)

L	O	N	G	J	O	B

15. DATAFLDD (Hex)

D 9	C 9	C 7	C 8	E 3

(Character)

R	I	G	H	T

16. DATAFLDE (Hex)

F 1	F 6	4 0	E 6	C 5	E 2	E 3

(Character)

1	6	(blank)	W	E	S	T

17. DATAFLDF (Hex)

C 7	F 2	C 7	F 1	C 7	E 6

(Character)

G	2	G	1	G	W

DATAFLDG (Hex)

C 6	C 9	D 5	C 9	E 2

(Character)

F	I	N	I	S

GLOSSARY OF TERMS

absolute value　A value that is self-defining, one whose decimal characteristics denote its intended arithmetic value.

adcon　An address constant; any one of the particular group of constants that have an address as their contents.

address　The absolute identity of a position of storage.

address adjusting　The action of modifying an address; to modify the address pointed to by a label by stating that label name in conjunction with an increment, i.e. FIELDA + 6 which would address a point in storage six bytes beyond FIELDA.

alphameric　Alphanumeric.

alphanumeric　A mixture of alphabetic and numeric digits, usually in 8-bit character form.

base-2　(See Powers-Of-2); A number system comprised of ones and zeros. These digits are arranged in a contiguous row in order to express a numeric value. Each digit position has a potential value of twice that of the digit position to its right. The actual value of each position is effective only if it contains a one-bit.

base-16　The hexadecimal number system, represented by a total of sixteen digits consisting of 0 through 9 and A through F. When multiple digits are expressed, each digit has a value range of 0^{16} to 15^{16} greater than the digit position to its right.

base register　A general register that has been assigned as an addressing base within a program. This base is then used as part of a "base and displacement" addressing form for referencing any point within the next contiguous 4096 bytes of storage.

BDAM　The Basic Direct Access Method. It is used to randomly or directly retrieve data records from a data set that resides on a direct access storage device.

binary　A number system consisting of ones and zeros, the representation of the base-2 number system. Values are expressed in a contiguous row of ones and zeros.

A data configuration in which the data is expressed in the bit form of ones and zeros. This configuration represents character data, numeric values, or special representations.

binary comparison　A type of comparison in which the data is compared on the basis of the contents of each bit position, regardless of the intended interpretation of the data field itself. Thus, a numeric value in any form could be compared against a field that is considered to contain alphanumeric characters.

binary format　The bit-by-bit configuration of any field regardless of the intended representation or interpretation of that field.

BISAM　The Basic Indexed Sequential Access Method. The basic version of the access method that is capable of contiguous sequential, random sequential, or random processing of data records. The access method creates its own indexing structures based on keys associated with each record.

bit　A single bit is the smallest definable segment of any type of data. Multiple bits comprise the binary system of data representation.

A single bit may be represented within a bit position by either a one or a zero.

bit configuration   The configuration of any data as expressed in individual bits.

bit position   The individual position of bits within any data when it is expressed in binary or bit form.

bit switch   An indicator or logic switch consisting of one bit position. It is considered to represent one of two conditions, such as yes/no, on/off, etc.

block of records   A group of records that is considered to be one physical segment of data for the purpose of recording that data on a storage device. Certain data management routines can collect these records into blocks or extract them individually from the blocks.

BOS   The Basic Operating System of System/360.

boundary alignment   Any position of core that constitutes a valid alignment for a fixed-point field of a halfword, a fullword, or a double-word. A core address which is evenly divisable by 2, 4, or 8.

BPAM   The Basic Partitioned Access Method of System/360.

branch   To redirect the route of the program logic to a given instruction statement, as opposed to the natural flow of logic through sequential statements.

BSAM   The Basic Sequential Access Method of System/360.

byte   A measurement of space in System/360. A byte consists of 8 binary bit positions, representing the size of an EBCDIC alphanumeric character or symbol. The combinations of bit configurations for a byte can be any one of 256 possible configurations. A byte is also the smallest addressable segment of storage.

byte-switch   An indicator or logic switch requiring one byte of storage within the problem program. Its contents may represent one of several conditions such as yes/no, on/off, etc., but it can represent 256 different conditions, the maximum number of bit configurations for a single byte.

call   A program function that requests, extracts, or activates an external logic module or routine. An independent program or routine may be available to, and called by, any other program that wishes to use it.

Carriage Control Symbol   A one-byte EBCDIC character, appearing as the first byte of a data field that is to be printed, that is used to control the vertical spacing and skipping on the printed output form.

channel   A data transmission channel; an electrical cable over which pulses, representing data, may be passed between units of hardware of the computer system.

character   Any one of the standard EBCDIC character representations; alphabetics, numerics, and other characters and symbols such as $, #, *, %, &, ?, etc.

character-switch   A byte-switch.

compiler   A program that takes in the source coding of a programming language, interprets the coded statements, and creates a program module or deck containing the machine-language equivalent of the source language statements.

complement   The opposite value (negative or positive) of a value or configuration. The complement of $+250$ is -250, the complement of -786 is $+786$, etc.

conditional branch   A branch within the program logic that is taken only when certain processing conditions have been met.

Condition Code   An internal indicator of the computer operating system, consisting of two bit positions within the Program Status Word. Any one of the four possible bit configurations (00, 01, 10, 11) may reside within the Condition Code bit positions as a result of the execution of an instruction.

constant   A labeled field of data that is defined for the purpose of multiple references throughout the program. Unless the contents of that field are explicitly altered by the program, the data within the defined constant will not change.

control block   A logical collection of specific parameter data, formatted and used by an operating system.

core   A term used to refer to the memory storage units of the computer hardware.

core dump   A listing of the data contents of core storage at any given point in time. A core dump is usually created whenever the abnormal termination of a program occurs; it is then used by the programmer as an aid in interpreting the problem area within the program that might have caused the termination.

CPU The Central Processing Unit of a computer system; that portion of the hardware containing the basic memory units, logic modules, and arithmetic function modules.

DASD A reference to a direct access storage device; sometimes used as a direct referral to the IBM 2311 disk storage unit.

DASF A direct access storage facility; used to identify or make reference to the IBM 2314 disk storage system.

Data Control Block An operating system control block containing the identifying attributes of a data set. Such information is provided by the DCB parameters specified by the program and consists of the record length, blocking factor, record form, system options, buffering techniques to be used, etc.

data cell A large-volume storage device, in particular the IBM 2321 data cell. In this particular device data is stored magnetically on flexible tape strips within bins. As information is to be read or stored, data strips are extracted and passed by read/write heads.

data management routines Supporting softward programs that provide the functions of file organization, file structure, and input/output tasks.

data set One or more data records comprising a logical grouping of information that may be referred to by a unique name. Data sets are usually considered to reside on a storage device such as a disk, drum, or magnetic tape.

Data Set Control Block A control block entry of the Volume Table of Contents (VTOC) on a direct access storage device. The Data Set Control Block contains information regarding the location and organization of a single data set. Each data set has its own DSCB within the overall Volume Table of Contents.

DCB Data Control Block

delimiter card A card that is used to signal either the end of a function or the end of input card data.

delimiter segment A segment that is used within a problem program table or index, indicating the end of data or space assigned to that area.

Digit Select Character One of the unprintable characters that are a functional part of the editing process generated by the Edit and the Edit & Mark instructions. It is represented by the hexadecimal digits "20". The Digit Select Characters, residing within the edit pattern, indicate those 1-byte positions within the pattern that are to be supplied with numeric characters from the source field or with fill characters from the edit pattern.

direct access device Any one of a group of data storage devices capable of performing random or direct data retrieval and access.

direct access volume A removable unit of data storage; a portion of a direct access device. When used to refer to a disk pack of a disk storage unit, the direct access volume is considered to have a unique volume serial number or identity by which it may be addressed or referred to.

directory The internal index of a Partitioned Data Set, pointing to the associated data set members.

direct processing A mode of data record processing. Records are sent to or retrieved from a direct access device via a relative location and/or identity key. One or more records may be written on the file without regard to their logical or physical sequence.

disk (disc) Any one of the storage devices that record data on platters resembling phonograph records.
A single platter within a disk storage device.

displacement The actual distance, measured in bytes, between two locations of storage.

display unit A device that is used to enter or retrieve and visually display data that is being transmitted between that unit and another device. Although it can be a typewriter-style of device, a display unit is usually thought of as presenting the data on a cathode ray tube similar to a television picture tube.

DOS The Disk Operating System of System/360.

doubleword An eight-byte field residing at a decimal core address evenly divisible by eight. Although a doubleword may contain data of any type, they are primarily intended for floating-point arithmetic purposes.

doubleword boundary Any storage position address which, in decimal form, is evenly divisable by 8.

drum A direct access storage device, such as the IBM 2301 or 2303 drums. The data is recorded on the outside surface of a cylindrical drum, each data track having a fixed read/write head.

DSCB A Data Set Control Block

DSD A disk storage device; a general reference to any of the group of disk storage device, but often used as a particular reference to the IBM 2311 disk storage unit.

dummy records Format records; pseudo-records; simulated records created for the purpose of formatting or padding a data set, used particularly on those data sets that are created or retrieved by direct access techniques.

dump A core dump; a printed listing of the partial or complete contents or core storage.

duplication factor A specification element of a Define Constant (DC) or Define Storage (DS) statement. It indicates how many copies (duplicates) of the defined constant or storage area should be created by the language compiler.

EBCDIC The Extended Binary Coded Decimal Interchange Code. A system of bit representations for standard alphanumeric characters, punctuation symbols, and special characters, using 8 bit positions to represent each character or symbol.

edit pattern A field containing an arrangement of the control characters that are used by the Edit and the Edit & Mark instructions. The packed decimal data is edited into this field, replacing the pattern in its entirety.

end-of-file condition A condition that exists whenever the end of a data set (file) volume is encountered. The condition setting is activated by the data management routines whenever an I/O task detects an end-of-volume marker or trailer label on a storage device.

end-of-volume condition A condition that exists whenever the end of a storage device volume is encountered. The condition setting is activated by the data management routines whenever an I/O task detects an end-of-volume marker or trailer label on a storage device.

EOF The end-of-file condition or the situation resulting from encountering an end-of-file.

EOV The end-of-volume condition or the situation resulting from encountering an end-of-volume.

equate An Assembler Language instruction that will define a label (symbol) so as to represent a decimal value or expression, either of which may be absolute (self-defining) or relocatable. The equate statement might appear as . . . REG2 EQU 2. In this case the label REG2 could now be used anywhere that the decimal "2" might be used as a register symbol. REG2 could be used equally as well wherever the programmer desired to indicate a parameter value of 2, such as . . . MVC FIELD(REG2,REG2),INPUT. In this instance the first REG2 indicates the length of the data being moved and the second REG2 specifies the base register assigned to FIELD.

even-numbered register Any one of the general registers whose reference is an even number, such as register 2, register 4, register 6, register 8, etc.

explicit attributes The specified characteristics of a constant as stated within a Define Constant (DC) statement.

fall through Reference to the action of the program logic processing encountering a conditional branch statement and passing on to the next sequential statement without taking the branch.

Field Separator Character One of the control characters used by the Assembler Language instructions of Edit and Edit & Mark. The Field Separator Character is used in multiple field edits to reset the Significant Trigger to an "off" condition between adjoining edited fields.

file organization The organization or structure of a data set. In most instances the file organization is directly related to the access method that was used to create the data set. For example, an indexed sequential file organization is created by the Indexed Sequential Access Method (ISAM).

fill character The first (left-most) character in an edit pattern. The editing function uses the fill character to replace those Digit Select Characters in the edit pattern that do not receive digits from the source field. The fill character is only transmitted to those pattern positions when the Significant Trigger (S-Trigger) is in an "off" condition.

fixed-length records Describing the contents of a data set or collection of data records in which all records are of equal fixed size.

fixed-point Specifically, the fixed-point arithmetic concept. Fixed-point numeric values are expressed in binary powers-of-two bit configuration wherein the single high-order bit position identifies the negative or positive representation of that value.

forced branch   A branch statement which, when encountered, will always cause an effective branch. The processing logic will never fall through a forced branch unless the branch itself is to that next sequential instruction statement.

fullword   A four-byte data field residing at a decimal core address evenly divisable by 4. The contents of a fullword are considered to be in fixed-point arithmetic form, although the fullword may contain data of any type.

fullword boundary   Any storage position which, in decimal form, is evenly divisably by 4.

GAM   A reference to the Graphic Access Macros. These macros (macro-instructions) are used within the System/360 Operating System for the purpose of programming cathode ray display terminals such as the IBM 2260 Display Terminal.

half-byte   Either half of a byte; either the left-most or right-most 4 bit positions of a byte; a nibble.

halfword   Two bytes of data having a storage position address that is evenly divisible by 2. The contents of a halfword are considered to be in a fixed-point arithmetic form, although the halfword may contain data of any type.

halfword boundary   Any storage position address which, in decimal form, is evenly divisable by 2.

hardware   Any of the computer system units or related devices which comprise the overall physical portion of the computer. This would include the central processing unit, magnetic tape drives, storage devices, printers, and appropriate control units, as well as many other physical units.

header label   A data set label that appears at the beginning of a data set or at the beginning of a continuation of a data set residing on one or more separate storage volumes.

hex   A general reference to the hexadecimal configuration of a field or to a single hexadecimal digit.

hexadecimal   The complete base-16 number system or any one of the hexadecimal digits that are a part of that system.

hexadecimal digit   A single digit of the base-16 hexadecimal number system. Four bit positions (one half-byte) comprise one hexadecimal digit, creating a configuration that provides a range of digits from 0 through 9 and A through F.

high-order   The single position within a field that is to the extreme left of that field; that portion of a configuration that is to the left of the right-most position or positions of a field.

housekeeping   A set of instruction statements or logic that is usually performed at the beginning of a program. These statements perform base register initialization, save initial register contents, initialize data areas, and other functions that the programmer may wish to accomplish prior to entering the main logic of the program.

immediate character   A self-expressing byte of data used as an operand in any one of the Assembler Language "immediate" instruction statements. An immediate character may be expressed as a character, as two hexadecimal digits, or as eight binary bits.

implied attributes   The attributes or characteristics of a Define Constant (DC) statement, which, by their omission, are implied by the data contents of the constant.

insertion character   The fill character of an edit pattern.

instruction   A keyword or logical operator of a programming language; identifies a specific type of action that is to be accomplished.

integer   The decimal value that is expressed by a fixed-point numeric field; it is construed to consist of all of the bit positions of that field except for the single high-order sign-bit position.

integer-bit   Any one of the bits comprising the integer portion of a fixed-point value or field.

inter-record gap   A nonrecorded area separating physical groups of data on a storage device.

I/O   Input/output; used in reference to the task of transmitting or receiving data between devices.

K   A symbol used to represent a decimal value of 1024; an expression of "4K" is interpreted to represent a decimal value of 4096. There are some exceptions in technical manuals where "K" is used to represent an even value of 1000.

key   The identity field or identifier of a record. A name or value associated with a particular record for the purpose of unique identification of that record or to synonomously associate it with other records.

label   A symbolic reference to an address within a program.
A data set label; the unique name identifying a particular data set.

language   In computer terminology a language is a written code, words, or statements that are used to program the action of a computer. The language is written according to the action desired, entered into the computer via punched cards, and translated into executable machine-coding by a compiler (translator) program for that particular language. The results of this translation, an object module or object deck, are used as the executable program.

length modifier   The length specification for a Define Constant (DC) statement or a Define Storage (DS) statement. The specified length attribute assigned to a constant, literal, or storage area.

literal   A constant that is created as the second operand of an executable instruction statement, rather than by a Define Constant statement. The format of this type of constant is the same as for regular constants except that it must be preceded by an equal sign (=).

logical comparison   A comparison, between two characters or fields, in which the compare is made between corresponding bit positions of each field, from left to right. The comparison terminates as soon as two unlike bits are compared. The signed arithmetic value or character representation of the fields are not taken into consideration.

looping   The technique for contiguous repetition of the execution of a group of instruction statements for a controlled number of times. The number of times that the loop is executed is determined by a "count control" or by one or more conditions that are tested within the loop. This technique is often used in performing table searches and scanning data fields.

low-order   The single position within a field that is to the extreme right; that portion of a configuration that is to the right of the leftmost position or positions of the field; the units position of a whole decimal value.

machine-language   The level of coding that may be directly executed by the computer without further translation; the type of coding generated by a language compiler. System/360 machine-language code is represented in hexadecimal form and may be directly interpreted by the operating system.

macro   A macroinstruction; a type of language that is used to write macroinstructions.

macroinstruction   A keyword, label, or name that will activate a macro-language routine as identified by that reference. The macro-language routine will contain a group of statements for performing a specific function. Macro-language routines generally reside in a macro-library; their use may be invoked within a program by stating the name of the routine that is to be performed.

magnetic tape   A data storage media. A reel of magnetic tape consists of a plastic film base that is coated on one side with an oxide compound. Data is magnetically stored on the oxide surface in groups of parallel bits which are represented by the magnetic rearrangement of the oxide material.

mask   A field of data (one or more bytes) that is used to test or alter another data field. The bit or byte representation of the mask causes a reaction upon each corresponding bit or byte of the field being acted upon.

mask operand   An instruction statement operand that is used as a mask by that statement.

member   A logical group of records within a partitioned data set; the member name that identifies a particular set of data records.

module   A self-contained set of program instructions which may be in source, object, or executable form; a program, routine, or subroutine.

nibble   The left-most 4 bits or right-most 4 bits of a byte; one-half byte.

object deck   A deck of punched cards containing the machine-language interpretations of a program; the output deck from a compiled program.

object module   The machine-language coding, either in card deck form or in stored data form, that results from a program compilation.

odd-numbered register   Any of the general registers whose reference is an odd number, such as register 1, register 3, register 5, register 7, etc.

one-bit   A binary bit represented by a digit of 1.

op code   The mnemonic representation of an Assembler Language instruction. More generally, the logical operator or keyword of any computer language.

operand A label, value, or symbolic reference that is used within an instruction statement in order to identify a field or value.

operating system Any one of the supervisory systems that control the operation of a configuration of computer hardware. For System/360 these include the Basic Operating System (BOS), the Disk Operating System (DOS), the Tape Operating System (TOS), and the full Operating System (OS).

Operating System The largest of the four System/360 operating systems, capable of supporting any of the System/360 computer hardware. It requires a computer system whose Central Processing Unit (CPU) has a minimum of 65,536 bytes of core storage.

OS The full Operating System of System/360.

overflow Arithmetic overflow; the result of an arithmetic operation in which the resulting field value is larger than the field allotted to that result.

Overflow record; a record that has been moved into one of the overflow areas of an indexed sequential data set.

Track overflow/record overflow; a hardware-software feature that allows the automatic continuance of a data record between two contiguous tracks on a direct access device.

pack To compress an EBCDIC numeric character value into packed decimal form.

A disk pack for a direct access storage device.

packed decimal One of the arithmetic systems of System/360. Numeric values are represented in multiple hexadecimal digits, each with a potential self-defining value of 0 through 9. The hexadecimal digits, as expressed, represent the decimal interpretation of the value. The value may be signed by the existence of a hex digit of "A" through "F" in the right-most half-byte of the field.

parameter A field, a value, or a set of characters that must be stated explicitly in order to supply a set of characteristics to a language statement. Such items would be the operands of an Assembler Language instruction statement, the operand fields of a macroinstruction, or the control information on a Job Control Language card.

Partitioned Data Set A data set that has been created by the Basic Partitioned Access Method data management routines. The physical organization of the data set consists of a directory (an index) and the data set members (the collections of records). The directory entries point to the location of current data set members.

PDS A Partitioned Data Set.

pointer An address, symbol, or label that is used for the purpose of specifying any given address point within storage or on a storage device.

powers-of-two The ascending scale of value of the base-2 (binary) numeric system, used to define the potential value of contiguous bit positions from right to left. Each bit position to the left of its right-hand neighbor has a potential value equal to twice as much as that neighboring bit position.

printer Any one of a group of output devices that create printed output. This group includes system typewriters, but the term "printer" is more often used to define a device that uses a type-bar or type-chain and prints several complete lines in less than one second.

problem program A program that is executed to perform a particular task or service as an end in itself. Although this program may call or invoke other programs and routines, the calling program is considered to be the main program or the problem program.

program interrupt The interruption of a program as a result of planned or unplanned circumstances that prevent logic processing from continuing without additional intervening program logic or operator action.

Program Status Word A doubleword field (64 bit positions) within the controlling section of an operating system. It contains status indicators, addresses, error indicators, and other data regarding the status of the executing program. The Program Status Word is reset each time a machine instruction is executed.

PSW The Program Status Word.

QISAM The Queued Indexed Sequential Access Method; an access method or set of data management routines that are utilized in creating and accessing a data set arranged in an indexed sequential mode of organization.

QSAM The Queued Sequential Access Method; an access method that is used to process a sequentially organized data set in a contiguously sequential manner.

query byte A byte that is used to create an

argument (comparator) for a comparison; a byte that references an address point within a translate table.

quorem   A programmer-created work area for an arithmetic divide operation. After the divide operation is completed, the *quo*tient and *rema*inder occupy this work area, hence the name "quorem."

record overflow   Track overflow; a hardware/software feature that allows the automatic continuance of a data record between two contiguous tracks on a direct access device.

register   A fixed-location 32-bit field (one full-word) that is used by System/360 for address storage and address reference. There are 16 general registers, numbered from 0 through 15. These registers are also available to the Assembler Language programmer for use as data retention units, work areas for fixed-point arithmetic operations, and as address bases for problem program addressing linkage.

relative position   The location of any item in relationship to some other point. If a set of data consisted of "ABCDE" in character form, then the relative position of "B" to "A" would be 1, the relative position of "E" to "A" would be 4, etc. This is used to refer to the position or address of a record within a data set residing on a direct access device, in lieu of using a true physical address. Such reference would be that although record "XYZ" was the 3296th record within the data set, it would actually be the 3295th record relative to the beginning of the data set. The first physical record in the data set would be relative record 0 (zero), relative to the beginning of the data set.

relocation factor   A value representing the difference between the first addressable byte of core storage and the address of the storage point at which a program or routine is physically located; a value representing the number of bytes of storage between two specific addresses.

segment   A portion of a table or index, representing the groups of data that comprise that set of data. Any one of the entries or values within a table or index.

self-defining   A value or character that is presented in the form that it is intended to represent. Data whose intended character representation or value can be visually understood without further interpretation.

sequential processing   The mode of processing data records in which each successive record is examined or processed in the sequence of its physical storage or input location.

short block   A block of data that contains fewer logical records or bytes than specified for blocks on the data set to which it belongs.

sign   That portion of an arithmetic field that defines the plus/positive or minus/negative value of that field.

sign-bit   The single high-order bit of a fixed-point value, used to define the positive or negative configuration of that value.

significant   A bit, a hexadecimal digit, or a numeric character whose individual decimal value is greater than zero.

Significant Start Character   One of the non-printable characters that are a functional part of the editing process. It is represented by the hexadecimal digits '21'. The Significant Start Character is placed into the edit pattern to signal the termination of zero suppression. If zero suppression has not been terminated prior to encountering a Significant Start Character in the edit pattern, the editing process inspects that character and sets the Significant Trigger to an "on" condition.

Significant Trigger   A logic switch that is a part of the editing function. It has a setting of either "on" or "off". If the Significant Trigger is "off", zero suppression takes place and fill characters are used to replace non-significant source digits in the Digit Select Character positions of the edit pattern. If the Significant Trigger is "on", source field digits replace the Digit Select Characters in the edit pattern.

software   Any program or series of programs designed to aid in the execution of a problem program; the supervisory control programs of an operating system; a program designed to perform special functional operations for any other program that requires those services.

source deck   A deck of punched cards containing the EBCDIC character representation of the uncompiled coded statements for a program.

source field   A data field that supplies information, characters, or values to an instruction during the execution of a statement. If data is being moved from field "B" to field "A", then the source field is field "B", the sending field.

statement An instruction statement; a language instruction presented in its operational form along with any or all operands or keywords required for the execution of that instruction.

storage area The areas of core storage utilized by executable programs or routines.

S-Trigger The Significant Trigger of the editing functions.

subroutine One or more instruction statements that comprise a logic portion of a program, usually set apart from the straight-line coding logic of the body of the program. A logic routine that is secondary to the main logic of the program.

switch A bit, a byte, or a data field of storage that is used to signal a condition or situation of processing. It may be logically altered or configurated by the program logic, by the result of the processing action, or by the operating system of the computer.

symbol A label, tag, name, or reference; an identifier that represents a value. A symbol may be used to represent the address of a field, a register, a statement, or any other addressable point within the program.

symbolic label A name, tag, or identity that is used to reference an address point within a program. The symbolic label effectively creates an address in base and displacement form, corresponding to that segment of the program to which it was assigned.

Sysgen A system generation; the process of creating an operating system or a version of an operating system.

system generation The process of creating (generating) an operating system; a merge and organization of the data management routines, supervisory programs, and related computer systems programs, all arranged and defined for a specific hardware configuration on which the operating system is to be used.

table A group of data, often arranged in some type of logical pattern, containing specific information or a cross-reference to other data. A table usually consists of a quantity of data segments of equal length.

table segment One of the sections or elements of a table, usually containing a unique value or set of characters in order to identify it from the other segments within the table.

tape A general reference to magnetic tape; a means of data storage.

tape volume A single reel of magnetic tape, normally assigned a unique serial number. Although one reel of tape is considered to be an individual tape volume, a logical set of data, identified by one name, may reside contiguously across several reels of tape.

terminal Any type of input/output device that is used for entering, receiving, transmitting and/or interpreting data, rather than for the purpose of storing data. Such terminal units would be cathode ray display units, computer typewriter units, etc.

TOS The Tape Operating System of System/360

track overflow Record overflow; a feature of the 2314 DASF that allows a logical data block to commence on one physical track and extend through one or more contiguous tracks. Certain other direct access devices also have this capability.

trailer label A data set label or control block that appears at the end of the data set. It contains information relative to the data set including the number of data blocks within that file.

translate table A 256-byte table utilized by the Translate and the Translate & Test instructions.

truncated block A recorded data block that contains a lesser quantity of data bytes than the quantity stated as the block length for that data set.

two's complement notation A value expressed in negative fixed-point binary form.

unconditional branch A forced branch; an instruction statement, which, when entered, will always create a logic branch to another portion of the executing program or programs.

undefined records Data records whose length and format are not known.

variable-length records Data set records whose record length is not necessarily consistent throughout the overall data set. Each record contains a four-byte prefix specifying the total length of that record including the prefix bytes.

volume The quantity of records within a data set.
A complete unit of storage for a data storage

device; a disk pack, a drum, a bin of a data cell, or a reel of magnetic tape.

volume label   An identity control block for a data storage volume. The volume label usually appears as the first data on such a volume. It contains the volume serial number in order to create a unique identity for that particular volume.

volume table of contents   The data set labels for a direct access storage volume, also known as a VTOC. The volume table of contents serves as an informational data reference and index for the data sets residing on the volume. Each uniquely-named VTOC entry consists of Data Set Control Blocks for that specific data set.

VTOC   The volume table of contents for a data storage volume.

word   A measure of data or storage, equal to four bytes; a shortened form of reference to a fullword.

zero-bit   A zero digit representing a binary bit.

zero-suppression   The means or technique of creating an EBCDIC numeric value in which all non-significant leading zeros are replaced by either a blank or by a special character.

zoned decimal   A decimal value in EBCDIC character form; the units position consists of an alphabetic character representing the sign of the value.

INDEX